KT-178-666

LES ŒUVRES COMPLETES DE VOLTAIRE

50

THE VOLTAIRE FOUNDATION
TAYLOR INSTITUTION
OXFORD
1986

THE COMPLETE WORKS OF VOLTAIRE

50

THE VOLTAIRE FOUNDATION
TAYLOR INSTITUTION
OXFORD
1986

ISBN 0 7294 0334 3

PRINTED IN ENGLAND
AT THE ALDEN PRESS
OXFORD

under the sponsorship of

sous le haut patronage de

L'ACADÉMIE FRANÇAISE

L'ACADÉMIE ROYALE DE LANGUE ET DE LITTÉRATURE FRANÇAISES DE BELGIQUE

THE AMERICAN COUNCIL OF LEARNED SOCIETIES

THE BRITISH ACADEMY

L'UNION ACADÉMIQUE INTERNATIONALE

prepared with the kind co-operation of

réalisée avec le concours gracieux de

THE SALTYKOV-SHCHEDRIN STATE PUBLIC LIBRARY OF LENINGRAD

1760

I

TABLE OF CONTENTS

List of illustrations xiii
List of abbreviations xv
Key to the critical apparatus xvii
Preface xix

Le Droit du seigneur
Critical edition by W. D. Howarth 1
Introduction
1. The 'jus primae noctis' before Voltaire 3
2. Voltaire and the 'jus primae noctis' 8
3. The 'jus primae noctis' and the eighteenth-century theatre 14
4. Genesis and composition 18
5. Theatrical fortunes 22
6. Publication 25
7. Critical reception 29
8. Manuscripts 32
9. Editions 35
10. Editorial principles 58

LE DROIT DU SEIGNEUR 63
Acteurs 64
Le Droit du seigneur, comédie 65
Appendix 201

L'Ecossaise
Critical edition by Colin Duckworth 221
Acknowledgements 223

TABLE OF CONTENTS

Introduction
1. Genesis, sources and composition 225
2. Title, attribution and publication 242
3. Palissot's *Les Philosophes* and *L'Ecossaise* at the Comédie-Française 246
4. The fortunes of *L'Ecossaise* after summer 1760 274
5. Four 'petites poétiques': 283
'Préface' 283
'Requête à MM. les Parisiens' 289
'Epître dédicatoire' 290
'Avertissement' 292
6. Conclusions 293
7. Manuscripts 296
8. Editions 298
9. *A messieurs les Parisiens* 331
10. Editorial principles 335

LE CAFÉ OU L'ÉCOSSAISE 341
Epître dédicatoire du traducteur 343
A messieurs les Parisiens 347
Avertissement 352
Préface 355
Acteurs 361
Le Café ou l'Ecossaise, comédie 363
Appendix 469

Anecdotes sur Fréron
Edition critique par Jean Balcou 471
Introduction
1. Le dossier Thiriot (août 1760) 473
2. Les deux éditions de 1761 474
3. *Les Choses utiles et agréables* 476
4. Le mémoire Royou 477
5. Enquête 480
6. Réactions 481

7. La conspiration du silence 483
8. Fabulation 484
9. Appendices 485
10. Le texte 487
11. Principes de cette édition 491

ANECDOTES SUR FRÉRON 495
Appendice I 519
Appendice II 521

List of works cited 523

Index 529

LIST OF ILLUSTRATIONS

1. *Le Droit du seigneur*: a page of MS1 (II.i.49-69), with alterations and notes by the actors. 36

Comédie-Française, Paris.

2. *Le Droit du seigneur*: a page of MS1 (III.v-vi.271-288), with a marginal note by the censor, Crébillon. 37

Comédie-Française, Paris.

3. *Le Droit du seigneur*: a page of MS3 (II.iii.144-170), with a holograph addition. 38

Comédie-Française, Paris.

4. *Le Droit du seigneur*: a page from Voltaire's corrected copy of the *encadrée*, W75G* (III.x.506-518), with a revision by Wagnière. 39

Saltykov-Shchedrin State Public Library, Leningrad.

5. *Le Droit du seigneur*: title-page of the octavo issue of the first edition (63G8), published in Paris by Duchesne. 61

Taylor Institution, Oxford.

6. *L'Ecossaise*: holograph (MS1) of additional lines (II.ii.16-26) first published in W68 and T67. 297

Bibliothèque nationale, Paris.

7. *Le Café ou l'Ecossaise*: the title-page of the first edition (siglum 60), published in Geneva by Cramer. 339

Taylor Institution, Oxford.

8. *Anecdotes sur Fréron*: the first page of the holograph manuscript of the 'Avis de l'éditeur'. 486

Bibliothèque municipale, Grenoble.

9. *Anecdotes sur Fréron*: the first page of the 1770 edition (siglum 70), with a holograph annotation by Voltaire. 490

Saltykov-Shchedrin State Public Library, Leningrad.

LIST OF ABBREVIATIONS

Al Fréron, *L'Année littéraire*
Arsenal Bibliothèque de l'Arsenal, Paris
Austin Humanities Research Center Library, University of Texas at Austin
Bachaumont *Mémoires secrets*, 1777-1789
Bengesco *Voltaire: bibliographie de ses œuvres*, 1882-1890
Best *Voltaire's correspondence*, 1953-1965
Beuchot *Œuvres de Voltaire*, 1829-1840
Bh Bibliothèque historique de la ville de Paris
BL British Library, London
Bn Bibliothèque nationale, Paris
Bn F Bn, Manuscrits français
Bn N Bn, Nouvelles acquisitions françaises
Bodleian Bodleian Library, Oxford
Bpu Bibliothèque publique et universitaire, Geneva
Br Bibliothèque royale, Brussels
BV *Bibliothèque de Voltaire: catalogue des livres*, 1961
CLT Grimm, *Correspondance littéraire*, 1877-1882
D Voltaire, *Correspondence and related documents*, Voltaire 85-135, 1968-1977
Desnoiresterres *Voltaire et la société française*, 1867-1876
Diderot *Œuvres complètes*, 1975-
Essai Voltaire, *Essai sur les mœurs*, 1963
Havens and Torrey *Voltaire's catalogue of his library at Ferney*, 1959
ImV Institut et musée Voltaire, Geneva
Kehl *Œuvres complètes de Voltaire*, 1784-1789
Leningrad Saltykov-Shchedrin State Public Library, Leningrad
M *Œuvres complètes de Voltaire*, 1877-1885
Mlr *Modern language review*
Palissot *Œuvres de Voltaire*, 1792-1797
Rdm *Revue des deux mondes*

LIST OF ABBREVIATIONS

Registres H. C. Lancaster, *The Comédie française, 1701-1774*, 1951
Rhl *Revue d'histoire littéraire de la France*
Stockholm Kungliga Biblioteket, Stockholm
Studies *Studies on Voltaire and the eighteenth century*
Taylor Taylor Institution, Oxford
Toronto Thomas Fisher Rare Book Library, University of Toronto
Uppsala Universitetsbiblioteket, Uppsala
VM Leningrad, Voltaire library manuscripts
Voltaire *Œuvres complètes de Voltaire / Complete works of Voltaire*, 1968- [the present edition]

KEY TO THE CRITICAL APPARATUS

The critical apparatus, printed at the foot of the page, gives variant readings from those manuscripts and editions listed on pages 58, 337-38 and 491 below. Each variant consists of some or all of the following elements:

- The number of the text line or lines to which the variant relates; headings, character names and stage directions bear the number of the preceding text line, plus a, b, c, etc.
- The sigla of the sources of the variant, as given on p.32-57, 296-335 and 487-91. Simple numbers, or numbers followed by letters, generally stand for separate editions of the work in question; letters followed by numbers are normally collections of one sort or another, W being reserved for collected editions of Voltaire's works and T for collected editions of his theatre; an asterisk after the siglum indicates a specific copy of the edition, usually containing manuscript corrections.
- Editorial explanation or comment.
- A colon, indicating the start of the variant; any editorial remarks after the colon are enclosed within square brackets.
- The text of the variant itself, preceded and followed, if appropriate, by one or more words from the base text, to indicate its position.

Several signs and typographic conventions are employed:

- Angle brackets ⟨ ⟩ encompass deleted matter.
- Beta β stands for the base text.
- The paragraph sign ¶ indicates the start of a new paragraph.
- The forward arrow → means 'followed by', in the case of manuscript corrections subsequently adopted in print.
- Up ↑ and down ↓ arrows precede text added above or below the line, with $^{+}$ to terminate the addition, where necessary .

– A superior V precedes text in Voltaire's hand, W indicating that of Wagnière.
– A pair of slashes // indicates the end of a paragraph or other section of text.

Thus, 'il ⟨allait⟩ W↑⟨courait⟩+ donc V↓β' indicates that 'allait' was deleted, that Wagnière added 'courait' over the line, that 'courait' was deleted and that Voltaire inserted the reading of the base text below the line. The notation 'W75G* (→K)' indicates that a manuscript correction to the *encadrée* edition was followed in the Kehl editions.

PREFACE

1760 was as busy a year as any in Voltaire's literary career – too busy, he frequently complains in the course of his voluminous correspondence that year, which comprises more than 800 letters. It saw the first publication of only one older work, the *Histoire d'un bon bramin*, written a few months earlier. Much of his energy clearly went into the creation of the works included in this volume and the one that follows it: many of them directly related to the polemics of the moment, and printed as soon as ready. These writings however represent little more than the tip of the iceberg of his literary activities during the year. What follows is an attempt to indicate the outlines of what lay below the public surface, visible only at times to certain of his correspondents.

To begin with the theatre, Voltaire was working this year on four other plays in addition to *L'Ecossaise* and *Le Droit du seigneur*. There are references in May and June to revision of *Socrate*, published the previous year (D8933, 8951, 8959, 8972). In the autumn he similarly returned to *Oreste*, of ten years earlier (D9346, 9370, 9408), and sent d'Argental a new version on 22 December (D9485), which was published in 1761. The greater part of his theatrical energies, however, were devoted to *Zulime*, mostly referred to at this date as either *Médime* or, more frequently, *Fanime*; and above all to *Tancrède*. The former tragedy (see Voltaire 18), first performed in 1740, was revised, and staged in Voltaire's private theatre at Tournay in the autumn (D9236, 9317), then further revised in November and December (D9425, 9485); he was still dissatisfied with the play in June 1761 (D9820), and much distressed by the appearance in Paris in that month of an unauthorised edition (D9840, 9843). *Tancrède*, substantially conceived in 1759 (see Voltaire 49), first produced at the Comédie-Française on 3 September 1760 and published early in 1761, is the subject of constant discussion in correspondence with the d'Argentals from March onwards, with numerous proposals for emending the text and much evidence of concern about the details of the stage presentation (28 references in letters between 3 March and 22 December, D8785-D9485).

La Pucelle was not neglected: two extra cantos (now VIII and XXI) were sent in April to d'Argental (D8836) and to the Elector Palatine (D8893). And later in the year there is evidence that Voltaire may for a time have contemplated a new burlesque epic ridiculing the *anti-philosophes*, in the manner of Pope's *Dunciad*: in July he mentions the idea to Thiriot, and asks him (D9044) and d'Alembert (D9047) for relevant information and suitable anecdotes about their common foes. This ambitious scheme, however, seems to have turned into what Voltaire calls later in the year 'la capilotade'; in early January 1761 he announces to d'Alembert that this piece, now ready, will form a new canto of *La Pucelle*, 'par voie de prophétie' (D9523). It duly figured, as canto XVIII, in the 1773 edition, after having appeared in 1764 in the *Contes de Guillaume Vadé* as a 'chant détaché d'un poème épique, de la composition de Jérôme Carré'.

Two historical works bulk large. The *Essai sur les mœurs* is in course of revision for Cramer's new edition of 1761, with ten additional chapters written by August 1760, apparently (D9159). And throughout the year, as well as struggling with official obstructions and practical difficulties over the circulation of the first volume of his *Histoire de l'empire de Russie sous Pierre le Grand*, printed in 1759, he is at work on the second volume, requesting additional memoranda and documentation at frequent intervals from his Russian correspondents (it did not appear until 1763).

Voltaire's contributions to alphabetical works also figure. There is a mention of his articles for the *Encyclopédie* in January (D8702), and references to work destined for his own *Dictionnaire philosophique* in February and later (D8764, 8816, 8859, 8911). And August sees Voltaire agreeing to assist in the project of a new *Dictionnaire de l'Académie*, by providing part of the entries for the letter *T* (D9135, 9289), and committing himself to having his copy ready by the end of the year (D9340, 9423).

Finally, mention must be made of two 'lettres ostensibles',

written by Voltaire in 1760, but published in this edition with the texts to which they relate: the *Lettre civile et honnête, à l'auteur malhonnête de la 'Critique de l'histoire universelle'*, a reply to an attack on an early version of the *Essai sur les mœurs* (Voltaire 27); and the *Lettre de monsieur de Voltaire, sur plusieurs sujets intéressants, adressée à monsieur le marquis Albergati Capacelli, sénateur de Bologne*, which Voltaire himself included in the first authorised edition of *Tancrède*, 1761.

W. H. B.

Le Droit du seigneur

critical edition

by

W. D. Howarth

INTRODUCTION

Le Droit du seigneur was performed at the Comédie-Française (under the title *L'Ecueil du sage*) in 1762, and published in 1763. It was written quickly – in a fortnight, if Voltaire's own claim is to be taken literally (D8933, D8959) – during the early months of 1760. Its style and theme link the play to earlier sentimental comedies like *Nanine* (1749), with which it also has in common the decasyllabic verse-form; and the playwright can be seen once more paying practical tribute to the *larmoyant* fashion which, although he affected to despise it,[1] he never ceased to attempt to exploit to his own advantage.[2] At the same time, however, he chose for his new play a subject with a definite polemical interest: an interest that he had himself done more than any of his contemporaries to foster; and it is this fact that puts *Le Droit du seigneur* into a somewhat different category, lending it – ostensibly, at any rate – a propaganda value that his other comedies do not possess.

1. *The 'jus primae noctis' before Voltaire*

The so-called *jus primae noctis*, the overlord's right to the first night with his vassal's bride, which provides the starting-point not only for Voltaire's play but also for a much more distinguished comedy by Beaumarchais, is almost certainly a myth with no historical

[1] 'La Comédie larmoyante, qui, à la honte de la nation, a succédé au seul vrai genre comique, porté à sa perfection par l'inimitable Molière' (to Sumarokov, 26 February 1769; D15488).

[2] See L. Willens, *Voltaire's comic theatre: composition, conflict and critics*, Studies 136 (1975), especially chapters 1 and 4.

foundation.[3] Nevertheless, it has exercised a strong appeal to the imagination of the credulous, from the Renaissance down to the twentieth century, and in the eighteenth and nineteenth centuries it became the subject of some violently partisan propaganda.

In order to explain the origins, and account for the vogue, of this bizarre belief it may perhaps not be necessary to explore the parallel, much loved by anthropologists, with the custom of ritual defloration reported by travellers to various parts of the globe as a feature of the marriage-rites of primitive peoples. On the other hand, such accounts were quite common in the sixteenth century (for a second-hand version of one of them, see Montaigne's essay 'De la coutume et de ne changer aisément une loi reçue'[4]), and it can be shown that a passage describing the marriage-ceremonies of ancient Peru was the source of the first known use of the motif of the *jus primae noctis* in imaginative literature. For it appears in 1617 in Cervantes' novel *Persiles y Sigismunda*, and thence was borrowed by Fletcher and Massinger for their play *The Custom of the country* (1622).[5] Cervantes, however, had stayed close enough to his source to retain the notion of 'multiple' defloration by the male wedding-guests (even though he transposed the Peruvian custom into a European setting), and it was Fletcher who took the decisive step of changing the custom into a 'droit du seigneur' vested in an individual. It may well be that the disclaimer contained in the preface:

> No lord nor lady have we taxed; nor state
> Nor any private person

indicates Fletcher's own scepticism about the authenticity of such a custom; but it seems legitimate to assume from his willingness

[3] See my article, '*Droit du seigneur*: fact or fantasy?', *Journal of European studies* 1 (1971), p.291-312. The most detailed and comprehensive treatment of the subject remains K. Schmidt, *Jus primae noctis: eine geschichtliche Untersuchung* (Freiburg im Breisgau 1881).

[4] *Essais*, I.xxiii; ed. Pléiade [1958], p.140.

[5] See my article, 'Cervantes and Fletcher: a theme with variations', *Mlr* 56 (1961), p.563-66.

to exploit it as a plot-motif that the legend already had a certain currency in the form in which he presents it: that is, the overlord's right to the first night with his vassal's bride, which had at some stage been commuted into a money payment.

And indeed, there is ample evidence that by the end of the sixteenth century belief in the factual existence of the *jus primae noctis* (always situated in the past, and usually in a location geographically remote) was current in several European countries. The principal source for such a belief can be identified as a history of the early kings of Scotland, published in 1526 by Hector Boece (Boethius), whose fanciful account attributes to Evenus III various acts of debauchery and vice, including the conferring of the *jus* on his nobles. Having remained in force for a thousand years, says Boethius, the practice was commuted into a money payment called *mercheta mulierum*; and his explanation of these feudal dues was repeated by later authorities, almost without question, for over two centuries. Boswell's *Journal of a tour to the Hebrides* (1785), for instance, still gives the same explanation of the *mercheta*, linking it with the custom known as Borough English 'by which the eldest child does not inherit, from a doubt of his being a son of the tenant'.[6] There is, of course, a perfectly acceptable alternative explanation of the *mercheta*, and of similar customs located elsewhere in Europe: namely the fact that under the feudal system the children of a serf were the overlord's property, and when they married and left his domains, he was entitled to compensation for loss of their services. This fee can be seen as deriving directly from the conditions of serfdom, and there is no evidence that its derivation from an iniquitous seigneurial right was ever anything more than a gratuitous flight of fancy.

In France, the earliest mentions of the *jus primae noctis* occur in the sixteenth century, some locating it in various parts of France, though the most circumstantial accounts tend to follow Boethius

[6] Ed. R. W. Chapman (Oxford 1924), p.129.

and situate it in Scotland. The legal historian Jean Papon in his *Recueil d'arrêts notables des cours souveraines de France* (Lyon 1568) and Antoine Du Verdier in his *Diverses leçons* (Lyon 1577) provide important links in the transmission of belief in the existence of the custom; and Du Verdier's text (p.89) already gives the key to the inordinate interest that eighteenth-century *philosophes* were to take in the subject:

Je me suis laissé dire qu'il n'y a pas longtemps, qu'aucuns seigneurs mêmes ecclésiastiques avaient droit par ancienne coutume de mettre une jambe dans le lit où couchait l'épousée la première nuit de ses noces. Il y en eut un lequel voulant outrepasser les limites de son devoir, et abuser de son privilège, poussé d'une effrénée lubricité fit perdre cette coutume au prix de sa vie.

Where Montaigne and most other sixteenth-century collectors of human eccentricities had seen merely another bizarre example of the unpredictable variety of human behaviour, and where Furetière[7] and Bayle[8] found material for a display of curious erudition, Voltaire and his contemporaries were to pay the custom a very different kind of attention. In their eyes, it was no longer an idle curiosity, but the very symbol of an inhuman system of power and privilege – particularly, for Voltaire, of the perversion of ecclesiastical power. For a large number of the medieval documents that had now been brought to light, and could be interpreted as supporting the authenticity of the *jus primae noctis*, dealt with money payments, similar to the *mercheta mulierum* but payable to the ecclesiastical authorities. This fact, like the existence of the *mercheta*, has a much more prosaic explanation, since such payments represent an indulgence, or dispensation from the ecclesiastical ban, occasionally and locally enforced, on the consummation of a marriage on the first night after the ceremony. This ban, originally ordained by the Council of Carthage in 298, was said to derive its justification from a passage in the Book of Tobit (chapter 8) dealing with the marriage of Tobias:

[7] *Dictionnaire universel* (La Haye, Rotterdam 1690), *s.v.* 'Dépuceler'.
[8] *Dictionnaire historique et critique* (Rotterdam 1697), *s.v.* 'Sixte IV', note H.

After they were both shut in together, Tobias rose up from the bed, and said, Sister, arise, and let us pray that the Lord may have mercy on us [...] O Lord, I take not this my sister for lust, but in truth: command that I may find mercy and grow old with her. And she said with him, Amen. And they slept both that night.

Whenever this prohibition was renewed throughout the Middle Ages, bishops and abbots were found who were willing to sell indulgences. Any document in which such a dispensation was regularised, and the injunction waived in favour of a money payment, naturally lent itself to the same sort of misinterpretation as those requiring payment to a secular overlord; but the fact is that 'mener la mariée au moustier' had a less sinister significance than many eighteenth-century writers were willing to see in it.

This alternative explanation of such practices was already current at the time at which Voltaire was writing. Boucher d'Argis, for instance, the author of the two articles in the *Encyclopédie* in which the topic is dealt with ('Culage, Cullage ou Culiage' and 'Droit', sub-heading 'Droits abusifs'), while expressing moral indignation at the existence of the 'droits, même honteux et injustes [...] tels que la coutume infâme qui donnait à [certains] seigneurs la première nuit des nouvelles mariées', is able at the same time to write:

On voit encore plusieurs seigneurs en France et ailleurs, auxquels il est dû un droit en argent pour le mariage de leurs sujets; lequel droit pourrait bien avoir la même origine que celui de culage. Mais il y en a beaucoup aussi qui perçoivent ces droits seulement à cause que leurs sujets ne pouvaient autrefois se marier sans leur permission, comme sont encore les serfs et mortaillables dans certaines coutumes.

L'évêque d'Amiens exigeait aussi autrefois un droit des nouveaux mariés, mais c'était pour leur donner congé de coucher avec leurs femmes la première, seconde et troisième nuits de leurs noces. (iv.548)

Montesquieu, for his part, does not seem to have been taken in by the legend, and his witticism on the subject is typical enough of the writer and his age:

On ne pouvait pas coucher ensemble la première nuit des noces, ni même les deux suivantes, sans en avoir acheté la permission: c'était bien ces trois nuits-là qu'il fallait choisir; car, pour les autres, on n'aurait pas donné beaucoup d'argent.[9]

For Voltaire, on the other hand, the *jus primae noctis* was a subject that could not simply be dismissed with a *bon mot*: his attitude to the custom represents a completely different aspect of Enlightenment thought, and he can be seen returning to it almost obsessively during the years immediately preceding and following the appearance of *Le Droit du seigneur*.

2. *Voltaire and the 'jus primae noctis'*

Nevertheless, when we come to examine Voltaire's treatment of the subject in detail, there is a clear distinction to be drawn between the way in which it is handled in the historical or polemical writings, and the tone of certain comments in private references to his friends. In his public utterances, Voltaire displays the same moral indignation as we have seen in the case of Boucher d'Argis, with no sign of the encyclopaedist's recognition that some at any rate of the documentary evidence under discussion may have related to quite different practices; in his letters, on the other hand, the prevailing tone is a cavalier matter-of-factness, with an occasional flippancy which seems to belie the moral earnestness of the references elsewhere.

The first mention is in the *Essai sur les mœurs* (1756), in a passage dealing with examples of thirteenth-century anarchy and brigandage:

Les usages les plus ridicules et les plus barbares étaient alors établis. Les seigneurs avaient imaginé le droit de cuissage, de marquette, de prélibation; c'était celui de coucher la première nuit avec les nouvelles mariées leurs vassales roturières. Des évêques, des abbés, eurent ce

[9] *De l'esprit des lois*, xxviii, 41.

droit en qualité de hauts barons; et quelques-uns se sont fait payer, au dernier siècle, par leurs sujets, la renonciation à ce droit étrange, qui s'étendit en Ecosse, en Lombardie, en Allemagne, et dans les provinces de France. Voilà les mœurs qui régnaient dans le temps des croisades. (*Essai*, i.543)

The last sentence demonstrates clearly enough why the *droit du seigneur* has been included in this chapter: it fits into Voltaire's picture of the Middle Ages darkened by violence and crime to which the Church was a party. Earlier in the same chapter he shows that 'les croisades, les persécutions contre les Albigeois, épuisaient toujours l'Europe [...] la querelle de la couronne impériale et de la mitre de Rome, [...] les haines des Allemands et des Italiens, troublaient le monde plus que jamais', and in citing the *droit du seigneur* as a particular iniquity he seems to be saying: *this* is the Christendom that our crusaders were defending.

In default of more precise evidence as to the dating of specific articles that were to appear in Voltaire's alphabetical writings, we may perhaps reasonably assume that the articles in which the subject of the *jus primae noctis* recurs are roughly contemporary with the writing and performance of *Le Droit du seigneur*. (This is certainly the case with the handful of references to the custom in the correspondence). An article in the *Questions sur l'Encyclopédie*, 'Cuissage ou culage', insists dogmatically on the existence of the *jus* in the Middle Ages, with no supporting evidence beyond the vaguest of references to the supposed Scottish origins:

Il est étonnant que dans l'Europe chrétienne on ait fait très longtemps une espèce de loi féodale, et que du moins on ait regardé comme un droit coutumier, l'usage d'avoir le pucelage de sa vassale. La première nuit des noces de la fille au vilain appartenait sans contredit au seigneur [...] On prétend que cette jurisprudence commença en Ecosse; je le croirais volontiers: les seigneurs écossais avaient un pouvoir encore plus absolu sur leurs clans que les barons allemands et français sur leurs sujets. Il est indubitable que des abbés, des évêques s'attribuèrent cette prérogative en qualité de seigneurs temporels: et il n'y a pas bien longtemps que des prélats se sont désistés de cet ancien privilège pour des redevances en argent, auxquelles ils avaient autant de droit qu'aux pucelages des filles. (M.xviii.300)

However, the purpose of this article becomes clear in the following paragraphs; it is to proclaim, apropos of the so-called *droit du seigneur*, a favourite principle of Voltaire's: 'qu'il n'y a jamais eu de peuple un peu civilisé qui ait établi des lois formelles contre les mœurs [...] Des abus s'établissent, on les tolère; ils passent en coutume; les voyageurs les prennent pour des lois fondamentales'. The 'droit de cuissage', then, was an 'excès de tyrannie [qui] ne fut jamais approuvé par aucune loi publique'. And the article concludes with a stirring profession of rationalist faith: 'Des lois absurdes, ridicules, barbares, vous en trouverez partout; des lois contre les mœurs, nulle part'.

Throughout the article 'Taxe', Voltaire attempts to give his argument a basis of documentary evidence; but in the case of those paragraphs dealing with the *jus primae noctis*, this only serves to show up the more clearly his prejudice and lack of scholarly method:

> Un arrêt du parlement de Paris, du 19 mai 1409, rendu à la poursuite des habitants et échevins d'Abbeville, porte que chacun pourra coucher avec sa femme sitôt après la célébration du mariage, sans attendre le congé de l'évêque d'Amiens, et sans payer le droit qu'exigeait ce prélat pour lever la défense qu'il avait faite de consommer le mariage les trois premières nuits des noces [...] Quelques théologiens ont prétendu que cela était fondé sur le quatrième concile de Carthage, qui l'avait ordonné pour la révérence de la bénédiction matrimoniale. Mais comme ce concile n'avait point ordonné d'éluder sa défense en payant, il est plus vraisemblable que cette taxe était une suite de la coutume infâme qui donnait à certains seigneurs la première nuit des nouvelles mariées de leurs vassaux. Buchanan croit que cet usage avait commencé en Ecosse, sous le roi Even.[10]

[10] M.xx.488; first published in the Kehl edition. It seems plausible to suppose that another of the examples quoted ('Les seigneurs de Prelley et de Parsanny en Piémont appelaient ce droit *carragio*') supplied Voltaire with the name of the hero of *Le Droit du seigneur*, le Marquis du Carrage.

'Quand nos prélats eurent des fiefs', says Voltaire, 'ils crurent avoir comme évêques ce qu'ils n'avaient que comme seigneurs'. However valid this remark might be in other contexts, in this instance the alternative explanation of the origin of the indulgences seems to be rejected out of hand for no other reason than that the issue has been prejudged.

Voltaire returns to the subject in chapter 2 of the *Défense de mon oncle* (1767), 'Apologie des dames de Babylone'. Rejecting Herodotus's account of ritual prostitution (according to which every Babylonian woman was required to give herself once in her lifetime to a stranger), he declares that if the author of the *Supplément à la Philosophie de l'histoire* (to which the *Défense* is a reply) was looking for customs of that nature:

S'il avait voulu justifier la paillardise par de grands exemples, il aurait pu choisir ce fameux droit de prélibation, de marquette, de jambage, de cuissage, que quelques seigneurs de châteaux s'étaient arrogé dans la chrétienté, dans le commencement du beau gouvernement féodal. Des barons, des évêques, des abbés devinrent législateurs, et ordonnèrent que dans tous les mariages autour de leurs châteaux, la première nuit des noces serait pour eux. Il est bien difficile de savoir jusqu'où ils poussaient leur législation, s'ils se contentaient de mettre une cuisse dans le lit de la mariée [...] ou s'ils y mettaient les deux cuisses. Mais ce qui est avéré, c'est que ce droit de cuissage qui était d'abord un droit de guerre, a été vendu enfin aux vassaux par les seigneurs soit séculiers soit réguliers, qui ont sagement compris qu'ils pourraient avec l'argent de ce rachat avoir des filles plus jolies. (Voltaire 64, p.200-201)

Once again, no doubt is cast on the authenticity of the custom, and this is all the more striking by contrast with Voltaire's scepticism with regard to Herodotus. The reason is clear enough: to believe Herodotus would be an outrage to human nature – 'le faiseur de contes Hérodote a pu amuser les Grecs de cette extravagance; mais nul homme sensé n'a dû le croire' (Voltaire 64, p.198) – whereas the tradition of the *jus primae noctis* receives ready acceptance as one more stick with which to beat the feudal system.

To sum up, these references show a complete absence of

the critical caution that Voltaire elsewhere commends to the historian,[11] and of the scholarly method that he himself not infrequently makes a praiseworthy effort to observe.[12] It seems difficult not to conclude that in writing on this topic, the historian in him gave way to the propagandist – an impression that is reinforced when we come to compare the passages quoted with references to the custom in his private correspondence.

For when writing to his friends, Voltaire never seems to take the subject very seriously. There are, as we shall see, certain aspects of his play about which he held strong views, but these do not appear to have included the custom which provided its *point de départ*. Although he may urge Damilaville to press the actors to restore the original title, *Le Droit du seigneur*, alongside the one they had substituted (*L'Ecueil du sage*), 'car les Bellecours[13] et ejusdem farinae homines ne savent pas qu'autrefois les seigneurs séculiers et prêtres avaient dans leurs domaines le droit de cuissage, le droit de prélibation[14]', he rather gives the game away by explaining that 'cette partie du sujet ignorée des comédiens perd de son piquant aux yeux de ceux qui n'en sont pas instruits' (D9887). Similarly, in confessing to Albergati that he is the author of a play 'dont le sujet est le droit qu'avaient autrefois les seigneurs de coucher avec les nouvelles mariées le premier soir de leurs noces', his only recommendation of the play is that it contains 'du comique et de l'intérêt' (D10303). In other letters, the tone becomes positively jocular. He writes to Chauvelin:

> Le titre [*Le Droit du seigneur*] en est beau, je l'avoue, mais je tiens avec vous monsieur l'ambassadeur qu'il vaut mieux être possesseur de madame de Chauvelin que d'avoir le droit des prémices de touttes les filles de village. (D10808)

[11] See for instance *Questions sur l'Encyclopédie*, article 'Vérité', subheading 'Vérité historique' (M.xx.558-61).

[12] E.g. in *Le Pyrrhonisme de l'histoire*, or in other parts of *La Défense de mon oncle*.

[13] The actor Gilles Colson was called Bellecour.

[14] Misprinted as 'prélitation' in D9887.

and to the d'Argentals, referring to a possible revival of the play:

Je serai fort aise qu'on jouât le droit du seigneur, quoique je ne sois guère homme à jouir d'un si beau droit. Vous pensez bien que je ne connais mad[lle] d'Epinay que par le droit que les premiers gentilshommes ont sur les actrices. Pour mes anges ils ont des droits inviolables sur mon cœur pour jamais. (D11714)

Finally, in a letter to Richelieu, written at the time of the 1762 publication, there are references which must seem remarkably cynical when compared with the moral earnestness Voltaire showed on the same topic when he was writing for publication:

Je vous exhorte à voir le droit du seigneur qu'on a sottement appellé l'écueil du sage. On dit qu'on en a retranché beaucoup de bonnes plaisanteries, mais qu'il en reste assez pour amuser le seigneur de France qui a le plus usé de ce beau droit [...] Je vous avertis que mademoiselle Corneille est une laidron extrêmement piquante et que si vous voulez jouir du droit du seigneur avant qu'on la marie, il faut faire un petit tour aux Délices. (D10288)

It may well be the case that a certain ambivalence in Voltaire's attitude, revealed in this contrast between his public and his private writings on the subject of the *jus primae noctis*, helps to explain the feebleness of *Le Droit du seigneur* from the didactic, or polemical, point of view; for the play is remarkably anodyne when compared with the uncompromising vigour of the passages from the *Essai sur les mœurs*, the *Questions sur l'Encyclopédie* and the *Défense de mon oncle*. However, it must be remembered that the theme expressed in the title was only one aspect of the play, which was conceived as a sentimental comedy, not as a *drame* (and still less as a *pièce à thèse* in the manner of Dumas *fils*); and that in any case, in writing for the theatre, Voltaire was subject to certain constraints which necessarily diluted the force of any propagandist message. It goes without saying that it would have been impossible for a playwright writing in 1760 to portray the sufferings of a young bride actually forced to submit to the outrage of the *jus primae noctis*; and we may be equally certain that the censor would have objected to any suggestion of an ecclesiastical, rather than a temporal, overlord attempting to exercise the custom. Inevitably, therefore, Voltaire was thrown back, as Beaumarchais was to be in his turn, on a treatment of the *droit du seigneur* that made of it little more than a mechanical plot-device. In Voltaire's play, indeed, it does not even serve (as it does in *Le Mariage de Figaro*) as a variant on the conventional obstacle separating the lovers, since the author represents the custom as having been commuted into a harmless ceremonial. From the point of view of plot, the *jus primae noctis*, in its bowdlerised form, serves to get Voltaire's play under way, and that is all.

3. *The 'jus primae noctis' and the eighteenth-century theatre*

The earliest reference to the theme that has been discovered in French imaginative literature is in Dufresny's *La Noce interrompue* (1699) where, although the custom cannot be said to contribute to the plot, explicit mention is made of it in the closing *couplets*:

> L'honneur et le premier hommage
> Sont dûs par l'habitant au seigneur du village
> Mais par malheur il exige souvent
> De l'habitante la plus sage
> L'honneur et le premier hommage.

This is followed by *Le Droit du seigneur*, an anonymous play of 1732 of which the manuscript bears the subtitle 'Comédie en un acte pour les Comédiens Français, année 1732' (Bn F9295), though it appears neither to have been performed at that theatre nor to have been published. In scene 9, Eraste's valet opens his master's eyes to a threat to the latter's love for Henriette:

La Brie: J'ai tout découvert. Mr votre père a trouvé dans ses archives qu'autrefois dans de certains pays, le seigneur d'un village quand son vassal se mariait... le seigneur, le premier jour de ses noces... m'entendez-vous?

Eraste: Point du tout.
La Brie: Je m'explique. Mathurin est vassal de votre père. Ce soir il épouse Henriette, ils sont convenus ensemble qu'après la cérémonie le vassal pour cent pistoles céderait...
Eraste: N'achève pas. Il faut que la cervelle lui ait tourné.

This slight work has one considerable claim on our interest, since its title provides the first traceable instance of the use of the formula 'le droit du seigneur' as a name for the custom. It is nowhere found in documents, and seems to have been an eighteenth-century invention;[15] compared with the picturesque names used by the historians ('cuissage', 'culage', 'jambage' and the like), its decorousness made it eminently suitable for use in a theatre subject to the censor and Voltaire's play is one of at least five that were produced during the period 1730-1785 with the same title.[16] Apart from the anonymous one-acter just mentioned, the others are: *Le Droit du seigneur ou le mari retrouvé et la femme fidèle* by L. de Boissy, a one-act parody of Le Blanc's tragedy *Aben-saïd* performed at the Foire Saint-Laurent in 1735 (Bn F9322); a lost one-act *Le Droit du seigneur* by P. J. B. Nougaret, performed in the provinces in 1763; and finally *Le Droit du seigneur, comédie en trois actes mêlée d'ariettes* by Desfontaines. This last play, performed at Fontainebleau in 1783 and published at Paris in the same year, was still being played half a century later.[17]

In addition to these specific links with a tradition of theatrical

[15] '*Droit du seigneur* est un non-sens qui ne peut être employé [...] Il n'y en a nulle trace dans aucun texte', A. de Barthélemy, 'Le droit du seigneur', *Revue des questions historiques* 1 (1866), p.102. In the nineteenth century, Louis Veuillot was to advance the fanciful explanation that the title could be accounted for by deriving it from the ecclesiastical ban on immediate consummation of marriage, which he suggests was known as 'le droit du Seigneur (Dieu)'. See L. Veuillot, *Le Droit du seigneur au Moyen Age* (Paris 1854), p.137ff.

[16] See C. D. Brenner, *A bibliographical list of plays in the French language, 1700-1789* (New York 1979).

[17] For a more detailed discussion of these and other plays, see my article 'The theme of the "droit du seigneur" in the eighteenth-century theatre', *French studies* 15 (1961), p.228-39.

versions of the *droit du seigneur* theme, Voltaire's play can be related to a more widespread fictional motif common in the eighteenth century: that of a love-match between an enlightened member of the nobility and a member of the lower classes – a theme to which the publication of the French translation of Richardson's *Pamela* in 1741 had given a considerable impetus. Voltaire had himself, of course, in his *Nanine* (1749), adopted this theme of 'le préjugé vaincu', in spite of his clearly expressed disapproval of both Richardson[18] and La Chaussée (see D10287, D10289), whose version of *Pamela* had been given only one performance at the Comédie-Française in 1743. In the earliest mentions of *Le Droit du seigneur* in correspondence with his friends, we find him keen to stress that the new play is not just another variation on the same theme: 'Il [the author] n'y voit pas la moindre ressemblance avec Nanine' (D8972).[19] In fact, the central situation is very close to that of the earlier play, and the relationship between the Marquis and Acante is a copy of that between the Comte d'Olban and Nanine: both noblemen are enlightened in matters of class, paternalistic towards the respective heroines; while the heroines themselves are both well educated (Acante is an enthusiastic, but discriminating, reader of novels, while Nanine seems to have read *Pamela* in the original), and both have been 'formed' by the particular attentions of a lady of quality. But here the similarity stops – and insofar as fictional representation of noblemen in love defying the conventions possessed any power at all to persuade, it must be said that the example of Nanine's lover is a good deal more positive than that of the hero of *Le Droit du seigneur*. For in *Nanine* the heroine really is of humble – though 'honnête' – parentage; whereas the denouement of the later play establishes that Acante, if of illegitimate birth,[20] is

[18] See D8846 (where *Clarissa Harlowe* is described as 'neuf volumes entiers, dans lesquels on ne trouve rien du tout') and D14179.

[19] See also D8880, D8959, D9451.

[20] The details are not very clear. We are told that Acante's mother Laure 'crut l'hymen légitime' (IV.ix.346); and although the use of the phrase 'faire casser l'hymen' (IV.ix.375-376) might suggest a legal marriage subsequently

nevertheless descended from the same noble line as the Marquis himself. In other words, where the final scene of *Nanine* had shown a willingness on the hero's part to defy convention that was just as unequivocal as the attitude to which Richardson had finally brought his hero, in *Le Droit du seigneur* the social issue is badly blurred, and prejudice is not so much overcome as sidestepped.

By the same token, any social message implicit in the theme of the *droit du seigneur* itself is completely invalidated by the way the subject is treated. The custom has been 'civilised', and is now quite innocuous: the tyrannical abuse of power has been reduced to a fifteen-minute interview of an improving character (see I.i.83-86; III.iv.228ff).[21] Even the Chevalier's attempt to kidnap Acante – an action for which we are invited to blame headstrong youth rather than aristocratic corruption[22] – is more than outweighed by the idealised example of the enlightened Marquis. Beaumarchais was to make much more tendentious use of the *droit*, by showing Almaviva as a despotic overlord trying to exploit his privilege in order to have his way with Suzanne; moreover, *Le Mariage de Figaro* presents a class struggle in simple terms of right and wrong.

dissolved, elsewhere it is stated that 'l'amant de Laure' (IV.viii.328) 'la trompa' (IV.ix.347), and that the marriage was 'un hymen que réprouvent nos lois' (IV.viii.324). The three-act version of the play is even more cryptic, the above references being replaced by the couplet: 'Et mes parents par un zèle inhumain / Avaient puni cet hymen clandestin' (III.525-26). A propos of this passage, Flaubert was to complain: 'Jamais d'adultère, toujours le mariage secret' (*Le Théâtre de Voltaire*, Studies 50-51, 1967, ii.632); but as Maurice Descotes has shown, at this time 'il reste rigoureusement interdit de présenter un adultère [...], interdit d'évoquer des rapports charnels entre deux personnes non mariées: ainsi s'explique dans la dramaturgie du XVIIIe siècle la fréquence du 'mariage secret': il est une convention bienséante pour désigner, tout simplement, une liaison' (*Le Public de théâtre et son histoire*, Paris 1964, p.182-83).

[21] This is evidently the origin of Beaumarchais's 'certain quart d'heure, seul à seule' (*Le Mariage de Figaro*, I.i).

[22] In fact the Chevalier, with his self-satisfied manner and complete lack of principle, contributes the only realistic touch to the play: the scene with Champagne in which the abduction of Acante is planned (II.vi) is – stilted language apart – all too credible.

The egalitarian tirades spoken by Mathurin are something grafted on to Voltaire's play as an *hors d'œuvre*; and in any case they are tame indeed, compared with Figaro's act 5 soliloquy some twenty years later. As for Voltaire's idealised aristocrat, and the conversion of his repentant libertine, these are clichés representing the sentimental humanitarianism of the age; and to include *Le Droit du seigneur* among the plays of the period 1759-1767 which 'reflect the militancy of his works in general'[23] seems to be very wide of the mark. Voltaire's own comment in a letter of 1763 (D11042) is a good deal more perceptive:

J'aime assez le droit du seigneur, je vous l'avoue; mais je voudrais qu'il y eût un peu plus de ces honnêtes libertés que le sujet comporte, et que les femmes aiment beaucoup quoi qu'elles disent.

Contemporaries looking for audacities of any sort must have found the play disappointingly tame. Indeed, writing in the following year, Voltaire does not even pretend to have been motivated by the provocative nature of the subject: *Le Droit du seigneur* is one of the plays, he tells the d'Argentals, that his friends have constantly forced him to write for the amusement of Paris audiences: 'c'est vous qui avez fait l'orphelin de la Chine, Tancrède, le droit du seigneur, Olimpie et les Rouez' (D11799).[24]

4. *Genesis and composition*

It seems from the first mentions in correspondence with d'Argental that the play was finished in April 1760; and from the beginning Voltaire was concerned to weave a web of *mystification* round it. It was 'une pièce de Jodele ajustée par un petit Hurtaud' (D8845),

[23] Willens, *Voltaire's comic theatre*, p.123.

[24] On the subject of eighteenth-century drama as an expression of *philosophe* propaganda, see my article 'The playwright as preacher: didacticism and melodrama in the French theatre of the Enlightenment', *Forum for modern language studies* 14 (1978), p.97-115.

and nobody must suspect Voltaire's hand in the matter. Reactions from the d'Argentals were lukewarm to begin with: as well as considering the situation a copy of that presented in *Nanine*, a view that Voltaire energetically contested (D8959, D8972, D9451), they evidently found weaknesses in the third, fourth and fifth acts; on the latter score, Voltaire excused himself on the grounds of hasty composition, and promised to rewrite the offending passages:

On pourrait rendre le droit du seigneur très intéressant au 3e acte. Cette pièce fut jetée en sable, elle n'a jamais coûté que quinze jours. (D8933)

N'abandonnons point le droit de cuissage. Il me semble qu'on en peut faire quelque chose de très intéressant. Le 4 et le 5 étaient à la glace mais en quinze jours on ne peut avoir un feu égal dans son fournau. (D8959)

Later letters, up to the early months of 1761, analyse the characters and relationships of the new play in an attempt to convert his friends, to whom Voltaire writes in February 1761 that Mme Denis is 'toujours folle du droit du seigneur' (D9630). In March 1761 a series of letters develops the idea behind the false attribution of authorship. Not only, it appears, is Voltaire anxious (as will emerge later) about the treatment *Le Droit du seigneur* may receive at the hands of the Comédie-Française if he is known to be its author,[25] he also plans to benefit 'une personne de mérite qui est dans la pauvreté', he tells the d'Argentals (D9706); and the same day he writes to Octavie Belot, the person in question:

Madame, vous n'ètes pas riche, voicy ce que j'ay imaginé [...] Un jeune magistrat de Dijon a fait une comédie; et il veut être ignoré à cause des fleurs de lis et de la grave sottise de Mr son père le président [...] On vous fera tenir la pièce. Vous partagerez les honoraires de la représentation et de L'impression. Je crois que la comédie aura du succez. (D9707)

In April, Thiriot is enlisted to present the play to the Comédie-

[25] And also that the reception of his *tragedies* might suffer (to Mlle Clairon, 27 August 1761; D9973).

Française as the work of 'un magistrat de Dijon, jeune et de baucoup d'esprit' (D9747); and in May Voltaire is still trying to persuade the d'Argentals, assuring them of considerable changes from the text they had first seen (D9765). By mid-June, to his great pleasure, they have relented and approved the play (D9820), which Voltaire now insists is by 'un homme de l'Académie de Dijon' (D9823 to Damilaville) – the sole element of truth in all this *mystification*, since Voltaire himself had recently become a member of that body (D9823, note).

In August 1761 the author is for the first time named as 'Mr le Goust, jeune maître des comptes de Dijon, et de plus académicien de Dijon' (D9964); but by the following month Voltaire has rejected this name in favour of Picardet, on learning that there was a real Le Goust (D9991);[26] and this choice, or its variant Picardin (e.g. D10008) remains the definitive *nom de plume*, with the curious exception of a passing reference to the supposed authorship of Mellin de Saint-Gelais (D10039).

As regards the reception of the play by the censor and the *comédiens* Voltaire himself volunteers certain objections. In the very first letter referring to the play, for instance, he writes that he expects the censor to object to the use of the word 'sacrement' (D8845): he was later to substitute the term 'engagement'.[27] Again, he feels (D9823) that certain 'jeunes demoiselles' might blush at hearing the Bailli ask Colette if she is pregnant: 'je prierai mon Dijonnais d'adoucir l'interrogatoire'.[28] But once negotiations begin with the Comédie-Française – the play was read to the *comité de lecture* in August 1761 (D9973, dated 27 August) and

[26] This is somewhat puzzling, for not only had Voltaire earlier taken steps to find the name of a genuine lawyer at Dijon (D9823), but it seems that Picardin was equally real (D9991).

[27] Although the substitution, at line 57 of act 1, is made in MS1 (in Crébillon's hand), it does not seem to have been adopted in any printed text.

[28] See act 2, scene 1 for evidence of a slight modification of the text at this point.

again, with textual changes, on 9 October[29] – he expresses repeated concern that his text may be subjected to unauthorised changes, either for reasons of taste (as with the substitution of the title *L'Ecueil du sage*, which he pleads with Damilaville to get reversed; D9887), or because of the actors' vanity: 'Mad^elle^ Dangeville est fâchée que son rôle de Colette ne soit pas le premier rôle. On aura de la peine à l'appaiser' (D9925). In the latter instance he found it politic to add some extra lines (D9931); and on 24 August 1761 he writes to both d'Argental and Damilaville (D9964, D9965), enclosing an additional passage for act 3, scene 1, a set-piece containing the definition of a *philosophe*:[30] 'cela fera plaisir aux cacouacs'. In October he complains (D10069, 10070) of the activities of Crébillon as censor: the latter, he suggests, has not been deceived by the attempts at anonymity, and has taken vengeance on Voltaire for outshining him in the field of tragedy; this letter is followed shortly afterwards by another to Damilaville (D10148), informing him that a new scene has been despatched to meet the requirements of the *comédiens*. Through the remainder of the year, and into January 1762, we can see Voltaire becoming increasingly anxious about the reception his play will receive, requesting a copy of the text adopted by the Comédie-Française, and complaining of unauthorised cuts (D10171, D10271).

[29] The archives of the Comédie-Française have preserved no reference to the earlier reading, though the *procès-verbal* of the meeting of 9 October reads: 'la troupe s'est assemblée pour arrêter les corrections nécessaires à faire à la pièce de l'*Ecueil du sage*'. There is evidence that Diderot lent a helping hand in the matter: he writes to Damilaville 'que ce jour j'avois remis la copie en question [presumably the corrected copy] à Mr Girard, c'est le nom de l'homme qui se mêle de cette affaire; que Mr Girard alla droit à la Comédie françoise pour y trouver Belcour; que la pièce est selon toute apparence entre les mains de Belcour; que la lecture s'en fera peut-être demain' (*Correspondance*, ed. Roth-Varloot, iii.356-57; incorrectly dated December 1761). I am grateful to Mlle Sylvie Chevalley, former archiviste-bibliothécaire of the Comédie-Française, for information about the reception of the play.

[30] The insertion corresponds to act 3, lines 79-88 of our text.

Crébillon's 'approbation' as censor was finally given on 26 November 1761,[31] and the play was put into rehearsal.

5. *Theatrical fortunes*

Bachaumont writes, early in the new year 1762: 'On commence à parler beaucoup de *L'Ecueil du sage*, comédie philosophique et en vers de dix syllabes, de M. de Voltaire. On espère qu'elle triomphera des scrupules de la censure et de la police, et que nous la verrons enfin représenter'.[32] The play was in fact performed on 18 January, together with Regnard's *La Sérénade*. Since the *registre-journal* of the Théâtre-Français does not specify which actors took part in which play, it is impossible to draw up a precise cast-list for *Le Droit du seigneur*; but among the principal roles those of the Marquis and the Chevalier were taken respectively by Grandval and Molé (CLT, v.42), and that of Colette by Mlle Dangeville (D9925); and it seems to be a reasonable assumption that Mlle Gaussin played Acante.[33] Although correspondents assured Voltaire that his play had been well received – Thibouville, for instance, wrote:

> Elle eut les plus grands applaudissements, et elle les mérite. C'est un composé de la plus agréable plaisanterie, de la plus belle morale, des plus grands sentiments. (D10275)

–we find Voltaire himself writing to Mme de Fontaine in February that three acts of it have been 'mutilés [...] à la police', the effect of Crébillon's work (D10302). In particular he complains (D10305) of the cutting of the Marquis's 'ai-je perdu la gageure?',

[31] See below, p.32-33, MS1.

[32] Dated 7 January 1762 (Bachaumont, i.15; see also p.23).

[33] The remainder of the cast-list (for the outstanding roles of Voltaire's play and the eight roles of *La Sérénade*) consisted of Paulin, Préville, Brizard, Blainville, Durancy, Dauberval; and Mlles Drouin, Préville, Durancy *mère* and Durancy *fille*.

which he had already told d'Argental was 'si fort dans la nature' (D10282).[34] Finally, having received the text as performed in Paris, Voltaire writes to the d'Argentals:

Mme Denis est indignée, elle ne peut concevoir qu'on n'ait siflé d'un bout à l'autre cette rapsodie mutilée, tronquée, sans suitte, sans liaison, sans dialogue et privée de tout l'intérest que le dialogue et la liaison des scènes y avaient mis quand elle sortit de mes mains. (D10333)

and he follows this shortly after with a letter (2 March 1762; D10353) complaining of unspecified changes imposed by the censor, which had affected the character of Acante.

Earlier, Voltaire had instructed Damilaville (D10305) to ensure that half the profit from performances of *Le Droit du seigneur* should be banked for 'celui à qui il est promis', whilst the other half should go to Thiriot; but when the run of the play came to an end on 3 February after eight performances, Damilaville received instructions (D10315) that Thiriot was now to receive the whole profit.[35] And on 3 March (D10357) Thiriot writes to Voltaire, giving him an account of the play's financial success, and thanking him for his gift of 1000 francs.

Meanwhile, the correspondence shows that preparations had been in hand for some time for a private performance of *Le Droit du seigneur* by the author's own household. Rehearsals had begun before the end of 1761, and Mme Denis wrote to Lekain (D10238), suggesting he visit Ferney for a performance in the spring. This in fact took place at the beginning of March 1762, with Voltaire himself in the role of Le Bailli and Mlle Corneille as Colette (D10366, D10367); and the author lost no time in sending the

[34] Though reference is made to the 'gageure' at various points in the dialogue, neither manuscript nor printed versions contain the phrase in the form quoted in D10305. The nearest approximation is the Marquis's 'j'ai perdu la gageure' in the three-act version (III.640). See also 'Ai-je perdu?' in MS1 (critical apparatus to V.282-295a).

[35] Voltaire's text reads '9 représentations', but the *Registres* of the Comédie-Française (p.803a) record only eight. Takings for the eight performances were as follows: 3664, 2780, 3341, 2212, 2166, 2379, 1355 and 1513 *livres*.

d'Argentals the text used in his own production, in the hope that the *comédiens* might be induced to adopt an authorised text for a Paris revival. As seen through the author's eyes, the defects of the text used for the Paris production are reflected in the comment:

Depuis l'effet que cette pièce a fait sur mes Suisses et sur mes Savoiards, j'aurai bien mauvaise opinion de vos pauvres Français s'ils ne rient pas, et s'ils ne sont pas touchez. Je veux qu'une comédie soit intéressante, mais je la tiens un monstre si elle ne fait pas rire. (D10373)

He writes to Lekain to this same end in June 1762 (D10482), and in the same month, in writing to Damilaville, goes into details of changes the censor may possibly require:

Je prie mon cher frère de me mander quels sont les endroits scabreux qu'il faut retrancher ou adoucir dans la scène du bailli et de Colette; mais prenons garde que la prétendue décence ne fasse grand tort au plaisant. (D10509)

Many letters from this period and from later years, right up to 1778 when, within months of his death, he was busy discussing casting details for a proposed new production (D21061), refer hopefully to the possibility of a revival by the Comédie-Française; but *Le Droit du seigneur* was not to be performed again professionally during its author's lifetime. It had, however, been revived at Ferney – 'avec un prodigieux succès', according to a letter from Voltaire to Chauvelin in November 1762 (D10791).

For the posthumous Paris production in June 1779, the text used was Voltaire's own shortened three-act version, on which he had been working during the last year of his life. Why this reduction should have been undertaken is not clear, though the first suggestion of the desirability of such a rewriting seems to have been contained in a hint from d'Alembert: 'J'y voudrois un autre cinquième acte; la pièce eût été meilleure en quatre, ou même en trois' (D10291). However, throughout the subsequent correspondence dealing with negotiations for a possible revival, there is no sign of Voltaire accepting this hint until the final revision, completed in February 1778, when he tells d'Argental of a *Droit du seigneur* 'qui est entièrement changé' (D21061). Quite soon after the play's original appearance on stage and in print, however, a shortened version had appeared, the work of one La Ribadière: *L'Ecueil du sage, comédie de M. de Voltaire, réduite à 3 actes pour le service de la cour de Vienne*, which was published at Vienna in 1764.[36]

The author's own abridged version of *Le Droit du seigneur* had six performances in 1779, the first being given together with *Agathocle* on 12 June; the cast was as follows:

Le Marquis		Molé
Le Chevalier		Fleury
Le Bailli		Dugazon
Maturin		Des Essarts
Dignant		Vanhove
Champagne		Dazincourt
Acante	Mmes	Doligny
Colette		Luzy
Berthe		La Chassaigne

The play has not been revived at the Comédie-Française since that date.

6. *Publication*

If Voltaire had cause to be displeased with the treatment of his text by the actors, this was even more the case when *Le Droit du seigneur* appeared in print. As regards the authorised publication,

[36] La Ribadière's adaptation retains, in effect, the last three acts of Voltaire's play, with the addition of the last scene of act 2. For the most part it presents Voltaire's own text, with a small number of minor textual changes, mainly affecting a single word or phrase. There is, however, a slight abridgement, since La Ribadière's text consists of 1220 lines against the 1248 of the corresponding section of the five-act version in its definitive form. The edition is described below, p.44, under the siglum 64V.

all was well. This had been mentioned in a letter to the d'Argentals in February 1763, in which Voltaire suggests a project for issuing *Le Droit du seigneur* together with certain other plays:

Je pense qu'il ne serait pas mal de faire un petit volume de Zulime, Mariamne, Olimpie, le droit du seigneur, et d'exiger du libraire qu'il donnât une somme honnête à m^elle^ Clairon et à Lekain. (D10999)

On 10 May, in a letter to Gabriel Cramer, the play is again associated with *Zulime* (D11202); and in June, profits from sales of the new play are again linked with the name of Mlle Clairon – though this time with no mention of Lekain as co-beneficiary (D11265). There are references in the correspondence both to a preface (D9988, D9991, D10008), and to 'une drôle de dédicace pour m^r^ de Choiseul' (D10526): neither of these is extant,[37] but it is to be presumed that they were at some stage designed to be incorporated in the Cramer edition. Any comment that the actual appearance of this edition, later in 1763, may have occasioned on Voltaire's part has not survived in the published correspondence; though its authenticity is proclaimed in a letter from Wagnière to Pierre Guy, Duchesne's manager, of June 1764, urging the latter to follow it in any re-issue (D11905). For the Duchesne edition, which also appeared in 1763, had been vehemently denounced by Voltaire, who complained in a letter of 23 August to the d'Argentals: 'On a imprimé mon pauvre droit du seigneur tout délabré' (D11378), and enclosed a copy of a statement bearing the same date, and due to appear in the *Mercure de France* in the following month, in which among various matters affecting other literary works, he informed readers of the defective state of the published text of *Le Droit du seigneur* (see Voltaire 54, p.2-3). On the same day, he wrote to Damilaville and to Thiriot in more or less identical terms:

J'aprends qu'un forban de libraire de Paris vient d'imprimer le droit du

[37] With regard to the dedication, Besterman suggests that 'Voltaire may have drawn on it for the dedication of the *Scythes* in 1767' (D10526, note).

seigneur tout défiguré, d'après quelque copie informe faitte à la comédie. (D11379; see D11380)

In January 1764 he complains to Gabriel Cramer of Duchesne's conduct in the matter (D11610), and on the same day writes to Pierre Guy, ostensibly about a proposal on the latter's part to publish *La Henriade*:

La dédicace que vous voulez bien m'en faire m'est très honorable. Mais en me dressant ce petit autel, je vous prie d'y brûler en sacrifice vôtre Zulime et vôtre Droit du seigneur, que vous avez imprimés sous mon nom, et qui ne sont point du tout mon ouvrage. Vous avez été trompé par ceux qui vous ont donné les manuscrits, et celà n'arrive que trop souvent. C'est le moindre des inconvénients de la Littérature. (D11611)

However, by May of the same year we find Wagnière writing to Guy to make an offer on Voltaire's part:

Il me charge de vous dire qu'il est très sensible au soin que vous prenez d'imprimer ses ouvrages; mais il sait que vous avez eu de très infidèles copies de la Tragédie de Zulime, et de la comédie du droit du Seigneur; il vous serait très aisé de substituer, les deux véritables pièces, aux fausses, dont vous vous êtes malheureusement chargé. Il entrera avec plaisir dans les frais que vous coûtera cette petite entreprise. (D11882)

Wagnière's letter is backed up in the following month by the one already referred to, repeating the exhortation to adopt the text published by Cramer:

Il n'y a certainement d'autre remède que de substituer dans vôtre recueil, la bonne édition à la mauvaise, en vous servant de l'édition Cramer. M^r^ De Voltaire vous offre de vous dédommager de vos frais, et il se flatte que vous ne ferez aucune difficulté de prendre un parti si raisonnable. (D11905)

The offer was not accepted, however; and Voltaire's relations with the Duchesnes over this play followed the same course as they did in respect of other dramatic works: witness the 'Avis au lecteur' to the 1767 edition of *Les Scythes*, denouncing 'la plupart [des] tragédies imprimées à Paris chez Duchesne, au Temple du Goût, en 1764' as 'point du tout conformes à l'original', and the long letter written in April 1767 by the widow of Nicolas Bonaventure Duchesne (who had died in July 1765), appealing to Voltaire to give his approval to further publishing ventures by the Duchesne house.

Changes made in subsequent editions between the authorised original and the *encadrée* edition of 1775 are textual modifications of little substance; and the *encadrée* itself is with a few minor exceptions a corrected version of the original edition of 1763 (OD63). On the other hand, the effect of Voltaire's annotations to his own copy of the *encadrée* was to produce a radical revision of his text, reducing it from the 1964 lines of the original (1958 in the *encadrée*) to the 1472 lines of the three-act version referred to above. This revised version, which Voltaire hoped, in the year of his death, to have accepted at the Comédie-Française, is the one to which he refers in the final mention of the play in his correspondence, two months before his death, when he writes to d'Argental:

> Songez que je meurs; songez qu'en mourant j'ai achevé, Irène, Agatocle, le droit du Seigneur [...] Songez que Molé m'a mutilé indignement, sottement et insolemment; qu'il ne veut point jouer son rôle dans le droit du Seigneur. (D21117)

The Kehl editors, respecting Voltaire's final intentions, published the three-act version of *Le Droit du seigneur* as the substantive text, but give the original form of the end of act 3, and of acts 4 and 5, as a continuous text in an appendix. We have preferred to restore the text of the play as originally written for performance and publication, for in the three-act version *Le Droit du seigneur* almost entirely loses what psychological interest it originally possessed. The sentimental 'intérêt' of which Voltaire repeatedly speaks (e.g. D9007, D9975, D9990, D10287) derives almost wholly from the struggle in the mind of the Marquis, who finally overcomes his hesitation and offers his hand to Acante; in the five-act version this development is not without a certain subtlety, and the sentimental appeal combines quite attractively with the more conventional comic effects. In the shortened version, however, since it is the last three acts that have been so drastically telescoped, the corresponding development is quite unsubtle, and practically devoid of psychological interest.

7. *Critical reception*

Contemporary criticism was far from flattering to *Le Droit du seigneur*. Indeed, there is no record of any favourable reaction, and it seems likely that the play would not have received the attention it did receive had it not been for the newsworthiness of the author's name.

For Bachaumont, for instance, the only interest is an anecdotal one. He tells a story – for which there appears to be no known authority – of an unknown young man presenting a new play to the Comédie-Française under the title of *Le Droit du seigneur*; he is treated condescendingly, and although the play is finally read, it is rejected unanimously. Only later, says Bachaumont, when the same play was offered by Voltaire himself with the title changed to *L'Ecueil du sage*, was it accepted (Bachaumont, i.15-16).

Grimm gives a sustained critical account of the play itself: 'L'*Ecueil du sage* est en deux mots une mauvaise pièce de M. de Voltaire'; and although he concedes that 'une mauvaise pièce de M. de Voltaire vaut encore mieux que les bons ouvrages de nos auteurs médiocres', he declares roundly that 'M. de Voltaire n'a jamais trop réussi dans la comédie'. This latest example, he says, suffers from a lack of logical cohesion in the plot (the subject of the 'droit du seigneur' is an irrelevance), the character of Gernance lacks psychological conviction, and the 'rôles subalternes' are weak. Altogether 'il faut regarder [cette pièce] comme une de ces productions auxquelles M. de Voltaire se livre dans ses moments perdus, et qu'il nous abandonne ensuite sans les avoir relues'. In the theatre, 'la partie comique' (that is, the first two acts) 'n'a point du tout réussi, et [...] la partie larmoyante' (the last three) 'a reçu les plus grands applaudissements'; and although act 4 was 'sans contredit' the worst of the five, 'c'est cet acte qui a fait le succès de la pièce'. Two scenes singled out by Grimm for approval are the scene between the Bailli and Colette (II.i)[38] and the 'tableau de la noce' in act 3 (CLT, v.39-43).

Act 2, scene 1 is analysed in greater detail by Fréron, and receives a double-edged compliment: 'cette scène prolixe, qui serait mieux placée dans une parade, est cependant une des moins mauvaises de cette comédie'. The word-play on *abuser* here, and on *débouter* in the following scene, comes in for criticism, and the latter example is quite fairly judged by Fréron to be an inferior imitation of Regnard: 'cette plaisanterie est ressassée au dégoût; on sent que c'est une copie maladroite d'*interloquée*'.[39] In spite of a limited approval of the play's sentimental appeal (in the scene between the Marquis and the Chevalier, in which the latter recounts his treatment at the hands of Acante), Fréron is a severe critic – the more effectively so in that what he says about *Le Droit du seigneur* is the product of judicious analysis, not of the sort of subjective prejudice one might have expected Fréron to show after Voltaire's savage attack on him in *L'Ecossaise*. The irrelevance of the 'droit du seigneur' to the plot; the imitation of Richardson in Gernance's abduction of Acante; the repetition of theme and characters from *Nanine*; the uninspired versification: these are all objects of a fair and well substantiated critique.[40]

Another example of contemporary criticism of Voltaire's play is contained in the anonymous *Lettre de M. D. R. à M. de S. R. sur la Zulime de M. de Voltaire et sur l'Ecueil du sage du même auteur*.[41] Grimm described this little pamphlet as 'du badinage en vingt-huit pages' (CLT, v.47), but as well as amusing, it makes a

[38] Grimm sent out the text of this scene to his subscribers; see U. Kölving and J. Carriat, *Inventaire de la Correspondance littéraire*, Studies 225 (1984), no. 62:034 (15 février 1762), and below, p.35, manuscripts CL1 and CL2.

[39] See Regnard, *Le Légataire universel*, III.viii.

[40] *Al* (1763), v.289-318 (letter 13, dated 4 September 1763).

[41] Geneva 1762. Of the 28 pages, the first 22 deal with *Zulime* and other tragedies, the last six with *Le Droit du seigneur*.

number of valid points. A good deal of the author's criticism bears on the similarity between *Nanine* and the new play, which as he says is more or less the three-act comedy of 1749 amplified by the addition of the 'droit du seigneur' motif. However, the latter brings little dramatic action with it; and for the rest:

C'est du Nanine tout pur, avec quelques scènes comiques qui ne touchent en rien au dénouement, et des aventures merveilleuses, qui ne sont rien moins qu'amenées. Nanine est enlevée, Nanine dit des maximes, Nanine n'ose s'avouer qu'elle aime Monseigneur, Nanine, destinée à Blaise, épouse Monseigneur, et le public se contente de deux ou trois scènes nouvelles pour se dire à lui-même: *Ah! la jolie pièce! Quel génie créateur!*

An unsatisfactory feature of the play in this reviewer's eyes is the treatment of Laure, who proves to be Acante's mother. Why, he says, does Laure herself not appear – possibly instead of Dormène? This would have made the recognition scene, which as it is is a failure, much more effective. Dignant is another character who comes in for criticism. He should be 'un homme simple, comme Mathurin qui le tutoie'; but is he? 'Point du tout, il parle avec noblesse, dit des sentences'. The concluding verdict is that this is a 'pièce sans invention, dont l'intrigue est compliquée et sans vraisemblance [...] une pièce toute contraire à la principale règle du théâtre'.

Surviving critical comment, therefore, reflects the lack of success of *Le Droit du seigneur* on the stage – and in Fréron's case, the mediocre effect it produced in print as well:

Ce drame, mort presque subitement au théâtre, renaît pour mourir peut-être encore par la voie de l'impression. (*Al*, 1763, v.289)

On the other hand, if *Le Droit du seigneur* was roughly handled by the critics, Voltaire could take some consolation from the fact that his play was both translated and imitated. The translation, into German, by Johann Friedrich Schmid, was published by Korn at Breslau in 1765 under the title *Das Herrenrecht oder die Klippe des Weisen, ein Lustspiel ... in 5 Handlungen*; there is no evidence as to whether this version was performed. However, Favart's *Les Moissonneurs, comédie en trois actes et en vers, mêlée d'ariettes*, published

(Paris, veuve Duchesne) in 1768, was performed at the Comédie-Italienne in January of that year, the musical score being contributed by M. Duni. Favart's play is a blatant copy of Voltaire's plot, reduced to the most elementary terms possible: characterisation hardly exists, and simplistic clichés of 'honnêteté' and 'bienfaisance' abound. The spirit of this feeble play is summed up in the epigraph quoted on the title-page, a couplet spoken by the enlightened nobleman Candor (corresponding to Voltaire's Marquis) with reference to Rosine (the counterpart of Acante):

> Laisse tomber beaucoup d'épis
> Pour qu'elle en glane davantage.

8. *Manuscripts*

Three complete manuscripts of *Le Droit du seigneur* have survived: one connected with the first staging of the five-act version, in 1762, and two giving the text of the three-act version, one of which was used for performances in 1779. The first scene of the second act appeared in the *Correspondance littéraire*, under the date of 15 February 1762; two manuscripts of this issue of Grimm's journal are known.

MS1

L'Ecueil du sage / Comedie en cinq Actes / Et en Vers. /

Contemporary copy in several hands, with numerous corrections by Crébillon, d'Argental (?) and others, and remarks for production such as 'bon' and 'à changer'; 195 x 263 mm (acts 1-3), 186 x 242 mm (acts 4-5).

Act 1, paginated 1-26: 6 sheets folded and gathered to form one section of 12 leaves with one additional leaf at the end (p.25-26); leaves 4 and 5 were removed and replaced by two separate leaves in another hand (p.7-10); p.1 title, as above, endorsed 'Le Role de Maturin pour [*illegible*]' (deleted), and 'Une copie de piece / bien pressée'; p.2 Acteurs.

Act 2, paginated 1-22: 6 sheets folded and gathered to form one section of 12 leaves; leaf 3 removed and replaced (p.5-6), the stub of the leaf removed being endorsed 'a lais[ser] blanc'; leaf 12 partly removed and folded over to the front of the section; p.15 and 17 both numbered 'vingt' by Crébillon, p.19 'vingt et un' and p.21 'vingt trois'.

Act 3, paginated 1-31: 8 sheets folded and gathered to form one section of 16 leaves; leaf 6 removed and replaced (p.11-12); p.31 not numbered by Crébillon.

Act 4, paginated 1-27: 7 sheets folded and gathered to form one section of 14 leaves; slips bearing additional text attached to p.17; p.27-28 blank.

Act 5, paginated 1-22: 6 sheets folded and gathered to form one section of 12 leaves; leaf 12 removed; slips bearing additional text attached to p.9 and 20.

Comédie-Française: MS 227.

This is the copy submitted by the *comédiens* to the censor Crébillon, and official approval is recorded on the verso of the final leaf (p.22 of act 5), as follows:

> J'ay lu par ordre de Monsieur le Lieutenant Général de Police l'*Ecueil du Sage* et je crois que l'on peut en permettre la représentation. Ce 26 9bre 1761. Crébillon
>
> Vû L'aprobation Permis de representer ce 28 9bre 1761. de Sartine

The textual changes incorporated in this manuscript provide some justification for Voltaire's fears about the accuracy of the text used for stage performance.[42]

MS2

Le Droit du Seigneur / Comedie / En trois actes. / Acte premier. /

Contemporary copy, corrected by Voltaire and Wagnière, and endorsed by the latter on the title-page 'Bon Original'; format unknown; 45 leaves, subsequently foliated 156-200; f.156*r* title, as above; f.156*v* Acteurs; f.157-200 text.

[42] See Voltaire to Pierre Guy, 4 June 1764: 'On avait horriblement mutilé à la comédie le droit du seigneur par des scrupules chimériques qui ont disparu depuis' (D11905).

Leningrad: VM i.156-200.

This manuscript is probably one of the 'copies' referred to on the title-page of MS3. The text of both manuscripts is close to that of the corrected *encadrée* (see below, W75G*), but they contain important corrections, especially MS3 which presumably reflects further changes made for the stage performance in 1779.

MS3

Le droit du seigneur / Comédie / en trois actes. / Acte premier. / Bonne copie collationé / Mr Pankouke et Wagniere / en ont chacun une semblable. / 1er. Acte / Maturin / Le Bailli / Colette / Agante / Dignant / Me. Berthe /

Contemporary copy in the same hand as MS2, with corrections by Wagnière and Voltaire (p.10, 13, 43 and 92), and with numerous alterations in ink and pencil from later periods (these alterations have not been taken into account in the present edition); 188 x 239 mm; 55 leaves, paginated 1-107.

Act 1, paginated 1-32: 8 sheets folded and gathered to form one section of 16 leaves; p.1 title, as above, endorsed by Wagnière 'copie originale' (the three lines beginning 'Bonne copie collationé' are also in his hand); p.2 Acteurs, possibly in the hand of d'Argental; p.3-30 text; p.31-32 blank.

Act 2, paginated 33-60: 7 sheets folded and gathered to form one section of 14 leaves; p.33-59 text; p.60 blank.

Act 3, paginated 61-107: 12 sheets folded and gathered to form one section of 24 leaves; leaf 21 removed and replaced with a new leaf in another hand (p.101-102), followed by an additional leaf (p.103-104) in a third hand, pinned in; p.61-107 text; p.107 approbation, as below; p.[108-110] blank.

Comédie-Française: MS 305.

Official approval is recorded on p.107:

> Lu et aprouvé les changemens. A Paris le 8 juin 1779. Suard.
>
> Vu l'aprobation, Permis de representer et d'imprimer ce 9 juin 1779. Lenoir.

The text of this manuscript incorporates the corrections in MS2.

CL1

The copy of the *Correspondance littéraire* sent to Louisa Ulrica. At the end of his notice on the *Droit du seigneur*, Grimm presents the text of II.i, introduced by the following remarks:

'La police a fait gâter la scene la plus plaisante par les retranchemens qu'elle a ordonnés, et, comme il ne sera pas, peut être, permis de rétablir à l'impression les endroits supprimés, je profiterai de l'occasion que j'ai eu de me procurer cette scene toute entiere, pour la conserver ici. Elle ne tient pas d'ailleurs au fond de la piece et l'on peut la regarder comme un fragment entièrement détaché.'

The readings thus provided by Grimm are included in the variants to the present edition.

Kungliga Biblioteket, Stockholm: Vu 29:3, p.43-50.

CL2

A secondary copy, similar to CL1, probably made in Gotha, perhaps from the copy of the *Correspondance littéraire* sent to Studnitz. See Kölving and Carriat, i.XLV-XLVI.

Forschungsbibliothek Gotha: 1138 D, f.223*v*-26*r*.

9. *Editions*

The first editions of *Le Droit du seigneur* were those published by Duchesne in Paris (siglum 63G) and by Cramer in Geneva (OD63), the latter being part of the fifth volume of the *Ouvrages dramatiques* in the *Collection complette* of 1756-1772. Both editions were copied by a number of unidentified publishers (three separate editions in 1763, two or three in 1764 and one each in 1770 and 1777), and one text or the other was reproduced in most collective editions (W64R, T64P, T66, W52, T70 and T76X following Duchesne, with OD70 and OD72 reprinting Cramer's OD63). Voltaire effected a few minor changes for the quarto edition (W68), which was in turn copied by W71 and W72P. The *encadrée* (W75G), based on the

Le Bailly

Non plus qu'eux tous, je n'ay donc rien à dire.
Votre complainte en droit ne peut suffire,
On ne produit ni temoins, ni billets,
On ne vous a rien fait, rien ecrit...

Collette

Mais
Un Mathurin aura donc l'insolence
Impunement d'abuser l'innocence!

Le Bailly

Oh oh mais, s'il est en ainsy, ce cas
est autre chose et vous n'en parliés pas
(il ecrit)
Instrumentons... dit en notre presence
que maturin usant de violence
~~Contre~~ malgré les loix, ~~contre~~ malgré l'honnêteté
~~[illegible]~~
~~amoureusement sur icelle attente~~
~~[illegible]~~
~~[illegible]~~
~~[illegible]~~
~~[illegible]~~

+ à changer

Collette

Rayez cela. Je ne veux pas qu'on dise
Dans le pays une telle sottise:
On n'a rien fait de semblable et pour peu
Qu'on l'eût osé l'on auroit vû beau jeu

Le Bailly

Que pretendez-vous donc?

1. *Le Droit du seigneur*: a page of MS1 (II.i.49-69), with alterations and notes by the actors (Comédie-Française, Paris).

Mais pourra t'il me blamer de me rendre
chez cette Dame, et si noble et si tendre,
Qui fuit le monde; et qu'en ce triste jour,
J'implorerai pour le sien à mon tour.
Ou suis-je? on ouvre à peine j'envisage
Celui qui vient. – je ne vois qu'un nuage.

Scene sixieme

Le marquis Acante!

Le marquis.

Bien aimable ~~Essayez vous lorsqu'~~ quand icy je vous vois
C'est le plus beau le plus cher de mes droits.
J'ai commandé qu'on porte a votre pere
Les foibles dons qu'il convient de vous faire.
Ils paroitront bien indignes de vous.

Acante (~~seigneur~~)

Trop de bontez se répandent sur nous
J'en suis confuse et ma reconnoissance
N'a pas besoin de tant de bienfaisance
Mais avant tout il est de mon devoir
De vous prier de daigner recevoir
Ces vieux papiers que mon pere presente,
Tres humblement.

2. *Le Droit du seigneur*: a page of MS1 (III.v-vi.271-288), with a marginal note by the censor, Crébillon (Comédie-Française, Paris).

que ce marquis, ce beau seigneur qui tient
dans le païs, le rang, l'état d'un prince,
de sa présence honora la province?
il s'est passé juste un an et deux mois
depuis qu'il vint pour cette seule fois.
t'en souvient-il? nous le vîmes à table;
il m'accueillit; ah! qu'il était affable!
tous ses discours étaient des mots choisis,
que l'on n'entend jamais dans ce païs.
C'était colette, une langue nouvelle,
supérieure, et pourtant naturelle;
j'aurais voulu l'entendre tout le jour.

Colette.

tu l'entendras sans doute à son retour.

acante.

Ce jour, colette, occupe la mémoire,
où Monseigneur tout raïonnant de gloire,
dans nos forêts suivi d'un peuple entier,
le fer en main courait le sanglier?

Colette.

oui, quelque idée et confuse et légère,
peut m'en rester.

acante.

je l'ai distincte et claire.

te souvient il combien l'eco des bois
retentissait da plus de mille voix
jay tort peutetre; il faut que je convienne
mais je crus voir quil distinguait la mienne

3. *Le Droit du seigneur*: a page of MS3 (II.iii.144-170), with a holograph addition (Comédie-Française, Paris).

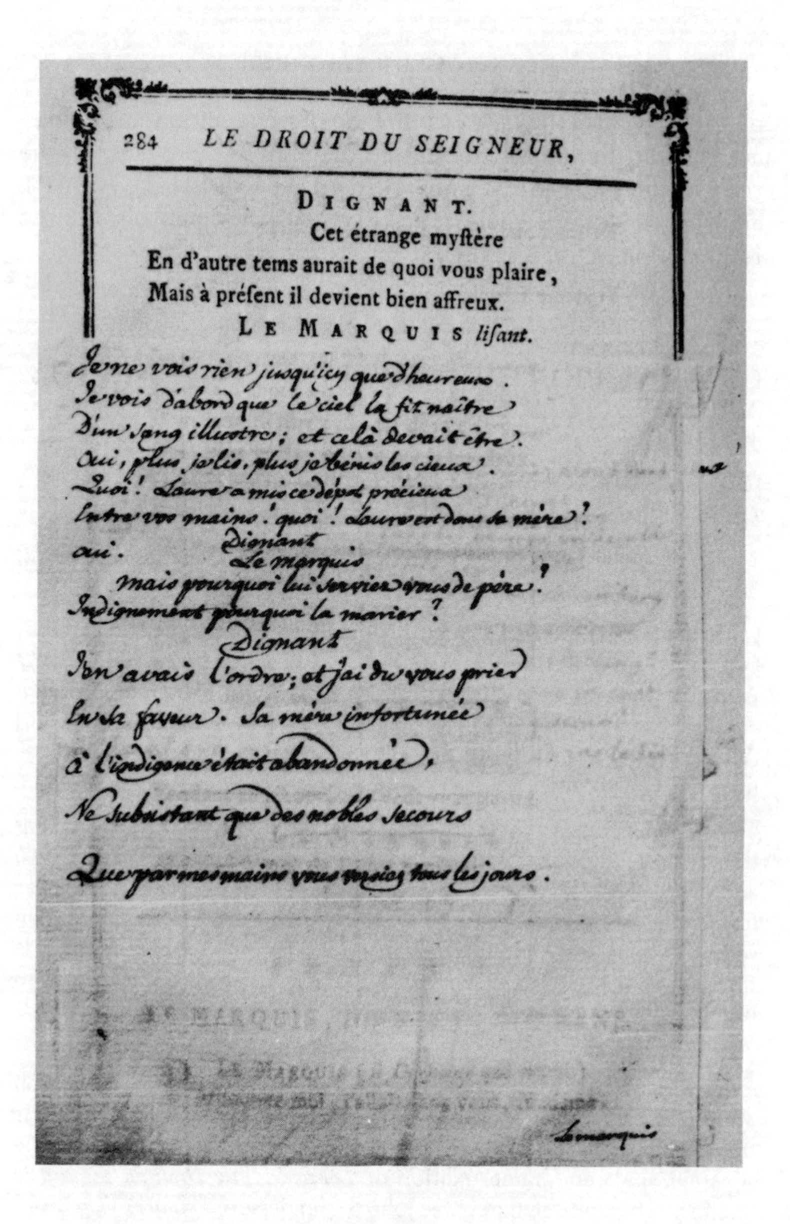

284 LE DROIT DU SEIGNEUR,

DIGNANT.

Cet étrange myſtère
En d'autre tems aurait de quoi vous plaire,
Mais à préſent il devient bien affreux.

LE MARQUIS *liſant.*

Je ne vois rien jusqu'icy que d'heureux.
Je vois d'abord que le ciel la fit naître
D'un sang illustre; et celà devait être.
Oui, plus je lis, plus je bénis les cieux.
Quoi! Laure a mis ce dépôt précieux
Entre vos mains! quoi! Laure est donc sa mère?
oui.

Dignant

Le marquis

mais pourquoi lui serviez vous de père?
Indignement pourquoi la marier?

Dignant

J'en avais l'ordre; et j'ai du vous prier
En sa faveur. Sa mère infortunée
à l'indigence était abandonnée,
Ne subsistant que des nobles secours
Que par mes mains vous versiez tous les jours.

Le marquis

4. *Le Droit du seigneur*: a page from Voltaire's corrected copy of the *encadrée*, W75G* (III.X.506-518), with a revision by Wagnière (Saltykov-Shchedrin State Public Library, Leningrad).

quarto, provides the base text for the present edition of the five-act version. Voltaire then reduced the play to three acts, on the copy of the *encadrée* that he marked up for Panckoucke (W75G*), and this version (see below, p.201-19) was first published in the Kehl edition of 1784.

OD63

OUVRAGES / DRAMATIQUES, / *AVEC* / LES PIÉCES RELATIVES / A CHACUN. / *TOME CINQUIEME.* / [*woodcut, lyre and trumpets, 74 x 61 mm*] / [*thick-thin rule, 69 mm*] / M. DCC. LXIII. /

[*half-title*] COLLECTION / COMPLETTE / DES / ŒUVRES / DE / M^R^. *DE VOLTAIRE.* / TOME DIXIEME, / *SECONDE PARTIE.* /

8°. sig. *⁸ A-Ff⁸ Gg⁴; pag. [*16*] 471 [472]; $4 signed, arabic (– *1-2, P4, Gg4); direction line '*Théatre* Tom.V.'; page catchwords.

[*1*] half-title; [*2*] blank; [*3*] title; [*4*] blank; [*5-16*], [1]-324 other texts; [325] X3*r* 'LE DROIT / DU / SEIGNEUR, / *COMÉDIE* / EN CINQ ACTES. / [*rule, 74 mm*] / Elle a été jouée à Paris ſous le nom de / *L'Ecueil du Sage*, qui n'était pas ſon / véritable titre. / X3 *ACTEURS.*'; [326] Acteurs; [327]-471 Le Droit du seigneur, comédie; [472] Pièces contenues dans ce volume.

This volume was produced by or for Cramer in Geneva, to supplement the various editions and impressions of his *Collection complette* dated 1756 and 1757. It also served as part of the 1764 edition, and does not appear to have been reprinted until 1770 (see below, OD70). The preparation of this volume is mentioned in D10999, D11034 and D11202, and it is referred to in D11265 (13 June 1763) as if it had been or was about to be published. It provided the first authorised edition of the *Droit du seigneur*.

Copies also exist (Merton College, Oxford: 36 f 13) with the collation π^2 *⁴ (– *1) **² A-G⁸ (G8 blank) H-Ff⁸ Gg⁴: in these copies, sig. π is from a different printing and leaves *1 through G8 consist of the separate, undated Cramer edition of *Tancrède*. The *Droit du seigneur* is unaffected by these changes. See John S. Henderson, *Voltaire's 'Tancrède'*, Studies 61 (1968).

Bn: Rés. Z Beuchot 21 (11); Taylor: V1 1770G/2 (10.ii).

63G8

LE DROIT / DU / SEIGNEUR, / *COME'DIE EN VERS*, / PAR M. DE VOLTAIRE: / *Repréſentée pour la premiere fois, sous le titre de* / *l'*Ecueil du Sage, *par les Comédiens François* / *Ordinaires du Roi, le* 18 *Janvier* 1762. / [*rule, 52 mm*] / Le prix eſt de trente ſols. / [*rule, 50 mm*] / [*woodcut, basket of fruit and flowers, 37 x 22 mm*] / A GENEVE, / *CHEZ LES FRERES ASSOCIÉS.* / [*thick-thin rule, 45 mm*] / M. DCC LXIII. /

8°. sig. A-G⁸ H⁴; pag. 119; $4 signed, roman (– A1, H2-3; in the Rés. Z Bengesco 94 copy, F1 is signed 'Fii' and F3 'Fiv'; in Yf 7191, the first 'i' of 'Fiii' is inverted; the ImV copy is correctly signed); sheet catchwords.

[1] title; [2] Acteurs; [3]-119 Le Droit du seigneur, comédie.

This is the Duchesne edition, which was also issued as a duodecimo (see the entry next below). The woodcut head-piece on p.[3], which represents a lake, trees and buildings, is also to be found in T64P (v.291) and in a 1765 edition of *Adélaïde Du Guesclin* reliably attributed to Duchesne (siglum 65PA).

Voltaire alleged that this edition was based upon a corrupt manuscript used at the Comédie-Française: this is unlikely to have been true, for although the text of 63G is indeed marred by a fair number of mistakes and apparent mis-readings, it rarely differs substantially from OD63, and has nothing in common with any of the surviving manuscripts. Two departures from the OD63 text are worthy of note: II.227-228 and V.66-67.

This edition was announced in the *Catalogue hebdomadaire* on 20 August 1763, at 1 *livre*, 10 *sous* (année 1763, reprinted Paris 1776, Livres étrangers, no.14, item 1).

Bn: Rés. Z Bengesco 94, Yf 7191; Arsenal: Rf 14536 (uncut and largely unopened); Taylor: V3 D6 1763; ImV: D Droit 1763/2; Austin: PQ 2077 D6 1763.

63G12

As 63G8, except:

12°. sig. A-E¹²; pag. 119; $6 signed, roman (– A1, A3; D5 signed 'Dvv' in some copies, E5 'Evj'); sheet catchwords.

[1] title; [2] Acteurs; [3]-119 Le Droit du seigneur, comédie.

This is a duodecimo reimposition of 63G8, from the same setting of type. There are a few typographic and textual differences between the two issues: these were probably introduced when reimposition took place, but some could also be due to press corrections during the printing of either version. For example, on p.74 (in the copies we have seen) the duodecimo has no vertical space after '[*Il fonne*]', and on line 5 of p.26 it reads 'Phlippe' against the 'Philippe' of the octavo. One obvious error of the octavo is corrected at I.94, but a new one is introduced at I.120.

Copies of the duodecimo were still being sold by Duchesne in 1784, as the last item in volume D12 of the *Bibliothèque des théâtres*.

Bn: Rés. Z Bengesco 977 (uncut; sig. B bound after D); Bpu: Hf 5002* (in the *Bibliothèque des théâtres*); Comédie-Française (marked up by Delaporte, the *souffleur*, to record the readings of OD63).

63X

LE DROIT / DU / SEIGNEUR, / *COME'DIE EN VERS*, / PAR M. DE VOLTAIRE: / *Repréfentée pour la premiere fois, sous le titre de* / *l'*Ecueil du Sage, *par les Comédiens François* / *Ordinaires du Roi, le* 18 *Janvier* 1762. / [*rule, 48 mm*] / Le prix eft de trente fols. / [*rule, 49 mm*] / [*woodcut, small basket of flowers above floral motif, 24 x 22 mm*] / A GENEVE, / *CHEZ LES FRERES ASSOCIÉS*. / [*thick-thin composite rule composed of three elements, 43 mm*] / M. DCC. LXIII. /

8°. sig. A-G^8 H^4; pag. 119; $4 signed, roman (– A1, H3-4); sheet catchwords.

[1] title; [2] Acteurs; [3]-119 Le Droit du seigneur, comédie.

This is a close imitation or reprint of the Duchesne edition, 63G8. The woodcut on the title is different, as are the rules; there is a period after 'DCC' in the date; the woodcut headpiece on p.[3] represents a stag hunt; there is a period after 'Mde' in the catchword on p.80; there is no period after 'Acante' in that on p.112; the misprint 'MATHUDIN' appears on p.11.

Two obvious errors of 63G8 are corrected, at I.94 ('S'est' becomes 'C'est') and at III.c (the comma in 'LE CHEVALIER, GERNANCE' is removed).

Taylor: V3 A2 1764 (20); Austin: PQ 2077 D6 1763b; ImV: D Droit 1763/1.

63PC

LE DROIT / DU / SEIGNEUR, / *COMÉDIE* / EN CINQ ACTES. / *Représentée à Paris ſous le nom de* l'Écueil / du Sage, *qui n'étoit pas ſon véritable / titre.* / [*woodcut, winged angel with trumpet and sun, 68 x 46 mm*] / A PARIS, / Aux dépens de la Compagnie. / [*treble rule, 65 mm*] / M. DCC. LXIII. /

8°. sig. A-L^4; pag. 86 (the '3' of folio 83 inverted); $1 signed (– A1; A2 signed 'A'); sheet catchwords.

[1] title; [2] Acteurs; [3]-86 Le Droit du seigneur, comédie.

The text of this edition follows that of OD63 (with the errors at I.169 and V.80), but makes a number of changes and corrections, at I.14, III.6, 99, 399, IV.83, 236, 251 and V.31. At IV.247 it gives a reading apparently in advance of its time. Could this be the edition referred to by Voltaire in D11232, where he appears to be asking Cramer for six copies of a separate *Droit du seigneur*? It does not look like a Cramer production, but part of his output was produced for him by other printers, some of them at a fair distance from Geneva. It is also quite possible that this edition, of which only one copy is known, was produced well after the date given on the title.

Arsenal: Rf 14537 (lacks L4, presumed blank).

63PD

LE DROIT / DU SEIGNEUR, / *COMÉDIE* / EN CINQ ACTES, / *Par Monſieur de VOLTAIRE.* / [*woodcut, eagle in cartouche, signed* 'J.R. 1761', *68 x 56 mm*] / A PARIS, / Chez DUCHESNE, Libraire, rue Saint / Jacques, au-deſſous de la Fontaine Saint-Benoît, / au temple du goût. / [*thick-thin rule, 72 mm*] / *Avec Approbation & privilége du Roi.* 1763. /

8°. sig. A-K^4; pag. 79 (p.51 numbered '15'); $2 signed, arabic (– A1, B2, G2; A2 signed 'Aij', C2 'C3'); sheet catchwords.

[1] title; [2] Acteurs; [3]-79 Le Droit du seigneur, comédie.

There is no reason to accept the accuracy of this edition's imprint: the name of Duchesne was frequently borrowed by provincial publishers. The woodcut on the title is also found in a 1771 edition of the *Ecossaise* (siglum 71L).

The text follows that of OD63, including the errors at I.169 and V.80, but has 'Philipe' throughout.

Arsenal: GD 9353 (p.[47-48] damaged, with loss of text and folios); Austin: PQ 2077 D6 1763c.

64G

LE DROIT / *DU* / SEIGNEUR, / *COMÉDIE* / EN CINQ ACTES. / [*rule, 84 mm*] / Elle a été jouée à Paris ſous le nom de *L'Ecueil* / *du Sage*, qui n'était pas ſon véritable titre. / [*woodcut, includes two baskets of flowers, 49 x 31 mm*] / A GENEVE, / Chez les Freres CRAMER, Imprimeurs-Libraires. / [*thick-thin rule, 40 mm*] / M. DCC. LXIV /

8°. sig. A-L^4; pag. 88; $2 signed, arabic (– A1, L2); sheet catchwords.

[1] title; [2] Acteurs; 3-88 Le Droit du seigneur, comédie.

Part of p.86 and all of 87-88 are set in smaller type. Sig. I4 (p.71-72) is printed out of true, and may be a cancel.

The text reproduces that of OD63, including the errors at I.169, IV.251 and V.80.

Arsenal: Rf 14538; Toronto: Volt V65 D754 1764.

64V

L'ECUEIL / DU SAGE, / *COMÉDIE* / DE / M. DE VOLTAIRE, / REDUITE à 3. ACTES / POUR LE SERVICE DE LA COUR DE / VIENNE / PAR / M. DELARIBADIERE. / [*woodcut, shell or leaf motif with foliage, 34 x 22 mm*] / [*thick-thin rule, 58 mm*] / *VIENNE EN AUTRICHE*, / Dans l'Imprimerie de Ghelen 1764. /

8°. sig. A-D^8 E^4; pag. 72; $5 signed, arabic (– A1, E4; B5 signed 'A5', D5 'C5'); page catchwords.

[1] title; [2] Acteurs; [3]-72 L'Ecueil du sage, comédie.

This adaptation has not been taken into account in the present edition.

Bn: Rés. Z Bengesco 95; Arsenal: Rf 14539, Rf 14540.

T64G

LE / THÉATRE / DE MONSIEUR / *DE VOLTAIRE*. / NOUVELLE ÉDITION, / *QUI contient un Récueil complet de tou-* / *tes les Piéces que l'Auteur a données / jusqu'à ce jour.* / TOME SIXIEME. / [*woodcut, two cherubs and suspended globe, 28 x 22 mm*] / *A GÉNÉVE*, / Chez les Freres CRAMER, Libraires. / [*thick-thin rule, composed of 3 elements, 46 mm*] / M. DCC. LXIV. /

12°. sig. A-Cc^6 Dd^2; pag. 315 [316] (p.129 numbered '229'; folios 131-132 used twice; folios 179-180 not used); $3 signed, roman (– A1-2; + E4; B2 signed 'Cij', E4 'Eiij', Bb3 'Bbij'); direction line '*Tome VI.*'; sheet catchwords.

[1] title; [2] blank; [3]-211 other texts; [212] blank; [213] S4*r* '*LE DROIT* / DU SEIGNEUR, / *COMEDIE.*'; [214] Acteurs; 215-315 Le Droit du seigneur, comédie; [316] Table des pièces contenues dans le VI volume.

The text is close to that of OD63.

Arsenal: Rf 14092 (6) (sigs E3 and E4 transposed).

T64P

ŒUVRES / *DE* / THÉATRE / *DE* / M. DE VOLTAIRE, / *De l'Académie Françaiſe, de celle de Berlin,* / *& de la Société Royale de Londres, &c.* / TOME QUATRIEME. / [*woodcut, sunrise within cartouche, 29 x 22 mm*] / A PARIS, / Chez DUCHESNE, Libraire, rue Saint Jacques, / au-deſſous de la Fontaine Saint Benoît, / au Temple du Goût. / [*thick-thin rule, 47 mm*] / M. DCC. LXIV. / *Avec Approbation & Privilége du Roi.* / [*lines 1, 3, 5, 8, 9 and 13 in red*]

[*half-title*] THÉATRE / *DE* / M. DE VOLTAIRE. / *TOME IV.* /

12°. sig. π^2 $1\pi^1$ A-C^{12} D^6 E-K^{12} L^6 M-Z^{12}; pag. [*6*] 528 (p.238-240 numbered '240', '241', '242'); $6 signed, arabic (– D4-6, L4-6); direction line '*Tome IV.*'; sheet catchwords.

[*1*] half-title; [*2*] blank; [*3*] title; [*4*] blank; [*5*] Table des pièces contenues dans ce quatrième volume; [*6*] blank, but for catchword 'ROME'; [1]-432 other texts; [433] V1*r* 'LE DROIT / DU / SEIGNEUR, / *COMÉDIE* / En Vers, en cinq Actes; / *Repréſentée pour la première fois, ſous* / *le titre de l'*Ecueil du Sage, *par les Co-* / *médiens Français ordinaires du Roi,* / *le* 18 *Janvier* 1762. / *Tome IV.* V'; 434 Acteurs; [435]-528 Le Droit du seigneur, comédie.

This Duchesne edition was often decried by Voltaire. It follows 63G, but with corrections in the first three acts at I.20, 94, II.16, 205, III.C, 182). It invents a line at I.78, to replace that omitted by 63G.

Bn: Yf 4255.

W64R

COLLECTION / *COMPLETE* / DES ŒUVRES / *de Monsieur* / DE VOLTAIRE, / NOUVELLE ÉDITION, / *Augmentée de ſes dernieres Pieces de Théâtre*, / *& enrichie de 61 Figures en taille-douce.* / TOME DIX-HUITIEME, / SECONDE *P*ARTIE. / [*typographic ornament*] / *A AMSTERDAM*, / AUX DÉPENS DE LA COMPAGNIE. / [*thick-thin rule, 48 mm*] / M. DCC. LXIV. /

12°. sig. π^2 R8-12 S-Ee^{12} Ff^6 Gg-Ii^{12} Kk^4 (Kk has vertical chain lines); pag. [2] 387-[672] [2] [673]-748 [749] (p.399 numbered '396'); $6 signed, arabic (– Y4, Ff4-6, Kk3-4; Bb2 signed 'B2', Cc6 'C6'); direction line '*Tome XVIII.*'; sheet catchwords.

[*1-2*] blank; [*3*] title; [*4*] blank; [387]-670 other texts; 671 Table des pièces contenues dans ce dix-huitième tome; [672] blank; [*1*] Gg1*r* 'LE DROIT / *DU* / SEIGNEUR, / *COMEDIE EN VERS*, / PAR M. DE VOLTAIRE, / *Repreſentée pour la premiere fois, ſous le titre* / *de l'*Ecueil du Sage, *par les Comédiens* / *Français Ordinaires du Roi, le 18 Janvier* / *1762.* / *Tome XVIII.* Gg'; [2] Acteurs; [673]-748 Le Droit du seigneur, comédie; [749] Table des pièces contenues dans ce dix-huitième tome.

The signatures and pagination of this volume are continuous with those of the first part of volume 18. The 'Table' on p.671 excludes the *Droit du seigneur*, and no doubt that leaf (Ff6) should have been removed by the binder. The standing type of the play was used to print a separate edition, with new pagination and signatures: see below, 64R.

The text of this edition follows 63G8.

Bn: Rés. Z Beuchot 26 (18.ii).

64R

LE DROIT / *DU* / SEIGNEUR, / *COMEDIE EN VERS*, / PAR M. DE VOLTAIRE, / *Repreſentée pour la premiere fois, ſous le titre* / *de l'*Ecueil du Sage, *par les Comédiens* / *Français Ordinaires du Roi, le 18 Janvier* / *1762.* / A /

12°. sig. A-C^{12} D^4 (D4 blank); pag. 78 (p.51 not numbered); $6 signed, arabic (– D3-4); sheet catchwords.

[1] title; [2] Acteurs; [3]-78 Le Droit du seigneur, comédie.

A separate issue of W64R: see the entry next above. The last line on the title page is the signature of that leaf: there is no publisher, place or date.

Arsenal: GD 9354.

T66

[*within ornamented border*] LE / THÉATRE / DE / M. DE VOLTAIRE. / *NOUVELLE ÉDITION.* / Qui contient un Recueil complet de toutes / les Piéces de Théâtre que l'Auteur a / données juſqu'ici. / TOME CINQUIEME. / [*woodcut, floral cartouche, 31 x 18 mm*] / *A AMSTERDAM*, / Chez FRANÇOIS-CANUT RICHOFF, / près le Comptoir de Cologne. / [*thick-thin rule, 40 mm*] / M. DCC. LXVI. /

12°. sig. π^2 A-I^{12} K^8 L-O^{12} (π1 blank); pag. [*4*] 328; $6 signed, arabic (– K5-6; C4 signed 'C'); direction line '*Théâtre. Tom. V.*'; sheet catchwords.

[*1-2*] blank; [*3*] title; [*4*] blank; [1]-231 other texts; [232] blank; [233] L1*r* 'LE DROIT / DU / SEIGNEUR, / *COMÉDIE: / Repréſentée, pour la premiere fois, ſous / le titre de l'*Ecueil du Sage, *par les / Comédiens François Ordinaires / du Roi, le 18 Janvier 1762. / Théâtre. Tome V.* L' ; [234] Acteurs; 235-328 Le Droit du seigneur, comédie.

The *Droit du seigneur* was probably added at a late stage in the production of the volume, perhaps necessitating the removal of an original table of contents which may well have occupied one of the last leaves of sig. K. This printing was reissued two years later: see T68 below.

The text follows that of the 63G12, with corrections at III.182 and IV.413.

University of Aberdeen Library: MH 84256 T (5).

T67

ŒUVRES / *DE THÉATRE* / DE / M. DE VOLTAIRE, / Gentilhomme Ordinaire du Roi, de / l'Académie Françaiſe, / &c. &c. / *NOUVELLE ÉDITION*, / *Revûe & corrigée exactement ſur l'Édition / de Genève in-4°.* / TOME QUATRIÈME. / [*typographic ornament*] / *A PARIS*, / Chez la Veuve DUCHESNE, Libraire, rue Saint- / Jacques, au-deſſous de la Fontaine Saint- / Benoît, au Temple du Goût. / [*thick-thin rule, 54 mm*] / M. DCC. LXVII. /

12°. sig. π^2 A-C^{12} D^6 E-K^{12} L^6 M-Z^{12} (± I8, K4, L1-6; + K4*); pag.

[*4*] 212 211*bis* 212*bis* 213-528; $6 signed, arabic (– D4-6, L4-6); direction line '*Tome IV.*'; sheet catchwords.

[*1*] title; [*2*] blank; [*3*] Table des pièces contenues dans ce quatrième volume; [*4*] Errata; [1]-432 other texts; [433] V1*r* half-title to Le Droit du seigneur (as T64P); 434 Acteurs; [435]-528 Le Droit du seigneur, comédie.

Sheets A to K and M to Z are from the same printing as those in T64P, but K4 is a cancel, followed by an additional leaf (K4*, numbered 211*bis* and 212bis). The effect of this cancel is to shorten scene 5 of act 3 of *L'Orphelin de la Chine* and to add scene 6. Sheet L is completely reset. The text of *Le Droit du seigneur* is unaffected by these changes, and is therefore identical to that of T64P.

Bn: Rés. Yf 3390; BL: C 69 b 10 (4).

T68

LE / THÉATRE / *DE* / M. DE VOLTAIRE. / *NOUVELLE ÉDITION.* / Qui contient un Recueil complet de toutes / les Pieces de Théâtre que l'Auteur a / données jusqu'ici. / *TOME CINQUIEME.* / [*woodcut, stylised cartouche, 33 x 28 mm*] / *A AMSTERDAM*, / Chez FRANÇOIS CANUT RICHOFF, / près le Comptoir de Cologne. / [*ornamented rule, 38 mm*] / M. DCC. LXVIII. /

A reissue of the sheets of T66 under a new title page.

Bn: Yf 4261.

W68

THÉATRE / Complet / DE / *M^R. DE VOLTAIRE.* / [*rule, 124 mm*] / TOME CINQUIÉME. / [*rule, 125 mm*] / *CONTENANT* / LE DROIT DU SEIGNEUR, LA FEMME QUI / A RAISON, L'ECOSSAISE, PANDORE, SAMSON, / LA PRINCESSE DE NAVARRE, LE TEMPLE / DE LA GLOIRE, SOCRATE, CHARLOT, avec / toutes les piéces rélatives à ces Drames. / [*rule, 119 mm*] / *GENEVE.* / [*thick-thin rule, 119 mm*] / M. DCC. LXVIII. /

[*half-title*] COLLECTION / Complette / DES / *ŒUVRES* / DE / M^R. DE VOLTAIRE. / [*thick-thin rule, 118 mm*] / *TOME SEPTIÉME.* / [*thin-thick rule, 120 mm*] /

4°. sig. π^2 A-Bbbb⁴ (Bbbb3-4 blank); pag. [*4*] 564; $3 signed, roman

(– Bbbb3); direction line '*Tom.* VII [or 'VI'] *& du Théâtre le cinquiéme.*'; sheet catchwords.

[*1*] half-title; [*2*] blank; [*3*] title; [*4*] blank; [1] A1*r* 'LE DROIT / DU / SEIGNEUR, / *COMEDIE* / EN CINQ ACTES. / [*rule, 118 mm*] / *Elle a été jouée à Paris ſous le nom de l'*ECUEIL DU SAGE, / *qui n'était pas ſon véritable titre.* / [*rule, 119 mm*] / *Tom.* VII. [or 'VI.'] *& du Théâtre le cinquiéme.* A'; [2] Acteurs; 3-108 Le Droit du seigneur, comédie; [109]-563 other texts; 564 Table des pièces contenues dans ce septième [*or* sixième] volume.

The title of the 'Table' and the direction lines were altered on press so that purchasers of the edition could choose whether to place the volume containing the *Histoire de Charles XII* before or after the theatre.

This edition, produced by Cramer, follows OD63 apart from corrections at I.14, IV.251 and V.80, and new readings at IV.168, 175 and 247.

Bn: Z 4934 ('*Tom.* VII.' in direction line); Rés. m Z 587 (7) ('*Tom.* VI.').

70P

LE DROIT / DU / *SEIGNEUR*, / COMÉDIE / *EN CINQ ACTES.* / Par M. DE VOLTAIRE. / *Repréſentée à Paris ſous le nom de* l'Ecueil du Sage, / *qui n'étoit pas ſon véritable titre.* / NOUVELLE ÉDITION. / [*woodcut, fountain flanked by semi-human figures, 64 x 42 mm*] / A PARIS, / Par la Compagnie des Libraires. / [*thick-thin rule, 49 mm*] / M. DCC. LXX. /

8°. sig. A-K⁴ L²; pag. 84; $2 signed, roman (– L2; I2 signed 'Ii'); sheet catchwords.

[1] title; [2] Acteurs; [3]-84 Le Droit du seigneur, comédie.

The text appears to be based largely upon 63PC.

Bibliothèque Sainte-Geneviève, Paris: Y 8° 2336 Inv 4505 F.A. (5).

OD70

OUVRAGES / DRAMATIQUES, / *AVEC* / LES PIÉCES RELATIVES / A CHACUN. / *TOME CINQUIEME.* / [*woodcut, theatrical emblems, 80 x 49 mm*] / [*thick-thin rule, 70 mm*] / M. DCC. LXX. /

[*half-title*] COLLECTION / COMPLETTE / DES / ŒUVRES / DE / MR. *de VOLTAIRE.* / DERNIERE EDITION. / *TOME DIXIEME*, / Seconde partie. /

8°. sig. A-Bb[8] Cc[2]; pag. 402 [403]; $4 signed, arabic (– A1-2, Cc2); direction line '*Théatre*. Tom.V.'; page catchwords.

[1] half-title; [2] blank; [3] title; [4] blank; [5]-291 other texts; [292] blank; [293] T3*r* 'LE DROIT / DU / SEIGNEUR, / *COMÉDIE* / EN CINQ ACTES. / [*rule, 75 mm*] / Elle a été jouée à Paris ſous le nom de / *L'Ecueil du Sage*, qui n'était pas ſon / véritable titre. / T3'; [294] Acteurs; [295]-402 Le Droit du seigneur, comédie; [403] Pièces contenues dans ce volume.

A Cramer reprint of his OD63, ignoring the changes made for W68.

Taylor: V1 1770G/1 (10.ii); Bn: Z 24696.

T70

LE / THEATRE / *DE* / M. DE VOLTAIRE. / *NOUVELLE ÉDITION*, / Qui contient un Recueil complet de toutes / les Pieces de Théatre que l'Auteur a don- / nées juſqu'ici. / *TOME CINQUIEME*. / [*woodcut, a bunch of flowers, 32 x 23 mm*] / *A AMSTERDAM*, / Chez FRANÇOIS CANUT RICHOEF, / près le Comptoir de Cologne. / [*thick-thin rule, 47 mm*] / M. DCC. LXX. /

12°. sig. π[1] A-I[12] K[8] L-O[12]; pag. [2] 328; $6 signed, arabic; direction line '*Théâtre. Tome V.*'; sheet catchwords.

[*1*] title; [2] blank; [1]-231 other texts; [232] blank; [233] L1*r* 'LE DROIT, / *DU* / SEIGNEUR, / *COMÉDIE*, / *Repréſentée, pour la premiere fois, ſous* / *le titre de l'*Ecueil du Sage, *par les Comé-* / *diens François ordinaires du Roi, le* 18 / *Janvier* 1762. / *Théâtre. Tome V.* L'; [234] Acteurs; 235-328 Le Droit du seigneur, comédie.

This is a new edition of T66, and gives a similar text.

Bn: Yf 4267.

W52 (1770)

OEUVRES / DE / Mr. DE VOLTAIRE, / *NOUVELLE ÉDITION* / RE-VUE, CORRIGÉE / ET CONSIDERABLEMENT AUGMENTÉE / PAR L'AUTEUR. / TOME NEUVIEME. / [*typographic ornament*] / [*treble rule, 62 mm*] / *à DRESDE, 1770.* / CHEZ GEORGE CONRAD WALTHER, / LIBRAIRE DE LA COUR. / *AVEC PRIVILEGE*. / [*lines 1, 3, 5, 8, 10 and 12 in red*]

12°. sig. π² A-Ss⁸ʼ⁴ Tt²; pag. [*4*] 255 [*2*] 256-381 [*2*] 382-494 [495-496]; $5,3 signed, arabic (– K3, Tt2; K2 signed 'K3', Ee3 'Ee5', Hh3 'Hh5'); direction line 'VOLT. Tom. !X.'; page catchwords.

[*1*] title; [*2*] blank; [*3-4*] Avertissement de l'éditeur; [1] A1*r* 'LE DROIT / DU / SEIGNEUR, / *COMÉDIE* / EN CINQ ACTES. / [*rule, 65 mm*] / Elle a été jouée à Paris sous le nom de / *L'Ecueil du Sage*, qui n'était pas son / véritable titre. / VOLT. Tom. IX. A *ACTEURS*.'; [2] Acteurs; [3]-110 Le Droit du seigneur, comédie; [111]-494 other texts; 494-[495] Table du tome neuvième.

W. H. Trapnell (*Studies* 77, p.131-32) separates this volume from his entry for the rest of W52D (under the siglum 70X), since it differs in appearance from the earlier volumes. The typographic changes are imputable to Walther's use of a different printer, however, and there is no reason to think that this ninth volume was not published by him. The 'Avertissement de l'éditeur' (quoted by Bengesco, iv.49-50), plaintively attacks Cramer's 1756 edition: even after fourteen years, Walther was still bemoaning the loss of Voltaire's patronage.

The text of this edition follows that of OD63, but with the omission of line I.135. See also the entry next below.

Bn: Rés. Z Beuchot 30 (9).

70D

[*within ornamented border*] LE DROIT / DU / SEIGNEUR, / *COMÉDIE* / EN CINQ ACTES, / *par Mr. de VOLTAIRE.* / [*thick-thin rule, 35 mm*] / [*typographic ornament*] / [*line of typographic ornaments, 58 mm*] / à DRESDE, 1770. / CHEZ GEORGE CONR. WALTHER, / *Libraire de la Cour.* /

12°. sig. A-H⁸ʼ⁴ I⁸ (– I8); pag. 110; $5,3 signed, arabic; page catchwords.

[1] title; [2] Acteurs; [3]-110 Le Droit du seigneur, comédie.

A separate printing from the standing type of W52.

Staatsbibliothek, Bamberg: L fr. o 108 c.

W70L (1772)

THÉATRE / COMPLET / *DE* / Mᴿ. DE VOLTAIRE. / Le tout revû & corrigé par l'Auteur même. / TOME SEPTIEME, / *CONTENANT* / LE DROIT DU SEIGNEUR, LA PRUDE, / OU L'HOMME AU FRANC

PROCÉDÉ, / LE DÉPOSITAIRE, / ET LA FEMME QUI A RAISON. / [*woodcut, musical and military emblems, signed* 'Beugnet', *42 x 35 mm*] / *A LAUSANNE*, / Chez FRANÇ. GRASSET et Comp. / [*ornamented rule, 79 mm*] / M. DCC. LXXII. /

[*half-title*] *COLLECTION* / COMPLETTE / *DES* / ŒUVRES / *DE* / M^R^. DE VOLTAIRE. / [*ornamented rule, 80 mm*] / *TOME VINGTIEME.* / [*ornamented rule, 80 mm*] /

8°. sig. π^2 $*^2$ A-Cc^8; pag. [2] vi 416; $5 signed, arabic (*2 signed '3*', since π1, blank, is not counted, and π2 is regarded as *1); direction line '*Théâtre*. Tom.VII.' (sigs B, G, K, O, R, T, X, Y and Cc: '*Théâtre*. Tome VII.'; sig. F: '*Théâtre* Tom.VII.'); sheet catchwords.

[*1-2*] blank; [i] half-title; [ii] blank; [iii] title; [iv] blank; [v]-vi Table des pièces contenues dans ce volume; [1] A1*r* 'LE DROIT / DU / SEIGNEUR, / *COMÉDIE*, / EN CINQ ACTES. / [*rule, 78 mm*] / Elle a été jouée à Paris ſous le nom de / *L'Ecueil du Sage*, qui n'était pas ſon / véritable titre. / *Théâtre*. Tom. VII. A'; [2] Acteurs; [3]-114 Le Droit du seigneur, comédie; [115]-416 other texts.

The text of this edition follows OD63, corrects I.14, IV.251 and V.80 and ignores the new readings of W68. Voltaire's revisions and corrections were limited to two lines, at I.49-50.

Also issued with the half-title: 'THÉATRE / COMPLET / DE / M^R^. DE VOLTAIRE. / [*thick-thin rule, 80 mm*] / *TOME SEPTIEME.* / [*thick-thin rule, 79 mm*]'.

Taylor: V1 1770L (20).

W71 (1772)

THEATRE / *COMPLET* / DE / *M. DE VOLTAIRE*, / [*rule, 69 mm*] / TOME CINQUIEME. / [*rule, 68 mm*] / *CONTENANT* / Le Droit du Seigneur, la Femme qui / a raison, l'Ecossaise, Pandore, Samson, la / Princesse de Navarre, le Temple de la Gloire, / Socrate, Charlot, avec toutes les piéces rélatives / à ces Drames. / [*woodcut, winged head, 28 x 17 mm*] / *GENEVE.* / [*ornamented rule, 36 mm*] / M. DCC. LXXII. /

[*half-title*] COLLECTION / *COMPLETTE* / DES / *ŒUVRES* / DE / M^R^. DE VOLTAIRE. / [*ornamented rule, 74 mm*] / *TOME SIXIEME.* / [*ornamented rule, 74 mm*] /

12°. sig. π^2 A-T^{12} V^4; pag. [*4*] 464; $6 signed, arabic (– V3-4; H3 signed

'H*3*', S3 'S*3*'); direction line '*Tome VI. & du Théâtre le cinquiéme.*' (sig. S '*Tome.* VI. *& du Théâtre le cinquiéme.*'; sig. T '*Tome* VI. *& du Théâtre le cinquiéme.*'); sheet catchwords.

[*1*] half-title; [*2*] blank; [*3*] title; [*4*] blank; [1] A1*r* 'LE DROIT / DU / SEIGNEUR, / *COMEDIE* / EN CINQ ACTES. / [*ornamented rule, 68 mm*] / *Elle a été jouée à Paris ſous le nom de l'*ECUEIL / DU SAGE, *qui n'était pas ſon véritable titre.* / [*ornamented rule, 68 mm*] / *Tome VI. & du Théâtre le cinquiéme.* A'; [2] Acteurs; [3]-83 Le Droit du seigneur, comédie; [84] blank; [85]-464 other texts; 464 Table des pièces contenues dans ce sixième volume.

This edition was printed at Liège, by or for Plomteux. According to Bengesco (iv.90-91), it reproduces 'tome pour tome, l'édition in-4° des Cramer', and consequently possesses no more than 'la valeur très relative d'une réimpression'. This appears to be the case.

Uppsala: Litt. fransk.

OD72

OUVRAGES / DRAMATIQUES / *AVEC* / LES PIÉCES RELATIVES / A CHACUN. / *TOME CINQUIEME.* / [*woodcut, mussels on a rock, 53 x 27 mm*] / [*thick-thin rule, 61 mm*] / M. DCC. LXXII. /

[*half-title*] COLLECTION / COMPLETTE / DES / ŒUVRES / DE / MR. *de VOLTAIRE.* / DERNIERE ÉDITION. / *TOME DIXIEME*, / Seconde Partie. /

8°. sig. A-Bb⁸ (B7 blank); pag. 396 [397-400] (p.243 numbered '143', 281 '241'; the folio on p.221 is on the left); $4 signed, arabic (– A1-2; Q3 signed 'O3'); direction line '*Théâtre.* Tom. V.'; page catchwords.

[1] half-title; [2] blank; [3] title; [4] blank; [5]-291 other texts; [292] blank; [293] T3*r* 'LE DROIT / DU / SEIGNEUR, / *COMÉDIE* / EN CINQ ACTES. / [*thick-thin rule, 74 mm*] / Elle a été jouée à Paris ſous le nom de / *L'Ecueil du Sage*, qui n'était pas / ſon véritable titre. / T3'; [294] Acteurs; [295]-396 Le Droit du seigneur, comédie; [397-399] blank; [400] Pièces contenues dans ce volume.

A reprint of OD63 and OD70 intended to form part of W72X. It was not necessarily produced by or for Cramer.

Bn: 16° Z 15081 (10.ii).

W72P (1773)

ŒUVRES / *DE M. DE VOLTAIRE.* / [*thick-thin rule, 76 mm*] / THÉATRE. / TOME SEPTIÈME, / *Contenant* / *LA FEMME QUI A RAISON, LE CAFFÉ,* / *ou L'ÉCOSSAISE, SOCRATE, CHARLOT,* / *ou LA COMTESSE DE GIVRI, LE DROIT* / *DU SEIGNEUR.* / [*woodcut, man bearing spear, within roundel of foliage, 27 x 25 mm*] / *A NEUFCHATEL.* / [*ornamented rule, 62 mm*] / M. DCC. LXXIII. /

[*half-title*] *ŒUVRES* / DE THÉATRE / *DE M. DE VOLTAIRE.* / TOME SEPTIÈME. /

12°. sig. π² A-R¹²; pag. [*4*] 408; $6 signed, roman; direction line 'Th. *Tome VII.*'; sheet catchwords.

[*1*] half-title; [*2*] blank; [*3*] title; [*4*] blank; [1]-294 other texts; [295] N4*r* 'LE DROIT / *DU* / SEIGNEUR, / *COMÉDIE* / EN CINQ ACTES. / [*rule, 72 mm*] / *Elle a été jouée à Paris ſous le nom de* / *l'*ECUEIL DU SAGE, *qui n'était pas ſon* / *véritable titre.* / [*rule, 70 mm*] / N iv'; 296 Personnages; 297-408 Le Droit du seigneur, comédie.

This edition, published by Panckoucke, follows w68.

Arsenal: Rf 14095 (7).

W75G

[*within ornamented border*] OUVRAGES / *DRAMATIQUES,* / PRÉCÉDÉS ET SUIVIS / DE TOUTES LES PIÉCES QUI LEUR / SONT RELATIFS. / [*rule, 74 mm*] / TOME SEPTIÉME. / [*rule, 74 mm*] / *M. DCC. LXXV.* /

[*half-title, within ornamented border*] TOME HUITIÉME. /

8°. sig. π² A-Cc⁸ Dd² (Dd2 blank); pag. [*4*] 418; $4 signed, roman; direction line '*Théatre*. Tom. VII.'; sheet catchwords.

[*1*] half-title; [*2*] blank; [*3*] title; [*4*] blank; [1]-206 other texts; [207] N8*r* 'LE DROIT / DU / SEIGNEUR, / *COMÉDIE* / EN CINQ ACTES. / [*rule, 75 mm*] / *Elle a été jouée à Paris ſous le nom de l'*ECUEIL / DU SAGE, *qui n'était pas ſon véritable titre.* / [*rule, 73 mm*]'; [208] Acteurs; 209-316 Le Droit du seigneur, comédie; [317]-417 other texts; 418 Table des pièces contenues dans ce volume.

This is the *encadrée* edition, published by Cramer under Voltaire's supervision, which provides the base text for our edition (in conjunction with the relevant corrections to W75G*). It follows the quarto edition (W68), ignores the one new reading in W70L, and introduces a few new errors. The play ends, in strange anticipation of Voltaire's plans, with 'Fin du troisième & dernier acte'.

The theatre volumes of the *encadrée* were reissued with a new title page, dated 1776 (Westfield College, London). The corner ornament used on this title page is that employed throughout W75X.

Taylor: VF.

W75G*

The Leningrad copy of the *encadrée* was extensively altered by Voltaire and Wagnière to produce the three act version, and full details are given by S. S. B. Taylor, 'The definitive text of Voltaire's works: the Leningrad *encadrée*', *Studies* 124 (1974), p.48-55, and see p.39 above, figure 4. This revised version provides the base text for the appendix, p.201-19 below.

Leningrad: BV, no.3472, 11-11 (8).

W75X

[*within ornamented border*] OUVRAGES / DRAMATIQUES, / PRÉCÉDÉS ET SUIVIS / *DE TOUTES LES PIÉCES QUI LEUR / SONT RELATIVES.* / [*rule, 75 mm*] / TOME SEPTIÈME. / [*rule, 73 mm*] / [*typographic ornament*] / [*ornamented rule, 79 mm*] / *M. DCC. LXXV.* /

[*half-title, within ornamented border*] ŒUVRES / DE / *M^R. DE VOLTAIRE.* / [*rule, 70 mm*] / TOME HUITIÈME. / [*rule, 70 mm*] /

8°. sig. π^2 A-Cc^8 Dd^2 (Dd2 blank); pag. [4] 418 (p.234 numbered '134', 313 '113', 418 '814'); $4 signed, roman; direction line '*Théatre.* Tom. VII.' (sig. Aa '*Théatre.* Tom. IX.'); sheet catchwords.

[*1*] half-title; [*2*] blank, but for border; [*3*] title; [*4*] blank; [1]-206 other texts; [207] N8*r* 'LE DROIT / *DU* / SEIGNEUR, / *COMÉDIE* / EN CINQ ACTES, / [*rule, 78 mm*] / *Elle a été jouée à Paris ſous le nom de l'*ECUEIL / DU SAGE, *qui n'était pas ſon véritable titre.* / [*rule, 78 mm*]'; [208] Acteurs; 209-316 Le Droit du seigneur, comédie; [317]-417 other texts; 418 Table des pièces contenues dans ce volume.

This is a counterfeit or reprint of Cramer's *encadrée* edition.

Bn: Z 24887.

T76X

THEATRE / COMPLET / DE MONSIEUR / DE VOLTAIRE. / TOME CINQUIEME. / *Contenant* LA PRUDE *ou* GARDEUSE DE / CASSETTE, LE DROIT DU SEIGNEUR, LA / FEMME QUI A RAISON, LE CAFFÉ *ou* / L'ÉCOSSAISE, PANDORE, LA PRINCESSE / DE NAVARRE, / *avec toutes les Pièces relatives / à ces Drames.* / [*woodcut, two birds within cartouche, 42 x 32 mm*] / [*ornamented rule, 51 mm*] / M. DCC. LXXVI. / [*lines 1, 3, 5 and date in red*]

8°. sig. π^1 A-Nn^8; pag. [2] 576; $4 signed, roman (F2 signed 'Fi', V3 'Vviij'); direction line '*Théatre. Tome V.*'; sheet catchwords.

[*1*] title; [2] blank; [1]-118 La Prude; [119] H4*r* 'LE DROIT / *DU* / SEIGNEUR, / *COMÉDIE* / EN CINQ ACTES. / [*rule, 73 mm*] / *Elle a été jouée à Paris ſous le nom de l'*ECUEIL DU / SAGE, *qui n'était pas ſon véritable titre.* / [*rule, 72 mm*] / H iv'; [120] Acteurs; 121-231 Le Droit du seigneur, comédie; [232] blank; [233]-575 other texts; 576 Table des pièces contenues dans ce cinquième volume.

Arsenal: Rf 14096 (5).

77N

LE DROIT / DU / SEIGNEUR, / *COMÉDIE.* / EN CINQ ACTES. / Par Mr. DE VOLTAIRE. / [*treble rule, 74 mm*] / LE PRIX EST DE 20. GRAINS. / [*treble rule, 74 mm*] / [*typographic ornament*] / NAPLES / DE L'IMPRIMERIE DE JEAN GRAVIER. / MDCCLXXVII. / [*rule, 26 mm*] / *AVEC APPROBATION ET PRIVILEGE.* /

8°. not collated; pag. 108; $4 signed, arabic; page catchwords.

[1] title; [2] Acteurs; 3-108 Le Droit du seigneur, comédie.

Biblioteca centrale della regione siciliana, Palermo.

T77

THÉATRE / *COMPLET* / DE M. DE VOLTAIRE; / *NOUVELLE ÉDITION,* / *Revue & corrigée par l'AUTEUR.* / TOME NEUVIÈME, / *CONTENANT* / LE DROIT DU SEIGNEUR, / LE DÉPOSITAIRE, L'ÉCOSSAISE. / [*woodcut, thistle, 20 x 20 mm*] / *A AMSTERDAM,* / Chez les LIBRAIRES ASSOCIÉS. / [*thick-thin rule, 49 mm*] / M. DCC. LXXVII. /

12°. sig. π^1 A-P^{12}; pag. [2] 358 [359]; $6 signed, arabic (– A6; B4 signed 'B'); direction line '*Tome IX.*'; sheet catchwords.

[*1*] title; [*2*] blank; [1] A1*r* 'LE DROIT / *DU* / SEIGNEUR, / *COMÉDIE*, / EN CINQ ACTES. / [*rule, 57 mm*] / *Elle a été jouée à Paris ſous le nom de l'*Écueil / du Sage, *qui n'était pas ſon véritable nom.* / [*rule, 58 mm*] / *Tome IX.* A'; [2] Acteurs; 3-114 Le Droit du seigneur, comédie; [115]-358 other texts; [359] Table des pièces contenues dans le neuvième volume.

This edition follows W70L.

Stockholm: Litt. fr. dram.

K

OEUVRES / COMPLETES / DE / VOLTAIRE. / TOME HUITIEME. / [*swelled rule, 41 mm*] / DE L'IMPRIMERIE DE LA SOCIÉTÉ LITTÉ-RAIRE- / TYPOGRAPHIQUE. / 1785. /

[*half-title*] OEUVRES / COMPLETES / DE / VOLTAIRE. /

8°. sig. π^2 a^2 A-Ee^8; pag. [*2*] iv 447; $4 signed, arabic (– a2); direction line '*Théâtre.* Tome VIII.'; sheet catchwords.

[*1*] half-title; [*2*] blank; [*3*] title; [*4*] blank; [i] a1*r* 'THEATRE.'; [ii] blank; [iii]-iv Table des pièces contenues dans ce volume; [1]-107 other texts; [108] blank; [109] G7*r* 'LE DROIT / DU / SEIGNEUR, / *COMEDIE.* / Repréſentée à Paris, en 1762, en cinq actes, / ſous le nom de l'ECUEIL DU SAGE, qui / n'était pas ſon véritable titre; remiſe au / théatre en 1778, en trois actes, après la / mort de l'auteur.'; [110] Personnages; [111]-187 Le Droit du seigneur, comédie; [188]-221 Variantes du Droit du seigneur (recording the text given below at II.229-232, III.338-345 and III.414-V.298); [222] blank; [223]-447 other texts.

The Kehl edition, which gives the text of the three-act version from Voltaire's manuscripts.

This is the revised version of the volume, of which the first printing dates from 1784, and all the faults listed in the first version of the errata (in volume 70) have been corrected. The 1784 title-pages are sometimes found with 1785 versions of the text, and 1784 texts sometimes carry 1785 title-pages. The two settings of this volume may be most easily distingished by the 'août' (1784) and 'auguſte' (1785) on p.[1], the half-title to *L'Ecossaise*, and by '&' (1784) and 'et' (1785).

The duodecimo edition of 1785 has not been taken into account.

Taylor: VF.

10. *Editorial principles*

Our reasons for the choice of the five-act version, rather than that in three acts, have already been indicated (see above, p.28-29). As the most authoritative of the editions in five acts, the *encadrée* (W75G) has been chosen as the base text.

Variants, modernised, are given from MS1, MS2 and MS3, from the extract included in the *Correspondance littéraire* (CL), and from the more significant editions: OD63, 63G8 and 63G12 (the last two collectively designated, where appropriate, as 63G), 63PC, T64P, W68, W70L, W75G* and K. Variations in punctuation are not recorded.

Corrections and additions to the Leningrad copy of the *encadrée* (W75G*) have been recorded in the critical apparatus up to and including act 3, scene 7, but are thereafter regarded as forming part of the three-act version, and figure only in the appendix.

Simple misprints are not recorded in the apparatus, and we have made the following silent corrections to the base text: I.169, 'le' for 'les'; I.237, 'royal' for 'rayal'; I.314, 'comme' for 'conme'; IV.118, 'd'autres' for 'd'autre'.

Modernisation of the base text

The spelling of names of persons and places has been respected, as has the original punctuation.

The following aspects of orthography and grammar in the base text have been modified to conform to modern usage:

1. Consonants

- the consonant *p* was not used in: tems, nor in its compound: longtems
- the consonant *t* was not used in syllable endings *–ans* and *–ens*: enfans, parens, descendans, etc.
- double consonants were used, in: allarmes, annoblit, appaise, s'appellait, appercevant, muguetter, rejettait, verreux
- a single consonant was used in: courier, couroux, hupés, poura, pourait (also: pourrait)

– archaic forms were used, as in: appas, baillif, batise, bienfaicteur, dixmes, domter, guères, promtement, me quarre, vuide

2. Vowels

– *y* was used in place of *i* in: asseye, ayeux, enyvré

– *i* was used in place of *y* in: fuions, fuiez, stile

– *ai* was used in place of *é* in: tremblai-je

– archaic forms were used, as in: agréra, avanture, godelurau

3. Accents

The acute accent

– was used in place of the grave in: enlévement, relévera, siége, troisiéme

– was not used in: deplait, deshonneur, deshonore, replique, reprimant, reprouver

– was used in: asséyez-vous, s'asséyant

– was used hesitantly in: désespérer, désespoir

The grave accent

– was not used in: déja

The circumflex accent

– was used in place of the acute in: pêtri

– was not used in: ame, bacler, benet, chaine, coute, enjoler, fraiche, grace, parait, passates, plait

– was used in: lû, sû, toûjours, vîte

The dieresis

– was used in: conjouïssance, ébloui̇̈, évanouïe, jouïr, obéïs, païs, réjouïr

4. Capitalisation

– initial capitals were attributed to: Baillif, Chevalier, Comte, Cour, Dame, Déesse, Diable, Empereur, Grec (le), Latin (adj.), Madame, Magister, Marquis, Monseigneur, Monsieur, Notaire, Picard (adj.), Prince, Roi, Seigneur

– and to adjectives denoting nationality: Français, Germain, Vénétien

5. Points of grammar

– agreement of the past participle was not consistent

– the cardinal number *cent* was invariable
– the final *–s* was not used in the second person singular of the imperative: convien, croi, di, fai, plain, pren, reçoi, sui, voi
– the plural in *–x* was used in: loix

6. Various

– rhyme and metre influenced orthography in several instances:
  1. the final *-s* in the first person, present tense : Je croi / moi (II.211, 212), je crois / autrefois (III.327, 328), je vous vois / de mes droits (III.277, 278), je le voi / vient à moi (IV.203, 204)
  2. the circumflex as an artifice in the future tense : avoûrai, marîrez, oublîra, oublîrez - these and similar incidences have been modernised
  3. *baillif* has been retained in the present edition in the following three cases: plaintif / baillif (I.401, 402 and II.87, 88), and pensif / baillif (III.425, 426)
– monsieur was abbreviated: Mr.; madame: Mad.
– the ampersand was used
– the hyphen was used in: à-peu-près, au-lieu-de, aussi-tôt, bon-jour, champ-part, par-là, si-tôt, tout-à-l'heure
– the hyphen was not used in: ce fou là, ces cas là, petit maître, sang froid, sur le champ.[43]

[43] The editor acknowledges with gratitude the valuable assistance of Ulla Kölving and Andrew Brown in the description of manuscripts and editions, and in the establishing of the critical apparatus of this edition.

LE DROIT
DU
SEIGNEUR,
COMEDIE EN VERS,
PAR M. DE VOLTAIRE:
Représentée pour la premiere fois, sous le titre de l'Ecueil du Sage, *par les Comédiens François Ordinaires du Roi, le 18 Janvier 1762.*

Le prix est de trente sols.

A GENEVE,
CHEZ LES FRERES ASSOCIES.

M. DCC LXIII.

5. *Le Droit du seigneur*: title-page of the octavo issue of the first edition (63G8), published in Paris by Duchesne (Taylor Institution, Oxford).

LE DROIT DU SEIGNEUR,

COMÉDIE EN CINQ ACTES

Elle a été jouée à Paris sous le nom de l'Ecueil du sage, qui n'était pas son véritable titre.

ACTEURS

Le marquis du CARRAGE.[1]
Le chevalier GERNANCE.
Le bailli.
MATURIN, fermier.
DIGNANT, ancien domestique. 5
ACANTE, élevée chez Dignant.
BERTHE, seconde femme de Dignant.
DORMÈNE.
COLETTE.
CHAMPAGNE. 10
Domestiques.

Les deux premiers actes se passent sous les arbres du village; les trois derniers dans le vestibule du château.

La scène est supposée en Picardie, et l'action du temps de Henri second. 15

a K: Personnages
2 K: Le chevalier de Gernance
3 W75G* (→ MS2, MS3, K): ⟨Le bailli⟩ VMétaprose, bailli
8 W75G* (→ MS3, K): ⟨DORMÈNE⟩
12-13 K, absent
MS2, MS3: *le dernier dans*
13 MS1: *dans le château*
14 K: *est en Picardie*
14-15 MS1, absent

[1] For the source of this name, see above, p.10, n.10.

ACTE PREMIER

SCÈNE PREMIÈRE

MATURIN, LE BAILLI

MATURIN

Ecoutez-moi, monsieur le magister;
Vous savez tout, du moins vous avez l'air
De tout savoir; car vous lisez sans cesse
Dans l'almanach. D'où vient que ma maîtresse
S'appelle Acante, et n'a point d'autre nom? 5
D'où vient cela?

LE BAILLI

Plaisante question!
Et que t'importe?

MATURIN

Oh! cela me tourmente,
J'ai mes raisons.

LE BAILLI

Elle s'appelle Acante.
C'est un beau nom, il vient du grec *Antos*,
Que les Latins ont depuis nommé *Flos*. 10
Flos se traduit par *Fleur*; et ta future
Est une fleur que la belle nature
Pour la cueillir façonna de sa main;

7 MS1-3, OD63-W70L: Eh! que

Elle fera l'honneur de ton jardin.
Qu'importe un nom? chaque père à sa guise 15
Donne des noms aux enfants qu'on baptise.
Acante a pris son nom de son parrain,
Comme le tien te nomma Maturin.

MATURIN

Acante vient du grec?

LE BAILLI

Chose certaine.

MATURIN

Et Maturin d'où vient-il?

LE BAILLI

Ah! qu'il vienne 20
De Picardie, ou d'Artois, un savant
A ces noms-là s'arrête rarement.
Tu n'as point de nom, toi, ce n'est qu'aux belles
D'en avoir un, car il faut parler d'elles.

MATURIN

Je ne sais, mais ce nom grec me déplaît. 25
Maître, je veux qu'on soit ce que l'on est:
Ma maîtresse est villageoise, et je gage
Que ce nom-là n'est pas de mon village.
Acante, soit. Son vieux père Dignant
Semble accorder sa fille en rechignant; 30

14 MS1, OD63, 63G, T64P: Elle sera l'honneur
16 MS1: ⟨aux enfants qu'on baptise⟩ ↑⟨soit Acante ou Belise⟩ [but first reading restored by 'bon' in the margin]
26 MS2: ⟨que l'on⟩ V↑ qu'on

Et cette fille, avant d'être ma femme,
Paraît aussi rechigner dans son âme.
Oui, cette Acante, en un mot, cette fleur,
Si je l'en crois, me fait beaucoup d'honneur,
De supporter que Maturin la cueille. 35
Elle est hautaine, et dans soi se recueille,
Me parle peu, fait de moi peu de cas;
Et quand je parle, elle n'écoute pas:
Et n'eût été Berthe sa belle-mère,
Qui haut la main régente son vieux père, 40
Ce mariage en mon chef résolu,
N'aurait été, je crois, jamais conclu.

LE BAILLI

Il l'est enfin: et de manière exacte
Chez ses parents je t'en dresserai l'acte;
Car si je suis le magister d'ici, 45
Je suis bailli, je suis notaire aussi;
Et je suis prêt dans mes trois caractères
A te servir dans toutes tes affaires.
Que veux-tu? dis.

MATURIN

Je veux qu'incessamment
On me marie.

LE BAILLI

Ah! vous êtes pressant. 50

MATURIN

Et très pressé… Voyez-vous? l'âge avance.

35 63G, T64P: De supposer que
49-50 W70L: Je veux incessamment / Avoir Acante.

J'ai dans ma ferme acquis beaucoup d'aisance;
J'ai travaillé vingt ans pour vivre heureux;
Mais l'être seul!... il vaut mieux l'être deux.
Il faut se marier avant qu'on meure. 55

LE BAILLI

C'est très bien dit: et quand donc?

MATURIN

Tout à l'heure.

LE BAILLI

Oui; mais Colette à votre sacrement,[2]
Mons' Maturin, peut mettre empêchement.
Elle vous aime avec quelque tendresse,
Vous et vos biens; elle eut de vous promesse 60
De l'épouser.

MATURIN

Oh bien, je dépromets.
Je veux, pour moi, m'arranger désormais,
Car je suis riche, et coq de mon village.
Colette veut m'avoir par mariage,
Et moi je veux du conjugal lien 65
Pour mon plaisir, et non pas pour le sien.
Je n'aime plus Colette: c'est Acante,
Entendez-vous? qui seule ici me tente.
Entendez-vous, magister trop rétif?

57 MS1, MS3: ⟨sacrement⟩ ↑engagement
58 MS2: ⟨peut⟩ veut

[2] See above, p.20 and note.

LE BAILLI

Oui, j'entends bien: vous êtes trop hâtif; 70
Et pour signer vous devriez attendre
Que monseigneur daignât ici se rendre;
Il vient demain, ne faites rien sans lui.

MATURIN

C'est pour cela que j'épouse aujourd'hui.

LE BAILLI

Comment?

MATURIN

Eh oui: ma tête est peu savante; 75
Mais on connaît la coutume impudente
De nos seigneurs de ce canton picard.
C'est bien assez qu'à nos biens on ait part,
Sans en avoir encore à nos épouses.
Des Maturins les têtes sont jalouses. 80
J'aimerais mieux demeurer vieux garçon,
Que d'être époux avec cette façon.
Le vilain droit!

LE BAILLI

Mais il est fort honnête.
Il est permis de parler tête à tête
A sa sujette, afin de la tourner 85
A son devoir, et de l'endoctriner.

MATURIN

Je n'aime point qu'un jeune homme endoctrine

79-82 MS1, absent
83 MS1: ⟨Le vilain droit!⟩ ↓Sans avoir droit / LE BAILLI / ⟨Mais il⟩ ↑Ce droit est

Cette disciple à qui je me destine;
Cela me fâche.

LE BAILLI

Acante a trop d'honneur
Pour te fâcher. C'est le droit du seigneur; 90
Et c'est à nous, en personnes discrètes,
A nous soumettre aux lois qu'on nous a faites.

MATURIN

D'où vient ce droit?

LE BAILLI

Ah! depuis bien longtemps,
C'est établi... ça vient du droit des gens.

MATURIN

Mais sur ce pied, dans toutes les familles 95
Chacun pourrait endoctriner les filles.

LE BAILLI

Oh! point du tout... c'est une invention
Qu'on inventa pour les gens d'un grand nom.
Car vois-tu bien, autrefois les ancêtres
De monseigneur s'étaient rendus les maîtres 100
De nos aïeux, régnaient sur nos hameaux.

MATURIN

Ouais! nos aïeux étaient donc de grands sots!

89-92 MS1, absent
90 63G, T64P: Pour se fâcher
93-132 MS1, struck out, restored by a series of 'bon' in the margin
94 63G8: S'est établi

LE BAILLI

Pas plus que toi. Les seigneurs du village
Devaient avoir un droit de vasselage.

MATURIN

Pourquoi cela? sommes-nous pas pétris 105
D'un seul limon, de lait comme eux nourris?
N'avons-nous pas comme eux des bras, des jambes?
Et mieux tournés, et plus forts, plus ingambes?
Une cervelle avec quoi nous pensons
Beaucoup mieux qu'eux, car nous les attrapons? 110
Sommes-nous pas cent contre un? ça m'étonne
De voir toujours qu'une seule personne
Commande en maître à tous ses compagnons,
Comme un berger fait tondre ses moutons.
Quand je suis seul, à tout cela je pense 115
Profondément. Je vois notre naissance,
Et notre mort, à la ville, au hameau,
Se ressembler comme deux gouttes d'eau.
Pourquoi la vie est-elle différente?
Je n'en vois pas la raison: ça tourmente. 120
Les Maturins et les godelureaux,
Et les baillis, ma foi sont tous égaux.

LE BAILLI

C'est très bien dit, Maturin, mais je gage,
Si tes valets te tenaient ce langage,
Qu'un nerf de bœuf appliqué sur le dos 125
Réfuterait puissamment leurs propos.
Tu les ferais rentrer vite à leur place.

110 W75G* (→ MS2): qu'eux⟨,⟩? […] attrapons⟨?⟩.
113 MS3: à $^{V\uparrow}$tous^{+} ses
120 T64P: ça m'tourmente
63G12: ça me tourmente

MATURIN

Oui, vous avez raison; ça m'embarrasse;
Oui, ça pourrait me donner du souci.
Mais palsambleu, vous m'avouerez aussi, 130
Que quand chez moi mon valet se marie,
C'est pour lui seul, non pour ma seigneurie,
Qu'à sa moitié je ne prétends en rien,
Et que chacun doit jouir de son bien.

LE BAILLI

Si les petits à leurs femmes se tiennent, 135
Compère, aux grands les nôtres appartiennent.
Que ton esprit est bas, lourd et brutal!
Tu n'as pas lu le code *féodal*.

MATURIN

Féodal! qu'est-ce?

LE BAILLI

Il tient son origine
Du mot *fides* de la langue latine: 140
C'est comme qui dirait...

MATURIN

Sais-tu qu'avec
Ton vieux latin et ton ennuyeux grec,
Si tu me dis des sottises pareilles,
Je pourrais bien frotter tes deux oreilles.

133 63G, T64P: moitié moi je ne prétends rien
133-134 MS1, absent
135-136 MS1, absent
137 63G, T64P: bas, sourd et
144 63G, T64P: Je pourrai bien

(*Il menace le bailli, qui parle toujours en reculant;*
et Maturin court après lui.)

LE BAILLI

Je suis bailli, ne t'en avise pas. 145
Fides veut dire *foi*. Conviens-tu pas
Que tu dois foi, que tu dois plein hommage
A monseigneur le marquis du Carrage?
Que tu lui dois dîmes, champart, argent?
Que tu lui dois…

MATURIN

Bailli outrecuidant, 150
Oui, je dois tout; j'en enrage dans l'âme;
Mais palsandié je ne dois point ma femme,
Maudit bailli!

LE BAILLI (*en s'en allant.*)

Va, nous savons la loi;
Nous aurons bien ta femme ici sans toi.

144a-b MS1: *reculant.*//
150 MS1: Bailli trop suffisant,
154 MS1: ⟨Nous aurons bien ta femme⟩ ↑⟨Et nous saurons la suivre⟩ ↓Nous saurons bien la suivre
MS2, MS3: ⟨aurons bien⟩ V↑ jugerons

SCÈNE II

MATURIN *seul.*

Chien de bailli! que ton latin m'irrite! 155
Ah! sans latin marions-nous bien vite;
Parlons au père, à la fille surtout,
Car ce que je veux, moi, j'en viens à bout.
Voilà comme je suis… J'ai dans ma tête
Prétendu faire une fortune honnête, 160
La voilà faite. Une fille d'ici
Me tracassait, me donnait du souci,
C'était Colette, et j'ai vu la friponne
Pour mes écus mugueter ma personne;
J'ai voulu rompre, et je romps: j'ai l'espoir 165
D'avoir Acante, et je m'en vais l'avoir,
Car je m'en vais lui parler. Sa manière
Est dédaigneuse, et son allure est fière;
Moi je le suis: et dès que je l'aurai,
Tout aussitôt je vous la réduirai; 170
Car je le veux. Allons…

166 63G, T64P: vais la voir
169 OD63: Moi je les suis
W75G*: ⟨les⟩ $^{W\uparrow}$le^{+} suis: ⟨et dès que⟩ $^{V\uparrow}$⟨et aussi quand je l'aurai⟩

SCÈNE III

MATURIN, COLETTE (*courant après.*)

COLETTE

Je t'y prends, traître.

MATURIN (*sans la regarder.*)

Allons.

COLETTE

Tu feins de ne me pas connaître?

MATURIN

Si fait... bonjour.

COLETTE

Maturin! Maturin!
Tu causeras ici plus d'un chagrin.
De tes bonjours je suis fort étonnée, 175
Et tes bonjours valaient mieux l'autre année.
C'était tantôt un bouquet de jasmin,
Que tu venais me placer de ta main;
Puis des rubans pour orner ta bergère;
Tantôt des vers que tu me faisais faire 180
Par le bailli qui n'en entendait rien,
Ni toi, ni moi; mais tout allait fort bien:
Tout est passé, lâche! tu me délaisses?

171b MS1: *courant après lui*
178 63G, omitted
T64P: Tantôt d'œillets, de roses et de thym
181 W75G* (→MS2, MS3, K): qui n'⟨en entendait⟩ W↑ y comprenait

MATURIN

Oui, mon enfant.

COLETTE

Après tant de promesses,
Tant de bouquets acceptés et rendus, 185
C'en est donc fait? je ne te plais donc plus?

MATURIN

Non, mon enfant.

COLETTE

Et pourquoi, misérable?

MATURIN

Mais, je t'aimais; je n'aime plus. Le diable
A t'épouser me poussa vivement,
En sens contraire il me pousse à présent; 190
Il est le maître.

COLETTE

Eh va, va, ta Colette
N'est plus si sotte, et sa raison s'est faite.
Le diable est juste, et tu diras pourquoi
Tu prends les airs de te moquer de moi.
Pour avoir fait à Paris un voyage, 195
Te voilà donc petit-maître au village?
Tu penses donc que le droit t'est acquis
D'être en amour fripon comme un marquis?
C'est bien à toi d'avoir l'âme inconstante!

187 MS1: ⟨Eh pourquoi, misérable⟩ ↑Cela n'est pas croyable
188 MS1: ⟨Mais⟩ ↑Si

Toi, Maturin, me quitter pour Acante! 200

MATURIN

Oui, mon enfant.

COLETTE

Et quelle est la raison?

MATURIN

C'est que je suis le maître en ma maison:
Et pour quelqu'un de notre Picardie
Tu m'as paru un peu trop dégourdie.
Tu m'aurais fait trop d'amis, entre nous; 205
Je n'en veux point, car je suis né jaloux.
Acante, enfin, aura la préférence.
La chose est faite. Adieu, prends patience.

COLETTE

Adieu! non pas, traître, je te suivrai,
Et contre ton contrat je m'inscrirai. 210
Mon père était procureur: ma famille
A du crédit, et j'en ai, je suis fille;
Et monseigneur donne protection,
Quand il le faut, aux filles du canton;
Et devant lui nous ferons comparaître 215
Un gros fermier qui fait le petit-maître,
Fait l'inconstant, se mêle d'être un fat.
Je te ferai rentrer dans ton état.
Nous apprendrons à ta mine insolente,
A te moquer d'une pauvre innocente. 220

204 T64P: Tu me parais un
MS1: Tu m'as semblée un peu
W75G*: paru$^{V\uparrow}$e^{+}
210 MS1: contre le contrat

MATURIN

Cette innocente est dangereuse; il faut
Voir le beau-père, et conclure au plus tôt.

SCÈNE IV

MATURIN, DIGNANT, ACANTE, COLETTE

MATURIN

Allons, beau-père, allons bâcler la chose.

COLETTE

Vous ne bâclerez rien, non, je m'oppose
A ses contrats, à ses noces, à tout. 225

MATURIN

Quelle innocente!

COLETTE

Oh! tu n'es pas au bout.
Gardez-vous bien, s'il vous plaît, ma voisine,
De vous laisser enjôler sur sa mine.
Il me trompa quatorze mois entiers.
Chassez cet homme.

222c MS1: Maturin *à Dignant.*
225 63G, T64P: A ces contrats, à ces noces
226 MS1: Quelle impudente!
W75G* (→MS2, MS3, K), added between 226-227: (*à Acante*) [W75G*: W]

ACANTE

Hélas! très volontiers. 230

MATURIN

Très volontiers!... tout ce train-là me lasse;
Je suis têtu; je veux que tout se passe
A mon plaisir, suivant mes volontés;
Car je suis riche... Or, beau-père, écoutez;
Pour honorer en moi mon mariage, 235
Je me décrasse, et j'achète au bailliage
L'emploi brillant de receveur royal
Dans le grenier à sel; ça n'est pas mal.
Mon fils sera conseiller; et ma fille
Relèvera quelque noble famille. 240
Mes petits-fils deviendront présidents.
De monseigneur un jour les descendants
Feront leur cour aux miens: et quand j'y pense,
Je me rengorge, et me carre d'avance.

DIGNANT

Carre-toi bien; mais songe qu'à présent 245
On ne peut rien sans le consentement
De monseigneur; il est encor ton maître.

MATURIN

Et pourquoi ça?

DIGNANT

Mais, c'est que ça doit être.
A tous seigneurs tous honneurs.

248-249 MS1, struck out, restored by 'bon' in the margin

COLETTE (*à Maturin.*)

Oui, vilain.

Il t'en cuira, je t'en réponds.

MATURIN

Voisin, 250

Notre bailli t'a donné sa folie.
Eh! dis-moi donc, s'il prend en fantaisie
A monseigneur d'avoir femme au logis,
A-t-il besoin de prendre ton avis?

DIGNANT

C'est différent: je fus son domestique 255
De père en fils dans cette terre antique.
Je suis né pauvre, et je deviens cassé.
Le peu d'argent que j'avais amassé
Fut employé pour élever Acante.
Notre bailli dit qu'elle est fort savante, 260
Et qu'entre nous, son éducation
Est au-dessus de sa condition.
C'est ce qui fait que ma seconde épouse,
Sa belle-mère, est fâchée et jalouse,
Et la maltraite, et me maltraite aussi. 265
De tout cela je suis fort en souci.
Je voudrais bien te donner cette fille,
Mais je ne puis établir ma famille
Sans monseigneur; je vis de ses bontés,
Je lui dois tout; j'attends ses volontés; 270
Sans son aveu nous ne pouvons rien faire.

ACANTE

Ah! croyez-vous qu'il le donne, mon père?

251-266 MS1, struck out, restored by 'bon' in the margin.

COLETTE

Eh bien, fripon, tu crois que tu l'auras?
Moi je te dis que tu ne l'auras pas.

MATURIN

Tout le monde est contre moi, ça m'irrite. 275

SCÈNE V

LES ACTEURS PRÉCÉDENTS, MADAME BERTHE

MATURIN (*à Berthe qui arrive.*)

Ma belle-mère, arrivez, venez vite.
Vous n'êtes plus la maîtresse au logis.
Chacun rebèque, et je vous avertis,
Que si la chose en cet état demeure,
Si je ne suis marié tout à l'heure, 280
Je ne le serai point, tout est fini,
Tout est rompu.

BERTHE

Qui m'a désobei?
Qui contredit, s'il vous plaît, quand j'ordonne?
Serait-ce vous, mon mari? vous?

DIGNANT

Personne;
Nous n'avons garde; et Maturin veut bien 285

275b MS1: Mad[e] Berthe, et les acteurs précédents.
275c MS1: *à Mad[e] Berthe.*

Prendre ma fille à peu près avec rien;
J'en suis content; et je dois me promettre
Que monseigneur daignera le permettre.

BERTHE

Allez, allez, épargnez-vous ce soin;
C'est de moi seule ici qu'on a besoin; 290
Et quand la chose une fois sera faite,
Il faudra bien, ma foi, qu'il la permette.

DIGNANT

Mais…

BERTHE

Mais il faut suivre ce que je dis.
Je ne veux plus souffrir dans mon logis,
A mes dépens, une fille indolente, 295
Qui ne fait rien, de rien ne se tourmente,
Qui s'imagine avoir de la beauté,
Pour être en droit d'avoir de la fierté.
Mademoiselle avec sa froide mine,
Ne daigne pas aider à la cuisine; 300
Elle se mire, ajuste son chignon,
Fredonne un air en brodant un jupon,
Ne parle point, et le soir en cachette
Lit des romans que le bailli lui prête.
Eh bien voyez, elle ne répond rien. 305
Je me repens de lui faire du bien.
Elle est muette ainsi qu'une pécore.

MATURIN

Ah c'est tout jeune, et ça n'a pas encore

292 63G, T64P: qu'il le permette.
294 MS1: plus nourrir dans

L'esprit formé; ça vient avec le temps.

DIGNANT

Ma bonne, il faut quelques ménagements 310
Pour une fille; elles ont d'ordinaire
De l'embarras dans cette grande affaire;
C'est modestie, et pudeur que cela.
Comme elle, enfin, vous passâtes par là;
Je m'en souviens, vous étiez fort revêche. 315

BERTHE

Eh! finissons. Allons, qu'on se dépêche:
Quels sots propos! Suivez-moi promptement
Chez le bailli.

COLETTE

N'en fais rien, mon enfant.

BERTHE

Allons, Acante.

ACANTE

O ciel! que dois-je faire?

COLETTE

Refuse tout, laisse ta belle-mère, 320
Viens avec moi.

BERTHE

Quoi donc! sans sourciller?

309 MS1: L'esprit ouvert
318a MS1, W75G* (→ MS2, MS3, K): COLETTE (*à Acante*) [W75G*: [V]]
320 MS1: Refuse-les;
321a W75G* (→ MS2, MS3, K): BERTHE (*à Acante*) [W75G*: [W]]

Mais parlez donc.

ACANTE

A qui puis-je parler?

DIGNANT

Chez le bailli, ma bonne, allons l'attendre,
Sans la gêner; et laissons-lui reprendre
Un peu d'haleine.

ACANTE

Ah! croyez que mes sens 325
Sont pénétrés de vos soins indulgents;
Croyez qu'en tout je distingue mon père.

MATURIN

Madame Berthe, on ne distingue guère
Ni vous, ni moi: la belle a le maintien
Un peu bien sec, mais cela n'y fait rien; 330
Et je réponds, dès qu'elle sera nôtre,
Qu'en peu de temps je la rendrai toute autre.

(*ils sortent.*)

ACANTE

Ah! que je sens de trouble et de chagrin!
Me faudra-t-il épouser Maturin?

332a MS1, no stage direction

SCÈNE VI

ACANTE, COLETTE

COLETTE

Ah! n'en fais rien, crois-moi, ma chère amie. 335
Du mariage aurais-tu tant d'envie?
Tu peux trouver beaucoup mieux… que sait-on?
Aimerais-tu ce méchant?

ACANTE

Mon Dieu non.
Mais vois-tu bien, je ne suis plus soufferte
Dans le logis de la marâtre Berthe; 340
Je suis chassée, il me faut un abri,
Et par besoin je dois prendre un mari.
C'est en pleurant que je cause ta peine.
D'un grand projet j'ai la cervelle pleine;
Mais je ne sais comment m'y prendre; hélas! 345
Que devenir?… Dis-moi, ne sais-tu pas
Si monseigneur doit venir dans ses terres?

COLETTE

Nous l'attendons.

ACANTE

Bientôt?

COLETTE

Je ne sais guères

335 MS1: Non, n'en fais

Dans mon taudis les nouvelles de cour.
Mais s'il revient, ce doit être un grand jour. 350
Il met, dit-on, la paix dans les familles;
Il rend justice, il a grand soin des filles.

ACANTE

Ah! s'il pouvait me protéger ici!

COLETTE

Je prétends bien qu'il me protège aussi.

ACANTE

On dit qu'à Metz il a fait des merveilles, 355
Qui dans l'armée ont très peu de pareilles;
Que Charles-Quint a loué sa valeur.

COLETTE

Qu'est-ce que Charles-Quint?

ACANTE

Un empereur
Qui nous a fait bien du mal.

COLETTE

Et qu'importe?
Ne m'en faites-pas, vous, et que je sorte 360
A mon honneur du cas triste où je suis.

349 MS1: En ce pays des nouvelles
355-357 MS3, β pasted over and replaced by:
On dit qu'à Metz il s'est couvert de gloire;
Que c'est à lui ⟨qu'on⟩ ↑que+ l'on doit la victoire,
Et Charles-Quint a loué sa valeur.

ACANTE

Comme le tien mon cœur est plein d'ennuis.
Non loin d'ici quelquefois on me mène
Dans un château de la jeune Dormène...

COLETTE

Près de nos bois?... ah! le plaisant château! 365
De Maturin le logis est plus beau;
Et Maturin est bien plus riche qu'elle.

ACANTE

Oui, je le sais; mais cette demoiselle
Est autre chose; elle est de qualité;
On la respecte avec sa pauvreté. 370
Elle a près d'elle une vieille personne
Qu'on nomme Laure, et de qui l'âme est bonne.
Laure est aussi d'une grande maison.

COLETTE

Qu'importe encor?

ACANTE

Les gens d'un certain nom,
J'ai remarqué cela, chère Colette, 375
En savent plus, ont l'âme autrement faite,
Ont de l'esprit, des sentiments plus grands,
Meilleurs que nous.

363 MS1: ⟨Non loin⟩ ↑Tout près
371 W75G* (→ MS2, MS3, K): Elle a ⟨près d'⟩ V↑ chez
372 W75G* (→ MS2, MS3, K): ⟨et de qui l'âme est bonne⟩ V↑ et dont l'âme est si bonne

COLETTE

Oui, dès leurs premiers ans,
Avec grand soin leur âme est façonnée;
La nôtre, hélas! languit abandonnée. 380
Comme on apprend à chanter, à danser,
Les gens du monde apprennent à penser.

ACANTE

Cette Dormène, et cette vieille dame,
Semblent donner quelque chose à mon âme;
Je crois en valoir mieux quand je les vois; 385
J'ai de l'orgueil, et je ne sais pourquoi;
Et les bontés de Dormène et de Laure
Me font haïr, mille fois plus encore,
Madame Berthe, et monsieur Maturin.

COLETTE

Quitte-les tous.

ACANTE

Je n'ose; mais enfin 390
J'ai quelque espoir: que ton conseil m'assiste.
Dis-moi d'abord, Colette, en quoi consiste
Ce fameux droit du seigneur?

COLETTE

Oh! ma foi,
Va consulter de plus doctes que moi.

378 w75G* (→ MS2, MS3): Oui⟨,⟩;
386 w75G* (→ MS2, MS3): l'orgueil⟨,⟩; [...] pourquoi⟨;⟩.
391-400 MS1:

COLETTE

Eh que crains-tu; n'avons-nous pas ma mère
Elle est alerte, et conduit cette affaire;

Je ne suis point mariée: et l'affaire, 395
A ce qu'on dit, est un très grand mystère.
Seconde-moi, fais que je vienne à bout
D'être épousée, et je te dirai tout.

ACANTE

Ah! j'y ferai mon possible.

COLETTE

Ma mère
Est très alerte, et conduit mon affaire: 400
Elle me fait, par un acte plaintif,
Pousser mon droit par devant le baillif.
J'aurai, dit-elle, un mari par justice.

ACANTE

Que de bon cœur j'en fais le sacrifice!
Chère Colette, agissons bien à point, 405
Toi pour l'avoir, moi pour ne l'avoir point.
Tu gagneras assez à ce partage,
Mais en perdant, je gagne davantage.

Fin du premier acte.

ACTE II

SCÈNE PREMIÈRE

LE BAILLI, PHLIPE SON VALET

LE BAILLI

Ma robe, allons… du respect… vite Phlipe.
C'est en bailli qu'il faut que je m'équipe.
J'ai des clients qu'il faut expédier.
Je suis bailli; je te fais mon huissier.
Amène-moi Colette à l'audience. 5

(*il s'assied devant une table,*
et feuillette un grand livre.)

L'affaire est grave, et de grande importance.
De Matrimonio… chapitre deux.
Empêchements… Ces cas-là sont véreux.
Il faut savoir de la jurisprudence.

(*à Colette.*)

Approchez-vous… faites la révérence, 10
Colette; il faut d'abord dire son nom.

COLETTE

Vous l'avez dit, je suis Colette.

LE BAILLI *écrit.*

Bon,

c MS1, 63G, T64P: Philippe [throughout]
MS2, MS3: Ph⟨i⟩lipe
1 MS1: Ma robe ⟨allons⟩ Et du respect… Allons, vite Philippe
CL: Ma robe, et du respect… Philippe
6 CL, omitted

Colette… Il faut dire ensuite son âge.
N'avez-vous pas trente ans, et davantage?

COLETTE

Fi donc, monsieur, j'ai vingt ans tout au plus. 15

LE BAILLI (*écrivant.*)

Çà, vingt ans, passe: ils sont bien révolus?

COLETTE

L'âge, monsieur, ne fait rien à la chose;
Et jeune ou non, sachez que je m'oppose
A tout contrat qu'un Maturin sans foi
Fera jamais avec d'autres que moi. 20

LE BAILLI

Vos oppositions seront notoires.
Çà, vous avez des raisons péremptoires?

COLETTE

J'ai cent raisons.

LE BAILLI

Dites-les… Aurait-il…

COLETTE

Oh! oui, monsieur.

16 63G: Ça vingt ans passés. Ils
T64P: Vingt ans passés. Ils
20 MS1: avec d'autre que
23 CL: Dites-les, vous a-t-il?…

LE BAILLI

Mais vous coupez le fil,
A tout moment, de notre procédure. 25

COLETTE

Pardon, monsieur.

LE BAILLI

Vous a-t-il fait injure?

COLETTE

Oh tant! j'aurais plus d'un mari sans lui;
Et me voilà pauvre fille aujourd'hui.

LE BAILLI

Il vous a fait sans doute des promesses?

COLETTE

Mille pour une, et pleines de tendresses. 30
Il promettait, il jurait que dans peu
Il me prendrait en légitime nœud.

LE BAILLI (*écrivant.*)

En légitime nœud... quelle malice!
Çà, produisez ses lettres en justice.

COLETTE

Je n'en ai point, jamais il n'écrivait, 35
Et je croyais tout ce qu'il me disait.
Quand tous les jours on parle tête à tête
A son amant d'une manière honnête,
Pourquoi s'écrire? à quoi bon?

LE BAILLI

Mais du moins,
Au lieu d'écrits, vous avez des témoins? 40

COLETTE

Moi? point du tout: mon témoin c'est moi-même.
Est-ce qu'on prend des témoins quand on s'aime?
Et puis, monsieur, pouvais-je deviner
Que Maturin osât m'abandonner?
Il me parlait d'amitié, de constance; 45
Je l'écoutais, et c'était en présence
De mes moutons, dans son pré, dans le mien;
Ils ont tout vu, mais ils ne disent rien.

LE BAILLI

Non plus qu'eux tous je n'ai donc rien à dire.
Votre complainte en droit ne peut suffire. 50
On ne produit ni témoins, ni billets,
On ne vous a rien fait, rien écrit…

COLETTE

Mais,
Un Maturin aura donc l'insolence
Impunément d'abuser l'innocence?

LE BAILLI

En abuser! mais vraiment, c'est un cas 55

48 MS1: Ils ⟨ont tout vu:⟩ ↑sont muets ⟨mais ils ne disent⟩ ↑ainsi ne diront rien

52 MS2: fait, ⟨ni⟩ ↑rien

55 MS1: Oh oh mais s'il en est ainsi, ce cas

CL: Ah, si de vous il abusa, ce cas

Epouvantable, et vous n'en parliez pas!
Instrumentons… Laquelle nous remontre
Que Maturin en plus d'une rencontre,
Se prévalant de sa simplicité,
A méchamment contre icelle attenté: 60
Laquelle insiste, et répète dommages,
Frais, intérêts, pour raison des outrages
Contre les lois faits par le suborneur,
Dit Maturin, à son présent honneur.

COLETTE

Rayez cela; je ne veux pas qu'on dise 65
Dans le pays une telle sottise.
Mon honneur est très intact; et pour peu
Qu'on l'eût blessé, l'on aurait vu beau jeu.

LE BAILLI

Que prétendez-vous donc?

56-60 MS1, CL:
Est autre chose et vous n'en parliez pas
(*il écrit*)
Instrumentons… dit en notre présence
Que Maturin usant de violence
⟨Contre⟩ ↑Malgré+ les lois, ⟨contre⟩ ↑malgré+ l'honnêteté
[CL: Contre les lois, contré l'honnêteté]
⟨Contre Colette il a fait⟩
A méchamment sur icelle attenté

56 63G, T64P: n'en parlez pas

61-62 MS1, struck out

63-64 MS1:
⟨Et torts griefs, faits malgré sa pudeur
Par Maturin à son présent honneur.⟩ [in the margin: à changer]
CL: Brèches, assauts faits malgré sa pudeur
Par Mathurin à son présent honneur

67 MS1: On n'a rien fait de semblable et pour peu
CL: On ne m'a rien fait de pareil; pour peu

68 MS1, CL: Qu'on l'eût osé, l'on aurait vu beau jeu.

COLETTE

Etre vengée.

LE BAILLI

Pour se venger il faut être outragée; 70
Et par écrit coucher en mots exprès,
Quels attentats encontre vous sont faits;
Articuler les lieux, les circonstances,
Quis, *quid*, *ubi*, les excès, insolences,
Enormités sur quoi l'on jugera. 75

COLETTE

Ecrivez donc tout ce qu'il vous plaira.

LE BAILLI

Ce n'est pas tout: il faut savoir la suite
Que ces excès pourraient avoir produite.

COLETTE

Comment produite? Eh rien ne produit rien.

77-78 MS1, CL:
Ce n'est pas tout: Pour fonder vos poursuites,
De ces excès il faut savoir les suites.

78a-84 MS1, CL:
⟨Devant la cour prouver son attentat [CL: constater votre état]
Bien consulter, constater votre état [CL: comment cet attentat]
Et quelle suite eut enfin son audace. [CL: Aura produit une apparente trace,]
Examiner…

COLETTE

Et vous m'osez en face
Tenir à moi cet insolent discours!
Si vous n'étiez bailli, jour de mes jours,
A poings fermés de mes dix doigts…

LE BAILLI

Ma bonne

Traître bailli, qu'entendez-vous?

LE BAILLI

Fort bien, 80

Laquelle fille a dans ses procédures,
Perdu le sens, et nous dit des injures;
Et n'apportant nulle preuve du fait,
L'empêchement est nul, de nul effet.

(*il se lève.*)

Depuis une heure en vain je vous écoute. 85
Vous n'avez rien prouvé, je vous déboute.[3]

COLETTE

Me débouter, moi?

LE BAILLI

Vous.

COLETTE

Maudit baillif!

Je suis déboutée?

LE BAILLI

Oui, quand le plaintif

S'il est ainsi, la cour vous abandonne;
Vous n'apportez nulle preuve du fait,
Et vos prétentions sont sans effet.〉

85 MS1, CL: Depuis longtemps en vain
87a MS1: LE BAILLI (*se levant*)
87 MS1, CL: Traître bailli!

[3] This passage is based on a similar play with the verb 'interloquer' in a well-known passage from Regnard's comedy *Le Légataire universel* (1708). See above, p.30.

Ne peut donner des raisons qui convainquent,
On le déboute, et les adverses vainquent. 90
Sur Maturin n'ayant point action,
Nous procédons à la conclusion.

COLETTE

Non, non, bailli, vous aurez beau conclure,
Instrumenter, et signer, je vous jure
Qu'il n'aura point son Acante.

LE BAILLI

Il l'aura; 95
De monseigneur le droit se maintiendra.
Je suis bailli, et j'ai les droits du maître:
C'est devant moi qu'il faudra comparaître.
Consolez-vous, sachez que vous aurez
A faire à moi quand vous vous marierez. 100

COLETTE

J'aimerais mieux le reste de ma vie
Demeurer fille.

LE BAILLI

Oh je vous en défie.

97 63G, T64P: j'ai le droit du

SCÈNE II

COLETTE *seule.*

Ah! comment faire? où reprendre mon bien?
J'ai protesté, cela ne sert de rien.
On va signer. Que je suis tourmentée! 105

SCÈNE III

COLETTE, ACANTE

COLETTE

A mon secours! me voilà déboutée.

ACANTE

Déboutée!

COLETTE

Oui, l'ingrat vous est promis.
On me déboute.

ACANTE

Hélas! je suis bien pis.
De mes chagrins mon âme est oppressée;
Ma chaîne est prête, et je suis fiancée, 110
Ou je vais l'être au moins dans un moment.

COLETTE

Ne hais-tu pas mon lâche?

112 MS1: Mais tu hais le perfide?

ACANTE

Honnêtement.
Entre nous deux, juges-tu sur ma mine
Qu'il soit bien doux d'être ici Maturine?

COLETTE

Non pas pour toi; tu portes dans ton air, 115
Je ne sais quoi de brillant et de fier;
A Maturin cela ne convient guère,
Et ce maraud était mieux mon affaire.

ACANTE

J'ai par malheur de trop hauts sentiments.
Dis-moi, Colette, as-tu lu des romans? 120

COLETTE

Moi? non; jamais.

ACANTE

Le bailli Métaprose
M'en a prêté... Mon Dieu la belle chose!

COLETTE

En quoi si belle?

118 MS1: Et ce fermier était
122a-132 MS1:
<Chère Colette, on y voit des amants
Pleins de vertu, courageux, et galants
Sachant unir la gloire à la tendresse,
Servant leur prince, adorant leur maîtresse,
Victorieux des plus fameux guerriers,
A nos genoux apportant des lauriers.
COLETTE
Ma chère enfant, je suis toute interdite;
Et les romans t'ont vraiment bien instruite.

ACANTE

On y voit des amants,
Si courageux, si tendres, si galants!

COLETTE

Oh Maturin n'est pas comme eux.

ACANTE

Colette, 125
Que les romans rendent l'âme inquiète!

COLETTE

Et d'où vient donc?

ACANTE

Ils forment trop l'esprit.
En les lisant le mien bientôt s'ouvrit.
A réfléchir que de nuits j'ai passées!
Que les romans font naître de pensées! 130
Que les héros de ces livres charmants
Ressemblent peu, Colette, aux autres gens!
Cette lumière était pour moi féconde;
Je me voyais dans un tout autre monde.
J'étais au ciel… Ah! qu'il m'était bien dur 135
De retomber dans mon état obscur!
Le cœur tout plein de ce grand étalage,
De me trouver au fond de mon village!
Et de descendre après ce vol divin,

Ah! je vois bien qu'ils donnent de l'esprit!
ACANTE
En les lisant le mien bientôt s'ouvrit;⟩

134 MS1: dans tout un autre
139 63G, T64P: après un vol

Des Amadis à maître Maturin! 140

COLETTE

Votre propos me ravit; et je jure
Que j'ai déjà du goût pour la lecture.

ACANTE

T'en souvient-il, autant qu'il m'en souvient,
Que ce marquis, ce beau seigneur qui tient
Dans le pays le rang, l'état d'un prince, 145
De sa présence honora la province?
Il s'est passé juste un an et deux mois
Depuis qu'il vint pour cette seule fois.
T'en souvient-il? nous le vîmes à table;
Il m'accueillit; ah! qu'il était affable! 150
Tous ses discours étaient des mots choisis,
Que l'on n'entend jamais dans ce pays.
C'était, Colette, une langue nouvelle,
Supérieure, et pourtant naturelle;
J'aurais voulu l'entendre tout le jour. 155

COLETTE

Tu l'entendras sans doute à son retour.

ACANTE

Ce jour, Colette, occupe ta mémoire,
Où monseigneur tout rayonnant de gloire,
Dans nos forêts suivi d'un peuple entier,
Le fer en main courait le sanglier? 160

141 MS1: ravit, je vous jure
143 MS1: Te souvient-il
154 MS1: Toute étonnante, et
160 MS1: ⟨courait⟩ ↓percer↑ ce sanglier

COLETTE

Oui, quelque idée et confuse, et légère,
Peut m'en rester.

ACANTE

Je l'ai distincte et claire.
Je crois le voir avec cet air si grand,
Sur ce cheval superbe et bondissant;
Près d'un gros chêne il perce de sa lance 165
Le sanglier qui contre lui s'élance.
Dans ce moment j'entendis mille voix,
Que répétaient les échos de nos bois;
Et de bon cœur (il faut que j'en convienne)
J'aurais voulu qu'il démêlât la mienne. 170
De son départ je fus encor témoin;
On l'entourait, je n'étais pas bien loin.
Il me parla... Depuis ce jour, ma chère,
Tous les romans ont le don de me plaire.
Quand je les lis, je n'ai jamais d'ennui; 175
Il me paraît qu'ils me parlent de lui.

COLETTE

Ah qu'un roman est beau!

ACANTE

C'est la peinture

163-170 MS2, MS3:
⟨β⟩↑ [MS3: V]
Te souvient-il combien l'écho des bois
Retentissait de plus de mille voix
J'ai tort peut-être, il faut que j'en convienne
Mais je crus voir qu'il distinguait la mienne.

170 MS1: qu'on démêlât

171 63G, T64P: je suis encor

174 63G, T64P: le droit de

Du cœur humain, je crois, d'après nature.

COLETTE

D'après nature!... Entre nous deux, ton cœur
N'aime-t-il pas en secret monseigneur? 180

ACANTE

Oh non, je n'ose; et je sens la distance
Qu'entre nous deux mit son rang, sa naissance.
Crois-tu qu'on ait des sentiments si doux
Pour ceux qui sont trop au-dessus de nous?
A cette erreur trop de raison s'oppose. 185
Non, je ne l'aime point, mais il est cause
Que l'ayant vu je ne peux à présent
En aimer d'autre, et c'est un grand tourment.

COLETTE

Mais de tous ceux qui le suivaient, ma bonne,
Aucun n'a-t-il cajolé ta personne? 190
J'avouerai moi, que l'on m'en a conté.

ACANTE

Un étourdi prit quelque liberté;
Il s'appelait le chevalier Gernance;
Son fier maintien, ses airs, son insolence,
Me révoltaient, loin de m'en imposer. 195

180a-185 MS1:
⟨β⟩ ↑Tu m'en dis tant de bien.
ACANTE
Oh! non je n'ose

182 63G, T64P: deux met son
186 W75G*: point⟨,⟩
188 W75G*: d'autre⟨,⟩
193 63G: Germance
194 63G, T64P: maintien, son air, son

Il fut surpris de se voir mépriser;
Et réprimant sa poursuite hardie,
Je lui fis voir combien la modestie
Etait plus fière, et pouvait d'un coup d'œil
Faire trembler l'impudence et l'orgueil. 200
Ce chevalier serait assez passable,
Et d'autres mœurs l'auraient pu rendre aimable.
Ah! la douceur est l'appât qui nous prend.
Que monseigneur, ô ciel, est différent!

COLETTE

Ce chevalier n'était donc guère sage? 205
Cà, qui des deux te déplaît davantage,
De Maturin, ou de cet effronté?

ACANTE

Oh Maturin!... c'est sans difficulté.

COLETTE

Mais monseigneur est bon: il est le maître;
Pourrait-il pas te dépêtrer du traître? 210
Tu me parais si belle.

ACANTE

Hélas!

COLETTE

Je crois

200 63G, T64P: l'imprudence et
201 63G, T64P: assez capable
202 MS1: Et, plus modeste, il pourrait être aimable.
205 63G: n'étant donc
211 MS1: ACANTE / Ah! Ah!

Que tu pourras mieux réussir que moi.

ACANTE

Est-il bien vrai qu'il arrive?

COLETTE

Sans doute,

Car on le dit.

ACANTE

Penses-tu qu'il m'écoute?

COLETTE

J'en suis certaine, et je retiens ma part 215
De ses bontés.

ACANTE

Nous le verrons trop tard;
Il n'arrivera point; on me fiance,
Tout est conclu, je suis sans espérance.
Berthe est terrible en sa mauvaise humeur;
Maturin presse, et je meurs de douleur. 220

COLETTE

Eh moque-toi de Berthe.

213-216 MS1, struck out
217 MS1: ⟨β⟩↑Nous le verrons trop tard: on
220a-223 MS1:
Je m'en vais prendre un parti.
COLETTE
Prends donc vite.
Et quel est-il?
ACANTE
C'est celui de la fuite.

ACANTE

Hélas Dormène,
Si je lui parle, entrera dans ma peine.
Je vais prier Dormène de m'aider
De son appui, qu'elle daigne accorder
Aux malheureux: cette dame est si bonne! 225
Laure, surtout, cette vieille personne,
Qui m'a souvent montré tant d'amitié,
De moi, sans doute, aura quelque pitié,
Me donnera des conseils.

223 W75G* (→ MS2, MS3, K): ⟨vais⟩ W↑ veux
227 W75G* (→ MS2, MS3, K): ⟨souvent⟩ W↑ toujours
227-228 63G, T64P:
Par le malheur sensible à la pitié,
Qui m'a souvent montré tant d'amitié
229-232 W75G* (→ MS2, MS3, K), added by Wagnière on a slip of paper:

COLETTE

Oui, oui, va t'en; c'est le meilleur parti.
Je t'aime bien, mais plus ailleurs qu'ici.
Ici tu rends Maturin infidèle;
Quand tu n'y seras plus je serai belle.

ACANTE

Je vais prier

Car, sais-tu bien que cette dame Laure
Très tendrement de ses bontés m'honore?
Entre ses bras elle me tient souvent,
Elle m'instruit, et pleure en m'instruisant.

COLETTE

Pourquoi pleurer?

ACANTE

Mais de ma destinée.
Elle voit bien que je ne suis pas née
Pour Maturin. – crois-moi, Colette, allons
Lui demander des conseils, des leçons. –
Veux-tu me suivre?

COLETTE

Ah oui, ma chère Acante,
Enfuyons-nous, la chose est très prudente.
Viens, je connais des chemins détournés
Tout près d'ici.

COLETTE

A notre âge,
Il faut de bons amis, rien n'est plus sage. 230
Tu trembles?

ACANTE

Oui.

COLETTE

Par ces lieux détournés
Viens avec moi.

SCÈNE IV

ACANTE, COLETTE, BERTHE,
DIGNANT, MATURIN

BERTHE (*arrêtant Acante.*)

Quel chemin vous prenez!
Etes-vous folle? et quand on doit se rendre
A son devoir, faut-il se faire attendre?
Quelle indolence! et quel air de froideur! 235
Vous me glacez: votre mauvaise humeur
Jusqu'à la fin vous sera reprochée.
On vous marie, et vous êtes fâchée!
Hom l'idiote! allons, çà, Maturin,

229a-230 MS1:

COLETTE

Pour bien faire
Viens-t'en d'abord te cacher chez ma mère.

Soyez le maître, et donnez-lui la main. 240

MATURIN *approche sa main, et veut l'embrasser.*

Ah! palsamdié…

BERTHE

Voyez la malhonnête!
Elle rechigne et détourne la tête!

ACANTE

Pardon, mon père, hélas! vous excusez
Mon embarras, vous le favorisez,
Et vous sentez quelle douleur amère 245
Je dois souffrir en quittant un tel père.

BERTHE

Et rien pour moi?

MATURIN

Ni rien pour moi non plus?

COLETTE

Non, rien, méchant, tu n'auras qu'un refus.

MATURIN

On me fiance.

COLETTE

Et va, va, fiançailles
Assez souvent ne sont pas épousailles. 250

240a MS1: *approchant sa main et voulant l'embrasser*

Laisse-moi faire.

DIGNANT

Eh! qu'est-ce que j'entends?
C'est un courrier: c'est je pense un des gens
De monseigneur; oui, c'est le vieux Champagne.

SCÈNE V

LES ACTEURS PRÉCÉDENTS, CHAMPAGNE

CHAMPAGNE

Oui, nous avons terminé la campagne,
Nous avons sauvé Metz, mon maître et moi, 255
Et nous aurons la paix. Vive le Roi!
Vive mon maître!... il a bien du courage,
Mais il est trop sérieux pour son âge:
J'en suis fâché. Je suis bien aise aussi,
Mon vieux Dignant, de te trouver ici. 260
Tu me parais en grande compagnie.

DIGNANT

Oui... vous serez de la cérémonie.
Nous marions Acante.

CHAMPAGNE

Bon! tant mieux!
Nous danserons, nous serons tous joyeux.

253 MS3: ⟨vieux⟩ ↑bon
253b MS1: Champagne, et les acteurs précédents

Ta fille est belle… Ah ah, c'est toi, Colette, 265
Ma chère enfant, ta fortune est donc faite,
Maturin est ton mari?

COLETTE

Mon Dieu, non.

CHAMPAGNE

Il fait fort mal.

COLETTE

Le traître, le fripon,
Croit dans l'instant prendre Acante pour femme.

CHAMPAGNE

Il fait fort bien; je réponds sur mon âme, 270
Que cet hymen à mon maître agréera,
Et que la noce à ses frais se fera.

ACANTE

Comment! il vient?

CHAMPAGNE

Peut-être ce soir même.

DIGNANT

Quoi! ce seigneur, ce bon maître que j'aime,
Je puis le voir encore avant ma mort? 275
S'il est ainsi, je bénirai mon sort.

272 MS1: ⟨β⟩↑Et qu'à la noce il se divertira

ACANTE

Puisqu'il revient, permettez, mon cher père,
De vous prier (devant ma belle-mère)
De vouloir bien ne rien précipiter
Sans son aveu, sans l'oser consulter. 280
C'est un devoir dont il faut qu'on s'acquitte,
C'est un respect, sans doute, qu'il mérite.

MATURIN

Foin du respect.

DIGNANT

Votre avis est sensé,
Et comme vous en secret j'ai pensé.

MATURIN

Et moi, l'ami, je pense le contraire. 285

COLETTE (*à Acante.*)

Bon, tenez ferme.

MATURIN

Est un sot qui diffère.
Je ne veux point soumettre mon honneur,
Si je le puis, à ce droit du seigneur.

277 MS1: permettez-moi, mon père
MS3: ⟨mon cher⟩ ↑moi, mon
278 MS1: prier (et vous ma
285-286 MS1, struck out, restored by 'bon' in the margin
287-288 MS1:
⟨Je ne veux point attendre monseigneur
Et son retour augmente ma frayeur⟩
[restored by 'bon' in the margin]

BERTHE

Eh pourquoi tant s'effaroucher? la chose
Est bonne au fond, quoique le monde en cause, 290
Et notre honneur ne peut s'en tourmenter.
J'en fis l'épreuve; et je peux protester
Qu'à mon devoir quand je me fus rendue,
On s'en alla dès l'instant qu'on m'eut vue.

COLETTE

Je le crois bien.

BERTHE

Cependant, la raison 295
Doit conseiller de fuir l'occasion.
Hâtons la noce, et n'attendons personne.
Préparez tout, mon mari, je l'ordonne.

MATURIN (*à Colette, en s'en allant.*)

C'est très bien dit. Eh bien, l'aurai-je enfin?

COLETTE

Non, tu ne l'auras pas, non, Maturin. 300

(*Ils sortent.*)

CHAMPAGNE

Oh, oh, nos gens viennent en diligence.
Eh quoi, déjà le chevalier Gernance?

289-296 MS1, absent
300b MS1: Champagne (*seul.*)

SCÈNE VI

LE CHEVALIER, CHAMPAGNE

CHAMPAGNE

Vous êtes fin, monsieur le chevalier,
Très à propos vous venez le premier.
Dans tous vos faits votre beau talent brille. 305
Vous vous doutez qu'on marie une fille;
Acante est belle, au moins.

LE CHEVALIER

Eh oui vraiment,
Je la connais; j'apprends en arrivant
Que Maturin se donne l'insolence
De s'appliquer ce bijou d'importance; 310
Mon bon destin nous a fait accourir
Pour y mettre ordre: il ne faut pas souffrir
Qu'un riche rustre ait les tendres prémices
D'une beauté qui ferait les délices
Des plus huppés, et des plus délicats. 315
Pour le marquis, il ne se hâte pas;
C'est, je l'avoue, un grave personnage,
Pressé de rien, bien compassé, bien sage,
Et voyageant comme un ambassadeur.
Parbleu, jouons un tour à sa lenteur. 320
Tiens, il me vient une bonne pensée,

309 MS1: ⟨β⟩↑Qu'un Maturin veut avoir l'insolence
310 MS1: ⟨s'appliquer⟩ ↑⟨marchander⟩ ↑se donner
313-314 MS1:
Que ce lourdaud fasse ainsi son partage
De doux appas, qui méritent l'hommage
319 T64P: En voyageant

C'est d'enlever *presto* la fiancée,
De la conduire en quelque vieux château,
Quelque masure.

CHAMPAGNE

Oui, le projet est beau.

LE CHEVALIER

Un vieux château, vers la forêt prochaine, 325
Tout délabré, que possède Dormène,
Avec sa vieille…

CHAMPAGNE

Oui, c'est Laure, je crois.

LE CHEVALIER

Oui.

CHAMPAGNE

Cette vieille était jeune autrefois,
Je m'en souviens: votre étourdi de père
Eut avec elle une certaine affaire 330
Où chacun d'eux fit un mauvais marché.
Ma foi, c'était un maître débauché,
Tout comme vous, buvant, aimant les belles,
Les enlevant, et puis se moquant d'elles.
Il mangea tout, et ne vous laissa rien. 335

LE CHEVALIER

J'ai le marquis, et c'est avoir du bien.

325-326 MSI:
Non loin d'ici, vers la forêt prochaine
Dans un réduit, il est une Dormène,

Sans nul souci je vis de ses largesses.
Je n'aime point l'embarras des richesses.
Est riche assez qui sait toujours jouir.
Le premier bien, crois-moi, c'est le plaisir. 340

CHAMPAGNE

Et que ne prenez-vous cette Dormène?
Bien plus qu'Acante elle en vaudrait la peine;
Elle est très fraîche: elle est de qualité;
Cela convient à votre dignité.
Laissez pour nous les filles du village. 345

LE CHEVALIER

Vraiment Dormène est un très doux partage;
C'est très bien dit. Je crois que j'eus un jour,
S'il m'en souvient, pour elle un peu d'amour.
Mais entre nous elle sent trop sa dame.
On ne pourrait en faire que sa femme. 350
Elle est bien pauvre, et je le suis aussi;
Et pour l'hymen j'ai fort peu de souci.
Mon cher Champagne, il me faut une Acante;
Cette conquête est beaucoup plus plaisante.
Oui, cette Acante aujourd'hui m'a piqué. 355
Je me sentis l'an passé provoqué
Par ses refus, par sa petite mine.
J'aime à dompter cette pudeur mutine.
J'ai deux coquins, qui font trois avec toi,

347-354 MS1, absent
354 63G, T64P: Cette coquette est
355 MS1: Mais cette Acante
358 MS1, between 358-359:
Et l'enlever est un vrai passetemps.
Notre Dormène a des airs importants,
Et, quoique pauvre, elle sent trop sa dame.
On ne pourrait en faire que sa femme.

Déterminés, alertes comme moi; 360
Nous tiendrons prêt à cent pas un carrosse,
Et nous fondrons tous quatre sur la noce.
Cela sera plaisant; j'en ris déjà.

CHAMPAGNE

Mais croyez-vous que monseigneur rira?

LE CHEVALIER

Il faudra bien qu'il rie, et que Dormène 365
En rie encor, quoique prude et hautaine;
Et je prétends que Laure en rie aussi.
Je viens de voir à cinq cents pas d'ici
Dormène et Laure en très mince équipage,
Qui s'en allaient vers le prochain village, 370
Chez quelque vieille. Il faut prendre ce temps.

CHAMPAGNE

C'est bien pensé; mais vos déportements
Sont dangereux, je crois, pour ma personne.

LE CHEVALIER

Bon! l'on se fâche, on s'apaise, on pardonne.
Tous les gens gais ont le don merveilleux 375
De mettre en train tous les gens sérieux.

CHAMPAGNE

Fort bien.

367 MS1: ⟨l'autre⟩ ↑Laure
374 MS2: ⟨l'on⟩ V↑on
377-379 MS1:
Fort bien.

LE CHEVALIER

Portons des perdrix, des bouteilles,

LE CHEVALIER

L'esprit le plus atrabilaire
Est subjugué quand on cherche à lui plaire.
On s'épouvante, on crie, on fuit d'abord,
Et puis l'on soupe, et puis l'on est d'accord. 380

CHAMPAGNE

On ne peut mieux: mais votre belle Acante
Est bien revêche.

LE CHEVALIER

Et c'est ce qui m'enchante.
La résistance est un charme de plus;
Et j'aime assez une heure de refus.
Comment souffrir la stupide innocence 385
D'un sot tendron faisant la révérence,
Baissant les yeux, muette à mon aspect,
Et recevant mes faveurs par respect?
Mon cher Champagne, à mon dernier voyage,
D'Acante ici j'éprouvai le courage. 390
Va, sous mes lois je la ferai plier.
Rentre pour moi dans ton premier métier,
Sois mon trompette, et sonne les alarmes.
Point de quartier, marchons, alerte, aux armes,
Vite.

CHAMPAGNE

Je crois que nous sommes trahis; 395

Un bon pâté, des truffes.

CHAMPAGNE

A merveilles!

LE CHEVALIER

On s'épouvante,

388 MS1: mes douceurs par

C'est du secours qui vient aux ennemis;
J'entends grand bruit, c'est monseigneur.

LE CHEVALIER

N'importe:

Sois prêt ce soir à me servir d'escorte.

Fin du second acte.

ACTE III

SCÈNE PREMIÈRE

LE MARQUIS, LE CHEVALIER GERNANCE

LE MARQUIS

Cher chevalier, que mon cœur est en paix!
Que mes regards sont ici satisfaits!
Que ce château qu'ont habité nos pères,
Que ces forêts, ces plaines me sont chères!
Que je voudrais oublier pour toujours 5
L'illusion, les manèges des cours!
Tous ces grands riens, ces pompeuses chimères,
Ces vanités, ces ombres passagères,
Au fond du cœur laissent un vide affreux.
C'est avec nous que nous sommes heureux. 10
Dans ce grand monde où chacun veut paraître,
On est esclave, et chez moi je suis maître.
Que je voudrais que vous eussiez mon goût!

LE CHEVALIER

Eh oui, l'on peut se réjouir partout,
En garnison, à la cour, à la guerre, 15
Longtemps en ville, et huit jours dans sa terre.

c 63G: LE MARQUIS, LE CHEVALIER, GERMANCE
T64P: LE MARQUIS, LE CHEVALIER
MS1, with stage direction: *Le théâtre représente une salle du château*
2 63G, T64P: regards ici sont satisfaits
5 MS1: Que j'y voudrais
6 63PC: le manège des

LE MARQUIS

Que vous et moi nous sommes différents!

LE CHEVALIER

Nous changerons peut-être avec le temps.
En attendant vous savez qu'on apprête
Pour ce jour même une très belle fête? 20
C'est une noce.

LE MARQUIS

Oui, Maturin vraiment
Fait un beau choix, et mon contentement
Est tout acquis à ce doux mariage.
L'époux est riche, et sa maîtresse est sage;
C'est un bonheur bien digne de mes vœux, 25
En arrivant de faire deux heureux.

LE CHEVALIER

Acante encore en peut faire un troisième.

LE MARQUIS

Je vous reconnais là, toujours vous-même.
Mon cher parent, vous m'avez fait cent fois
Trembler pour vous par vos galants exploits. 30
Tout peut passer dans des villes de guerre;
Mais nous devons l'exemple dans ma terre.

LE CHEVALIER

L'exemple du plaisir apparemment?

LE MARQUIS

Au moins, mon cher, que ce soit prudemment;

22 MS1, 63G, T64P, MS3: mon consentement

Daignez en croire un parent qui vous aime. 35
Si vous n'avez du respect pour vous-même,
Quelque grand nom que vous puissiez porter,
Vous ne pourrez vous faire respecter.
Je ne suis pas difficile et sévère,
Mais entre nous songez que votre père, 40
Pour avoir pris le train que vous prenez,
Se vit au rang des plus infortunés,
Perdit ses biens, languit dans la misère,
Fit de douleur expirer votre mère,
Et près d'ici mourut assassiné. 45
J'étais enfant; son sort infortuné
Fut à mon cœur une leçon terrible,
Qui se grava dans mon âme sensible.
Utilement témoin de ses malheurs,
Je m'instruisais en répandant des pleurs. 50
Si comme moi cette fin déplorable
Vous eût frappé, vous seriez raisonnable.

LE CHEVALIER

Oui, je veux l'être un jour, c'est mon dessein;
J'y pense quelquefois, mais c'est en vain;
Mon feu m'emporte.

LE MARQUIS

Eh bien, je vous présage 55
Que vous serez las du libertinage.

LE CHEVALIER

Je le voudrais; mais on fait comme on peut.
Ma foi, n'est pas raisonnable qui veut.

38 T64P: Vous ne pouvez
57 63G, T64P: mais l'on fait

LE MARQUIS

Vous vous trompez, on est un peu son maître;
J'en fis l'épreuve, est sage qui veut l'être; 60
Et croyez-moi, cette Acante, entre nous,
Eut des attraits pour moi comme pour vous:
Mais ma raison ne pouvait me permettre
Un fol amour qui m'allait compromettre.
Je rejetai ce désir passager, 65
Dont la poursuite aurait pu m'affliger,
Dont le succès eût perdu cette fille,
Eût fait sa honte aux yeux de sa famille,
Et l'eût privée à jamais d'un époux.

LE CHEVALIER

Je ne suis pas si timide que vous. 70
La même pâte, il faut que j'en convienne,
N'a point pétri votre branche et la mienne.
Quoi, vous pensez être dans tous les temps
Maître absolu de vos yeux, de vos sens?

LE MARQUIS

Et pourquoi non?

LE CHEVALIER

Très fort je vous respecte, 75
Mais la sagesse est tant soit peu suspecte.
Les plus prudents se laissent captiver,
Et le vrai sage est encore à trouver.

59 W75G* (→ MS2, MS3, K): ⟨on est un peu son⟩ ↑V de son cœur on est
63 MS1: ⟨pouvait⟩ ↑pouvant
71-72 MS1:
⟨β⟩↑Je vais au fait. En amour comme en guerre
La hardiesse est un point nécessaire
72 K: point formé votre

Craignez surtout le titre ridicule
De philosophe.

LE MARQUIS

O l'étrange scrupule![4] 80
Ce noble nom, ce nom tant combattu,
Que veut-il dire? amour de la vertu.
Le fat en raille avec étourderie,
Le sot le craint, le fripon le décrie;
L'homme de bien dédaigne les propos 85
Des étourdis, des fripons et des sots:
Et ce n'est pas sur les discours du monde
Que le bonheur et la vertu se fonde.
Ecoutez-moi. Je suis las aujourd'hui
Du train des cours où l'on vit pour autrui; 90
Et j'ai pensé, pour vivre à la campagne,
Pour être heureux, qu'il faut une compagne.
J'ai le projet de m'établir ici,
Et je voudrais vous marier aussi.

LE CHEVALIER

Très humble serviteur.

LE MARQUIS

Ma fantaisie 95
N'est pas de prendre une jeune étourdie.

LE CHEVALIER

L'étourderie a du bon.

84 MS1: ⟨le fripon⟩ ↑⟨l'ignorant⟩ ↑le méchant
86 MS1: ⟨fripons⟩ ↑méchants

[4] See above, p.21.

LE MARQUIS

Je voudrais
Un esprit doux, plus que de doux attraits.

LE CHEVALIER

J'aimerais mieux le dernier.

LE MARQUIS

La jeunesse,
Les agréments n'ont rien qui m'intéresse. 100

LE CHEVALIER

Tant pis.

LE MARQUIS

Je veux affermir ma maison,
Par un hymen qui soit tout de raison.

LE CHEVALIER

Oui, tout d'ennui.

LE MARQUIS

J'ai pensé que Dormène
Serait très propre à former cette chaîne.

LE CHEVALIER

Notre Dormène est bien pauvre.

LE MARQUIS

Tant mieux. 105

99 63PC: les derniers.
105 63G, T64P: Votre Dormène

C'est un bonheur si pur, si précieux,
De relever l'indigente noblesse,
De préférer l'honneur à la richesse!
C'est l'honneur seul qui chez nous doit former
Tout notre sang: lui seul doit animer 110
Ce sang reçu de nos braves ancêtres,
Qui dans les camps doit couler pour ses maîtres.

LE CHEVALIER

Je pense ainsi: les Français libertins
Sont gens d'honneur. Mais dans vos beaux desseins,
Vous avez donc, malgré votre réserve, 115
Un peu d'amour?

LE MARQUIS

Qui, moi? Dieu m'en préserve!
Il faut savoir être maître chez soi;
Et si j'aimais, je recevrais la loi.
Se marier par amour, c'est folie.

LE CHEVALIER

Ma foi, marquis, votre philosophie 120

115-123 MS1:
Par vos courriers avez-vous à la dame
Fait quelque part de votre froide flamme?
LE MARQUIS
Non; je mûris mon projet et je veux,
Bien peser tout, n'étant point amoureux.
LE CHEVALIER
Pesez, pesez.
LE MARQUIS
Il faut d'abord connaître
Son monde à fonds; et je penserais être,
Un fou fieffé si j'allais épouser,
Ce que j'estime avant d'y bien penser.
LE CHEVALIER
Moi je pense fort peu; mais j'imagine

Me paraît toute à rebours du bon sens;
Pour moi, je crois au pouvoir de nos sens.
Je les consulte en tout, et j'imagine
Que tous ces gens si graves par la mine,
Pleins de morale et de réflexions, 125
Sont destinés aux grandes passions.
Les étourdis esquivent l'esclavage,
Mais un coup d'œil peut subjuguer un sage.

LE MARQUIS

Soit; nous verrons.

LE CHEVALIER

Voici d'autres époux;
Voici la noce; allons, égayons-nous. 130
C'est Maturin, c'est la gentille Acante,
C'est le vieux père, et la mère, et la tante,
C'est le bailli, Colette et tout le bourg.

SCÈNE II

LE MARQUIS, LE CHEVALIER, LE BAILLI
à la tête des habitants

LE MARQUIS

J'en suis touché. Bonjour, enfants, bonjour.

LE BAILLI

Nous venons tous avec conjouissance, 135

121 63G, T64P: tout à rebours

Nous présenter devant Votre Excellence,
Comme les Grecs jadis devant Cyrus…
Comme les Grecs.

LE MARQUIS

Les Grecs sont superflus.
Je suis Picard; je revois avec joie
Tous mes vassaux.

LE BAILLI

Les Grecs de qui la proie… 140

LE CHEVALIER

Ah finissez!… Notre gros Maturin,
La belle Acante est votre proie enfin?

MATURIN

Ouida, monsieur, la fiançaille est faite,
Et nous prions que monseigneur permette
Qu'on nous finisse.

COLETTE

Oh tu ne l'auras pas; 145
Je te le dis, tu me demeureras.
Oui, monseigneur, vous me rendrez justice;
Vous ne souffrirez pas qu'il me trahisse;
Il m'a promis…

MATURIN

Bon, j'ai promis en l'air.

145 MS1: COLETTE / On ne finira pas.

LE MARQUIS

Il faut, bailli, tirer la chose au clair. 150
A-t-il promis?

LE BAILLI

La chose est constatée.
Colette est folle, et je l'ai déboutée.

COLETTE

Ça n'y fait rien, et monseigneur saura
Qu'on force Acante à ce beau marché-là,
Qu'on la maltraite, et qu'on la violente 155
Pour épouser.

LE MARQUIS

Est-il vrai, belle Acante?

ACANTE

Je dois d'un père avec raison chéri
Suivre les lois; il me donne un mari.

MATURIN

Vous voyez bien qu'en effet elle m'aime.

LE MARQUIS

Sa réponse est d'une prudence extrême; 160
Eh bien chez moi la noce se fera.

LE CHEVALIER

Bon, bon, tant mieux.

LE MARQUIS (*à Acante.*)

Votre père verra

Que j'aime en lui la probité, le zèle,
Et les travaux d'un serviteur fidèle.
Votre sagesse à mes yeux satisfaits 165
Augmente encor le prix de vos attraits.
Comptez, amis, qu'en faveur de la fille
Je prendrai soin de toute la famille.

COLETTE

Et de moi donc?

LE MARQUIS

De vous, Colette, aussi.
Cher chevalier, retirons-nous d'ici; 170
Ne troublons point leur naïve allégresse.

LE BAILLI

Et votre droit, monseigneur, le temps presse.

MATURIN

Quel chien de droit! Ah me voilà perdu.

COLETTE

Va, tu verras.

171a-178 MS1:

LE BAILLI *au marquis que veut s'en aller*
Mais songez-vous...? monseigneur, le temps presse.
MATURIN
Maudit bavard, et pourquoi parles-tu?
Il oubliait... Ah, me voilà perdu.
LE BAILLI
Vous savez bien que cet antique usage...
LE MARQUIS
Arrangez tout, bailli, en homme sage,
Car de mes droits je ne veux disposer
Qu'avec décence

BERTHE

Maturin, que crains-tu?

LE MARQUIS

Vous aurez soin, bailli, en homme sage, 175
D'arranger tout suivant l'antique usage;
D'un si beau droit je veux m'autoriser
Avec décence, et n'en point abuser.

LE CHEVALIER

Ah quel Caton! mais mon Caton, je pense,
La suit des yeux, et non sans complaisance. 180
Mon cher cousin.

LE MARQUIS

Eh bien?

LE CHEVALIER

Gageons tous deux
Que vous allez devenir amoureux.

LE MARQUIS

Moi! mon cousin.

LE CHEVALIER

Oui, vous.

LE MARQUIS

L'extravagance!

178 MS1, with stage direction after 178: *ils s'en vont*
182 63G, 'Que vous' omitted

LE CHEVALIER

Vous le serez, j'en ris déjà d'avance.
Gageons, vous dis-je, une discrétion. 185

LE MARQUIS

Soit.

LE CHEVALIER

Vous perdrez.

LE MARQUIS

Soyez bien sûr que non.

SCÈNE III

LE BAILLI, LES AUTRES ACTEURS

MATURIN

Que disent-ils?

LE BAILLI

Ils disent que sur l'heure
Chacun s'en aille et qu'Acante demeure.

MATURIN

Moi, que je sorte?

LE BAILLI

Oui sans doute.

COLETTE

Oui, fripon.

Oh! nous aimons la loi, nous.

MATURIN (*au bailli.*)

Mais doit-on?... 190

BERTHE

Eh quoi, benêt, te voilà bien à plaindre!

DIGNANT

Allez, d'Acante on n'aura rien à craindre.
Trop de vertu règne au fond de son cœur;
Et notre maître est tout rempli d'honneur.

(*à Acante.*)

Quand près de vous il daignera se rendre, 195
Quand sans témoin il pourra vous entendre,
Remettez-lui ce paquet cacheté,

(*lui donnant des papiers cachetés.*)

C'est un devoir de votre piété,
N'y manquez pas... O fille toujours chère!...
Embrassez-moi.

ACANTE

Tous vos ordres, mon père, 200
Seront suivis, ils sont pour moi sacrés;
Je vous dois tout... D'où vient que vous pleurez?

DIGNANT

Ah! je le dois... de vous je me sépare,

191 MS1: Et oui vraiment, te
191a MS1: DIGNANT (*à Maturin*)
197a MS1: *il lui donne des papiers*

C'est pour jamais: mais si le ciel avare,
Qui m'a toujours refusé ses bienfaits, 205
Pouvait sur vous les verser désormais,
Si votre sort est digne de vos charmes,
Ma chère enfant, je dois sécher mes larmes.

BERTHE

Marchons, marchons, tous ces beaux compliments
Sont pauvretés qui font perdre du temps. 210
Venez, Colette.

COLETTE (*à Acante.*)

Adieu, ma chère amie.
Je recommande à votre prud'hommie
Mon Maturin; vengez-moi des ingrats.

ACANTE

Le cœur me bat… que deviendrai-je, hélas!

SCÈNE IV

LE BAILLI, MATURIN, ACANTE

MATURIN

Je n'aime point cette cérémonie, 215
Maître bailli, c'est une tyrannie.

LE BAILLI

C'est la condition, *sine qua non.*

212-214, 216 MS1, absent

MATURIN

Sine qua non; quel diable de jargon!
Morbleu ma femme est à moi.

LE BAILLI

Pas encore:
Il faut premier que monseigneur l'honore 220
D'un entretien, selon les nobles us
En ce châtel de tous les temps reçus.

MATURIN

Ces maudits us quels sont-ils?

LE BAILLI

L'épousée
Sur une chaise est sagement placée;
Puis monseigneur dans un fauteuil à bras, 225
Vient vis-à-vis se camper à six pas.

MATURIN

Quoi, pas plus loin?

LE BAILLI

C'est la règle.

MATURIN

Allons, passe.
Et puis après?

223 63G, T64P: Les maudits
225 63G, T64P: dans une chaise à bras
226 MS1: se placer à

LE BAILLI

Monseigneur avec grâce
Fait un présent de bijoux, de rubans,
Comme il lui plaît.

MATURIN

Passe pour des présents. 230

LE BAILLI

Puis il lui parle, il vous la considère,
Il examine à fond son caractère;
Puis il l'exhorte à la vertu.

MATURIN

Fort bien;
Et quand finit, s'il vous plaît, l'entretien?

LE BAILLI

Expressément la loi veut qu'on demeure 235
Pour l'exhorter l'espace d'un quart d'heure.

MATURIN

Un quart d'heure est beaucoup. Et le mari
Peut-il au moins se tenir près d'ici,
Pour écouter sa femme?

LE BAILLI

La loi porte
Que s'il osait se tenir à la porte, 240
Se présenter avant le temps marqué,
Faire du bruit, se tenir pour choqué,

237-244 MS1, absent

S'émanciper à sottises pareilles,
On fait couper sur-le-champ ses oreilles.

MATURIN

La belle loi! les beaux droits que voilà! 245
Et ma moitié ne dit mot à cela?

ACANTE

Moi j'obéis, et je n'ai rien à dire.

LE BAILLI

Déniche, il faut qu'un mari se retire:
Point de raisons.

MATURIN (*sortant.*)

Ma femme heureusement
N'a point d'esprit, et son air innocent, 250
Sa conversation ne plaira guère.

LE BAILLI

Veux-tu partir?

MATURIN

Adieu donc, ma très chère;
Songe surtout au pauvre Maturin,
Ton fiancé.

(*il sort.*)

ACANTE

J'y songe avec chagrin.

246 MS1, 63G, T64P: ne dit rien à
249-252 MS1, absent

Quelle sera cette étrange entrevue? 255
La peur me prend, je suis tout éperdue.

LE BAILLI

Asseyez-vous; attendez en ce lieu
Un maître aimable et vertueux. Adieu.

SCÈNE V

ACANTE *seule.*

Il est aimable... ah! je le sais sans doute.
Pourrai-je hélas! mériter qu'il m'écoute? 260
Entrera-t-il dans mes vrais intérêts,
Dans mes chagrins, et dans mes torts secrets?
Il me croira du moins fort imprudente,
De refuser le sort qu'on me présente;
Un mari riche, un état assuré. 265
Je le prévois, je ne remporterai
Que des refus, avec bien peu d'estime;
Je vais déplaire à ce cœur magnanime;
Et si mon âme avait osé former
Quelque souhait, c'est qu'il pût m'estimer. 270
Mais pourra-t-il me blâmer de me rendre
Chez cette dame et si noble et si tendre,
Qui fuit le monde, et qu'en ce triste jour
J'implorerai pour le fuir à mon tour?...
Où suis-je?... on ouvre?... à peine j'envisage 275
Celui qui vient... je ne vois qu'un nuage.

258 MS1, with stage direction after 258: *Il s'en va*
271-274 MS2 (→ MS3), struck out
275 MS2: ⟨où suis-je? on ouvre?⟩ $^{V\uparrow}\beta$ [restores]

SCÈNE VI[5]

LE MARQUIS, ACANTE

LE MARQUIS

Asseyez-vous. Lorsqu'ici je vous vois,
C'est le plus beau, le plus cher de mes droits.
J'ai commandé qu'on porte à votre père
Les faibles dons qu'il convient de vous faire; 280
Ils paraîtront bien indignes de vous.

ACANTE (*s'asseyant.*)

Trop de bontés se répandent sur nous;
J'en suis confuse; et ma reconnaissance
N'a pas besoin de tant de bienfaisance;
Mais avant tout il est de mon devoir 285
De vous prier de daigner recevoir
Ces vieux papiers que mon père présente
Très humblement.

LE MARQUIS (*les mettant dans sa poche.*)

Donnez-les, belle Acante,
Je les lirai; c'est sans doute un détail
De mes forêts: ses soins et son travail 290
M'ont toujours plu; j'aurai de sa vieillesse

281a MS1: ⟨*s'asseyant*⟩
288a MS1: (*les prend et les met dans sa poche*)

[5] At the head of this scene, MS1 is annotated by the censor, Crébillon, as follows: 'Il ne faut point de fauteuils dans cette scène; ce serait donner les idées que l'on veut écarter, il ne doit être question que d'un simple examen. Laisser imaginer quelque chose de plus ce serait insulter le public.' This observation was later struck out.

Les plus grands soins; comptez sur ma promesse.
Mais est-il vrai qu'il vous donne un époux
Qui vous causant d'invincibles dégoûts,
De votre hymen rend la chaîne odieuse? 295
J'en suis fâché… Vous deviez être heureuse.

ACANTE

Ah! je le suis un moment, monseigneur,
En vous parlant, en vous ouvrant mon cœur;
Mais tant d'audace est-elle ici permise?

LE MARQUIS

Ne craignez rien; parlez avec franchise; 300
Tous vos secrets seront en sûreté.

ACANTE

Qui douterait de votre probité?
Pardonnez donc à ma plainte importune.
Ce mariage aurait fait ma fortune,
Je le sais bien, et j'avouerai surtout 305
Que c'est trop tard expliquer mon dégoût;
Que dans les champs élevée et nourrie,
Je ne dois point dédaigner une vie
Qui sous vos lois me retient pour jamais;
Et qui m'est chère encor par vos bienfaits. 310
Mais après tout, Maturin, le village,
Ces paysans, leurs mœurs, et leur langage,
Ne m'ont jamais inspiré tant d'horreur;
De mon esprit c'est une injuste erreur;
Je la combats, mais elle a l'avantage. 315
En frémissant je fais ce mariage.

LE MARQUIS (*approchant son fauteuil.*)

Mais vous n'avez pas tort.

316a MS1: ⟨*s'approchant*⟩

ACANTE (*à genoux.*)

J'ose à genoux
Vous demander, non pas un autre époux,
Non d'autres nœuds, tous me seraient horribles,
Mais que je puisse avoir des jours paisibles; 320
Le premier bien serait votre bonté,
Et le second de tous la liberté.

LE MARQUIS (*la relevant avec empressement.*)

Eh! relevez-vous donc... Que tout m'étonne
Dans vos desseins, et dans votre personne,

(*Ils s'approchent.*)

Dans vos discours si nobles, si touchants, 325
Qui ne sont point le langage des champs!
Je l'avouerai, vous ne paraissez faite
Pour Maturin, ni pour cette retraite.
D'où tenez-vous, dans ce séjour obscur,
Un ton si noble, un langage si pur? 330
Partout on a de l'esprit; c'est l'ouvrage
De la nature, et c'est votre partage:
Mais l'esprit seul sans éducation
N'a jamais eu ni ce tour, ni ce ton,
Qui me surprend,... je dis plus, qui m'enchante. 335

ACANTE

Ah! que pour moi votre âme est indulgente!
Comme mon sort, mon esprit est borné.
Moins on attend, plus on est étonné.
Un peu de soins, peut-être, et de lecture,

323a MS1: *avec empressement*
324a MS1: ⟨*ils s'approchent*⟩
325 MS1: si nobles et si
339-346 W75G* (→ MS2, MS3, K), on paper slip: [W]LE MARQUIS

Ont pu dans moi corriger la nature; 340
C'est vous surtout, vous qui dans ce moment
Formez en moi l'esprit, le sentiment,
Qui m'élevez, qui dans moi faites naître
L'ambition d'imiter un tel maître.

LE MARQUIS

Je n'y tiens plus; son mérite inouï 345
M'a plus encor pénétré qu'ébloui.
Quoi, dans ces lieux la nature bizarre
Aura voulu mettre une fleur si rare,
Et le destin veut ailleurs l'enterrer!
Non, belle Acante, il vous faut demeurer. 350

(*il s'approche.*)

ACANTE

Pour épouser Maturin?

LE MARQUIS

Sa personne
Mérite peu la femme qu'on lui donne,
Je l'avouerai.

ACANTE

Mon père quelquefois
Me conduisit au-delà de vos bois,
Chez une dame aimable et retirée, 355
Pauvre, il est vrai, mais noble et révérée,
Pleine d'esprit, de sentiments, d'honneur;

344a MS1: LE MARQUIS ⟨*s'approchant*⟩
350a MS1, no stage direction
354 W75G* (→ MS2, MS3, K): ⟨conduisit au-delà⟩ W↑ conduisait tout auprès
355-356 63G, T64P, two lines conflated: Chez une dame aimable et révérée

Elle daigne m'aimer: votre faveur,
Votre bonté peut me placer près d'elle.
Ma belle-mère est avare et cruelle, 360
Elle me hait, et je hais malgré moi
Ce Maturin qui compte sur ma foi.
Voilà mon sort, vous en êtes le maître.
Je ne serai point heureuse peut-être;
Je souffrirai, mais je souffrirai moins, 365
En devant tout à vos généreux soins.
Protégez-moi, croyez qu'en ma retraite
Je resterai toujours votre sujette.

LE MARQUIS

Tout me surprend. Dites-moi, s'il vous plaît;
Celle qui prend à vous tant d'intérêt, 370
Qui vous chérit, ayant su vous connaître,
Serait-ce point Dormène?

ACANTE

Oui.

LE MARQUIS

Mais peut-être...
Il est aisé d'ajuster tout cela.
Oui... votre idée est très bonne... oui, voilà
Un vrai moyen de rompre avec décence 375
Ce sot hymen, cette indigne alliance.
J'ai des projets... en un mot, voulez-vous
Près de Dormène un destin noble et doux?

ACANTE

J'aimerais mieux la servir, servir Laure,

372 MS2: Serait-ce V↑ point+ Dormène?

Laure si bonne, et qu'à jamais j'honore, 380
Manquer de tout, goûter dans leur séjour
Le seul bonheur de vous faire ma cour,
Que d'accepter la richesse importune
De tout mari qui ferait ma fortune.

LE MARQUIS

Acante, allez... vous pénétrez mon cœur; 385
Oui, vous pourrez, Acante, avec honneur
Vivre auprès d'elle... et dans mon château même.

ACANTE

Auprès de vous! ah ciel!

LE MARQUIS (*s'approche un peu.*)

Elle vous aime,
Elle a raison... J'ai, vous dis-je, un projet,
Mais je ne sais s'il aura son effet. 390
Et cependant vous voilà fiancée,
Et votre chaîne est déjà commencée,
La noce prête, et le contrat signé.
Le ciel voulut que je fusse éloigné,
Lorsqu'en ces lieux on parait la victime; 395
J'arrive tard, et je m'en fais un crime.

ACANTE

Quoi! vous daignez me plaindre? ah qu'à mes yeux
Mon mariage en est plus odieux!
Qu'il le devient chaque instant davantage!

388a MS1: ⟨*s'approchant*⟩
63G, T64P: *s'approchant un peu*
399 63PC: chaque fois davantage

LE MARQUIS (*Ils s'approchent.*)

Mais après tout, puisque de l'esclavage 400

(*Il s'approche.*)

Avec décence on pourra vous tirer…

ACANTE (*s'approchant un peu.*)

Ah! le voudriez-vous?

LE MARQUIS

J'ose espérer…

Que vos parents, la raison, la loi même,

Et plus encor votre mérite extrême…

(*Il s'approche encore.*)

Oui, cet hymen est trop mal assorti. 405

(*Elle s'approche.*)

Mais… le temps presse, il faut prendre un parti.

Ecoutez-moi…

(*Ils se trouvent tout près l'un de l'autre.*)

ACANTE

Juste ciel! si j'écoute!

399a MS1: ⟨*Ils s'approchent*⟩
400a MS1, no stage direction
63G, T64P: *Le marquis s'approche*
401a MS1: ⟨*ils s'approchent*⟩ ACANTE ⟨*s'approchant*⟩
404a MS1: ⟨*il s'approche*⟩
405a MS1: ⟨*elle s'approche*⟩
63G, T64P: *Acante s'approche*
407a MS1: ⟨*il s'approche*⟩

SCÈNE VII

LE MARQUIS, ACANTE, LE BAILLI, MATURIN

MATURIN (*entrant brusquement.*)

Je crains, ma foi, que l'on ne me déboute.
Entrons, entrons, le quart d'heure est fini.

ACANTE

Eh quoi! si tôt?

LE MARQUIS (*tirant sa montre.*)

Il est vrai, mon ami. 410

MATURIN

Maître bailli, ces sièges sont bien proches;
Est-ce encore un des droits?

LE BAILLI

Point de reproches,
Mais du respect.

MATURIN

Mon Dieu! nous en aurons;
Mais aurons-nous ma femme?

LE MARQUIS

Nous verrons.[6]

411-414 MS1, struck out, restored by 'bon' in the margin

[6] From this point onwards, where the text of the three-act version diverges from that in five acts, the continuous text of W75G* is shown in an appendix (see p.201-19). Variants with the siglum K (app) refer to acts 4 and 5 of the Kehl text, given in an appendix in that edition.

Eh!

(*il sonne.*)

UN DOMESTIQUE

Monseigneur!

LE MARQUIS

Que l'on remène Acante 415

Chez ses parents.

MATURIN

Ouais! ceci me tourmente.

ACANTE (*s'en allant.*)

Ciel! prends pitié de mes secrets ennuis.

LE MARQUIS (*sortant d'un autre côté.*)

Sortons, cachons le désordre où je suis.

Ah! que j'ai peur de perdre la gageure![7]

415 T64P: ramène

416a-418 MS1, struck out

419 MS1: ⟨Le chevalier doit perdre la gageure⟩

[7] See the introduction, p.23 and note.

SCÈNE VIII

MATURIN, LE BAILLI

MATURIN

Dis-moi, bailli, ce que cela figure? 420
Notre seigneur est sorti bien sournois:
Il me parlait poliment autrefois;
J'aimais assez ses honnêtes manières,
Et même à cœur il prenait mes affaires;
Je me marie... il s'en va tout pensif! 425

LE BAILLI

C'est qu'il pense beaucoup.

MATURIN

Maître baillif,
Je pense aussi. Ce, *nous verrons*, m'assomme;
Quand on est prêt, *nous verrons*! Ah quel homme!
Que je fis mal, ô ciel! quand je naquis
Chez mes parents de naître en ce pays! 430

420 MS1, struck out
426 MS1: MATURIN / Avec motif
428 63G, T64P: on est près, *nous*
428 MS1, between 428-429:
⟨Maître bailli?
LE BAILLI
Quoi?
MATURIN
Ces sièges voisins
N'ont rien de bon... tous deux font mes chagrins
J'aurais dessein de n'aimer plus Acante
Je l'aime encor pourtant, ça me tourmente⟩
429-436 MS1, struck out

J'aurais bien dû choisir quelque village,
Où j'aurais pu contracter mariage
Tout uniment, comme cela se doit,
A mon plaisir, sans qu'un autre eût le droit
De disposer de moi-même à mon âge, 435
Et de fourrer son nez dans mon ménage!

LE BAILLI

C'est pour ton bien.

MATURIN

Mon ami Baillival,
Pour notre bien on nous fait bien du mal.

Fin du troisième acte.

437-438 MS1:

MATURIN
Nous verrons! Ah ce mot
Fera du mal ou je ne suis qu'un sot.

ACTE IV

SCÈNE PREMIÈRE

LE MARQUIS *seul.*

Non, je ne perdrai point cette gageure.[8]
Amoureux! moi! quel conte! ah je m'assure
Que sur soi-même on garde un plein pouvoir;
Pour être sage, on n'a qu'à le vouloir.
Il est bien vrai qu'Acante est assez belle... 5
Et de la grâce! ah! nul n'en a plus qu'elle...
Et de l'esprit!... quoi, dans le fond des bois!
Pour avoir vu Dormène quelquefois,
Que de progrès! qu'il faut peu de culture
Pour seconder les dons de la nature! 10
J'estime Acante: oui, je dois l'estimer;
Mais, grâce au ciel, je suis très loin d'aimer.

(*Il s'assied à une table.*)

Ah! respirons. Voyons, sur toute chose,
Quel plan de vie enfin je me propose...
De ne dépendre en ces lieux que de moi, 15
De n'en sortir que pour servir mon roi,
De m'attacher, par un sage hyménée,
Une compagne agréable et bien née,

1 MS1: ⟨Non⟩ je ne perdrai ⟨point⟩ ↑jamais
6 MS1: ⟨β⟩↑Qui jamais eut autant de grâce qu'elle,
7 MS1: ⟨Et de l'⟩ ↑Autant d'
10 63G, T64P: Pour cultiver les

[8] Again, see the comment in the introduction on the theme of the 'gageure', p.23.

Pauvre de bien, mais riche de vertu,
Dont la noblesse et le sort abattu, 20
A mes bienfaits doivent des jours prospères:
Dormène seule a tous ces caractères;
Le ciel pour moi la réserve aujourd'hui.
Allons la voir… d'abord écrivons-lui
Un compliment… mais que puis-je lui dire? 25
Acante est là* qui m'empêche d'écrire;

**en se cognant le front avec la main*

Oui je la vois; comment la fuir? par où?

(*Il se relève.*)

Qui se croit sage, ô ciel! est un grand fou.
Achevons donc… Je me vaincrai sans doute.

21 MS1: devront des
27a MS1: (*il se lève en se frappant le front*)
29-37 MS1:

<SCÈNE II
LE MARQUIS, UN DOMESTIQUE

UN DOMESTIQUE
Monseigneur?…

LE MARQUIS
Non – je me vaincrai sans doute.

LE DOMESTIQUE
Monseigneur…

LE MARQUIS
Hem! – je sais bien qu'il en coûte
(*il se met à écrire*)
Mais – (*au domestique*) qu'on me laisse. Examinons-nous bien.

LE DOMESTIQUE
Je vous apprends…

LE MARQUIS
Qu'on ne m'apprenne rien.
Retirez-vous – Si pourtant la décence,
La probité – je m'y perds quand j'y pense.

LE DOMESTIQUE
Mais monseigneur, Acante…

LE MARQUIS (*se levant*)
Acante! Eh quoi?
Demeure – Acante, eh bien, parle, dis-moi…

(*Il finit sa lettre.*)

Holà! quelqu'un... Je sais bien qu'il en coûte. 30

SCÈNE II

LE MARQUIS, UN DOMESTIQUE

LE MARQUIS

Tenez, portez cette lettre à l'instant.

LE DOMESTIQUE

Où?

LE MARQUIS

Chez Acante.

LE DOMESTIQUE

Acante? mais vraiment...

LE MARQUIS

Je n'ai point dit Acante, c'est Dormène
A qui j'écris... on a bien de la peine
Avec ses gens... tout le monde en ces lieux 35
Parle d'Acante; et l'oreille et les yeux
Sont remplis d'elle, et brouillent ma mémoire.

Qu'a-t-elle fait?

LE DOMESTIQUE

Ce qu'on a peine à croire.〉

[this whole scene is struck out, and the rest of the scenes in act 4 are renumbered]

SCÈNE III

LE MARQUIS, DIGNANT, MME BERTHE, MATURIN

MATURIN

Ah! voici bien pardienne une autre histoire!

LE MARQUIS

Quoi?

MATURIN

Pour le coup c'est le droit du seigneur;
On m'a volé ma femme.

BERTHE

Oui, votre honneur 40
Sera honteux de cette vilenie;
Et je n'aurais pas cru cette infamie
D'un grand seigneur, si bon, si libéral.

LE MARQUIS

Comment? qu'est-il arrivé?

BERTHE

Bien du mal.

MATURIN

Vous le savez comme moi.

38 MS1, after 38:
A ces façons mettez-vous votre gloire?
41 MS1: ⟨vilenie⟩ ↑⟨volerie⟩ ↑⟨félonie⟩ ↑tromperie

LE MARQUIS

Parle, traître, 45
Parle.

MATURIN

Fort bien, vous vous fâchez, mon maître;
Oh c'est à moi d'être fâché.

LE MARQUIS

Comment?
Explique-toi.

MATURIN

C'est un enlèvement.
Savez-vous pas qu'à peine chez son père
Elle arrivait pour finir notre affaire, 50
Quatre coquins, alertes, bien tournés,
Effrontément me l'ont prise à mon nez,
Tout en riant, et vite l'ont conduite
Je ne sais où.

LE MARQUIS

Qu'on aille à leur poursuite…
Holà! quelqu'un… ne perdez point de temps; 55
Allez, courez, que mes gardes, mes gens
De tous côtés marchent en diligence.

55-56 MS1:
⟨β⟩↑Que faites-vous vous autres plantés là,
M'entendez-vous? Volez, secourez-la.
57 MS1: De tous côtés ⟨volent après Acante⟩ ↑β
MS1, after 57:
⟨Qu'on la ramène et qu'on me la présente,
Que le tocsin sonne dans tout le bourg;
Qu'on soit armé, qu'aux châteaux d'alentour
Avant la nuit on aille en diligence;⟩

Volez, vous dis-je, et s'il faut ma présence,
J'irai moi-même.

BERTHE (*à son mari.*)

Il parle tout de bon;
Et l'on croirait, mon cher, à la façon 60
Dont monseigneur regarde cette injure,
Que c'est à lui qu'on a pris sa future.

LE MARQUIS

Et vous son père, et vous qui l'aimiez tant,
Vous qui perdez une si chère enfant,
Un tel trésor, un cœur noble, un cœur tendre, 65
Avez-vous pu souffrir, sans la défendre,
Que de vos bras on osât l'arracher?
Un tel malheur semble peu vous toucher.
Que devient donc l'amitié paternelle?
Vous m'étonnez.

DIGNANT

Tout mon cœur est pour elle, 70
C'est mon devoir; et j'ai dû pressentir
Que par votre ordre on la faisait partir.

LE MARQUIS

Par mon ordre?

DIGNANT

Oui.

58-62 MS1:

⟨β⟩ ↑BERTHE (*à son mari*)
A la façon dont il prend cette injure
Il semblerait qu'il y perd sa future.

63 63G, 63PC, T64P: l'aimez tant

LE MARQUIS

Quelle injure nouvelle!
Tous ces gens-ci perdent-ils la cervelle?
Allez-vous-en, laissez-moi, sortez tous. 75
Ah! s'il se peut, modérons mon courroux...
Non, vous, restez.

MATURIN

Qui? moi?

LE MARQUIS (*à Dignant.*)

Non, vous, vous dis-je.

SCÈNE IV

LE MARQUIS *sur le devant,* DIGNANT *au fond*

LE MARQUIS

Je vois d'où part l'attentat qui m'afflige.
Le chevalier m'avait presque promis
De se porter à des coups si hardis. 80
Il croit au fond que cette gentillesse
Est pardonnable au feu de sa jeunesse.
Il ne sait pas combien j'en suis choqué,
A quel excès ce fou-là m'a manqué,
Jusqu'à quel point son procédé m'offense. 85
Il déshonore, il trahit l'innocence;
Il perd Acante: et pour percer mon cœur,

79 MS1: ⟨m'avait⟩ ↑s'était
83 63PC: je suis choqué

Je n'ai passé que pour son ravisseur!
Un étourdi, que la débauche anime,
Me fait porter la peine de son crime! 90
Voilà le prix de mon affection
Pour un parent indigne de mon nom!
Il est pétri des vices de son père,
Il a ses traits, ses mœurs, son caractère;
Il périra malheureux comme lui. 95
Je le renonce, et je veux qu'aujourd'hui
Il soit puni de tant d'extravagance.

DIGNANT

Puis-je en tremblant prendre ici la licence
De vous parler?

LE MARQUIS

Sans doute, tu le peux.
Parle-moi d'elle.

DIGNANT

Au transport douloureux 100
Où votre cœur devant moi s'abandonne,
Je ne reconnais plus votre personne.
Vous avez lu ce qu'on vous a porté,
Ce gros paquet qu'on vous a présenté?

LE MARQUIS

Eh mon ami! suis-je en état de lire? 105

DIGNANT

Vous me faites frémir.

LE MARQUIS

Que veux-tu dire?

DIGNANT

Quoi, ce paquet n'est pas encore ouvert?

LE MARQUIS

Non.

DIGNANT

Juste ciel! ce dernier coup me perd!

LE MARQUIS

Comment!... j'ai cru que c'était un mémoire
De mes forêts.

DIGNANT

Hélas! vous deviez croire 110
Que cet écrit était intéressant.

LE MARQUIS

Eh lisons vite... Une table à l'instant;
Approchez donc cette table.

DIGNANT

Ah mon maître!
Qu'aura-t-on fait, et qu'allez-vous connaître?

LE MARQUIS *assis examine le paquet.*

Mais ce paquet qui n'est pas à mon nom, 115
Est cacheté des sceaux de ma maison?

DIGNANT

Oui.

114a MS1, 63G, T64P: *assis, examinant le paquet*

LE MARQUIS

Lisons donc.

DIGNANT

Cet étrange mystère
En d'autres temps aurait de quoi vous plaire,
Mais à présent il devient bien affreux.

LE MARQUIS *lisant.*

Je ne vois rien jusqu'ici que d'heureux. 120
Je vois d'abord que le ciel la fit naître
D'un sang illustre: et cela devait être.
Oui, plus je lis, plus je bénis les cieux.
Quoi! Laure a mis ce dépôt précieux
Entre vos mains! quoi! Laure est donc sa mère? 125
Mais pourquoi donc lui serviez-vous de père?
Indignement pourquoi la marier?

DIGNANT

J'en avais l'ordre, et j'ai dû vous prier
En sa faveur.

UN DOMESTIQUE

En ce moment Dormène
Arrive ici, tremblante, hors d'haleine, 130
Fondant en pleurs: elle veut vous parler.

LE MARQUIS

Ah! c'est à moi de l'aller consoler.

119a MS1, no stage direction

SCÈNE V

LE MARQUIS, DIGNANT, DORMÈNE

LE MARQUIS (*à Dormène qui entre.*)

Pardonnez-moi, j'allais chez vous, madame,
Mettre à vos pieds le courroux qui m'enflamme.
Acante... à peine encore entré chez moi, 135
J'attendais peu l'honneur que je reçois...
Une aventure assez désagréable...
Me trouble un peu... Que Gernance est coupable!

DORMÈNE

De tous mes biens il me reste l'honneur;
Et je ne doutais pas qu'un si grand cœur 140
Ne respectât le malheur qui m'opprime,
Et d'un parent ne détestât le crime.
Je ne viens point vous demander raison
De l'attentat commis dans ma maison...

LE MARQUIS

Comment? chez vous?

DORMÈNE

C'est dans ma maison même 145
Qu'il a conduit le triste objet qu'il aime.

LE MARQUIS

Le traître!

DORMÈNE

Il est plus criminel cent fois

Qu'il ne croit l'être… Hélas! ma faible voix
En vous parlant expire dans ma bouche.

LE MARQUIS

Votre douleur sensiblement me touche; 150
Daignez parler, et ne redoutez rien.

DORMÈNE

Apprenez donc…

SCÈNE VI

LE MARQUIS, DORMÈNE, DIGNANT; *quelques* DOMESTIQUES *entrent précipitamment avec* MATURIN

MATURIN

Tout va bien, tout va bien,
Tout est en paix, la femme est retrouvée;
Votre parent nous l'avait enlevée:
Il nous la rend; c'est peut-être un peu tard, 155
Chacun son bien. Tudieu, quel égrillard!

LE MARQUIS (*à Dignant.*)

Courez soudain recevoir votre fille,
Qu'elle demeure au sein de sa famille.
Veillez sur elle: ayez soin d'empêcher
Qu'aucun mortel ose s'en approcher. 160

MATURIN

Excepté moi?

152 MS1: Tout va bien, tout est bien,

LE MARQUIS

Non; l'ordre que je donne
Est pour vous-même.

MATURIN

Ouais! tout ceci m'étonne.

LE MARQUIS

Obéissez…

MATURIN

Par ma foi tous ces grands
Sont dans le fond de bien vilaines gens.
Droit du seigneur, femme que l'on enlève! 165
Défense à moi de lui parler… Je crève.
Mais je l'aurai, car je suis fiancé.
Consolons-nous, le plus fort est passé.

(*Il sort.*)

LE MARQUIS

Elle revient; mais l'injure cruelle
Du chevalier retombera sur elle; 170
Voilà le monde: et de tels attentats
Faits à l'honneur ne se réparent pas.

(*à Dormène.*)

161a-163 MS1:

LE MARQUIS

Non; l'ordre est pour vous-même;
J'ai déclaré ma volonté suprême.
Obéissez…

165-168 MS1, struck out

168 MS1: ⟨tout le mal⟩ ↑le plus fort
OD63, 63G, 63PC, T64P, W70L, K (app): nous, tout le mal est

Eh bien parlez, parlez; daignez m'apprendre
Ce que je brûle et que je crains d'entendre.
Nous sommes seuls.

DORMÈNE

Il le faut bien, monsieur? 175

Apprenez donc le comble du malheur:
C'est peu qu'Acante en secret étant née
De cette Laure illustre infortunée,
Soit sous vos yeux prête à se marier
Indignement à ce riche fermier; 180
C'est peu qu'au poids de sa triste misère
On ajoutât ce fardeau nécessaire.
Votre parent qui voulait l'enlever,
Votre parent qui vient de nous prouver
Combien il tient de son coupable père, 185
Gernance enfin...

LE MARQUIS

Gernance!

DORMÈNE

Il est son frère.

LE MARQUIS

Quel coup horrible! O ciel! qu'avez-vous dit?

DORMÈNE

Entre vos mains vous avez cet écrit,
Qui montre assez ce que nous devons craindre:
Lisez, voyez combien Laure est à plaindre. 190

175 MS1, OD63, 63G, 63PC, T64P, W70L, K (app): faut donc, monsieur?
178 63G, T64P: illustre fortunée

(*Le marquis lit.*)

C'est ma parente; et mon cœur est lié
A tous ses maux que sent mon amitié.
Elle mourra de l'affreuse aventure
Qui sous ses yeux outrage la nature.

LE MARQUIS

Ah! qu'ai-je lu? que souvent nous voyons 195
D'affreux secrets dans d'illustres maisons!
De tant de coups mon âme est oppressée;
Je ne vois rien, je n'ai point de pensée.
Ah pour jamais il faut quitter ces lieux:
Ils m'étaient chers; ils me sont odieux. 200
Quel jour pour nous! quel parti dois-je prendre?
Le malheureux ose chez moi se rendre!
Le voyez-vous?

DORMÈNE

Ah monsieur, je le vois,
Et je frémis.

LE MARQUIS

Il passe, il vient à moi.
Daignez rentrer, madame, et que sa vue 205
N'accroisse pas le chagrin qui vous tue;
C'est à moi seul de l'entendre, et je crois
Que ce sera pour la dernière fois.
Sachons dompter le courroux qui m'anime.

(*en regardant de loin.*)

Il semble, ô ciel! qu'il connaisse son crime. 210
Que dans ses yeux je lis d'égarement!

198 63G, T64P: n'ai plus de
205 63G, T64P: madame, que

Ah l'on n'est pas coupable impunément.
Comme il rougit! comme il pâlit… le traître!
A mes regards il tremble de paraître.
C'est quelque chose.

(*Tandis qu'il parle, Dormène se retire en regardant attentivement Gernance.*)

SCÈNE VII

LE MARQUIS, LE CHEVALIER

LE CHEVALIER (*de loin se cachant le visage.*)

Ah! Monsieur.

LE MARQUIS

Est-ce vous? 215

Vous, malheureux?

LE CHEVALIER

Je tombe à vos genoux…

LE MARQUIS

Qu'avez-vous fait?

LE CHEVALIER

Une faute, une offense,
Dont je ressens l'indigne extravagance,
Qui pour jamais m'a servi de leçon,
Et dont je viens vous demander pardon. 220

LE MARQUIS

Vous des remords! vous! est-il bien possible?

LE CHEVALIER

Rien n'est plus vrai.

LE MARQUIS

Votre faute est horrible,
Plus que vous ne pensez: mais votre cœur
Est-il sensible à mes soins, à l'honneur,
A l'amitié? Vous sentez-vous capable 225
D'oser me faire un aveu véritable,
Sans rien cacher?

LE CHEVALIER

Comptez sur ma candeur;
Je suis un libertin, mais point menteur;
Et mon esprit que le trouble environne,
Est trop ému pour abuser personne. 230

LE MARQUIS

Je prétends tout savoir.

LE CHEVALIER

Je vous dirai,
Que de débauche et d'ardeur enivré,
Plus que d'amour, j'avais fait la folie
De dérober une fille jolie
Au possesseur de ses jeunes appas, 235

228 MS1, with pencilled alternative:
J'ai toujours eu le mensonge en horreur
234 MS1: ⟨D'escamoter⟩ ↑De dérober

(Qu'à mon avis, il ne mérite pas.)
Je l'ai conduite à la forêt prochaine,
Dans ce château de Laure et de Dormène;
C'est une faute, il est vrai, j'en conviens,
Mais j'étais fou, je ne pensais à rien. 240
Cette Dormène, et Laure sa compagne,
Etaient encor bien loin dans la campagne.
En étourdi je n'ai point perdu temps;
J'ai commencé par des propos galants.
Je m'attendais aux communes alarmes, 245
Aux cris perçants, à la colère, aux larmes;
Mais qu'ai-je vu! la fermeté, l'honneur,
L'air indigné, mais calme avec grandeur.
Tout ce qui fait respecter l'innocence
S'armait pour elle, et prenait sa défense. 250
J'ai recouru dans ces premiers moments,
A l'art de plaire, aux égards séduisants,
Aux doux propos, à cette déférence,
Qui fait souvent pardonner la licence.
Mais pour réponse, Acante à deux genoux 255

236 63PC: ne méritait pas
239-245 MS1:

⟨β⟩ ↑LE MARQUIS
Le crime en est plus affreux et plus grand.
C'est insulter et Dormène et son rang.
Pourquoi lui faire une semblable offense?
Qui vous permet d'outrager l'innocence?
LE CHEVALIER
C'est une faute, il est vrai, j'en conviens,
Mais j'étais fou.
LE MARQUIS
Ne me cachez donc rien.
LE CHEVALIER
Je m'attendais

247 MS1, OD63, 63G, T64P, W70L, K (app): qu'ai-je ouï
249-252 MS1, struck out
251 OD63: J'ai reconnu
253 MS1: ⟨Aux doux propos⟩ ↑Je recourus

M'a conjuré de la rendre chez vous;
Et c'est alors que ses yeux moins sévères
Ont répandu des pleurs involontaires.

LE MARQUIS

Que dites-vous?

LE CHEVALIER

Elle voulait en vain
Me les cacher de sa charmante main; 260
Dans cet état, sa grâce attendrissante
Enhardissait mon ardeur imprudente;
Et tout honteux de ma stupidité,
J'ai voulu prendre un peu de liberté.
Ciel! comme elle a tancé ma hardiesse! 265
Oui, j'ai cru voir une chaste déesse,
Qui rejetait de son auguste autel
L'impur encens qu'offrait un criminel.

LE MARQUIS

Ah! poursuivez.

LE CHEVALIER

Comment se peut-il faire
Qu'ayant vécu presque dans la misère, 270
Dans la bassesse, et dans l'obscurité,
Elle ait cet air et cette dignité,
Ces sentiments, cet esprit, ce langage,
Je ne dis pas au-dessus du village,
De son état, de son nom, de son sang, 275
Mais convenable au plus illustre rang?

260 63G, T64P: Me le cacher dans
265 MS1: ⟨tancé⟩ reçu
276 MS1: Mais au-dessus des femmes d'un haut rang!

Non, il n'est point de mère respectable,
Qui condamnant l'erreur d'un fils coupable,
Le rappelât avec plus de bonté
A la vertu dont il s'est écarté; 280
N'employant point l'aigreur et la colère,
Fière et décente, et plus sage qu'austère.
De vous surtout elle a parlé longtemps.

LE MARQUIS

De moi?...

LE CHEVALIER

Montrant à mes égarements
Votre vertu, qui devait, disait-elle, 285
Etre à jamais ma honte ou mon modèle.
Tout interdit, plein d'un secret respect,
Que je n'avais senti qu'à son aspect,
Je suis honteux, mes fureurs se captivent.
Dans ce moment les deux dames arrivent; 290
Et me voyant maître de leur logis,
Avec Acante, et deux ou trois bandits,
D'un juste effroi leur âme s'est remplie;
La plus âgée en tombe évanouie.
Acante en pleurs la presse dans ses bras; 295
Elle revient des portes du trépas.
Alors sur moi fixant sa triste vue,
Elle retombe, et s'écrie éperdue,
Ah! je crois voir Gernance... c'est son fils,

277-280 MS1, struck out, restored by 'bon' in the margin
284-286 MS1:
⟨β⟩↑De moi; grand Dieu! dans ces affreux moments
Elle y pensait... Eh mais, qu'en disait-elle?
LE CHEVALIER
Elle m'offrait vos vertus pour modèle.
299 63G, T64P: mon fils

C'est lui… je meurs… à ces mots je frémis; 300
Et la douleur, l'effroi de cette dame,
Au même instant ont passé dans mon âme.
Je tombe aux pieds de Dormène, et je sors,
Confus, soumis, pénétré de remords.

LE MARQUIS

Ce repentir dont votre âme est saisie, 305
Charme mon cœur, et nous réconcilie.
Tenez, prenez ce paquet important,
Lisez-le seul, pesez-le mûrement;
Et si pour moi vous conservez, Gernance,
Quelque amitié, quelque condescendance, 310
Promettez-moi, lorsqu'Acante en ces lieux
Pourra paraître à vos coupables yeux,
D'avoir sur vous un assez grand empire,
Pour lui cacher ce que vous allez lire.

LE CHEVALIER

Oui, je vous le promets, oui.

LE MARQUIS

Vous verrez 315
L'abîme affreux d'où vos pas sont tirés.

LE CHEVALIER

Comment?

LE MARQUIS

Allez, vous tremblerez, vous dis-je.

306 MS1: Augmentera; j'en réponds sur ma vie,
311 MS1: ⟨Permettez⟩ ↑Promettez

SCÈNE VIII

LE MARQUIS *seul.*

Quel jour pour moi! tout m'étonne et m'afflige.
La belle Acante est donc de ma maison!
Mais sa naissance avait flétri son nom; 320
Son noble sang fut souillé par son père;
Rien n'est plus beau que le nom de sa mère;
Mais ce beau nom a perdu tous ses droits,
Par un hymen que réprouvent nos lois.
La triste Laure, ô pensée accablante! 325
Fut criminelle en faisant naître Acante;
Je le sais trop, l'hymen fut condamné;
L'amant de Laure est mort assassiné.
De maux cruels quel tissu lamentable!
Acante hélas! n'en est pas moins aimable, 330
Moins vertueuse; et je sais que son cœur
Est respectable au sein du déshonneur;
Il anoblit la honte de ses pères;
Et cependant, ô préjugés sévères!
O loi du monde! injuste et dure loi! 335
Vous l'emportez…

320 63G, T64P: Mais la naissance
333 K (app): ennoblit

SCÈNE IX

LE MARQUIS, DORMÈNE

LE MARQUIS

Madame, instruisez-moi.

Parlez, madame, avez-vous vu son frère?

DORMÈNE

Oui, je l'ai vu, sa douleur est sincère.
Il est bien étourdi; mais entre nous,
Son cœur est bon, il est conduit par vous. 340

LE MARQUIS

Eh! mais Acante!

DORMÈNE

Elle ne peut connaître
Jusqu'à présent le sang qui la fit naître.

LE MARQUIS

Quoi, sa naissance illégitime!

DORMÈNE

Hélas!
Il est trop vrai.

LE MARQUIS

Non, elle ne l'est pas.

DORMÈNE

Que dites-vous?

LE MARQUIS (*relisant un papier qu'il a gardé.*)

Sa mère était sans crime; 345

Sa mère au moins crut l'hymen légitime;
On la trompa, son destin fut affreux.
Ah! quelquefois le ciel moins rigoureux
Daigne approuver ce qu'un monde profane
Sans connaissance avec fureur condamne. 350

DORMÈNE

Laure n'est point coupable, et ses parents
Se sont conduits avec elle en tyrans.

LE MARQUIS

Mais marier sa fille en un village!
A ce beau sang faire un pareil outrage!

DORMÈNE

Elle sans biens, l'âge, la pauvreté, 355
Un long malheur abaisse la fierté.

LE MARQUIS

Elle est sans biens! votre noble courage
La recueillit.

DORMÈNE

Sa misère partage
Le peu que j'ai.

LE MARQUIS

Vous trouvez le moyen,

354 63G, T64P: Au plus beau sang
355 63G, T64P: Elle est sans bien
356 MS1: malheur ôte la
63G, T64P: abaissent

Ayant si peu, de faire encor du bien. 360
Riches et grands, que le monde contemple,
Imitez donc un si touchant exemple.
Nous contentons à grands frais nos désirs;
Sachons goûter de plus nobles plaisirs.
Quoi! pour aider l'amitié, la misère, 365
Dormène a pu s'ôter le nécessaire;
Et vous n'osez donner le superflu?
O juste ciel! qu'avez-vous résolu?
Que faire enfin?

DORMÈNE

Vous êtes juste et sage.
Votre famille a fait plus d'un outrage 370
Au sang de Laure, et ce sang généreux
Fut par vous seuls jusqu'ici malheureux.

LE MARQUIS

Comment? comment?

DORMÈNE

Le comte votre père,
Homme inflexible en son humeur sévère,
Opprima Laure, et fit par son crédit 375
Casser l'hymen; et c'est lui qui ravit
A cette Acante, à cette infortunée,
Les nobles droits du sang dont elle est née.

LE MARQUIS

Ah! c'en est trop... mon cœur est ulcéré.
Oui, c'est un crime... il sera réparé, 380
Je vous le jure.

372 63PC: vous seul jusqu'ici

DORMÈNE

Et que voulez-vous faire?

LE MARQUIS

Je veux...

DORMÈNE

Quoi donc?

LE MARQUIS

Mais... lui servir de père.

DORMÈNE

Elle en est digne.

LE MARQUIS

Oui... mais je ne dois pas
Aller trop loin.

DORMÈNE

Comment, trop loin?

LE MARQUIS

Hélas!...
Madame, un mot: conseillez-moi de grâce; 385
Que feriez-vous, s'il vous plaît, à ma place?

DORMÈNE

En tous les temps je me ferais honneur
De consulter votre esprit, votre cœur.

LE MARQUIS

Ah!...

DORMÈNE

Qu'avez-vous?

LE MARQUIS

Je n'ai rien… mais, madame,
En quel état est Acante?

DORMÈNE

Son âme 390
Est dans le trouble, et ses yeux dans les pleurs.

LE MARQUIS

Daignez m'aider à calmer ses douleurs.
Allons, j'ai pris mon parti: je vous laisse;
Soyez ici souveraine maîtresse,
Et pardonnez à mon esprit confus, 395
Un peu chagrin, mais plein de vos vertus.

(*il sort.*)

SCÈNE X

DORMÈNE *seule.*

Dans cet état quel chagrin peut le mettre?

389-390 MS1:
⟨β⟩↑LE MARQUIS
Moi je n'ai rien madame.
Que fait Acante en ce moment?

397-410 MS1:
⟨Ou je me trompe, ou ce cœur magnanime
Pour notre Acante a plus que de l'estime⟩
[the whole soliloquy is struck out, so that act 4 concludes with the exit of the Marquis]

Qu'il est troublé! j'en juge par sa lettre;
Un style assez confus, des mots rayés,
De l'embarras, d'autres mots oubliés. 400
J'ai lu pourtant le mot de mariage.
Dans le pays il passe pour très sage.
Il veut me voir, me parler, et ne dit
Pas un seul mot sur tout ce qu'il m'écrit!
Et pour Acante il paraît bien sensible! 405
Quoi! voudrait-il?... cela n'est pas possible.
Aurait-il eu d'abord quelque dessein
Sur son parent?... demandait-il ma main?
Le chevalier jadis m'a courtisée,
Mais qu'espérer de sa tête insensée? 410
L'amour encor n'est point connu de moi;
Je dus toujours en avoir de l'effroi;
Et le malheur de Laure est un exemple
Qu'en frémissant tous les jours je contemple:
Il m'avertit d'éviter tout lien: 415
Mais qu'il est triste, ô ciel! de n'aimer rien!

Fin du quatrième acte.

413 63G, T64P: de l'autre est

ACTE V

SCÈNE PREMIÈRE

LE MARQUIS, LE CHEVALIER

LE MARQUIS

Faisons la paix, chevalier, je confesse
Que tout mortel est pétri de faiblesse,

1-70 MS1 contains no scenes corresponding to scenes 1 and 2 of the text as published; this act opens with a lengthier version of scene 3:

ACANTE, COLETTE

COLETTE

Si les romans te plaisent, chère Acante
De celui-ci tu dois être contente!

ACANTE

J'ai peu sujet de l'être.

COLETTE

Eh mais pourtant
Rien n'est plus beau que ton enlèvement
N'aime-t-on pas les gens qui nous enlèvent?

ACANTE

Ah! Contre moi tous mes sens se soulèvent!
Du chevalier je déteste l'amour.

COLETTE

N'est-ce donc rien de se voir en un jour
De Maturin pour jamais délivrée
D'un beau seigneur poursuivie, adorée
Un mariage en un seul mot cassé.
Par monseigneur un autre commencé
Si ce roman n'a pas de quoi te plaire
Tu me parais difficile ma chère.

ACANTE

Quoi! – que dis-tu? l'on aurait aujourd'hui
Rompu l'hymen de Maturin?

COLETTE

Eh oui.

Que le sage est peu de chose; entre nous,
J'étais tout prêt de l'être moins que vous.

LE CHEVALIER

Vous avez donc perdu votre gageure? 5
Vous aimez donc?

LE MARQUIS

Oh non, je vous le jure:

ACANTE

Et depuis quand?

COLETTE

Mais depuis tout à l'heure.

ACANTE

Est-il bien vrai?

COLETTE

Du fonds de ma demeure
J'étais en hâte accourue au château
⟨Pour implorer contre mon friponneau⟩
↑Dans le dessein d'implorer de nouveau
De monseigneur la puissante assistance;
Le scélérat vient avec confiance,
Lui présenter ton contrat à signer,
Mais le marquis sans le voir, sans daigner
Sur Maturin jeter un œil affable
Et me regardant moi d'un œil aimable
A déchiré le contrat en morceaux.

ACANTE

Oui!

COLETTE

Comme il est maître de ses vassaux
Qu'il est surtout maître de ses vassalles
Il a voulu, (que ses lois sont loyales!)
Il a voulu que maître Maturin
A ma main blanche unit sa lourde main
Sans dire un mot de mon amie Acante.

ACANTE

Mais…

COLETTE

Il me donne une dot opulente,

Mais par l'hymen, tout prêt de me lier,
Je ne veux plus jamais me marier.

LE CHEVALIER

Votre inconstance est étrange et soudaine.
Passe pour moi: mais que dira Dormène? 10
N'a-t-elle pas certains mots par écrit,
Où par hasard le mot d'hymen se lit?

LE MARQUIS

Il est trop vrai; c'est là ce qui me gêne.
Je prétendais m'imposer cette chaîne;
Mais à la fin m'étant bien consulté, 15
Je n'ai de goût que pour la liberté.

LE CHEVALIER

La liberté d'aimer?

LE MARQUIS

Eh bien, si j'aime,
Je suis encor le maître de moi-même;
Et je pourrai réparer tout le mal.
Je n'ai parlé d'hymen qu'en général, 20
Sans m'engager, et sans me compromettre.
Car en effet, si j'avais pu promettre,
Je ne pourrais balancer un moment.
A gens d'honneur promesse vaut serment.
Cher chevalier, j'ai conçu dans ma tête 25
Un beau dessein, qui paraît fort honnête,
Pour me tirer d'un pas embarrassant;
Et tout le monde ici sera content.

24 63G, T64P: promesses sont serment

LE CHEVALIER

Vous moquez-vous? contenter tout le monde!
Quelle folie!

LE MARQUIS

En un mot, si l'on fronde 30
Mon changement, j'ose espérer au moins
Faire approuver ma conduite et mes soins.
Colette vient, par mon ordre on l'appelle;
Je vais l'entendre, et commencer par elle.

SCÈNE II

LE MARQUIS, LE CHEVALIER, COLETTE

LE MARQUIS

Venez, Colette.

COLETTE

Oh j'accours, monseigneur, 35
Prête en tout temps, et toujours de grand cœur.

LE MARQUIS

Voulez-vous être heureuse?

COLETTE

Oui, sur ma vie;
N'en doutez pas, c'est ma plus forte envie.

31 63PC: du moins

Que faut-il faire?

LE MARQUIS

En voici le moyen.
Vous voudriez un époux, et du bien? 40

COLETTE

Oui, l'un et l'autre.

LE MARQUIS

Eh bien donc, je vous donne
Trois mille francs pour la dot, et j'ordonne
Que Maturin vous épouse aujourd'hui.

COLETTE

Ou Maturin, ou tout autre que lui;
Qui vous voudrez, j'obéis sans réplique. 45
Trois mille francs! ah l'homme magnifique!
Le beau présent! que monseigneur est bon!
Que Maturin va bien changer de ton!
Qu'il va m'aimer! que je vais être fière!
De ce pays je serai la première. 50
Je meurs de joie.

LE MARQUIS

Et j'en ressens aussi,
D'avoir déjà pleinement réussi;
L'une des trois est déjà fort contente.
Tout ira bien.

COLETTE

Et mon amie Acante
Que devient-elle? on va la marier, 55
A ce qu'on dit, à ce beau chevalier.

Tout le monde est heureux, j'en suis charmée,
Ma chère Acante!

LE CHEVALIER (*en regardant le marquis.*)

Elle doit être aimée,
Elle le sera.

LE MARQUIS (*au chevalier.*)

La voici, je ne puis
La consoler en l'état où je suis. 60
Venez, je vais vous dire ma pensée.

(*Ils sortent.*)

SCÈNE III

ACANTE, COLETTE

COLETTE

Ma chère Acante, on t'avait fiancée,
Moi déboutée, on me marie.

ACANTE

A qui?

COLETTE

A Maturin.

ACANTE

Le ciel en soit béni.
Et depuis quand?

COLETTE

Eh depuis tout à l'heure. 65

ACANTE

Est-il bien vrai?

COLETTE

Du fond de ma demeure
J'ai comparu par devant monseigneur.
Ah! la belle âme! ah qu'il est plein d'honneur!

ACANTE

Il l'est, sans doute!

COLETTE

Oui, mon aimable Acante;
Il m'a promis une dot opulente, 70
Fait ma fortune; et tout le monde dit
Qu'il fait la tienne, et l'on s'en réjouit.
Tu vas, dit-on, devenir chevalière,
Cela te sied, car ton allure est fière.
On te fera dame de qualité, 75
Et tu me recevras avec bonté.

ACANTE

Ma chère enfant, je suis fort satisfaite
Que ta fortune ait été si tôt faite.
Mon cœur ressent tout ton bonheur… Hélas!

66-67 63G, T64P:
Comment cela?
COLETTE
Du fond de ma demeure
J'ai comparu devant mon bon seigneur.

Elle est heureuse, et je ne le suis pas! 80

COLETTE

Que dis-tu là? qu'as-tu donc dans ton âme?
Peut-on souffrir quand on est grande dame?

ACANTE

Va, ces seigneurs qui peuvent tout oser,
N'enlèvent point, crois-moi, pour épouser.
Pour nous, Colette, ils ont des fantaisies, 85
Non de l'amour; leurs démarches hardies,
Leur procédés montrent avec éclat
Tout le mépris qu'ils font de notre état:
C'est ce dédain qui me met en colère.

COLETTE

Bon, des dédains! c'est bien tout le contraire; 90

80 OD63, 63PC: ne la suis
86 63G, T64P: leurs demandes hardies
89 63G, T64P: C'est le dédain
MS1: ce mépris qui
90-110 MS1:
On dit ici que toute cette affaire
Est de l'aveu de monsieur le marquis
Que c'est Champagne un de ses favoris
Qui par son ordre enlevait ta personne.
ACANTE
Quoi! jusque-là le marquis m'abandonne!
J'avais compté sur sa protection
Ah! Désormais à qui se fiera-t-on?
COLETTE
Si tu te plains, je suis toute honteuse
Ma chère enfant de me voir seule heureuse.
ACANTE
Que deviendrai-je hélas!
COLETTE
Ce chevalier
Marche vers toi d'un air tout familier

Rien n'est plus beau que ton enlèvement;
On t'aime, Acante, on t'aime assurément.
Le chevalier va t'épouser, te dis-je,
Tout grand seigneur qu'il est:... cela t'afflige?

ACANTE

Mais monseigneur le marquis qu'a-t-il dit? 95

COLETTE

Lui? rien du tout.

ACANTE

Hélas!

COLETTE

C'est un esprit
Tout en dedans, secret, plein de mystère;
Mais il paraît fort approuver l'affaire.

ACANTE

Du chevalier je déteste l'amour.

COLETTE

Oui, oui, plains-toi de te voir en un jour 100
De Maturin pour jamais délivrée,
D'un beau seigneur poursuivie, adorée;
Un mariage en un moment cassé

Et tu pourrais n'être pas tant à plaindre.

ACANTE

Allons, fuyions.

103-104 63G:

en un moment cassé,
Par monseigneur un autre commencé

Par monseigneur, un autre commencé.
Si ce roman n'a pas de quoi te plaire, 105
Tu me parais difficile, ma chère…
Tiens, le vois-tu, celui qui t'enleva?
Il vient à toi, n'est-ce rien que cela?
T'ai-je trompée? es-tu donc tant à plaindre?

ACANTE

Allons, fuyons.

SCÈNE IV

ACANTE, COLETTE, LE CHEVALIER

LE CHEVALIER

Demeurez sans me craindre. 110
Le marquis veut que je sois à vos pieds.

COLETTE (*à Acante.*)

Qu'avais-je dit?

LE CHEVALIER (*à Acante.*)

Eh quoi! vous me fuyez?

ACANTE

Osez-vous bien paraître en ma présence?

LE CHEVALIER

Oui, vous devez oublier mon offense;

105 63G, T64P: Si cet amant n'a
110 63G, T64P: sans rien craindre

Par moi, vous dis-je, il veut vous consoler. 115

ACANTE

J'aimerais mieux qu'il daignât me parler.

(*à Colette qui veut s'en aller.*)

Ah! reste ici: ce ravisseur m'accable.

COLETTE

Ce ravisseur est pourtant fort aimable.

LE CHEVALIER (*à Acante.*)

Conservez-vous au fond de votre cœur
Pour ma présence une invincible horreur? 120

ACANTE

Vous devez être en horreur à vous-même.

LE CHEVALIER

Oui, je le suis, mais mon remords extrême
Répare tout, et doit vous apaiser.
Ma folle erreur avait pu m'abuser.
Je fus surpris par une indigne flamme; 125
Et mon devoir m'amène ici, madame.

ACANTE

Madame! à moi! quel nom vous me donnez!
Je sais l'état où mes parents sont nés.

COLETTE

Madame!... oh oh! quel est donc ce langage?

120 63G, T64P: Pour ma personne une
124 MS1: ⟨Ma folle erreur avait⟩ ↑Mes sentiments avaient

ACANTE

Cessez, monsieur, ce titre est un outrage; 130
C'est s'avilir que d'oser recevoir
Un faux honneur qu'on ne doit point avoir.
Je suis Acante, et mon nom doit suffire,
Il est sans tache.

LE CHEVALIER

Ah! que puis-je vous dire?
Ce nom m'est cher: allez, vous oublierez 135
Mon attentat, quand vous me connaîtrez:
Vous trouverez très bon que je vous aime.

ACANTE

Qui? moi, monsieur!

COLETTE (*à Acante.*)

C'est son remords extrême.

LE CHEVALIER

N'en riez point, Colette, je prétends
Qu'elle ait pour moi les plus purs sentiments. 140

ACANTE

Je ne sais pas quel dessein vous anime;
Mais commencez par avoir mon estime.

140 MS1, between 140-141:

COLETTE

Je ne ris point et comme vous je pense
Qu'elle doit avoir un peu plus d'indulgence.
Vous n'aviez pas dessein de la fâcher.

LE CHEVALIER

Par mes remords je saurai la toucher.

141 63G, T64P: quel destin vous

LE CHEVALIER

C'est le seul but que j'aurai désormais;
J'en serai digne, et je vous le promets.

ACANTE

Je le désire, et me plais à vous croire. 145
Vous êtes né pour connaître la gloire;
Mais ménagez la mienne, et me laissez.

LE CHEVALIER

Non, c'est en vain que vous vous offensez.
Je ne suis point amoureux, je vous jure;
Mais je prétends rester.

COLETTE

Bon, double injure. 150
Cet homme est fou, je l'ai pensé toujours.
Dormène vient, ma chère, à ton secours.
Démêle-toi de cette grande affaire;
Ou donne grâce, ou garde ta colère.
Ton rôle est beau, tu fais ici la loi. 155
Tu vois les grands à genoux devant toi.
Pour moi je suis condamnée au village.
On ne m'enlève point, et j'en enrage.
On vient, adieu, suis ton brillant destin,
Et je retourne à mon gros Maturin. 160

(*Elle sort.*)

SCÈNE V

ACANTE, LE CHEVALIER, DORMÈNE, DIGNANT

ACANTE

Hélas, madame, une fille éperdue
En rougissant paraît à votre vue.
Pourquoi faut-il, pour combler ma douleur,
Que l'on me laisse avec mon ravisseur?
Et vous aussi, vous m'accablez, mon père! 165
A ce méchant au lieu de me soustraire,
Vous m'amenez vous-même dans ces lieux;
Je l'y revois; mon maître fuit mes yeux.
Mon père, au moins, c'est en vous que j'espère!

DIGNANT

O cher objet! vous n'avez plus de père! 170

ACANTE

Que dites-vous?

DIGNANT

Non, je ne le suis pas.

DORMÈNE

Non, mon enfant, de si charmants appas
Sont nés d'un sang dont vous êtes plus digne.
Préparez-vous au changement insigne
De votre sort; et surtout pardonnez 175
Au chevalier.

161 63G, T64P: une fille perdue

ACANTE

Moi, madame?

DORMÈNE

Apprenez,
Ma chère enfant, que Laure est votre mère.

ACANTE

Elle!…Est-il vrai?

DORMÈNE

Gernance est votre frère.

LE CHEVALIER

Oui je le suis, oui vous êtes ma sœur.

ACANTE

Ah! je succombe. Hélas! est-ce un bonheur? 180

LE CHEVALIER

Il l'est pour moi.

ACANTE

De Laure je suis fille!
Et pourquoi donc faut-il que ma famille
M'ait tant caché mon état et mon nom?
D'où peut venir ce fatal abandon?
D'où vient qu'enfin daignant me reconnaître, 185
Ma mère ici n'a point osé paraître?
Ah! s'il est vrai que le sang nous unit,

177-178 MS1: […] mère. / Tout est connu. Gernance est votre frère.
185-188 MS1, struck out

Sur ce mystère éclairez mon esprit.
Parlez, monsieur, et dissipez ma crainte.

LE CHEVALIER

Ces mouvements dont vous êtes atteinte 190
Sont naturels, et tout vous sera dit.

DORMÈNE

Dans ce moment, Acante, il vous suffit
D'avoir connu quelle est votre naissance.
Vous me devez un peu de confiance.

ACANTE

Laure est ma mère, et je ne la vois pas! 195

LE CHEVALIER

Vous la verrez, vous serez dans ses bras.

DORMÈNE

Oui, cette nuit je vous mène auprès d'elle.

ACANTE

J'admire en tout ma fortune nouvelle.
Quoi! j'ai l'honneur d'être de la maison
De monseigneur!

LE CHEVALIER

Vous honorez son nom. 200

199-200 MS1:
⟨β⟩↑Quoi je serais de l'illustre maison
Du marquis!… moi.

ACANTE

Abusez-vous de mon esprit crédule?
Et voulez-vous me rendre ridicule?
Moi de son sang! ah! s'il était ainsi,
Il me l'eût dit, je le verrais ici.

DIGNANT

Il m'a parlé... je ne sais quoi l'accable: 205
Il est saisi d'un trouble inconcevable.

ACANTE

Ah! je le vois.

SCÈNE DERNIÈRE

ACANTE, DORMÈNE, DIGNANT, LE CHEVALIER,
LE MARQUIS (*au fond.*)

LE MARQUIS (*au chevalier.*)

Il ne sera pas dit
Que cette enfant ait troublé mon esprit.
Bientôt l'absence affermira mon âme.
(*apercevant Dormène.*)
Ah pardonnez: vous étiez là, madame! 210

LE CHEVALIER

Vous paraissez étrangement ému!

206 MS1, line given to the Chevalier
206a-210 MS1, struck out
208 63G, T64P: Que cet enfant

LE MARQUIS

Moi!... point du tout. Vous serez convaincu
Qu'avec sang-froid je règle ma conduite.
De son destin Acante est-elle instruite?

ACANTE

Quel qu'il puisse être, il passe mes souhaits. 215
Je dépendrai de vous plus que jamais.

LE MARQUIS

Permets, ô ciel! qu'ici je puisse faire
Plus d'un heureux!

LE CHEVALIER

C'est une grande affaire.
Je ferai, moi, tout ce que vous voudrez;
Je l'ai promis.

LE MARQUIS

Que vous m'obligerez! 220

(*à Dormène.*)

Belle Dormène, oubliez-vous l'offense,
L'égarement du coupable Gernance?

DORMÈNE

Oui, tout est réparé.

218-220 MS1:

LE CHEVALIER

Il n'est pas ordinaire
De contenter à la fois tous les goûts

LE MARQUIS

Essayons donc et commençons par vous

LE MARQUIS

Tout ne l'est pas.
Votre grand nom, vos vertueux appas
Sont maltraités par l'aveugle fortune. 225
Je le sais trop; votre âme non commune
N'a pas de quoi suffire à vos bienfaits;
Votre destin doit changer désormais.
Si j'avais pu d'un heureux mariage
Choisir pour moi l'agréable esclavage, 230
C'eût été vous (et je vous l'ai mandé)
Pour qui mon cœur se serait décidé.
Voudriez-vous, madame, qu'à ma place
Le chevalier, pour mieux obtenir grâce,
Pour devenir à jamais vertueux, 235
Prît avec vous d'indissolubles nœuds?
Le meilleur frein pour ses mœurs, pour son âge,
Est une épouse aimable, noble et sage.
Daignerez-vous accepter un château
Environné d'un domaine assez beau? 240
Pardonnez-vous cette offre?

DORMÈNE

Ma surprise
Est si puissante, à tel point me maîtrise,
Que ne pouvant encor me déclarer,
Je n'ai de voix que pour vous admirer.

229-237 MS1:
Souffrirez-vous qu'un hymen convenable
Unisse à vous dans un état sortable
Ce gentilhomme?

LE CHEVALIER

Après ma folle erreur
Me croira-t-on digne d'un tel honneur?

LE MARQUIS

Le meilleur frein pour ses mœurs ⟨est⟩ ↑et+ son âge

LE CHEVALIER

J'admire aussi: mais je fais plus, madame; 245
Je vous soumets l'empire de mon âme.
A tous les deux je devrai mon bonheur.
Mais seconderez-vous mon bienfaiteur?

DORMÈNE

Consultez-vous, méritez mon estime,
Et les bienfaits de ce cœur magnanime. 250

LE MARQUIS

Et… vous… Acante…

ACANTE

Eh bien! mon protecteur…

LE MARQUIS (*à part.*)

Pourquoi tremblé-je en parlant?

ACANTE

Quoi, monsieur…

LE MARQUIS

Acante… vous… qui venez de renaître,
Vous qu'une mère ici va reconnaître,
Vivez près d'elle; et de ses tristes jours 255

245 MS1: ⟨β⟩↑Tant de bontés me confondent, madame
247 MS1: ⟨β⟩↑Je sens hélas! le prix de votre cœur.
249-250 MS1:
Il est le mien: cette grâce est insigne,
⟨je la reçois, mais rendez-vous en digne⟩
↓Mais c'est à vous à vous en rendre digne
253-256 MS1, struck out

Adoucissez et prolongez le cours.
Vous commencez une nouvelle vie,
Avec un frère, une mère, une amie.
Je veux... Souffrez qu'à votre mère, à vous,
Je fasse un sort indépendant et doux. 260
Votre fortune, Acante, est assurée;
L'acte est passé, vous vivrez honorée,
Riche... contente... autant que je le peux.
J'aurais voulu... mais goûtez toutes deux,
Dormène et vous, les douceurs fortunées 265
Que l'amitié donne aux âmes bien nées...
Un autre bien que le cœur peut sentir
Est dangereux... Adieu... je vais partir.

LE CHEVALIER

Eh quoi! ma sœur, vous n'êtes point contente?
Quoi! vous pleurez?

ACANTE

Je suis reconnaissante, 270
Je suis confuse... Ah c'en est trop pour moi.
Mais j'ai perdu plus que je ne reçois...
Et ce n'est pas la fortune que j'aime...
Mon état change, et mon âme est la même;
Elle doit être à vous... Ah permettez 275
Que le cœur plein de vos rares bontés,
J'aille oublier ma première misère,
J'aille pleurer dans le sein de ma mère.

LE MARQUIS

De quel chagrin vos sens sont agités?
Qu'avez-vous donc? qu'ai-je fait?

258 63G, T64P: Avec un père, une

ACANTE

Vous partez. 280

DORMÈNE

Ah! qu'as-tu dit?

ACANTE

La vérité, madame;

La vérité plaît à votre belle âme.

LE MARQUIS

Non, c'en est trop pour mes sens éperdus…

282-295a MS1:

La vérité plaît à votre belle âme.
⟨Il est permis de montrer sa douleur
Lorsqu'à jamais on perd un bienfaiteur

LE MARQUIS

Acante, ô sort! que dis-je? ô Providence,
Qui règles tout, tiens tout sous ta puissance.
Conduis mon cœur et mes sens éperdus. 5*v*
Acante!

ACANTE

Hélas!

LE MARQUIS

Ne partirai-je plus?

LE CHEVALIER

Mon cher parent, de Laure elle est la fille,
Elle retrouve un frère, une famille,
Et moi je trouve un mariage heureux
Mais je voudrais ⟨que vous en fissiez deux⟩
↑pour combler tous mes vœux 10*v*

ACANTE

Que dites-vous?

LE CHEVALIER

Je voudrais […]

[12*v*-17*v* on pasted-down paper slip covering 10*v*-11*v* and some illegible text]

⟨Mais je voudrais pour combler tous mes vœux

Acante…

ACANTE

Hélas!…

LE MARQUIS

Expliquez-vous

LE CHEVALIER

Mais je voudrais qu'Acante
Dans les liens d'une union constante
Pût éprouver le charme et la douceur 15*v*
D'être à celui dont on fait le bonheur.

LE MARQUIS

De qui?

LE CHEVALIER

D'un homme, etc…⟩ [20*v*]
[end of pasted-down slip]
⟨Du vrai mérite et dont le noble cœur
Fût au-dessus de sa rare valeur

LE MARQUIS

Qui donc?

LE CHEVALIER

D'un homme à la fleur de son âge, 20*v*
Sensible et noble, homme d'esprit et sage,
Ferme en son choix, respectable en aimant
Et qui surtout ⟨sait payer⟩ s'acquitte noblement,
Quand par malheur il perd une gageure.

LE MARQUIS

Ai-je perdu?

LE CHEVALIER

La chose est assez sure 25*v*

LE MARQUIS

Je ne suis point l'homme que vous peignez
(*à Acante*)
J'en ai des traits; j'aime. Eh bien donc régnez.⟩
[2*v*-27*v* deleted and replaced by 28*v*-31*v*]

LE MARQUIS

Ah! c'en est trop je ne résiste plus
Les préjugés sont ici superflus.
Régnez sur moi – courrons chez votre mère 30*v*
Je lui dirai combien vous m'êtes chère.
[295a follows]

LE MARQUIS

Ne partirai-je plus?

LE CHEVALIER

Mon cher parent, de Laure elle est la fille; 285
Elle retrouve un frère, une famille;
Et moi je trouve un mariage heureux.
Mais je vois bien que vous en ferez deux.
Vous payerez, la gageure est perdue.

LE MARQUIS

Je vous l'avoue... oui, mon âme est vaincue. 290
Dormène et Laure, Acante, et vous, et moi,
Soyons heureux... Oui... recevez ma foi,
Aimable Acante; allons que je vous mène
Chez votre mère... elle sera la mienne,
Elle oubliera pour jamais son malheur. 295

ACANTE

Ah! je tombe à vos pieds...

LE CHEVALIER

Allons, ma sœur:
Je fus bien fou: son cœur fut insensible;
Mais on n'est pas toujours incorrigible.

Fin du cinquième et dernier acte.

296 MS1, after 296:
⟨Vous épouser est le droit du seigneur⟩
↑ Que votre hymen achève son bonheur

298a W75G: troisième et dernier

APPENDIX

The text reproduced below is that of the three-act version performed in 1779 and first published in 1784, from the point at which this diverges from the text of W75G. Though many of the lines are common to both versions, the remainder of the three-act version is given as a continuous text for the convenience of the reader. The text is that of W75G*, with the manuscript element modernised for the sake of uniformity.

[ACTE III]

[*SCÈNE VII*]

[LE MARQUIS, ACANTE, LE BAILLI, MATURIN]

MATURIN

Ce nous verrons, est d'un mauvais présage. 415
Qu'en dites-vous bailli?

LE BAILLI

L'ami, sois sage.

MATURIN

Que je fis mal ô ciel! quand je naquis

414a-418a W75G*, added by Wagnière on a slip of paper covering the bottom of p.274; p.275-76 removed

De naître hélas! le vassal d'un marquis!

(*ils sortent.*)

SCÈNE VIII

LE MARQUIS (*seul.*)

Non, je ne perdrai point cette gageure...
Amoureux! moi! quel conte! ah je m'assure 420
Que sur soi-même on garde un plein pouvoir;
Pour être sage, on n'a qu'à le vouloir.
Il est bien vrai qu'Acante est assez belle...
Et de la grâce! ah! nul n'en a plus qu'elle...
Et de l'esprit!... quoi, dans le fond des bois! 425
Pour avoir vu Dormène quelquefois,
Que de progrès! qu'il faut peu de culture
Pour seconder les dons de la nature!
J'estime Acante: oui, je dois l'estimer;
Mais, grâce au ciel, je suis très loin d'aimer. 430
A fuir l'amour j'ai mis toute ma gloire.

418b-419 W75G*, added by Wagnière on a slip of paper
421 MS2: sur moi-même on
MS3: ⟨moi⟩ soi-même
431 MS2, MS3: ⟨j'ai mis toute⟩ ↑je mets un peu [MS2: W]
W75G*, added by Wagnière on a slip of paper covering the bottom of p.277

SCÈNE IX

LE MARQUIS, DIGNANT, MADAME BERTHE, [MATURIN]

BERTHE

Ah! voici bien pardienne une autre histoire.

LE MARQUIS

Quoi?

BERTHE

Pour le coup c'est le droit du seigneur.
On nous enlève Acante.

LE MARQUIS

Ah!

BERTHE

Votre honneur
Sera honteux de cette vilenie; 435
Et je n'aurais pas cru cette infamie
D'un grand seigneur si bon, si libéral.

431a-439 W75G*, added by Wagnière on slips of paper covering p.278-79 and the top of p.280
431d MS3: ⟨M[de] Berthe⟩ ↑Maturin
433a MS3: ⟨M[de] Berthe⟩ ↑Maturin
434 MS3: Ah! Ah!
435 MS3: ⟨vilenie⟩ ↑perfidie

LE MARQUIS

Comment? qu'est-il arrivé?

BERTHE

Bien du mal…
Savez-vous pas qu'à peine chez son père
Elle arrivait pour finir notre affaire, 440
Quatre coquins, alertes, bien tournés,
Effrontément me l'ont prise à mon nez,
Tout en riant, et vite l'ont conduite
Je ne sais où.

LE MARQUIS

Qu'on aille à leur poursuite…
Holà! quelqu'un… ne perdez point de temps; 445
Allez, courez, que mes gardes, mes gens
De tous côtés marchent en diligence.
Volez, vous dis-je, et s'il faut ma présence,
J'irai moi-même.

BERTHE (*à son mari.*)

Il parle tout de bon;
Et l'on croirait, mon cher, à la façon 450
Dont monseigneur regarde cette injure,
Que c'est à lui qu'on a pris la future.

LE MARQUIS

Et vous son père, et vous qui l'aimiez tant,

438-439 MS3:
Comment? qu'est-il arrivé?

MATURIN

Bien du mal.

M[DE] BERTHE

Savez-vous pas…

452 W75G*: ⟨sa⟩ la future

Vous qui perdez une si chère enfant,
Un tel trésor, un cœur noble, un cœur tendre, 455
Avez-vous pu souffrir, sans la défendre,
Que de vos bras on osât l'arracher?
Un tel malheur semble peu vous toucher.
Que devient donc l'amitié paternelle?
Vous m'étonnez.

DIGNANT

Mon cœur gémit sur elle, 460
Mais je me trompe, ou j'ai dû pressentir
Que par votre ordre on la faisait partir.

LE MARQUIS

Par mon ordre?

DIGNANT

Oui.

LE MARQUIS

Quelle injure nouvelle!
Tous ces gens-ci perdent-ils la cervelle?
Allez-vous-en, laissez-moi, sortez tous. 465
Ah! s'il se peut, modérons mon courroux...
Non, vous, restez.

MATURIN

Qui? moi?

460 W75G*: ⟨Tout mon cœur est pour elle⟩ $^{W\uparrow}$β
461 W75G*: ⟨C'est mon devoir; et⟩ $^{W\uparrow}$β
466 MS2, MS3, with stage direction after 466: *à Dignant* [MS3: ^{V}]
467a MS2, MS3: ⟨DIGNANT⟩ $^{\uparrow}$MATURIN

LE MARQUIS (*à Dignant.*)

Non, vous, vous dis-je.

SCÈNE X

LE MARQUIS *sur le devant*, DIGNANT *au fond.*

LE MARQUIS

Je vois d'où part l'attentat qui m'afflige.
Le chevalier m'avait presque promis
De se porter à des coups si hardis. 470
Il croit au fond que cette gentillesse
Est pardonnable au feu de sa jeunesse.
Il ne sait pas combien j'en suis choqué,
A quel excès ce fou-là m'a manqué,
Jusqu'à quel point son procédé m'offense. 475
Il déshonore, il trahit l'innocence;
Voilà le prix de mon affection
Pour un parent indigne de mon nom!
Il est pétri des vices de son père,
Il a ses traits, ses mœurs, son caractère; 480
Il périra malheureux comme lui.
Je le renonce, et je veux qu'aujourd'hui
Il soit puni de tant d'extravagance.

DIGNANT

Puis-je en tremblant prendre ici la licence
De vous parler? 485

467b MS2, MS3, no stage direction

LE MARQUIS

Sans doute, tu le peux.
Parle-moi d'elle.

DIGNANT

Au transport douloureux
Où votre cœur devant moi s'abandonne,
Je ne reconnais plus votre personne.
Vous avez lu ce qu'on vous a porté,
Ce gros paquet qu'on vous a présenté? 490

LE MARQUIS

Eh mon ami! suis-je en état de lire?

DIGNANT

Vous me faites frémir.

LE MARQUIS

Que veux-tu dire?

DIGNANT

Quoi, ce paquet n'est pas encore ouvert?

LE MARQUIS

Non.

DIGNANT

Juste ciel! ce dernier coup me perd!

LE MARQUIS

Comment!... j'ai cru que c'était un mémoire 495
De mes forêts.

DIGNANT

Hélas! vous deviez croire
Que cet écrit était intéressant.

LE MARQUIS

Eh lisons vite… Une table à l'instant;
Approchez donc cette table.

DIGNANT

Ah mon maître!
Qu'aura-t-on fait, et qu'allez-vous connaître? 500

LE MARQUIS *assis examine le paquet.*

Mais ce paquet qui n'est pas à mon nom,
Est cacheté des sceaux de ma maison?

DIGNANT

Oui.

LE MARQUIS

Lisons donc.

DIGNANT

Cet étrange mystère
En d'autres temps aurait de quoi vous plaire;
Mais à présent il devient bien affreux. 505

LE MARQUIS *lisant.*

Je ne vois rien jusqu'ici que d'heureux.
Je vois d'abord que le ciel la fit naître

506-532 w75G*, added by Wagnière on slips of paper covering p.284-85, the top of p.286 and the top of p.289; p.287-88 removed

D'un sang illustre; et cela devait être.
Oui, plus je lis, plus je bénis les cieux.
Quoi! Laure a mis ce dépôt précieux 510
Entre vos mains! quoi! Laure est donc sa mère?

DIGNANT

Oui.

LE MARQUIS

Mais pourquoi lui serviez-vous de père?
Indignement pourquoi la marier?

DIGNANT

J'en avais l'ordre; et j'ai dû vous prier
En sa faveur. Sa mère infortunée 515
A l'indigence était abandonnée,
Ne subsistant que des nobles secours
Que par mes mains vous versiez tous les jours.

LE MARQUIS

Il est trop vrai: je sais bien que mon père
Fut envers elle autrefois trop sévère... 520
Quel souvenir!... que souvent nous voyons
D'affreux secrets dans d'illustres maisons!...
Je le savais: le père de Gernance
De Laure hélas! séduisit l'innocence,
Et mes parents par un zèle inhumain 525
Avaient puni cet hymen clandestin.
Je lis, je tremble, ah douleur trop amère!
Mon cher ami! quoi! Gernance est son frère!

519 W75G*: ⟨trop⟩ V↑bien
523 W75G*: ⟨Tu le sais trop⟩ V↑Je le savais
527 MS2, MS3:
J'aurais été moins dur et moins austère.

DIGNANT

Tout est connu.

LE MARQUIS

Quoi! c'est lui que je vois!…
Ah! ce sera pour la dernière fois… 530
Sachons dompter le courroux qui m'anime.
Il semble ô ciel! qu'il connaisse son crime.
Que dans ses yeux je lis d'égarement!
Ah l'on n'est pas coupable impunément.
Comme il rougit! comme il pâlit… le traître! 535
A mes regards il tremble de paraître.
C'est quelque chose.

528a-534 MS2, added by Voltaire:

DIGNANT

Oui.

(*Le chevalier paraît de loin*)

LE MARQUIS

Quoi! c'est lui qui revient tout honteux!
Il a l'air humble, il baisse enfin les yeux!
Dès qu'à l'honneur on a fait quelque outrage
Il y paraît aussitôt au visage
Comme il rougit!

MS3: DIGNANT

Oui.

(*Le chevalier paraît de loin*)

LE MARQUIS

⟨Quoi! C'est lui⟩ ↑Le voilà+ qui revient tout honteux!
Il a l'air humble, il baisse enfin les yeux!
Dès qu'à l'honneur ⟨on a⟩ ↑il a+ fait ⟨quelque⟩ outrage
⟨[*variant*]⟩ ↑D'un cœur bien né la honte est le partage.
Comme il rougit!

SCÈNE XI

LE MARQUIS, LE CHEVALIER

LE CHEVALIER (*de loin se cachant le visage.*)

Ah! Monsieur.

LE MARQUIS

Est-ce vous?
Vous, malheureux?

LE CHEVALIER

Je tombe à vos genoux…

LE MARQUIS

Qu'avez-vous fait?

LE CHEVALIER

Une faute, une offense,
Dont je ressens l'indigne extravagance, 540
Qui pour jamais m'a servi de leçon,
Et dont je viens vous demander pardon.

LE MARQUIS

Vous des remords! vous! est-il bien possible?

LE CHEVALIER

Rien n'est plus vrai.

LE MARQUIS

Votre faute est horrible,

Plus que vous ne pensez: mais votre cœur 545
Est-il sensible à mes soins, à l'honneur,
A l'amitié? Vous sentez-vous capable
D'oser me faire un aveu véritable,
Sans rien cacher?

LE CHEVALIER

Comptez sur ma candeur;
Je suis un libertin, mais point menteur; 550
Et mon esprit que le trouble environne,
Est trop ému pour abuser personne.

LE MARQUIS

Je prétends tout savoir.

LE CHEVALIER

Je vous dirai,
Que de débauche et d'ardeur enivré,
Plus que d'amour, j'avais fait la folie 555
De dérober une fille jolie
Au possesseur de ses jeunes appas,
(Qu'à mon avis, il ne mérite pas.)
Je l'ai conduite à la forêt prochaine,
Dans ce château de Laure et de Dormène; 560
C'est une faute, il est vrai, j'en conviens,
Mais j'étais fou, je ne pensais à rien.
Cette Dormène, et Laure sa compagne,
Etaient encor bien loin dans la campagne.
En étourdi je n'ai point perdu temps; 565
J'ai commencé par des propos galants.
Je m'attendais aux communes alarmes,
Aux cris perçants, à la colère, aux larmes;

550 MS3: Je ⟨suis⟩ ↑fus

Mais qu'ai-je vu! la fermeté, l'honneur,
L'air indigné, mais calme avec grandeur. 570
Tout ce qui fait respecter l'innocence
S'armait pour elle, et prenait sa défense.
J'ai recouru dans ces premiers moments,
A l'art de plaire, aux égards séduisants,
Aux doux propos, à cette déférence, 575
Qui fait souvent pardonner la licence.
Mais pour réponse, Acante à deux genoux
M'a conjuré de la rendre chez vous;
Et c'est alors que ses yeux moins sévères
Ont répandu des pleurs involontaires. 580

LE MARQUIS

Que dites-vous?

LE CHEVALIER

Elle voulait en vain
Me les cacher de sa charmante main;
Dans cet état, sa grâce attendrissante
Enhardissait mon ardeur imprudente;
Et tout honteux de ma stupidité, 585
J'ai voulu prendre un peu de liberté.
Ciel! comme elle a tancé ma hardiesse!
Oui, j'ai cru voir une chaste déesse,
Qui rejetait de son auguste autel
L'impur encens qu'offrait un criminel. 590

573-91 MS2, MS3:
A son ton noble, à son charmant aspect,
J'étais surpris de sentir du respect.
LE MARQUIS
Que dites-vous?
LE CHEVALIER
Comment se peut-il faire

LE MARQUIS

Ah! poursuivez.

LE CHEVALIER

Comment se peut-il faire
Qu'ayant vécu presque dans la misère,
Dans la bassesse, et dans l'obscurité,
Elle ait cet air et cette dignité,
Ces sentiments, cet esprit, ce langage, 595
Je ne dis pas au-dessus du village,
De son état, de son nom, de son sang,
Mais convenable au plus illustre rang?
Non, il n'est point de mère respectable,
Qui condamnant l'erreur d'un fils coupable, 600
Le rappelât avec plus de bonté
A la vertu dont il s'est écarté;
N'employant point l'aigreur et la colère,
Fière et décente, et plus sage qu'austère.
De vous surtout elle a parlé longtemps. 605

LE MARQUIS

De moi?...

LE CHEVALIER

Montrant à mes égarements
Votre vertu, qui devait, disait-elle,
Etre à jamais ma honte ou mon modèle.

594 MS2, MS3: Elle ait toujours cet air de dignité
595-98 MS2, MS3, absent
608 MS2, MS3: honte et mon

Tout interdit, plein d'un secret respect,
Que je n'avais senti qu'à son aspect, 610
Je suis honteux, mes fureurs se captivent.
Dans ce moment les deux dames arrivent;
Et me voyant maître de leur logis,
Avec Acante, et deux ou trois bandits,
D'un juste effroi leur âme s'est remplie; 615
La plus âgée en tombe évanouie.
Acante en pleurs la presse dans ses bras;
Elle revient des portes du trépas.
Alors sur moi fixant sa triste vue,
Elle retombe, et s'écrie éperdue, 620
Ah! je crois voir Gernance... c'est son fils,
C'est lui... je meurs... à ces mots je frémis;
Et la douleur, l'effroi de cette dame,
Au même instant ont passé dans mon âme.
Je tombe aux pieds de Dormène, et je sors, 625
Confus, soumis, pénétré de remords.

609-11 MS2, MS3:

LE MARQUIS

Est-il bien vrai?

LE CHEVALIER

Tandis qu'elle parlait [MS3: partait],
Le repentir dans mon cœur descendait,
Mes sentiments, mes fureurs se captivent

613 MS2: de leur taudis

613-14 MS3:
Et ⟨me⟩ nous voyant maîtres de leur maison
⟨Avec Acante et comme en garnison⟩
↑Moi, mes valets, Acante, avec raison

616 MS3, MS2: Madame Laure en tombe

619 MS3, MS2: Laure sur moi fixe sa

622-24 MS3, MS2:
Le trouble alors s'empare du logis,
Nous pleurons tous. La douleur de la dame
Au même instant a passé dans mon âme

LE MARQUIS

Ce repentir dont votre âme est saisie
Charme mon cœur, et nous réconcilie.
Tenez, prenez ce paquet important,
Lisez bien vite, et pesez mûrement… 630
Pauvre jeune homme! hélas! comme il soupire!
(*Il lui montre l'endroit où il est dit qu'il est frère d'Acante.*)
Tenez, c'est là, là surtout qu'il faut lire.

LE CHEVALIER

Ma sœur Acante!…

LE MARQUIS

Oui, jeune libertin.

LE CHEVALIER

Oh! par ma foi je ne suis pas devin.
Il faut tout réparer. Mais par l'usage 635
Je ne saurais la prendre en mariage,
Je suis son frère, et vous êtes cousin,
Payez pour moi.

630-666a W75G*, added by Wagnière on a slip of paper covering part of p.293; p.294-316 removed, and replaced by one leaf in Wagnière's hand
631 MS3: ⟨β⟩ ↑De vos excès concevez le délire
631a W75G*, MS2, MS3, stage direction added (W75G*: V)
634-38 MS3:
⟨Ah! pardonnez, je ne suis pas devin,
Il faut pourtant réparer ma folie,
Marquis, Acante est sage, elle est jolie,
Je suis son frère, elle n'est plus mon fait
C'est donc à vous…⟩ ↑Ah, cher Marquis…
LE MARQUIS
Comment finir enfin

LE MARQUIS

Comment finir enfin
Honnêtement cette étrange aventure?...
Ah! la voici... j'ai perdu la gageure. 640

SCÈNE DERNIÈRE

LES ACTEURS PRÉCÉDENTS, ACANTE, ET COLETTE

ACANTE

Où suis-je hélas! et quel nouveau malheur!

639 MS2, MS3, with stage direction after 639: *Acante vient*
640C K: ACANTE, COLETTE
641 MS2: Où suis-je! où suis-je! et
641-54 MS3:
Où suis-je, où suis-je
[followed by a text identical to that of W75G*, but struck out and replaced by the following, in a different hand, on a separate sheet]
Où suis-je, hélas! et quel nouveau malheur!
Je vois mon père et mon persécuteur!
GERNANCE
Il ne l'est plus... vous n'avez plus de père.
Vous saurez tout... mais un coupable frère,
Que le remords amène à vos genoux,
Madame, est-il enfin digne de vous?
ACANTE
Madame! un frère? est-il vrai? Quel mystère!
LE MARQUIS
Il est bien grand: le sort longtemps contraire
Répare tout: tout éprouve en ce jour
Les coups du sort et surtout de l'amour.
Je me soumets à leur pouvoir suprême.
Et quel mortel fait son destin soi-même?
Faites le mien: acceptez un époux.

Je vois mon père avec mon ravisseur!

DIGNANT

Madame, hélas! vous n'avez plus de père.

ACANTE

Madame à moi! qu'entends-je? quel mystère!

LE MARQUIS

Il est bien grand. Tout éprouve en ce jour 645
Les coups du sort, et surtout de l'amour.
Je me soumets à leur pouvoir suprême.
Eh quel mortel fait son destin soi-même!...
Nous sommes tous, madame, à vos genoux.
Au lieu d'un père acceptez un époux. 650

ACANTE

Ciel! est-ce un rêve?

LE MARQUIS

On va tout vous apprendre.
Mais à nos vœux commencez par vous rendre;

ACANTE

Vous épouser! qui! moi! Monsieur?

LE MARQUIS

Oui, vous.
Vous que j'ai craint d'aimer, vous que j'adore!

ACANTE

Quoi! je serais à vous! j'ai peine encore
A concevoir un tel excès d'honneur.
J'étais bien loin d'y prétendre, et mon cœur,
Qui combattait le penchant le plus tendre,
Et vos vertus peut donc enfin le rendre
Il vous doit tout, mais ses purs sentiments
Ont prévenu le sort et vos présents.

Et par régner pour jamais sur mon cœur.

ACANTE

Moi! comment croire un tel excès d'honneur.

LE MARQUIS

Vous libertin, je vais vous rendre sage. 655
Et dès demain je vous mets en ménage
Avec Dormène. Elle s'y résoudra.

LE CHEVALIER

J'épouserai tout ce qu'il vous plaira.

COLETTE

Et moi donc?

LE MARQUIS

Toi! ne crois pas, ma mignonne
Qu'en faisant tous les lots je t'abandonne. 660
Ton Maturin te quittait aujourd'hui;
Je te le donne; il t'aura malgré lui.
Tu peux compter sur une dot honnête...
Allons danser, et que tout soit en fête.
J'avais cherché la sagesse; et mon cœur 665
Sans rien chercher a trouvé le bonheur.

Fin

654 W75G*: ⟨Je n'ose⟩ V↑Moi! comment
655 MS3: Vous, ⟨libertin, je vais⟩ ↑mon cousin, je veux
658 MS3: ⟨ce qu'il⟩ ↑comme il
658a MS2: COLETTE (*arrivant*)

L'Ecossaise

critical edition

by

Colin Duckworth

ACKNOWLEDGMENTS

It gives me great pleasure to acknowledge my grateful appreciation to the following, who have in various ways contributed to the successful completion of this edition: the late Dr Theodore Besterman; Mlle Sylvie Chevalley; the late Professor J. S. Spink; Professor Robert Niklaus; Mlle H. Frémont; M. Marcel Thomas; M. Georges Colin; M. Charles Wirz; the late Professor Werner Krauss; Dr Martin Fontius; Mme I. F. Grigorieva and Mme L. L. Albina of the Saltykov-Shchedrin State Public Library of Leningrad; the Research Collections Librarian of McMaster University Library; Mr L. Koritz; Miss Sylvie Duff, for painstaking help with variants; Miss Eileen Gillies, for secretarial assistance; and my wife, for her unfailing encouragement and patient research assistance.

I owe a great debt of gratitude to Andrew Brown and Ulla Kölving of the Voltaire Foundation for additional information relating to editions and variants.

My thanks are also due to the universities of London, Auckland and Melbourne for grants towards travel and research expenses.

Colin Duckworth

INTRODUCTION

1. *Genesis, sources and composition*

L'Ecossaise was a work born out of sheer exasperation. We must therefore expect it to possess all the weaknesses and the interest peculiar to *œuvres de circonstance*. It was written in haste; it was not intended for public performance; its object was to rid Voltaire and the *encyclopédistes* of a troublesome adversary, Fréron, once and for all, without any aesthetic pretentions. But for one fact, it would long ago have been relegated to the ranks of minor works with which only the most devoted scholars would trouble to claim acquaintance. That one fact is that it has the mark of Voltaire upon it. His ire inspired it. It is very much a part of his own life, a modest shot in his struggle to keep at bay the *anti-philosophe* movement which seemed to be gathering strength during the late 1750s. The brunt of his attack was borne by Fréron who, for Voltaire, was not simply a biting critic: the editor of *L'Année littéraire* wielded a great influence over public opinion. It was therefore important to all the *philosophes* that he should be ridiculed and discredited. Fréron himself called the first performance of *L'Ecossaise* 'la grande bataille', with misplaced irony (*Al*, 1760, v.209-16). The evening of 26 July 1760 at the Comédie-Française was more than a *cause célèbre*, as numerous letters from and to Voltaire during that summer reveal. If Voltaire lowered himself to the level of personal vituperation, it was because much more was at stake than his own defence. Whether he was justified or not in using the theatre to excoriate an individual must be judged in the light of Fréron's own part in the waning fortunes of the philosophic movement at the end of the decade.

The first questions that pose themselves in establishing the background to the creation of *L'Ecossaise* are related not only to Voltaire's private dispute with Fréron but also to the intellectual climate of the time: namely, what precipitated Voltaire's scathing satire on Fréron? In deciding upon his basic plot, why did he revert to the genre of sentimental drama and to the *Pamela* situation he had already used for *Nanine* ten years earlier? Finally, having written *L'Ecossaise*, why did he ascribe it to the Scottish playwright John Home?

During the two years immediately prior to *L'Ecossaise*, there was an active exchange of pamphlets and satires between Fréron, Palissot, Moreau and the 'cacouacs', which culminated in the resignation of d'Alembert as co-editor of the *Encyclopédie*, the defection of Duclos and Marmontel from this great enterprise of enlightened minds, and finally the suppression on 8 March 1759 of the existing volumes (A-H), followed shortly after (3 September) by the condemnation of the *Encyclopédie* by pope Clement XIII.

Days were dark indeed in the autumn of 1759 for the *philosophes*. In the previous year, Voltaire had already foreseen the outcome, and had suggested that the encyclopaedists should publish from Lausanne while there was time; but, he commented, 'ils n'en sauront jamais jusques là. Ils resteront à Paris, persécutez et mal payez' (to d'Alembert, 7 March 1758; D7666). The persistent attacks on d'Alembert and the *Encyclopédie* by Fréron in *L'Année littéraire* were as much a source of anger to the *philosophes* as they were a source of irritation and embarrassment to Malesherbes.[1] Thus, when Fréron came under direct attack in the character of Wasp (or Frélon), the harassed director of the *librairie* was in no mood to sympathise with him, as we shall see. Voltaire was subjected to Fréron's critical gaze several times in the latter's *Lettres de madame la comtesse* in 1745 and 1746. Voltaire responded with an oblique reference, in his third verse discourse (on *Envie*) to 'un lourd frelon méchamment imbécile, / Qui vit du mal qu'il fait, et nuit sans être utile' (M.ix.397). These are the features (real

[1] See Pierre Grosclaude, *Malesherbes, témoin et interprète de son temps* (Paris 1962), ch.6.

or imaginary) of Fréron's character that Voltaire develops in *L'Ecossaise*.

Voltaire commented on Fréron's particular style of destructive criticism in 1749, to Marmontel,[2] whose tragedy *Aristomène* had been pulled to pieces in the recently established *Lettres sur quelques écrits de ce temps* (ii.289-321). He allowed himself private expressions of distaste for Fréron, to his correspondents, in response to Fréron's published calumnies, and was reduced to seeking the good offices of Berryer de Ravenoville (the *lieutenant de police*) and of the comte d'Argenson to stop Fréron printing his odious libels every fortnight, in order to forestall 'les querelles violentes qui naîtront infailliblement d'une pareille licence' (15 March 1750; D4123). Only when these requests to remonstrate with Fréron fell on deaf ears did he have recourse to Mairan (secretary for life of the Académie des sciences, who had influence with the chancellor, Daguesseau), pointing out that Fréron was printing without permission (22 March 1750; D4130). Action was finally taken by the new director of the *librairie*, Malesherbes, who was obliged to suppress Fréron's *Lettres* in 1752. Voltaire immediately wrote to Malesherbes asking him not to deprive Fréron of his livelihood (D4911), although there is little doubt that he was delighted at being left in peace for six months.

Fréron treated Voltaire with circumspection in the first few volumes of *L'Année littéraire*, from 1754 to 1758. However, his inability to distinguish between literary criticism and scurrilous personal attacks on writers led the *encyclopédistes* to defend themselves in the articles 'Cependant' and 'Critique'. Fréron complained to Malesherbes about these in a letter of 27 January 1758, seeing a reference to himself where Marmontel, in the article

[2] D4075, *c.* 15 June 1749. One cannot help wondering whether Voltaire would not have made his satirical representation of Fréron less harsh and caricatural if he had recalled his own words in this letter: 'Les satires passent, dit le grand Racine, et les bons écrits qu'elles attaquent demeurent. Mais il demeure aussi quelque chose de ces satires. C'est la haine et le mépris que leurs auteurs accumulent sur leurs personnes'.

'Critique', quotes Voltaire's description of 'the ignorant critic': 'Les derniers de cette classe sont ceux qui *attaquent tous les jours ce que nous avons de meilleur, qui louent ce que nous avons de plus mauvais et font de la noble profession des lettres, un métier aussi lâche et aussi méprisable qu'eux-mêmes* (M. de Voltaire dans les *Mensonges imprimés*)'. Fréron was right to recognise himself; corroboration of his fears was given later by Voltaire when he used the same expressions in the *Relation du jésuite Berthier*, *L'Ecossaise* and *Candide*. Tension between *philosophes* and *anti-philosophes* increased after the publication of Helvétius's *De l'esprit* in July 1758, and its condemnation to be burnt (10 August 1758) encouraged Fréron to turn his attention again to his old enemy.[3] *Candide* gave him a good opportunity to irritate Voltaire (which the latter reciprocated in good measure in his celebrated addition to chapter 22 of the novel in 1761).[4] It was Fréron's review of the *reprise* of *La Femme qui a raison* (first performed in 1749) which seemed to make Voltaire decide that open warfare was the only means of defence left to him.[5] He asked Thiriot to send him a copy of the play (which he claimed, in his usual fashion, not to know) and of 'la malsemaine dans laquelle Freron répand son venin de Crapaud' (15 December 1759; D8665). Thiriot sent them off by 29 December, and Voltaire was soon reading Fréron's imputations of 'grossièreté tudesque, de bassesse et d'indécence' in *La Femme qui a raison*. On 4 January 1760 Voltaire showed he was reacting warmly to the hostile comments of 'cet autre animal de Fréron qui [...] saisit la chose comme un dogue affamé qui ronge le premier os qu'on luy présente' (to Thiriot; D8694). At the same time, Voltaire wrote a long open letter[6] denouncing all those who set themselves up as judges of literary works instead of writing

[3] *Al* (1758), viii.312, viii.356; (1759), ii.203-10, iii.242-55, iv.81 ss, v.71, v.133, vi.137 and viii.3-25 (on *La Femme qui a raison*).

[4] See *Candide*, Voltaire 48, p.212-13.

[5] 30 November 1759 (*Al*, viii.3-25).

[6] D8696. First published in the *Journal encyclopédique* (1760, i.i.110-16), and shortly after in the *Mercure de France* (1760, ii.143-48).

good ones themselves, and expressing his contempt for those who write in that 'pitoyable genre' called satire, 'que je n'en fais point'. Not, he explains, that he has in mind the author of *L'Année littéraire*, of which he knows nothing except that he has heard it is a work in which the most celebrated men of letters are often outrageously attacked.

One might think that this was enough protest; too much, even, for as Voltaire repeatedly says in his letters at this time, France had more serious things to think about in those critical days of strife. He himself had several preoccupations which should have taken his mind off Fréron: continuous attempts to bring the Seven Years' War to an end by acting as intermediary and mediator between Frederick the Great and Choiseul; preparing a plan for freeing Gex from the salt monopoly; performing the tasks of lord of the manor, such as giving medical treatment to the people of Gex (after seeking Tronchin's advice); trying to buy Tournay from the président de Brosses; rebuilding Ferney; cultivating – and improving – his garden at Les Délices; and trying to keep warm during that bitterly cold winter of 1759-1760. However, he did not spend very long on what he fondly hoped would be the *coup de grâce* that would 'faire donner Fréron au Diable' (D9010). In fact, it was written in eight days.[7]

How is it that he was able to dash off this comedy so quickly? It is partly explained by his determination to see his *anti-fréronnade* in print at the earliest possible moment. This lent wings to his pen, certainly, but the absence of hesitation in the process of creation is accounted for by the curiously hybrid nature of its sources and inspiration. We shall now attempt to reconstruct this process by showing the extent to which Voltaire brought together various elements – his own plays, others' plays, and his personal experiences – in the rapid and highly professional construction of the plot and characters. The elements of the main plot – the story of the unknown virtuous girl reunited with her father and her

[7] So Voltaire says in his *Commentaire historique sur les œuvres de l'auteur de la Henriade* (M.i.100). It was less than eight days according to D9113.

beloved despite the efforts of a scheming rival – were quickly assembled from his own *Nanine* (1749) and from a play which his niece, Mme Denis, was writing in 1759. This was *Pamela*, an adaptation of Goldoni's *Pamela nubile*.[8] Voltaire's attention was drawn to the '45 Scottish rebellion by Mme Denis's play, in which Pamela becomes the daughter of a Scottish nobleman, Count Astaingue, 'un rebelle, qui souleva l'Ecosse contre l'Angleterre, pour soutenir le parti du prétendant' (III.viii). Whereas Goldoni's chieftain, Count Auspingh, had taken up arms in the Jacobite rising of 1715, Mme Denis brings the action of her play forward to the repressive period following the '45 rebellion. This is, of course, the background to *L'Ecossaise*. Voltaire easily transformed Astaingue into Monrose, and was thus provided with an excellent reason for putting his young heroine in a vulnerable situation without repeating the setting which had been used in every stage

[8] See C. R. Duckworth, 'Madame Denis's unpublished *Pamela*: a link between Richardson, Goldoni and Voltaire', *Studies* 76 (1970), p.37-53. In his article on *L'Ecossaise* in *Studies* 182 (1979), p.253-71, Jack Yashinsky states: 'the reference to the eight days required for the composition of *L'Ecossaise* is misleading. There are numerous allusions to the play in the author's correspondence showing that he was constantly revising and polishing it between October 1759 and the date of its première, July 1760' (p.258). The fact remains that there is only one reference to the play in the correspondence in 1759 (Mr Yashinsky has kindly confirmed that he is not aware of any others). That reference is in the letter from Voltaire to Vernes, dated '22 or 26 October 1759' in Best. 7826. Dr Besterman told me he thought this date was in fact 'too early' (the letter is tentatively redated 'September 1760' in D9228). Whilst Mr Yashinsky is right in saying that Voltaire meticulously revised the play, the revisions were all of a minor nature; the play was *sous presse* before 9 February 1760 (according to Cramer), complete in structure, dialogue, and characterisation. Whilst subsequent omissions and additions (see the variants) made for performance are not unimportant, they are in no instance fundamental or substantial enough to make one revise the view that the overall composition was in a complete state for publication well before 9 February. Mr Yashinsky's scepticism about Voltaire's claim to rapidity is partly explained by the fact that his article was written between 1970 and 1973; publication was delayed until 1979, but he did not revise it in the light of the new information about Mme Denis's *Pamela* in my 1970 article, whose arguments, he generously concedes, are 'convincing' (letter of 14 May 1980).

adaptation of *Pamela* (including his own *Nanine*) – the master's household.

Jean Balcou[9] has claimed that 'c'est Fréron lui-même qui impose à Voltaire le thème historique de la pièce: en 1742, en effet, avec l'abbé de Marsy, il avait publié l'*Histoire de Marie Stuart, reine d'Ecosse et de France*. Or l'histoire des Stuart sert de toile de fond à *l'Ecossaise*'. This was a worthy speculation at the time, but Mme Denis's play makes it unnecessary. It was never very likely that Voltaire would have re-read a book by Fréron whose subject was Scottish politics of two hundred years before. On the other hand, if one is looking for evidence of Voltaire's acquaintance with the history of the Stuarts, what could be more convincing than the certainty that he possessed and knew the *History of Great Britain under the house of Stuart*, published only a short time (1754-1757) before *L'Ecossaise*, by David Hume, kinsman of the John Home to whom Voltaire attributed *L'Ecossaise*?[10]

Thus the foundations were laid for a sentimental drama in the style of its precursors – *Nanine* and *Pamela* – with an up-to-date setting in the mid-1750s (Monrose was 'condamné depuis onze ans à perdre la tête', III.iii.108-109; and Lindane was ten years old when her brother was killed in battle, IV.vi.198-199).

It is misleading to refer to the 'historical' background to the play, as it was the contemporary interest of the subject that appealed to Voltaire. Only ten years earlier he had been very emotionally involved in the fate of Prince Charles, and was filled with sorrow and disgust when the prince was arrested and expelled from France. Voltaire, according to Longchamp (*Mémoires*, ii.224-28), had just written that chapter (7) of his *Histoire de la guerre de*

[9] 'L'affaire de l'*Ecossaise*', *Information littéraire* (mai-juin 1969), p.111-15.

[10] Voltaire refers to 'l'histoire des Stuarts' by 'mon ami Hume [...] le cousin de l'auteur de l'Ecossaise' in letters to Mme Du Deffand in 1760 (D9248 and D9297). Hume's *History of Great Britain* (1754) and *Histoire de la maison des Stuart* (Londres 1760) are both in Voltaire's library in Leningrad (BV, no.1703 and 1701). There is no copy of Fréron's *Histoire de Marie Stuart* in the library. Voltaire said he preferred Hume's *History* to the *History of Scotland during the reigns of Queen Mary and King James VI* by William Robertson (1759); see D12089.

1741 which recounts the defeat of Prince Charles and the horrors of the executions of Jacobites.[11] He describes therein (M.xv.300) the wanderings of the prince in Lochaber (where Lindane was born, IV.vi). He recounts (p.303) the treachery of John Murray (one of Prince Charles's secretaries) nicknamed 'le Judas des Jacobites', who bought his life by revealing secrets of a plot against the king, thus causing the execution of the aged Lord Lovat (p.304). Thus, the reason why Voltaire chose the name Murray for the man who had had Lindane Monrose's father condemned is not difficult to see.[12] In this same chapter Voltaire relates Drummond's landing at Montrose, and the publication there of his manifesto stating he was sent by the king of France – a manifesto Voltaire wrote out in French in 1745.[13] The Scottish background to *L'Ecossaise*, then, was an intimate reminiscence of Voltaire's own personal experience. It needed no history book by Fréron to bring it back to life.

But why did Voltaire choose to set his play in a London coffee-house? Fréron seized on this unlikely setting straight away in his first review of the first edition of the play: 'N'est-il pas d'abord bien étrange qu'une fille sage & vertueuse, telle que *Lindane*, qu'une fille qui veut vivre dans la retraite & se cacher à tous les yeux, se loge dans un Caffé, dans une maison ouverte au premier venu, où, par conséquent, elle est exposée à toute heure aux

[11] It became chapter 25 of the *Précis du siècle de Louis XV* ('Suite des aventures du prince Charles-Edouard. Sa défaite, ses malheurs, et ceux de son parti'). See M.xv.305-306.

[12] It seems unlikely therefore that Voltaire had in mind Lord George Murray, which would have made political nonsense. The second Duke of Montrose, on the other hand, was among those Whigs who met on 10 September 1745 to encourage the raising of loyalist regiments to oppose Prince Charles; they failed to arouse enthusiasm (Andrew Lang, *A history of Scotland*, iv.472).

[13] *Manifeste du roi de France en faveur du prince Charles-Edouard* (M.xxiii.203-204).

regards qu'elle vouloit éviter'.[14] Fréron's concern about *vraisemblance* is well founded – in real life, a girl like Lindane would obviously have chosen private lodgings – but Voltaire's dramatic sense in choosing such a setting was pointed out by Grimm (in a review that was not entirely eulogistic): 'M. de Voltaire a très bien choisi le lieu de la scène; un café offre une multitude de tableaux vrais'.[15] Indeed, the public nature of the setting provided Voltaire with the answer to d'Argental's query about another apparent *invraisemblance*: 'Pourquoi', wrote Voltaire in this irritated letter of 14 July 1760, 'avez-vous la cruauté de vouloir que Lindane ennuie le public de la manière dont elle a fait Connaissance avec Murrai? Ce Murrai venait au Caffé; ce coquin de Frélon qui y vient aussi y a bien vû Lindane, pourquoi mylord Murrai ne l'aurait-il pas vüe? Ce sont ces petites misères, qu'on appelle en France bienséances, qui font languir la plus part de nos Comédies' (D9062).

It has been suggested that Voltaire did have in mind a real live model for his heroine, Lindane:[16] Suzanne-Catherine Gravet de Corsembleu de Livry (or Livri), the actress, who later became the wife of Voltaire's friend the marquis de Gouvernet. Mlle de Livry was a *protégée* and mistress of Voltaire, who probably met her first in 1716 at Sully. To Voltaire's annoyance, she was not a success at the Comédie-Française in 1719, and she joined a troupe of actors going to London. According to Bengesco this was in 1723-1724, but the Latreille manuscript of London playbills[17] has no record of a visiting French company for that period. In the previous year and in 1724-1725 there were French

[14] *Al* (3 June 1760), iv.98. G. E. Lessing also objects to the coffee-house lodging (*Hamburgische Dramaturgie*, ed. O. Mann, Stuttgart 1958, p.52), preferring the furnished rooms of Mrs Goodman in Colman's adaptation of *L'Ecossaise* (*The English merchant*).

[15] CLT (15 June 1760), iv.247. The only two comedies by Voltaire which Grimm reviewed after 1753 were *L'Ecossaise* and *Le Droit du seigneur*.

[16] Renouard, in his edition of Voltaire's works (1819), xi.62-63; Bengesco, *Les Comédiennes de Voltaire* (1912), p.290-326; M.v.402; Desnoiresterres, i.406.

[17] BL Add. mss. 32249-32252.

companies at 'The Little Theatre in the Haymarket' (which became known as the French Theatre). However, on 4 February 1720 the *Daily post* pre-reviewed the company which Jean-Baptiste Grimberghs (de Grimbergue) was due to bring to London in March. A 'Mlle de Livrey' was one of the company, which returned (with or without her) on 26 December 1720. On 21 January 1721 the *London journal* reported that the French company was discouraged and was going home. De Grimbergue denied this, and they stayed at the Haymarket until 4 May 1721.[18] All this is merely circumstantial support for Renouard's story,[19] that Mlle de Livry, when stranded in London through the failure of the troupe, took refuge in the house of a Frenchman who kept a coffee-house (one of the many haunts of French *émigrés* no doubt, such as 'The Rainbow' in Marylebone). M. de Gouvernet, so the story goes, frequented the *café*. 'C'était un homme bienfesant, mais un peu brusque'. He fell in love with Mlle de Livry but she refused him, so he resorted to a ruse by means of which she was led to believe she had won a large sum in a state lottery (whereas it was really M. de Gouvernet's money that was being given to her). 'Alors', Renouard continues, 'il lui persuada que résister à son empressement c'était refuser de l'enrichir: elle céda'. He concludes that this episode 'a fourni les rôles de Lindane, de Freeport et de Fabrice'.

Of how much of all this can we be certain? That she went to act in London; that she did win 'dix mille livres de rente' in a lottery in 1724 (D220); that she did marry the marquis de Gouvernet in England; that Voltaire remained very attached to her and to his memories of her throughout his lifetime;[20] that she kept the portrait of him painted by Largillière in 1718, until he

[18] See S. Rosenfeld, *Foreign theatrical companies in Great Britain in the 17th and 18th centuries* (1955).

[19] Which he was told by 'M. de Desprez' (either the architect, or Desprez de Crassier, or – more probably – Desprez de Boissy).

[20] See, for example, his affectionate letter (D1059), written in 1736, mentioning the 'sentiments tendres et respectueux' he still had for her.

asked her to send it to Mme de Villette in 1778; and that he still had her in his mind as 'Mlle de Livry' in the early 1760s, when he referred to her by this name (see D11094). So far as the genesis of *L'Ecossaise* is concerned, the episode in the Frenchman's *café* adds verisimilitude to the setting, and perhaps gave Voltaire the idea of making Freeport not only generous towards Lindane, but on the point of falling in love with her.

Did Voltaire read Goldoni's *Bottega del caffè* and borrow the setting from there? Lessing suggests this,[21] although Gaiffe dismisses the possibility on the grounds that the only striking similarity is between the characters of Don Marzio and Frélon: 'il n'avait pas besoin du théâtre de Goldoni pour camper sur la scène la caricature de son infatigable ennemi'.[22] This is not quite the point, however. In the process of creation, Voltaire had the problem of finding quickly a dramatic action in which he could make a malicious *écrivain de feuilles* play a contemptible role. Don Marzio, in Goldoni's coffee-house play, is a boorish, back-biting, slandering scandal-monger who cannot keep a secret or be trusted. He is trying to find out – from Rodolfo, the keeper of the coffee-house, Fabrice's counterpart – all about the ballet dancer, Lisaura, who lives next door. There the similarities end, for Goldoni's play is concerned with gambling and marital infidelities. But turn Don Marzio into a hack critic instead of a gambling-house keeper, make Lisaura an apparently orphaned Scots girl stranded in London, and present the play as an English sentimental comedy, and there was Voltaire's revenge accomplished with – he hoped – anonymity adroitly assured.

Quite apart from these similarities, Voltaire's debt to Goldoni is made more certain by his frequently expressed admiration for this *pittor della natura*, and by his claim, in the preface to *L'Ecossaise*, that his comedy 'a la naïveté et la vérité de l'estimable Goldoni'; more precisely relevant is the fact that Voltaire possessed several

[21] *Hamburgische Dramaturgie*, p.51.

[22] F. Gaiffe, *Le Drame en France au XVIIIe siècle* (Paris 1910), p.42-43.

volumes of Goldoni's *Commedie*[23] and that he refers to the character of Don Marzio in a letter of 24 September 1760 (D9259). With his niece working on *Pamela nubile* beside him in 1759, Voltaire would not even have to search on his bookshelves for Goldoni's comedies – not only *Pamela nubile* and *La Bottega del caffè*, but even perhaps *La Locandiera* in which the *cameriere di locanda* is called Fabrizio – a fairly obvious source of Voltaire's 'maître Fabrice'. Fréron points out in the third of his four articles devoted to *L'Ecossaise* (*Al*, 1760, v.282), still searching for evidence of plagiarism, that the character of Freeport greatly resembles that of Ripafratta, 'homme brusque et sauvage'. Here again, as with Don Marzio, Ripafratta may have given Voltaire the idea not of the character but of the *placing* of the character in the setting of the main action; that is to say, the introduction of a forthright honest man into a plot played out in a lodging-house. Equally possibly, he may have realised from *Pamela nubile* the dramatic need for a character who would contrast strongly with Frélon, someone utterly devoid of finesse and cunning. This contrast is provided in *Pamela nubile* by Sire Curbrech, who is a foil to the unpleasant and untrustworthy Cavaliere Ernold. Admittedly Mme Denis omitted Sire Curbrech from her *Pamela*, but as this is one of the major changes in her adaptation, it is possible that this very suppression made him a subject of some discussion between her and Voltaire. Ripafratta/Sire Curbrech... the blunt man showing up the devious cunning of Don Marzio/Fréron. But to conceive the personalities of both Freeport and Frélon as theatrical entities, Voltaire had only to recall two plays of his own: *La Prude* (1740) and *L'Envieux* (1738).[24]

[23] Eleven volumes, of the Turin (1756) edition, according to Havens and Torrey, *Voltaire's catalogue of his library at Ferney*, Studies 9 (1959), p.162. In Voltaire's library in Leningrad there are still volumes 1 (containing *La Bottega del caffè*), 2 and 7-13 of the *Commedie* (Torino: R. Fantino, 1756-1758; BV, no.1482). For Voltaire's views on Goldoni, see D8756, D8990, D9079, D9257, D9760, D10126, D11199, D11854, D17677.

[24] The conception of Freeport did not, then, depend any more on *La Locandiera* than on Dufresny's *Faux honnête homme*, Brueys's *Muet*, or Boissy's *Français à*

In adapting Wycherley's *Plain dealer* under the title *La Dévote* (later, *La Prude*) Voltaire made the close acquaintance of 'l'homme au franc procédé', captain Manly, whom he renamed Blanford. His character is described in terms that fit Freeport exactly:

> [...] son humeur et son austérité [...]
> Il est souvent trop confiant, trop bon;
> Et son humeur gâte encor sa franchise. (I.i)

Although Freeport gives the impression of being a much older man (Blanford is hardly thirty), he considers himself an eligible suitor for Lindane, and comes as close as his gruffness will allow him to making an avowal of love ('j'ai conçu pour vous beaucoup d'estime et d'affection', V.i.36-37).[25] Voltaire had ready-made, in Blanford, Freeport's misanthropy; the sea-captain airs his views on mankind in his very first speech:

> [...] j'ai vu force fripons
> De tous les rangs, de toutes les façons,
> D'honnêtes gens dont la molle indolence
> Tranquillement nage dans l'opulence,
> Blasés en tout, aussi durs que polis,
> Toujours sûrs d'eux, ou d'eux seuls tout remplis [...]
> Et je voudrais qu'ainsi que mon vaisseau
> Le genre humain fût abîmé dans l'eau. (I.ii)

Freeport does likewise in his first scene:

> Les hommes ne sont pas bons à grand'chose, fripons ou sots: voilà pour les trois quarts; et pour l'autre quart il se tient chez soi. (II.v.135-137)[26]

Although Voltaire maintains the sea-going connections (Freeport has just returned from Jamaica), he makes Freeport a 'gros négociant de Londres', showing his acquaintance with the respect-

Londres. In all of these plays, Fréron says, the features of Freeport are to be found (*Al*, 3 June 1760, iv.104).

[25] The Gravelot engravings for *L'Ecossaise* in w68 and w75G show Freeport as a young man.

[26] The resemblance between Freeport and Alceste is not surprising, as the main source of Wycherley's *Plain dealer* was *Le Misanthrope*.

ful treatment accorded to the merchant class in English 'sentimental comedy' after about 1730, in contrast to the Restoration antimercantile bias which was only too obvious in the stratified social picture and stereotyped caricatures of the merchant character in the plays of Congreve, Vanbrugh and Farquhar.[27] The social bias of *L'Ecossaise* is ambiguous and hesitant, however, reflecting the conflicting ideals of the main sources, Italian and English. On the one hand, Voltaire found in Goldoni's and Mme Denis's *Pamela* plays a rapidly adaptable dénouement making the orphan girl of noble extraction. At the end it is the aristocrat who gets the girl. So Voltaire was obliged to reject the egalitarian stance he had taken up in *Nanine*, and thus reverted to a treatment of the theme of merchant-gentry opposition more akin to that of seventeenth-century English drama, in which the social penetration of genteel society by rich citizens was treated unsympathetically. Freeport is an outsider at the end of the play, and his sad admission that 'cette demoiselle n'était pas faite pour moi' has the implication of social as well as personal incompatibility.

In contrast to this, Voltaire, not content to make Freeport a simple *bourru bienfaisant*, uses him to express very definite social attitudes, first towards the dignity of poverty, which Freeport makes the substance of a compliment to Lindane, who is bitterly ashamed of her lack of resources: 'Ecoutez. Je ne suis point homme à compliments; on m'a dit de vous… le plus grand bien qu'on puisse dire d'une femme: vous êtes pauvre et vertueuse' (II.vi.200-203). Secondly, Freeport is made to reveal a strong antipathy for nobility and fashionable ways: 'Je n'aime pas plus les grands seigneurs que les mauvais écrivains' (IV.i.39-40); 'Ce milord-là […] est si beau et si bien mis, qu'il me déplaît souverainement' (V.ii.44-45); 'Quoi! verrai-je toujours ce maudit milord? que cet homme me choque avec ses grâces!' (V.vi.148-149). He even goes so far as to deny the majesty of kings: as he reads from the gazette that 'le roi est venu en haute personne', he exclaims,

[27] See J. Loftis, *Comedy and society from Congreve to Fielding* (Stanford 1959), chapters 3 and 5.

'Eh, malotru! qu'importe que sa personne soit haute ou petite? Dis le fait tout rondement' (II.vi.230-231).

There can be little doubt that these anti-establishment prejudices stem from the original Freeport, Sir Andrew Freeport, whom Steele created in the second issue of the *Spectator* (Friday 2 March 1711). It is in no.174 (19 September 1711) that Steele's Freeport makes a long and impassioned speech in defence of the 'merchant' as being of very much more benefit to society than the 'hunting nobleman' personified by Sir Roger de Coverley; all very much in the spirit with which Voltaire imbues his merchant, and at variance with the more conciliatory attitude of George Lillo's London merchant, Thorowgood, who says, 'As the Name of Merchant never degrades the Gentleman, so by no means does it exclude him' (I.ii).[28]

There can be little doubt that Voltaire's own celebrated eulogy of the English merchant in the *Lettres philosophiques* has a part in his conception of Freeport; there we find the same self-assurance of the useful, working citizen who considers himself the equal (at least) of the powdered lord.

The quality that distinguishes Voltaire's blunt man from his dramatic predecessors is the very one that would seem to be inconsistent with misanthropy – his generosity and charity. This inconsistency would, in our post-Strindbergian era, be acceptable as a quite plausible multiplicity of personality, but in the case of Voltaire's Freeport it is the result of his hybrid origins – Alceste/Blanford, M. de Gouvernet, and the *Spectator*'s Sir Andrew who, whilst holding firm to his belief that 'we Merchants, who live by Buying and Selling, ought never to encourage Beggars', is equally disposed to perform acts of charity, as the performance of a duty towards himself. However, his utter dislike of idleness

[28] The first French translation (*Le Marchand de Londres*) was published in 1748; it was made suitably 'decent' for French taste. Voltaire thought little of *Orphanis*, Blin de Sainmore's adaptation of *Barnwell*: 'cela est très digne du siècle où nous sommes. Tout me dégoûte du théâtre, et pièces et comédiens' (30 December 1773; D18710).

is uncompromising: 'an industrious Man shall submit to the hardest Labour and coarsest Fare, rather than endure the Shame of taking Relief from the Parish, or asking it in the street' (no.232, 26 November 1711). We can thus see why Lindane appeals so much to Freeport, for Voltaire creates his young heroine in this image, by endowing her with great dignity in her refusal to accept charity.[29] It is quite consistent with his predecessor in the *Spectator* that he should be generous to such a person.

The sub-plot of *L'Ecossaise* is concerned with Lady Alton's efforts to prevent her former lover, Murray, from transferring his affections to Lindane. The relationships between the three characters are taken from *Nanine*: the Comte d'Olban/Baronne de l'Orme/Nanine triangle became the Murray/Lady Alton/Lindane triangle.[30] But we must not jump to the conclusion that Voltaire simply adapted his earlier play in a fit of self-recollection. The connection lies in Mme Denis's *Pamela* and, through her, in Richardson's novel (of which *Nanine* was, of course, Voltaire's very free adaptation). The snobbish villainess of each piece respectively is Lady Davers (in Richardson's *Pamela*), the Baronne de l'Orme (in *Nanine*), Lady Clifort (in Mme Denis's play), and Lady Alton.[31] All four are very anxious to prevent the hero from marrying below him, and in all but *Nanine* they are seconded by an unpleasant and villainous male: in Richardson's novel, it is Lady Davers's nephew, Jack (the 'tinsell'd boy'), in Mme Denis's *Pamela*, it is Sir Charles (her dandified, lecherous Foppington-esque version of Goldoni's Cavaliere Ernold). In *L'Ecossaise*, it is Frélon. Frélon's counterpart is not to be found in Voltaire's own

[29] Lindane's extreme modesty (which Freeport criticises as pride) is reminiscent of Addison's article on modesty in the number of the *Spectator* immediately preceding no. 232: 'Modesty is not only an Ornament, but also a Guard to Virtue' (no.231).

[30] Especially *Nanine*, I.i and *L'Ecossaise*, IV.iv.

[31] Voltaire's Baronne de Croupillac (*L'Enfant prodigue*, 1736) is also an 'assez grande épouseuse', and schemes to prevent the marriage of Lise and Fierenfat. Fréron thought Voltaire had *réchauffé* this character as Lady Alton (*Al*, 3 June 1760, iv.101).

Pamela play *Nanine*; but in his niece's *Pamela* he found, in 1759, exactly the slot he needed into which he could fit his own particular villain: Fréron. Structurally, Frélon takes over the part of Sir Charles, aiding and abetting the overbearing obstacle to the triumph of love. Psychologically, however, the original of Frélon is to be found, not in Fréron or in Sir Charles, but in Zoïlin, the villain of *L'Envieux*.

It was in this play that Voltaire, in 1738, had done for Desfontaines what he now intended to do for Fréron: ridicule him to death.[32] Zoïlin, 'écrivain de feuilles littéraires périodiques', was resuscitated in Voltaire's memory by the obvious similarities of circumstances; twenty years earlier he had had to defend himself in *L'Envieux* against a poisonous scandalmonger, one of those 'lâches esprits tout remplis de venin' (I.viii). He had referred in that play to

> [...] les cafés où ces pestes publiques
> Vont, dit-on, quelquefois faire les beaux esprits,
> Ramasser les poisons qu'on voit dans leurs écrits. (I.viii)

Here, then, is the germ of the idea that took shape quickly in Voltaire's mind in 1759 for the setting of *L'Ecossaise*; Goldoni's *Bottega del caffè* was but a catalyst, a trigger, prompting the creative memory to action. Voltaire now had the plot, sub-plot, main characters, setting, all beginning to take shape. By incorporating his earlier prototype of the libellous hack-writer, however, Voltaire weakened his play and his attack; for whereas Zoïlin's activities as a sub-literary purveyor of libels had been central to *L'Envieux* (Ariston – Voltaire – loses his credit because of the 'affreux écrits' attributed to him by Zoïlin), the activities of the

[32] He was foiled in 1738 by Mme Du Châtelet, who persuaded Voltaire not to lower himself by attacking publicly such an unworthy opponent. *L'Envieux* was neither printed nor performed during Voltaire's lifetime. He was therefore quite justified (from an artistic point of view) in making use of his own earlier material.

Zoïle[33] in *L'Ecossaise* are irrelevant to the plot. He could be a clerk or an actor, and still fulfil the same perfidious role he is given in the action of *L'Ecossaise*. As a caricature of Fréron, therefore, he is much less effective than Zoïlin was as a caricature of the author of *La Voltairomanie*. Naturally Voltaire realised that Frélon was not really part of the plot.[34] We are now in a position to understand why *L'Ecossaise* has this structural defect. What is remarkable, however, is not so much that it does have these structural and tactical weaknesses, as that a play conceived in such a hasty manner and in response to such inartistic basic motivation should have continued to be performed in Paris, the provinces and abroad, long after the initial *succès de scandale*, despite the additional disadvantage of having been published before performance.

2. *Title, attribution and publication*

The play has a title and sub-title which for several years and through many editions were interchangeable. All the early editions that have come to our notice bear the title *Le Caffé ou l'Ecossaise*, with the exception of 60AM and 63CR. These two have *L'Ecossaise ou le Caffé*. The quarto edition (w68) was the first to spell *Le Café* thus; but still gave the setting precedence over the heroine.

The first mention of the play occurs in a letter of 29 February 1760, from Gabriel Cramer to Grimm (D8780): 'Notre maître a

[33] The connection between the portrayal of Zoïlin and Frélon is clear from the 'Avertissement' to *L'Ecossaise*: 'Les zoïles ne sont soutenus qu'un temps', and from these lines of *Le Pauvre diable*: 'Vermisseau né du cul de Des Fontaines / Digne en tous sens de son extraction, / Lâche Zoïle, autrefois laid giton: / Cet animal se nommait Jean Fréron' (M.x.103).

[34] 'Si j'avais pu prévoir ce petit succez, si en barbouillant l'écossaise en moins de huit jours j'avais imaginé, qu'on dût me l'attribuer et qu'elle pût être jouée, je l'aurais travaillée avec plus de soin, et j'aurais mieux cousu le cher Freron à l'intrigue', Voltaire wrote to d'Argental on 3 August 1760 (D9113).

fait une Comédie en 5 actes en prose, intitulée le Caffé, ou l'Ecossaise, elle est sous presse'. The first letter by Voltaire to refer to it dates from *c.* 10 March 1760 (D8801), mentioning the 'Préface'; a little later (April?) he wrote complaining to Cramer that he had not yet received 'la préface de l'Ecaissaize' (D8857).

The 'Grand livre' of the Cramer brothers[35] records the *envoi* of '60 *Caffé Comédie* en avril 1760' and the cost of '*Le Caffé ou l'Ecossaise* 12 sols'.[36] Voltaire's habit, in his letters, is always to refer to it as *L'Ecossaise*. It would seem, then, that because Voltaire's manuscript put *Le Café* first, the early editions inevitably followed this; but Voltaire soon changed his mind. Why? Partly, no doubt, because his correspondents (and even Fréron) referred to it as *L'Ecossaise*; and partly because *L'Ecossaise* was a much more distinctive title than *Le Café*, which invited comparison and confusion with other plays set in cafés and coffee-shops – particularly Goldoni's *Bottega del caffè*.[37]

Why did Voltaire choose John Home (or Hume) as the putative author of *L'Ecossaise*?[38] For a number of very good reasons. Home's *Douglas* had had a resounding success at Covent Garden in 1757.[39] Garrick had thus been persuaded to put on *Agis* at Drury Lane in 1758. John Home was, therefore, 'in the news', an active and successful playwright whose name on a title-page would attract the public. Furthermore, *Douglas* had two features

[35] Archives d'Etat de Genève, cote Commerce F57.

[36] See B. Gagnebin, *Lettres inédites à son imprimeur Gabriel Cramer* (1952), p.xxiv and xxviii.

[37] J.-B. Rousseau's *Le Café* (1695) portrays the marriage of a humble coffee-girl and an officer-gentleman. On this theme, see Lucy Stuart Sutherland, *A London merchant, 1695-1774* (1933), p.5-6; and J. Loftis, *Comedy and society from Congreve to Fielding*, p.125. Fréron lists a number of English coffee-house plays in his first review of *L'Ecossaise*, admitting that they bear no similarity to Voltaire's play.

[38] In Horn-Monval's *Répertoire bibliographique des traductions et des adaptations* (1958-1967), v.3287-98, it is listed as an apocryphal work of *David* Hume!

[39] After an enthusiastic reception at the Canongate Theatre, Edinburgh, to the cry of 'Whaur's Wully Shakespeare noo?' (A. Lang, *A history of Scotland*, iv.415).

in common with the play Voltaire was attributing to him – features which make it quite plausible that the Scottish dramatist could have been its author. Namely, a long-lost child, and warring Scottish houses. If it is true[40] that in inventing the story of Norval, Home may have had in mind the story of Perdita in the *Winter's tale*, Voltaire has simply reverted to the earlier Shakespearian situation in making the child a girl.

The subject and background of Voltaire's play are akin to those of *Douglas*. Nevertheless there is one very good reason why *L'Ecossaise* should not have been attributed to Home: in 1745 he volunteered to serve in the loyalist ranks against the Jacobites – and was, indeed, taken prisoner at the battle of Falkirk. No man with this record could have written a play as sympathetic to the rebel cause as is *L'Ecossaise*. Fréron did not draw attention to this in his short list of reasons why Home could not be the author of *L'Ecossaise* (*Al*, 1760, iv.108-10). His reasons are that Home had told the princess of Wales he would never write a comedy since he knew nothing about the genre; that the play did not exist in English; and that there are two errors of fact of which 'un auteur Anglois'(!) would have been incapable. Fréron also claimed, tongue in cheek, that it could not possibly be by Voltaire: 'Quelle apparence, en effet, qu'une aussi médiocre production soit sortie d'une aussi belle plume?' (p.110).

Why, indeed, did Voltaire resort to such pointless anonymity? Grimm was led to deal with this question in his second review of *L'Ecossaise* on 15 July 1760 (CLT, iv.260-63). He had begun his first review (15 June) by naming Voltaire as 'le véritable auteur', and Voltaire knew it was common knowledge even though he continued to maintain for some time that he was not the author – even after the play was produced at the Comédie-Française in July 1760.[41] Grimm noted that false attribution of

[40] As F. S. Boas suggests in his *An introduction to eighteenth-century drama 1700-1780* (Oxford 1953), p.266.

[41] See D8918 (19 May 1760), D8920 (20 May), D9120 (6 August), D9138 (13 August), D9173 and D9176 (29 August).

authorship was a growing tendency, for various possible reasons – diffidence, fear of persecution, fear of personal attack by hostile critics, hope that critics will be kinder if they fear the author might be their master, hope that 's'il y a dans son ouvrage un peu de style et d'idées, il sera d'abord attribué à M. de Voltaire ou à quelque autre écrivain estimé et connu, et que cette prévention passagère en fera le succès' (iv.260). As Grimm points out, the anonymous writer is freer to say what he thinks, and the government can claim ignorance of the identity of an anonymous author when it pleases. In Voltaire's case, it was not only a question of his habitual caution, but also of his belief that *L'Ecossaise* must be taken as an English play, as we shall see.

Grimm was certain Voltaire was the author of *L'Ecossaise* for the simple reason that Cramer had told him so whilst it was *sous presse* (D8780). The printer admitted he was 'un peu embarrassé' because although he wanted to send copies to the bookseller Lambert, he hesitated to do so (in view of Lambert's connection with *L'Année littéraire*); 'cependant, cet auteur [Fréron] n'est point nommé, son journal non plus; la scène est à Londres, la pièce est suposée traduitte de l'Anglois, & elle est tout à fait dans le goût Anglois. Que dois-je donc faire mon cher Monsieur? Je prie M. Lambert de passer chez vous, ayez la bonté de luy dire sur cela ce que vous jugerez convenable au bien des choses'. In this letter he tells Grimm he thinks the play 'sera reçeue avidement'. In May he is able to write to him, 'Je suis enchanté du succès de L'Ecossaise', adding that it would deserve even greater success if it had been more *soignée*: 'mais dès qu'on eût trouvé ce bienheureux *Frêlon*, on n'eût rien de plus pressé que d'en faire part à tout le monde; et vite & vite, il falut imprimer, sans rien retoucher, sans relire' (D8911).

Cramer's remarks seem to apply to Voltaire's manuscript rather than to the first edition which, whilst far from being a masterpiece of book production, is noticeably superior to the duodecimo *contrefaçon* that made its appearance very quickly, with exactly the same pagination.[42] The Cramer records (p.21) give April as the date of publication (in the sense of technical completion). Distribution to booksellers naturally took a few days.

As soon as it had been disseminated Choiseul wrote to Voltaire (on 12 May) the earliest surviving letter to mention the first edition.[43] Only four days earlier he had written a long letter to Voltaire (D8896) making no reference to the play. On 6 May d'Alembert had written to Voltaire (D8894) a letter which would most certainly have mentioned *L'Ecossaise* had it been published by then. Hence the date of publication (in the sense of availability to the public) can be narrowed down to between 8 (possibly 6) May and 12 May 1760. That is to say, a week or so after the first performance at the Comédie-Française of Charles Palissot's *Les Philosophes*.

3. *Palissot's 'Les Philosophes' and 'L'Ecossaise' at the Comédie-Française*

Within one week the public was confronted with two plays representing the extremes of *philosophe* and *anti-philosophe* interest. If either had been a riposte to the other their coincidence would have been more understandable, but such neatness is only for those who have chosen to ignore simple chronology[44] by labelling *L'Ecossaise* as a riposte to *Les Philosophes*.

The effect of *Les Philosophes* was twofold: it led to, and justified,

[42] For description, see below, p.299.

[43] 'Il y a une pièce intitulée *L'Ecossaise* que l'on dit de vous et qui court le monde; on assure qu'elle est intéressante, je trouve moi que vous êtes trop grand pour dire des injures personnelles à Fréron; j'aime un peu ce Fréron, j'ai été au collège avec lui et, quoique je n'approuve pas ces satires, je suis fâché que vous ne les méprisiez pas' (D8904).

[44] Such as, for example, Geoffroy, Monselet, Deschanel, Lintilhac, F. C. Green, Gaiffe, and J. Stern. Moland gives the correct sequence of events (M.v.399).

the performance of *L'Ecossaise*, which Voltaire had not intended (had he done so, he would not have published it first, since this risked killing a play on stage);[45] and it widened Voltaire's attack from the particular (Fréron) to the general (the *anti-philosophes*), as can be seen from certain changes he made in the text for performance. Voltaire realised immediately on reading Palissot's play that its aim was not simply to ridicule the *philosophes*, but to drive a wedge between him and them by excluding him from the satire. He feared even that they might accuse him of complicity. How else could he avoid being attacked alongside Diderot, Helvétius, Grimm, Duclos, d'Alembert and Rousseau? As Gabriel Cramer reported to Grimm, 'nôtre maitre est au désespoir de n'y être pas maltraitté' (D8911).

The strategy almost succeeded. Voltaire's immediate reaction to *Les Philosophes* was certainly less vehement than it would have been had he been personally attacked. D'Alembert had told him on 6 May (D8894) that the aim of the play was to represent the *philosophes* not simply as ridiculous people 'mais comme des gens de sac et de corde, sans principes, et sans mœurs'. He had pleaded with Voltaire to take action, to avenge the honour of the outraged *philosophes*, by withdrawing from the Comédie-Française *Zulime* (alias *Médime*) which was in rehearsal at that moment. As d'Alembert no doubt shrewdly guessed, this would have a profound effect not only on the actors (through their pockets) but also and above all on the morale of the beleaguered *philosophes*. He hoped to spur Voltaire on by pointing out that the only 'protecteur *déclaré*' of *Les Philosophes* was his own arch-enemy, Fréron.[46]

Voltaire's reaction was to ponder, wait to be sent a copy of

[45] D'Argental was astounded that 'cette écossoise que vous aviés fait imprimer ne la jugeant pas digne de la représentation, cette écossoise que vous n'avés pas daigné corriger' should have succeeded (27 July 1760; D9091). By 1769 it had become the fashion to publish plays before performance, but Voltaire claimed that *L'Ecossaise* was the only such play to have been accepted by the Comédie-Française (12 July 1769; D15745).

[46] In fact Collé tells us, as 'un fait bien certain', that it was Fréron who presented and read *Les Philosophes* to the Comédiens (*Journal*, ii.236).

Palissot's play, and recommend the 'brothers' to laugh the insults off and to remain above all else united.

The old alliances were taking up their familiar battle positions.[47] In 1757 Palissot had published a violent condemnation of the *philosophes*, and in particular of Diderot's dramatic theory, in his *Petites lettres sur de grands philosophes*;[48] he returned to the attack against Diderot in the following year in the *Supplément d'un important ouvrage*. Malesherbes considered Palissot 'un assez mauvais sujet' who had never 'passé pour ce qu'on appelle un homme de bien'.[49] However, he had enough powerful support at court to be granted permission for this play containing personal attacks on respectable citizens; it was above all Fréron's protector, Choiseul, angered by two libellous pamphlets vilifying Mme de Robecq (one of his mistresses) who was instrumental in authorising it. The alleged writer of the libels was Diderot, who was now the victim of reprisal.[50]

The duc de Choiseul was too quick to proclaim his non-involvement to Voltaire: 'Quoiqu'on en dise, je ne protège ni l'auteur ni la pièce, à moins que ce ne soit protéger que d'avoir lu la pièce qui m'a paru écrite à merveille et' (oh, ingenuousness!) 'comme je suis bête, je n'y ai reconnu personne'.[51] Choiseul was

[47] By August Voltaire was able to summarise the position succinctly: 'Le public voit d'un côté Palissot, Freron et Pompignan a la tête de la relligion, et de l'autre les hommes les plus éclairez qui respectent cette relligion encor plus que les Frerons ne la déshonorent' (to Thiriot, 20 August 1760; D9159).

[48] Lettre II, p.29 and 43.

[49] Quoted by Grosclaude, *Malesherbes*, p.158.

[50] It is strange that this affair should have been resuscitated after two years. The two libels appeared in the form of *dédicaces* to two Goldoni plays translated as *Le Véritable ami* and *Le Père de famille* (Avignon et Liège 1757, in-8°). The revival of interest in the libels was no doubt machinated by Palissot (and perhaps a mutual friend of his and Choiseul's, such as Fréron) in order to gain protection for a play that would otherwise have been disallowed.

[51] D8904, 12 May 1760. In this same letter Choiseul illogically took to task the author of *L'Ecossaise* for insulting Fréron: 'j'aime un peu ce Fréron, j'ai été au collège avec lui.' A month later he was more understanding: 'cette critique [de *La Femme qui a raison*] vous a fâché; vous le maltraitez; à la bonne heure, je vous le livre; j'en fait de même de Palissot' (16 June 1760; D8983).

in a different position since he needed to retain Voltaire's goodwill, to ensure the continuance of the peace negotiations with Frederick which were being conducted through Voltaire. It has even been suggested[52] that Choiseul was deliberately fanning the flames of petty controversy in Paris in order to deflect public attention from his political failures. This was the view of the président de Brosses, who wrote colourfully of 'cette vilaine dispute' that 'le ministre n'en étoit peutêtre pas trop fâché. C'est le tonneau jetté à la baleine' (D9037). He was not necessarily well informed, since he believed *L'Ecossaise* was by Diderot (even though it was July when he wrote this). By Choiseul's own admission, however, we are left in little doubt that he took advantage of these literary quarrels. His letter to Voltaire of 16 June 1760 (D8983) makes his position quite clear: 'tout ce train d'auteur [...] ne m'est bon que pour faire diversion dans la tête des badauds de Paris à la guerre véritable'.[53] Voltaire used the same words to Elie Bertrand a couple of weeks later referring to the public effect of the whole *Philosophes-Ecossaise* affair and 'la guerre des brochures': 'Cela amuse les badauts de Paris qui s'occupent plus de ces bagatelles que de ce qui se passe en Silésie' (D9038). Voltaire shared the view that the authorities found what Mme Du Deffand referred to as 'la guerre des rats et des grenouilles' a useful diversion; but for the 'niaiseries' of Palissot, Pompignan, Joly de Fleury 'on ne parlerait que de remontrances', he wrote on 6 August (D9121) to Mme Du Deffand, who had unsuccessfully attempted to persuade Voltaire not to involve himself (D9041).

Voltaire continued to believe that Choiseul was not protecting 'les Polissots et les Frélons', but d'Alembert thought Voltaire was

[52] By Jean Balcou, 'L'affaire de l'*Ecossaise*', p.113.

[53] A very successful diversion too; Clément and de La Porte (*Anecdotes dramatiques*, ii.67-68) claimed that 'depuis la fondation du théatre on n'avait peut-être jamais vu à la Comédie-Française un concours de monde aussi prodigieux'. The takings confirm this (*Registres*, p.797), but according to d'Alembert (D8894) at least 450 complimentary tickets were given away for the first performance of *Les Philosophes*.

being taken in by Choiseul, and he was annoyed with him for not flatly refusing to give any credence to the idea that Diderot had written the *dédicaces*.[54] Palissot was even claiming, he complained, that he had shown Voltaire *Les Philosophes* before production and that he had approved the play.[55]

Just as d'Alembert was penning this letter accusing Voltaire of *lèse-philosophie*, Voltaire, who was tired of playing Don Quixote, harassed by letters urging him to be 'le réparateur des torts, pour que je vange le public de l'infamie du téâtre' (D8912), finally decided to respond to d'Alembert's plea, to take action in defence of the *philosophes*: *Médime* would be withdrawn, and *L'Ecossaise* would be performed instead. He had read only a couple of pages of *Les Philosophes* (D8936), but these were apparently so distasteful

[54] Voltaire's enquiries, through d'Argental, enabled him to squash Palissot's accusations indisputably, which was very much more effective than a mere declaration of faith in Diderot's innocence. D'Alembert's impatience, and his reference to the ladies supporting Palissot (including the princesse de Robecq) as *catins* and *putains* (D8894) were counter-productive, and made Voltaire cautious. What is more, from the reports he received of *Les Philosophes*, he could not really take it seriously. He was highly amused by the lettuce-eating satire on Rousseau; and then, Palissot had impressed on Voltaire in 1756 that he was a great admirer of his (D6780). His caricature of Rousseau in *Le Cercle* (1755) made Voltaire think of him as something of an ally – and allies had to be nurtured. Hence his outrage at Morellet's *Vision de Charles Palissot* (published at the end of May), which alienated Choiseul even further at a critical time: 'l'insulte faitte à son amie mourante est le tombeau ouvert pour les frères' he wrote in despair to d'Alembert (20 June; D8993). 'Il est absurde de mêler les dames dans des querelles d'auteurs' he wrote to Thiriot ten days later (D9017).

[55] D8937, 26 May 1760. F. C. Green states in his chapter on 'Voltaire's greatest enemy', in *Eighteenth-century France* that Voltaire was 'secretly in correspondence' with Palissot (p.139), had made 'overtures' to him as part of his 'projected attack on Fréron' (p.140). In fact, there is no surviving letter of 1760 from Voltaire to Palissot written before 4 June (D8958), when Voltaire rebuked Palissot in strong terms. Professor Green, in his anxiety to turn everything to Voltaire's disadvantage, imagined that *L'Ecossaise* was not published until 'early in June', after the performance of *Les Philosophes*. He also thought *Le Pauvre diable* was really published in 1758 (p.138) and that Voltaire only 'pretended to withdraw his *Médime* from the Comédie-Française' (p.139).

that he reacted immediately.[56] 'Si vous avez la probité et le courage de faire jouer ce bon pasteur Hume', he wrote to d'Argental, 'il n'y a qu'à donner à Fréron le nom de Guèpe au lieu de Frelon [...] Très bonne idée, excellente idée de reculer Medime'. Thus, he continued, he would have time to polish it up without losing anything, since he would have given the proceeds to the actors (as usual) and, furthermore, would enjoy 'la gloire de n'avoir pas voulu que les comédiens profitassent de ma pièce après s'être déshonorés en se prêtant pour de l'argent au déshonneur de la nation' (D8933).

On 28 May Palissot sent Voltaire a copy of *Les Philosophes*, with a flattering letter (D8943) expressing his admiration for 'les vrais philosophes' such as Voltaire, and assuring him *Les Philosophes* was aimed only at 'les faux philosophes' such as Diderot. Voltaire's reply (4 June; D8958) was unequivocal: he associated himself with the *philosophes* Palissot had attacked; although he did not know Diderot, he said, he thought him incapable of writing the libels against the comtesse de La Marck and the princesse de Robecq. He expected to receive irrefutable proof of the accusation immediately if any existed; and even if Diderot were guilty, he asked, why pillory all the *encyclopédistes*?

[56] The contents of D9694 (dated 25 and 26 May), D8934 and D8936 would seem to indicate that Voltaire had approved the idea of staging *L'Ecossaise* the day before he read *Les Philosophes*, but decided to withdraw *Médime* only on the day he looked at Palissot's play. Something changed Voltaire's attitude very markedly and suddenly, for on 21 May he was still telling d'Alembert not to take *Les Philosophes* seriously since it was 'un ridicule méprisable qui sera bientôt oublié' (D8926). One new factor was the news that Mlle Clairon was ill and would not be able to play Médime – but Voltaire insists more than once that he had taken the decision to withdraw it before he heard she was ill. On 26 May Fréron possibly furnished another motive for Voltaire's sudden change of heart by publishing a satirical review of the letter Voltaire had misguidedly had printed in the *Journal encyclopédique*. This would certainly have stiffened Voltaire's resolve to push his attack further, but it does seem unlikely that he would have read Fréron's piece as soon as 26 May. It seems clear that the decisive factor was his reading of Palissot's play.

Thus Voltaire rejected Palissot's divisive tactics[57] which he was able to reduce to nought in his final letter on 12 July 1760: 'N.b. que madame la comtesse de la Mark nie formellement qu'elle se soit jamais plainte (ou qu'elle ait eu à se plaindre) de Diderot' (D9058).[58] The affair was *éclaircie*. But the affair of *L'Ecossaise* which it had precipitated was about to come to a head.

Although *L'Ecossaise* had been performed privately several times at Ferney,[59] Voltaire had very divided feelings about exposing his hastily written comedy to the merciless criticism it would be subjected to if, performed on the professional stage. On 13 June he told d'Argental (D8972) that the revised version of *L'Ecossaise* was ready, and that M. Hume did not wish to change the character of 'cet animal' Frélon, lest the latter should think he was afraid of him. He could be called M. Guèpe – but Wasp would not do in Paris. Voltaire had by then had his ire against Fréron replenished by the review of *L'Ecossaise* in *L'Année littéraire* on 3 June. What is more, from 28 May (possibly earlier) to about 20 June Voltaire had Marmontel staying at Les Délices. As it was Marmontel who had written the article 'Critique' in the *Encyclopédie*, in which Fréron saw himself as the 'critique ignorant', we may safely assume the staging of *L'Ecossaise* was frequently discussed, and that Voltaire was actively encouraged by him to pursue Fréron further.[60] However, by the end of June, after Marmontel's departure, his opinion apparently became modified,

[57] In fact, Palissot gave sound advice in II.iii, where Théophraste tells the other *philosophes*, 'nous sommes perdus, si nous nous divisons'. This was Voltaire's reiterated advice to them, through d'Alembert.

[58] The series of letters which ensued up to 12 July 1760 were published, with omissions, by Palissot without Voltaire's consent – a procedure which was 'ni de la philosophie ni du monde', he complained (24 September 1760; D9262). These *Lettres et réponses de Mr Palissot et de Mr de Voltaire* were included in the *Recueil des facéties parisiennes* (1760), with annotations by Voltaire; the disculpation of Diderot quoted above was not printed in this edition.

[59] This detail is given in Wagnière's manuscript 'Notes et remarques' (see *Studies* 77, p.50).

[60] See D8963. Marmontel's enthusiastic report on the play in performance is in D9116.

for he wrote to Mme d'Epinay, 'On veut jouer L'Ecossaise à Paris et ce n'est pas mon avis. Le public s'intéresse à l'humiliation des philosophes qu'il respecte malgré luy, mais il ne prendra aucun plaisir à voir un fripon qu'il méprise' (30 June; D9014).

By 6 July he had recovered his confidence again, and tried to persuade d'Argental to keep the name Frélon: 'Esce la faute de Hume s'il y a un cuistre dans Paris qui porte un nom lequel a un raport éloigné au mot de frélon?' (D9043).

Throughout May, June and July, Voltaire was correcting *L'Ecossaise*, eradicating some of the weaknesses which were the result of hasty composition, and making it more suitable for performance.[61] Apart from the alterations which can be termed purely dramatic, there were several which seem to stem from his reactions to *Les Philosophes*, Grimm's review of *L'Ecossaise* in the *Correspondance littéraire* (15 June), and Fréron's review in *L'Année littéraire* (3 June). Voltaire's attention was no doubt brought by d'Argental and Mme d'Epinay to points raised in the reviews, but the incorporation of references to the *philosophes* in act 1 scene 3 of the stage version can be seen as his attempt to make it fulfil an additional function as a reply to Palissot's play: 'La philosophie est bien dangereuse [...] c'est elle qui nous a fait perdre L'Ile de Minorque';[62] 'les philosophes font baisser les fonds publics'; 'Il y a beaucoup à craindre cette année pour la Jamaïque, ces Philosophes la feront reprendre'. The fact that these ridiculous references to the supposed evils wrought by *philosophes* made no sense in an English

[61] These alterations, mostly recorded in the 'Additions et corrections' in the Cramer 1760 edition (60CR) were not all retained in W75G. M. Balcou ('L'affaire de l'*Ecossaise*', p.113) has been misled into believing that the Comédie-Française manuscript prompt copy of *L'Ecossaise* was written at this stage in the preparation of the play for performance. However, this manuscript, in the hand of Caron Du Chanset, dates from many years later, and will be dealt with in its proper place.

[62] A timely reminder to the duc de Richelieu that in 1756 he had not lost faith in him despite the delay in capturing Port Mahon (see D6854, D6915, D6918, D6926), and a tactful prompt in the ear of his old friend and ally that a little reciprocated moral support was expected by the poet on the eve of his battle against *his* enemy, Fréron.

play set in London was of secondary importance to Voltaire, intent merely on satirising – in the ironic manner he had adopted in a letter written the previous year[63] – remarks in *Les Philosophes* such as 'la Philosophie endurcit trop les cœurs'; *philosophes* are unpatriotic ('Préférant à l'honneur de servir leur pays, / L'état de colporteurs de la philosophie'), and immoral ('J'en prévois pour les mœurs d'étranges catastrophes, / Et je suis alarmé de tant de Philosophes').

Voltaire disingenuously suggested to Mme d'Epinay that Hume must have included Frélon, 'sans doute quelque ennemi de la philosofie anglaise', simply 'pour peindre un coquin à qui il en voulait' (D9014). Mme d'Epinay had been advising Voltaire to make Frélon less odious by giving Fabrice the devil's role – an idea she had perhaps culled from Grimm, who had quite skilfully rewritten act I scene I,[64] putting most of Frélon's unpleasant words into Fabrice's mouth, and ending with the suggestion: 'Vous gagnez déjà quelque chose à dire du mal; si vous pouvez parvenir à en faire, votre fortune est faite'. Voltaire thought this a poor idea, as one would then have two *coquins* instead of one and that was too many (D9014). He took heed of Grimm's warning that Frélon's inadvertently self-accusing remarks were unconvincing, to the extent of suppressing the most outrageous one: 'Il faut siffler la pièce qui réussit, et ne pas souffrir qu'il se fasse rien de bon' (I.i.119-120*v*). If one wanted to make something out of this play, he told Mme d'Epinay, 'je conseillerais au traducteur de Hume de retrancher absolument ce misérable qui d'ailleurs ne sert en rien au dénouement' (D9014). Only three days before, his doubts about the play were obvious, for similar

[63] To Mme d'Epinay, 19 October 1759 (D8546): 'N'est ce pas une chose honteuse que des Anglais qui ne croient pas en Jesus Christ, prennent Surate et aillent prendre Quebec [...] Nos péchés en sont la cause. C'est l'encyclopédie qui attire visiblement la colère céleste sur nous'.

[64] CLT, iv.246-47. Gaiffe is unjust to Grimm in accusing him (p.111) of not expressing any objection to 'la sanglante caricature de Fréron'. In fact, Grimm thought that Frélon and Lady Alton 'gâtent tout', and that Voltaire was wrong to base Frélon on Fréron: 'cela lui a fait gâter son tableau'.

reasons (expressed to d'Argental): 'Il faudrait [...] refondre l'Ecossaise; changer absolument le caractère de Frélon, en faire un balourd de bonne volonté, qui gâterait tout en voulant tout réparer.' The play would be bearable on stage only on condition that it were taken for a 'Comédie véritablem[t] anglaise' (27 June; D9010). Voltaire thus rejected Grimm's opinion that Frélon should be 'un fourbe profond', betraying Lindane, Lady Alton and Murray beneath a mask of honesty. Quite the contrary, in fact: Voltaire made Frélon less odious in the stage version – under pressure, no doubt. 'Frélon' had to become 'Wasp' on police orders. The word 'fripon' was removed from the attributes of Wasp, not only in the list of characters, but also in act 4, scene 1 (being replaced by 'délateur' twice, 11-12*v*, 13*v*, and 'mauvais sujet' once, 37*v*). 'Cœur de boue' was softened to 'un homme dangereux' (I.v.200*v*); Lady Alton's snide remark to Frélon, 'tu n'es pas un imbécile, comme on le dit' (II.iii.92-93*v*) was omitted. But the longest single outburst of vituperation against Frélon, spoken by Lady Alton, in act 2 scene 4 remained with only one modification: 'le plus impudent et le plus lâche coquin' became 'le plus méchant homme' (106-107*v*) – this change was no doubt imposed on Voltaire as a result of Fréron's complaint to Malesherbes on 14 June about being taken to task for ending his notice of *L'Ecossaise* on 3 June with an irrelevant reference to the ancient rumour that he (Fréron) had been sent to the galleys.[65]

There were, however, other modifications introduced into the text which show that Voltaire not only read Fréron's review of 3 June but also took advantage of it to improve his revised text. Fréron, his self-confidence unpricked by the publication of *L'Ecossaise*, suggested that if the Comédiens Français really

[65] 'Lambert a engagé mon censeur que je ne connois pas [it was Coqueley de Chaussepierre] à vous écrire au sujet de la petite anecdote qui me concerne à la fin de mon extrait de *L'Ecossoise*. C'est bien la moindre chose, Monsieur, que je réponde par une gaité à un homme qui m'appelle *fripon*, *coquin*, *impudent*, *dogue*, &c. Il est très certain (et vous le sçavez mieux que personne, Monsieur), que *L'Ecossoise* est de M. *de Voltaire*. *M. d'Argental* en convient publiquement' (D8977).

intended to put it on, they should persuade the author to 'corriger les défauts qu'on vient de relever, & à supprimer aussi les mauvaises plaisanteries, les pitoyables jeux de mots qui lui sont échappés'.[66] The examples he then gives were all subjected to revision before performance, as follows:

I.vi. Fabrice's most inelegant line: 'C'est moi qui voudrais bien que vous voulussiez avoir quelque volonté' was modified to '... que vous eussiez quelque volonté' (266*v*).

II.i. Lady Alton says to Fabrice: 'Vous me mettez toute hors de moi-même'. Voltaire altered his reply: 'Eh bien, madame, rentrez donc toute dans vous-même' to '... revenez à vous' (3*v*).

II.v. Fabrice says of Lindane: 'elle vit plus retirée que jamais'; Freeport's answer: 'J'aime qu'on se retire: je me retirerai avec elle' was mercifully changed to 'J'aime les personnes de cette humeur, je hais la cohue aussi bien qu'elle' (168*v*).

II.viii. Fréron drew attention to the unlikely exchange in this scene, where Fabrice says of Monrose: 'cet homme ne se soucie pas des filles qui s'évanouissent'. Voltaire omitted not only this comment but also the preceding remarks by Monrose which had justified Fabrice's impression that he was a selfish, hard-hearted old man (378a-387*v*).

IV.iii. Murray gives money to Polly, saying: 'Tiens, voilà pour l'évanouissement où tu as eu envie de tomber'. In the corrected version he thanks her for 'le service que tu lui as rendu' (to Lindane, that is; 91*v*).

In addition to these fairly minor changes (none of which he retained in W75G) Voltaire made others more important, relating to plot and characterisation, which Fréron had listed as being necessary. The critic was worried by the lack of explanatory exposition: what brought Lindane to this *café*? Why does the proscribed Monrose go to such a public place? How did Lindane meet Murray? 'Les questions ne finiroient pas; rien n'est préparé, expliqué, motivé, amené' (IV.101).

[66] Page 107. In his article of 4 August (*Al*, V.287), Fréron ended by noting that the author had taken his advice – but that this had not made a better play.

The first of these questions had already occurred to d'Argental; Voltaire assured him on 25 May: 'Quant au petit procès verbal des raisons pourquoi cette Lindane est à Londres, c'est l'affaire d'un moment' (D8933). The English are quite indifferent to this sort of *procès verbal* so dear to the French,[67] he explains. 'Mais si vous exigez ces préliminaires vous serez servi, et vite'. On 13 June he assured d'Argental that 'tout le procès verbal du voyage de Lindane à Londres et de ce qu'elle y fait ne tiendra pas dix lignes' (D8972). But 'Hume' was rather dilatory, and d'Argental had to write to Voltaire on 30 June that 'on attend avec la plus vive impatience vos corrections de l'Ecossoise [...] L'Ecossoise, l'Ecossoise et vite' (D9018). It was not until 9 July that the problem was duly – and neatly – solved: 'quand le chevalier Montrose sort, et qu'avant de finir la scène 3ème [...] il demande au maître du caffé si ce lord vient souvent dans la maison, le caffetier répond, *il y vient quelquefois*,[68] il doit répondre: *il y venait avant son voiage d'Espagne*' (I.iii.142). Voltaire then goes on to explain what this simple detail will establish: 'Cette petite particularité est nécessaire 1° p^{r} faire voir que Monrose ne vient pas sans raison se loger dans ce caffé là, 2° qu'il a besoin de Falbridge, 3° pour prévenir les esprits sur la mort de ce Falbridge, 4° pour fonder la demeure de Lindane près d'un caffé où ce L. Faldbridge vient quelquefois. C'est un rien, mais c'est baucoup' (to d'Argental; D9048).

Voltaire also noticed that in the first edition Monrose unwit-

[67] Collé's criticisms of the lack of detailed explanation in *L'Ecossaise* exemplify the pre-Stendhalien demand for all the gaps to be filled in, leaving nothing to the reader's or spectator's intelligence or imagination. 'Il faut que les personnes qui ont trouvé de l'intérêt dans cette rapsodie aient composé en eux-mêmes le roman, pour s'attendrir dessus' (Collé, *Journal*, ii.252). Hence his disapproval of what he calls this 'amas froid et confus d'énigmes et de logogriphes qu'on donne à deviner aux spectateurs'. How far away from Jaspers's 'beating of the other wing' we are here. Voltaire's attitude foreshadows that of Victor Hugo: only seventy years later Hernani and Doña Sol were to meet in unexplained and inexplicable circumstances.

[68] The first edition reading remained unchanged in all editions until Beuchot corrected it on the basis of this letter.

tingly voices Fréron's criticism about the public nature of the *café*: 'Il faut sortir d'ici, la maison est trop publique' (III.iii.14). He therefore cut out this remark. With respect to Fréron's objection to the improbability that Lindane could have become acquainted with Murray, however, Voltaire was much less obliging. D'Argental also thought this detail important (no doubt being anxious to cut as much ground as possible from under Fréron's feet before his review of the performance), and earned himself an irritated rebuke from Voltaire on 14 July: 'Pourquoi avez vous la cruauté de vouloir que Lindane ennuie le public de la manière dont elle a fait Connaissance avec Murrai? Ce Murrai venait au Caffé; ce coquin de Frelon qui y vient aussi y a bien vû Lindane, pourquoi mylord Murrai ne l'aurait-il pas vûe? Ce sont ces petites misères, qu'on appelle en France bienséances, qui font languir la plus part de nos Comédies' (D9062). That, he continues, is why French plays cannot be put on in Italy or England, since it is action and not explanation that is required there.

Finally, Voltaire took good note of Fréron's criticism of Murray's complacent inconstancy; in act 4 scene 4, Murray was made to say that he was not *fâché* at appearing to be a monster in Lady Alton's eyes, that he had promised to marry her but had changed his mind (for very good reasons, it must be admitted). Voltaire omitted both these potentially offensive remarks from the acting version (117-118*v*, 118-128*v*).

Whereas d'Argental feared that the publication of *L'Ecossaise* before production would seriously detract from its success, it did in fact induce Fréron to make a great tactical mistake: he allowed his heavy artillery fire to be drawn before the battle was really engaged. When he entitled his review of the first performance *Relation d'une grande bataille* he realised its important position in the sequence of events. It should have been his finest, most polished and elegant essay in destructive criticism; but he left so many things unsaid, spent so much time on trivia, that he had to have two more shots at finishing off his prey, each one less telling than the last. Favart reported that 'Fréron s'est assez mal défendu dans sa dernière feuille [...] au lieu de l'attaquer sérieusement, il s'est épuisé en plaisanteries froides et forcées',[69] but did not perceive that Fréron had not only left himself with little to say (apart from abuse) but had also given Voltaire a good deal of valuable advice which he was not too proud to take.

D'Argental's anxiousness about Voltaire's corrections, which he expressed in his letter of 30 June, was caused by the fact that the Théâtre Italien wanted to perform *L'Ecossaise* – or rather, as he said, massacre it. M. d'Aumont, the administrator of the Comédie-Française, gave priority to the Comédiens Français who, according to Monselet, were anxious to perform *L'Ecossaise* in revenge for Fréron's criticisms of them.[70] They had to take up the option quickly in order to avoid doing an injustice to the Italiens.[71] Voltaire was amused by this rivalry for his play,[72] but by 14 July he was irritated not only by the Murray problem just mentioned, but also by d'Argental's inability to cope with the simple problem of providing a set which would represent two rooms on the stage. 'Vous me faites enrager sur L'Ecossaise', he wrote. 'Où est donc la difficulté de diviser en deux pièces le fonds du théâtre? de pratiquer une porte dans une Cloison qui avance de 4 ou 5 pieds. L'avant-scène est alors suposée tantôt le caffé, tantôt la chambre de Lindane'.[73]

On 25 July, the day before the first performance, Voltaire published his riposte to Fréron's review. The first surviving reference to this *Requête à messieurs les Parisiens, par B. Jérôme Carré*

[69] *Mémoires et correspondance* (1808), i.77.

[70] *Fréron ou l'illustre critique* (Paris 1864), p.43.

[71] D'Argental to Voltaire, 30 June; D9018. The Théâtre Italien first performed the verse adaptation of *L'Ecossaise* in September 1760.

[72] To d'Argental, D9048, and to Mme d'Epinay, D9049 (both dated 9 July).

[73] D9062. In fact, a drop-curtain was raised and lowered as the action moved from the *café* to Lindane's room and back. Despite Voltaire's disapproval of this (he thought the room and the *café* should have been side by side, as in Lyon, Marseille and elsewhere) the curtain continued to be used in Paris. In the manuscript 'Mémoires des Décorations peintes à la Comédie-Française depuis l'ouverture du Théâtre de 1769 jusques à la Clôture de 1769', by Brunetti, is the following entry: 'Pour l'Ecossaise un grand Rideau Représentant un Caffé Anglâis avec tous les Accessoires Relatifs entièrement Repeint...200^ll'.

dates from 9 July 1760.[74] In writing it, was he afraid the play would not stand by itself? Certainly he was far from confident about 'cette misère' (as he called *L'Ecossaise*), but his main reason – apart from pouring a little more ridicule on Fréron – can be deduced from his letter to d'Argental of 27 June (D9010), in which he says that the play 'ne pourait être supportée au Théâtre, qu'en cas qu'on la prit pour une Comédie véritablem[t] anglaise. Elle ressemble aux toiles peintes de Hollande, qui ne sont de débit, que quand elles passent pour être des Indes'. He may well have been misjudging the situation, for the public was likely to be much less interested in an English play than in M. de Voltaire's reply to Fréron. Be that as it may, his statement to d'Argental may be taken at its face value. He genuinely believed it, hence his attempt to establish the reality of B. Jérôme Carré as the translator of Hume's play and the irrefutability of Hume's authorship. He even quotes from a letter he has received from M. Hume chastising him for the 'many a blunder' in his translation. Carré says he has cut out as much as possible of Wasp's part[75] and complains of the irrelevance of Fréron's anecdote (in his article of 3 June) about the rumour spread by a certain man of letters to the effect that he (Fréron) had been condemned to the galleys.[76]

Whether any member of the public was taken in or not by this hoax *Requête*, it was good publicity; its good-humoured tone was intended to make the spectators of the play, 'messieurs les parisiens [...] bien disposez en sa faveur' (D9060). The import-

[74] To Mme d'Epinay; D9049. Beuchot's statement that the *Requête* was 'composée dès le mois de juin' (M.v.413) arose from incorrect dating of this letter.

[75] The smallness of Frélon's part is obvious from a count of lines spoken by each major character: Lindane 360; Monrose 270; Freeport 247; Fabrice 240; Polly 240; Murray 170; Wasp 152 (*Catalogue des pièces choisies du répertoire de la Comédie Française*, Paris 1775, p.47-48).

[76] See D9077 to d'Argental, 19 July 1760: 'il serait pourtant plaisant de présenter la requête aux Parisiens la veille de L'Ecossaise. Il me parait qu'un homme qui prétend que la pièce n'est pas anglaise, parce que le bruit a couru qu'il avait été aux galères, est une des bonnes choses des plus comiques qu'on Connaisse'.

ance Voltaire attached to the *Requête* comes out in his letter to d'Argental dated 14 July (D9062), where he makes the point that whereas it is 'très plaisant' to play *L'Ecossaise*, 'il faut absolument imprimer deux ou trois jours auparavant' Carré's *Requête*.

Voltaire heard that Fréron was objecting to the play's being performed on the grounds that he had sometimes been called Frélon (by Piron). 'Quelle chicanne!' he protested to d'Argental, 'Ne sera t'il permis qu'à l'illustre Palissot de jouer d'honnêtes gens!' (13 July; D9060). Behind his indignation lay real fears that the performance would not be permitted. The *Requête* would, he hoped, make it clear that Frélon in fact counted for little in the play. Nevertheless, on 25 July, the day before the first performance, he was still not sure it would be performed. With customary irony he enquired from d'Argental: 'Jouera t'on L'écossaise? ne sera ce point un crime de mettre Frélon sur le téâtre après qu'il a été permis d'y jouer Diderot par son nom'.[77] His fear that a just reprisal would elude him at the last moment was, of course, unfounded.

One should begin to re-create that first night, with its atmosphere so strikingly prefiguring that of the *bataille d'Hernani*, with reference to an unelaborate and neutral report, such as that given by the chevalier de Mouhy: 'Le 26 Juillet 1760, les Comédiens donnèrent pour la première fois l'*Ecossaise*, Comédie du célèbre Voltaire; jamais pièce n'a fait plus de bruit, ni n'a été plus suivie,

[77] D9089. Not true, of course, but Palissot's Dortidius had been fairly transparent. According to Fréron himself (*Al*, 27 July 1760, v.215-16) he asked the *comédiens* to keep the name 'Frélon' or even use 'Fréron'. This might seem unlikely in view of Fréron's indignation in his letters to Malesherbes at being named in the *Requête* and named 'à une lettre près' in the first edition of the play. On the other hand, Fréron no doubt realised that he had nothing to lose and something to gain by being named on stage: everyone knew Wasp was a caricature of himself, but without being named he could not attack Voltaire by name in the way he wished, for his right of reply was severely restricted by Coqueley and Malesherbes. According to d'Argental it was 'le vieux Crébillon' who would not 'passer le nom de Frélon' (D9091).

et essuyé tant de critiques'.[78] The audience on the first night, in fact, counted 289 fewer spectators than at the first performance of *Les Philosophes* (1150 and 1439 respectively); receipts were 3760 francs (*Les Philosophes*: 4379 francs).

Much of what passed for dramatic criticism of the play in performance concentrated on the personification of Fréron. In *L'Observateur littéraire*, La Porte commented that no one had ever been so universally 'honni, bafoué, hué, sifflé, moqué, conspué que ce M. Wasp; c'est que chaque trait était suivi des applaudissements de tous les spectateurs; qu'ils en exigeaient la répétition; qu'ils y joignaient souvent de nouveaux sarcasmes'.[79] Grimm did not review the performance until 15 August, and even then very briefly (CLT, iv.276-77). He was surprised at its success, in view of the fact that its novelty had been diminished by prior publication. The performance did not please him: 'Nos acteurs me paraissent encore bien éloignés de la vérité et de la simplicité que demande le genre de cette comédie. Ils ont, dans leur jeu, je ne sais quoi de faux et de maniéré qui tue tout'. He thought Mlle Gaussin had divested the role of Lindane of 'tout ce qu'il a de touchant'.

Favart, on the contrary, thought the play was 'jouée supérieurement: mademoiselle Gaussin rend son rôle avec tant d'intérêt et de naïveté, qu'elle fait illusion sur son âge; elle ne paraît pas plus de dix-huit ans' (*Mémoires*, i.78). Grimm considered that Mlle Dangeville made the role of Polly even worse than in the text; that Mme Préville (Lady Alton) was not unpleasant enough; Armand failed to understand his role as Fabrice 'qui, bien joué, doit plaire infiniment'. Brizard did not play Monrose badly, thought Grimm, but Sarrazin would have done it better. As for Préville,

[78] *Abrégé de l'histoire du Théâtre-Français* (1780), iii.70. The exactitude of his description is somewhat marred by his comment on *Les Philosophes*, only two paragraphs earlier: 'Jamais Pièce n'a tant fait de bruit, n'a tant été applaudie, et ne s'est tant attiré de critiques'.

[79] *L'Observateur littéraire* (31 juillet 1760), iii.287. See also *Le Mercure* (août 1760), ii.185, and *Les Spectacles de Paris* (1761), p.134.

he had 'ni la figure ni la voix de Freeport', but, Grimm remarks, he is so popular with the *parterre* that he can succeed in any part.[80] D'Argental, whose opinion is not to be disdained, thought the acting of Préville and Mlle Gaussin superior: 'M. Frieport a ravi [...] les rosles de Lindane et de Frieport ont beaucoup gagnés à la représentation', he wrote to Voltaire on 27 July (D9091). He was delighted with the play's production and reception, and stressed the dual effect on the audience of the satire and the pathos, which did not counteract each other. Armand, he says, was 'un bon Fabrice', Bellecour played Murray 'avec feu et noblesse', Brizard played Monrose 'avec vérité', Mme Préville 'n'a point été mauvaise dans miladi Alton'; Mlle Dangeville was 'au dessus des éloges' and brought out Polly's role 'qui n'est pas le rosle le plus brillant de la pièce'. The final scene, he added, 'a transporté'.

Collé thought the play and Fréron equally detestable. Only Freeport pleased him in this 'mauvais roman qui veut être une comédie' which he suspected was by Diderot (*Journal*, ii.251-52). Diderot thought its 'petit pathétique [...] mince et chétif' was far inferior to his own adaptation of *The Gamester* and prophesied it would be a failure.[81]

One person who attracted great interest at the first performance was Mme Fréron who, according to Collé and Favart, was seated in the front row of the amphitheatre 'pour exciter par sa jolie figure les partisans de son mari contre la pièce' (Favart, i.73). She almost fainted away, he says, and when a friend reassured her that Wasp did not resemble her husband, made the unfortunate reply, 'on a beau dire, on le reconnaîtra toujours'. Thiriot noticed her there: '[elle] soutint fort bien son rôle, ayant été fort sérieuse

[80] Préville was then 38, and had just created the role of Crispin in *Les Philosophes*. According to E.-D. de Manne (*Galerie historique des comédiens français de la troupe de Voltaire*, 1877, p.160-61) his judgement about the character of Freeport was so sure that he submitted to Voltaire 'quelques observations que celui-ci accueillit et dont il fit son profit'.

[81] *Correspondance*, ed. Roth-Varloot, iii.39.

dans les endroits qui regardoient son Mari, et applaudissant sans affectation à tout le reste' (D9100). In this letter, written on the day of the third performance, Thiriot comments that the play's success was without exaggeration equal to that of *Mérope*. 'Courage, s'écria un avocat, c'est un Maître qui venge bien ses disciples [...] Tout en a été bien senti, et a fait son effet'.

Palissot was also at the first night, 'en grande loge avec un air radieux qui s'obscurcissait à mesure que le succès augmentait', according to Favart.[82] Mme Du Deffand, reported d'Alembert to Voltaire, thought it 'une bien mauvaise pièce [...] elle applaudit fort à une mauvaise critique qu'on dit que Freron en a faite' (D9034). And yet she took great pains to assure Voltaire of her admiration for *Tancrède* and *L'Ecossaise*, with an interesting slip of the pen: 'Préville est charmant dans le rôle de Fripon, enfin vous m'avez fait rire et pleurer' (5 September 1760; D9197).

On 3 August d'Alembert reiterated the 'succez prodigieux' of the play and reported that at the fourth performance there were more people than at the first (there were fifteen fewer in fact). Marmontel's comments are recorded in his letter to Voltaire of 5 August (D9116): 'Vous ne sauriez croire combien sur le théâtre le spectacle en est vrai, l'action vive et intéressante; on pleure comme à Zaïre, et aplaudi des pieds et des mains'. Voltaire suggested to d'Argental on 6 August that the play should not be performed three times a week – twice is enough (D9119) – but also asked Marmontel, with studied indifference, how Fréron was taking his thrice-weekly punishment at the Comédie-Française (D9142).

F. G. F. Desfontaines was present at the twelfth, thirteenth, fourteenth, fifteenth and sixteenth performances, and said he derived more pleasure from the play each time. Freeport made him want to be English; his tears for Lindane and Monrose were

[82] *Mémoires*, i.73. D'Alembert told Voltaire that Palissot thought *L'Ecossaise* 'une chose atroce' (D9114). This was no doubt true at the time, but he had changed his mind when he wrote his preface to the play in his edition of Voltaire's works (1792), as we shall see.

such that only he (Voltaire) and Racine were capable of calling forth.[83]

We shall see the reactions of the chief adversary shortly. Let us note for the moment that when Fréron's review eventually appeared (after many difficulties) attendance picked up, whereas the attraction of *Les Philosophes* had steadily declined. As the fortunes of these two plays are so closely linked, and as attendance is not unconnected with public interest (or indifference) and feeling (whether sympathy or indignation), the attendance figures for the first run of each play are given on the following page.[84]

These figures lend some support to d'Alembert's contention that a large number of complimentary tickets were given away for the first performance of *Les Philosophes* (the attendance was 308 higher than the average for the next four performances). On the other hand, d'Argental's statement that at the first night of *L'Ecossaise* 'nous n'avions aucun secours étranger, pas la moindre cabale en notre faveur, aucune belle dame n'avoit achepté le parterre, les freronistes ont eû la liberté entière d'y venir et d'y faire de leur mieux'[85] seems to be borne out by the closer correlation between attendance on the first night and the following four nights (120 higher only), and by a comparison of average receipt per spectator at each first performance: 3.04 at *Les Philosophes*, as against 3.26 at *L'Ecossaise*. All this is quite contrary to the impression gained and given by Fréron, who wrote to Malesherbes on 21 August that the only reason why the play had been

[83] D9183, 1 September 1760. Desfontaines was wanting Voltaire to help him find a post as secretary at this time.

[84] *Registres*, p.797-98. Clément, in his *Anecdotes dramatiques* (i.289), states that if *Les Philosophes* had not been authorised, *L'Ecossaise* would certainly not have been permitted. Collé thought Fréron had been thrown to the wolves by his supporters at court (*Journal*, ii.251n). It must not be forgotten that from the theatre's point of view this controversy was very good business; between them *Les Philosophes*, *L'Ecossaise* and *Tancrède* accounted for one fifth of the total receipts for 1760-61, which was a fairly good year (Cl. Alasseur, *La Comédie-Française au 18e siècle*, Paris 1967, p.62).

[85] To Voltaire, 27 July 1760; D9091.

Attendance figures for

Les Philosophes and *L'Ecossaise*

	LES PHILOSOPHES			L'ÉCOSSAISE		
Perf. No.	*Date: May*	*Spectators*	*Receipts*	*Date: July*	*Spectators*	*Receipts*
1	2	1439	4379	26	1150	3760
2	3	1189	3658	28	953	2730
3	5	1159	3688	30	1026	2984
				Aug.		
4	7	1094	3339	2	1135	3526
5	10	1083	3258	4	1005	2662
6	12	924	2375	6	984	2705
7	14	802	1749	9	1053	2894
8	17	869	2073	11	813	1947
9	19	769	1662	13	810	1848
10	21	846	1947	16	974	2189
11	24	651	1230	18	580	1253
12	26	891	1822	20	794	2003
13	28	661	1283	23	747	1648
14	31	462	971	25	916	1821
		12839	33434		12940	33970
15	—	—	—	27	605	1244
16	—	—	—	30	738	1540

received so enthusiastically at its first performance was that the audience was so full of his enemies (D9163). This was also the picture he painted in the article he published in *L'Année littéraire* (dated 27 July)[86] purporting to be a *Relation d'une grande bataille*

[86] *Al* (1760), v.209-16. Reprinted in D.app.190. Marivaux was in the audience (it was he who told Collé Mme Fréron felt ill), and so was Malesherbes, according to Collé. Fréron confirms that Malesherbes was present (D9163).

which had been sent to him, and which he had at first (he pretended) refused to insert in his *feuilles*.

Fréron's *Relation* tells how, on Saturday 26 July, at half past five in the afternoon, 'il se donna au Parterre de la Comédie Françoise une des plus mémorables batailles dont l'Histoire Littéraire fasse mention'. The whole piece is rendered in military terms, and aims at relating the antics of an army whose vanguard consisted of all the 'rimailleurs et *prosailleurs* ridiculisés dans *l'Année littéraire*', led by 'une espèce de *Savetier* appelé *Blaise* [Sedaine]'. In the midst of the élite of the troops (the typographers, booksellers and shop-boys working for the *Encyclopédie*) stood the wild-eyed, shaggy-haired, frenetic and redoubtable General Dortidius (Diderot). Two regiments of 'Clercs de Procureurs et d'Ecrivains sous les Charniers' were under the command of a '*Prophète de Boëhmischbroda*' (Grimm); reserve troops of lackeys and Savoyards were receiving orders from 'un petit prestolet' (La Porte). These were the front line soldiers, all well drilled in firing volleys of well-timed applause. But the grave senators of the 'république des philosophes' stayed in the rear with 'le sage *Tacite*' (d'Alembert) and 'le prudent *Théophraste*' (d'Argental or Duclos), anxiously pacing up and down in the Tuileries.

The philosophic army (so the *Relation* tells) went into action as soon as the curtain was raised, with clapping and stamping. At the end, 'le faible Détachement du Goût fut écrasé par la supériorité du nombre, et les Barbares se virent maîtres du champ de bataille'. The barbarian army marched rejoicing to the Tuileries to announce their victory. After much self-congratulation, mutual back-slapping and speechifying, they all went to a philosophic ball and banquet which lasted until eight the next morning. The senators gave orders for re-assembly the following evening to sing a *Te Voltarium*.

This piece of whimsy is harmless enough, and indeed, rather

Monselet's dramatisation of this first performance represents caricatural *philosophes* baying at a noble Fréron (*Fréron ou l'illustre critique*, p.21-42).

pointless.[87] But for that we must not blame Fréron, who had prepared a much more scathing report. To his fury, much of it was suppressed as indecent, libellous or irrelevant by Coqueley de Chaussepierre (his unknown censor) and Malesherbes, whose dislike of defamatory and personal polemics made him regard the *Ecossaise* affair as acutely embarrassing. His policy was to allow Fréron to reply strictly to the extent that he had been attacked, and no more.[88] This was not acceptable to Fréron, who wrote indefatigably complaining of his censor's refusal to pass his *Relation*. Coqueley de Chaussepierre, having suppressed part of Fréron's *feuille* 'parce que cela m'a paru très indécent' (D9101) wrote again to Malesherbes on the same day (31 July) asking him to read on pages 209 to 215 inclusive 'une relation qui vous amusera peutêtre et faites moy l'amitié de décider Vous même de son sort'. He puts the matter into perspective with the comment that 'La censure des feüilles devient une affaire furieusement difficile depuis les poüilles qu'on permet sur la scène' (D9103). Fréron's long letter in defence of his *Relation* (D9102) adopted the same line as his letter of 18 July (D9076) asking for 'un peu plus d'indulgence que par le passé pour quelques traits de pure plaisanterie qui pourront m'échapper dans mes feuilles sur ce fou de Voltaire'. In this letter he was preparing the way for his reviews of *L'Ecossaise* in performance. Finding the 'indulgence' withheld, he now adopted the same tone of injured innocence: 'Si je disois dans mes feuilles que Voltaire et les Encyclopédistes sont des coquins, des fripons, des faquins et des scélérats (ce qu'il me seroit très aisé de prouver) mon censeur, malgré les preuves, auroit raison de ne pas me permettre ces vérités. Mais au torrent d'injures et d'atrocités dont on m'accable, je n'oppose qu'une pure

[87] Marmontel, La Porte and d'Alembert denied the accuracy of Fréron's account. See Desnoiresterres, v.488-500, for a detailed reconstruction of the battle.

[88] Grosclaude, *Malesherbes*, p.156. This was not, of course, the opinion of Brunetière in his study of 'La direction de la Librairie sous Malesherbes', *Rdm* (1er février 1882), p.567-612.

plaisanterie, qu'une gaité très innocente.' He repeats the same device several times, contrasting the vileness, abomination, calumnious vomit and infamy of Voltaire, Grimm, Diderot and d'Alembert, with his own gaiety, slight mockery, sense of fun, and badinage. However, if one compares the public and private styles of Fréron and Voltaire one is struck by the contrast: Fréron is all outraged innocence in private, venom in public; Voltaire is cruelly contemptuous and abusive in private, the master of controlled deflation in public.

Malesherbes demanded that all proper names be suppressed in the *Relation*; Fréron very reluctantly complied, pleading to have the final *Te Voltarium* left in, refusing to take seriously the censor's apprehension that the priests would object to it as a parody of the *Te Deum* (D9107).

No sooner had the *Relation* been passed than Fréron submitted his 4 August review of *L'Ecossaise* for approval (v.278-88). Coqueley was driven to distraction: 'Encor du Freron, Encor du caffé, de l'Ecossaise & cela va arriver à chaque ordinaire. Cet homme devient fou. Si j'étois le maitre je rayerois tout l'article, *non bis in idem* et cecy est la 3e fois' (D9117). So he wrote to Malesherbes on or about 5 August. It would be far less trouble, he added, if he had 'carte Blanche pr Rayer sans appel'. Failing this, would Malesherbes please find another censor for Fréron? Malesherbes's attitude is revealed in his reply to Coqueley, dated 10 August: 'Je crois, Monsieur, que Freron se fera plus de tort qu'à personne en parlant de l'Ecossoise, d'autant plus que ce qu'il en dit n'est pas trop bon. Cependant il n'est pas juste de lui interdire sur cela la critique Littéraire. Ce qu'il dit à la fin de M. de Voltaire et de M. D'Alembert n'est plus Littéraire, mais quant à M. de Voltaire ce seroit trop blesser la Loy du Talion que de ne pas permettre à M. Wasp de lui retorquer quelques personalités'.[89]

[89] D9129. The reference to d'Alembert was suppressed in the article printed. Voltaire was not named in it, but the reference to 'le fond de sa retraite forcée' was left in by the censor as a compromise providing an adequate clue to Voltaire's identity as the object of Fréron's remarks.

Malesherbes's sense of fair play is clearly demonstrated here; the article does not do much harm, he goes on to say, but one must keep to a rule – even though they departed from it in passing the *Relation* 'parce que dans ce moment là le pauvre Fréron étoit dans une crise qui exigeoit quelque indulgence'. As with all people whose function is to conciliate and referee, Malesherbes's efforts to be fair were not appreciated by either side. 'Je doute fort', wrote Voltaire to d'Argental (no doubt after reading Fréron's article of 4 August) 'que Mr de Mallesherbes me rende d'importants services'.[90]

Does Fréron's article of 4 August offer anything new? It is *bis in idem* in that it covers the same ground as in his 3 June review of the published text, in praising the character of Freeport and criticising the stock recognition scene. In between times, however, he had gone source-hunting *chez* Goldoni (with little success).[91] So far as the attack on himself is concerned, he points out that he is in good company with Boileau, who had to suffer the same indignity from Boursault. The play is more like an Italian or Spanish farce, Fréron continues, complaining that 'le cœur & l'esprit sont blessés à chaque Acte de ce mélange de bouffonneries & de pathétique, contre lequel le Goût réclame depuis si longtemps'.[92] D'Argental's impression on this score was quite

[90] D9128, 10 August 1760. On 20 August he asked Thiriot who was 'l'approbateur des feuilles de Fréron' (D9159). He had probably read Fréron's *fourth* article on *L'Ecossaise*, dated 7 August, and was beginning to wonder, no doubt, how long they were going to go on. Fréron considered it right to keep up his attack for as long as *L'Ecossaise* was being performed (21 August 1760; D9163).

[91] Favart reported in his *Mémoires* (1 August 1760): [Fréron] 'm'a emprunté le théâtre de Goldoni, pour disputer à Voltaire le mérite de l'invention; il épluche *la Locandiera*, *il filosofo inglese*, *il Cavaliere e la dama* et *la Bottega del Caffè*' (i.77-78). Favart comments that the similarities are too remote to accuse Voltaire of plagiarism.

[92] *Al* (1760), v.286. Fréron also points out that the line 'Je ne le parierais pas, mais j'en jurerais' (II.iii) was not original, having been used by Piron. With incredibly heavy pedantry he returned to this in his *feuille* on 7 August and devoted three pages to it! In this article he plagiarises Piron's letter to Baculard d'Arnaud (D9108) and falsifies the crucial quotation in order to try and justify his charge of plagiarism against Voltaire (see act 2, note 5).

different: 'Les plaisanteries, les rires vrays qu'elles ont excités n'ont fait aucun tort au pathétique des scènes ny à l'effet des situations' (D9091).

Voltaire did not see Fréron's *Relation d'une grande bataille* until 17 August, deducing from it that 'le pauvre homme est si blessé qu'il ne peut rire' (D9154). The literary war, he commented, is apparently not approaching its end; only when the public is tired of it will it end. He seemed to be strangely out of touch, judging by his questions to Thiriot on 20 August (D9159): 'Quel est le *savetier Blaise* [...] Quel est ou qui est, le *petit abbé*, le petit *prestolet*? Qui est l'auteur de l'avant coureur?'[93] He ends by wanting to know who is the *approbateur* of Fréron's *feuilles*. No doubt he had been feeling that Fréron had been allowed too much leash; he was quite unaware, of course, of the despair to which Fréron was driving Coqueley and Malesherbes; quite unaware that on that very day, 20 August, Fréron was pleading with Malesherbes again to reverse his censor's decision, and allow him to publish yet another article attacking Voltaire. One can appreciate Fréron's frustration: 'Il est bien triste pour moi d'être joué par Voltaire dans une comédie et sur le théâtre de la nation, et de ne pouvoir plaisanter à son sujet' (D9161). This had been Voltaire's own argument for *L'Ecossaise*, of course, as he had pointed out to d'Argental only three days earlier: but for Jérôme Carré (among a number of pseudonymous personages) the Pompignans, the Palissots, Frérons and Joly de Fleurys would have made the *philosophes* look like 'une trouppe de gens sans honneur et sans raison' (D9154).

Malesherbes, caught in the middle once more, refused to 'se mesler de toutes les infamies faites pour et contre les Wasp, les contes de Tournay, &^{a}', and told Fréron to publish his article as a separate brochure. 'Au fond', he concluded, 'il faudra incessamment que tout cela finisse' (D9162). Undaunted, Fréron wrote to him the following day, explaining at length that he did not have

[93] The *Avant-coureur* was edited by C. P. Jonval.

time to write separate brochures. By now, of course, he was feeling he had a right to reprisals not only for *L'Ecossaise* (yet again) but also for *Le Pauvre diable* and *Le Russe à Paris*.

What happened to this article about which Fréron felt so strongly that he wrote two long, pleading and argumentative letters to Malesherbes? There is evidence from the style and contents of an anonymous brochure entitled *Lettre sur la comédie de l'Ecossaise*[94] that this is Fréron's work: as in Fréron's 4 August article, its author stresses the unworthiness of the play in comparison with ancient classical drama, criticises the violation of the unity of place and compares it to the Spanish and Italian farces. This *Lettre* objects to the 'mélange bizarre d'intérêt, de Bouffonnerie, & de Satyre' where Fréron's article of 4 August refers to 'ce mélange de bouffonneries & de pathétique'. In this article Fréron remarks that 'nos grands hommes ont travaillé pendant un siècle à purger l'Art Dramatique de tout ce qui le deshonorait' and that one man (the author of *L'Ecossaise*) had put the art back a hundred and fifty years; the *Lettre* contains the same thought: 'Voilà donc où nous ont conduit deux siècles de travaux, à ramener sur la Scène l'indécence, les contradictions, la barbarie'. But the *Lettre* then goes on to berate Voltaire by name (which Malesherbes had forbidden Fréron to do in *L'Année littéraire*) at considerable length. The argument is that Voltaire is a great writer who has stooped to writing a scandalous libel against a man for saying that '*La Femme qui a raison* est une méchante pièce'. The *Lettre* contrasts the 'plaisanterie si légitime' of *Les Philosophes* (which was 'une critique, à la fois profonde et comique de plusieurs systèmes tristement dangereux [...] un tableau fort gai des ridicules, des travers de quelques Sages Modernes') and, on the other hand, 'ce drame monstrueux et diffamatoire' that is *L'Ecossaise*. 'O honte! ô contradiction!' it ends, 'les Français qui ont ri à l'*Ecossaise* sont-ils donc les mêmes qui ont pleuré à *Mérope*?' In the absence of any better claim this brochure may be attributed

[94] Mentioned by Beuchot (M.v.403) as 'une satire très-violente dont l'auteur m'est inconnu'. The shelf-mark of the Arsenal copy is Rf 14503.

to Fréron, or at least to one of his associates prompted by his guidance.

The anonymous brochure entitled *La Wasprie ou l'ami Wasp* is a very different matter. It is an extended complaint about Wasp's attacks on its author who has committed 'un crime de *lèze-Wasp*' – writing in praise of Voltaire – which Wasp can never forgive. He pities Wasp in his hour of humiliation: 'Avec quelle douleur n'ai-je point vu la petite figure de M. *Wasp* pendu sans égard près de celle de l'Abbé *Coste* à toutes les cheminées de Paris, avec cette honnête inscription: joué aux Français, berné à la Foire, écorché aux Italiens'. Grimm refers to this brochure as 'deux volumes d'injures contre Fréron, par M. Le Brun, qui a joué un rôle dans l'histoire de Mlle Corneille'.[95]

Finally, there is one anonymous pamphlet of 1761, 'un monument de sagesse et d'équité' as Grimm called it, which deserves more than passing attention.[96] It is the *Discours sur la satyre contre les philosophes représentée, par une troupe qu'un poète philosophe fait vivre, et approuvée par un académicien qui a des philosophes pour collègues*.[97] Its author, who (greatly to Grimm's surprise; iv.303) was eventually revealed to be l'abbé Coyer, begins by quoting some of the judgements on *L'Ecossaise* expressed by Fréron, 'l'infatigable Aristarque de Quimper, qui prononce sur plus d'Ouvrages en un mois, que Dandin ne jugea de procès dans toute sa vie'. He suggests that if public opinion is at variance with Fréron's it is because the public found in *L'Ecossaise* what was

[95] CLT, iv.442 (15 July 1761). *La Wasprie ou l'ami Wasp, revu et corrigé*, was published 'A Berne [Paris?]. Aux dépens de M. Wasp. M.DCC.LXI' (British Library: 11825 bb 23). The passages quoted are from pt.1, p.132 and pt.2, p.125. P. D. E. Le Brun ('Pindare') was the author of *L'Ane littéraire ou les âneries de Me Aliboron, dit Fr*... (Paris 1761). *La Wasprie* is generally attributed to him.

[96] And there is one which does not: an *Epître à un ami dans sa retraite, à l'occasion des Philosophes et de l'Ecossaise*, attributed to Dorat (ImV: R fac 1713). Grimm rightly calls it 'bavardage d'enfant' (CLT, iv.280).

[97] 'Athènes [Paris], chez le libraire antiphilosophe', 1760, in-12°, p.86-91 (ImV: 1701). The *poète philosophe* is Voltaire, the *académicien*, Crébillon.

not in *Les Philosophes*: 'de l'action, de la chaleur & de l'intérêt'. He continues:

[*L'Ecossaise*] amusera encore le Public, lorsque la Pièce des Philosophes sera ensevelie dans l'oubli [...] Les tenèbres commencent à se dissiper: mais ne sçauroit-on faire bien sans y mêler le mal? La lumière, en nous arrivant de Genève à chaque poste,[98] blesse toujours quelqu'un de nos Citoyens. *L'Ecossaise*, par exemple, traduite aux portes de cette Ville Suisse, n'est pas en tout un amusement innocent, tel que la Comédie devroit toujours être. Un grand Ecrivain de petites feuilles y est personnellement joué [...] Mais les erreurs fréquentes où la fragilité humaine le fait tomber, ne donnent pas le droit de l'outrager [...] M. Hume! vous avez tort, d'autant plus tort, qu'Hercule n'employoit pas la Massue à écraser des Guèpes.

L'abbé Coyer ends his *Discours* with a warning:

Deux comédies personnelles sur le même Théâtre en trois mois! Citoyens, en quelque rang que vous soyez, prenez garde à vous. L'Ordre des Lettrés, qui gouverne à la Chine dans la plus grande union, & qui rampe en France dans la discorde, se lassera peut-être de se déchirer lui-même. Sur qui se jettera-t-il?

This clearly implies an awareness of Choiseul's ploy, but the suggestion that intellectuals were being sidetracked ignores the fact that *L'Ecossaise* was part of a very much larger battle. The numerous attempts to trivialise the play into a purely personal satire do not alter the fact that the *philosophes* themselves considered it to be vital to their cause as a counter-attack against the formidable alliance between the court, Fréron and Palissot, the aim of which was to discredit them and suppress the *Encyclopédie* for good.

4. *The fortunes of 'L'Ecossaise' after summer 1760*

The day after the end of the five-week summer run of *L'Ecossaise*,

[98] *Post tenebras lux*, as the motto of the Ville de Genève has it.

Voltaire wrote to express his gratitude to d'Argental: 'Permettez moi de vous remercier encor d'avoir vangé le public en donnant L'Ecossaise; vous avez décrédité ce malheureux Fréron dans Paris et dans les provinces, et il était nécessaire qu'il fut décrédité' (D9180). Voltaire had already heard of the successful performances in Lyon, Bordeaux and Marseille (D9173, D9175), and was delighted about them – with reason, for they were evidence that the play had a dramatic interest and not merely a satirical one. The same is true of the major temporal and geographical extensions of interest taking the form of *reprises* in Paris throughout the century and foreign translations and performances.

The Comédiens Français decided at the end of its summer run that they wanted to revive the play for the winter season, pleasing news which d'Alembert transmitted to Voltaire on 2 September (D9184). As its last performance (on 30 August) drew 738 spectators its run would probably have been extended then and there but for the fact that *Tancrède* was scheduled to be put on.[99] During the autumn the repercussions of *L'Ecossaise* were still to be felt, through the inevitable parodies and the Théâtre Italien's adaptation in verse. *L'Ecosseuse* was first off the mark, on 4 September, at the Opéra-Comique de la Foire Saint-Laurent. The conventional parodic tricks are used – vulgarisation of characters, slang, songs, and deformation of names (Frélon / Moucheron, *chansonnier*; Monrose / La Rose, *vieux contrebandier*; Lady Alton / La Grand'Jeanneton, *fruitière*; Murray / Furet; Freeport / Francport, *marchand de bœufs*). Its authors are given on the title-page as 'Mrs. P... & A...', which Brenner (following Bengesco, ii.84, n.1) interprets as Panard and Anseaume.[100] It is really of little moment whether these gentlemen wrote it, or Poinsinet *jeune* and Davesne

[99] First performed 3 September 1760, with much the same team: Argire: Brizard (Monrose), Tancrède: Lekain (Interlocuteur), Lorédan: Bellecour (Murray), Catane: Dauberval (Messager), Aldamon: Dubois (Wasp), Fanie: Mme Préville (Lady Alton).

[100] *A bibliographical list of plays in the French language 1700-1789* (New York 1979). Voltaire asked Thiriot to send him a copy of *L'Ecosseuse* if it was 'plaisante comme on me mande' (23 September 1760; D9253).

as Beuchot believed (M.v.403), but for one detail. Poinsinet (*le Petit* or *le Mystifié* as he was affectionately known), whom Voltaire met in Berlin in 1755, was Palissot's brother-in-law and, like him, one of Fréron's collaborators on *L'Année littéraire*. This rather diminishes his case for the doubtful honour, since Moucheron is an even more ridiculous and odious character than Frélon.[101]

The Comédiens Italiens, who had been thwarted in August by the Français, performed M. de La Grange's *L'Ecossaise mise en vers* on 20 September. This line-by-line verse rendering deserves to be read as it makes one appreciate even more, by contrast, the economy of Voltaire's prose. Here, Frélon becomes Mordant, and André is transformed into 'Arlequin, laquais de Lord Murrai'. That the original production by the other house was very much in the minds of the Italian company seems clear from the following comments by d'Origny:[102]

Quand l'*Ecossaise* de *Voltaire*, mise en vers par M. de la Grange, occupa la scène (20 septembre) le public en fut plus étonné que mécontent. L'Ecossaise ne peut être mieux que dans sa parure naturelle; mais sa beauté brillait encore sous les ornements étrangers qui la couvraient. Avant la pièce, Mlle Catinon, chargée du rôle de Lindane, adressa aux spectateurs le discours suivant: Messieurs, oser remettre sous vos yeux un drame que le premier théâtre du monde vous a déjà présenté, avec ses succès ordinaires, est une entreprise dont nous ne pouvons dissimuler le danger. Il semble que, séduits par quelques applaudissements dont vos bontés daignent chaque jour encourager notre faiblesse, nous voulions entrer en concurrence avec la Scène Française. Non, Messieurs, cet esprit

[101] Léris and Favart, however, attribute it to Poinsinet (*Mémoires*, i.95). A comic opera, *Les Nouveaux Calotins*, attributed by Quérard and Brenner to Lesage and Harny, by Beuchot to Harny alone, was first performed on 19 September. It is 'moins une parodie qu'une pièce faite à l'occasion de la comédie de Voltaire' (M.v.403). Taconet's parody, *La Petite Ecosseuse*, was not performed, according to Beuchot.

[102] *Annales du Théâtre Italien*, Duchesne (1788), i.299-300. Voltaire possessed a copy of Lagrange's (or La Grange's) version (BV, no.1859). It is misleadingly entered in Havens and Torrey (3034) simply as '*L'Ecossaise*, comédie, Paris 1761'. BV gives correct details: '*L'Ecossaise*, comédie en 5 actes, traduite de l'Anglais et mise en vers par M. de Lagrange, Paris, Duchesne (1761), p.108'.

de rivalité ne nous amène pas aujourd'hui devant vous; l'ambition de vous plaire nous anime seule, et nous ne craignons, à cet égard, aucune supériorité. Nous avons cru qu'un ouvrage qui avait déjà pu vous amuser, pourrait, à la faveur du langage de la Poésie, piquer encore votre curiosité.

Voltaire was delighted to hear in December 1760 that his *Ecossaise* had been performed at Versailles, 'et que mon ami Fréron est fort connu à la cour' (D9443). He goes on to express to the d'Argentals his hope that there will be a *reprise* at the Comédie-Française. Again one notices how out of touch he was kept regarding the Comédie's plans, for only six days later it was performed.[103] Between 1760 and 1788 it was repeated every year except 1777, 1786, and 1787, for a total of 112 performances.[104]

Even in 1765, when Voltaire feared that it might be among the plays prohibited by 'le tyran du tripot' (the duc de Richelieu) it was performed four times.[105] In that year it was performed before Fréron in Rennes, in circumstances which, if Marin and Trublet reported the matter correctly, indicate that Fréron was either brazen or brave (D12931). Or perhaps he was by now able to view the whole affair with equanimity and enjoy the notoriety.

Of the eighteenth-century foreign adaptations and translations of *L'Ecossaise*, the Portuguese, Italian and English ones deserve comment. *L'Ecossaise* was the first of Voltaire's plays to be translated into Portuguese.[106] Under the title *A Loja do café ou a Escocesa*, it appeared in 1762, published by Francisco Luís Ameno.[107] This

[103] The play was performed five times that winter (11, 15, 17, 20 December, 18 January). Cideville reported to Voltaire that the duc de Duras had ordered a performance to celebrate his wedding, and two other performances were given by public demand, 'au grand dépit de Fréron, qui en mouroit de honte, si c'étoit son genre de mort' (27 December 1760; D9500). In October 1761 Voltaire planned to begin Mlle Clairon's visit to him at Ferney with a performance of *L'Ecossaise* in his new private theatre (D10052).

[104] *Registres*, and Joannidès, *La Comédie-Française, 1680-1900* (Paris 1901).

[105] D12993 (February 1765). Voltaire had not heard about the performance given on 1 January.

[106] See *Voltaire et la culture portugaise* (Paris 1969), p.88.

[107] Arsenal, Rf 14502.

is a prose version attributed like the first French editions to M. Hume. A verse adaptation was performed in Lisbon in 1805 but was never published.[108]

Goldoni was one of the first to read *L'Ecossaise* in Venice, and wanted to translate it straight away; but he found it necessary to adapt it 'alla foggia italiana' both to make it acceptable to the Italian public and to avoid the charge of plagiarism.[109] *La Scozzese* was commented on by Lessing[110] for its deviation from the original. He pointed out that Voltaire claimed he had omitted the final punishment of Frélon as it detracted from the main interest in the play. 'The Italian did not deem this excuse sufficient, he completed the punishment of Frélon [or M. de La Cloche, as Goldoni renames him] out of his own head, for the Italians are great lovers of poetical justice'. M. de La Cloche is not so much punished, in fact, as sent off by Lindana with a flea in his ear. Goldoni's villain is not a journalist; he betrays Lindana not for gain, but out of pique.

About the other Italian translation, by Casanova, we have considerable circumstantial information, thanks to his *Mémoires*.[111] Casanova had played Murray in a private performance of *L'Ecossaise* at Soleure in May 1760, before a brilliant company of four hundred at the residence of the French ambassador to the Corps helvétique, Chevignard de Chavigny (*Mémoires*, ch.16, p.393-402). Whilst he was there M. de Chavigny showed him a letter from Voltaire (who was a fairly frequent visitor at Soleure), in which 'cet homme célèbre lui témoignait sa reconnaissance pour le rôle de Monrose qu'il avait joué dans l'*Ecossaise*' (p.402).[112]

[108] According to *Voltaire et la culture portugaise*, the autograph manuscript was in the possession of Inocêncio Francisco da Silva, author of the *Dicionário bibliográfico português*.

[109] *La Scozzese*. For a comparative analysis of *L'Ecossaise* and *La Scozzese* see *Il Teatro moderno applaudito* (Venezia 1799), xxxiv.

[110] *Hamburgische Dramaturgie* (1958), p.53 (quoted from the English translation, New York 1962, p.38).

[111] Ed. R. Abirached (Paris 1959), ii.

[112] The letter is not in D.

Casanova visited Voltaire on 21 August 1760; he found his host knew all about the performances of *L'Ecossaise* at Soleure. Voltaire offered to invite Mme de ... (to whom Casanova had been paying court at Soleure) to come to Les Délices to play Lindane again; he himself would play Monrose. The young lady was not available, and the performance did not take place (*Mémoires*, ch.21, p.505). Casanova's acquaintance with the play's success encouraged him to make it known in Italy. He therefore translated *L'Ecossaise* as soon as he arrived in Genoa, 'pour la faire jouer par les comédiens qui étaient à Gênes et qui m'avaient paru assez bons' (ch.27, p.653). He offered the translation *gratis* to Pietro Rossi,[113] the director of the troupe of actors, who had it performed under Casanova's own direction.[114] The rehearsals, incidentally, as at Soleure, were an inseparable part of Casanova's amorous intrigues. A week before the first performance, the following announcement was made: '*Nous donnerons* l'Ecossaise *de M. de Voltaire, traduite par une plume inconnue, et nous la jouerons sans souffleur*' (p.659).

The play was well received at Genoa, 'portée aux nues', as Casanova relates. 'Le théâtre, très grand, était encombré par tout ce que la ville avait de mieux. Les comédiens, sans souffleur, se surpassèrent et furent vivement applaudis'. There were five more performances before full houses. Thus encouraged, Casanova sent a copy of his translation to Voltaire, who sent back a message saying he thought it bad (p.672). It was in this way that Voltaire incurred Casanova's bitter enmity for many years. Writing his *Mémoires* after Voltaire's death, Casanova sagely commented that the only one to be hurt by his 'faibles piqûres' was himself, and

[113] Who also acted in Goldoni's adaptation of *L'Ecossaise*. M. Abirached notes that no trace of Casanova's translation has been found (*Mémoires*, ii.1192).

[114] His methods were very sound: at the first reading (which lasted only an hour and a quarter) he refused to tell the actors which parts they would be playing. 'Je savais que d'ordinaire les acteurs paresseux ou insouciants ne s'occupent que de leur rôle spécial, sans s'attacher à l'esprit de l'ensemble; d'où vient qu'une pièce, quoique bien sue dans ses parties, est mal rendue dans son entier' (*Mémoires*, p.656).

regretted that 'la postérité me mettra au nombre des Zoïles que l'impuissance déchaîna contre ce grand génie' (p.673).

When George Colman the Elder adapted *L'Ecossaise* in 1767, he may have had in mind his own 'Zoïle'. In *The English merchant* Frélon becomes Mr Spatter, apropos of whom Colman was taken to task by William Kenrick, who was 'greatly injured by Colman's having insinuated that there was the least resemblance' between them.[115] *The English merchant* was first performed at the Theatre Royal, Drury Lane, on 21 February 1767. It is recorded[116] that the play was received with great applause for several nights, 'but many Admirers of Mr *Colman* as a Dramatic Writer, were sorry he adhered so closely to *Voltaire*, and wished he had done more from himself, which would, undoubtedly, have been better for the Play, the Author, and the Public'. This rather astounding judgement leads one to suppose that the 'many admirers' did not know Voltaire's play, for Colman's adaptation contains many changes in plot and characterisation,[117] which led Voltaire to comment to Colman, 'Vous avez furieusement embelli l'Ecossaise que vous avez donnée sous le nom de Fréeport, qui est en effet le meilleur personnage de la pièce' (15 November 1768; D15317). Colman, he says, had done what he had not dared to do – punished his Fréron at the end of the play. 'J'avais quelque répugnance à faire paraître plus longtems ce polisson sur le théâtre'. In this letter Voltaire savours his revenge on Fréron in Paris and in 'tous les théâtres de l'Europe depuis Petersbourg[118] jusqu'à Bruxelles',

[115] R. B. Peake, *Memoirs of the Colman family* (1841), p.220. Of Kenrick, the *Biographica dramatica* has this to say: 'Few persons were ever less respected by the world, still fewer have created so many enemies, or dropped into the grave so little regretted by their contemporaries'.

[116] B. Victor, *A history of the theatres of London* (1761-1771), iii.100-101.

[117] These are analysed in K. M. Lynch, '*Pamela nubile*, *L'Ecossaise*, and *The English Merchant*', *Mln* 47 (1932), p.94-96.

[118] Catherine II was to write to Voltaire the following month recommending some excellent *spécifiques*: 'C'est de se faire lire l'Ecossaise, Candide, l'Ingénu, l'hoṁe aux quarante écus, et la Princesse de Babilone, il n'i a pas moyen après cela de sentir le moindre mal' (D15396).

which drew from George Colman the Younger the remark that 'the celebrated and lively Frenchman' wrote it 'with his vanity floating on the surface', for 'he cannot help informing the Author who has built upon his ground-work of the great success of his *own* play... and of the admirable portrait he has drawn in it, of an original whom he never saw'. The phrase 'furieusement embelli' is interpreted by the younger Colman as 'a little like a sneer, couched in the compliments bestowed upon the English poet'.[119]

Voltaire referred to Colman's adaptation in slightly disapproving terms in about 1770 [120] as 'la traduction, ou plutôt l'imitation de la comédie de l'Ecossaise & de Fréron', adding: 'Elle a eu autant de succès à Londres qu'à Paris, parce que par tout pays on aime la vertu des Lindanes & des Friports, & qu'on déteste les folliculaires qui barbouillent du papier, & mentent pour de l'argent'. To Fréron's claim that the play succeeded in Paris only because he (Fréron) was so disliked there, Voltaire simply offers the evidence of its success throughout Europe (once again). The reason for his apparently vain insistence on its European vogue lies in his determination to prove the play's worth over and above mere personal satire, since he was well aware that in many quarters he was accused of stooping to crush. He concludes his open letter: 'Personne n'en voulait à Pourceaugnac, quand Pourceaugnac fit rire l'Europe'.

Inevitably the shadow of Fréron has become blurred with time behind the figure of Frélon-Wasp. Perhaps we should leave the last word on this controversy not to Voltaire, who never was able

[119] *Posthumous letters addressed to F. Colman and G. Colman the Elder etc.*, by George Colman the Younger (London 1820), p.91-93.

[120] In an open letter to Damilaville printed in the *Questions sur l'Encyclopédie* (1770), i.265-72; D.app.328. Voltaire felt honoured that 'l'illustre Garrick' wrote an epilogue for *The English merchant*. Garrick mentions it in a letter (n.d.) to Colman: 'My Wife has persuaded me to stay [at Hampton] till Wed^y when I hope to wait upon the *English merchant* with all my wits & Spirits about Me [...] You must write to me, & say if I am to furnish an Epilogue for the Merchant – I will certainly do my best if you are not provided' (*Posthumous letters*, p.300).

to forgive Fréron,[121] but to the author of *Les Philosophes*. Not the Palissot who, throughout Voltaire's lifetime, showed an almost pathetic need to retain the patriarch's good opinion (perhaps because he feared receiving the same treatment as Fréron) but the Palissot who edited Voltaire's works in 1792, when his fear of Voltaire had been replaced by his fear of being remembered as a defender of throne and altar, as the caricaturist of Diderot and Rousseau:

Fréron abusait depuis longtemps de son métier d'écrivain folliculaire, pour décrier, s'il l'avait pu, ceux des gens de lettres qui s'étaient le plus distingués par leurs talents. Il avait surtout fatigué Voltaire de ses critiques injurieuses. Ce grand homme, que le mépris eut beaucoup mieux vengé, ne dédaigna pas de descendre dans l'arène avec l'écrivain de feuilles [...] Aujourd'hui pourtant ce n'est plus le personnage de Wasp qui paraît attirer les spectateurs, mais celui de Lindane, et surtout celui de Freeport, caractère vraiment original et digne de la bonne comédie [...] L'auteur l'écrivit très vite; mais il savait imprimer sur les ouvrages même qu'il avait le moins travaillés, un cachet qui n'appartenait qu'à lui.[122]

[121] In 1764, for example, he wrote to Palissot (D11812) telling him that as he was very ill his Jesuit chaplain had made him ask God's forgiveness for being uncharitable towards Fréron and Lefranc de Pompignan. He ends by assuring Palissot: 'Il faut absolument que nous demandions pardon à Dieu, et que nous fassions pénitence'. But the sting, as always, is in the rear: 'Je consens même d'aller en purgatoire, à condition que Fréron sera damné'. See also D12016, again to Palissot, on the need for unity among 'gens de la même communion', against Fréron 'qui a commencé ce beau combat'. Gaiffe (p.378) opens up an interesting field of enquiry (beyond the scope of a critical edition) when he remarks: 'Une caricature aussi outrée que celle de Fréron dans l'*Ecossaise* n'offre d'intérêt psychologique qu'à celui qui veut étudier les effets de la haine aveugle chez Voltaire'. On the lack of psychological interest in *drames* of this period, see R. Niklaus, *A literary history of France: the eighteenth century, 1715-1789*, ch.12.

[122] Palissot's preface to *L'Ecossaise*, *Œuvres de Voltaire* (1792), vi.173-74.

5. *Four 'petites poétiques'*

Voltaire's prefaces to his plays, said Grimm in his second review of *L'Ecossaise* (15 July 1760), are 'de petites poétiques dont les principes sont ajustés à la justification du poème qui suit'. Each of the four pieces attached to the play has a separate function. Two of them were published before the Comédie-Française production of summer 1760, and two after. We shall deal with each in the probable order of composition.

Préface

Voltaire's aims in writing this sole accompaniment to the original edition are fivefold: to establish the identity of the putative author, M. Hume; to pay tribute to Diderot's theory of conditions and maintain the importance of Frélon as a personification of the *condition* of the journalist; to pay homage to the *Encyclopédie*; to define the genre of his play; and to defend the theatre as a valuable institution which should not be persecuted.

The attribution of the play to John Hume has already been discussed in chapter 2.[123] As for Voltaire's contention that Frélon is intended to represent a social condition, this is deliberate nonsense – the core of Frélon consists of his 'caractère lâche et odieux', not his social function. Even if one accepts the possibility that Voltaire's intention was to make Frélon represent a certain sub-species of journalist, the 'Arétins subalternes qui gagnent

[123] Not only does Voltaire stress its English origin; he claims for it two qualities that make it superior among English plays. First, the unities are respected; secondly, the stage is never left empty. The 'Frenchness' of the first characteristic does not require comment, except that Fréron was to deny that *L'Ecossaise* respects the unity of place (*Al*, 4 August 1760, v.286). The second had been claimed by Voltaire in 1748 as something which great modern (French) dramatists could have taught the Greeks: 'cet art imperceptible qui ne laisse jamais le théâtre vide, et qui fait venir et sortir avec raison les personnages' ('Dissertation sur la tragédie ancienne et moderne', *Sémiramis*; M.iv.494).

leur pain à dire et à faire du mal', as he describes him in the preface, it still remains true that Frélon's role in the play is not that of a journalist, but of a hired villain. Voltaire's professed adherence to the theory of conditions can be considered as a fragile attempt to provide an unnecessary justification of his caricature of Fréron. However, much more important is the fact that Voltaire sees fit to give public support to Diderot by paraphrasing ideas contained in the *Entretiens sur le Fils naturel* and the *Discours sur la poésie dramatique*. By doing this he was simply waging the same war on another front; for Fréron and Palissot, Diderot's theories of *drame* and *philosophie* were one and the same thing.[124] Conversely, sympathy for Diderot's theories was, so far as Voltaire was concerned, a second form of attack on Fréron. So far as the *philosophes* were concerned, it was above all a reply to Palissot's attacks on them, and particularly on Diderot, during the previous three years.

Voltaire's praise for the simplicity and truth to life in Goldoni's plays and in English drama is merely a stepping-stone to his personal objective: 'Il n'importe aux Anglais que le sujet soit bas, pourvu qu'il soit vrai'. Lower than Frélon one cannot get, is the implication. But to the wounded *philosophes* his homage to foreign drama must have seemed a welcome rejoinder to Palissot's accusation that because the *philosophes* admired foreign writers and ideas they were disloyal to France.

The term *drame* is not mentioned in the preface (although it is in the *Requête*). Voltaire stresses the mixed genre of his play, however: 'il est dans le haut comique, mêlé au genre de la simple comédie'. A judicious evocation of a 'sourire de l'âme' (not a guffaw) and an effortless appeal to tender response:[125] this is the

[124] See Gaiffe, p.85-87.

[125] Fréron criticises Voltaire's statement, 'Malheur à celui qui tâche', as not being French (*Al*, 1760, iv.111); but the sense seems clear enough to be a motto for all who aspire to effortless artistry. Fréron goes on to suggest that the only reason why Voltaire states a preference for the smile over the laugh is that his play is not funny. He disagrees with Voltaire's view that 'celui qui vous émeut ne songe point à vous émouvoir' by asking, 'Est-ce par hazard que Corneille,

mixture Voltaire is presenting to his public. As we have seen, several people remarked on the successful co-existence of humour and pathos in performance. It was on this point, however, that Voltaire parted company not only with Fréron – open disagreement with him about dramatic theory was part of the larger battle – but also with Diderot. Both Fréron and Diderot, believing that different types of comedy should be kept separate, were at variance with the author of *L'Enfant prodigue*, *Nanine* and *L'Ecossaise*. In 1738 and 1749 Voltaire had expressed ideas on the 'mélange de sérieux et de plaisanterie, de comique et de touchant',[126] on the ability of comedy to 'se passionner, s'emporter, s'attendrir, pourvu qu'ensuite elle fasse rire les honnêtes gens'. Purely *larmoyante* comedy, he added, would be 'un genre très vicieux et très désagréable'.[127] Hence Voltaire's warning, in the preface to *L'Ecossaise*, against deliberate, studied pathos. The pathetic reality of the situation of the heroine must eschew the rhetorical. If this is to be a comedy, the *vis comica* must have its place alongside the gravity and moral value he claims for it. In emphasising the appeal of the play for *l'honnête homme* and *les honnêtes gens*, Voltaire joins forces once more with Diderot. But are we to take seriously Voltaire's claims that the play is 'd'une excellente morale [...] digne de la gravité du sacerdoce dont l'auteur est revêtu', and that 'la comédie ainsi traitée est un des plus utiles efforts de l'esprit humain'? These two paragraphs of the preface are drawn as directly from the *Discours sur la poésie dramatique*[128] as is his comment about 'les conditions et les états

Racine, M[rs.] de Crébillon et de Voltaire ont mis du pathétique dans leurs pièces? Peut-on supposer qu'ils nous ont émus sans songer à nous émouvoir?' (iv.112). There is a *malentendu* here: Voltaire is referring to characters, not to dramatists, as Fréron assumes.

[126] Preface to *L'Enfant prodigue* (M.iii.443).

[127] Preface to *Nanine* (M.v.10).

[128] For example: 'Ce qu'on objecte contre ce genre, ne prouve qu'une chose; c'est qu'il est difficile à manier, que ce ne peut être l'ouvrage d'un enfant, et qu'il suppose plus d'art, de connaissances, de gravité et de force d'esprit, qu'on n'en a communément quand on se livre au théâtre' (*De la poésie dramatique*; Diderot, x.334).

des hommes'; does he really intend *L'Ecossaise* to be a didactic *comédie sérieuse* with a moral appeal through the emotions? Beaumarchais certainly thought so in 1767, classifying it alongside *L'Enfant prodigue*, *Nanine*, La Chaussée's *Mélanide*, Mme de Graffigny's *Cénie*, Sedaine's *Le Philosophe sans le savoir*, and Diderot's *Le Père de famille*, all plays which, he says, 'ont déjà fait connaître de quelles beautés le genre sérieux est susceptible, et nous ont accoutumés à nous plaire à la peinture touchante d'un malheur domestique'.[129] Do we find, in *L'Ecossaise*, the objective designated by Diderot for the *comédie sérieuse*? For virtue, we have no further to look than Lindane. For the fulfilment of duties, what better example than Freeport? 'En effet', asks Diderot, 'qu'est-ce qui nous affecte comme le récit d'une action généreuse? Où est le malheureux qui puisse écouter froidement la plainte d'un homme de bien?' (Diderot, x.337). Murray's self-abasement before his father's enemy, Freeport's generosity, Monrose's and Lindane's lamentable plight are all meant to tug at our heart-strings quite unashamedly and consistently with the preference Voltaire was to express (in the *Appel à toutes les nations*, and in his article 'Art dramatique' in the *Questions sur l'Encyclopédie*) for tragedies that speak to the heart rather than the mind. Indeed, it was because Voltaire feared that Frélon would 'mêler un peu de froideur' with the moving pathos of the dénouement that he cut short Frélon's part (or so he says). If we are to accept Grimm's judgement on this character, the part he plays in the action had to be curtailed because he was portrayed too weakly; Grimm sees him as 'trop mince, trop ridicule, trop faible, pour se tenir au milieu des autres'. He should have been made more 'lâche' and 'odieux' to be really theatrical (CLT, iv.261). Nevertheless, it is quite clear, from Voltaire's intentions in portraying Frélon, that he is fully qualified to figure in *la comédie gaie* ('qui a pour objet le ridicule et le vice' according to Diderot's formula), but not in *la comédie sérieuse*. The inclusion of this character, 'plus dégoûtant que comique' as

[129] *Essai sur le genre dramatique sérieux* (*Théâtre complet*, 1973, p.8).

Voltaire describes him, in a play depicting the trials of virtue and calling forth our tears, would clearly explain why Diderot disliked *L'Ecossaise*. For Voltaire's views on dramatic contrast, as expressed in the preface, are diametrically opposed to those of Diderot – in fact, one could say Voltaire set out deliberately to refute them. 'Je veux que les caractères soient différents', Diderot states, 'mais je vous avoue que le contraste m'en déplaît' (Diderot, x.376). The English, Voltaire replies, say that 'tout ce qui est dans la nature doit être peint', that 'nous avons une fausse délicatesse', and that 'l'homme le plus méprisable peut servir de contraste au plus galant homme'. Diderot goes on to draw an analogy with painting: 'Voulez-vous qu'un tableau soit d'une composition désagréable et forcée, méprisez la sagesse de Raphaël, strapassez, faites contraster vos figures' (x.376). Voltaire, on the contrary, claims that the author of *L'Ecossaise* 'a imité ces peintres qui peignent un crapaud, un lézard, une couleuvre, dans un coin du tableau, en conservant aux personnages la noblesse de leur caractère'.

On this aesthetic point then, one of the major ones to be developed by Hugo seventy years later, the two *philosophes* are in radical disagreement. What is curious is that Voltaire should have chosen to emphasise this difference of opinion just when disunity within the brotherhood of *philosophes* was what he was repeatedly warning them to avoid in this time of crisis. However, Voltaire does attenuate the effect of contrast by stressing that M. Hume 'a l'art de ne présenter son Frélon que dans des moments où l'intérêt n'est pas encore vif et touchant'. Can one, then, agree with Grimm when he maintains that what Voltaire says about 'le comique pathétique' in this preface is precisely the opposite of what he says in *Le Pauvre diable*? 'J'aime assez qu'on rie', he wrote in the latter, 'Souvent je baille au tragique bourgeois' (M.x.108). This does not seem to conflict with anything Voltaire says in the preface. In the first place, nowhere in it does he mention 'le comique pathétique' (he uses the word 'pathétique' only to warn against an excess of it). Secondly, Voltaire's opinions of *tragédie bourgeoise* are quite irrelevant to *L'Ecossaise* and its preface. Confusion between *comédie* and *drame*, during that period of dramatic innovation, was frequent enough,[130] but there was nothing confusing about Voltaire's opinion of *tragédie bourgeoise*: it was uncompromisingly scornful and disapproving. The only mixture of genres he tolerated was in the comic mode; but he did not include *comédie larmoyante* (as distinct from *le comique larmoyant*)[131] in this category, for whereas 'on ne travaille dans le goût de la comédie larmoyante que parce que ce genre est plus aisé',[132] comedy of the type found in *L'Ecossaise* was, he claimed, 'un art très difficile'. The degradation of tragedy and unrelieved lacrymosity were what he could not stomach and, as Raymond Naves has demonstrated, his position on this question remained quite consistent.[133]

We come now to Voltaire's final objective in this preface. Here his attention turns away from Fréron to Rousseau (although he is not named), for it was the *Lettre à d'Alembert sur les spectacles* which had greatly offended both Diderot and Voltaire two years previously. Although Voltaire seems to be appealing to higher authority by merely quoting at length from Montaigne, he succeeds in this way in eliminating any trace of personal difference of opinion, which would have been extremely difficult to achieve had he set down his own reactions to Rousseau's views on the immorality of the theatre. Why should he wish to avoid expressing his own views on this matter? Why fight shy of adding just one more to the many replies – by d'Alembert himself, Marmontel and Dancourt, for example – which Rousseau's *Lettre* inspired? The disapproval of theatre by the civil and religious authorities of Geneva had become stronger as a result of Rousseau's *Lettre* (Desnoiresterres, v.191-92); their unwelcome attentions to his

[130] 'Le titre de *comédie* appliqué à *L'Ecossaise* ne doit pas nous faire illusion: c'est si bien un drame que l'on [Lintilhac] a pu fort justement y retrouver les éléments essentiels de tout bon mélo composé suivant la formule' (Gaiffe, p.159).

[131] Simon Iraílh, in his *Querelles littéraires* (1761), ii.380, says that Voltaire approved of 'le comique larmoyant' but rejected 'le tragique bourgeois'.

[132] 'Art dramatique', *Questions sur l'Encyclopédie* (M.xvii.420).

[133] *Le Goût de Voltaire* (1967), p.269-72.

rehearsals at Les Délices and performances at Tournay were to culminate in prohibition at the end of 1760 (D.app.199). Voltaire, realising that his insistence, in 1758, that d'Alembert should include in his article 'Genève' support for the establishment of a theatre in Geneva had backfired as a result of Rousseau's intervention, was probably not anxious, at the time of writing the preface to *L'Ecossaise*, to aggravate the authorities further by stating his case. Far better to allow his assertion of the morality and sacerdotal gravity of his comedy to lead on naturally to a quotation from one of the most revered names in the history of ideas and of literature. Montaigne, at least, could not be accused of special pleading or immorality.

Requête à MM. les Parisiens

The death of that mythical personage Jérôme Carré was announced in 1769, in the 'Discours historique et critique' preceding *Les Guèbres*. It is a pity he (and Guillaume Vadé) are no more, said Voltaire regretfully; 'ils auraient peut-être un peu servi à débarbouiller ce siècle' (M.vi.503). There is less *débarbouillage* in the *Requête* than in the *Appel à toutes les nations*, which Carré 'wrote' a few months later. Voltaire's motives in the *Requête* have already been discussed (p.259-61). They are, very briefly, to assert the English origins of the play, to expose Fréron to more ridicule, and to enlist public support for its performance as a counter to the pressures being applied (he believed) in order to prevent the Comédie-Française from putting it on. Maynard (*Voltaire*, ii.350) maintains that it is 'une réponse embarrassée à la lettre de Fréron'. There is a certain embarrassment over the mistake he had made in calling the dramatist and the philosopher Hume brothers, but it stops there. It is hardly a reply to Fréron's article of 3 June – had this been his aim he would certainly have drawn attention to Fréron's strange opinion that characters like Lady Alton should not be represented on stage because they do not do credit to the 'sexe plein de douceur et de charmes' (iv.102); and to Fréron's unwarranted assumption that Freeport is a Quaker (iv.105). Rather than reply to Fréron's criticisms, he satirises a few quirks of his style (only one of which – 'sur le ton' – appears in the article of 3 June). In criticising Fréron for misspelling Hume's name as Home, Voltaire makes a double error, of course: Fréron does not call him Home, but had he done so he would have been correct.

In this *Requête* Voltaire is not concerned with serious matters. The tone and content are facetious. We should note, however, that in reply, as it were, to Fréron's comment that 'ce Drame n'est point une Comédie' (iv.106), Voltaire changes its genre and refers to it as a 'drame anglais', and 'mon petit drame'. So the argument as to whether it is a comedy or not is neatly side-stepped.

Epître dédicatoire

The part played by Louis Félicité de Brancas, comte de Lauraguais, physicist, inventor, 'le plus grand chimiste de France' (D10045) in bringing about a radical change in the history of French theatre is too well known to require a detailed account here. What have to be established are the reasons why Voltaire chose a re-edition of *L'Ecossaise* in 1761 as the occasion for paying homage to him for his generosity, which enabled the Comédie-Française to afford to expel spectators from the stage.

So far as we know, Voltaire first became conscious of Lauraguais's existence in 1755, when the young nobleman was twenty-two years of age. He wrote a flattering letter to Voltaire praising *L'Orphelin de la Chine*, which encouraged the dramatist to think well of him: 'Cultivez de cet esprit là tout ce que vous pourrez', he told Du Marsais, 'c'est un service que vous rendez à la nation' (12 October 1755; D6536). Two years later Voltaire read his two reports on the chemistry of porcelain with interest and admiration (D7310). The young scientist was elected to the Académie des sciences on 19 March 1758 .

In early April 1759, when Voltaire first heard the excellent news that 'les blancs poudrez et les talons rouges ne se mêleront plus avec les Augustes et les Cléopatres', he saw clearly that 'le théâtre de Paris va changer de face'. He went on, in this letter to d'Argental (D8249) to expatiate on the advantages of the freeing of the stage as an acting area in terms which are almost a first draft of the fourth paragraph of the *Epître*: 'Les tragédies ne seront plus des conversations en cinq actes au bout des quelles on aprendra pour la bienséance tragique qu'il y a eu un peu de sang répandu. On voudra de la pompe, du spectacle, du fracas'.[134] You will have something stronger than *Fanime*, he promised him (i.e. *Tancrède*). *Rome sauvée* and *Oreste* could be performed to console and encourage him in the meantime. The theatrical potentialities he envisages all relate to tragedies, both in this letter and in the *Epître*. Why then did he preface a comedy with these thoughts?

The primary – and simpler – reason was that *L'Ecossaise* was the first *new* play by Voltaire to be performed at the Comédie-Française since the relegation of fashionable spectators to the auditorium.[135] By pure coincidence it was the kind of play which benefited greatly from the clearing of the stage, one of the new 'natural' plays in contemporary costume. Previously it had been impossible to distinguish between actors and spectators in modern dress plays. Furthermore, by having the whole of the acting area at their disposal the actors were able to experiment with the use of a curtain to denote the removal of the action from one room to another.[136]

[134] Jérôme Carré makes the point again in his *Appel à toutes les nations*, applauding the demise of declamation.

[135] It was during the Easter recess (1-22 April 1759) that the new seating and *loges* were installed. The chevalier de Mouhy recalls that when the curtain went up on the first night of the new season, 'un applaudissement général et réitéré avec transport partit [...] à l'aspect de la Scène, devenue libre par le retranchement des balustrades' (*Abrégé de l'histoire du Théâtre-Français*, 1780, iii.65-66). According to E.-D. de Manne (*Galerie historique*, p.126) it was Lekain 'qui provoqua la suppression des banquettes'.

[136] Voltaire disapproved of this – see note to the beginning of act 1, scene 1, and above, p.259.

A less obvious, but in fact more cogent reason why Voltaire included Lauraguais in this *recueil* of writings aimed at the *anti-philosophes* is to be found in the count's own relationships with the *philosophes*. The supper-parties and *conciliabules* to which he invited several of them – notably Morellet – twice a week *chez* Sophie Arnould caused him considerable trouble and embarrassment in June 1760, when l'abbé Morellet's virulent satire against Palissot and his protectress, the princesse de Robecq, entitled *La Vision de Charles Palissot* was published. Thiriot reported to Voltaire on the eighteenth of that month (D8988) that the comte de Lauraguais was 'aussi vexé et tourmenté par tous ses parens que les Philosophes le sont par la police et par les ordres de la Cour'.

In taking advantage of the publication of his 'petite bagatelle' in the *Seconde suite des mélanges* (SS61) to dedicate it to this cultivated young man of science and protector of letters, Voltaire was thus saluting not only the liberator of the stage of France's first theatre, but also the enlightened aristocrat who was willing to brave the scowls of his relatives in order to show his sympathy with the *philosophes*.

Avertissement

This imaginary account of the first performance was intended as a corrective to Fréron's *Relation d'une grande bataille*. Its main interest is as an expression of Voltaire's ambiguous attitude towards Fréron and his caricature of him. On the one hand, he takes great pains to stress yet again the smallness and insignificance of Frélon's part in the play (implying that he pays scant attention to the original). On the other hand, his obsessional desire to punish Fréron further, to keep the flame burning, leads him to exaggerate his action to quixotic proportions. In this, his final public word on the *Ecossaise* affair, he brings a historical perspective into play, hoping that posterity will see him as fighting the same external battle against criticasters as Pope. But at the same time, he is destroying his other thesis – that the play's success has nothing to do with Frélon's part in it.

This appeal to an example of high repute was less happy in its effects than the one he made to Montaigne at the end of the *Préface*. For the example of Pope was followed only three years later by Palissot, whose *Dunciade* earned him a period of exile which failed to chasten him. Rightly, Palissot replied (D11926) to Voltaire's suggestion (in D11812) that men of letters should not satirise each other, by saying that if Voltaire himself were to renounce satire, he would have to sacrifice a goodly part of his works – everything that had displeased the Maupertuis, Desfontaines, Frérons, Trublets and so on, of this world. One may regret that Voltaire attacked Fréron in this and other writings. Voltaireans will agree with Mme Du Bocage: 'Il faut rendre justice à Voltaire, il n'attaque pas le premier; mais comme le lion quand il est blessé, il fait sentir sa supériorité'.[137]

6. *Conclusions*

L'Ecossaise was destined to remain in the living theatrical repertory for barely half a century. The reasons why it has failed to transcend the socio-literary circumstances surrounding its composition and initial success are complex. Perhaps its strategic importance in the troubled mid-eighteenth century, when the *philosophes* looked to Voltaire for leadership and took courage from the popularity of *L'Ecossaise*, has led critics and public alike to ignore its dramatic qualities. Voltaire realised full well that if you 'Peignez un faquin, vous ne réussirez qu'auprès de quelques personnes: intéressez, vous plairez à tout le monde'. Was his optimism about the play's intrinsic merits ill-founded? This has been the general view of nineteenth-century criticism, regarding this play and Voltaire's theatre as a whole. But M. Lioure's re-appraisal of Voltaire's place

[137] Quoted in commentary to D9013.

as a precursor of Romantic drama[138] has been ably matched by Mr Yashinsky's more recent re-examination of *L'Ecossaise* (*Studies* 182, p.253-71), in which he attempts to get above and beyond consideration of the play as an *œuvre de circonstance*. As a result, he convincingly rehabilitates it as 'remarkable for its innovations, characterisations, staging, and popularity in eighteenth-century France as well as abroad' (p.253). Briefly, *L'Ecossaise* is closer to English Restoration comedy than anything previously seen at the Comédie-Française;[139] it was the first to use the entire stage space; it gives far more detailed stage directions than was customary; its structure is 'modern' in its lack of explicit exposition (this roused both d'Argental and Fréron to object, since it flouted the classical norm); and it is a demonstration of Voltaire's generally underestimated desire to reform theatrical practice and promulgate mixed genre plays.

All this is well argued and supported by deft studies of the characters: the engaging 'English' gruffness of Freeport, the shockingly emancipated Lady Alton, effectively counterbalanced by the retiring nature of Lindane (who, nevertheless, like Polly, is prevented from becoming *fade* by her courage and forthrightness), and even Frélon himself, a prototype of the villain so dear to melodrama, and endowed with vigour (as Flaubert saw) which comes from his utter devotion to evil and nastiness.

It would need a good deal of courage to undertake a professional revival of *L'Ecossaise* today – but that would be true of almost any other play of this period. We take more pleasure in adaptations of fiction: not *Le Père de famille*, but *Le Neveu de Rameau*; not *Zaïre*, but *Zadig*; not *Le Café ou l'Ecossaise*, but *Candide ou l'optimisme*.

However, if the short extract from *L'Ecossaise* included in the tercentenary programme of the Comédie-Française in 1980 is anything to go by, it could still *passer la rampe*. In showing how

[138] *Le Drame* (Paris 1967).

[139] *Le Comte de Boursoufle* (1735) would merit this award if it had been staged at the Comédie-Française, as it retains much English Restoration flavour from its origins (Vanbrugh's *The Relapse*).

it was integrated into *Simul et singulis: la Comédie-Française racontée par ses comédiens*, we can leave the last word to the great *tripot* itself, as is right and proper:[140]

COLLÉ

Le samedi 26, je fus à la première représentation de 'L'Ecossaise', donnée sous le nom de M. de Voltaire.

Dans cette comédie, comme dans celle des Philosophes, j'ai été indigné de la licence scandaleuse qui s'introduit actuellement, de jouer le citoyen sur le théâtre; de personnifier les gens sur la scène, et d'y voir exposer les gens de lettres comme des bêtes féroces qui combattent pour le divertissement des spectateurs: je ne ris point de cela, j'en gémis. Fréron était à cette représentation, au milieu de l'orchestre.

FRÉRON

Il n'y a dans cette prétendue comédie ni liaison, ni intérêt, ni marche, ni chaleur, ni action.

Monsieur, je passe ma vie au café, j'y compose des brochures, des feuilles: je sers les honnêtes gens. Si vous avez quelque ami à qui vous vouliez donner des éloges, ou quelque ennemi dont on doive dire du mal, quelque auteur à protéger ou à décrier, il n'en coûte qu'une pistole par paragraphe. Si vous voulez faire quelque connaissance utile ou agréable, je suis encore votre homme.

VOLTAIRE

Et vous ne faites point d'autre métier dans la ville?

FRÉRON

Monsieur, c'est un très bon métier.

VOLTAIRE

Et on ne vous a pas encore montré en public, le cou décoré d'un collier de fer de quatre pouces de hauteur?

FRÉRON

Voilà un homme qui n'aime pas la littérature.

140 *Simul et singulis* (Paris 1980), p.182-83.

7. *Manuscripts*

One complete manuscript of the play has survived, and one fragment.

MS1

Le Caffé ou L'Ecossaise. / Comedie / De Monsieur Hume traduite en François / par Monsieur de Voltaire. / Representée par les Comediens François / ordinaires du Roi. / À Paris /

Prompt copy in the hand of Caron Du Chanset with corrections and additions by Delaporte, the *secrétaire-souffleur* (for example, p.86, 'Il appelle, Polly, Polly') and Bouthier Darcourt (for example, p.29, 'à part'); 195 x 273 mm; 30 sheets folded and gathered to form 5 sections each of 12 leaves, paginated 1-118, p.[119-120] blank; sewn and bound in contemporary limp vellum.

Comédie-Française, MS 223.

L'Ecossaise was taken out of the repertory on 12 May 1788, and was revived in 1792-1793 (at the time of Palissot's edition). It seems most likely that this copy was made for this *reprise*, since Bouthier Darcourt assisted Delaporte and Bonneval with the copying of plays from December 1788. On the other hand, Caron could have written it out during his trial period as assistant *secrétaire-souffleur* between 1770 and 1772 (his handwriting was considered insufficiently elegant to justify his permanent employment) – but there is no question of its predating 1770.

The text appears to be based on 60AM (even to the point of wrongly numbering II.v), but other sources were also involved. It is not clear if the manuscript took readings from 71L*, or if this corrected edition was based on the manuscript: many of the passages deleted from 71L* do not appear in MS1 (the reference to Minorca, for example, at I.iii.105-110*v*).

MS2

dans l'ecossaise / acte 2 / scene 2 /

Holograph fragment of II.ii.16-26; 182 x 240 mm; one leaf.

Bn: N 24342, f.49.

44

49

dans l'écossaise

acte 2

Scene 2

lindane/qui peut frapper ainsi et que vois-je

lady alton

connaissez vous les grandes passions mademoiselle?

lindane

helas, madame — voila une étrange question.

ladi alton

connaissez vous lamour véritable? je ne dis pas l'amour insipide, lamour langoureux — mais cet amour — là — qui fait qu'on voudrait empoisoner sa rivale, tuer son amant et se jetter ensuitte par la fenetre?

lindane

mais, cest la rage dont vous me parlez là.

ladi alton

je veux bien que vous sachiez que je n'aime point autrement, que je suis jalouse furieuse implacable.

lindane

tant pis pour vous madame.

ladi alton

répondez moy mylord murray nest il pas venu etc comme dans l'imprimé

6. *L'Ecossaise*: holograph (MS1) of additional lines (II.ii.16-26) first published in W68 and T67 (Bibliothèque nationale, Paris).

This fragment gives a version of the addition first made in W68, and executed by a cancel in T67 (see the critical apparatus). It ends 'n'est-il pas venu etc comme dans l'imprimé'. See figure 6.

8. *Editions*

The textual history of the *Ecossaise* is complex, largely due to the influence of several different stage versions.

The first edition (siglum 60) was published by Cramer, for Voltaire, before the play was performed. It was followed, directly or indirectly, by some 16 editions (60X, 60L1, 60L2, 60L3, 60L4, 60L5, 60CR, 60AV, 60LH, 60S, 61L2, PR62, T62, 64D, T66, 68V and T70). Edition 60CR was then revised, by the insertion of six pages of 'Additions et corrections', to reflect the changes made by Voltaire, and others, for the performances in Paris. This edition was followed by 61L1 and W64R.

An unidentified source lies behind the 'Amsterdam' edition, 60AM, which offers many unique variants, while yet another source, or group of sources, was drawn upon by the publisher of 60Y (an edition followed by 63AV, 65B, 72P2, 75M and 77N).

The second edition produced under Voltaire's control (SS61, volume 5, part 2 of the Cramer *Collection complète* of 1756 and following years) was also printed in 1760, but published in 1761. Its text, which is close to the final version, was followed by 63G, SS64, T64P, SS70 and SS72. The quarto edition (W68) incorporated Voltaire's last substantive revisions, and was followed by a cancel in T67 (the re-issue of T64P) and by 71L, W71, 72P1, W72P, W75G (our base text), W75X, 85P and K. The cancel in T67 also included an exchange between Lady Alton and Fabrice which appears only in one other edition, W70L (I.312-314*v*).

Three copies of the play carry manuscript alterations or additions: 60X*, 60CR* and 71L*.

60

LE CAFFÉ, / OU / L'ECOSSAISE, / *COMEDIE*, / Par Mr. HUME, traduite en / Français. / [*typographic ornament*] / *LONDRES*, / [*thick-thin rule, 46 mm*] / MDCCLX. /

[*half-title*] LE CAFFÉ, / OU / L'ECOSSAISE, / *COMEDIE.* /

12°. sig. A^{12} ($A2 + \chi^6$) B-H^{12} I^6; pag. [*4*] XII [5]-204; $6 signed, arabic (– A1-2, I5-6); page catchwords.

[*1*] half-title; [*2*] blank; [*3*] title; [*4*] Acteurs; [I]-XII Préface; [5]-204 Le Café, ou l'Ecossaise, comédie.

Scenes 6, 7 and 8 of act 2 are misnumbered 5, 6 and 7.

This is in all probability the original edition printed by Cramer in Geneva in April 1760. The 'Grand livre' of the Cramer brothers (Archives d'Etat, Genève: cote Commerce F57) contains these details: '60 *Caffé Comédie* en avril 1760 [...] *Le Caffé ou L'Ecossaise*, 12 sols' (see B. Gagnebin, *Lettres inédites à son imprimeur Gabriel Cramer*, p.xxiv, xxviii).

This edition was reissued in Copenhagen in 1767: see below, edition 67.

Bn: Yf 7212; Br: FS 42A; Bpu: Hf 5014/2; Taylor: V3 C2 1760 (3); Bodleian: G Pamph 100 (3).

60x

LE CAFFÉ, / OU / L'ECOSSAISE, / *COMEDIE.* / Par Mr. HUME, traduite en / Français. / [*typographic ornament*] / *LONDRES*, / [*thick-thin rule, 48 mm*] / MDCCLX. /

[*half-title*] LE CAFFÉ, / OU / L'ECOSSAISE, / *COMEDIE.* /

12°. sig. A^{12} ($A2 + \chi^6$) B-H^{12} I^6; pag. [*4*] *XII* [5]-204 (p.199 numbered '299' in some copies); $6 signed, arabic (– A1-2, I3, I5-6); page catchwords.

[*1*] half-title; [*2*] blank; [*3*] title; [*4*] Acteurs; [*I*]-*XII* Préface; [5]-204 Le Café, ou l'Ecossaisse [*sic*], comédie.

A counterfeit of 60, with the same misnumbering of scenes. It may be distinguished by the mis-spelling of 'L'ECOSSAISSE' on p.5, and by the one textual variant of any significance, at II.328.

Bn: Fb 19508 (in a volume of 26 items related to *Les Philosophes*);

Yf 12315; London Library: 54036; King's College, Cambridge (p.199 misnumbered).

60x*

This is a copy of 60x with numerous manuscript corrections and additions in an unknown hand. Some of the corrections appear to derive from 60CR:AC, others are similar to those found in 60CR*. The effect of the alterations is recorded in the critical apparatus to the present edition.

Bn: Yth 2503 (lacking the preface, and with p.77-110 bound between 140 and 141).

60L1

LE CAFFÉ, / *OU* / L'ÉCOSSAISE, / *COMÉDIE*, / Par M. HUME, traduite en Français. / [*woodcut, motto* 'SERERE NE DUBITES', *68 x 50 mm*] / *LONDRES*. / [*thick-thin rule, 59 mm*] / MDCCLX. /

8°. sig. A-H⁴; pag. [2] IV 3-42 45-62; $1 signed (– A1; C1 signed 'B'); sheet catchwords.

[*1*] title; [2] Acteurs; [I]-IV Préface [3]-42, 45-62 Le Café, ou l'Ecossaise, comédie.

A similar, possibly identical, ornament is found on the title page of *Tancrède*, 1760, 'Paris, Prault' (Taylor: V3 Z3 1772 (3)) and on that of Dancourt's *La Maison de campagne*, 1760, 'Bruxelles, chez Josse de Grieck, Marchand Libraire, proche la Steen-Porte' (Taylor: Vet Fr II B 930). Pierre-Josse De Grieck is recorded as 'éditeur' from 1757 to 1768 in the *Histoire du livre et de l'imprimerie en Belgique* (Bruxelles 1923-1934), iv.40; a Pierre-Joseph De Grieck traded as 'imprimeur' from 25 August 1751 to 1774.

The printer of this edition (which follows the text of 60) also produced 61L2, below.

Arsenal: Rf 14491; Comédie-Française; Bodleian: Vet D5 e 386.

60L2

LE CAFFÉ, / OU / L'ECOSSAISE, / *COMEDIE*, / Par Monf. HUME, / traduite en Français. / [*woodcut*] / [*rule, 66 mm*] / *LONDRES*, / [*rule, 66 mm*] / MDCCLX. /

8°. sig. π^6 A-F^8 G^2; pag. [12] 100; $5 signed, arabic ($\pi$2-4 signed respectively '2', '3' and '4'); page catchwords.

[1] title; [2] blank; [3]-11 Préface; [12] Acteurs; [1]-100 Le Café, ou l'Ecossaise, comédie.

The typographic style of this edition suggests a German or Dutch origin.

Br: FS 43A.

60L3

LE / CAFFÉ, / *OU* / L'ÉCOSSOISE, / *COMÉDIE.* / PAR M. DE VOLTAIRE. / [*rule, 58 mm*] / *Prix* 30 *fols.* / [*rule, 59 mm*] / [*typographic ornament*] / A LONDRES. / [*thick-thin rule, 63 mm*] / *M. DCC. LX.* /

12°. sig. A-E^{12} F^6 (– F6); pag. [xii] 117; $5 signed, roman (– A1, A4, F4-5); sheet catchwords.

[i] title; [ii] blank; iij-xj Préface; [xii] Acteurs; [1]-117 Le Café, ou l'Ecossaise, comédie.

This is one of the earliest editions to carry Voltaire's name on the title-page. The text is that of the first edition, 60.

Bn: Rés. Z Beuchot 126; Br: FS 44A.

60L4

LE CAFFÉ, / *OU* / L'ECOSSAISE, / *COMÉDIE,* / Par Mr. HUME, traduite en français. / [*woodcut, flowers and foliage, 55 x 49 mm*] / *LONDRES.* / [*thick-thin rule, 62 mm*] / M. DCC. LX. /

8°. sig. A-H^4; pag. 64; $2 signed, arabic (– A1); sheet catchwords.

[1] title; [2] Acteurs; 3-64 Le Café, ou l'Ecossaise, comédie.

Another edition based on 60.

Bn: Rés. Z Beuchot 125.

60L5

LE CAFFÉ, / *OU* / L'ÉCOSSAISE, / *COMÉDIE,* / Par M^r. HUME, traduite en Français. / [*typographic ornament*] / *LONDRES.* / [*thick-thin rule, 53 mm*] / M. DCC. LX. /

[*half-title*] LE CAFFÉ, / *OU* / L'ECOSSAISE, / COMÉDIE. /

8°. sig. a⁸ B-E⁸; pag. *viij* 9-79 (folio of p.36 inverted); $3 signed, arabic (sig. a signed roman, – a1-2; a3 signed 'aij', a4 'aiij'); sheet catchwords.

[i] half-title; [ii] blank; [iii] title; [iv] Acteurs; *v-viij* Préface; 9-79 Le Café, ou l'Ecossaise, comédie.

The text follows 60, with the omission of lines 38-45 of the 'Préface' (from 'L'un' to 'des hommes.').

Arsenal: Rf 14490.

60Y

LE CAFFÉ, / *OU* / L'ECOSSAISE, / *COMÉDIE*, / PAR Mr. HUME PRETRE ECOSSAIS, / *Traduite en Français par JEROME CARRE'*, / Nouvelle Edition avec des Additions & des Corrections, / & telle qu'on doit la donner au Théatre de la / Comédie Françaiſe à Paris. / [*woodcut, 42 x 33 mm*] / *LONDRES*, / [*thick-thin rule, 48 mm*] / M. DCC. LX. /

8°. sig. A-I⁴; pag. VI 66; $2 signed, roman (– A1, I2); sheet catchwords.

[I] title; [II] Acteurs; III-VI Préface; 1-66 Le Café, ou l'Ecossaise, comédie.

Sheets H and I are set in smaller type.

The text of this edition is enigmatic, and may well be correctly described as 'telle qu'on *doit* la donner', a formula that suggests access to manuscripts (or marked-up editions) in use at the Comédie-Française. It is difficult to determine what part Voltaire may have played in its publication, if any, and to what extent it follows or precedes 60CR:AC. The textual tradition it established (including the Jérôme Carré formula on the title-page) was followed by 63AV, 65B, 72P2, 75M, 77N, 77P and 80P (Voltaire's name replacing that of Carré in the last two).

Bn: Rés. Z Beuchot 127; Taylor: V3 C2 1760 (2); Bibliothèque municipale, Grenoble: E29525.

60CR and 60CR:AC

[*first state*] LE CAFFÉ, / OU / L'ECOSSAISE, / *COMÉDIE*, / Par Mr. HUME, traduite en / Français par Mr. DE VOLTAIRE. / *Nouvelle Edition*. / [*rule, 65 mm*] / Le prix eſt de 30 ſols. / [*rule, 64 mm*] / [*typographic ornament*] / LONDRES. / [*thick-thin rule, 44 mm*] / M. DCC. LX. /

[*second state*] LE CAFFÉ, / *OU* / L'ECOSSAISE, / *COMÉDIE.* / EN CINQ ACTES. / Par Mr. HUME, traduite en / Français / *Par M.* DE *VOLTAIRE.* / Réprésentée pour la premiere fois par les / Comédiens Français ordinaires du Roi, / le 26 Juillet 1760. / *Nouvelle édition, à laquelle on a joint / par ſupplément les corrections & aug- / mentations faites aux Répréſentations.* / [*rule, 52 mm*] / Le prix eſt de 30. ſols. / [*rule, 52 mm*] / [*typographic ornament*] / *A GENEVE*, / Chez les Freres CRAMER. / [*thick-thin rule, 58 mm*] / M. DCC LX./

12°. A12 (± A1, ± π^4) B-E12; pag. first state, XII 108 (p.IV numbered 'iv'); pag. second state, viij [III]-XII 108 (p.iii numbered 'v', p.IV 'iv'); $6 signed, roman (– A1; A7 signed 'Aij'); sheet catchwords.

First state: [I] title; [II] Acteurs; [III]-XII Préface; [1]-108 Le Café, ou l'Ecossaise, comédie.

Second state: [i] title; [ii] Acteurs [named]; [iii]-viij Additions et corrections; [III]-XII Préface; [1]-108 Le Café, ou l'Ecossaise, comédie.

The second state differs from the first in the cancellation of the original title leaf and its replacement by an unsigned, octavo gathering of four leaves, printed on different paper in a different typographic style. This gathering contains the new title, a list of named actors, and the 'Additions et corrections' derived from the changes made for the performances in July 1760. The latter are designated in the critical apparatus to the present edition by the siglum 60CR:AC.

The catchword on p.viij appears variously as 'PRE'FACE' (Z Bengesco 973, Z Beuchot 123, Br) and 'FRE'FACE' (Yth 2495, Z Bengesco 81).

The reference to p.177 on p.vij of the 'Additions et corrections' should be to p.95: p.177 is the relevant page of 60 and 60X.

The text of this edition (leaving aside the 'Additions et corrections') follows that of 60, with minor variants at II.244 and V.35-36.

Taylor: V3 C2 1760 (1) (first state); Leningrad: BV, no.3498, 11-140 (see 60CR* below); Bn: Yth 2495, Rés. Z Bengesco 81, Rés. Z Bengesco 973, Rés. Z Beuchot 123; Arsenal: Rf 14493; Br FS 45A.

60CR*

The copy of 60CR in Voltaire's library passed through the hands of Joannes de Roqueville, and contains his handwritten corrections in the margins (derived partly from the 'Additions et corrections') and a slip pasted on p.12. No doubt de Roqueville is the actor who played the father in Voltaire's *Tancrède* in August 1761 (see D9945 and Max Fuchs, *Lexique des troupes de comédiens au XVIIIe siècle*, Paris 1944, p.180).

Leningrad: BV, no.3498, 11-140.

60AM

L'ECOSSAISE, / *OU* / LE CAFFE', / *COMEDIE*, / En cinq Actes & en Profe. / *De M. HUME*. / Traduite en Français / *Par M.* DE *VOLTAIRE*. / DERNIERE ÉDITION, / Telle qu'elle a été repréfentée pour la / premiére fois par les Comédiens Français, / ordinaires du Roi, le 26 Juillet 1760. / [*rule, 49 mm*] / Le prix eft de trente fols. / [*rule, 48 mm*] / [*typographic ornament*] / A AMSTERDAM, / [*thick-thin rule, 44 mm*] / M. DCCLX. /

12°. sig. A^{12} B^{12} (± B4) C-E^{12}; pag. [xii] 108 (p.vi numbered '6', vii '7', 71 '77'); $6 signed, roman (– A1); sheet catchwords.

[i] title; [ii] blank; [iii]-xi Préface; [xii] Acteurs; [1]-108 L'Ecossaise, comédie.

This was the first edition to invert the titles of the play (Voltaire always referred to it as *L'Ecossaise* in correspondence). It incorporates all the amendments listed in 60CR, and even follows the same pagination as 60CR. For this reason, Beuchot used it (but not exclusively) as his base text. It contains other variations of text (in comparison with 60, SS61 and W75G) which cannot be explained. One reason for doubting its Voltairean authenticity is that it prints 'WASP' for 'FRÉLON', to which Voltaire would not have agreed, but the cancellation of B4 introduces the variant at I.245-251, to which Voltaire was party (see D8933).

Bn: 8° Yth 5710 (uncancelled), Rés. Z Beuchot 234 (cancelled).

60AV

LE CAFFÉ, / *OU* / L'ÉCOSSAISE, / *COMÉDIE*. / Par M. HUME, traduite en Français par / M. de VOLTAIRE. / [*typographic ornament*] / A AVIGNON, / Chez *LOUIS CHAMBEAU*, Imprimeur-Libraire, / près les R. R. P. P. Jéfuites. / [*triple rule, 40 mm*] / M. DCC. LX. /

8°. sig. A-G^4; pag. 55; $2 signed, arabic (–A1, E2; G2 signed 'G3'); sheet catchwords.

[1] title; [2] Acteurs; [3]-55 Le Café, ou l'Ecossaise, comédie.

The text follows that of 60, but corrects the misnumbering of the scenes.

Bn: 8° Yk 1048.

60LH

LE CAFFÉ, / OU / L'ECOSSAISE, / *COMEDIE*, / Par Mr. HUME, traduite en / Français. / [*rule, 67 mm*] / Prix 12 sols. / [*rule, 65 mm*] / [*woodcut, three cherubs on a cloud, 56 x 41 mm*] / *A LA HAYE*, / Chez H. CONSTAPEL, Libraire. / MDCCLX. /

8°. sig. A-G⁸; pag. 112 (p.15 numbered '51'); $5 signed, arabic (– A1); page catchwords.

[1] title; [2] Acteurs; [3]-10 Préface; [11]-112 Le Café, ou l'Ecossaise, comédie.

Also issued with separate La Haye editions of *L'Yvrogne corrigé* (1760), *Momus exilé* (1758) and *Les Magots, parodie de l'Orphelin de la Chine* (1758) under a collective title: NOUVEAU / THEATRE / DE LA / HAYE. / TOME SIXIEME, & *dernier.* / *Contenant des Piéces mêlées d'Arriettes,* & / *autres.* / [*intaglio device, plate size 58 x 46 mm*] / *A LA HAYE*, / Chez H. CONSTAPEL, Libraire. / *M. DCC. LXI.* / [*lines 2, 4, 8 and 10 in red*]. This title (verso blank), is followed by a leaf for the list of contents, 'Pieces contenue dans le tome sixieme, & dernier' (verso blank).

This edition was kindly drawn to our attention by M. Jean-Daniel Candaux.

Arsenal: Rec 31 VI (31); Stockholm: Litt. fr. dram. saml. ex. A.

60S

LE CAFFÉ, / OU / L'ECOSSAISE, / *COMEDIE*, / Par Mr. *Hume*, traduite en / François. / Par Mr. DE VOLTAIRE. / [*typographic ornament*] / à STOCKHOLM, / [*rule, 78 mm*] / Chez CHARLES THÉOPHILE ULFF, / Marchand Libraire dans la Grande Rue Neuve. / MDCCLX. /

8°. sig. A⁸ (– A5 + χ^2) B-F⁸; pag. 8 [*4*] [11]-95 [96]; $5 signed, arabic (– A1); page catchwords.

[1] title; [2] blank; [3]-8 Préface; [*1-3*] Avertissement de l'éditeur de cette nouvelle édition; [*4*] Acteurs; [11]-95 Le Café, ou l'Ecossaise, comédie; [96] Fautes à corriger; [imprint] 'à STOCKHOLM, / IMPRIMÉ CHEZ PIERRE HESSELBERG. / 1760.'

The 'Avertissement', composed by or for Ulff, justifies the publication of a Stockholm edition of the *Ecossaise* ('Tout ce qui sort de la plume de Mr. de Voltaire, porte une empreinte du vrai beau & du talent décidé, contre laquelle les envieux se déchaineront vainement') and promises the production of an edition of *Tancrède*.

Stockholm: Litt. fr. 1700-1829; Uppsala: Litt. romansk.

60V

An edition catalogued as 'L'écossaise. Comédie par Mr. Hume traduite en françois. Vienne en Autriche, impr. de Ghelen, 1760, cm. 17.5, pp.120' is held by the Biblioteca nazionale of Naples, but has been inaccessible since the 1980 earthquake. For another Ghelen edition, see below, 68V.

SS61

SECONDE SUITE / DES / MELANGES / DE / LITTERATURE, / D'HISTOIRE, / DE PHILOSOPHIE &c. / [*woodcut, inverted, theatrical emblems with manacles, 79 x 48 mm*] / [*thick-thin rule, 55 mm*] / *MDCCLXI.* / [*lines 3, 5, 7 and thick-thin rule in red*]

[*half-title*] COLLECTION / COMPLETTE / DES / ŒUVRES / *de Mr. de* .... / TOME CINQUIEME. / *SECONDE PARTIE.* /

8°. sig. π^2 A-Cc^8 Dd^2 Ee-Ff^8 (± Bb1; Ff8 is blank); pag. [*4*] 449; $4 signed, arabic (– Dd2); no direction line; page catchwords.

[*1*] half-title; [*2*] blank; [*3*] title; [*4*] blank; [1]-6 Epître dédicatoire du traducteur de l'Ecossaise, à monsieur le comte de Lauraguais; [7]-10 A messieurs les Parisiens; 11-14 Avertissement; [15]-20 Préface; [21] B3*r* 'LE CAFFÉ, / OU / L'ECOSSAISE, / *COMEDIE*, / Par Monſieur HUME, / *Traduite en Français par Jérôme Carré,* / Repréſentée à Paris au mois d'Août 1760. / *NOUVELLE EDITION* / corrigée & augmentée. / [*rule, 77 mm*] *J'ai vengé l'Univers autant que je l'ai pû.* / [*rule, 76 mm*] / B3 *AC-*'; [22] Acteurs; [23]-130 Le Café, ou l'Ecossaise, comédie; [131]-418 other texts; 419-420 Table des pièces contenues dans ce volume; [421] Ee1*r* 'SUPPLEMENT / A LA / *SECONDE SUITE* / DES / MELANGES / DE / LITTERATURE, &c. / Ee'; [422] blank; [423]-437 Le Pauvre diable; [438]-441 La Vanité; 442-448 Le Russe à Paris; 449 Table des pièces contenues dans ce supplément.

It is no doubt to this edition that Voltaire's letter to Cramer of 3

September 1760 refers: 'Voicy L'Ecossaise; il faut commencer par imprimer L'Epitre dédicatoire; ensuitte la Lettre de Jerôme Carré aux Parisiens, que Monsieur Cramer doit avoir dans le petit recueil que je n'ai point, parce que le relieur ne me l'a pas encor rendu' (D9187). According to B. Gagnebin (*Lettres inédites à son imprimeur Gabriel Cramer*, p.49) the *Seconde suite*, 'datée de 1761', was 'en grande partie imprimée en 1760'. This is the first edition containing the 'Epître', 'A MM. les Parisiens' and the 'Avertissement', and was designed to supplement the Cramer *Collection complète* of 1756 or 1757. Reprints appeared in 1764, 1770 and 1772 (see below).

This edition differs from the final text (W75G) at I.46b, II.16a-26, III.40-41, 79b and IV.3a.

Bn: Z 27377*bis* (5,II.1), 8° Z 10397 (lacks π1, half-title); BL: 12238 e 5 (lacks π1).

61L1

LE / CAFFÉ / *OU* / L'ÉCOSSAISE, / *COMÉDIE.* / Par Mr. HUME, traduite en Français. / *Repréſentée pour la premiere fois par les Comédiens / Français ordinaires du Roi, le 26 Juillet* 1760. / [*intaglio portrait of Voltaire*] / A LONDRES. / [*thick-thin rule, 51 mm*] / *M. DCC. LXI.* /

[*half-title*] LE CAFFÉ / *OU* / L'ÉCOSSAISE, / *COMÉDIE.* /

8°. sig. *⁸ A-G⁸ (– G7-8); pag. [xvi] 107; $4 signed, arabic (– *1-2); sheet catchwords.

[i] half-title; [ii] blank; [iii] title; [iv] blank; [v]-xj Préface; [xii]-xv Avis au lecteur (with additions and corrections as in 60CR); [xvi] Acteurs (named); [1]-107 Le Café, ou l'Ecossaise, comédie.

The text is similar to that of 60CR.

Bn: Rés. Z Beuchot 128, Yth 2502; Taylor: V3 A2 1764 (27); Toronto: Volt V65 C344 1761.

61L2

LE CAFFÉ, / *OU* / L'ÉCOSSAISE, / *COMÉDIE,* / Par M. HUME, traduite en Français. / [*woodcut, motto* 'SERERE NE DUBITES', *68 x 50 mm*] / *LONDRES.* / [*double rule, 59 mm*] / MDCCLXI. /

8°. sig. A-H⁴; pag. 64 (p.32 numbered '22', 57 '75'); $1 signed (– A1); sheet catchwords.

[*1*] title; [*2*] Acteurs; [I]-IV Préface; [7]-64 Le Café ou l'Ecossaise, comédie.

Produced by the same printer as 60L1 and using the same woodcuts on p.IV and p.[7]; the type was re-set between the two editions.

ImV: D Ecossaise 1761/1; Bibliothèque municipale, La Rochelle; Austin: PQ 2077 C2 1761 HRC.

PR62

QUATRIEME RECUEIL / DE / NOUVELLES PIECES / FUGITI-VES / DE / MR. DE VOLTAIRE. / [*typographic ornament*] / *À GENEVE, / ET SE TROUVE À PARIS, /* CHEZ *DUCHESNE* RUE S. JACQUES / *AU TEMPLE DU GOUT.* / [*thick-thin rule, 74 mm*] / *M DCC LXII.* /

8°. sig. A-H^8 I^1; pag. CXXX; \$5 signed, arabic (– A1, D5; B4 signed 'A4'); page catchwords.

[i] title; [ii] blank; [iii] A2*r* '*LE CAFFÉ, / OU / L'ECOSSAISE, / COME-DIE. / Par Mr. HUME, traduite en Français.* / A2'; [iv] Acteurs; V-X Préface; XI-CX Le Café, ou l'Ecossaise, comédie; [cxi] G8*r* '*TRÉS HUMBLE / REQUÊTE / A / MESSIEURS LES PARISIENS.*'; [cxii] blank; CXIII-CXVI A messieurs les Parisiens; [cxvii]-CXXVIII Prédiction sur la Nouvelle Heloïse roman de J. J. Rousseau; CXXIX Table des pièces contenues dans ce volume; CXXIX-CXXX Avertissement.

The text is close to that of 60.

Taylor: V2 1762 (4).

T62 (1763)

[*within ornamented border*] / *SUITE* / DU / THÉATRE / DE / M. DE VOL-TAIRE. / *NOUVELLE ÉDITION*, / Qui contient un Recuëil complet de toutes / les Pièces de Théatre que l'Auteur a / données jusqu'ici. / TOME CINQUIÉME. / [*woodcut, basket of flowers within cartouche, 26 x 20 mm*] / *A AMSTERDAM*, / Chez FRANÇOIS-CANUT RICHOFF, / près le Comptoir de Cologne. / [*thick-thin rule, 54 mm*] / M. DCC. LXIII. /

8°. sig. π^2 A-O^8 P^2 Q-S^8; pag. [*4*] 276 (p.176 numbered '276', 124 '224'); \$4 signed, arabic; sheet catchwords (– P).

[*1*] title; [*2*] blank; [*3*] Table; [*4*] blank; [1]-140 other texts; [141] I7*r* 'LE CAFFÉ, / OU / L'ECOSSAISE, / *COMEDIE.*'; [142] Acteurs; 143-148

Préface; 149-228 Le Café, ou l'Ecossaise, comédie; [229]-276 La Femme qui a raison.

La Femme qui a raison (sheets Q-S) does not appear in the 'Table', is not preceded by a catchword and was probably added as an after-thought.

The text of *L'Ecossaise* follows that of 60.

Bn: Rés. Z Bengesco 123 (5).

63G

L'ÉCOSSAISE, / *OU* / LE CAFFÉ, / *COMÉDIE* / EN CINQ ACTES / ET EN PROSE; / *Telle qu'elle a été repréſentée par les Comédiens / Français Ordinaires du Roi, le 26 Juillet 1760.* / Traduite de l'Anglais de M. HUME. / Par M. DE VOLTAIRE. / NOUVELLE ÉDITION. / J'ai vengé l'Univers autant que je l'ai pû. / [*thick-thin rule, 70 mm*] / Le prix eſt de 30 ſols. / [*thick-thin rule, 70 mm*] / [*typographic ornament*] A GENEVE, / Chez les Freres CRAMER. / [*double rule, 55 mm*] / M. DCC. LXIII. /

12°. sig. A-E^{12}; pag. 120; $6 signed, arabic (– A1); direction line, sigs B-D '*Tome V.*'.

[1] title; [2] blank; 3-8 Epître dédicatoire du traducteur de l'Ecossaise, à monsieur le comte de Lauraguais; 9-16 A messieurs les Parisiens; 17-20 Avertissement; 21-28 Préface; [29] B3*r* 'L'ECOSSAISE, / *OU* / LE CAFFÉ; / *COMÉDIE.* / EN CINQ ACTES, / ET EN PROSE. / B3'; 30 Acteurs; 31-120 L'Ecossaise, ou le café, comédie.

This is not a separate edition, but an issue of T64P, using sheets printed at the same time (in 1763); the title-page (section title in T64P) differs only in the addition of the imprint and date, while the indication '*Tome V.*', proper to T64P, remains in the direction line of signatures B, C and D of 63G. The various issues of T64P ignore many of the additions and corrections printed in 60CR:AC and the text of *L'Ecossaise* is close to that of SS61, except for the addition of a number of stage directions in the first three acts.

Bn: Rés. Z Beuchot 235, Rés. Z Bengesco 83; Arsenal: GD 23153; Austin: PQ 2077 C2 1763 HRC.

63AV

LE CAFFÉ, / *OU* / L'ÉCOSSAISE, / *COMÉDIE.* / PAR MR. HUME PRÊTRE ÉCOSSAIS, / *Traduit en François par JEROME CARRÉ,* / Nouvelle Édition avec des Additions & des Correc- / tions, & telle qu'on doit la donner au Théatre / de la Comédie Françoise, à Paris. / [*woodcut, roses and foliage, 60 x 53 mm*] / A AVIGNON, / Chez *Louis Chambeau*, Imprimeur-Libraire, / près les RR. PP. Jésuites. / [*triple rule, 50 mm*] / M. DCC. LXIII. /

8°. sig. A-G[4] (G4 blank); pag. 54; $2 signed, arabic (– A1, G2; the 'G' on G1 inverted); sheet catchwords.

[1] title; [2] Acteurs; [3]-54 Le Café, ou l'Ecossaise, comédie.

The woodcut on the title is found also in an Avignon 1766 *Adélaïde Du Guesclin* (siglum 66A).

This edition is based upon 60Y.

ImV: D Ecossaise 1763/1; Toronto: Volt pam V65 C344 1763; Austin: PQ 2077 C2 1763b HRC (G4 present).

64D

LE / CAFFE / OU / L'ECOSSAISE, / *COMEDIE* / PAR / Mons. HUME, / TRADUITE EN FRANÇOIS. / Représentée par les Comédiens françois de / la Cour sur le nouveau Théatre de S. A. / Electorale de Saxe, à Dresde. / [*woodcut, cherub with book and wreath above cartouche, 50 x 32 mm*] / [*rule, 76 mm*] / *Avec l'Approbation de la Cour.* / [*rule, 78 mm*] / Dans la Librairie de Gröll. / 1764. /

[*half-title*] LE CAFFE / OU / L'ÉCOSSAISE, / *COMEDIE.* /

8°. sig. a-f[8]; pag. 95; $5 signed, roman (– a1-2); page catchwords.

[1] half-title; [2] blank; [3] title; [4] Acteurs; [5]-95 Le Café, ou l'Ecossaise, comédie.

The text is close to that of 60, except that the 'Acteurs' are given as in the first state of 60CR.

Bn: Musique Th. 504; Stockholm: Litt. fr. dram. pjes.

SS64

SECONDE SUITE / DES / MÉLANGES / DE / LITTÉRATURE, / D'HISTOIRE, / DE PHILOSOPHIE &c. / [*woodcut, as* SS61, *but not inverted*] / [*thick-thin rule, 56 mm*] / *MDCCLXIV.* /

[*half-title*] COLLECTION / COMPLETTE / DES / ŒUVRES / *de Mr. de .... / DERNIERE EDITION. / TOME CINQUIEME,* / *Seconde partie.* /

8°. sig. A-Cc^{8} Dd^{4}; pag. 423 [424]; $4 signed, arabic (– A1-2, Dd3-4); direction line '*Seconde Suite des Mélanges &c.*'; page catchwords.

[1] half-title; [2] blank; [3] title; [4] blank; [5]-8 Epître dédicatoire du traducteur de l'Ecossaise à monsieur le comte de Lauraguais; [9]-12 A messieurs les Parisiens; 13-16 Avertissement; [17]-22 Préface; [23] B4*r* 'LE CAFFE, / OU / L'ECOSSAISE, / *COMÉDIE*, / Par Monſieur HUME; / *Traduite en Français par Jérôme Carré*; / Repréſentée à Paris au mois d'Août 1760. / *NOUVELLE EDITION* / corrigée & augmentée. / [*rule, 75 mm*] / *J'ai vengé l'univers autant que je l'ai pû.* / [*rule, 74 mm*] / B4 *AC-*'; [24] Acteurs; [25]-121 Le Café, ou l'Ecossaise, comédie; [122]-423 other texts; [424] Table des pièces contenues dans ce volume.

A Cramer reprint of the 1761 *Seconde suite*, SS61.

ImV: 6063*bis*.

T64A

[*within ornamented border*] / *SUITE* / DU / THEATRE / DE / M. DE VOLTAIRE. / *NOUVELLE EDITION*. / Qui contient un Recuëil complet de toutes / les Piéces de Théâtre que l'Auteur a / données juſqu'ici. / TOME CINQUIÉME. / [*woodcut, cupid in cartouche, 34 x 25 mm*] / *A AMSTERDAM*, / Chez FRANÇOIS-CANUT RICHOFF, / près le Comptoir de Cologne. / [*thick-thin rule, 52 mm*] / M. DCC. LXIV. /

12°. sig. a^{2} A-Aa^{8,4} Bb^{4}; pag. [*4*] 238 [*2*] [239]-291 [292-293]; $4,2 signed, arabic (– Bb2; a2 signed 'aij', Bb4 signed 'aij'); direction line '*Théâtre. Tome V.*'; sheet catchwords (– V4*v*).

[*1*] title; [*2*] blank; [*3*] Table des ouvrages dramatiques contenus en ce volume: avec les pièces qui sont rélatives à chacun (excludes *La Femme qui a raison*); [*4*] blank; [1]-149 other texts; [150] blank; [151] N4*r* 'LE CAFFÉ, / OU / L'ECOSSAISE, / *COMÉDIE*. / N4'; [152] blank; 153-157 Préface; [158] Acteurs; 159-238 Le Café, ou l'Ecossaise, comédie; [*1-2*] blank; [239] X1*r* 'LA / *FEMME* / QUI A RAISON, / *COMEDIE*. / EN TROIS ACTES, EN VERS. / *Donnée ſur le Théâtre de Caronge, / près Genève. / Théâtre. Tome I.* X'; [240] blank; 241-291 La Femme qui a raison, comédie; [292] blank; [293] Table des ouvrages dramatiques contenus en ce volume: avec les pièces qui sont rélatives à chacun (includes *La Femme qui a raison*).

La Femme qui a raison (sheets X-Bb) does not appear in the first 'Table' and was clearly added as an after-thought. The 'Table' on Bb4 was intended to replace that on a2, and the blank at V8 should have been removed.

BL: 11735 aa 1 (5).

T64P

ŒUVRES / *DE* / THÉATRE / *DE* / M. DE VOLTAIRE, / *De l'Académie Françaiſe, de celle de Berlin,* / *& de la Société Royale de Londres, &c.* / TOME CINQUIEME. / [*woodcut, lyre and trumpets, 24 x 20 mm*] / A PARIS, / Chez DUCHESNE, Libraire, rue Saint Jacques, / au-deſſous de la Fontaine Saint Benoît, / au Temple du Goût. / [*thick-thin rule, 47 mm*] / M. DCC. LXIV. / *Avec Approbation & Privilége du Roi.* / [*lines 1, 3, 5, 8, 9 and 13 in red*]

[*half-title*] THÉATRE / *DE* / M. DE VOLTAIRE. / *TOME V.* /

12°. sig. π^2 $1\pi^1$ A-I^{12} a^4 K-Q^{12} R^6 S-V^{12}; pag. [*6*] 216 viij [217]-396 [337]-400 [401-406]; signed $6 arabic; direction line '*Tome V.*'; sheet catchwords.

[*1*] half-title; [*2*] blank; [*3*] title; [*4*] blank; [*5*] Table des pièces contenues dans ce cinquième et dernier volume; [*6*] blank, but for catchword 'L'ÉCOSSAISE'; [1] A1*r* 'L'ÉCOSSAISE, / *OU* / LE CAFFÉ, / *COMÉDIE* / EN CINQ ACTES / ET EN PROSE; / *Telle qu'elle a été repréſentée par les Comédiens* / *Français Ordinaires du Roi, le 26 Juillet 1760.* / Traduite de l'Anglais de M. HUME. / Par M. DE VOLTAIRE. / NOUVELLE ÉDITION. / [*thick-thin rule, 70 mm*] / J'ai vengé l'Univers autant que je l'ai pû. / [*thin-thick rule, 70 mm*] / *Tome V.* A'; [2] blank; [3]-8 Epître dédicatoire du traducteur de l'Ecossaise, à monsieur le comte de Lauraguais; 9-16 A messieurs les Parisiens; 17-20 Avertissement; 21-28 Préface; [29] B3*r* 'L'ECOSSAISE, / *OU* / LE CAFFÉ; / *COMÉDIE.* / EN CINQ ACTES, / ET EN PROSE. / B3'; [30] Acteurs; [31]-120 L'Ecossaise, ou le café, comédie; [121]-216, [i]-viij, [217]-396, [337]-[406] other texts.

The complexities of this edition are beyond the scope of the present study, but see 63G above and T67 below.

Bn: Yf 4256.

W64R

COLLECTION / *COMPLETE* / DES ŒUVRES / *de Monsieur* / DE VOLTAIRE, / NOUVELLE ÉDITION, / *Augmentée de ſes dernieres Pieces de*

Théâtre, / *& enrichie de 61 Figures en taille-douce.* / TOME DIX-HUITIEME. / [*typographic ornament*] / *A AMSTERDAM*, / AUX DÉPENS DE LA COMPAGNIE. / [*thick-thin rule, 48 mm*] / M. DCC. LXIV. /

12°. sig. π^2 A-G^{12} H^6 I-R^{12} (– R8-12); pag. [2] 386 (p.47 numbered '74', 300 '260'); $6 signed, arabic (– A1, H4-6, M3; A2 signed 'A', A3 'A2', A4 'A3', A5 'A4', A6 'A5'); direction line '*Tome XVIII.*'; sheet catchwords (– H).

[*1*] title; [*2*] blank; [1]-168 other texts; [169] H1*r* 'LE CAFFÉ / *ou* / L'ECOSSAISE, / *COMÉDIE.* / *Tome XVIII.* H'; [170] blank; [171]-176 Préface; 177-179 Avis au lecteur (with additions and corrections as in 60CR); 180 Acteurs; [181]-250 Le Café ou l'Ecossaise, comédie; [251]-386 other texts.

The text follows 61L1.

Bn: Rés. Z Beuchot 26 (18,i).

65B

LE CAFFE, / *OU* / L'ÉCOSSOISE, / *COMÉDIE.* / PAR M. HUME, PRÊTRE ÉCOSSOIS, / *Traduite en François par JEROME CARRÉ.* / Nouvelle édition avec des additions & des corrections, / & telle qu'on doit la donner au Théâtre de la / Comédie Françoiſe à Paris. / [*typographic ornament*] / *A BESANÇON*, / Chez FANTET, Libraire, plus haut que / la Place Saint Pierre. / [*rule composed of three elements, 49 mm*] / M. DCC. LXV. / *AVEC PERMISSION.* /

8°. sig. A-G^4 H^2; pag. 60; $2 signed, arabic; sheet catchwords.

Contents: [1] title; [2] Acteurs; [3]-60 Le Café, ou l'Ecossaise, comédie.

Based upon 60Y.

Bn: Rés. Z Beuchot 129.

T66

[*within ornamented border*] LE / THEATRE / DE / M. DE VOLTAIRE. / *NOUVELLE ÉDITION.* / Qui contient un Recueil complet de toutes / les Piéces de Théâtre que l'Auteur a / données juſqu'ici. / TOME SIXIEME. / [*woodcut, bracket, foliage and basket, 30 x 25 mm*] / *A AMSTERDAM*, / Chez FRANÇOIS-CANUT RICHOFF, / près le Comptoir de Cologne. / [*thick-thin rule, 43 mm*] / M. DCC. LXVI. /

12°. sig. π² *a*⁴ *A-F*¹² G-H¹² I⁸; pag. [*4*] [viii] 208; $6 signed, arabic (– *a*3-4; D1-3 signed '*C*', '*C2*', '*C3*'; E1-6 signed '*D*', '*D2*', '*D3*', '*D4*', '*D5*', '*D6*'); direction line sig. G '*Théâtre. Tome V.*'; sigs H and I '*Théâtre. Tome VI.*'; sheet catchwords.

[*1-2*] blank; [*3*] title; [*4*] blank; [i-viii] 1-45 Socrate, tragédie; [46] blank; [47] *B12r* 'LE CAFFÉ, / *OU* / L'ÉCOSSAISE, / *COMÉDIE.*'; [48] blank, but for the catchword '*PRÉFACE.*'; 49-56 Préface; [57] blank, but for signature '*C5*'; [58] Acteurs; 59-144 Le Café, ou l'Ecossaise, comédie; [145]-207 Zulime, tragédie; 208 Table des pièces contenues dans ce sixième volume.

The text of this edition is closely based upon 60CR.

University of Aberdeen Library: MH 84256 T (6).

67

LE CAFFÉ, / *OU* / L'ÉCOSSAISE, / *COMEDIE*, / PAR MONSIEUR HUME. / *TRADUITE DE L'ANGLAIS*, / PAR MR. DE VOLTAIRE. / *Repréſentée ſur le Théâtre de la Cour, par les* / *Comédiens François ordinaires du Roi, le 7* / *Nov.* 1767. / [*woodcut, fruit and foliage, 41 x 23 mm*] / [*double rule, 81 mm* / *Se trouve* / *A COPENHAGUE*, / Chez CL. PHILIBERT, / Imprimeur-Libraire. / [*rule, 82 mm*] / M. DCC. LXVII. /

This is a re-issue of the first edition of the play (60), with a new title leaf, and constitutes unique evidence of the transfer of the greater part of Cramer's stock to Claude Philibert in 1767 (see John R. Kleinschmidt, *Les Imprimeurs et libraires de la république de Genève, 1700-1798*, Genève 1948, p.93).

The verso of the title, 'Acteurs', gives the names of those involved in the Copenhagen performances.

Stockholm: Litt. fr. dram. pjes.

T67

ŒUVRES / *DE THEATRE* / DE / M. DE VOLTAIRE, / Gentilhomme Ordinaire du Roi, de / l'Académie Françaiſe, / &c. &c. / *NOUVELLE ÉDITION*, / *Revûe & corrigée exactement ſur l'Édition* / *de Genève in-4°.* / TOME CINQUIÈME. / [*typographic ornament*] / *A PARIS*, / Chez la Veuve DUCHESNE, Libraire, rue Saint- / Jacques, au-deſſous de la Fontaine

Saint- / Benoît, au Temple du Goût. / [*thick-thin rule, 52 mm*] / M. DCC. LXVII./

12°. sig. π^2 A-B^{12} C^{12} (± C1,2) D-H^{12} I^{12} (– I11,12) K-V^{12} $^{\pi}$S-$^{\pi}$V^{12}; pag. [*4*] 212 [*3*] 220-479 [*3*] 339-400 [401-406]; $6 signed, arabic; direction line '*Tome V*'; sheet catchwords.

[*1*] title; [*2*] blank; [*3*] Table des pièces contenues dans ce cinquième volume; [*4*] Errata de ce cinquième volume; [1]-120 contents as T64P; [121]-[406] other texts.

This edition is a reissue of T64P (and, in the case of *L'Ecossaise*, of 63G also), using the same sheets. Some leaves were cancelled, however, some sheets reprinted, and an errata added, in order to fulfil the promise of the title, 'revue et corrigée exactement'. Changes in *L'Ecossaise* are limited to the cancel in sig. C, which incorporates a reading from the quarto edition at II.16a-26, and a variant to I.312-314 which is found only in this edition and in W70L.

Bn: Rés. Yf 3391.

68V

L'ECOSSAISE, / COMÉDIE / *PAR MR. HUME*, / TRADUITE EN FRANÇOIS. / [*typographic ornament*] / *A VIENNE*, / DE L'IMPRIMERIE DES DE GHÉLEN. / [*ornamented rule, 49 mm*] / MDCCLXVIII. /

8°. sig. A-E^8 F^6; pag. 89; $5 signed, arabic (– F4); sheet catchwords.

[1] title; [2] Acteurs; [3]-89 L'Ecossaise, comédie.

Quérard, *Supercheries* (1870), ii.319 cites a related, and perhaps the same edition: 'Vienne (en Autriche) de l'impr. de J.-Th. Trattern, 1768, in 8.'

This edition follows 60CR:AC.

Taylor: V3 C2 1768 (lacks F6, presumed blank).

T68

LE / THÉATRE / *DE* / M. DE VOLTAIRE. / *NOUVELLE ÉDITION.* / Qui contient un Recueil complet de toutes / les Pieces de Théatre que l'Auteur a / données jusqu'ici. / *TOME SIXIEME.* / [*woodcut, flowers and foliage, 21 x 23 mm*] / *A AMSTERDAM*, / Chez FRANÇOIS CANUT RICHOFF, / près le Comptoir de Cologne. / [*ornamented rule, 38 mm*] / M. DCC. LXVIII. /

A reissue of the sheets of T66 under a new title-page.

Bn: Yf 4262.

W68

THÉATRE / Complet / DE / *M*[R]. *DE VOLTAIRE.* / [*rule, 124 mm*] / TOME CINQUIÉME. / [*rule, 125 mm*] / *CONTENANT* / LE DROIT DU SEIGNEUR, LA FEMME QUI / A RAISON, L'ECOSSAISE, PANDORE, SAMSON, / LA PRINCESSE DE NAVARRE, LE TEMPLE / DE LA GLOIRE, SOCRATE, CHARLOT, avec / toutes les piéces rélatives à ces Drames. / [*rule, 119 mm*] / *GENEVE.* / [*thick-thin rule, 119 mm*] / M. DCC. LXVIII. /

[*half-title*] COLLECTION / Complette / DES / *ŒUVRES* / DE / M[R]. DE VOLTAIRE. / [*thick-thin rule, 118 mm*] / *TOME SEPTIÉME.* / [*thin-thick rule, 120 mm*] /

4°. sig. π^2 A-Bbbb[4] (Bbbb3-4 blank); pag. [*4*] 564; $3 signed, roman (–Bbbb3); direction line '*Tom.* VII [or 'VI'] *& du Théâtre le cinquiéme.*'; sheet catchwords.

[*1*] half-title; [*2*] blank; [*3*] title; [*4*] blank; [1]-164 other texts; [165] X3*r* 'LE CAFFÉ, / OU / L'ECOSSAISE, / *COMÉDIE.* / [*rule, 118 mm*] / Par Monſieur HUME; traduite en Français par JÉRÔME / CARRÉ; / repréſentée à Paris au mois d'Août 1760. / [*rule, 118 mm*] / J'ai vengé l'univers autant que je l'ai pû. / [*rule, 119 mm*] / Xiij'; [166] blank; 167-169 Epître dédicatoire du traducteur de l'Ecossaise, à monsieur le comte de Lauraguais; 170-172 A messieurs les Parisiens; 173-175 Avertissement; 176-179 Préface; [180] Acteurs; 181-254 Le Café ou l'Ecossaise, comédie; [255]-563 other texts; 564 Table des pièces contenues dans ce septième [*or* sixième] volume.

This, the quarto edition published by Cramer, follows SS61 apart from changes at I.46b, II.16a-26, III.40-41, 79b and IV.3a. The resulting text is virtually identical to that of W75G, our base text.

The plates drawn by Gravelot for this edition include one for *L'Ecossaise* (engraved by Godefroy), illustrating act 2, scene 6: 'Voilà ma dette de cinq cent guinées payée. Point de remerciement…'. The caption links the plate to scene 6 of act *3*, an error perpetuated by the reversed copy of the plate in W75G.

For the variation in volume numbers see above, p.49.

Bn: Z 4934, Rés. m Z 587 (7); BL: 94 f 6.

SS70

SECONDE SUITE / DES / MELANGES / DE / LITTÉRATURE, / D'HISTOIRE, / DE PHILOSOPHIE &c. / [*woodcut, foliage, signed* 'IRS' *45 x 35 mm*] / [*thick-thin rule, 57 mm*] / M. DCC. LXX. /

[*half-title*] COLLECTION / COMPLETTE / DES / ŒUVRES / DE / MR. *de VOLTAIRE.* / DERNIERE EDITION. / *TOME CINQUIEME.* / *Seconde partie.* /

8°. sig. A-Cc⁸ Dd⁴; pag. 423 [424]; $4 signed, arabic (– A1-2, Dd3-4); direction line '*Seconde Suite des Mélanges, &c.*'; page catchwords.

[1] half-title; [2] blank; [3] title; [4] blank; [5]-8 Epître dédicatoire du traducteur de l'Ecossaise à monsieur le comte de Lauraguais; [9]-12 A messieurs les Parisiens; 13-16 Avertissement; [17]-22 Préface; [23] B4*r* 'LE CAFFE, / OU / L'ECOSSAISE, / *COMÉDIE*, / Par Monſieur HUME; / *Traduite en Français par Jérôme Carré;* / Repréſentée à Paris au mois d'Août 1760. / *NOUVELLE EDITION* / corrigée & augmentée. / [*rule, 74 mm*] / *J'ai vengé l'univers autant que je l'ai pû.* / [*rule, 76 mm*] / B4 *AC-*'; [24] Acteurs; [25]-121 Le Café, ou l'Ecossaise, comédie; [122]-423 other texts; [424] Table des pièces contenues dans ce volume.

A second Cramer reprint of the 1761 *Seconde suite*, SS61.

Bn: Z 24747.

T70

LE / THEATRE / *DE* / M. DE VOLTAIRE. / *NOUVELLE ÉDITION.* / Qui contient un Recueil complet de toutes / les Pieces de Théâtre que l'Auteur a don- / nées juſqu'ici. / *TOME SIXIEME.* / [*woodcut, stylised foliage, 23 x 20 mm*] / *A AMSTERDAM*, / Chez FRANÇOIS CANUT RICHOFF, / près le Comptoir de Cologne. / [*thick-thin rule, 47 mm*] / M. DCC. LXX. /

12°. sig. π^1 a⁴ A-H¹² I⁸ K-Q¹² (N11-12 and Q11-12 blank); pag. [2] [viii] 300 [*4*] 301-367; $6 signed, arabic (– a3-4, F3; C3 signed 'C4', F2 'G2', M2 'M', O2 'Oij', O3 'A3', O4 'Oiv', O6 'Ovj'; P and Q signed roman); direction line '*Théâtre. Tome VI.*'; sheet catchwords.

[*1*] title; [2] blank; [i]-[viii] 1-45 Socrate; [46] blank; [47] C8*r* 'LE CAFFÉ, / *OU* / L'ECOSSAISE, / *COMÉDIE.*'; [48] blank, but for the catchword '*PREFACE.*'; [49]-56 Préface; [57] blank, but for signature 'C5'; [58]

Acteurs; 59-144 Le Café, ou l'Ecossaise, comédie; [145]-300 [*4*] 301-366 other texts; [367] Table des pièces contenues dans ce sixième volume.

Les Scythes and *Charlot* were clearly added late in the production process, and no page references are given for them in the 'Table'. The errors in the signatures suggest that separate editions of one or both may have been printed off from the same type.

The text is similar to that of T66.

Bn: Yf 4268 (sig. a is bound between I4 and 5, where it was probably printed).

71L

LE CAFFÉ, / *OU* / L'ÉCOSSAISE, / *COMÉDIE*, / Par M. de VOLTAIRE. / *Conforme à l'édition in-4°. donnée par l'Auteur.* / [*woodcut, eagle in cartouche, signed* 'J.R. 1761.', *68 x 56 mm*] / *LONDRES.* / [*thick-thin rule, 48 mm*] / M. DCC. LXXI. /

8°. sig. A-G[4] H[1]; pag. 58; $2 signed, roman (– A1); sheet catchwords.

[1] title; [2] Acteurs; [3]-58 Le Café, ou l'Ecossaise, comédie.

The woodcut on the title appears also in an edition of the *Droit du seigneur* of 1763, published (spuriously) under the name of Duchesne (siglum 63PD).

As announced on the title-page, the text is that of w68.

Bodleian: Vet E5 e 343 (1); Stockholm: Litt. fr. dram. pjes.

71L*

A copy of 71L marked up and amended by J.-J.-B.-A. Dazincourt (who created the character of Figaro in *Le Mariage de Figaro*). Dazincourt was at the Comédie from 1776 to 1809 – so there is no question of this copy having been used for any performance earlier than 1776. The resulting text (which has not been taken into account in the present edition) is a mixture of readings from MS1 and 60AM.

Comédie-Française.

72PI

LE CAFÉ, / *OU* / L'ÉCOSSAISE, / *COMÉDIE* / EN CINQ ACTES ET EN PROSE, / Par M. HUME. / *Traduite en Français par JEROME*

CARRE'. / Repreſentée à Paris, au mois d'Août 1760. / NOUVELLE ÉDITION. / *Revue ſur celle* in-4°. *de Geneve.* / [*rule, 84 mm*] / J'ai vengé l'univers autant que je l'ai pu. / [*rule, 84 mm*] / [*ornamented rule, 59 mm*] / *Le prix eſt de* 12 *ſols.* / [*ornamented rule, 59 mm*] / [*woodcut, two cherubs, 30 x 21 mm*] / A PARIS, / *Et ſe vend à* TOULON, / Chez J. L. R. MALLARD, Imprimeur de la Marine & / Libraire, Place St. Pierre. / [*ornamented rule, 62 mm*] / M. DCC. LXXII. /

8°. sig. A-I^4 K^2; pag. 76; $2 signed, roman (– A1, K2); sheet catchwords.

[1] title; [2] Acteurs; [3]-76 Le Café, ou l'Ecossaise, comédie.

The text follows w68.

Arsenal: Rf 14496.

72P2

LE CAFFÉ, / *OU* / L'ÉCOSSAISE, / *COMÉDIE* / PAR MR. HUME, PRÊTRE ÉCOSSAIS. / [*ornamented rule, 87 mm*] / *Traduit en François par JÉROME CARRÉ.* / [*ornamented rule, 87 mm*] / Nouvelle Édition, avec des Additions & des Cor- / rections, & telle qu'on doit la donner au Théâtre / de la Comédie Françoiſe, à Paris. / [*typographic ornament*] / *A PARIS*, / Chez DIDOT l'aîné, Libraire & Imprimeur, rue Pavée, / près du Quai des Auguſtins. / [*ornamented rule, 70 mm*] / M. DCC. LXXII. /

8°. sig. A-G^4; pag. 56; $2 signed, roman (– A1); sheet catchwords.

[1] title; [2] Acteurs; [3]-56 Le Café, ou l'Ecossaise, comédie.

Another edition based upon 60Y.

Arsenal: Rf 14497.

SS72

SECONDE SUITE / DES / MÊLANGES / DE / LITTÉRATURE, / D'HISTOIRE, / DE PHILOSOPHIE, &c. / [*typographic ornament*] / [*thick-thin rule, 51 mm*] / M. DCC. LXXII. /

[*half-title*] COLLECTION / COMPLETTE / DES / ŒUVRES / DE / MR. *de VOLTAIRE*. / DERNIERE ÉDITION. / *TOME CINQUIEME.* / *Seconde partie.* /

8°. sig. π^4 A-Cc^8 (Cc8 blank); pag. viij 413 [414] (p.137 numbered '237', p.399 '299'); $4 signed, arabic (Q3 signed 'O3'); direction line '*Seconde ſuite des Mêlanges, &c.*'; page catchwords.

[i] half-title; [ii] blank; [iii] title; [iv] blank; [v]-viij, [1]-238 other texts; [239]-242 Epître dédicatoire du traducteur de l'Ecossaise, à monsieur le comte de Lauraguais; [243]-246 A messieurs les Parisiens; 247-250 Avertissement; [251]-256 Préface; [257] R1r 'LE CAFÉ, / OU / L'ÉCOSSAISE, / *COMÉDIE*, / Par Monſieur HUME; / *Traduite en Français par Jérôme Carré;* / Repréſentée à Paris au mois d'Août 1760. / *NOUVELLE ÉDITION* / corrigée & augmentée. / [*rule, 80 mm*] / *J'ai vengé l'univers autant que je l'ai pu.* / [*rule, 79 mm*] / *Seconde ſuite des Mêlanges, &c.* R *AC*-'; [258] Acteurs; [259]-355 Le Café, ou l'Ecossaise, comédie; [356]-413 Socrate; [414] Table des pièces contenues dans ce volume.

A third reprint of SS61, produced to accompany W72X, the 1772 reprint or counterfeit of W70G.

Stockholm: Litt. fr.; Bn: Yth 2505 (incomplete, sigs R-Cc only).

W70L (1772)

THÉATRE / COMPLET / *DE* / M^R^. DE VOLTAIRE. / Le tout revû & corrigé par l'Auteur même. / TOME SIXIEME, / *CONTENANT* / L'ENFANT PRODIGUE, L'INDISCRET, / NANINE OU L'HOMME SANS PRÉJUGÉ, / L'ÉCOSSAISE OU LE CAFFÉ, / ET SOCRATE. / [*woodcut, lyre, signed* 'Beugnet', *42 x 35 mm*] / *A LAUSANNE*, / CHEZ FRANÇ. GRASSET ET COMP. / [*ornamented rule, 79 mm*] / M. DCC. LXXII. /

[*half-title*] *COLLECTION* / COMPLETTE / *DES* / ŒUVRES / *DE* / M^{R}. DE VOLTAIRE. / [*ornamented rule, 80 mm*] / *TOME DIX-NEUVIEME*. / [*ornamented rule, 80 mm*] /

8°. sig. π^1 $*^2$ A-Cc^8 (Cc8 blank); pag. VI 414; $5 signed, arabic (*2 signed '*3'); direction line '*Théatre.* Tome VI.'; sheet catchwords.

[i] half-title; [ii] blank; [iii] title; [iv] blank; V-VI Table des pièces contenues dans ce volume; [1]-246 other texts; [247] Q4*r* 'L'ÉCOSSAISE, / *OU* / LE CAFFÉ, / *COMÉDIE*. / Repréſentée à Paris au mois d'Auguſte 1760. / NOUVELLE ÉDITION, / Corrigée & augmentée par l'auteur. / [*rule, 75 mm*] / *J'ai vengé l'univers autant que je l'ai pu.* / [*rule, 74 mm*] / Q4'; 248 Avertissement de l'éditeur; 249-252 Epître dédicatoire à monsieur le comte de Lauraguais; 253-259 Lettre à messieurs les Parisiens (including the 'Avertissement', run on without title); [260] Acteurs; 261-354 L'Ecossaise, ou le café, comédie; [355]-414 other texts.

Voltaire complained about this edition to d'Argental (4 January 1773,

D18119) and to Elie Bertrand (25 October 1773, D18599), but the theatre (at least) was 'revû and corrigé' by him to a certain extent. His hand is apparent in the 'Auguste' of the half-title to *L'Ecossaise*, in the 'Avertissement de l'éditeur' (reproduced below, p.469) and in the presence of a textual variant, at I.312-314, retrieved from T67.

Also issued with a different half-title (π), reading: THÉATRE / COMPLET / DE / M^R^. DE VOLTAIRE. / [*ornamented rule, 79 mm*] / *TOME SIXIEME.* / [*ornamented rule, 79 mm*] /

Bpu: Hf 6743; Taylor: V1 1770.

W71 (1772)

THEATRE / *COMPLET* / DE / *M. DE VOLTAIRE,* / [*rule, 69 mm*] / TOME CINQUIEME. / [*rule, 68 mm*] / *CONTENANT* / LE DROIT DU SEIGNEUR, LA FEMME QUI / A RAISON, L'ECOSSAISE, PANDORE, SAMSON, LA / PRINCESSE DE NAVARRE, LE TEMPLE DE LA GLOIRE, / SOCRATE, CHARLOT, avec toutes les piéces rélatives / à ces Drames. / [*woodcut, winged head, 28 x 17 mm*] / *GENEVE.* / [*ornamented rule, 36 mm*] / M. DCC. LXXII. /

[*half-title*] COLLECTION / *COMPLETTE* / DES / *ŒUVRES* / DE / M[R]. DE VOLTAIRE. / [*ornamented rule, 74 mm*] / *TOME SIXIEME.* / [*ornamented rule, 74 mm*] /

12°. sig. π^2 A-T^{12} V^4; pag. [*4*] 464; $6 signed, arabic (– V3-4; H3 signed 'H*3*', S3 'S*3*'); direction line '*Tome VI. & du Théâtre le cinquiéme.*' (sig. S '*Tome.* VI. *& du Théâtre le cinquiéme.*'; sig. T '*Tome* VI. *& du Théâtre le cinquiéme.*'); sheet catchwords.

[*1*] half-title; [*2*] blank; [*3*] title; [*4*] blank; [1]-128 other texts; [129] F5*r* 'LE CAFFÉ, / OU / L'ECOSSAISE, / *COMEDIE.* / [*ornamented rule, 68 mm*] / Par Monſieur HUME; traduite en Français par / JÉROME CARRÉ; repréſentée à Paris / au mois d'Août 1760. / [*rule, 69 mm*] / *J'ai vengé l'univers autant que je l'ai pû.* / [*ornamented rule, 68 mm*] / F5'; [130] blank; 131-133 Epître dédicatoire du traducteur de l'Ecossaise, à monsieur le comte de Lauraguais; 134-136 A messieurs les Parisiens; 137-139 Avertissement; 140-144 Préface; 144 Acteurs; 145-212 Le Café, ou l'Ecossaise, comédie; [213]-464 other texts; 464 Table des pièces contenues dans ce sixième volume.

This edition, published by Plomteux in Liège, follows W68 and has no independent authority.

Uppsala: Litt. fr.

W72P (1773)

ŒUVRES / *DE M. DE VOLTAIRE.* / [*thick-thin rule, 76 mm*] / THÉATRE. / TOME SEPTIÈME, / *Contenant* / *LA FEMME QUI A RAISON, LE CAFFÉ,* / *ou L'ÉCOSSAISE, SOCRATE, CHARLOT,* / *ou LA COMTESSE DE GIVRI, LE DROIT* / *DU SEIGNEUR.* / [*woodcut, man bearing spear within roundel of foliage, 27 x 25 mm*] / *A NEUFCHATEL.* / [*ornamented rule, 62 mm*] / M. DCC. LXXIII. /

[*half-title*] *ŒUVRES* / DE THÉATRE / *DE M. DE VOLTAIRE.* / TOME SEPTIÈME. /

12°. sig. π² A-R¹²; pag. [*4*] 408; $6 signed, roman; direction line 'Th. *Tome VII.*'; sheet catchwords.

[*1*] half-title; [*2*] blank; [*3*] title; [*4*] blank; [1]-58 other texts; [59] C6*r* 'LE CAFFÉ, / *OU* / L'ECOSSAISE, / *COMÉDIE;* / Par Monſieur HUME: traduite en Français / par JÉRÔME CARRÉ; repreſentée à Paris / au mois d'Août 1760. / [*rule, 72 mm*] / *J'ai vengé l'univers autant que je l'ai pu.* / [*rule, 71 mm*] / C vj'; 60 Avertissement de l'éditeur; 61-65 Epître dédicatoire du traducteur de l'Ecossaise à monsieur le comte de Lauraguais; 66-70 A messieurs les Parisiens; 71-75 Avertissement; 76-83 Préface; 84 Personnages; 85-176 Le Café, ou l'Ecossaise, comédie; [177]-408 other texts.

This edition, published in Paris by Panckoucke, follows the text of w68.

Arsenal: Rf 14095 (7).

75M

LE CAFFÉ, / *OU* / L'ECOSSAISE, / *COMÉDIE.* / PAR Mr. HUME, PRETRE ECOSSAIS. / *Traduite en Français par JEROME CARRÉ.* / Nouvelle Edition avec des Additions & des Cor- / rections, & telle qu'on doit la donner au / Théatre de la Comédie Françaiſe à Paris. / [*woodcut, floral cartouche, 45 x 40 mm*] / A MARSEILLE, / Chez JEAN MOSSY, Imprimeur du Roi, & de / la Marine, & Libraire, au Parc. / [*ornamented rule, 64 mm*] / M. DCC. LXXV. / *Avec Approbation & permiſſion.* /

8°. sig. A⁴ (± A1) B-H⁴ I²; pag. 67 [68]; $2 signed, arabic (– A1, I2); sheet catchwords.

[1] title; [2] Acteurs; [3]-67 Le Café, ou l'Ecossaise, comédie; [68] On trouve à Marseille, chez Jean Mossy, imprimeur-libraire, à la Canebiere, un assortiment de pièces de théatre, imprimées dans le même goût.

Page 67 bears: 'Permis d'imprimer, et distribuer, à Marseille le 8 février 1775. VITALIS P.D.R.D.P.'

This edition follows 60Y, and was reissued at Naples in 1777 (see below, 77N).

Arsenal: GD 6782, Rf 14498; Comédie-Française; Taylor: V3 C2 1775; Bodleian: Vet E5 e 343 (2).

W75G

[*within ornamented border*] OUVRAGES / *DRAMATIQUES,* / PRÉCÉDÉS ET SUIVIS / DE TOUTES LES PIÉCES QUI LEUR / SONT RELATIFS. / [*rule, 75 mm*] / TOME HUITIÉME. / [*rule, 75 mm*] / *M. DCC. LXXV.* /

[*half-title, within ornamented border*] TOME NEUVIÉME. /

8°. sig. π^2 A-Cc^8; pag. [*4*] 416; $4 signed, roman (H4 signed 'H' in some copies); direction line '*Théatre*. Tom. VIII.'; sheet catchwords.

[i] half-title; [ii] blank; [iii] title; [iv] blank; [1] A1*r* 'LE CAFFÉ, / OU / L'ECOSSAISE, / *COMÉDIE*. / [*rule, 75 mm*] / Par Monſieur HUME; traduite en Français par / JÉROME CARRÉ; repréſentée à Paris au mois / d'Août 1760. / [*rule, 72 mm*] / *J'ai vengé l'univers autant que je l'ai pu.* / [*rule, 71 mm*] / *Théatre*. Tom. VIII. A'; 2-5 Epître dédicatoire du traducteur de l'Ecossaise, à monsieur le comte de Lauraguais; 6-9 A messieurs les Parisiens; 10-13 Avertissement; 14-19 Préface; [20] Acteurs; 21-99 Le Café ou l'Ecossaise, comédie; [100] blank; [101]-415 other texts; 416 Table des pièces contenues dans ce volume.

This, the *encadrée* edition, was the last to be produced under Voltaire's supervision, and provides the base text for the present edition. The Leningrad copy bears no evidence of subsequent correction or revision to *L'Ecossaise*, although other plays in the same volume were revised.

The illustration to *L'Ecossaise*, engraved by Martinet, is a reduced and reversed copy of that in W68; the expressions on the faces of Lindane and Polly have been changed, from *boudeuses* to disapproving.

Taylor: VF.

W75X

[*within ornamented border*] OUVRAGES / *DRAMATIQUES,* / PRÉCÉDÉS ET SUIVIS / *DE TOUTES LES PIÉCES QUI LEUR / SONT RELATI-*

VES. / [*rule, 73 mm*] / TOME HUITIÈME. / [*rule, 72 mm*] / [*typographic ornament*] / [*ornamented rule, 79 mm*] / *M. DCC. LXXV.* /

[*half-title, within ornamented border*] ŒUVRES / DE / *M^R. DE VOLTAIRE.* / [*rule, 78 mm*] / TOME NEUVIÈME. / [*rule, 76 mm*] /

8°. sig. π^2 A-Cc^8; pag. [*4*] 416; $4 signed, arabic; direction line '*Théatre.* Tom. VIII.'; sheet catchwords.

[*1*] half-title; [*2*] blank, but for border; [*3*] title; [*4*] blank, but for border; [1] A1*r* 'LE CAFÉ, / *OU* / L'ECOSSAISE, / *COMÉDIE.* / [*rule, 78 mm*] / Par Monſieur HUME; traduite en français par / JÉROME CARRÉ; repréſentée à Paris au mois / d'Août 1760. / [*rule, 78 mm*] / *J'ai vengé l'univers autant que je l'ai pu.* / [*rule, 78 mm*] / *Théatre.* Tom. VIII. A'; 2-5 Epître dédicatoire du traducteur de l'Ecossaise, à monsieur le comte de Lauraguais; 6-9 A messieurs les Parisiens; 10-13 Avertissement; 14-19 Préface; [20] Acteurs; 21-99 Le Café, ou l'Ecossaise, comédie; [100] blank but for border; [101]-415 other texts; 416 Table des pièces contenues dans ce volume.

A reprint or counterfeit of W75G.

BN: Z 24888.

T76X

THEATRE / COMPLET / DE MONSIEUR / DE VOLTAIRE. / TOME CINQUIEME. / *Contenant* LA PRUDE *ou* GARDEUSE DE / CASSETTE, LE DROIT DU SEIGNEUR, LA / FEMME QUI A RAISON, LE CAFFÉ *ou* / L'ÉCOSSAISE, PANDORE, LA PRINCESSE / DE NAVARRE, / *avec toutes les Pièces relatives* / *à ces Drames.* / [*woodcut, two birds within cartouche, 42 x 32 mm*] / [*ornamented rule, 51 mm*] / M. DCC. LXXVI. / [*lines 1, 3, 5 and date in red*]

8°. sig. π^1 A-Nn^8; pag. [2] 576; $4 signed, roman (F2 signed 'Fi', V3 'Vviij'); direction line '*Théatre. Tome V.*'; sheet catchwords.

[*1*] title; [*2*] blank; [1]-293 other works; [294] blank; [295] T4*r* 'LE CAFÉ, / *OU* / L'ÉCOSSAISE, / *COMÉDIE* / [*rule, 72 mm*] / Par Monſieur HUME, traduite en français par JÉRÔME / CARRÉ; repréſentée à Paris au mois d'Août 1760. / [*rule, 72 mm*] / *J'ai vengé l'univers autant que je l'ai pû.* / [*rule, 72 mm*] / T iv'; [296] blank; 297-300 Epître dédicatoire du traducteur de l'Ecossaise, à monsieur le comte de Lauraguais; 301-305 A messieurs les Parisiens; 306-309 Avertissement; 310-316 Préface; 316 Acteurs;

317-399 Le Café, ou l'Ecossaise, comédie; [400] blank; [401]-575 other texts; 576 Table des pièces contenues dans ce cinquième volume.

Arsenal: Rf 14096 (5).

77N

LE CAFFE, / *OU* / L'ECOSSAISE, / *COMÉDIE*, / Par Mr. HUME, PRETRE ECOSSAIS. / *Traduite en Français par JEROME CARRÉ*. / [*triple rule, 74 mm*] / LE PRIX EST DE 20. GRAINS. / [*triple rule, 75 mm*] / [*typographic ornament*] / NAPLES / DE L'IMPRIMERIE DE JEAN GRAVIER. / MDCCLXXVII. / [*rule, 26 mm*] / *AVEC APPROBATION ET PRIVILEGE*. /

A re-issue of 75M with a new title-leaf, cancelling A1.

Taylor: V3 C2 1777 (lacking top third of A2).

77P

LE CAFFÉ, / *OU* / L'ÉCOSSAISE, / *COMÉDIE*. / EN CINQ ACTES, / *ET EN PROSE*. / Par M. HUME, Prêtre Ecoſſais. / *Traduite en François, par Mr. de VOLTAIRE*. / Avec des Additions & des Corrections, & telle qu'on / doit la donner au Théatre de la Comédie Françoiſe, / à Paris, ſur les principaux Théâtres de Province. / [*ornamented rule, 83 mm*] / *NOUVELLE ÉDITION*. / [*ornamented rule, 83 mm*] / [*woodcut, doves and foliage, 40 x 31 mm*] / *A PARIS*. / Chez RUAULT, Libraire, / rue de la Harpe. / [*ornamented rule, 65 mm*] / *M. DCC. LXXVII*. /

8°. sig. A-F^4 G^1; pag. 50; $2 signed, arabic (– A1); sheet catchwords.

[1] title; [2] Acteurs; [3]-63 Le Café, ou l'Ecossaise, comédie.

Bibliothèque municipale, Poitiers: E95 (8).

T77

THÉATRE / *COMPLET* / DE M. DE VOLTAIRE; / *NOUVELLE ÉDITION*, / *Revue & corrigée par l'AUTEUR*. / TOME NEUVIÈME, / *CONTENANT* / LE DROIT DU SEIGNEUR, / LE DÉPOSITAIRE, L'ÉCOSSAISE. / [*woodcut, thistle, 20 x 20 mm*] / *A AMSTERDAM*, / Chez les LIBRAIRES ASSOCIÉS. / [*thick-thin rule, 49 mm*] / M. DCC. LXXVII. /

12°. sig. π^1 A-P^{12}; pag. [2] 358 [359]; $6 signed, arabic (– A6; B4 signed 'B'); direction line '*Tome IX.*'; sheet catchwords.

[*1*] title; [*2*] blank; [1]-236 other texts; [237] K11*r* 'L'ÉCOSSAISE, / *OU* /

LE CAFÉ, / *COMÉDIE*; / Repréſentée à Paris au mois d'Août 1760. / [*rule, 59 mm*] / *J'ai vengé l'univers autant que je l'ai pu.* / [*rule, 59 mm*]'; 238 Avertissement de l'éditeur; 239-242 Epître dédicatoire à monsieur le comte de Lauraguais; 243-246 Lettre à messieurs les Parisiens; 247-250 Avertissement; 251-257 Préface; [258] Acteurs; 259-358 L'Ecossaise, ou le café, comédie; [359] Table des pièces contenues dans le neuvième volume.

This edition is based closely upon W70L.

Stockholm: Litt. fr. dram.

80P

LE CAFÉ, / OU L'ECOSSAISE, / *COMÉDIE* / EN CINQ ACTES ET EN PROSE; / Par M. HUME, Prêtre écoſſais. / *Traduite en français, par M. DE VOLTAIRE.* / Avec des additions & des corrections, & telle qu'on doit / la donner au théatre de la Comédie françaiſe, à Paris, / & ſur les principaux théatres de Province. / [*woodcut, flowers, 37 x 32 mm*] / *A PARIS*, / Chez la veuve DUCHESNE, Libraire, rue / Saint-Jacques, au Temple du Goût. / [*thick-thin rule, 55 mm*] / M. DCC. LXXX. / *Avec Approbation & Permiſſion.* /

8°. sig. A-H⁴; pag. 63; $2 signed, roman (– A1); sheet catchwords.

[1] title; [2] Acteurs; [3]-63 Le Café, ou l'Ecossaise, comédie.

A truncated version, not previously recorded. For example, I.iii consists only of lines 88a-97 and 133a-138.

Arsenal: Rf 14499.

85P

LE CAFÉ, / *OU* / L'ÉCOSSAISE, / *COMÉDIE* / EN CINQ ACTES ET EN PROSE, / *Par M. HUME.* / Traduite en François par JEROME CARRÉ. / *Repréſentée à Paris, au mois d'Août 1760.* / NOUVELLE ÉDITION. / *Revue ſur celle in 4°. de Geneve.* / [*ornamented rule, 89 mm*] / J'ai vengé l'univers autant que je l'ai pu. / [*ornamented rule, 89 mm*] / [*woodcut, inverted, fool's head, scroll and arrow, 53 x 33 mm*] / *A PARIS*, / Chez DIDOT, l'aîné, Imprimeur & Libraire. / [*ornamented rule, 54 mm*] / M. DCC. LXXXV.

8°. sig. A-F⁴ G¹; pag. 50; $1 signed (– A1); sheet catchwords.

[1] title; [2] Acteurs; [3]-50 Le Café, ou l'Ecossaise, comédie.

The text is that of w68.

Bn: Musique Th 565; Arsenal: Rf 14500; Taylor: V3 C2 1785.

K

OEUVRES / COMPLETES / DE / VOLTAIRE. / TOME HUITIEME. / [*swelled rule, 41 mm*] / DE L'IMPRIMERIE DE LA SOCIÉTÉ LITTÉ-RAIRE-/TYPOGRAPHIQUE./ 1785./

[*half-title*] OEUVRES / COMPLETES / DE / VOLTAIRE. /

8°. sig. π^2 a^2 A-Ee^8; pag. [2] iv 447; $4 signed, arabic (– a2); direction line '*Théâtre.* Tome VIII.'; sheet catchwords.

[*1*] title; [2] blank; [i] a1*r* 'THEATRE. / *Théâtre.* Tome VIII. a'; [ii] blank; [iii]-iv Table des pieces contenues dans ce volume; [1] A1*r* 'L'ECOSSAISE, / *COMEDIE.* / PAR M. HUME. / *TRADUITE EN FRANÇAIS* / PAR JEROME CARRÉ. / Repréſentée à Paris au mois d'auguſte 1760. / *J'ai vengé l'univers autant que je l'ai pu.* / *Théâtre.* Tome VIII. A'; [2] blank; [3]-6 Epître dédicatoire du traducteur à monsieur le comte de Lauraguais; [7]-10 A messieurs les Parisiens; [11]-14 Avertissement; [15]-21 Préface; [22] Personnages; [23]-106 L'Ecossaise, comédie; [107] Variantes de l'Ecossaise (recording those at I.108-110, 117-118, II.89 and V.177-178); [108] blank; [109]-447 other texts.

The Kehl edition, which follows w75G.

This is the revised version of the volume, of which the first printing dates from 1784, and all the faults listed in the first version of the errata (in volume 70) have been corrected. The 1784 title-pages are sometimes found with 1785 versions of the text, and 1784 texts sometimes carry 1785 title-pages. The two settings of this volume may be most easily distinguished by the 'août' (1784) and 'auguſte' (1785) on p.[1], the half-title to *L'Ecossaise*.

The duodecimo edition of 1785 has not been taken into account.

Taylor: VF.

88P

L'ÉCOSSAISE, / *OU* / LE CAFÉ, / *COMÉDIE* / EN CINQ ACTES, / EN PROSE, / DE VOLTAIRE; / *Repréſentée, pour la premiere fois, par les* /

Comédiens ordinaires du Roi, le 26 / Juillet 1760. / Nouvelle Édition, conforme à la / Repréſentation. / [*typographic ornament*] / A PARIS, / Chez la veuve DUCHESNE, Libraire, rue / St.-Jacques, au Temple du Goût. / [*swelled rule, 58 mm*] / 1788. /

12°. sig. A-E[12] F[4] (– F4); pag. 126; $6 signed, arabic (– C6, F2-4); sheet catchwords.

[1] title; [2] Personnages; [3]-126 L'Ecossaise, ou le café, comédie.

An extensively revised version, probably based in part upon 60x*. It has not been taken into account in the present edition.

Bn: Musique Th 2106.

Translations and adaptations[141]

1. English

The Coffee-house; or, fair fugitive, a comedy of five acts. London, J. Wilkie, 1760. 8°. pag. viii 95. (Bn: Rés. p Yf 355/1; BL: 164 g 32).

The English merchant. London 1767. 8°. pag. 69. Imitated by George Colman the Elder, with an epilogue by David Garrick. (BL: 643 h 14/2).

The Highland girl. Kendal, Titus Wilson, 1910. 8°. pag. xv 82. Translated by W. G. Collingwood. (BL: 11736 e 31).

2. Italian

Translated by Casanova in 1760, according to his *Histoire de ma vie*, VII.v.

[141] Sources include: Hans Fromm, *Bibliographie Deutscher Übersetzungen aus dem Französischen 1700-1948* (Baden-Baden 1953), vi.267; Theodore Besterman's three bibliographies, 'A provisional bibliography of Italian editions and translations of Voltaire', *Studies* 18 (1961), p.280-81, 'A provisional bibliography of Scandinavian and Finnish editions and translations of Voltaire', *Studies* 47 (1966), p.66, 'Provisional bibliography of Portuguese editions of Voltaire', *Studies* 76 (1970), p.22; Jeroom Vercruysse, 'Bibliographie provisoire des traductions néerlandaises et flamandes de Voltaire', *Studies* 116 (1973), p.32; A. Coimbra Martins, *Voltaire et la culture portugaise* (Paris 1969), p.88; Francisco Lafarga, *Voltaire en España (1734-1835)* (Barcelona 1975), p.225-26; and Christopher Todd, 'A provisional bibliography of published Spanish translations of Voltaire', *Studies* 161 (1976), p.97-98.

La Scozzese, in Carlo Goldoni, *Opere*. 1761-1764. Volume 13, 1761. (Bn: Yd 4634-4651).

The Coffee house. 1925. Translation of Goldoni's translation. (BL: 12205 v 19/1).

Il Caffè, o la Scozzese, commedia, in *Biblioteca teatrale italiana*. Lucca 1762-1765. Volume 1, 1762. 8°. Translated by O. Diodati. (Bn: Yd 5560).

Le Caffè ossia la Scozzese, commedia. Venezia 1825. 8°. pag. 64. (Biblioteca universitaria, Padua: Busta 103.4).

3. Spanish

La Escocesa, comedia en prosa, y en cinco actos. Madrid, Imprenta real de la Gazeta, 1769. 8°. pag. 94 ii. Translation attributed to Tomás de Iriarte. (Biblioteca nacional, Madrid).

Comedia nueva, la Escocesa, en cinco actos ... segunda impresion. Barcelona, Viuda Piferrer, s.d. 8°. pag. 35. Translation attributed to Ramón de la Cruz. (BL: 1342 e 4/21; a manuscript is in the Biblioteca municipal, Madrid, MS 111-13).

Comedia nueva, la Escocesa, en cinco actos ... segunda impresion. Barcelona, Carlos Gibert y Tutó, s.d. 8°. pag. 35. (University of North Carolina Library, Chapel Hill).

4. Portuguese

A Loja do café ou a Escoceza. Lisboa, Francisco Luís Ameno, 1762. 8°. pag. 102.

Another version, in verse, was performed in Lisbon in 1805. The (unpublished) manuscript belonged to Inocêncio Francisco da Silva, author of the *Dicionário bibliográfico portugês*.

5. German

Das Caffeehaus, ein rührendes Lustspiel. Hamburg 1760. Translated by J. J. C. Bode. (Fromm, no.26933).

Das Caffee-Haus oder die Schottländerinn, ein Lustspiel. Berlin, Stettin and Leipzig, Rüdiger, 1761. 8°. pag. 103. Translated by Bode. (BL: 11747 a 40/1).

Das Caffeehaus oder die Schottländerinn, ein Lustspiel. Wien, Krauss, 1765. 8°. pag. 104. Translated by Bode. In the *Neue Sammlung, von Schauspielen welche auf der Kaiserlich-Königlichen privil. deutschen Schaubühne zu Wien aufgeführet werden*, Wien 1764-1767. (BL: 11747 g 1).

Das Caffee-Haus, oder die Schottländerinn, ein Lustspiel. Berlin, Stettin and Leipzig, Rüdiger, 1766. 8°. pag. 103. Translated by Bode. (Fromm, no.26936).

Another edition, as above, but pag. 191. (Fromm, no.26937).

6. Dutch

De wedergevondene dochter, en edelmoedige minnaar, blyspel. Amsteldam, Izaak Duim, 1761. 8°. pag. vi 91 iii. (Universiteitsbibliotheek, Gand).

Another edition, dated 1775. 8°. pag. 96. (Universiteitsbibliotheek, Gand).

7. Scandinavian

Caffe-Huset, eller Skotlaenderinden, comedie i fem acter, in *Skuespil til brug for den danske skueplads*, volume 1. Kjøbenhavn, Gyldendal, 1775. 8°. pag. 89 iii. Translated by Andreas Charles Teilmann. (Bn: Yl 240; Kongelige Bibliotek, Copenhagen).

Skottländskan eller cafféhuset i London, comedie i fem acter. Stockholm, Kunglig. Tryckeriet, 1786. 8°. pag. iv 102. (Stockholm).

8. Russian

Вольной дом, или Шотландка, комедия г. Гума, переведена на французской язык. Москва 1763. 8°. pag. 84. Translated by Aleksandr Protasov. (Leningrad).

French parodies and adaptations

L'Ecossoise, comédie en cinq actes, traduite de l'Anglois, et mise en vers par M. de Lagrange. Paris, Duchesne, 1761. 12°. pag. 107. (Arsenal: Rf 14501).

L'Ecosseuse, parodie de l'Ecossaise, opéra-comique en un acte, par MM. P... et A... Paris, Cuissart, 1761. 8°. pag. 56. By Poinsinet jeune and Davesne, or (according to Brenner), Panard and Anseaume. (Arsenal: Rf 14503).

Les Nouveaux Calotins, opéra-comique, représentés [*sic*] *pour la première fois le 19 septembre 1760 et jours suivants*. Avignon, Chambeau, 1760. 8°. pag. 25. Attributed to Lesage and Harny (see above, p.276, n.101). Bengesco, no.1643.

La Petite Ecosseuse, parodie de l'Ecossaise. By T. G. Taconet. According to Beuchot (M.v.403), this was published but not performed.

9. *A messieurs les Parisiens*

Manuscript copies of this text circulated in Paris a few days before the first performance, quickly followed by several printed versions.[141]

MSR1

à Messieurs les parisiens / Messieurs

Contemporary copy with holograph heading; 140 x 220 mm; 2 leaves.

Bn: N 24342, f.63-64.

There are no variants of any consequence from SS61, except that the text ends at 'natif de Montauban'.

MSR2

A Messieurs Les Parisiens /

Contemporary copy; 100 x 125 mm; 2 leaves.

Bh: Rés. 2026, f.206-207.

A neat copy which departs but little from the text of MSR1: its writer, not understanding Voltaire's (erroneous) point about Hume and Home, puts 'il appelle Monsieur hume M. hume'. The 'soixante-et-treize journaux' become '17'.

[141] Collé, *Journal*, ii.254. Voltaire wrote on 29 August 1760 to Damilaville: 'Je n'ai point encore vu l'imprimé qui a pour titre *Requête de Jérôme Carré aux Parisiens*. Vous me feriez plaisir de me l'envoyer; on dit qu'il est différent de celui qui courait en manuscrit' (D9173). Thiriot had told him on 30 July (D9100) there were many printer's errors in this and other *facéties* that had been recently published. Bengesco refers to this shortened title as 'une troisième édition' (no.1646).

MSR3

Requeste aux Parisiens pour servir de Post-Préface à L'Ecossaise /

Contemporary copy; 100 x 125 mm; 2 leaves.

Bh: Rés. 2026, f.208-209.

A hastily written copy of no apparent textual value.

R1

[*drop-head title*] [*typographic head-piece, 65 x 12 mm*] / REQUÊTE / *ADRESSÉE à Meſſieurs les Pari- / ſiens, par B. Jerôme Carré, / natif de Montauban, Traduc- / teur de la Comédie intitulée,* Le / Caffé *ou* l'Ecoſſaiſe, *pour ſer- / vir de Poſt-Préface à ladite / Comédie.* / A MESSIEURS LES PARISIENS. /

8°. sig. A⁴; pag. 8; $1 signed; no catchwords.

This may well have been one of the earliest editions of the *Requête*, for its appears to have been designed to accompany the first edition of the play (60). The first page is reproduced in *Voltaire's correspondence* (Geneva 1953-1965), xlii.197, fig. 227. The copy cited below is accompanied by an engraving of Fréron, holding an issue of the *Année littéraire*, with the inscription: 'Les Francois m'ont Jouée / L'Opera Comique ma Chantée / et les Italiens m'ont / Ecorchée.'[142]

There are two errors on line 38 ('on ni parle' and 'd'Agie est de').

Bn: Yf 12129.

R2

[*drop-head title*] (1) / [*line of typographic ornaments, 77 x 4 mm*] / REQUETE / *DE* / JÉROME CARRÉ / *AUX PARISIENS*. /

8°. sig. A²; pag. 4; $1 signed; no catchwords.

Follows R1 except at lines 50, 72-73 and 78.

This edition was also issued, with other pamphlets, as part of the undated 'RECUEIL / *DE PIECES* / INTÉRESSANTES.'

Bn: Yf 12128 (separate), Rés. Z Beuchot 912 (in the *Recueil*).

[142] See the gloss on this inscription in *La Wasprie* (above p.273).

R3

[*drop-head title*] [1] / [*typographic head-piece, 91 x 19 mm*] / REQUÊTE / *ADRESSÉE à Meſſieurs les Pariſiens, par / B. Jerôme Carré, natif de Montauban, Tra- / ducteur de la Comédie intitulée,* Le Caffé *ou* / l'Ecoſſaiſe, *pour ſervir de Poſt-Preface à ladite / Comédie.* / A MESSIEURS LES PARISIENS. /

8°. sig. π^2; pag. 4; no catchwords.

Follows the text of R1.

Bn: Rés. Z Beuchot 785; Arsenal: Rf 14504.

R4

[*drop-head title*] [*typographical head-piece, 91 x 8 mm*] / REQUETE / DE / JEROME CARRÉ. / [*thick-thin rule, 93 mm*] / *AUX PARISIENS.* /

8°. sig. π^2; pag. 4; page catchwords.

Follows the text of R1 except at line 50.

Bn: Rés. Z Beuchot 786; Yf 12360.

R5

[*drop-head title*] 1 / [*typographic head-piece, 81 x 17 mm*] / REQUÊTE / *DE* / JÉROME CARRÉ / *AUX PARISIENS.* /

8°. sig. $*^2$; pag. 4; $1 signed; no catchwords.

Both copies seen appear in another 'RECUEIL / *DE PIÉCES* / INTERESSANTES.', similar to that associated with R2. The text is close to that of PD58.

Bn: Rés. Z Beuchot 741; Taylor: V2 1760 (3).

PD58 (1760)

LE / PAUVRE DIABLE. / [*thick-thin rule, 60 mm*] / *A PARIS.* / 1758. /

8°. sig. A-B^8; pag. 32; $4 signed, arabic (– A1); page catchwords.

[1] title; [2] blank; [3]-26 other texts; [27] B6*r* 'REQUÊTE / DE / JÉROME CARRÉ.'; [28] blank; [29]-32 Requête de Jérome Carré. Aux Parisiens.

Bn: Z 27377*bis* (5,ii) (4); Arsenal: 8° NF 5430 (3) (in a volume of Voltairiana put up by Laus de Boissy); Taylor: V4 P3 1760 (2).

RF60

RECUEIL / DES / FACETIES PARISIENNES, / *Pour les ſix premiers mois de / l'an* 1760. /

8°. sig. *a-r*^{8} *s*^{6} (*s*6 blank); pag. IV 5-282; $4 signed, arabic (– *a*1, *k*1); page catchwords.

[i] title; [ii] blank; [iii]-IV Préface; [5]-228 other texts; [229]-232 A messieurs les Parisiens; [233]-280 other texts; 281-282 Table des pieces contenues dans ce recueil.

This volume was published by Cramer shortly before October 1760.

Bn: Rés. Z Bengesco 375; Taylor: V4 O 1759 (2) (23).

JR60

LE JOLI / RECUEIL, / *OU* / L'HISTOIRE DE LA QUERELLE / LITTÉRAIRE, / Où les Auteurs s'amuſent *en amuſant / le Public.* / [*woodcut, four cherubs gardening, 56 x 39 mm*] / A GENEVE, / Chez les Libraires Aſſociés des Œuvres / du Grand Voltaire. / [*thick-thin rule, 44 mm*] / M. DCC. LX. /

[*half-title*] LE JOLI / RECUEIL. /

8°. sig. π^2 A-F^4 $^\pi$F^4 G-M^4; pag. [*4*] 104; signed $2 roman (+ Ciij, Liij; – F1, $^\pi$F1, L1); sheet catchwords.

[*1*] half-title; [*2*] Table des pieces contenues dans ce Recueil; [*3*] title; [*4*] blank; [1] A1*r* 'LETTRE / *A MESSIEURS* / LES PARISIENS. / A'; [2] blank; [3]-8 Lettre à messieurs les Parisiens; [9]-104 other texts.

The text of this edition presents a number of unique variants, which are recorded in the critical apparatus below.

Bn: Rés. Z Bengesco 482 (1).

PD60

LE PAUVRE / *DIABLE*, / POËME, / EN VERS AISÉS DE FEU M. VADÉ, / Mis en lumiére par CATHERINE VADÉ ſa Couſine; / *Dédié à maître ABRAHAM CHAUMEIX.* / [*woodcut, phoenix, 49 x 39 mm*] / A GENEVE. / [*thick-thin rule, 71 mm*] / *M. D. CC. LX.* /

[*half-title*] LE PAUVRE / *DIABLE.* /

8°. sig. π^2 a^1 A-B^4 C^4 (– C4) D^4; pag. [*6*] 30; $2 signed, arabic; sheet catchwords.

[*1*] half-title; [*2*] blank; [*3*] title; [*4*] blank; [*5-6*] 1-26 other texts; 27-30 Requête de Jérome Carré. Aux Parisiens.

The structure and presentation of this volume suggests that the *Requête*, sig. D, was added as an after-thought. It follows the text of PD58.

Bn: Rés. Z Bengesco 180.

SS61

The *Seconde suite des mélanges* (1761), pp.9-12, described above, p.306.

The *Requête* also appears in PR62, 63G, T64P, T67 (these last three being essentially the same edition), W68, SS70, SS72, W70L, W71, W72P, W75G, W75X and K. These editions are described above, p.308-309, 312, 314-17, 319-24, 327.

10. *Editorial principles*

The base text of the present edition is W75G, since Voltaire made no alterations to the play in the corrected *encadrée* volumes now in Leningrad.[143]

Modernisation of the base text

The spelling of names of persons and places has been respected. A compromise has been reached concerning the use of accents: we give Jérôme for Jérome. We have not followed the practice of W75G of printing the names of persons in italics.

The punctuation of W75G has been retained, with exception: hanging quotation marks at the beginning of each line have been replaced by opening and closing quotation marks.

The following details of orthography and grammar in the base text have been modified to conform to present-day usage:

[143] S. Taylor, 'The definitive text of Voltaire's works: the Leningrad *encadrée*', *Studies* 124 (1974), p.56.

1. Consonants
   - the consonant *p* was not used in: tems, nor in its compound: longtems
   - the consonant *t* was not used in syllable endings *–ans* and *–ens*: talens, vivans, etc.
   - double consonants were used in: allarme, appaiser, appellés, apperçoit, caffé, caffetier, imbécille, jetter, secrettement
   - a single consonant was used in: falait, falu, pourait, sabat
   - archaic forms were used, as in: cu, échaffaut, guères, hazard, hazarder, isle, patétique, solemnel

2. Vowels
   - *y* was used in place of *i* in: ayes, ayent, croye, ennuye, envoye, gaye, Mylord, Mylady, pardy, satyre
   - archaic forms were used, as in: avanture, avanturière, encor, plein pied, vuide

3. Accents

The acute
- was used in place of the grave in: cinquiéme, enlévera, quatriéme, piéce, siécle
- was used in: rélation, asséyez

The grave
- was not used in: déja, voila

The circumflex
- was used in place of the acute in: Chrêtien
- was not used in: ame, disgrace, grace, infame, Jérome, parait, théatre
- was used in: toûjours, vîte

The dieresis
- was used in: s'évanouït, poësie

4. Capitalisation
   - initial capitals were attributed to adjectives denoting nationality and creed, and to: Ambassadeur, Août, Archevêque, Avocat, Avril, Dame, Demoiselle, Jésuite, Lord, Madame, Mademoiselle, Ministre, Monsieur, Mylady, Mylord, Nation, Philosophe, Reine, Royaume, Seigneur, Théatre

– the initial capital was not used in the titles of works, nor in: dieu (singular), état (l')

5. Points of grammar

– agreement of the past participle was not consistent
– the cardinal number *cent* was invariable
– the final *-s* was not used in the second person singular of the imperative: di, pren, vi, etc.

6. Abbreviations

We have expanded all abbreviated forms found irregularly applied throughout the text of the play for Monsieur, Madame and Mademoiselle: these occurrences are not apparently in accord with the demands of space on the line:

– Monsieur was abbreviated only in acts I, II and V, but not in acts III and IV: 'Mr.' stands alone on several occasions, and precedes a name some twenty times
– 'Madame' was never abbreviated
– 'Mademoiselle' was seldom abbreviated, except on two occasions in acts III and IV, where the printer had retained 'Monsieur'.

7. Various

– the ampersand was used
– the hyphen was used in: aussi-bien, galant-homme, genre-humain, grand-merci, honnête-homme, mal-à-propos, mal-intentionné, tout-d'un-coup, tout-à-l'heure, très-aise, très-utile
– the hyphen was not used in: beaux arts, ce sentiment là, cu de sac, là haut.

Presentation of the variants

Variants are drawn from MS1, MS2 and from the following editions: 60, 60X (60 indicating both 60 and 60X unless otherwise stated), 60Y, 60CR, 60AM, 61L1, SS61, T64P, W68, W70L, K84. Misprints and differences in punctuation are not recorded.

The variants drawn from 60X*, 60CR:AC and 60CR* present only the results of the corrections contained in these editions, and not the processes involved.

Variants for *A messieurs les Parisiens* are also drawn from MSR1, R1, PD58, RF60, and JR60.

The variants to the other three prefatory items are of little editorial interest, consisting of misspellings, alterations to abbreviations and other discrepancies.

The variants to the text of the play, however, reflect the two main stages in composition:

1. the first version published by Voltaire, before performance (60);
2. the amended version published after the first production at the Comédie-Française, and incorporating changes made by Voltaire, or with his permission, for this production. These changes are listed at the beginning of 60CR under the heading 'Additions et corrections faites pour la représentation de la pièce' (p.v-viii, these particular pages being designated by the siglum 60CR:AC).

However, some changes made with Voltaire's permission were nevertheless made against his will (the substitution of 'Wasp' for 'Frélon' being the most important). These were all incorporated in 60AM. Ideally, the text should include only those changes which Voltaire willingly accepted, but this would result in a hybrid conflation. There is no edition, not even SS61 or W75G, incorporating simply the original edition and those corrections desired and authorized by Voltaire.

Variants are of four main types:

a. attempts to make Frélon less outrageously *méchant*;
b. political and philosophical references;
c. dramatic improvements (usually shortening);
d. more precise stage directions.

LE CAFFÉ,

OU

L'ECOSSAISE,

COMEDIE,

Par Mr. HUME, traduite en Français.

LONDRES,

MDCCLX.

7. *Le Café ou l'Ecossaise*: the title-page of the first edition (siglum 60), published in Geneva by Cramer (Taylor Institution, Oxford).

LE CAFÉ,
OU
L'ÉCOSSAISE,
COMÉDIE.

Par monsieur Hume;
traduite en français par Jérôme Carré;
représentée à Paris au mois d'août 1760.[1]

J'ai vengé l'univers[2] *autant que je l'ai pu.*

[1] In reality, 26 July 1760; the date is given correctly in many editions. This inexactitude (surprisingly perpetuated in W75G) originated in SS61.

[2] An obvious reference to Le Franc de Pompignan's pretentious *Mémoire présenté au roi* (11 May 1760), in which he boasts: 'Il faut que tout l'univers sache aussi qu'elles ont paru s'occuper de mon ouvrage.' In *La Vanité* (also published in SS61), Voltaire imagines Le Franc de Pompignan crying: 'L'univers doit venger mes injures!' On 6 August 1760 Voltaire wrote to Mme Du Deffand in terms that link this motto and the final paragraph of the 'Avertissement': 'il est assez plaisant d'envoïer du pied des Alpes à Paris des fusées volantes qui crèvent sur la tête des sots; il est vrai qu'on n'a pas visé précisément aux plus absurdes, et aux plus révoltans, mais patience, chacun aura son tour; il se trouvera quelque bonne âme que vangera l'univers' (D9121).

ÉPÎTRE DÉDICATOIRE DU TRADUCTEUR DE L'ÉCOSSAISE, A MONSIEUR LE COMTE DE LAURAGUAIS

Monsieur,

La petite bagatelle que j'ai l'honneur de mettre sous votre protection, n'est qu'un prétexte pour vous parler avec liberté.

Vous avez rendu un service éternel aux beaux-arts et au bon goût, en contribuant par votre générosité à donner à la ville de Paris un théâtre moins indigne d'elle. Si on ne voit plus sur la scène César et Ptolomée,[1] Athalie et Joad, Mérope et son fils entourés et pressés d'une foule de jeunes gens,[2] si les spectacles ont plus de décence, c'est à vous seul qu'on en est redevable. Ce bienfait est d'autant plus considérable, que l'art de la tragédie et de la comédie est celui dans lequel les Français se sont distingués davantage: il n'en est aucun dans lequel ils n'aient de très illustres rivaux, ou même des maîtres. Nous avons quelques bons philosophes; mais, il faut l'avouer, nous ne sommes que les disciples des Newtons, des Lockes, des Galilées. Si la France a quelques historiens, les Espagnols, les Italiens, les Anglais même nous disputent la supériorité dans ce genre. Le seul Massillon aujourd'hui passe chez les gens de goût pour un orateur agréable; mais qu'il est encore loin de l'archevêque Tillotson[3] aux yeux du reste

a-72 60, 60Y, 60CR, 60AM, 61L1, absent (first published in SS61)

[1] In Corneille's *La Mort de Pompée* (1643).

[2] Cf. Voltaire's disapproval of the same 'foule de jeunes gens qui laissaient à peine dix pieds de place aux acteurs' ('Dissertation sur la tragédie ancienne et moderne', prefacing *Sémiramis*, 1748; M.iv.500). It was, in effect, at this play that the famous appeal to make 'place à l'ombre' was made.

[3] John Tillotson (1630-1694), archbishop of Canterbury in 1691. Voltaire greatly admired his rhetoric.

de l'Europe! Je ne prétends point peser le mérite des hommes de génie; je n'ai pas la main assez forte pour tenir cette balance. Je vous dis seulement comment pensent les autres peuples; et vous savez, Monsieur, vous qui dans votre première jeunesse avez voyagé pour vous instruire, vous savez que presque chaque peuple a ses hommes de génie qu'il préfère à ceux de ses voisins. 20 25

Si vous descendez des arts de l'esprit pur à ceux où la main a plus de part, quel peintre oserions-nous préférer aux grands peintres d'Italie? C'est dans le seul art des Sophocles que toutes les nations s'accordent à donner la préférence à la nôtre; c'est pourquoi dans plusieurs villes d'Italie la bonne compagnie se rassemble pour représenter nos pièces, ou dans notre langue, ou en italien; c'est ce qui fait qu'on trouve des théâtres français à Vienne et à Pétersbourg. 30

Ce qu'on pouvait reprocher à la scène française, était le manque d'action et d'appareil. Les tragédies étaient souvent de longues conversations en cinq actes.[4] Comment hasarder ces spectacles pompeux, ces tableaux frappants, ces actions grandes et terribles, qui bien ménagées sont un des plus grands ressorts de la tragédie? Comment apporter le corps de César sanglant sur la scène?[5] Comment faire descendre une reine éperdue dans le tombeau de son époux, et l'en faire sortir mourante de la main de son fils, au milieu d'une foule qui cache et le tombeau et le fils et la mère, et qui énerve la terreur du spectacle par le contraste du ridicule?[6] 35 40

C'est de ce défaut monstrueux que vos seuls bienfaits ont purgé la scène; et quand il se trouvera des génies qui sauront allier la pompe d'un appareil nécessaire, et la vivacité d'une action également terrible et vraisemblable, à la force des pensées, et surtout à la belle et naturelle poésie, sans laquelle l'art dramatique 45

25 SS61, T64P: qu'elle préfère

[4] Voltaire's view since 1730 ('Discours sur la tragédie'; M.ii.314) and repeated in 1748 ('Dissertation sur la tragédie'; M.iv.500).
[5] *La Mort de César*, III.viii.
[6] *Sémiramis*, V.ii and viii.

n'est rien; ce sera vous, Monsieur, que la postérité devra remercier.[7] 50

Mais il ne faut pas laisser ce soin à la postérité; il faut avoir le courage de dire à son siècle, ce que nos contemporains font de noble et d'utile. Les justes éloges sont un parfum qu'on réserve pour embaumer les morts. Un homme fait du bien, on étouffe ce bien pendant qu'il respire; et si on en parle, on l'exténue, on le 55 défigure: n'est-il plus? on exagère son mérite pour abaisser ceux qui vivent.

Je veux du moins que ceux qui pourront lire ce petit ouvrage sachent qu'il y a dans Paris plus d'un homme estimable et

[7] Some of the notes which appear in eighteenth- and nineteenth-century editions are sufficiently interesting to warrant inclusion here. Kehl: 'Il y avait longtemps que M. de Voltaire avait réclamé contre l'usage ridicule de placer les spectateurs sur le théâtre, et de rétrécir l'avant-scène par des banquettes; lorsque M. le comte de Lauraguais donna les sommes nécessaires pour mettre les comédiens à portée de détruire cet usage.

M. de Voltaire s'est élevé contre l'indécence d'un parterre debout et tumultueux; et dans les nouvelles salles construites à Paris le parterre est assis. Ses justes réclamations ont été écoutées sur des objets importans. On lui doit en grande partie la suppression des sépultures dans les églises, l'établissement des cimetières hors des villes, la dimunition du nombre des fêtes, même celle qu'ont ordonnée des évêques qui n'avaient jamais lu ses ouvrages; enfin l'abolition de la servitude de la glèbe et celle de la torture. Tous ces changements se sont faits, à la vérité, lentement, à demi, et comme si l'on eût voulu prouver en les fesant qu'on suivait non sa propre raison, mais qu'on cédait à l'impulsion irrésistible que M. de Voltaire avait donnée aux esprits.

La tolérance qu'il avait tant prêchée s'est établie peu de temps après sa mort en Suède et dans les Etats héréditaires de la maison d'Autriche; et, quoi qu'on en dise, nous la verrons bientôt s'établir en France.'

Palissot: 'Depuis la date de cette lettre, toutes les salles de spectacles ont été renouvelées à Paris: mais c'est M. de Lauraguais qui, longtemps auparavant, avait fait cesser les abus contre lesquels Voltaire s'est si souvent élevé. Les comédiens, qui gagnèrent beaucoup à la suppression de ces abus, auraient dû, pour l'avantage de leur salle et pour la commodité du public, disputer à M. de Lauraguais cet honneur; mais ils lui laissèrent noblement payer tous les frais de ces réparations; et nous l'avons entendu souvent se plaindre de leur ingratitude.'

Beuchot: 'Il en coûta 30.000 francs au comte de Lauraguais pour la suppression des banquettes qui encombraient la scène, et dont Voltaire s'est plaint souvent. La suppression date du 23 avril 1759.'

malheureux secouru par vous; je veux qu'on sache que tandis que 60
vous occupez votre loisir à faire revivre par les soins les plus
coûteux et les plus pénibles un art utile perdu dans l'Asie qui
l'inventa,[8] vous faites renaître un secret plus ignoré, celui de
soulager par vos bienfaits cachés la vertu indigente.[9]

Je n'ignore pas qu'à Paris il y a dans ce qu'on appelle le monde, 65
des gens qui croient pouvoir donner des ridicules aux belles
actions, qu'ils sont incapables de faire; et c'est ce qui redouble
mon respect pour vous.

P. S. Je ne mets point mon inutile nom au bas de cette épître,
parce que je ne l'ai jamais mis à aucun de mes ouvrages; et quand 70
on le voit à la tête d'un livre ou dans une affiche, qu'on s'en
prenne uniquement à l'afficheur ou au libraire.

[8] Palissot: 'M. de Lauraguais ne crut pas déroger à ce qu'on appellait alors la dignité de son rang, en prenant des leçons d'anatomie et de chimie. Il devint même un assez habile chimiste pour faire la découverte d'une nouvelle espèce de porcelaine, et c'est à lui que la France doit en partie les belles manufactures que l'on y voit maintenant, et qui, dans ce genre d'industrie, ne paraissent pas inférieures à celles de la Chine et du Japon.'

[9] Kehl: 'M. le comte de Lauraguais avait fait une pension au célèbre du Marsais, qui sans lui eût traîné sa vieillesse dans la misère. Le gouvernement ne lui donnait aucun secours, parce qu'il était soupçonné d'être janséniste, et même d'avoir écrit en faveur du gouvernement contre les pretensions de la cour de Rome.'

Palissot: 'Le célèbre grammarien du Marsais, qui avait été obligé de faire des éducations pour vivre, et qui n'avait trouvé que des ingrats parmi ses élèves, serait mort de misère sans le secours de M. de Lauraguais, qui lui fit une pension. Du Marsais avait deux grands torts aux yeux du Gouvernement: une âme fière et noble, et une philosophie supérieure à tous les préjugés.'

A MESSIEURS LES PARISIENS[a]

Messieurs,

Je suis forcé par l'illustre M. F.....,[1] de m'exposer *vis-à-vis*[2] de vous. Je parlerai sur le *ton* du sentiment et du respect; ma plainte sera marquée au *coin* de la bienséance, et éclairée du *flambeau* de la vérité. J'espère que M. F..... sera confondu *vis-à-vis des* honnêtes gens qui ne sont pas accoutumés à se prêter aux méchancetés de ceux qui n'étant pas *sentimentés*,[3] font *métier et marchandise*[4] d'insulter *le tiers et le quart*, sans aucune *provocation*, comme dit Cicéron dans l'oraison *pro Murena*, page 4.[5]

[a] Cette plaisanterie fut publiée la veille de la représentation.

a-93 60, 60Y, 60CR, 60AM, 61L1, absent (first published in SS61)
n.*a* MSR1, R1, PD58, RF60, JR60, note *a* absent
2 MSR1, R1, PD58, JR60: M. Fréron [throughout]
9 JR60: *Murena*.//

[1] Despite Voltaire's complaint to Cramer (15 January 1761) to the effect that 'je ne conçois pas pourquoi on a mis une f au lieu de Fréron dans le volume qu'on a imprimé' – SS61 – later eighteenth-century editions (W68, W75G, K84 for example) continued to print F....., and an equally transparent truncation (M. L. F.... de P........) for Lefranc de Pompignan.

[2] Fréron frequently used *vis-à-vis de* for *avec*. Voltaire expressed his 'indignation académique' about this usage in a letter to d'Olivet on 22 January [1761] (D9566). Fréron saw himself as bearing 'le flambeau de la critique' in his *Lettres sur quelques écrits de ce temps* (ii.4).

[3] *Sentimentés*: a Voltairean invention?

[4] A parody of the line in *Tartuffe* (I.vi): 'Font de dévotion métier et marchandise.'

[5] *Provocatio* does not appear in Cicero's *Pro L. Murena Oratio*. It would have the sense of 'right of appeal' (as Cicero uses it in, for example, *De re publica*, II.xxxi.54). No doubt Voltaire is simply placing his own right of appeal, his own *Requête*, against anti-*philosophe* attacks by Le Franc de Pompignan, Fréron and Palissot under Ciceronian aegis, in a very oblique way.

Messieurs, je m'appelle Jérôme Carré, natif de Montauban;[6] je suis un pauvre jeune homme sans fortune; et comme la volonté me charge d'entrer dans Montauban, à cause que M. L. F.... de P........ m'y persécute, je suis venu implorer la protection des Parisiens. J'ai traduit la comédie de l'*Ecossaise* de M. Hume. Les comédiens français, et les Italiens, voulaient la représenter: elle aurait peut-être été jouée cinq ou six fois, et voilà que M. F..... emploie son autorité et son crédit, pour empêcher ma traduction de paraître; lui qui encourageait tant les jeunes gens quand il était jésuite, les opprime aujourd'hui: il a fait une feuille entière contre moi; il commence par dire méchamment que ma traduction vient de Genève, pour me faire *suspecter* d'être hérétique.[7] 10 15 20

Ensuite il appelle M. Hume, *M. Home*; et puis il dit que M. Hume le prêtre, auteur de cette pièce, n'est pas parent de M. Hume le philosophe. Qu'il consulte seulement le Journal Encyclopédique du mois d'avril 1758, journal que je regarde comme le premier des cent soixante et treize journaux qui paraissent tous les mois en Europe, il y verra cette annonce page 137. 25

L'auteur de Douglas est le ministre Hume, parent du fameux David Hume, si célèbre par son impiété.

Je ne sais pas si M. David Hume est impie: s'il l'est, j'en suis bien fâché, et je prie Dieu pour lui comme je le dois; mais il 30

11 JR60: et comme je me trouve forcé de m'exiler de ma patrie, à cause que

12 MSR1, R1, PD58, RF60, SS61, T64P: me change d'entrer
MSR1, R1, PD58, JR60: Lefranc de Pompignan

13-14 JR60: Parisiens. ¶J'ai

[6] Voltaire had established Jérôme Carré as an anglicist in his *Appel à toutes les nations* (1760). He regretfully announced the death of Carré (and of Guillaume Vadé) in the 'Discours' preceding *Les Guèbres* (1768): 'ils auraient peut-être un peu servi à débarbouiller ce siècle' (M.vi.503, n.3). The passing blows at Le Franc de Pompignan echo Voltaire's joyous *Extrait des nouvelles à la main de la ville de Montauban en Quercy* (1er juillet 1760).

[7] The adroit mixture of truth and insinuation in this paragraph does not merit any detailed comment. Clearly, in this battle no holds were barred on either side.

résulte que l'auteur de l'*Ecossaise* est M. Hume le prêtre, parent de M. David Hume; ce qu'il fallait prouver, et ce qui est très indifférent.[8]

J'avoue à ma honte que je l'ai cru son frère; mais qu'il soit frère ou cousin, il est toujours certain qu'il est l'auteur de l'*Ecossaise*. Il est vrai que dans le journal que je cite, l'*Ecossaise* n'est pas expressément nommée; on n'y parle que d'*Agis* et de *Douglas*; mais c'est une bagatelle. 35

Il est si vrai qu'il est l'auteur de l'*Ecossaise*, que j'ai en main plusieurs de ses lettres, par lesquelles il me remercie de l'avoir traduite; en voici une que je soumets aux lumières du charitable lecteur. 40

My dear translator, mon cher traducteur, *you have comitted many a blunder in yr. performancée,* vous avez fait plusieurs balourdises dans votre traduction: *you have quitte impoverish'd the caracter of Wasp, and you have blotted his chastitement at the end of the drama...* vous avez affaibli le caractère de Frélon, et vous avez supprimé son châtiment à la fin de la pièce. 45

Il est vrai, et je l'ai déjà dit, que j'ai fort adouci les traits dont l'auteur peint son Wasp, (ce mot *Wasp* veut dire *Frélon*;) mais je ne l'ai fait que par le conseil des personnes les plus judicieuses de Paris. La politesse française ne permet pas certains termes que 50

38 MSR1, R1, PD58: nommée expressément
45 PD58: *performann*
SS61, T64P: *performancee*
46 PD58: *quite impover sh'd*
47 PD58: *blolted vut his*
50 R1: fort admiré les

[8] On Hume, Home and similarities between *L'Ecossaise* and *Douglas*, see introduction, p.243-44. The *Journal encyclopédique* for 1 April 1758 reads: 'C'est le ministre Hume, parent du fameux David Hume, si célèbre par son esprit et son impiété'. Hence Voltaire's error regarding the spelling of John Home's name. His first play *Agis*, was rejected by Garrick, but was performed with great success in Edinburgh in 1756 and (thanks to Garrick) at Drury Lane in 1758. *Douglas* was a success in 1757 at Covent Garden, with Peg Woffington as Lady Randolph (later played by Mrs Siddons).

la liberté anglaise emploie volontiers. Si je suis coupable, c'est par excès de retenue; et j'espère que Messieurs les Parisiens, dont 55 je demande la protection, pardonneront les défauts de la pièce en faveur de ma circonspection.

Il semble que M. Hume ait fait sa comédie uniquement dans la vue de mettre son *Wasp* sur la scène, et moi j'ai retranché tout ce que j'ai pu de ce personnage; j'ai aussi retranché quelque chose 60 de milady Alton, pour m'éloigner moins de vos mœurs, et pour faire voir quel est mon respect pour les dames.

M. F....., dans la vue de me nuire, dit dans sa feuille page 114, qu'on l'appelle aussi *Frélon*, que plusieurs personnes de mérite l'ont souvent nommé ainsi. Mais, Messieurs, qu'est-ce que cela 65 peut avoir de commun avec un personnage anglais dans la pièce de M. Hume? Vous voyez bien qu'il ne cherche que de vains prétextes pour me ravir la protection, dont je vous supplie de m'honorer.

Voyez, je vous prie, jusqu'où va sa malice: il dit, pag. 115, que 70 le bruit courut longtemps qu'il *avait été condamné aux galères*; et il affirme, qu'en effet, pour la condamnation, elle n'a jamais eu lieu: mais, je vous en supplie, que ce monsieur ait été aux galères quelque temps, ou qu'il y aille, quel rapport cette anecdote peut-elle avoir avec la traduction d'un drame anglais? Il parle des 75 raisons qui *pouvaient*, dit-il, *lui avoir attiré ce malheur*.[9] Je vous jure, Messieurs, que je n'entre dans aucune de ces raisons; il peut y en

58 RI, PD58: fait la comédie

72-73 RI: lieu. ¶Mais

73-74 MSRI, RI, PD58, JR60: Mais, Messieurs, que M. Fréron ait été aux galères quelque temps, ou qu'il y aille, quel rapport, je vous en supplie, cette anecdote

76 MSRI, RI, PD58: *qui pouvaient lui avoir*, dit-il, *attiré*

[9] In *L'Année littéraire* (1760), iv.115, Fréron traces back the 'galleys rumour' to his unfavourable review of Voltaire's *Oreste* (1749). The rumour, betraying deep-seated wishful thinking on the part of the *philosophes*, was perpetuated on several occasions; Fréron's reference to it here was not only irrelevant but ill-advised.

avoir de bonnes, sans que M. Hume doive s'en inquiéter: qu'il aille aux galères ou non, je n'en suis pas moins le traducteur de l'*Ecossaise*. Je vous demande, Messieurs, votre protection contre lui. Recevez ce petit drame avec cette affabilité que vous témoignez aux étrangers. 80

J'ai l'honneur d'être avec un profond respect,

Messieurs,

Votre très humble et très obéissant serviteur, JÉRÔME CARRÉ, natif de Montauban, demeurant dans l'impasse de St Thomas du Louvre; car j'appelle *impasse*, Messieurs, ce que vous appelez *cul-de-sac*: je trouve qu'une rue ne ressemble ni à un cul ni à un sac: je vous prie de vous servir du mot d'*impasse*, qui est noble, sonore, intelligible, nécessaire, au lieu de celui de cul, en dépit du sieur Fr.... ci-devant J......[10] 85 90

78 RI: inquiéter. ¶Qu'il aille
86 MSRI, RI, PD58, JR60: Montauban.//

[10] The attack on *cul-de-sac* may seem parenthetical unless one links it with 1) Voltaire's letter to l'abbé d'Olivet of 20 August 1761 ('*impasse* que les Anglais ont imitée, & nous sommes réduits au mot bas & impertinent de *cul-de-sac*'; D9959); 2) the *rappel* of Jérôme Carré's apostrophe, in the *Discours aux Welches* (1764) and the *Supplément du Discours*, where *cul-de-sac* is judged 'horriblement Welche'; 3) the initial pederastic innuendo directed at *le sieur Fréron ci-devant jésuite*. The whole piece, at least, has a scurrilous unity, created by two apparent sets of irrelevances based on Voltaire's stylistic *bêtes noires*.

AVERTISSEMENT

Cette lettre de M. Jérôme Carré eut tout l'effet qu'elle méritait. La pièce fut représentée au commencement d'août 1760.[1] On commença tard, et quelqu'un demandant pourquoi on attendait si longtemps? *C'est apparemment*, répondit tout haut un homme d'esprit, *que F..... est monté à l'hôtel de ville*. Comme ce *F*..... avait eu l'inadvertance de se reconnaître dans la comédie de l'*Ecossaise*, quoique M. Hume ne l'eût jamais eu en vue, le public le reconnut aussi. La comédie était sue de tout le monde par cœur avant qu'on la jouât, et cependant elle fut reçue avec un succès prodigieux. F..... fit encore la faute d'imprimer dans je ne sais quelles feuilles, intitulées *l'Année Littéraire*, que l'*Ecossaise* n'avait réussi qu'à l'aide d'une cabale composée de douze à quinze cents personnes, qui toutes, disait-il, le haïssaient et le méprisaient souverainement. Mais M. Jérôme Carré était bien loin de faire des cabales: tout Paris sait assez qu'il n'est pas à portée d'en faire; d'ailleurs il n'avait jamais vu ce F.....[2] et il ne pouvait comprendre pourquoi tous les spectateurs s'obstinaient à voir F..... dans Frélon. Un avocat à la seconde représentation s'écria, Courage, M. Carré, vengez le public; le parterre et les loges applaudirent à ces paroles par des battements de mains qui ne finissaient point. Carré, au sortir du spectacle, fut embrassé par plus de cent personnes. Que vous êtes aimable, M. Carré, lui disait-on, d'avoir fait justice de cet homme, dont les mœurs sont encore plus odieuses que la plume! Eh, messieurs, répondit Carré, vous me faites plus d'hon-

a-74 60, 60Y, 60CR, 60AM, 61L1, absent (first published in SS61)

[1] This perpetuated error regarding the date of the first performance is inexplicable.

[2] Most probably true. In October 1750 Fréron wrote to Voltaire: 'Si j'étais connu de vous, monsieur' (D4284).

neur que je ne mérite; je ne suis qu'un pauvre traducteur d'une comédie pleine de morale et d'intérêt. 25

Comme il parlait ainsi sur l'escalier, il fut barbouillé de deux baisers par la femme de F......; Que je vous suis obligée, dit-elle, d'avoir puni mon mari! mais vous ne le corrigerez point. L'innocent Carré était tout confondu; il ne comprenait pas comment un personnage anglais pouvait être pris pour un Français nommé F.....; et toute la France lui faisait compliment de l'avoir peint trait pour trait. Ce jeune homme apprit par cette aventure combien il faut avoir de circonspection: il comprit en général que toutes les fois qu'on fait le portrait d'un homme ridicule, il se trouve toujours quelqu'un qui lui ressemble. 30 35

Ce rôle de Frélon était très peu important dans la pièce; il ne contribua en rien au vrai succès; car elle reçut dans plusieurs provinces les mêmes applaudissements qu'à Paris. On peut dire à cela que ce Frélon était autant estimé dans les provinces que dans la capitale: mais il est bien plus vraisemblable que le vif intérêt qui règne dans la pièce de M. Hume en a fait tout le succès. Peignez un faquin, vous ne réussirez qu'auprès de quelques personnes: intéressez, vous plairez à tout le monde. 40

Quoi qu'il en soit, voici la traduction d'une lettre de milord Boldthinker au prétendu Hume, au sujet de sa pièce de l'*Ecossaise*. 45

'Je crois, mon cher Hume, que vous avez encore quelque talent; vous en êtes comptable à la nation; c'est peu d'avoir immolé ce vilain Frélon à la risée publique, sur tous les théâtres de l'Europe, où l'on joue votre aimable et vertueuse *Ecossaise*: faites plus, mettez sur la scène tous ces vils persécuteurs de la littérature, tous ces hypocrites noircis de vices, et calomniateurs de la vertu; traînez sur le théâtre, devant le tribunal du public, ces fanatiques enragés, qui jettent leur écume sur l'innocence; et ces hommes faux, qui vous flattent d'un œil, et qui vous menacent de l'autre, qui n'osent parler devant un philosophe, et qui tâchent de le 50 55

28 SS61, T64P: par la f.... de F.....
29 SS61, T64P: puni mon m...! mais

détruire en secret: exposez au grand jour ces détestables cabales qui voudraient replonger les hommes dans les ténèbres.'

'Vous avez gardé trop longtemps le silence; on ne gagne rien à vouloir adoucir les pervers; il n'y a plus d'autre moyen de rendre les lettres respectables, que de faire trembler ceux qui les outragent: c'est le dernier parti que prit Pope avant de mourir: il rendit ridicules à jamais, dans sa *Dunciade*,[3] tous ceux qui devaient l'être: ils n'osèrent plus se montrer, ils disparurent; toute la nation lui applaudit; car si dans les commencements la malignité donna un peu de vogue à ces lâches ennemis de Pope, de Swift et de leurs amis, la raison reprit bientôt le dessus. Les Zoïles[4] ne sont soutenus qu'un temps. Le vrai talent des vers est une arme qu'il faut employer à venger le genre humain.[5] Ce n'est pas les Pantolabes et les Nomentanus seulement qu'il faut effleurer; ce sont les Anitus et les Mélitus qu'il faut écraser.[6] Un vers bien fait transmet à la dernière postérité la gloire d'un homme de bien, et la honte d'un méchant. Travaillez, vous ne manquerez pas de matière, etc.'

60

65

70

[3] Pope's satire (1742) was to be emulated by Palissot himself in 1763, with Fréron as one of the objects.

[4] The Alexandrian critic of Homer, Zoïlos, had already inspired the character of Zoïlin (see introduction, p.241).

[5] An echo of this is to be found in the alexandrine on the title page.

[6] Behind this pedantic façade is a call to action: it is not only minor villains such as Pantolabes and Nomentanus (Horace, *Eighth Satire*, I.10) (and Fréron) that should be attacked, but, more importantly, the enemies of the *philosophes* (symbolised by Socrates' opponents, whom Voltaire had recently dealt with in *Socrate*. Into the mouth of Anitus, Voltaire puts words echoed in *L'Ecossaise*, I.iii: 'ces philosophes sont d'une subtilité diabolique; ce sont eux qui ont troublé tous les Etats où nous apportions la concorde', *Socrate*, II.ix).

PRÉFACE

La comédie dont nous présentons la traduction aux amateurs de la littérature, est[a] de monsieur Hume,[1] pasteur de l'église d'Edimbourg, déjà connu par deux belles tragédies, jouées à Londres: il est parent et ami de ce célèbre philosophe M. Hume, qui a creusé avec tant de hardiesse et de sagacité les fondements de la métaphysique et de la morale; ces deux philosophes font également honneur à l'Ecosse leur patrie. 5

La comédie intitulée l'*Ecossaise*, nous parut un de ces ouvrages qui peuvent réussir dans toutes les langues, parce que l'auteur peint la nature, qui est partout la même: il a la naïveté et la vérité de l'estimable Goldoni, avec peut-être plus d'intrigue, de force, et d'intérêt. Le dénouement, le caractère de l'héroïne, et celui de Fréeport, ne ressemblent à rien de ce que nous connaissons sur les théâtres de France; et cependant, c'est la nature pure. Cette pièce paraît un peu dans le goût de ces romans anglais qui ont fait tant de fortune: ce sont des touches semblables, la même peinture des mœurs, rien de recherché, nulle envie d'avoir de l'esprit, et de montrer misérablement l'auteur, quand on ne doit montrer que les personnages: rien d'étranger au sujet; point de 10 15

[a] On sent bien que c'était une plaisanterie d'attribuer cette pièce à M. Hume.

n.*a* 60, note *a* absent
4 60, 60CR, 60AM: est le frère de ce célèbre
8 60, 60CR, 60AM: m'a paru un

[1] Palissot: 'Cette plaisanterie fut depuis renouvellée trop souvent par Voltaire. Il prenait tour-à-tour les noms de Jérôme Carré, de Guillaume Vadé, de Robert Covelle, de Fatéma, d'Eratou, &c. &c. sous lesquels il ne cherchait pas réellement à se cacher, mais qu'il adoptait par caprice, sans que nous puissions deviner ce qu'il trouvait de piquant dans ces espèces de travestissemens bisarres'.

tirade d'écolier, de ces maximes triviales qui remplissent le vide de l'action. C'est une justice que nous sommes obligés de rendre à notre célèbre auteur. 20

Nous avouons en même temps que nous avons cru, par le conseil des hommes les plus éclairés, devoir retrancher quelque chose du rôle de Frélon, qui paraissait encore dans les derniers actes: il était puni, comme de raison, à la fin de la pièce; mais cette justice qu'on lui rendait, semblait mêler un peu de froideur au vif intérêt qui entraîne l'esprit vers le dénouement. 25

De plus, le caractère de Frélon est si lâche, et si odieux, que nous avons voulu épargner aux lecteurs la vue trop fréquente de ce personnage, plus dégoûtant que comique. Nous convenons qu'il est dans la nature: car dans les grandes villes, où la presse jouit de quelque liberté, on trouve toujours quelques-uns de ces misérables qui se font un revenu de leur impudence, de ces Arétins subalternes qui gagnent leur pain à dire et à faire du mal, sous le prétexte d'être utiles aux belles-lettres, comme si les vers qui rongent les fruits et les fleurs pouvaient leur être utiles. 30 35

L'un des deux illustres savants, et pour nous exprimer encore plus correctement, l'un de ces deux hommes de génie, qui ont présidé au Dictionnaire Encyclopédique, à cet ouvrage nécessaire au genre humain, dont la suspension[2] fait gémir l'Europe; l'un de ces deux grands hommes, dis-je, dans des essais qu'il s'est amusé à faire sur l'art de la comédie,[3] remarque très judicieusement, que l'on doit songer à mettre sur le théâtre les conditions et les états des hommes. L'emploi du Frélon de M. Hume est une espèce 40 45

36 60AM: d'être utile aux

[2] The *Encyclopédie* had had its privilege revoked the previous year (8 March 1759).

[3] Diderot's *Entretiens sur le Fils naturel* (1757) and *Discours sur la poésie dramatique* (1758). On the 'Préface' and Diderot's theory of conditions, see introduction, p.283-87.

d'état en Angleterre: il y a même une taxe[4] établie sur les feuilles de ces gens-là. Ni cet état, ni ce caractère, ne paraissent dignes du théâtre en France; mais le pinceau anglais ne dédaigne rien; il se plaît quelquefois à tracer des objets, dont la bassesse peut révolter quelques autres nations. Il n'importe aux Anglais que le sujet soit bas, pourvu qu'il soit vrai. Ils disent que la comédie étend ses droits sur tous les caractères, et sur toutes les conditions; que tout ce qui est dans la nature doit être peint; que nous avons une fausse délicatesse, et que l'homme le plus méprisable peut servir de contraste au plus galant homme. 50 55

J'ajouterai, pour la justification de M. Hume, qu'il a l'art de ne présenter son Frélon que dans des moments où l'intérêt n'est pas encore vif et touchant. Il a imité ces peintres qui peignent un crapaud, un lézard, une couleuvre dans un coin du tableau, en conservant aux personnages la noblesse de leur caractère. 60

Ce qui nous a frappé vivement dans cette pièce, c'est que l'unité de temps, de lieu, et d'action y est observée scrupuleusement. Elle a encore ce mérite rare chez les Anglais, comme chez les Italiens, que le théâtre n'est jamais vide. Rien n'est plus commun et plus choquant, que de voir deux acteurs sortir de la scène, et deux autres venir à leur place sans être appelés, sans être attendus; ce défaut insupportable ne se trouve point dans l'*Ecossaise*. 65

Quant au genre de la pièce, il est dans le haut comique, mêlé au genre de la simple comédie. L'honnête homme y sourit de ce sourire de l'âme préférable au rire de la bouche. Il y a des endroits attendrissants jusqu'aux larmes; mais sans pourtant qu'aucun 70

59 60, 60CR, 60AM: un coin de tableau
60 60CR, 60AM: leurs caractères.

[4] An oblique reference to the tax levied on Fréron's *Année littéraire*. The proceeds were used to finance the *Journal des savants*, much to Voltaire's disgust: 'C'est une chose honteuse que m. de Malesherbes soutienne ce monstre de Fréron, et que le *Journal des savants* ne soit payé que du produit des feuilles scandaleuses d'un homme couvert d'opprobre' (Voltaire to Le Brun, 15 February 1761; D9629).

personnage s'étudie à être pathétique: car de même que la bonne plaisanterie consiste à ne vouloir point être plaisant, ainsi, celui qui vous émeut ne songe point à vous émouvoir; il n'est point rhétoricien, tout part du cœur. Malheur à celui qui tâche, dans quelque genre que ce puisse être! 75

Nous ne savons pas si cette pièce pourrait être représentée à Paris; notre état, et notre vie, qui ne nous ont pas permis de fréquenter souvent les spectacles, nous laissent dans l'impuissance de juger quel effet une pièce anglaise ferait en France. 80

Tout ce que nous pouvons dire, c'est que malgré tous les efforts que nous avons faits pour rendre exactement l'original, nous sommes très loin d'avoir atteint au mérite de ses expressions, toujours fortes, et toujours naturelles.

Ce qui est beaucoup plus important, c'est que cette comédie est d'une excellente morale, et digne de la gravité du sacerdoce, dont l'auteur est revêtu, sans rien perdre de ce qui peut plaire aux honnêtes gens du monde. 85

La comédie ainsi traitée est un des plus utiles efforts de l'esprit humain. Il faut convenir que c'est un art, et un art très difficile. Tout le monde peut compiler des faits et des raisonnements. Il est aisé d'apprendre la trigonométrie: mais tout art demande un talent, et le talent est rare. 90

Nous ne pouvons mieux finir cette préface que par ce passage de notre compatriote Montagne sur les spectacles. 95

'J'ai soutenu les premiers personnages ès tragédies latines de Bucanam, et de Guerante, et de Muret, qui se représentèrent à notre collège de Guienne avec dignité. En cela, Andreas Goveanus notre principal, comme en toutes autres parties de sa charge, fut sans comparaison le plus grand principal de France, et m'en tenait-on maître ouvrier. C'est un exercice que je ne mesloue point aux jeunes enfans de maison, et ai vu nos princes depuis s'y adonner en personne, à l'exemple d'aucuns des anciens, honnestement et louablement: il est loisible même d'en faire mestier aux gens d'honneur et en Grèce. *Aristoni tragico actori rem aperit: huic et genus, et fortuna honesta erant: nec ars, quia nihil tale apud* 100 105

Graecos pudori est, ea deformabat.[5] Car j'ai toujours accusé d'impertinence ceux qui condamnent ces esbatemens, et d'injustice ceux qui empeschent l'entrée de nos bonnes villes aux comédiens qui le valent, et envient au peuple ces plaisirs publics. Les bonnes polices prennent soin d'assembler les citoyens, et les rallier comme aux offices sérieux de la dévotion, aussi aux exercices et jeux. La société et amitié s'en augmente, et puis on ne leur concède des passetemps plus réglés que ceux qui se font en présence de chacun, et à la vue même du magistrat; et trouverais raisonnable que le prince à ses dépens en gratifiast quelquefois la commune; et qu'aux villes populeuses il y eût des lieux destinés, et desposés pour ces spectacles; quelque divertissement de pires actions et occultes. Pour revenir à mon propos, il n'y a tel que d'allécher l'appétit et l'affection, autrement on ne fait que des asnes chargés de livres; on leur donne à coups de fouet, en garde, leur pochette pleine de science; laquelle, pour bien faire, il ne faut pas seulement loger chez soi, il la faut épouser.'[6]

110

115

120

[5] Livy, xxiv.24. Voltaire copies Montaigne's reading, including omissions. 'He revealed the matter to the tragic actor Ariston. This man was distinguished in both birth and fortune; nor did his art spoil his position, since nothing of that sort is considered a disgrace by the Greeks.'

[6] 'De l'institution des enfants', *Essais*, ch.26 (ed. Pléiade [1958], p.212-13). This is the final paragraph of the essay.

ACTEURS

Maître FABRICE, tenant un café avec des appartements.

LINDANE, Ecossaise.

Le lord MONROSE, Ecossais.

Le lord MURRAI.

POLLY, suivante. 5

FRÉEPORT, *qu'on prononce* FRIPORT, gros négociant de Londres.

FRÉLON, écrivain de feuilles.

Lady ALTON, *on prononce* Lédy.

a K: PERSONNAGES

1 60CR, 60AM: FABRICE, maître du café. M. Armand

2 60CR, 60AM: L'ECOSSAISE ou LINDANE. Mlle Gaussin [60AM adds: ou Mme Tauvalegue]

3 60, 60Y: MONROSE, seigneur écossais

60CR, 60AM: MONROSE, père de Lindane. M. Brizard

4 60CR, 60AM: Milord MURRAI [60AM adds: amant de Lindane]. M. Bellecour

5 60CR, 60AM: POLLY, suivante de Lindane. Mlle Dangeville

6 60CR, 60AM: FRÉEPORT [...]. M. Préville

6-7 60, 60Y, 60CR, 60AM: négociant.//

8 60CR, 60AM: WASP, faiseur de feuilles périodiques. M. Dubois [with note: En français FRELON]

60, 60Y: écrivain de feuilles, et fripon

9 60CR, 60AM: Milady ALTON. Mlle Préville

Plusieurs Anglais qui viennent au café. 10

Domestiques.

Un messager d'Etat.

La scène est à Londres.

9 60CR, 60AM, between 9-10: ANDRÉ, valet. M. Duranci

10 60CR: Quatre interlocuteurs. MM. Le Kain, Bonneval, Paulin, Blainville

12 60CR, 60AM: Un messager. M. d'Auberval

60, absent

13 60CR, 60AM: *La scène* [60AM: *est à Londres, et le théâtre*] *représente tantôt une salle commune du café, et tantôt l'appartement de Lindane.*

ACTE PREMIER

SCÈNE PREMIÈRE

(*La scène représente un café et des chambres sur les ailes, de façon qu'on peut entrer de plain-pied des appartements dans le café.*)[a]

FRÉLON (*dans un coin, auprès d'une table sur laquelle il y a une écritoire et du café, lisant la gazette.*)

Que de nouvelles affligeantes! des grâces répandues sur plus de vingt personnes! aucunes sur moi! Cent guinées de gratification à un bas officier, parce qu'il a fait son devoir; le beau mérite! Une pension à l'inventeur d'une machine qui ne sert qu'à soulager des ouvriers! une à un pilote! des places à des gens de lettres! et à moi rien! Encore, encore, et à moi rien.[1] (*Il jette la gazette et se* 5

[a] On a fait hausser et baisser une toile au théâtre de Paris, pour marquer le passage d'une chambre à une autre; la vraisemblance et la décence ont été bien mieux observées à Lyon, à Marseille et ailleurs. Il y avait sur le théâtre un cabinet à côté du café. C'est ainsi qu'on aurait dû en user à Paris.

c-d 61L1, no stage direction
n.*a* 60, 60Y, 60CR, 60AM, T64P, MS1, note *a* absent
e 60CR:AC, 60CR*, 60X*, 60AM, MS1: WASP [throughout]
f 60AM: *écritoire et plusieurs papiers, lisant*
2 60Y: aucune sur moi!
2-5 60CR*, 60X*, 60AM, MS1: sur moi! des places à des gens

[1] Palissot: 'Ce refrain de Frélon, *Et à moi rien!* nous paraît caractériser parfaitement un envieux sans mérite, qui s'indigne intérieurement de toutes les récompenses accordées à des gens qui valent mieux que lui. Quelquefois même il leur arrive de laisser échapper ce sentiment honteux dans la société, et alors ils sont très plaisans.

Toutes les épigrammes de Fabrice dans cette scène sont d'autant plus piquantes qu'elles paraissent des naïvetés.'

promène.) Cependant, je rends service à l'Etat, j'écris plus de feuilles que personne, je fais enchérir le papier… et à moi rien! Je voudrais me venger de tous ceux à qui on croit du mérite. Je gagne déjà quelque chose à dire du mal; si je peux parvenir à en faire, 10
ma fortune est faite. J'ai loué des sots, j'ai dénigré les talents; à peine y a-t-il là de quoi vivre. Ce n'est pas à médire, c'est à nuire qu'on fait fortune.

(au maître du café.)

Bonjour, monsieur Fabrice, bonjour. Toutes les affaires vont bien, hors les miennes: j'enrage. 15

FABRICE

Monsieur Frélon, monsieur Frélon, vous vous faites bien des ennemis.

FRÉLON

Oui, je crois que j'excite un peu d'envie.

FABRICE

Non, sur mon âme, ce n'est point du tout ce sentiment-là que vous faites naître: écoutez; j'ai quelque amitié pour vous; je suis 20
fâché d'entendre parler de vous comme on en parle. Comment faites-vous donc pour avoir tant d'ennemis, monsieur Frélon?

FRÉLON

C'est que j'ai du mérite, monsieur Fabrice.

FABRICE

Cela peut être, mais il n'y a encore que vous qui me l'ayez dit;

7-9 60AM: *promène.)* Je voudrais me

9-10 60AM: ceux qui me veuillent du mal; je gagne déjà quelque chose à en dire; si je peux

18 60AM: un peu d'ennemis.

on prétend que vous êtes un ignorant; cela ne me fait rien; mais 25
on ajoute que vous êtes malicieux, et cela me fâche, car je suis bon
homme.

FRÉLON

J'ai le cœur bon; j'ai le cœur tendre; je dis un peu de mal des
hommes; mais j'aime toutes les femmes, monsieur Fabrice, pourvu
qu'elles soient jolies; et pour vous le prouver, je veux absolument 30
que vous m'introduisiez chez cette aimable personne qui loge chez
vous, et que je n'ai pu encore voir dans son appartement.

FABRICE

Oh pardi, monsieur Frélon, cette jeune personne-là n'est guère
faite pour vous; car elle ne se vante jamais, et ne dit de mal de
personne. 35

FRÉLON

Elle ne dit de mal de personne, parce qu'elle ne connaît personne. N'en seriez-vous point amoureux, mon cher monsieur Fabrice?

FABRICE

Oh non; elle a quelque chose de si noble dans son air, que je
n'ose jamais être amoureux d'elle: d'ailleurs sa vertu... 40

FRÉLON

Ah ah ah ah, sa vertu!...

FABRICE

Oui, qu'avez-vous à rire? est-ce que vous ne croyez pas à la
vertu, vous? Voilà un équipage de campagne qui s'arrête à ma

33-34 60AM: n'est pas faite

43-44 60AM: vous?... mais j'aperçois un valet qui porte une malle: il s'arrête à ma porte. C'est quelque

porte: un domestique en livrée qui porte une malle: c'est quelque seigneur qui vient loger chez moi. 45

FRÉLON

Recommandez-moi vite à lui, mon cher ami.

SCÈNE II

LE LORD MONROSE, FABRICE, FRÉLON

MONROSE

Vous êtes monsieur Fabrice, à ce que je crois?

FABRICE

A vous servir, monsieur.

MONROSE

Je n'ai que peu de jours à rester dans cette ville. O ciel! daigne m'y protéger... Infortuné que je suis!... On m'a dit que je serais 50 mieux chez vous qu'ailleurs, que vous êtes un bon et honnête homme.

FABRICE

Chacun doit l'être. Vous trouverez ici, monsieur, toutes les commodités de la vie, un appartement assez propre, table d'hôte si

46b 60, 60Y, 60CR, 60AM, SS61, T64P, W70L, MS1: LE CHEVALIER MONROSE
49 T64P: ville. (*A part.*) O ciel!
50 T64P: suis!... (*Haut.*) On
51 60AM: êtes bon et
54 60AM: vie, appartement

vous daignez me faire cet honneur, liberté de manger chez vous, 55
l'amusement de la conversation dans le café.

MONROSE

Avez-vous ici beaucoup de locataires?

FABRICE

Nous n'avons à présent qu'une jeune personne, très belle et très vertueuse.

FRÉLON

Eh oui, très vertueuse, eh, eh. 60

FABRICE

Qui vit dans la plus grande retraite.

MONROSE

La jeunesse et la beauté ne sont pas faites pour moi. Qu'on me prépare, je vous prie, un appartement où je puisse être en solitude... Que de peines!... Y a-t-il quelque nouvelle intéressante dans Londres? 65

FABRICE

Monsieur Frélon peut vous en instruire, car il en fait; c'est l'homme du monde qui parle et qui écrit le plus; il est très utile aux étrangers.

MONROSE (*en se promenant.*)

Je n'en ai que faire.

63 60AM: prie, quelqu'endroit où je
63-64 T64P: solitude... (*A part.*) Que
67 60AM: est fort utile

FABRICE

Je vais donner ordre que vous soyez bien servi. 70

(*Il sort.*)

FRÉLON

Voici un nouveau débarqué: c'est un grand seigneur sans doute, car il a l'air de ne se soucier de personne. Milord, permettez que je vous présente mes hommages, et ma plume.

MONROSE

Je ne suis point milord; c'est être un sot de se glorifier de son titre, et c'est être un faussaire de s'arroger un titre qu'on n'a pas. 75 Je suis ce que je suis; quel est votre emploi dans la maison?

FRÉLON

Je ne suis point de la maison, monsieur; je passe ma vie au café, j'y compose des brochures, des feuilles: je sers les honnêtes gens. Si vous avez quelque ami à qui vous vouliez donner des éloges, ou quelque ennemi dont on doive dire du mal, quelque auteur à 80 protéger ou à décrier, il n'en coûte qu'une pistole par paragraphe. Si vous voulez faire quelque connaissance agréable ou utile, je suis encore votre homme.

MONROSE

Et vous ne faites point d'autre métier dans la ville?

FRÉLON

Monsieur, c'est un très bon métier. 85

74 60AM: être sot
75-76 60X*, 60AM, MS1: n'a pas. Quel est votre
81-83 60, 60CR: par paragraphe.//
60CR:AC, 60CR*, last sentence added
82 60AM: faire quelques connaissances agréables ou utiles
83 60Y, 60CR:AC, 60CR*, 60AM, MS1: suis votre

MONROSE

Et on ne vous a pas encore montré en public, le cou décoré d'un collier de fer de quatre pouces de hauteur?

FRÉLON

Voilà un homme qui n'aime pas la littérature.[2]

SCÈNE III

FRÉLON (*se remettant à sa table.*) *Plusieurs personnes paraissent dans l'intérieur du café.* MONROSE *avance sur le bord du théâtre.*

MONROSE

Mes infortunes sont-elles assez longues, assez affreuses? errant, proscrit, condamné à perdre la tête dans l'Ecosse ma patrie: j'ai 90
perdu mes honneurs, ma femme, mon fils, ma famille entière: une fille me reste, errante comme moi, misérable, et peut-être déshonorée; et je mourrai donc sans être vengé de cette barbare famille de Murrai qui m'a persécuté, qui m'a tout ôté, qui m'a rayé du nombre des vivants! car enfin, je n'existe plus; j'ai perdu jusqu'à 95
mon nom, par l'arrêt qui me condamne en Ecosse; je ne suis qu'une ombre qui vient autour de son tombeau.

86-87 60CR*, 60X*, 60AM, MS1: MONROSE / Je fais peu de cas de vos talents; si tout le monde pensait comme moi, vos pareils auraient peu d'emploi.
88b 60AM: *Plusieurs interlocuteurs paraissent*
93-94 60AM: déshonorée. Ah barbare Murrai, qui m'a persécuté
93-97 60CR*, 60X*, MS1: déshonorée. Ah barbare Murrai.//

[2] Palissot: 'Ce trait de caractère peint à merveille la ridicule importance que se croit un folliculaire.'

(UN *de ceux qui sont entrés dans le café frappant sur l'épaule de Frélon qui écrit.*)

Eh bien, tu étais hier à la pièce nouvelle; l'auteur fut bien applaudi; c'est un jeune homme de mérite, et sans fortune, que la nation doit encourager. 100

UN AUTRE

Je me soucie bien d'une pièce nouvelle. Les affaires publiques me désespèrent; toutes les denrées sont à bon marché; on nage dans une abondance pernicieuse; je suis perdu, je suis ruiné.

FRÉLON (*écrivant.*)

Cela n'est pas vrai, la pièce ne vaut rien, l'auteur est un sot, et ses protecteurs aussi; les affaires publiques n'ont jamais été plus 105 mauvaises; tout renchérit; l'Etat est anéanti, et je le prouve par mes feuilles.

UN SECOND

Tes feuilles sont des feuilles de chêne;[3] la vérité est que la philosophie est bien dangereuse, et que c'est elle qui nous a fait perdre l'île de Minorque.[4] 110

97a 60X*: PREMIER INTERLOCUTEUR
100a 60X*: DEUXIÈME INTERLOCUTEUR
103 60AM: une profusion pernicieuse;
105-108 60CR*, 60AM: protecteurs aussi. / UN SECOND / La vérité est
105-110 60X*, MS1: aussi. / TROISIÈME INTERLOCUTEUR / La vérité est que la philosophie est bien dangereuse.//
108-110 60, 60CR: la vérité est que le grand Turc arme puissamment pour faire une descente à la Virginie, et que c'est ce qui fait tomber les fonds publics.

[3] 'Worthless articles without substance'; also possibly (here) a play on *feuille de chou*, 'rag'.

[4] This detail of local colour, with Englishmen bewailing the loss of Minorca, sets the play's action at the outbreak of the Seven Years' War (1756). Admiral Byng's fleet retired and allowed the maréchal duc de Richelieu to take Minorca in June 1756.

MONROSE (*toujours sur le devant du théâtre.*)

Le fils de milord Murrai me payera tous mes malheurs. Que ne puis-je au moins, avant de périr, punir par le sang du fils, toutes les barbaries du père!

UN TROISIÈME INTERLOCUTEUR (*dans le fond.*)

La pièce d'hier m'a paru très bonne.[5]

FRÉLON

Le mauvais goût gagne; elle est détestable. 115

LE TROISIÈME INTERLOCUTEUR

Il n'y a de détestable que tes critiques.

LE SECOND

Et moi je vous dis que les philosophes font baisser les fonds publics, et qu'il faut envoyer un autre ambassadeur à la Porte.[6]

110a 60AM: (*toujours sur le fond du théâtre.*)
111-112 60CR*, 60X*, 60AM, MS1: Tu es mort cruel Murrai, indigne ennemi; mais ton fils me reste. Que ne puis-je
112 60X*, 60AM: sang de ce fils
113a T64P, MS1, no stage direction
114a-116 60AM, absent
115a 60X*: QUATRIÈME INTERLOCUTEUR [throughout]
116 MS1: tes critiques. Si le prix de l'eau des Barbades ne baisse pas, la patrie est perdue.
116a 60X*: TROISIÈME INTERLOCUTEUR [throughout]
117-118 60, 60CR: dis que les fonds baissent, et qu'il faut [60CR*: β]

[5] Palissot: 'Cette peinture de ce qui se passe journellement dans les cafés plaît par son naturel et par sa vérité.'

[6] The *French* ambassador to Turkey (until 1785) was the comte de Saint-Priest; but we are here concerned with the *British* ambassador (Sir James Porter, who was ambassador at Constantinople 1746-1762). During his term of office there, 'the interests of our mercantile body were never better secured, nor the honour of our nation better supported' (Sir William Jones, *Works*, 1799, iv.5). An impeccable record – but on the other hand, his father's real name had been La Roche, and his mother was French; so a disgruntled patriot could realistically suspect him at the beginning of a war against France!

FRÉLON

Il faut siffler la pièce qui réussit, et ne pas souffrir qu'il se fasse rien de bon. 120

(*Ils parlent tous quatre en même temps.*)

UN INTERLOCUTEUR

Va, s'il n'y avait rien de bon, tu perdrais le plus grand plaisir de la satire. Le cinquième acte surtout a de très grandes beautés.

LE SECOND INTERLOCUTEUR

Je n'ai pu me défaire d'aucune de mes marchandises.

LE TROISIÈME

Il y a beaucoup à craindre cette année pour la Jamaïque; ces philosophes la feront prendre.[7] 125

FRÉLON

Le quatrième et le cinquième acte sont pitoyables.

MONROSE (*se retournant.*)

Quel sabbat!

118a-120 60AM, absent
119-120 60X*, MS1: Il faut siffler toute pièce qui réussit.//
120b 60X*: LE PREMIER INTERLOCUTEUR
121 60AM, MS1: Va, si rien ne réussissait, tu perdrais
123a-125 MS1, absent
124-125 60, 60CR: pour la Jamaïque.//
60CR:AC, 60CR*, last clause added
125 60AM: feront reprendre.
126 60CR, 60AM, MS1: actes

[7] Possibly an assimilation of French (*philosophes*) and British terms of reference, the latter being the Quakers, who were being strongly dissuasive at just this time, in England and America, regarding the slave trade, of which Jamaica was an important centre.

LE PREMIER INTERLOCUTEUR

Le gouvernement ne peut pas subsister tel qu'il est.[8]

LE TROISIÈME INTERLOCUTEUR

Si le prix de l'eau des Barbades[9] ne baisse pas, la patrie est perdue. 130

MONROSE

Se peut-il que toujours, et en tout pays, dès que les hommes sont rassemblés, ils parlent tous à la fois! quelle rage de parler, avec la certitude de n'être point entendu!

M. FABRICE (*arrivant avec une serviette.*)

Messieurs, on a servi; surtout, ne vous querellez point à table, ou je ne vous reçois plus chez moi. (*à Monrose.*) Monsieur veut-il 135 nous faire l'honneur de venir dîner avec nous?

MONROSE

Avec cette cohue? non, mon ami; faites-moi apporter à manger dans ma chambre. (*Il se retire à part et dit à Fabrice.*) Ecoutez, un mot, milord Falbrige est-il à Londres?

128a-130 MS1, absent
134 60AM: ne vous disputez point
136 60X: avec vous [corrected in 60X*]
138-146a 60, 60CR: dans ma chambre. (*Il se retire; les survenants sortent* [138-146 added in 60CR*]
138 60CR*, 60AM: (*Il tire Fabrice à part.*)
60X*: chambre. Ecoutez
60Y: (*Monrose se retire, et dit à part à Fabrice.*)

[8] The duke of Newcastle's government was very weak in 1755-1756, and was incapable of coping with an adverse war situation. The elder Pitt took over effective control in December 1756.

[9] Called *rhum* from the mid-eighteenth century.

FABRICE

Non, mais il revient bientôt. 140

MONROSE

Est-il vrai qu'il vient ici quelquefois?

FABRICE

Il m'a fait cet honneur.

MONROSE

Cela suffit: bonjour. Que la vie m'est odieuse!

(*Il sort.*)

FABRICE

Cet homme-là me paraît accablé de chagrins et d'idées. Je ne

141 60Y: qu'il vienne ici
142 60X*, MS1: Il me faisait cet honneur avant son voyage d'Espagne.
60Y, 60CR*: Il me fait cet
M: Il y venait avant son voyage d'Espagne.[10]
143-143a 60Y, 60CR*, MS1: bonjour. (*il sort.*) / FABRICE *seul.* / [60Y, '*seul*' absent]
60X*: bonjour. (*il sort.*) / SCÈNE / FABRICE, WASP / FABRICE, *à part*

[10] Beuchot makes this change following Voltaire's instruction in his letter of 9 July 1760 to d'Argental (D9048): 'N.b. dans l'Ecossaise, page 25, quand le chevalier Montrose sort, et qu'avant de finir la scène 3ème il demande à part à Fabrice, si mylord Falbridge est à Londres, et qu'il demande au maître du caffé si ce lord vient souvent dans la maison, le caffetier répond, *il y vient quelquefois*, il doit répondre, *il y venait avant son voiage d'Espagne*. Cette petite particularité est nécessaire 1° p^{r} faire voir que Monrose ne vient pas sans raison se loger dans ce caffé là, 2° qu'il a besoin de Falbridge, 3° pour prévenir les esprits sur la mort de ce Falbridge, 4° pour fonder la demeure de Lindane près d'un caffé où ce L. Faldbridge vient quelquefois. C'est un rien, mais rien, c'est baucoup.' Voltaire's instruction was not incorporated into 60AM, W56, W75G, or K; nor, indeed, into any other eighteenth-century edition collated.

serais point surpris qu'il allât se tuer là-haut; ce serait dommage, 145
il a l'air d'un honnête homme.

(*Les survenants sortent pour dîner. Frélon est toujours à la table où il écrit. Ensuite Fabrice frappe à la porte de l'appartement de Lindane.*)

SCÈNE IV

FABRICE, MLLE POLLY, FRÉLON.

FABRICE

Mademoiselle Polly, mademoiselle Polly!

POLLY

Eh bien, qu'y a-t-il, notre cher hôte?

FABRICE

Seriez-vous assez complaisante pour venir dîner en compagnie?

POLLY

Hélas je n'ose, car ma maîtresse ne mange point: comment 150
voulez-vous que je mange? Nous sommes si tristes!

FABRICE

Cela vous égayera.

POLLY

Je ne peux être gaie; quand ma maîtresse souffre, il faut que je souffre avec elle.

146a-b 60, 60Y, 60CR, 60AM: *il écrit. Fabrice frappe*
149 60AM: complaisante de venir

FABRICE

Je vous enverrai donc secrètement ce qu'il vous faudra. 155

(*Il sort.*)

FRÉLON (*se levant de sa table.*)

Je vous suis, monsieur Fabrice. Ma chère Polly, vous ne voulez donc jamais m'introduire chez votre maîtresse? vous rebutez toutes mes prières?

POLLY

C'est bien à vous d'oser faire l'amoureux d'une personne de sa sorte! 160

FRÉLON

Eh de quelle sorte est-elle donc?

POLLY

D'une sorte qu'il faut respecter: vous êtes fait tout au plus pour les suivantes.[11]

FRÉLON

C'est-à-dire que si je vous en contais, vous m'aimeriez?

POLLY

Assurément non. 165

FRÉLON

Et pourquoi donc ta maîtresse s'obstine-t-elle à ne me point recevoir, et que la suivante me dédaigne?

155 60AM: Je viens de vous envoyer secrètement ce qu'il vous faut.

[11] In 1750 Fréron had married his niece, who was his sister's servant.

POLLY

Pour trois raisons; c'est que vous êtes bel esprit, ennuyeux et méchant.

FRÉLON

C'est bien à ta maîtresse, qui languit ici dans la pauvreté, et qui 170 est nourrie par charité, à me dédaigner.

POLLY

Ma maîtresse pauvre! qui vous a dit cela, langue de vipère? ma maîtresse est très riche: si elle ne fait point de dépense, c'est qu'elle hait le faste: elle est vêtue simplement par modestie: elle mange peu, c'est par régime; et vous êtes un impertinent. 175

FRÉLON

Qu'elle ne fasse pas tant la fière: nous connaissons sa conduite; nous savons sa naissance; nous n'ignorons pas ses aventures.

POLLY

Quoi donc? que connaissez-vous? que voulez-vous dire?

FRÉLON

J'ai partout des correspondances.

POLLY

O ciel! cet homme peut nous perdre. Monsieur Frélon, mon 180 cher monsieur Frélon, si vous savez quelque chose, ne nous trahissez pas.

170-171 60CR:AC, 60X*, 60AM, MS1: la pauvreté, à me dédaigner
179 60AM: correspondances, moi.

FRÉLON

Ah ah, j'ai donc deviné, il y a donc quelque chose, et je suis le cher monsieur Frélon. Ah ça, je ne dirai rien; mais il faut...

POLLY

Quoi? 185

FRÉLON

Il faut m'aimer.

POLLY

Fi donc; cela n'est pas possible.

FRÉLON

Ou aimez-moi, ou craignez-moi: vous savez qu'il y a quelque chose.

POLLY

Non, il n'y a rien, sinon que ma maîtresse est aussi respectable 190 que vous êtes haïssable: nous sommes très à notre aise, nous ne craignons rien, et nous nous moquons de vous.

FRÉLON

Elles sont très à leur aise, de là je conclus qu'elles meurent de faim: elles ne craignent rien, c'est-à-dire qu'elles tremblent d'être découvertes... Ah je viendrai à bout de ces aventurières, ou je 195 ne pourrai. Je me vengerai de leur insolence. Mépriser monsieur Frélon!

(*Il sort.*)

183-184 60AM: suis à présent le cher
193-194 60CR:AC, 60CR*, 60X*, 60AM, MS1: conclus que tout leur manque: elles
196 60AM: vengerai bien de leur
196-197 60, 60CR: ne pourrai.//
60CR:AC, 60CR*, 60X*, last two sentences added

SCÈNE V

LINDANE (*sortant de sa chambre, dans un déshabillé des plus simples.*) POLLY

LINDANE

Ah ma pauvre Polly, tu étais avec ce vilain homme de Frélon: il me donne toujours de l'inquiétude: on dit que c'est un esprit de travers, et un cœur de boue, dont la langue, la plume et les dé- 200 marches sont également méchantes; qu'il cherche à s'insinuer partout pour faire le mal s'il n'y en a point, et pour l'augmenter s'il en trouve. Je serais sortie de cette maison qu'il fréquente, sans la probité et le bon cœur de notre hôte.

POLLY

Il voulait absolument vous voir! et je le rembarrais... 205

LINDANE

Il veut me voir; et milord Murrai n'est point venu! il n'est point venu depuis deux jours!

POLLY

Non, madame; mais parce que milord ne vient point, faut-il pour cela ne dîner jamais?

LINDANE

Ah! souviens-toi surtout de lui cacher toujours ma misère, et à 210

198-199 60CR*: homme: il me donne

199-200 60: de travers, un cœur

200 60CR:AC, 60CR*, 60X*, 60AM, MS1: travers, et un homme dangereux, dont

206 60X*, 60AM: Il voulait me voir

lui, et à tout le monde; je veux bien vivre de pain et d'eau; ce n'est point la pauvreté qui est intolérable, c'est le mépris: je sais manquer de tout, mais je veux qu'on l'ignore.

POLLY

Hélas, ma chère maîtresse, on s'en aperçoit assez en me voyant: pour vous, ce n'est pas de même; la grandeur d'âme vous soutient: 215 il semble que vous vous plaisiez à combattre la mauvaise fortune; vous n'en êtes que plus belle; mais moi je maigris à vue d'œil: depuis un an que vous m'avez prise à votre service en Ecosse, je ne me reconnais plus.

LINDANE

Il ne faut perdre ni le courage ni l'espérance: je supporte ma 220 pauvreté, mais la tienne me déchire le cœur. Ma chère Polly, qu'au moins le travail de mes mains serve à rendre ta destinée moins affreuse: n'ayons d'obligation à personne; va vendre ce que j'ai brodé ces jours-ci. (*Elle lui donne un petit ouvrage de broderie.*) Je ne réussis pas mal à ces petits ouvrages. Que mes mains te nourris- 225 sent et t'habillent: tu m'as aidée: il est beau de ne devoir notre subsistance qu'à notre vertu.

POLLY

Laissez-moi baiser, laissez-moi arroser de mes larmes ces belles mains qui ont fait ce travail précieux. Oui, madame, j'aimerais mieux mourir auprès de vous dans l'indigence, que de servir des 230 reines. Que ne puis-je vous consoler!

LINDANE

Hélas! Milord Murrai n'est point venu! lui que je devrais haïr, lui le fils de celui qui a fait tous nos malheurs! Ah! le nom de

211-212 60CR:AC, 60CR*, 60X*, 60AM, MS1: le monde; ce n'est point
216-217 60, 60CR: fortune; mais moi je [60X*: β]
233 60AM: fils de l'auteur de tous nos

Murrai nous sera toujours funeste: s'il vient, comme il viendra sans doute, qu'il ignore absolument ma patrie, mon état, mon infortune. 235

POLLY

Savez-vous bien que ce méchant Frélon se vante d'en avoir quelque connaissance?

LINDANE

Eh comment pourrait-il en être instruit, puisque tu l'es à peine? Il ne sait rien, personne ne m'écrit; je suis dans ma chambre comme dans mon tombeau: mais il feint de savoir quelque chose pour se rendre nécessaire. Garde-toi qu'il devine jamais seulement le lieu de ma naissance. Chère Polly, tu le sais, je suis une infortunée, dont le père fut proscrit dans les derniers troubles, dont la famille est détruite: il ne me reste que mon courage. Mon père est errant de désert en désert en Ecosse. Je serais déjà partie de Londres pour m'unir à sa mauvaise fortune, si je n'avais pas quelque espérance en milord Falbrige. J'ai su qu'il avait été le meilleur ami de mon père. Personne n'abandonne son ami. Falbrige est revenu d'Espagne, il est à Windsor; j'attends son retour. Mais hélas! Murrai ne revient point. Je t'ai ouvert mon cœur; songe que tu le perces du coup de la mort, si tu laisses jamais entrevoir l'état où je suis. 240 245 250

239 60AM: Comment pourrait-il
242 60AM: Garde-toi seulement qu'il devine jamais le lieu
245-251 60, 60CR: courage. Je t'ai ouvert [245-251 added in 60CR*, 60X*]
60AM cancel: courage. Milord Murrai est le fils de l'auteur de toutes mes infortunes; lui-même poursuit mon père avec la plus grande rigueur, lui seul enfin est cause que je reste à Londres inconnue et dans la misère où tu me vois: j'avais quelques espérances, elles sont vaines: Milord Murrai ne vient plus ici. Je t'ai ouvert
246-247 60CR*, 60X*, 60AM, MS1: Londres pour le chercher et [60X*, MS1: pour] m'unir à
247 60AM: si je n'avais quelque
249 60AM: Windsord
250-251 60X*, MS1: retour. Je t'ai ouvert
251 60, 60Y, 60CR, 60AM, MS1: cœur, mais songe

POLLY

Et à qui en parlerais-je? je ne sors jamais d'auprès de vous; et puis, le monde est si indifférent sur les malheurs d'autrui!

LINDANE

Il est indifférent, Polly,[12] mais il est curieux, mais il aime à 255
déchirer les blessures des infortunés: et si les hommes sont compatissants avec les femmes, ils en abusent; ils veulent se faire un droit de notre misère; et je veux rendre cette misère respectable. Mais hélas! Milord Murrai ne viendra point!

SCÈNE VI

LINDANE, POLLY, FABRICE (*avec une serviette.*)

FABRICE

Pardonnez... madame... mademoiselle... je ne sais comment 260
vous nommer, ni comment vous parler: vous m'imposez du respect. Je sors de table pour vous demander vos volontés... je ne sais comment m'y prendre.

LINDANE

Mon cher hôte, croyez que toutes vos attentions me pénètrent le cœur; que voulez-vous de moi? 265

[12] Palissot: 'Rien n'intéresse plus les belles âmes que la vertu souffrante et courageuse: ce personnage de Lindane est charmant.'

FABRICE

C'est moi qui voudrais bien que vous voulussiez avoir quelque volonté.[13] Il me semble que vous n'avez point dîné hier.

LINDANE

J'étais malade.

FABRICE

Vous êtes plus que malade, vous êtes triste… entre nous, pardonnez… il paraît que votre fortune n'est pas comme votre personne. 270

LINDANE

Comment? quelle imagination! je ne me suis jamais plainte de ma fortune.

FABRICE

Non, vous dis-je, elle n'est pas si belle, si bonne, si désirable que vous l'êtes. 275

LINDANE

Que voulez-vous dire?

FABRICE

Que vous touchez ici tout le monde, et que vous l'évitez trop.

266 60AM: que vous eussiez quelque
274-275 60AM: dis-je, il s'en faut bien qu'elle ne soit aussi belle, aussi bonne, aussi désirable que

[13] Palissot: *Je voudrais bien que vous voulussiez avoir une volonté*, est une phrase à la Marivaux, une phrase affectée, précieuse, et qui ne se concilie point avec la simplicité et la bonhommie de Fabrice. Il en est de même de celle-ci, qui se trouve quelques lignes plus bas: *deux afflictions mises ensemble peuvent devenir une consolation.*' The second phrase appears at I.vi.284-285.

Ecoutez; je ne suis qu'un homme simple, qu'un homme du peuple; mais je vois tout votre mérite, comme si j'étais un homme de la cour: ma chère dame, un peu de bonne chère: nous avons là-haut 280 un vieux gentilhomme avec qui vous devriez manger.

LINDANE

Moi, me mettre à table avec un homme, avec un inconnu?

FABRICE

C'est un vieillard qui me paraît tout votre fait. Vous paraissez bien affligée, il paraît bien triste aussi: deux afflictions mises ensemble peuvent devenir une consolation. 285

LINDANE

Je ne veux, je ne peux voir personne.

FABRICE

Souffrez au moins que ma femme vous fasse sa cour: daignez permettre qu'elle mange avec vous pour vous tenir compagnie. Souffrez quelques soins…

LINDANE

Je vous rends grâce avec sensibilité, mais je n'ai besoin de rien. 290

FABRICE

Oh je n'y tiens pas; vous n'avez besoin de rien, et vous n'avez pas le nécessaire.

280 60, 60Y, 60CR, 60AM, MS1: dame, un peu de société, un peu de bonne chère: nous

283 60CR:AC, 60CR*, 60X*, 60AM, MS1: me paraît [60AM: un] galant homme. Vous

291-292 60, 60Y, 60CR, 60AM, MS1: et vous manquez de tout.//

LINDANE

Qui vous en a pu imposer si témérairement?

FABRICE

Pardon!

LINDANE

Ah! Polly, il est deux heures, et milord Murrai ne viendra point! 295

FABRICE

Eh bien, madame, ce milord dont vous parlez, je sais que c'est l'homme le plus vertueux de la cour: vous ne l'avez jamais reçu ici que devant témoins; pourquoi n'avoir pas fait avec lui honnêtement, devant témoins, quelques petits repas que j'aurais fournis? C'est peut-être votre parent? 300

LINDANE

Vous extravaguez, mon cher hôte.

FABRICE (*en tirant Polly par la manche.*)

Va, ma pauvre Polly; il y a un bon dîner tout prêt dans le cabinet qui donne dans la chambre de ta maîtresse, je t'en avertis. Cette femme-là est incompréhensible. Mais qui est donc cette autre dame qui entre dans mon café comme si c'était un homme? elle a l'air 305 bien furibond.

294a-300 60CR:AC, 60CR*, 60X*, 60AM, MS1, omitted
301a 60, 60CR, no stage direction
60AM: FABRICE *à Polly*
303 60X*, MS1: avertis. (*à part*). Cette
304 60X*, MS1: incompréhensible. (*regardant vers la coulisse*). Mais
306 60AM: furibond. Voyons à qui elle en veut. (*Fabrice sort.*)
60CR*: furibond. Je vais voir ce qu'elle veut. (*il sort.*)
MS1, 60X*: furibond. Allons la recevoir. (*il sort.*)

POLLY

Ah! ma chère maîtresse, c'est milady Alton, celle qui voulait épouser milord; je l'ai vue une fois rôder près d'ici: c'est elle.

LINDANE

Milord ne viendra point, c'en est fait, je suis perdue: pourquoi me suis-je obstinée à vivre? 310

(*Elle rentre.*)

SCÈNE VII

LADY ALTON (*ayant traversé avec colère le théâtre et prenant Fabrice par le bras.*)

Suivez-moi, il faut que je vous parle.

FABRICE

A moi, madame?

309 60CR*: Ah! sortons. Milord ne viendra
310b-314 60CR*, 60X*, 60AM, MS1, omitted[14]
312-314 T67, W70L:

FABRICE

A moi, madame?

LADY ALTON

A vous, Fabrice, à vous [T67: A vous, malheureux!] que je ferai punir de l'affront que vous me faites.

FABRICE

Moi vous faire des affronts, madame? eh je n'ai pas l'honneur

[14] This scene was omitted by the actors at the first staging of the play. Voltaire wrote to d'Argental on 3 August 1760 (D9113) regretting its absence: 'J'oserais seulement désirer que madame Alton parût à la fin du premier acte. On s'y attendait. Je vous supplie de luy faire rendre son droit.'

LADY ALTON

A vous, malheureux.

FABRICE

Quelle diablesse de femme!

Fin du premier acte.

de vous connaître.

LADY ALTON

Bon, bon? on tue tous les jours des gens qu'on ne connaît pas. Vous me tuez, vous dis-je.

FABRICE

Je vous tue!

LADY ALTON

Oui, suivez-moi, malheureux!

FABRICE

Quelle diablesse de femme!

ACTE II

SCÈNE PREMIÈRE

LADY ALTON,[1] FABRICE

LADY ALTON

Je ne crois pas un mot de ce que vous me dites, monsieur le cafetier. Vous me mettez toute hors de moi-même.

FABRICE

Eh bien, madame, rentrez donc toute dans vous-même.

LADY ALTON

Vous m'osez assurer que cette aventurière est une personne d'honneur, après qu'elle a reçu chez elle un homme de la cour: 5 vous devriez mourir de honte.

FABRICE

Pourquoi, madame? Quand milord y est venu, il n'y est point venu en secret, elle l'a reçu en public, les portes de son appartement ouvertes, ma femme présente. Vous pouvez mépriser mon état, mais vous devez estimer ma probité; et quant à celle que vous 10

3 60CR:AC, 60CR*, 60X*, 60AM, MS1: Eh bien! [60AM,'bien' absent] madame, revenez à vous.
9 60, 60Y, 60CR, MS1: ma femme présente, sa suivante présente. Vous
60AM: ma femme présente, et sa suivante aussi. Vous

[1] Palissot: 'Ladi Alton est un personnage outré, dans la nature pourtant, mais peut-être plus commun en Angleterre qu'en France.'

appelez une aventurière, si vous connaissiez ses mœurs, vous les respecteriez.

LADY ALTON

Laissez-moi, vous m'importunez.

FABRICE

Oh quelle femme! quelle femme!

LADY ALTON (*elle va à la porte de Lindane, et frappe rudement.*)

Qu'on m'ouvre. 15

SCÈNE II

LINDANE, LADY ALTON

LINDANE

Eh qui peut frapper ainsi? et que vois-je?

LADY ALTON

Connaissez-vous les grandes passions, mademoiselle?

LINDANE

Hélas, madame, voilà une étrange question.

LADY ALTON

Connaissez-vous l'amour véritable, non pas l'amour insipide,

13a-14 60AM, absent
16 MS2: Qui peut
16a-26 60, 60Y, 60CR, 60AM, SS61, T64P, MS1, absent
19 MS2: véritable? je ne dis pas l'amour insipide

l'amour langoureux, mais cet amour-là,[2] qui fait qu'on voudrait 20
empoisonner sa rivale, tuer son amant, et se jeter ensuite par la fenêtre?

LINDANE

Mais c'est la rage dont vous me parlez là.

LADY ALTON

Sachez que je n'aime point autrement, que je suis jalouse, vindicative, furieuse, implacable. 25

LINDANE

Tant pis pour vous, madame.

LADY ALTON

Répondez-moi: milord Murrai n'est-il pas venu ici quelquefois?

LINDANE

Que vous importe, madame? et de quel droit venez-vous m'interroger? suis-je une criminelle? êtes-vous mon juge?

LADY ALTON

Je suis votre partie: si milord vient encore vous voir, si vous 30
flattez la passion de cet infidèle, tremblez: renoncez à lui, ou vous êtes perdue.

24 MS2: Je veux bien que vous sachiez que je n'aime
24-25 MS2: jalouse, furieuse

[2] Palissot: 'C'est l'amour de tempérament dont ladi Alton veut parler; Lindane, qui en éprouve un plus doux, lui répond très-plaisamment sans avoir envie d'être plaisante.'

LINDANE

Vos menaces m'affermiraient dans ma passion pour lui, si j'en avais une.

LADY ALTON

Je vois que vous l'aimez, que vous vous laissez séduire par un perfide; je vois qu'il vous trompe, et que vous me bravez: mais sachez qu'il n'est point de vengeance à laquelle je ne me porte. 35

LINDANE

Eh bien, madame, puisqu'il est ainsi, je l'aime.[3]

LADY ALTON

Avant de me venger, je veux vous confondre; tenez, connaissez le traître; voilà les lettres qu'il m'a écrites; voilà son portrait qu'il m'a donné; ne le gardez pas au moins, il faut le rendre, ou je... 40

LINDANE (*en rendant le portrait.*)

Qu'ai-je vu, malheureuse!... Madame...

LADY ALTON

Eh bien!...

40-41 60CR*, 60X*, MS1: m'a écrites.//
40-42 60AM: écrites, et son portrait... (*Elle le donne à Lindane*) / LINDANE / Que vois-je? Ah! malheureuse... Madame...
41 60CR:AC: donné. (*Elle le donne à Lindane.*)
41a 60CR*: (*en rendant la lettre*)
MS1, 60X*: (*après avoir lu bas*)

[3] Palissot: 'Cette réponse est très-noble. A la vue des lettres écrites à sa rivale, Lindane éprouve à son tour de la jalousie, mais c'est la jalousie d'une âme douce, tendre, sensible: ce sentiment n'est dangereux que pour la personne qui en est atteinte.'

LINDANE (*en rendant le portrait.*)

Je ne l'aime plus.

LADY ALTON

Gardez votre résolution et votre promesse: sachez que c'est un homme inconstant, dur, orgueilleux, que c'est le plus mauvais caractère... 45

LINDANE

Arrêtez, madame; si vous continuiez à en dire du mal, je l'aimerais peut-être encore. Vous êtes venue ici pour achever de m'ôter la vie; vous n'aurez pas de peine. Polly, c'en est fait; viens m'aider à cacher la dernière de mes douleurs. 50

POLLY

Qu'est-il donc arrivé, ma chère maîtresse, et qu'est devenu votre courage?

LINDANE

On en a contre l'infortune, l'injustice, l'indigence. Il y a cent traits qui s'émoussent sur un cœur noble; il en vient un qui porte enfin le coup de la mort. 55

(*Elles sortent.*)

43a 60X*, T64P, MS1, K, no stage direction
45 60X*: promesse: (*elle lui arrache la lettre*) sachez
50-56a 60CR:AC, 60CR*, 60X*, 60AM, MS1: peine. C'en est fait; allons cacher la dernière de mes douleurs. (*Elles sortent.*) [MS1, 60X*: (*Elle sort avec Polly*)]

SCÈNE III

LADY ALTON, FRÉLON

LADY ALTON

Quoi! être trahie, abandonnée pour cette petite créature! (*à Frélon.*) Gazetier littéraire, approchez;[4] m'avez-vous servie? avez-vous employé vos correspondances? m'avez-vous obéi? avez-vous découvert quelle est cette insolente qui fait le malheur de ma vie? 60

FRÉLON

J'ai rempli les volontés de votre grandeur; je sais qu'elle est Ecossaise, et qu'elle se cache.

LADY ALTON

Voilà de belles nouvelles!

FRÉLON

Je n'ai rien découvert de plus jusqu'à présent.

LADY ALTON

Et en quoi m'as-tu donc servie? 65

FRÉLON

Quand on découvre peu de chose, on ajoute quelque chose, et quelque chose avec quelque chose fait beaucoup. J'ai fait une hypothèse.

[4] Palissot: 'Le mépris que ladi Alton témoigne si ouvertement à Frélon en parlant à lui-même n'est pas sans vraisemblance: on n'outrage point celui dont on attend des services. Le plaisir de voir humilier Frélon pouvait couvrir ce défaut; c'était d'ailleurs un amusement que Voltaire donnait à sa vengeance: mais le défaut n'en est pas moins réel.'

LADY ALTON

Comment, pédant! une hypothèse!

FRÉLON

Oui, j'ai supposé qu'elle est malintentionnée contre le gouvernement. 70

LADY ALTON

Ce n'est point supposer, rien n'est posé plus vrai: elle est très malintentionnée, puisqu'elle veut m'enlever mon amant.

FRÉLON

Vous voyez bien que dans un temps de trouble, une Ecossaise qui se cache est une ennemie de l'Etat. 75

LADY ALTON

Je ne le vois pas; mais je voudrais que la chose fût.

FRÉLON

Je ne le parierais pas, mais j'en jurerais.[5]

LADY ALTON

Et tu serais capable de l'affirmer devant des gens de conséquence?

78-79 60CR:AC, 60X*, 60AM, MS1: de l'affirmer?//

[5] This quip which, as Palissot remarks, 'est devenu proverbe', occasioned an outburst of pedantic outrage in Fréron's *feuille* of August 1760 (p.315-17). The wording of this accusation that Voltaire plagiarised Piron's epigram is, itself, plagiarised from Piron's letter to Arnaud (D9108, [?1 August 1760]): 'Ce n'est pas d'aujourd'hui que le geai brille sous les plumes du paon' [Piron]; 'c'est le geai revêtu des plumes du Paon' [Fréron]. Other comments are also almost identical, except that Fréron changes the last line of the quotation from Piron's dialogue (from the original 'J'en jurerois bien sans doute, Mais je ne gagerois pas', to 'Mais je ne parierois pas'), in order to make Voltaire's allusion seem a blatant plagiarism.

FRÉLON

Je suis en relation avec des personnes de conséquence.[6] Je connais fort la maîtresse du valet de chambre d'un premier commis du ministre: je pourrais même parler aux laquais de milord votre amant, et dire que le père de cette fille, en qualité de malintentionné, l'a envoyée à Londres comme malintentionnée. Je supposerais même que le père est ici. Voyez-vous? cela pourrait avoir des suites, et on mettrait votre rivale, pour ses mauvaises intentions, dans la prison où j'ai déjà été pour mes feuilles. 80 85

LADY ALTON

Ah! je respire; les grandes passions veulent être servies par des gens sans scrupule; je veux que le vaisseau aille à pleines voiles, ou qu'il se brise. Tu as raison; une Ecossaise qui se cache dans un temps où tous les gens de son pays sont suspects, est sûrement une ennemie de l'Etat; tu n'es pas un imbécile, comme on le dit. Je croyais que tu n'étais qu'un barbouilleur de papier, mais je vois que tu as en effet des talents. Je t'ai déjà récompensé; je te récompenserai encore. Il faudra m'instruire de tout ce qui se passe ici. 90 95

FRÉLON

Madame, je vous conseille de faire usage de tout ce que vous saurez, et même de ce que vous ne saurez pas. La vérité a besoin de quelques ornements; le mensonge peut être vilain, mais la

86-87 60AM: votre rivale en prison.//
60CR:AC, 60CR*, 60X*, MS1: votre rival en prison, pour ses mauvaises intentions.//
89 60, 60Y, 60CR, 60AM, MS1: scrupule; je n'aime ni les demi-vengeances, ni les demi-fripons; je veux
92-93 60CR:AC, 60CR*, 60X*, 60AM, MS1: l'Etat. Je croyais

[6] Palissot: 'Frélon est moins ridicule qu'il ne le paraît. Il fut un temps, et ce temps n'est pas loin, où les valets d'un commis de ministre étaient véritablement des personnes de conséquence, souvent même très redoutables.'

fiction est belle;[7] qu'est-ce, après tout, que la vérité? la conformité 100
à nos idées: or ce qu'on dit est toujours conforme à l'idée qu'on a
quand on parle; ainsi il n'y a point proprement de mensonge.

LADY ALTON

Tu me parais subtil: il semble que tu aies étudié à St Omer.[a] [8]
Va, dis-moi seulement ce que tu découvriras, je ne t'en demande
pas davantage. 105

SCENE IV

LADY ALTON, FABRICE

LADY ALTON

Voilà, je l'avoue, le plus impudent, et le plus lâche coquin qui
soit dans les trois royaumes. Nos dogues mordent par instinct de

[a] Autrefois on envoyait plusieurs enfants faire leurs études au collège de St Omer.

103-104 60CR*, 60X*, 60AM, MS1: subtil. Va, dis-moi.
n.*a* 60CR*, 60X*, 60AM, MS1, note *a* absent
106-107 60X*, 60AM, MS1: l'avoue, le plus méchant homme qui soit dans

[7] Palissot: 'Rien de plus subtil en effet que la doctrine de Frélon sur le mensonge: un casuiste des Provinciales ne dirait pas mieux'.

[8] Fréron's education was received at the Collège Louis-le-Grand; but by introducing the English Jesuit college at Saint-Omer (established in the Pas-de-Calais in 1593 and destined to be removed from France with the Jesuits, in 1762), Voltaire deepens the ambiguous Anglo-French ambiance of the play's setting, whilst also, by this simple allusion, reinforcing the idea of Fréron's supposed Jesuitry, and indirectly ridiculing another *bête noire*: Omer Joly de Fleury.

courage, et lui par instinct de bassesse; à présent que je suis un peu plus de sang-froid, je pense qu'il me ferait haïr la vengeance. Je sens que je prendrais contre lui le parti de ma rivale: elle a dans son état humble une fierté qui me plaît: elle est décente; on la dit sage; mais elle m'enlève mon amant, il n'y a pas moyen de pardonner. (*à Fabrice, qu'elle aperçoit agissant dans le café.*) Adieu, mon maître, faisons la paix; vous êtes un honnête homme, vous; mais vous avez dans votre maison un vilain griffonneur. 110 115

FABRICE

Bien des gens m'ont déjà dit, madame, qu'il est aussi méchant que Lindane est vertueuse et aimable.

LADY ALTON

Aimable! tu me perces le cœur.

SCÈNE V

FRIPORT[9] (*vêtu simplement, mais proprement, avec un large chapeau*), FABRICE

FABRICE

Ah! Dieu soit béni, vous voilà de retour, monsieur Friport; comment vous trouvez-vous de votre voyage à la Jamaïque? 120

108-109 MS1: bassesse; il me ferait, je crois, haïr
112 60AM: sage; mais elle veut m'enlever mon amant
114-115 60CR*, 60X*, MS1: honnête homme, vous.//
116 60AM: Vous venez d'entretenir M. Wasp. Bien des gens
60CR*, 60X*, MS1: Vous venez d'entretenir M. Wasp, il vous aura peut-être prévenu contre Lindane. Mais ne vous en rapportez pas à lui. Bien des gens
116-117 60X*, MS1: méchant qu'elle est

[9] Palissot: 'Ce personnage de Fréeport est celui qui contribua le plus au succès de la pièce. Cette scène nous paraît de l'originalité la plus piquante, et doit réussir dans tous les temps, parce qu'elle est pleine de naturel, malgré sa singularité, et que rien n'est beau que le vrai'.

FRIPORT

Fort bien, monsieur Fabrice. J'ai gagné beaucoup, mais je m'ennuie. (*au garçon du café.*) Eh! du chocolat; les papiers publics; on a plus de peine à s'amuser qu'à s'enrichir.

FABRICE

Voulez-vous les feuilles de Frélon?

FRIPORT

Non, que m'importe ce fatras? Je me soucie bien qu'une araignée 125 dans le coin d'un mur marche sur sa toile pour sucer le sang des mouches. Donnez les gazettes ordinaires. Qu'y a-t-il de nouveau dans l'Etat?

FABRICE

Rien pour le présent.

FRIPORT

Tant mieux; moins de nouvelles, moins de sottises. Comment 130 vont vos affaires, mon ami? Avez-vous beaucoup de monde chez vous? Qui logez-vous à présent?

FABRICE

Il est venu ce matin un vieux gentilhomme qui ne veut voir personne.

FRIPORT

Il a raison: les hommes ne sont pas bons à grand'chose, fripons 135 ou sots: voilà pour les trois quarts; et pour l'autre quart il se tient chez soi.

129 60AM: Rien jusqu'à présent.

FABRICE

Cet homme n'a pas même la curiosité de voir une femme charmante que nous avons dans la maison.

FRIPORT

Il a tort. Et quelle est cette femme charmante? 140

FABRICE

Elle est encore plus singulière que lui; il y a quatre mois qu'elle est chez moi, et qu'elle n'est pas sortie de son appartement; elle s'appelle Lindane, mais je ne crois pas que ce soit son véritable nom.

FRIPORT

C'est sans doute une honnête femme, puisqu'elle loge ici. 145

FABRICE

Oh! elle est bien plus qu'honnête; elle est belle, pauvre et vertueuse: entre nous, elle est dans la dernière misère, et elle est fière à l'excès.

FRIPORT

Si cela est, elle a bien plus tort que votre vieux gentilhomme.

FABRICE

Oh point; sa fierté est encore une vertu de plus; elle consiste à 150 se priver du nécessaire, et à ne vouloir pas qu'on le sache: elle travaille de ses mains pour gagner de quoi me payer, ne se plaint jamais, dévore ses larmes; j'ai mille peines à lui faire garder pour ses besoins l'argent de son loyer; il faut des ruses incroyables pour faire passer jusqu'à elle les moindres secours; je lui compte tout 155

145 60AM: Il faut qu'elle soit une honnête femme, puisqu'elle
154-155 60AM: pour faire parvenir jusqu'à

ce que je lui fournis, à moitié de ce qu'il coûte: quand elle s'en aperçoit, ce sont des querelles qu'on ne peut apaiser, et c'est la seule qu'elle ait eue dans la maison: enfin, c'est un prodige de malheur, de noblesse et de vertu: elle m'arrache quelquefois des larmes d'admiration et de tendresse. 160

FRIPORT

Vous êtes bien tendre; je ne m'attendris point, moi; je n'admire personne, mais j'estime... Ecoutez; comme je m'ennuie, je veux voir cette femme-là, elle m'amusera.

FABRICE

Oh! monsieur, elle ne reçoit presque jamais de visites. Nous avions un milord qui venait quelquefois chez elle, mais elle ne 165 voulait point lui parler sans que ma femme y fût présente: depuis quelque temps il n'y vient plus, et elle vit plus retirée que jamais.

FRIPORT

J'aime qu'on se retire: je hais la cohue aussi bien qu'elle: qu'on me la fasse venir; où est son appartement?

FABRICE

Le voici de plain-pied au café. 170

FRIPORT

Allons, je veux entrer.

FABRICE

Cela ne se peut pas.

164 60X*, MS1: Oh! elle ne
168 60CR:AC, 60CR*, 60X*, 60AM, MS1: J'aime les personnes de cette humeur, je hais
168-169 60, 60CR: retire: je me retirerai avec elle: qu'on me
60AM: qu'elle. Je veux la voir; où est

FRIPORT

Il faut bien que cela se puisse; où est la difficulté d'entrer dans une chambre? Qu'on m'apporte chez elle mon chocolat et les gazettes. (*Il tire sa montre.*) Je n'ai pas beaucoup de temps à perdre, 175 mes affaires m'appellent à deux heures.

(*Il pousse la porte et entre.*)

SCÈNE VI

LINDANE *paraissant tout effrayée,* POLLY *la suit.*
FRIPORT, FABRICE

LINDANE

Eh mon Dieu! qui entre ainsi chez moi avec tant de fracas? Monsieur, vous me paraissez peu civil, et vous devriez respecter davantage ma solitude et mon sexe.

FRIPORT

Pardon. (*à Fabrice.*) Qu'on m'apporte mon chocolat, vous dis-je. 180

FABRICE

Oui, monsieur, si madame le permet.

(*Friport s'assied près d'une table, lit la gazette, et jette un coup d'œil sur Lindane et sur Polly: il ôte son chapeau et le remet.*)

176a 60, 60CR, MS1: (*Il enfonce la porte.*)
60AM, no stage direction
176b 60, 60Y, 60CR, 60AM, MS1, scene misnumbered: V
176c-d 60AM: *Le théâtre représente l'appartement de* LINDANE, *elle paraît effrayée.* POLLY, FRIPORT, FABRICE.

POLLY

Cet homme me paraît familier.

FRIPORT

Madame, pourquoi ne vous asseyez-vous pas quand je suis assis?

LINDANE

Monsieur, c'est que vous ne devriez pas l'être, c'est que je suis 185
très étonnée, c'est que je ne reçois point de visite d'un inconnu.

FRIPORT

Je suis très connu; je m'appelle Friport, loyal négociant, riche; informez-vous de moi à la bourse.

LINDANE

Monsieur, je ne connais personne en ce pays-là, et vous me feriez plaisir de ne point incommoder une femme à qui vous devez 190
quelques égards.

FRIPORT

Je ne prétends point vous incommoder; je prends mes aises, prenez les vôtres; je lis les gazettes, travaillez en tapisserie, et prenez du chocolat avec moi,... ou sans moi,... comme vous voudrez. 195

POLLY

Voilà un étrange original!

182 60AM: familier. (*Un garçon apporte du chocolat; Friport en prend sans en offrir; il parle et boit par reprises.*)

193 60X*: vôtres; je vais lire les

LINDANE

O ciel! quelle visite je reçois! Et milord ne vient point! Cet homme bizarre m'assassine, je ne pourrai m'en défaire; comment monsieur Fabrice a-t-il pu souffrir cela? Il faut bien s'asseoir.

(*Elle s'assied, et travaille à son ouvrage.*)

(*Un garçon apporte du chocolat, Friport en prend sans en offrir; il parle et boit par reprises.*)

FRIPORT

Ecoutez. Je ne suis pas homme à compliments; on m'a dit de vous... le plus grand bien qu'on puisse dire d'une femme: vous êtes pauvre et vertueuse; mais on ajoute que vous êtes fière, et cela n'est pas bien. 200

POLLY

Et qui vous a dit tout cela, monsieur?

FRIPORT

Parbleu, c'est le maître de la maison, qui est un très galant homme, et que j'en crois sur sa parole. 205

LINDANE

C'est un tour qu'il vous joue; il vous a trompé, monsieur; non pas sur la fierté, qui n'est que le partage de la vraie modestie; non pas sur la vertu, qui est mon premier devoir; mais sur la pauvreté, dont il me soupçonne. Qui n'a besoin de rien n'est jamais pauvre. 210

FRIPORT

Vous ne dites pas la vérité, et cela est encore plus mal que

197-198 60CR:AC, 60CR*, 60X*, 60AM, MS1: reçois! Cet homme
199b-c 60AM, no stage direction
200 60AM: ne suis pas complimenteur, moi; on

d'être fière: je sais mieux que vous que vous manquez de tout, et quelquefois même vous vous dérobez un repas.

POLLY

C'est par ordre du médecin.

FRIPORT

Taisez-vous; est-ce que vous êtes fière aussi vous? 215

POLLY

Oh l'original! l'original!

FRIPORT

En un mot, ayez de l'orgueil ou non, peu m'importe. J'ai fait un voyage à la Jamaïque, qui m'a valu cinq mille guinées; je me suis fait une loi (et ce doit être celle de tout bon chrétien) de donner toujours le dixième de ce que je gagne; c'est une dette que ma 220 fortune doit payer à l'état malheureux où vous êtes... oui, où vous êtes, et dont vous ne voulez pas convenir. Voilà ma dette de cinq cents guinées payée. Point de remerciement, point de reconnaissance; gardez l'argent et le secret.

(*Il jette une grosse bourse sur la table.*)

POLLY

Ma foi, ceci est bien plus original encore. 225

LINDANE (*se levant et se détournant.*)

Je n'ai jamais été si confondue. Hélas que tout ce qui m'arrive m'humilie! quelle générosité! mais quel outrage!

FRIPORT (*continuant à lire les gazettes, et à prendre son chocolat.*)

L'impertinent gazetier! le plat animal! peut-on dire de telles

212-213 60AM: et souvent même
224a-225 60CR*, omitted

pauvretés avec un ton si emphatique? *Le roi est venu en haute personne*. Eh malotru! qu'importe que sa personne soit haute ou petite? Dis le fait tout rondement. 230

LINDANE (*s'approchant de lui.*)

Monsieur...

FRIPORT

Eh bien?

LINDANE

Ce que vous faites pour moi me surprend plus encore que ce que vous dites; mais je n'accepterai certainement point l'argent que vous m'offrez: il faut vous avouer que je ne me crois pas en état de vous le rendre. 235

FRIPORT

Qui vous parle de le rendre?

LINDANE

Je ressens jusqu'au fond du cœur toute la vertu de votre procédé, mais la mienne ne peut en profiter; recevez mon admiration; c'est tout ce que je puis. 240

POLLY

Vous êtes cent fois plus singulière que lui. Eh! Madame, dans l'état où vous êtes, abandonnée de tout le monde, avez-vous perdu l'esprit, de refuser un secours que le ciel vous envoie par la main du plus bizarre et du plus galant homme du monde? 245

FRIPORT

Eh que veux-tu dire, toi? En quoi suis-je bizarre?

244 60CR, 60AM, MS1: par les mains

POLLY

Si vous ne prenez pas pour vous, madame, prenez pour moi; je vous sers dans votre malheur, il faut que je profite au moins de cette bonne fortune. Monsieur, il ne faut plus dissimuler; nous sommes dans la dernière misère, et sans la bonté attentive du 250 maître du café, nous serions mortes de froid et de faim. Ma maîtresse a caché son état à ceux qui pouvaient lui rendre service; vous l'avez su malgré elle, obligez-la malgré elle à ne pas se priver du nécessaire que le ciel lui envoie par vos mains généreuses.

LINDANE

Tu me perds d'honneur, ma chère Polly. 255

POLLY

Et vous vous perdez de folie, ma chère maîtresse.

LINDANE

Si tu m'aimes, prends pitié de ma gloire; ne me réduis pas à mourir de honte pour avoir de quoi vivre.

FRIPORT (*toujours lisant.*)

Que disent ces bavardes-là?

POLLY

Si vous m'aimez, ne me réduisez pas à mourir de faim par vanité. 260

LINDANE

Polly, que dirait milord, s'il m'aimait encore, s'il me croyait capable d'une telle bassesse? J'ai toujours feint avec lui de n'avoir

251 60CR:AC, 60CR*, 60X*, 60AM, MS1: mortes mille fois. Ma

258-260 60CR*, 60X*, 60AM, MS1: de quoi vivre. / POLLY / Si [60AM: Mais si] vous m'aimez

aucun besoin de secours, et j'en accepterais d'un autre, d'un inconnu?

POLLY

Vous avez mal fait de feindre, et vous faites très mal de refuser. 265
Milord ne dira rien, car il vous abandonne.

LINDANE

Ma chère Polly, au nom de nos malheurs, ne nous déshonorons point; congédie honnêtement cet homme estimable et grossier, qui sait donner, et qui ne sait pas vivre: dis-lui que quand une fille accepte d'un homme de tels présents, elle est toujours soupçonnée 270
d'en payer la valeur aux dépens de sa vertu.

FRIPORT (*toujours prenant son chocolat et lisant.*)

Hem, que dit-elle là?

POLLY (*s'approchant de lui.*)

Hélas, monsieur, elle dit des choses qui me paraissent absurdes; elle parle de soupçons; elle dit qu'une fille...

FRIPORT

Ah, ah! est-ce qu'elle est fille? 275

POLLY

Oui, monsieur, et moi aussi.

FRIPORT

Tant mieux; elle dit donc qu'une fille?...

266 60CR*, 60X*, 60AM, MS1: car nous ne le voyons plus.
268-269 60CR*, 60X*, 60AM, MS1: congédie-le honnêtement. Dis-lui que
270-271 60CR*, 60X*, 60AM, MS1: présens, sa vertu est toujours soupçonnée.//
273 60X*, MS1: Monsieur, elle
275a 60AM: POLLY *faisant la révérence.*

POLLY

Qu'une fille ne peut honnêtement accepter d'un homme.

FRIPORT

Elle ne sait ce qu'elle dit; pourquoi me soupçonner d'un dessein malhonnête, quand je fais une action honnête? 280

POLLY

Entendez-vous, mademoiselle?

LINDANE

Oui, j'entends, je l'admire, et je suis inébranlable dans mon refus. Polly, on dirait qu'il m'aime: oui, ce méchant homme de Frélon le dirait, je serais perdue.

POLLY (*allant vers Friport.*)

Monsieur, elle craint que vous ne l'aimiez. 285

FRIPORT

Quelle idée! comment puis-je l'aimer? je ne la connais pas. Rassurez-vous, mademoiselle, je ne vous aime point du tout. Si je viens dans quelques années à vous aimer par hasard, et vous aussi à m'aimer, à la bonne heure... comme vous vous aviserez je m'aviserai. Si vous vous en passez, je m'en passerai. Si vous dites 290 que je vous ennuie, vous m'ennuierez. Si vous voulez ne me revoir jamais, je ne vous reverrai jamais. Si vous voulez que je revienne, je reviendrai. Adieu, adieu. (*Il tire sa montre.*) Mon temps se perd, j'ai des affaires, serviteur.

LINDANE

Allez, monsieur, emportez mon estime et ma reconnaissance, 295

285 60CR:AC, 60CR*, 60X*, 60AM, MS1: craint qu'on [60AM: que l'on] ne dise que vous l'aimez.

291 60AM: je vous ennuie, je ne vous ennuierai pas. Si vous

mais surtout emportez votre argent, et ne me faites pas rougir davantage.

FRIPORT

Elle est folle.

LINDANE

Fabrice! monsieur Fabrice! à mon secours, venez.

FABRICE (*arrivant en hâte.*)

Quoi donc, madame? 300

LINDANE (*lui donnant la bourse.*)

Tenez, prenez cette bourse que monsieur a laissée par mégarde; remettez-la lui, je vous en charge; assurez-le de mon estime; et sachez que je n'ai besoin du secours de personne.

FABRICE (*prenant la bourse.*)

Ah! monsieur Friport, je vous reconnais bien à cette bonne action; mais comptez que mademoiselle vous trompe, et qu'elle 305 en a très grand besoin.

LINDANE

Non, cela n'est pas vrai. Ah! monsieur Fabrice! est-ce vous qui me trahissez?

FABRICE

Je vais vous obéir, puisque vous le voulez. (*bas à M. Friport.*) Je garderai cet argent, et il servira, sans qu'elle le sache, à lui procurer 310 tout ce qu'elle se refuse. Le cœur me saigne; son état et sa vertu me pénètrent l'âme.

304 60AM: Friport, que je vous reconnais

FRIPORT

Elles me font aussi quelque sensation; mais elle est trop fière. Dites-lui que cela n'est pas bien d'être fière. Adieu.

SCÈNE VII

LINDANE, POLLY

POLLY

Vous avez là bien opéré, madame; le ciel daignait vous secourir; 315 vous voulez mourir dans l'indigence; vous voulez que je sois la victime d'une vertu, dans laquelle il entre peut-être un peu de vanité; et cette vanité nous perd l'une et l'autre.

LINDANE

C'est à moi de mourir, ma chère enfant; milord ne m'aime plus; il m'abandonne depuis trois jours; il a aimé mon impitoyable et 320 superbe rivale; il l'aime encore sans doute; c'en est fait; j'étais trop coupable en l'aimant; c'est une erreur qui doit finir.

(*Elle écrit.*)

POLLY

Elle paraît désespérée; hélas! elle a sujet de l'être; son état est

313-314 60X*: fière. (*à Fabrice*). Ecoutez. Dites-lui
60X*: fière. (*à Lindane*). Adieu, mademoiselle.//
314a 60, 60Y, 60CR, 60AM, MS1, scene misnumbered: VI
320 60AM: m'abandonne; il a aimé
323 61L1: Elle me paraît

bien plus cruel que le mien; une suivante a toujours des ressources; mais une personne qui se respecte n'en a pas. 325

LINDANE (*ayant plié sa lettre.*)

Je ne fais pas un bien grand sacrifice. Tiens, quand je ne serai plus, porte cette lettre à celui…

POLLY

Que dites-vous?

LINDANE

A celui qui est la cause de ma mort: je te recommande à lui, mes dernières volontés le toucheront. Va. (*elle l'embrasse.*) Sois sûre 330 que de tant d'amertumes, celle de n'avoir pu te récompenser moi-même, n'est pas la moins sensible à ce cœur infortuné.

POLLY

Ah! mon adorable maîtresse! que vous me faites verser de larmes, et que vous me glacez d'effroi! Que voulez-vous faire? quel dessein horrible! quelle lettre! Dieu me préserve de la lui rendre 335 jamais! (*Elle déchire la lettre.*) Hélas! pourquoi ne vous êtes-vous pas expliquée avec milord? Peut-être que votre réserve cruelle lui aura déplu.

LINDANE

Tu m'ouvres les yeux; je lui aurai déplu sans doute; mais com-

324-325 60CR*, 60X*, 60AM, MS1: le mien. Sans mon extrême [60CR*, 60X* omit 'extrême'] attachement pour elle, une nouvelle condition pourrait me fournir des ressources; mais une personne comme elle est obligée de supporter ses malheurs pour se faire respecter.

328 60X: Que dites-vous, vous? [60X*: β]

335 60AM: horrible! Hélas! quelle

335-336 60, 60CR: horrible! hélas! pourquoi [60CR:AC, 60CR*, 60X*: β]
60Y: la lui jamais rendre.

336 60CR*: *Polly déchire*
MS1: jamais. Pourquoi ne vous êtes-vous

ment me découvrir au fils de celui qui a perdu mon père et ma 340
famille?

POLLY

Quoi, madame, ce fut donc le père de milord qui…[10]

LINDANE

Oui, ce fut lui-même qui persécuta mon père, qui le fit condamner à la mort, qui nous a dégradés de noblesse, qui nous a ravi notre existence. Sans père, sans mère, sans bien, je n'ai que ma 345
gloire et mon fatal amour. Je devais détester le fils de Murrai; la fortune qui me poursuit me l'a fait connaître; je l'ai aimé, et je dois m'en punir.

POLLY

Que vois-je! vous pâlissez, vos yeux s'obscurcissent…

LINDANE

Puisse ma douleur me tenir lieu du poison et du fer que 350
j'implorais!

POLLY

A l'aide! monsieur Fabrice, à l'aide! ma maîtresse s'évanouit.

FABRICE

Au secours! que tout le monde descende, ma femme, ma servante, monsieur le gentilhomme de là-haut, tout le monde…

(*La femme et la servante de Fabrice et Polly, emmènent Lindane dans sa chambre.*)

354a-b 60AM: (*Polly emmène Lindane dans sa chambre.*)

[10] Lindane has already told Polly this in I.V.232-233: the inconsistency of Polly's surprise here would be easily disposed of on stage by making Lindane's revelation in act I an *aparte*.

LINDANE (*en sortant.*)

Pourquoi me rendez-vous à la vie? 355

SCÈNE VIII

MONROSE, FABRICE

MONROSE

Qu'y a-t-il donc, notre hôte?

FABRICE

C'était cette belle demoiselle dont je vous ai parlé, qui s'évanouissait; mais ce ne sera rien.

MONROSE

Ces petites fantaisies de filles passent vite, et ne sont pas dangereuses: que voulez-vous que je fasse à une fille qui se trouve mal? 360 est-ce pour cela que vous m'avez fait descendre? Je croyais que le feu était à la maison.

FABRICE

J'aimerais mieux qu'il y fût, que de voir cette jeune personne en danger. Si l'Ecosse a plusieurs filles comme elle, ce doit être un beau pays. 365

MONROSE

Quoi! elle est d'Ecosse?

355a 60, 60Y, 60CR, 60AM, MS1, scene misnumbered: VII
358a-361 60CR:AC, 60CR*, 60X*, 60AM, MS1: MONROSE / Ah! tant mieux, mais [60AM, 'mais' absent] vous m'avez effrayé! je croyais

FABRICE

Oui, monsieur, je ne le sais que d'aujourd'hui; c'est notre faiseur de feuilles qui me l'a dit, car il sait tout, lui.

MONROSE

Et son nom, son nom?

FABRICE

Elle s'appelle Lindane. 370

MONROSE

Je ne connais point ce nom-là. (*Il se promène.*) On ne prononce point le nom de ma patrie que mon cœur ne soit déchiré. Peut-on avoir été traité avec plus d'injustice et de barbarie? Tu es mort, cruel Murrai, indigne ennemi! ton fils reste; j'aurai justice ou vengeance. O ma femme! ô mes chers enfants! ma fille! j'ai donc tout 375 perdu sans ressource! Que de coups de poignard auraient fini mes jours, si la juste fureur de me venger ne me forçait pas à porter dans l'affreux chemin du monde, ce fardeau détestable de la vie!

FABRICE (*revenant.*)

Tout va mieux, Dieu merci.

MONROSE

Comment? quel changement y a-t-il dans les affaires? quelle 380 révolution?

370 60CR*, 60X*: Lindane. Je vais savoir en quel état elle est à présent. [60X* adds '(*il sort*)']

370a 60X*: MONROSE, *seul*

371 60AM, MS1: connais point ce nom-là. / FABRICE / Je vais savoir en quel état elle est à présent. / SCÈNE VIII [misnumbered, read 'IX'] / MONROSE, *seul, se promenant.* / On ne prononce

373-375 60CR*, 60X*, MS1: barbarie? O ma femme!

378a-387 60CR*, 60X*, 60AM, MS1, omitted

FABRICE

Monsieur, elle a repris ses sens; elle se porte très bien; encore un peu pâle, mais toujours belle.

MONROSE

Ah, ce n'est que cela. Il faut que je sorte, que j'aille, que je hasarde… oui… je le veux. 385

(*Il sort.*)

FABRICE

Cet homme ne se soucie pas des filles qui s'évanouissent. S'il avait vu Lindane, il ne serait pas si indifférent.

Fin du second acte.

ACTE III

SCÈNE PREMIÈRE

LADY ALTON, ANDRÉ

LADY ALTON

Oui, puisque je ne peux voir le traître chez lui, je le verrai ici, il y viendra sans doute. Ce barbouilleur de feuilles avait raison; une Ecossaise cachée ici dans ce temps de trouble! Elle conspire contre l'Etat;[1] elle sera enlevée, l'ordre est donné: ah! du moins, c'est contre moi qu'elle conspire! c'est de quoi je ne suis que trop sûre. Voici André le laquais de milord; je serai instruite de tout mon malheur. André! vous apportez ici une lettre de milord, n'est-il pas vrai? 5

ANDRÉ

Oui, madame.

LADY ALTON

Elle est pour moi. 10

c 60X*, 'ANDRÉ' omitted
d 60X*: LADY ALTON, *seule*
2 60CR:AC, 60CR*, 60X*, 60AM, MS1: doute. Wasp avait raison
3 60X*, MS1: dans un temps
4 60X*, MS1: l'Etat; ah du moins
6 60X*: sûre. Elle sera enlevée, l'ordre est donné. / SCÈNE 2e / LADY ALTON, ANDRÉ / LADY ALTON / Voici André! [MS1 follows text of 60X*, but has no new scene]

[1] Frélon makes the comment to Lady Alton in II.iii.74-75: 'dans un temps de trouble, une Ecossaise qui se cache est une ennemie de l'Etat'. Fears of the Auld Alliance, no doubt.

ANDRÉ

Non, madame, je vous jure.

LADY ALTON

Comment? ne m'en avez-vous pas apporté plusieurs de sa part?

ANDRÉ

Oui, mais celle-ci n'est pas pour vous; c'est pour une personne qu'il aime à la folie.

LADY ALTON

Eh bien, ne m'aimait-il pas à la folie quand il m'écrivait? 15

ANDRÉ

Oh que non, madame, il vous aimait si tranquillement! mais ici ce n'est pas de même; il ne dort ni ne mange; il court jour et nuit; il ne parle que de sa chère Lindane; cela est tout différent, vous dis-je.

LADY ALTON

Le perfide! le méchant homme! N'importe, je vous dis que cette 20 lettre est pour moi; n'est-elle pas sans dessus?

ANDRÉ

Oui, madame.

LADY ALTON

Toutes les lettres que vous m'avez apportées n'étaient-elles pas sans dessus aussi?

ANDRÉ

Oui, mais elle est pour Lindane. 25

LADY ALTON

Je vous dis qu'elle est pour moi, et pour vous le prouver, voici dix guinées de port que je vous donne.

ANDRÉ

Ah oui, madame, vous m'y faites penser, vous avez raison, la lettre est pour vous, je l'avais oublié:… mais cependant, comme elle n'était pas pour vous, ne me décelez pas; dites que vous l'avez trouvée chez Lindane. 30

LADY ALTON

Laisse-moi faire.

ANDRÉ

Quel mal, après tout, de donner à une femme une lettre écrite pour une autre? il n'y a rien de perdu, toutes ces lettres se ressemblent. Si mademoiselle Lindane ne reçoit pas sa lettre, elle en recevra d'autres. Ma commission est faite. Oh! je fais bien mes commissions, moi! 35

(*Il sort.*)

LADY ALTON (*ouvre la lettre et lit.*)

Lisons: *Ma chère, ma respectable, ma vertueuse Lindane*… il ne m'en a jamais tant écrit… *il y a deux jours, il y a un siècle que je m'arrache au bonheur d'être à vos pieds, mais c'est pour vos seuls intérêts: je sais qui vous êtes, et ce que je vous dois: je périrai, ou les choses changeront. Mes amis agissent; comptez sur moi, comme sur l'amant le plus fidèle, et sur un homme digne peut-être de vous servir.* 40

(*après avoir lu.*)

27 60AM: guinées que je
32a 60AM: ANDRÉ *à part.*
37b MS1: LADY ALTON (*après qu'André est sorti*)
T64P: *la lettre.*//
40-41 60, 60Y, 60CR, 60AM, SS61, T64P, MS1: *mais c'est pour vous servir: je sais*

C'est une conspiration, il n'en faut point douter; elle est d'Ecosse, sa famille est malintentionnée; le père de Murrai a commandé en Ecosse; ses amis agissent; il court jour et nuit; c'est une conspiration. Dieu merci, j'ai agi aussi, et si elle n'accepte pas mes offres, elle sera enlevée dans une heure, avant que son indigne amant la secoure. 45

SCÈNE II

LADY ALTON, POLLY, LINDANE

LADY ALTON (*à Polly qui passe de la chambre de sa maîtresse dans une chambre du café.*)

Mademoiselle, allez dire tout à l'heure à votre maîtresse qu'il faut que je lui parle, qu'elle ne craigne rien, que je n'ai que des choses très agréables à lui dire; qu'il s'agit de son bonheur, (*avec emportement*) et qu'il faut qu'elle vienne tout à l'heure, tout à l'heure: entendez-vous? qu'elle ne craigne point, vous dis-je. 50

POLLY

Oh madame! nous ne craignons rien; mais votre physionomie me fait trembler. 55

LADY ALTON

Nous verrons, si je ne viens pas à bout de cette fille vertueuse, avec les propositions que je vais lui faire.

44-46 60X*, 60AM, MS1: point douter; ses amis agissent
46-47 60X*, MS1: agissent; j'ai agi
60CR:AC, 60CR*, 60AM: nuit; Dieu merci
49d 60AM: *dans la salle du café*
56a 60X*: SCÈNE / LADY ALTON, *seule.*

LINDANE (*arrivant toute tremblante soutenue par Polly.*)

Que voulez-vous, madame? venez-vous insulter encore à ma douleur? 60

LADY ALTON

Non, je viens vous rendre heureuse. Je sais que vous n'avez rien; je suis riche, je suis grande dame;[2] je vous offre un de mes châteaux sur les frontières d'Ecosse, avec les terres qui en dépendent; allez-y vivre avec votre famille, si vous en avez; mais il faut dans l'instant que vous abandonniez milord pour jamais, et qu'il 65 ignore toute sa vie votre retraite.

LINDANE

Hélas, madame, c'est lui qui m'abandonne; ne soyez point jalouse d'une infortunée; vous m'offrez en vain une retraite; j'en trouverai sans vous une éternelle, dans laquelle je n'aurai pas au moins à rougir de vos bienfaits. 70

LADY ALTON

Comme vous me répondez, téméraire!

LINDANE

La témérité ne doit point être mon partage; mais la fermeté doit l'être. Ma naissance vaut bien la vôtre; mon cœur vaut peut-être

58a 60x*: SCÈNE / LADY ALTON, LINDANE, POLLY
64 60x*: en avez une; mais

[2] Palissot: 'Les femmes de qualité ne disaient pas plus en Angleterre qu'en France, *je suis grande dame*. Cela est bon pour comtesse d'Escarbagnas, mais non pour ladi Alton'.

Nevertheless, in the context it is less ludicrous than, say, Lord Foppington's insistence (in *The Relapse*) on his being a 'man of quality'. Lady Alton is simply stating facts which enable her to make her offer to Lindane.

mieux; et quant à ma fortune, elle ne dépendra jamais de personne, encore moins de ma rivale. 75

(*elle sort.*)

LADY ALTON (*seule.*)

Elle dépendra de moi. Je suis fâchée qu'elle me réduise à cette extrémité. J'ai honte de m'être servie de ce faquin de Frélon; mais enfin, elle m'y a forcée. Infidèle amant! passion funeste! Je suffoque.

SCÈNE III

FRIPORT, MONROSE *paraissent dans le café avec* LA FEMME DE FABRICE, LA SERVANTE, LES GARÇONS DU CAFÉ, *qui mettent tout en ordre.* FABRICE, LADY ALTON

LADY ALTON (*à Fabrice.*)

Monsieur Fabrice, vous me voyez ici souvent, c'est votre faute. 80

FABRICE

Au contraire, madame, nous souhaiterions...

75a 60AM, MS1: (*Elle sort avec Polly.*)
77-78 60CR:AC, 60CR*, 60X*, 60AM, MS1: extrémité. Mais enfin
60, 60Y, 60CR: faquin d'écrivain; mais
78-79 60CR*, 60X*, MS1: m'y a forcée.//
60CR:AC, 60AM: passion funeste!//
79b 60, 60Y, 60CR, SS61, T64P: LE CHEVALIER MONROSE
79b-d 60AM: M. FRIPORT, LE CHEVALIER MONROSE, FABRICE, LADY ALTON
80 60AM: Adieu, monsieur Fabrice, vous

LADY ALTON

J'en suis fâchée plus que vous; mais vous m'y reverrez encore, vous dis-je.

(elle sort.)

FABRICE

Tant pis. A qui en a-t-elle donc? Quelle différence d'elle à cette Lindane, si belle et si patiente! 85

FRIPORT

Oui, à propos, vous m'y faites songer; elle est, comme vous dites, belle et honnête.

FABRICE

Je suis fâché que ce brave gentilhomme ne l'ait pas vue, il en aurait été touché.

MONROSE (*à part.*)

Ah! j'ai d'autres affaires en tête… Malheureux que je suis! 90

FRIPORT

Je passe mon temps à la bourse ou à la Jamaïque: cependant la vue d'une jeune personne ne laisse pas de réjouir les yeux d'un galant homme. Vous me faites songer, vous dis-je, à cette petite créature: beau maintien, conduite sage, belle tête, démarche noble. Il faut que je la voie un de ces jours encore une fois… C'est 95 dommage qu'elle soit si fière.

MONROSE (*à Friport.*)

Notre hôte m'a confié que vous en aviez agi avec elle d'une manière admirable.

84 60X*: Tant pis. / SCÈNE / FRIPORT, FABRICE, MONROSE / FABRICE / A qui

93-94 60AM: Vous m'y faites songer, vous dis-je. Beau maintien

FRIPORT

Moi? non:… n'en auriez-vous pas fait autant à ma place?

MONROSE

Je le crois si j'étais riche, et si elle le méritait. 100

FRIPORT

Eh bien, que trouvez-vous donc là d'admirable? (*il prend les gazettes.*) Ah ah, voyons ce que disent les nouveaux papiers d'aujourd'hui. Hom, hom, le lord Falbrige mort![3]

MONROSE (*s'avançant.*)

Falbrige mort! le seul ami qui me restait sur la terre! le seul dont j'attendais quelque appui! Fortune, tu ne cesseras jamais de me 105 persécuter!

FRIPORT

Il était votre ami? j'en suis fâché… *D'Edimbourg le 14 avril… On cherche partout le lord Monrose, condamné depuis onze ans à perdre la tête.*

MONROSE

Juste ciel! qu'entends-je! hem, que dites-vous? milord Monrose 110 condamné à…

107 60AM: fâché. (*Il lit.*) *D'Edimbourg le 14 juillet*

[3] Palissot: 'Cette manière si simple d'apprendre à Monrose la mort d'un personnage très-intéressant pour lui, mérite d'être remarquée. Il n'y a là aucune trace d'art, quoiqu'il y en ait un très grand; c'est la chose telle qu'elle a pu se passer. Il en est de même de la nouvelle plus accablante encore pour le lord Montrose, parce qu'elle lui annonce son extrême danger. C'est produire un grand intérêt avec un moyen qui a l'air de s'offrir de lui-même, mais qui est infiniment naturel. Nous avons remarqué que dans aucune de ses comédies, Voltaire n'avait mis autant de vérité, et c'est une de celles qui plaît le plus aux Anglais'.

FRIPORT

Oui parbleu, le lord Monrose:... lisez vous-même, je ne me trompe pas.

MONROSE *lit.*

(*froidement.*)

Oui cela est vrai... (*à part.*) Il faut sortir d'ici, la maison est trop publique... Je ne crois pas que la terre et l'enfer conjurés ensemble 115 aient jamais assemblé tant d'infortunes contre un seul homme, (*à son valet Jacq, qui est dans un coin de la salle.*) Eh! va faire seller mes chevaux, et que je puisse partir, s'il est nécessaire, à l'entrée de la nuit... Comme les nouvelles courent! comme le mal vole!

FRIPORT

Il n'y a point de mal à cela; qu'importe que le lord Monrose soit 120 décapité ou non? Tout s'imprime, tout s'écrit, rien ne demeure: on coupe une tête aujourd'hui, le gazetier le dit le lendemain, et le surlendemain on n'en parle plus. Si cette demoiselle Lindane n'était pas si fière, j'irais savoir comme elle se porte: elle est fort jolie, et fort honnête. 125

SCÈNE IV

LES ACTEURS PRÉCÉDENTS, UN MESSAGER D'ÉTAT

LE MESSAGER

Vous vous appelez Fabrice?

114-115 60CR:AC, 60CR*, 60X*, 60AM, MS1: d'ici. Je ne crois
117 60AM: (*à son valet Jacq.*) Eh!
123-124 60AM: le surlendemain il n'en est plus question. Si

FABRICE

Oui, monsieur; en quoi puis-je vous servir?

LE MESSAGER

Vous tenez un café, et des appartements?

FABRICE

Oui.

LE MESSAGER

Vous avez chez vous une jeune Ecossaise nommée Lindane? 130

FABRICE

Oui, assurément, et c'est notre bonheur de l'avoir chez nous.

FRIPORT

Oui, elle est jolie et honnête. Tout le monde m'y fait songer.

LE MESSAGER

Je viens pour m'assurer d'elle de la part du gouvernement; voilà mon ordre.

FABRICE

Je n'ai pas une goutte de sang dans les veines. 135

MONROSE (*à part.*)

Une jeune Ecossaise qu'on arrête! et le jour même que j'arrive! Toute ma fureur renaît. O patrie! ô famille! Hélas! que deviendra ma fille infortunée? elle est peut-être ainsi la victime de mes malheurs; elle languit dans la pauvreté ou dans la prison. Ah pourquoi est-elle née? 140

137-140 60CR:AC, 60CR*, 60X*, 60AM, MS1: Hélas!//

FRIPORT

On n'a jamais arrêté les filles par ordre du gouvernement; fi que cela est vilain! vous êtes un grand brutal, monsieur le messager d'Etat.

FABRICE

Ouais! mais si c'était une aventurière, comme le disait notre ami Frélon; cela va perdre ma maison;... me voilà ruiné. Cette 145 dame de la cour avait ses raisons, je le vois bien... Non, non, elle est très honnête.

LE MESSAGER

Point de raisonnement, en prison, ou caution; c'est la règle.

FABRICE

Je me fais caution, moi, ma maison, mon bien, ma personne.

LE MESSAGER

Votre personne, et rien, c'est la même chose; votre maison 150 ne vous appartient peut-être pas; votre bien, où est-il? il faut de l'argent.

FABRICE

Mon bon monsieur Friport, donnerai-je les cinq cents guinées que je garde, et qu'elle a refusées aussi noblement que vous les avez offertes? 155

FRIPORT

Belle demande! apparemment... Monsieur le messager, je dé-

143a-147 60AM, absent
144-146 60X*, MS1: une aventurière. Non, non
145-146 60CR*: ami Frélon. Non, non
156 60X*, MS1: Attendez: je vais arranger cela. – Monsieur le messager d'Etat, je dépose

pose cinq cents guinées, mille, deux mille, s'il le faut; voilà comme je suis fait. Je m'appelle Friport. Je réponds de la vertu de la fille,... autant que je peux;... mais il ne faudrait pas qu'elle fût si fière.

LE MESSAGER

Venez, monsieur, faire votre soumission. 160

FRIPORT

Très volontiers, très volontiers.

FABRICE

Tout le monde ne place pas ainsi son argent.

FRIPORT

En l'employant à faire du bien, c'est le placer au plus haut intérêt.[4]

(*Friport et le messager vont compter de l'argent, et écrire au fond du café.*)

158-159 60CR:AC, 60CR*, 60X*, 60AM, MS1: m'appelle Friport.//
164a 60AM: (*Friport et le messager sortent.*)
MS1, 60X*: *du café et sortent.*)

[4] On 21 July 1764 Voltaire wrote to the duc de Richelieu (D12002) to ask him his opinion of the Lally affair. He compares the French system of imprisoning a man before trial, with the English system of allowing bail first, and imprisoning the accused only if he is guilty 'comme dans la comédie de l'*Ecossaise*'. It is the system of bail which enables Freeport to prevent a gross miscarriage of justice: his willingness to risk up to two thousand guineas is intended by Voltaire to show how individual generosity can prevent unjustified imprisonment if the law makes provision for it.

SCÈNE V

MONROSE, FABRICE

FABRICE

Monsieur, vous êtes étonné peut-être du procédé de monsieur Friport, mais c'est sa façon. Heureux ceux qu'il prend tout d'un coup en amitié! Il n'est pas complimenteur; mais il rend service en moins de temps que les autres ne font des protestations de services. 165

MONROSE

Il y a de belles âmes... Que deviendrai-je? 170

FABRICE

Gardons-nous au moins de dire à notre pauvre petite le danger qu'elle a couru.

MONROSE

Allons, partons cette nuit même.

FABRICE

Il ne faut jamais avertir les gens de leur danger que quand il est passé. 175

MONROSE

Le seul ami que j'avais à Londres est mort!... Que fais-je ici?

FABRICE.

Nous la ferions évanouir encore une fois.

167-168 60CR:AC, 60CR*, 60X*, 60AM, MS1: mais il oblige en moins
175a T64: MONROSE, *à part*.

SCÈNE VI

MONROSE *seul.*

On arrête une jeune Ecossaise, une personne qui vit retirée, qui se cache, qui est suspecte au gouvernement! Je ne sais,… mais cette aventure me jette dans de profondes réflexions:… tout réveille l'idée de mes malheurs, mes afflictions, mon attendrissement, mes fureurs. 180

SCÈNE VII

MONROSE (*apercevant Polly qui passe.*)

Mademoiselle, un petit mot, de grâce… Etes-vous cette jeune et aimable personne née en Ecosse, qui…

POLLY

Oui, monsieur, je suis assez jeune; je suis Ecossaise, et pour aimable, bien des gens me disent que je le suis. 185

MONROSE

Ne savez-vous aucune nouvelle de votre pays?

POLLY

Oh non, monsieur, il y a si longtemps que je l'ai quitté!

MONROSE

Et qui sont vos parents, je vous prie?

185 60X*, MS1: Oui, monsieur, je suis Ecossaise
186 60AM, MS1: je la suis.

POLLY

Mon père était un excellent boulanger, à ce que j'ai ouï dire, et 190
ma mère avait servi une dame de qualité.

MONROSE

Ah, j'entends, c'est vous apparemment qui servez cette jeune personne dont on m'a tant parlé; je me méprenais.

POLLY

Vous me faites bien de l'honneur.

MONROSE

Vous savez sans doute qui est votre maîtresse? 195

POLLY

Oui, monsieur, c'est la plus douce, la plus aimable fille, la plus courageuse dans le malheur.

MONROSE

Elle est donc malheureuse?

POLLY

Oui, monsieur, et moi aussi; mais j'aime mieux la servir que
d'être heureuse. 200

MONROSE

Mais je vous demande si vous ne connaissez pas sa famille?

POLLY

Monsieur, ma maîtresse veut être inconnue; elle n'a point de famille; que me demandez-vous là? pourquoi ces questions?

190 60CR*, 60X*, 60AM, MS1: était un honnête artisan, à ce que

MONROSE

Une inconnue! O ciel, si longtemps impitoyable! s'il était possible qu'à la fin je pusse!… mais quelles vaines chimères! Dites-moi, je vous prie, quel est l'âge de votre maîtresse? 205

POLLY

Oh pour son âge, on peut le dire; car elle est bien au-dessus de son âge; elle a dix-huit ans.

MONROSE

Dix-huit ans!…[5] hélas ce serait précisément l'âge qu'aurait ma malheureuse Monrose, ma chère fille, seul reste de ma maison, 210 seul enfant que mes mains aient pu caresser dans son berceau: dix-huit ans?…

POLLY

Oui, monsieur, et moi je n'en ai que vingt-deux, il n'y a pas une si grande différence. Je ne sais pas pourquoi vous faites tout seul tant de réflexions sur son âge? 215

MONROSE

Dix-huit ans, et née dans ma patrie! et elle veut être inconnue: je ne me possède plus; il faut avec votre permission que je la voie, que je lui parle tout à l'heure.

203a T64P: MONROSE, *à part.*
205 T64P: chimères! (*A Polly.*) Dites
208a T64P: MONROSE, *à part.*
213-214 MS1: Oui, monsieur. Je ne sais
215a T64P: MONROSE, *à part.*
217 T64P: plus. (*A Polly.*) Il

[5] Palissot: 'L'intérêt du roman commence; mais, comme le dit l'auteur dans sa préface, ce roman est dans le goût anglais; il n'a rien de recherché, de merveilleux, ni d'invraisemblable; c'est une vraie peinture de mœurs.'

POLLY

Ces dix-huit ans tournent la tête à ce bon vieux gentilhomme. Monsieur, il est impossible que vous voyiez à présent ma maîtresse; elle est dans l'affliction la plus cruelle. 220

MONROSE

Ah! c'est pour cela même que je veux la voir.

POLLY

De nouveaux chagrins qui l'ont accablée, qui ont déchiré son cœur, lui ont fait perdre l'usage de ses sens. Hélas! elle n'est pas de ces filles qui s'évanouissent pour peu de chose. Elle est à peine 225 revenue à elle, et le peu de repos qu'elle goûte dans ce moment est un repos mêlé de trouble et d'amertume; de grâce, monsieur, ménagez sa faiblesse et ses douleurs.

MONROSE

Tout ce que vous me dites redouble mon empressement. Je suis son compatriote; je partage toutes ses afflictions; je les diminuerai 230 peut-être; souffrez qu'avant de quitter cette ville, je puisse entretenir votre maîtresse.

POLLY

Mon cher compatriote, vous m'attendrissez; attendez encore quelques moments. Les filles qui se sont évanouies sont bien longtemps à se remettre, avant de recevoir une visite. Je vais à elle. Je 235 reviendrai à vous.

224-225 60CR:AC, 60CR*, 60X*, 60AM, MS1: ses sens. Elle est à peine
233 60AM: Mon cher monsieur, vous
234-236 60CR:AC, 60CR*, 60X*, 60AM, MS1: quelques moments. Je vais à elle; et je reviens à vous. [60CR* adds: (*elle sort*)]

SCÈNE VIII

MONROSE, FABRICE

FABRICE (*le tirant par la manche.*)

Monsieur, n'y a-t-il personne là?

MONROSE

Que j'attends son retour avec des mouvements d'impatience et de trouble!

FABRICE

Ne nous écoute-t-on point? 240

MONROSE

Mon cœur ne peut suffire à tout ce qu'il éprouve.

FABRICE

On vous cherche…

MONROSE (*se retournant.*)

Qui? quoi? comment? pourquoi? que voulez-vous dire?

FABRICE

On vous cherche, monsieur. Je m'intéresse à ceux qui logent chez moi. Je ne sais qui vous êtes; mais on est venu me demander 245 qui vous étiez: on rôde autour de la maison, on s'informe, on entre, on passe, on repasse, on guette, et je ne serai point surpris si dans

237a T64P: MONROSE, *à part.*
240a T64P: MONROSE, *à part.*
245 60AM: Je n'ai pas l'honneur de vous connaître; mais

peu on vous fait le même compliment qu'à cette jeune et chère demoiselle, qui est, dit-on, de votre pays.

MONROSE

Ah! il faut absolument que je lui parle avant de partir. 250

FABRICE

Partez vite, croyez-moi; notre ami Friport ne serait peut-être pas d'humeur à faire pour vous ce qu'il a fait pour une belle personne de dix-huit ans.

MONROSE

Pardon... Je ne sais... où j'étais... je vous entendais à peine... Que faire? où aller, mon cher hôte? Je ne peux partir sans la voir... 255 Venez, que je vous parle un moment dans quelque endroit plus solitaire, et surtout que je puisse ensuite entretenir cette jeune Ecossaise.

FABRICE

Ah! je vous avais bien dit que vous seriez enfin curieux de la voir. Soyez sûr que rien n'est plus beau et plus honnête. 260

Fin du troisième acte.

248-249 60X*: cette jeune demoiselle

259-260 60CR*, 60X*, 60AM, MS1: de la voir. Mais je vous suis pour savoir ce que vous désirez de moi; je serai trop heureux si je puis vous être bon à quelque chose [60CR*, 60X*, MS1: rendre quelque service].

ACTE IV

SCÈNE PREMIÈRE

FABRICE, FRÉLON (*dans le café à une table.*)
FRIPORT *une pipe à la main au milieu d'eux.*

FABRICE

Je suis obligé de vous l'avouer, monsieur Frélon; si tout ce qu'on dit est vrai, vous me feriez plaisir de ne plus fréquenter chez nous.

FRÉLON

Tout ce qu'on dit est toujours faux; quelle mouche vous pique, monsieur Fabrice? 5

FABRICE

Vous venez écrire ici vos feuilles. Mon café passera pour une boutique de poisons.

FRIPORT (*se retournant vers Fabrice.*)

Ceci mérite qu'on y pense, voyez-vous?

FABRICE

On prétend que vous dites du mal de tout le monde.

c-d 60AM: FABRICE, WASP, FRIPORT.
3a 60, 60Y, 60CR, 60AM, SS61, T64P, MS1: FRIPORT
8 60AM: Ecoutez donc; ceci mérite
9 60CR*, 60X*, MS1: dites ici du mal de tout le monde. [60X*, MS1: et] Cela me fait tort.

FRIPORT (*à Frélon.*)

De tout le monde, entendez-vous? c'est trop. 10

FABRICE

On commence même à dire que vous êtes un délateur, un fripon; mais je ne veux pas le croire.

FRIPORT (*à Frélon.*)

Un fripon... entendez-vous? cela passe la raillerie.

FRÉLON

Je suis un compilateur illustre, un homme de goût.

FABRICE

De goût ou de dégoût; vous me faites tort, vous dis-je. 15

FRÉLON

Au contraire, c'est moi qui achalande votre café; c'est moi qui l'ai mis à la mode; c'est ma réputation qui vous attire du monde.

FABRICE

Plaisante réputation! celle d'un espion, d'un malhonnête homme, (pardonnez, si je répète ce qu'on dit) et d'un mauvais auteur! 20

9a-15 60CR*, 60X*, MS1, omitted
11-12 60CR:AC, 60AM: délateur, mais je
13 60AM: Un délateur, entendez-vous
18-19 60CR*, 60X*, MS1: réputation! celle d'un malhonnête homme, et d'un mauvais

FRÉLON

Monsieur Fabrice, monsieur Fabrice, arrêtez, s'il vous plaît;[1] on peut attaquer mes mœurs; mais pour ma réputation d'auteur, je ne le souffrirai jamais.

FABRICE

Laissez-là vos écrits; savez-vous bien, puisqu'il faut tout vous dire, que vous êtes soupçonné d'avoir voulu perdre mademoiselle Lindane? 25

FRIPORT

Si je le croyais, je le noyerais de mes mains, quoique je ne sois pas méchant.

FABRICE

On prétend que c'est vous qui l'avez accusée d'être Ecossaise, et qui avez aussi accusé ce brave gentilhomme de là-haut d'être Ecossais. 30

FRÉLON

Eh bien! quel mal y a-t-il à être de son pays?

FABRICE

On prétend que vous avez eu plusieurs conférences avec les

24 60AM: Savez-vous
25-28a 60CR*, 60X*, 60AM, MS1: mademoiselle Lindane. On prétend que c'est vous [omitting Friport's speech]
31-33 60AM: Ecossais. On ajoute même que vous [omitting Frélon's speech]
33 60CR:AC, 60CR*, 60X*, MS1: On ajoute que vous

[1] Palissot: 'Rien n'est plus plaisant que cette insouciance de Frélon pour sa réputation morale, et que la haute importance qu'il attache à la célébrité de son bel-esprit. Ces messieurs ressemblent aux femmes qui veulent bien qu'on les appelle catins, mais qui n'entendent jamais raillerie sur la laideur.'

gens de cette dame si colère qui est venue ici, et avec ceux de ce milord qui n'y vient plus; que vous redites tout, que vous envenimez tout. 35

FRIPORT (*à Frélon.*)

Seriez-vous un fripon en effet? je ne les aime pas, au moins.

FABRICE

Ah! Dieu merci, je crois que j'aperçois enfin notre milord.

FRIPORT

Un milord! Adieu. Je n'aime pas plus les grands seigneurs que les mauvais écrivains. 40

FABRICE

Celui-ci n'est pas un grand seigneur comme un autre.

FRIPORT

Ou comme un autre, ou différent d'un autre, n'importe. Je ne me gêne jamais, et je sors. Mon ami, je ne sais, il me revient toujours dans la tête une idée de notre jeune Ecossaise: je reviendrai incessamment; oui, je reviendrai, je veux lui parler sérieusement; serviteur. Cette Ecossaise est belle et honnête. Adieu. (*en revenant.*) Dites-lui de ma part que je pense beaucoup de bien d'elle. 45

37 60CR:AC, 60AM: un mauvais sujet, en effet?
60CR*: un malhonnête homme? je ne
60X*: un malhonnête homme en effet?
38 60AM: Ah! Dieu soit béni, je
45-46 60CR:AC, 60CR*, 60X*, 60AM, MS1: sérieusement. Adieu

SCÈNE II

LORD MURRAI (*pensif et agité.*) FRÉLON, *lui faisant la révérence, qu'il ne regarde pas.* FABRICE *s'éloignant par respect.*

LORD MURRAI (*à Fabrice, d'un air distrait.*)

Je suis très aise de vous revoir, mon brave et honnête homme; comment se porte cette belle et respectable personne que vous avez le bonheur de posséder chez vous? 50

FABRICE

Milord, elle a été très malade depuis qu'elle ne vous a vu: mais je suis sûr qu'elle se portera mieux aujourd'hui.

LORD MURRAI

Grand Dieu, protecteur de l'innocence, je t'implore pour elle; daigne te servir de moi pour rendre justice à la vertu, et pour tirer 55 d'oppression les infortunés. Grâce à tes bontés et à mes soins, tout m'annonce un succès favorable. Ami, (*à Fabrice*) laissez-moi parler en particulier à cet homme. (*en montrant Frélon.*)

FRÉLON (*à Fabrice.*)

Eh bien, tu vois qu'on t'avait bien trompé sur mon compte, et que j'ai du crédit à la cour. 60

FABRICE (*en sortant.*)

Je ne vois point cela.

LORD MURRAI (*à Frélon.*)

Mon ami!

53a T64P: LORD MURRAI, *à part.*
57 60x*: favorable. Mon ami
61a-62 60x*, omitted

FRÉLON

Monseigneur, permettez-vous que je vous dédie un tome?…

LORD MURRAI

Non: il ne s'agit point de dédicace. C'est vous qui avez appris à mes gens l'arrivée de ce vieux gentilhomme venu d'Ecosse; c'est vous qui l'avez dépeint, qui êtes allé faire le même rapport aux gens du ministre d'Etat. 65

FRÉLON

Monseigneur, je n'ai fait que mon devoir.

LORD MURRAI (*lui donnant quelques guinées.*)

Vous m'avez rendu service sans le savoir: je ne regarde pas à l'intention: on prétend que vous vouliez nuire, et que vous avez fait du bien; tenez, voilà pour le bien que vous avez fait: mais si vous vous avisez jamais de prononcer le nom de cet homme, et de mademoiselle Lindane, je vous ferai jeter par les fenêtres de votre grenier.[2] Allez. 70

FRÉLON

Grand merci, monseigneur. Tout le monde me dit des injures, et me donne de l'argent; je suis bien plus habile que je ne croyais. 75

62a 60X*: WASP, *s'inclinant profondément*
76 60AM, MS1: croyais. (*Wasp sort.*)

[2] Palissot: 'Nous ignorons si, en Angleterre, un membre de la chambre haute menacerait Frélon de le faire jeter par les fenêtres de son grenier; mais en France, le mépris de ceux qu'on nommait grands avait des formes plus polies.' Voltaire had early experience (thanks to the chevalier de Rohan) of French aristocrats' preference for employing thugs to do their dirty work for them.

SCENE III

LORD MURRAI, POLLY

LORD MURRAI, *seul un moment.*

Un vieux gentilhomme arrivé d'Ecosse, Lindane née dans le même pays! Hélas! s'il était possible que je pusse réparer les torts de mon père! si le ciel permettait!... Entrons. (*à Polly qui sort de la chambre de Lindane.*) Chère Polly, n'es-tu pas bien étonnée que j'aie passé tant de temps sans venir ici? deux jours entiers!... je ne me le pardonnerais jamais, si je ne les avais employés pour la respectable fille de milord Monrose; les ministres étaient à Vindsor, il a fallu y courir. Va, le ciel t'inspira bien quand tu te rendis à mes prières, et que tu m'appris le secret de sa naissance. 80 85

POLLY

J'en tremble encore, ma maîtresse me l'avait tant défendu! Si je lui donnais le moindre chagrin, je mourrais de douleur. Hélas! votre absence lui a causé aujourd'hui un assez long évanouissement, et je me serais évanouie aussi, si je n'avais pas eu besoin de mes forces pour la secourir. 90

LORD MURRAI

Tiens, voilà pour l'évanouissement où tu as eu envie de tomber.

76c T64P: *seul.//*
77 60AM: gentilhomme venu d'Ecosse
79 60AM: permettait! Mais entrons vite. (*à*
79-80 60X*: Entrons. (*il appelle*) Polly. Polly. / SCÈNE / LORD MURRAI, POLLY / LORD MURRAI / Chère Polly [MS1 has text of 60X*, but no new scene]
89-90 60CR:AC, 60CR*, 60X*, 60AM, MS1: et je ne sais comment j'ai eu [60CR*, 60X*, MS1: il m'est resté; 60CR:AC: il me reste] assez de force pour la secourir.
91 60CR:AC, 60CR*, 60X*, 60AM, MS1: voilà pour le service que tu lui as rendu.

POLLY

Milord, j'accepte vos dons; je ne suis pas si fière que la belle Lindane, qui n'accepte rien, et qui feint d'être à son aise, quand elle est dans la plus extrême indigence.

LORD MURRAI

Juste ciel! la fille de Monrose dans la pauvreté! malheureux que je suis! que m'as-tu dit? combien je suis coupable! que je vais tout réparer! que son sort changera! Hélas! pourquoi me l'a-t-elle caché? 95

POLLY

Je crois que c'est la seule fois de sa vie qu'elle vous trompera.

LORD MURRAI

Entrons, entrons vite, jetons-nous à ses pieds, c'est trop tarder. 100

POLLY

Ah! milord! gardez-vous-en bien, elle est actuellement avec un gentilhomme, si vieux, si vieux, qui est de son pays, et ils se disent des choses si intéressantes!

LORD MURRAI

Quel est-il ce vieux gentilhomme, pour qui je m'intéresse déjà comme elle? 105

POLLY

Je l'ignore.

LORD MURRAI

O destinée! Juste ciel! pourrais-tu faire que cet homme fût ce que je désire qu'il soit? Et que se disaient-ils, Polly?

102-103 60X*, MS1: gentilhomme bien vieux qui avait à lui parler.//
102 60AM: gentilhomme bien vieux, qui

POLLY

Milord, ils commençaient à s'attendrir; et comme ils s'attendrissaient, ce bon homme n'a pas voulu que je fusse présente, et je 110
suis sortie.

SCÈNE IV

LADY ALTON, LORD MURRAI, POLLY

LADY ALTON

Ah! je vous y prends enfin, perfide! me voilà sûre de votre inconstance, de mon opprobre, et de votre intrigue.

LORD MURRAI

Oui, madame, vous êtes sûre de tout. (*à part.*) Quel contretemps effroyable! 115

LADY ALTON

Monstre, perfide!

LORD MURRAI

Je peux être un monstre à vos yeux, et je n'en suis pas fâché;[3]

109-111 60x*, MS1: Milord, ce bonhomme avait des questions à lui faire, et il n'a pas voulu que je fusse présente.//
114-115 60x*, MS1: Eh bien, madame, vous êtes sûre de tout.//
117-118 60x*, MS1: à vos yeux, mais pour perfide

[3] Palissot: 'Le lord Murrai se défend comme, en pareil cas, un homme d'honneur doit se défendre envers une ladi Alton. Cette scène suspend l'action sans la rompre; en donnant à Murrai de vives inquiétudes, elle prépare les moyens du dénouement.'

mais pour perfide, je suis très loin de l'être, ce n'est pas mon caractère. Avant d'en aimer une autre, je vous ai déclaré que je ne vous aimais plus. 120

LADY ALTON

Après une promesse de mariage! scélérat, après m'avoir juré tant d'amour!

LORD MURRAI

Quand je vous ai juré de l'amour, j'en avais: quand je vous ai promis de vous épouser, je voulais tenir ma parole.

LADY ALTON

Eh qui t'a empêché de tenir ta parole, parjure? 125

LORD MURRAI

Votre caractère, vos emportements; je me mariais pour être heureux, et j'ai vu que nous ne l'aurions été ni l'un ni l'autre.

LADY ALTON

Tu me quittes pour une vagabonde, pour une aventurière.

LORD MURRAI

Je vous quitte pour la vertu, pour la douceur, et pour les grâces.

LADY ALTON

Traître, tu n'es pas où tu crois en être; je me vengerai plus tôt 130

118-128 60CR*, 60X*, 60AM, MS1: mon caractère. [60X*: de l'être.] Quand je vous ai juré de l'amour [60X*, MS1: dit que je vous aimais] j'étais de bonne foi; j'avais même dessein [60X*: conçu le dessein] de vous épouser, j'en conviens [60X* omits 'j'en conviens']. Mais votre caractère, vos emportements m'ont fait ouvrir les yeux; je voulais me marier pour être heureux, et j'ai vu que nous ne l'aurions jamais été ni l'un ni l'autre. / LADY ALTON / Tu me quittes pour une aventurière?

que tu ne penses.

LORD MURRAI

Je sais que vous êtes vindicative, envieuse plutôt que jalouse, emportée plutôt que tendre; mais vous serez forcée à respecter celle que j'aime.

LADY ALTON

Allez, lâche, je connais l'objet de vos amours mieux que vous; 135
je sais qui elle est, je sais qui est l'étranger arrivé aujourd'hui pour elle; je sais tout; des hommes plus puissants que vous sont instruits de tout; et bientôt on vous enlèvera l'indigne objet pour qui vous m'avez méprisée.

LORD MURRAI

Que veut-elle dire, Polly? elle me fait mourir d'inquiétude. 140

POLLY

Et moi de peur. Nous sommes perdus.

LORD MURRAI

Ah! madame, arrêtez-vous, un mot, expliquez-vous, écoutez...

LADY ALTON

Je n'écoute point, je ne réponds rien, je ne m'explique point. Vous êtes, comme je vous l'ai déjà dit, un inconstant, un volage, un cœur faux, un traître, un perfide, un homme abominable. 145

(*elle sort.*)

139 60x*: méprisée (*elle va pour sortir.*)

SCÈNE V

LORD MURRAI, POLLY

LORD MURRAI

Que prétend cette furie? Que la jalousie est affreuse! O ciel! fais que je sois toujours amoureux, et jamais jaloux. Que veut-elle? elle parle de faire enlever ma chère Lindane, et cet étranger; que veut-elle dire? sait-elle quelque chose?

POLLY

Hélas! il faut vous l'avouer, ma maîtresse est arrêtée par l'ordre du gouvernement; je crois que je le suis aussi; et sans un gros homme, qui est la bonté même, et qui a bien voulu être notre caution, nous serions en prison à l'heure que je vous parle: on m'avait fait jurer de n'en rien dire, mais le moyen de se taire avec vous? 150 155

LORD MURRAI

Qu'ai-je entendu? quelle aventure! et que de revers accumulés en foule! Je vois que le nom de ta maîtresse est toujours suspect. Hélas! ma famille a fait tous les malheurs de la sienne; le ciel, la fortune, mon amour, l'équité, la raison, allaient tout réparer; la vertu m'inspirait; le crime s'oppose à tout ce que je tente, il ne triomphera pas. N'alarme point ta maîtresse; je cours chez le ministre; je vais tout presser, tout faire. Je m'arrache au bonheur de la voir pour celui de la servir. Je cours, et je revole. Dis-lui bien que je m'éloigne parce que je l'adore. 160

(Il sort.)

146-147 60CR*, 60X*, 60AM, MS1: furie? Que veut-elle?
151-152 60CR:AC, 60X*, MS1: sans un homme
163 60X*: pour le plaisir de la
163-164 60X*: revole. Ah! Polly, dis-lui bien que je ne m'éloigne que pour elle, et parce que je l'adore.

POLLY *seule.*

Voilà d'étranges aventures! Je vois que ce monde-ci n'est qu'un 165
combat perpétuel des méchants contre les bons, et qu'on en veut
toujours aux pauvres filles.

SCENE VI

MONROSE, LINDANE, (POLLY *reste un moment, et sort à un signe que lui fait sa maîtresse.*)

MONROSE

Chaque mot que vous m'avez dit me perce l'âme. Vous née dans
le Locaber! et témoin de tant d'horreurs, persécutée, errante, et si
malheureuse avec des sentiments si nobles! 170

LINDANE

Peut-être je dois ces sentiments mêmes à mes malheurs; peut-être si j'avais été élevée dans le luxe et la mollesse, cette âme qui
s'est fortifiée par l'infortune, n'eût été que faible.

MONROSE

O vous! digne du plus beau sort du monde, cœur magnanime,
âme élevée, vous m'avouez que vous êtes d'une de ces familles 175
proscrites, dont le sang a coulé sur les échafauds dans nos guerres
civiles, et vous vous obstinez à me cacher votre nom et votre
naissance!

167b-c 60X*: MONROSE, LINDANE
168 60AM: Tout ce que vous m'avez
169 60CR, 60AM: Locabert
172 60X*, MS1: le luxe et dans la

LINDANE

Ce que je dois à mon père, me force au silence; il est proscrit lui-même; on le cherche; je l'exposerais peut-être si je me nommais; vous m'inspirez du respect et de l'attendrissement; mais je ne vous connais pas; je dois tout craindre. Vous voyez que je suis suspecte moi-même, que je suis arrêtée et prisonnière; un mot peut me perdre. 180

MONROSE

Hélas! un mot ferait peut-être la première consolation de ma vie. Dites-moi du moins quel âge vous aviez quand la destinée cruelle vous sépara de votre père, qui fut depuis si malheureux? 185

LINDANE

Je n'avais que cinq ans.

MONROSE

Grand Dieu! qui avez pitié de moi, toutes ces époques rassemblées, toutes les choses qu'elle m'a dites, sont autant de traits de lumière qui m'éclairent dans les ténèbres où je marche. O Providence! ne t'arrête point dans tes bontés. 190

LINDANE

Quoi! vous versez des larmes! Hélas! tout ce que je vous ai dit m'en fait bien répandre.

MONROSE (*s'essuyant les yeux.*)

Achevez, je vous en conjure. Quand votre père eut quitté sa famille pour ne plus la revoir, combien restâtes-vous auprès de votre mère? 195

186-187 60, 60Y, 60CR, 60AM, MS1: destinée si cruelle

LINDANE

J'avais dix ans quand elle mourut dans mes bras de douleur et de misère, et que mon frère fut tué dans une bataille.

MONROSE

Ah! je succombe! Quel moment, et quel souvenir! Chère et 200 malheureuse épouse!... fils heureux d'être mort, et de n'avoir pas vu tant de désastres! Reconnaîtriez-vous ce portrait? (*il tire un portrait de sa poche.*)

LINDANE

Que vois-je? est-ce un songe? c'est le portrait même de ma mère; mes larmes l'arrosent, et mon cœur qui se fend, s'échappe 205 vers vous.

MONROSE

Oui, c'est là votre mère, et je suis ce père infortuné dont la tête est proscrite, et dont les mains tremblantes vous embrassent.

LINDANE

Je respire à peine! Où suis-je? Je tombe à vos genoux! voici le premier instant heureux de ma vie... O mon père!... hélas! com- 210 ment osez-vous venir dans cette ville? je tremble pour vous au moment que je goûte le bonheur de vous voir.

MONROSE

Ma chère fille, vous connaissez toutes les infortunes de notre maison; vous savez que la maison des Murrai, toujours jalouse de

198 60AM: Je n'avais que dix ans
204-206 60X*, MS1: Que vois-je? c'est le portrait de ma mère.//
205-206 60AM: larmes l'arrosent.//
209-210 60X*: LINDANE / Vous, mon père! (*Elle tombe à ses genoux.*) Voici le premier
MS1: Vous, mon père! Je tombe à vous genoux: voici le premier

la nôtre, nous plongea dans ce précipice: toute ma famille a été 215
condamnée; j'ai tout perdu. Il me restait un ami, qui pouvait par
son crédit me tirer de l'abîme où je suis, qui me l'avait promis;
j'apprends en arrivant que la mort me l'a enlevé, qu'on me cherche
en Ecosse, que ma tête y est à prix; c'est sans doute le fils de mon
ennemi qui me persécute encore; il faut que je meure de sa main, 220
ou que je lui arrache la vie.

LINDANE

Vous venez, dites-vous, pour tuer milord Murrai?

MONROSE

Oui, je vous vengerai, je vengerai ma famille, ou je périrai; je
ne hasarde qu'un reste de jours déjà proscrits.

LINDANE

O fortune! dans quelle nouvelle horreur tu me rejettes! que 225
faire? quel parti prendre? Ah mon père!

MONROSE

Ma fille, je vous plains d'être née d'un père si malheureux.

LINDANE

Je suis plus à plaindre que vous ne pensez... Etes-vous bien
résolu à cette entreprise funeste?

MONROSE

Résolu comme à la mort. 230

LINDANE

Mon père, je vous conjure, par cette vie fatale que vous m'avez
donnée, par vos malheurs, par les miens qui sont peut-être plus
grands que les vôtres, de ne me pas exposer à l'horreur de vous

perdre, lorsque je vous retrouve;... ayez pitié de moi, épargnez votre vie et la mienne. 235

MONROSE

Vous m'attendrissez, votre voix pénètre mon cœur, je crois entendre celle de votre mère. Hélas! que voulez-vous?

LINDANE

Que vous cessiez de vous exposer, que vous quittiez cette ville si dangereuse pour vous... et pour moi... Oui, c'en est fait, mon parti est pris. Mon père, je renoncerai à tout pour vous,... oui, à 240 tout:... je suis prête à vous suivre: je vous accompagnerai, s'il le faut, dans quelque île affreuse des Orcades; je vous y servirai de mes mains; c'est mon devoir, je le remplirai... C'en est fait, partons.

MONROSE

Vous voulez que je renonce à vous venger? 245

LINDANE

Cette vengeance me ferait mourir; partons, vous dis-je.

MONROSE

Eh bien, l'amour paternel l'emporte, puisque vous avez le courage de vous attacher à ma funeste destinée; je vais tout préparer pour que nous quittions Londres avant qu'une heure se passe; soyez prête, et recevez encore mes embrassements et mes larmes. 250

SCÈNE VII

LINDANE, POLLY

LINDANE

C'en est fait, ma chère Polly, je ne reverrai plus milord Murrai, je suis morte pour lui.

POLLY

Vous rêvez, mademoiselle, vous le reverrez dans quelques minutes. Il était ici tout à l'heure.

LINDANE

Il était ici! et il ne m'a point vue! c'est là le comble. O mon malheureux père! que ne suis-je partie plus tôt? 255

POLLY

S'il n'avait pas été interrompu par cette détestable milady Alton…

LINDANE

Quoi! c'est ici même qu'il l'a vue pour me braver, après avoir été trois jours sans me voir, sans m'écrire! Peut-on plus indignement se voir outrager? Va, sois sûre que je m'arracherais la vie dans ce moment, si ma vie n'était pas nécessaire à mon père. 260

POLLY

Mais, mademoiselle, écoutez-moi donc; je vous jure que milord…

LINDANE

Lui perfide! c'est ainsi que sont faits les hommes! Père infortuné, je ne penserai désormais qu'à vous. 265

POLLY

Je vous jure que vous avez tort, que milord n'est point perfide, que c'est le plus aimable homme du monde, qu'il vous aime de tout son cœur, qu'il m'en a donné des marques.

LINDANE

La nature doit l'emporter sur l'amour; je ne sais où je vais; je ne sais ce que je deviendrai; mais sans doute je ne serai jamais si malheureuse que je le suis. 270

POLLY

Vous n'écoutez rien: reprenez vos esprits, ma chère maîtresse: on vous aime.

LINDANE

Ah Polly! es-tu capable de me suivre? 275

POLLY

Je vous suivrai jusqu'au bout du monde; mais on vous aime, vous dis-je.

LINDANE

Laisse-moi: ne me parle point de milord: hélas! quand il m'aimerait, il faudrait partir encore. Ce gentilhomme que tu as vu avec moi… 280

POLLY

Eh bien?

270 60X*, MS1: l'amour; je pars; je ne sais
272 60AM, MS1: je la suis

LINDANE

Viens, tu apprendras tout: les larmes, les soupirs me suffoquent.
Suis-moi, et sois prête à partir.

Fin du quatrième acte.

282 60CR:AC, 60X*, MS1: Tu apprendras
282-283 60CR:AC, 60CR*, 60X*, 60AM, MS1: suffoquent. Allons tout préparer pour notre [60X*: mon] départ.//

ACTE V

SCÈNE PREMIÈRE

LINDANE, FRIPORT, FABRICE

FABRICE

Cela perce le cœur, mademoiselle; Polly fait votre paquet; vous nous quittez.

LINDANE

Mon cher hôte, et vous, monsieur, à qui je dois tant, vous qui avez déployé un caractère si généreux, vous qui ne me laissez que la douleur de ne pouvoir reconnaître vos bienfaits, je ne vous oublierai de ma vie. 5

FRIPORT

Qu'est-ce donc que tout cela? qu'est-ce que c'est que ça? qu'est-ce que ça? Si vous êtes contente de nous, il ne faut point vous en aller; est-ce que vous craignez quelque chose? vous avez tort, une fille n'a rien à craindre. 10

FABRICE

Monsieur Friport, ce vieux gentilhomme qui est de son pays fait aussi son paquet. Mademoiselle pleurait, et ce monsieur pleurait aussi, et ils partent ensemble: je pleure aussi en vous parlant.

4 60CR:AC, 60CR*, 60X*, 60AM, MS1: généreux, car on m'a dit ce que vous avez fait pour moi; vous ne me laissez

5 60CR:AC, 60CR*, 60AM: bienfaits, mais je ne

11 60AM: Mon cher monsieur Friport, ce

FRIPORT

Je n'ai pleuré de ma vie; fi! que cela est sot de pleurer! les yeux n'ont point été donnés à l'homme pour cette besogne. Je suis affligé, je ne le cache pas; et quoiqu'elle soit fière, comme je le lui ai dit, elle est si honnête, qu'on est fâché de la perdre. Je veux que vous m'écriviez, si vous vous en allez, mademoiselle. Je vous ferai toujours du bien... Nous nous retrouverons peut-être un jour, que sait-on? ne manquez pas de m'écrire,... n'y manquez pas. 20

LINDANE

Je vous le jure avec la plus vive reconnaissance; et si jamais la fortune...

FRIPORT

Ah! mon ami Fabrice, cette personne-là est très bien née. Je serais très aise de recevoir de vos lettres. N'allez pas y mettre de l'esprit au moins. 25

FABRICE

Mademoiselle, pardonnez, mais je songe que vous ne pouvez partir, que vous êtes ici sous la caution de monsieur Friport, et qu'il perd cinq cents guinées si vous nous quittez.

LINDANE

O ciel! autre infortune! autre humiliation! quoi! il faudrait que je fusse enchaînée ici, et que milord,... et mon père... 30

FRIPORT (*à Fabrice.*)

Oh qu'à cela ne tienne; quoiqu'elle ait je ne sais quoi qui me

14-16 60X*, 60AM, MS1: pleurer! Je suis affligé
23-25 60, 60CR, 60AM, MS1: très bien née.//
26 60AM: mais songez que
29 60AM: O ciel! quelle nouvelle infortune! Quoi! il faudrait
60CR*, 60X*, MS1: autre infortune! quoi il

touche, qu'elle parte si elle en a envie; il ne faut point gêner les filles; je me soucie de cinq cents guinées comme de rien. (*bas à Fabrice.*) Fourre-lui encore les cinq cents autres guinées dans sa valise. Allez, mademoiselle, partez quand il vous plaira; écrivez-moi; revoyez-moi quand vous reviendrez,... car j'ai conçu pour vous beaucoup d'estime et d'affection. 35

SCÈNE II[1]

LORD MURRAI, ET SES GENS, *dans l'enfoncement.*
LINDANE, ET LES ACTEURS PRÉCÉDENTS, *sur le devant.*

LORD MURRAI (*à ses gens.*)

Restez ici vous: vous, courez à la chancellerie, et rapportez-moi le parchemin qu'on expédie dès qu'il sera scellé. Vous, qu'on aille préparer tout dans la nouvelle maison que je viens de louer. (*il tire* 40

32-33 60AM: envie; je me soucie
60CR:AC, 60CR*, 60X*, MS1: gêner les gens; je me
33 60AM: comme de ça. (*bas*
35-36 60CR, 60AM, MS1: écrivez-moi quand [60CR*: β]
37 60, 60Y, 60CR: beaucoup d'affection. [60CR*: β]
37-44 60CR:AC, 60AM: d'estime et d'affection. / *à part.* / (*Friport s'avance sur le bord du théâtre.*) [60CR, no stage direction] / Voilà encore! ce milord [60AM: il] vient toujours [followed by 44-54 as part of scene 1]
60X*, MS1: d'affection, d'estime, et... Encore ce milord! il vient toujours mal à propos [followed by 44-54 as part of scene 1]
40-55 60X*: que je viens de louer. Enfin donc,

[1] As the variants show, there is no short scene 2 in 60AM, since Murray's entrance ('Restez ici, vous...') is delayed until after Friport's 'Je me sens, vous dis-je, de la bonne volonté pour cette demoiselle'. This is dramatically preferable, since it avoids an awkward silence for Murray immediately on arrival.

un papier de sa poche et le lit.) Quel bonheur d'assurer le bonheur de Lindane!

LINDANE (*à Polly.*)

Hélas! en le voyant je me sens déchirer le cœur.

FRIPORT

Ce milord-là vient toujours mal à propos; il est si beau et si bien mis, qu'il me déplaît souverainement; mais après tout, que cela me fait-il? j'ai quelque affection,... mais je n'aime point, moi. Adieu, mademoiselle. 45

LINDANE

Je ne partirai point sans vous témoigner encore ma reconnaissance et mes regrets.

FRIPORT

Non, non, point de ces cérémonies-là, vous m'attendririez peut-être. Je vous dis que je n'aime point:... je vous verrai pourtant encore une fois: je resterai dans la maison, je veux vous voir partir. Allons, Fabrice, aider ce bon gentilhomme de là-haut. Je me sens, vous dis-je, de la bonne volonté pour cette demoiselle. 50

41-42 60CR:AC, 60CR*, 60AM: d'assurer celui de Lindane
42a-43 60CR:AC, 60CR*, omitted
43-55 60CR*, 60AM: déchirer le cœur. / LORD MURRAI / Enfin donc, je goûte
46 60X*, MS1: me fait-il? je n'aime point
54 60, 60CR: dis-je, quelque affection pour cette fille. [60CR:AC, 60CR*, 60X*: β]
60CR*, 60X*: demoiselle. (*il sort.*)

SCÈNE III

LORD MURRAI, LINDANE, POLLY

LORD MURRAI

Enfin donc, je goûte en liberté le charme de votre vue. Dans quelle maison vous êtes! elle ne vous convient pas; une plus digne de vous vous attend. Quoi! belle Lindane, vous baissez les yeux, et vous pleurez! quel est ce gros homme qui vous parlait? vous aurait-il causé quelque chagrin? il en porterait la peine sur l'heure. 55

LINDANE (*en essuyant ses larmes.*)

Hélas! c'est un bon homme, un homme grossièrement vertueux, qui a eu pitié de moi dans mon cruel malheur, qui ne m'a point abandonnée, qui n'a pas insulté à mes disgrâces, qui n'a point parlé ici longtemps à ma rivale en dédaignant de me voir, qui, s'il m'avait aimée, n'aurait point passé trois jours sans m'écrire. 60

LORD MURRAI

Ah! croyez que j'aimerais mieux mourir que de mériter le moindre de vos reproches. Je n'ai été absent que pour vous, je n'ai songé qu'à vous, je vous ai servie malgré vous. Si en revenant ici j'ai trouvé cette femme vindicative et cruelle qui voulait vous perdre, je ne me suis échappé un moment que pour prévenir ses desseins funestes. Grand Dieu! moi ne vous avoir pas écrit! 65 70

LINDANE

Non.

54a 60CR:AC, 60CR*, 60X*, 60AM, MS1: SCÈNE II / LORD MURRAI ET SES GENS *dans l'enfoncement*, LINDANE, POLLY / [followed by 38-43, 55]
58-59 60X*: pleurez! Cet homme qui vous parlait vous aurait-il
58 60CR:AC, 60CR*, 60AM, MS1: est cet homme
60 60CR:AC, 60X*, 60AM, MS1: homme vertueux

LORD MURRAI

Elle a, je le vois bien, intercepté mes lettres; sa méchanceté augmente encore, s'il se peut, ma tendresse: qu'elle rappelle la vôtre. Ah! cruelle, pourquoi m'avez-vous caché votre nom illustre, et l'état malheureux où vous êtes, si peu fait pour ce grand nom? 75

LINDANE

Qui vous l'a dit?

LORD MURRAI (*montrant Polly.*)

Elle-même, votre confidente.

LINDANE

Quoi! tu m'as trahie?

POLLY

Vous vous trahissiez vous-même; je vous ai servie.

LINDANE

Eh bien, vous me connaissez; vous savez quelle haine a toujours 80 divisé nos deux maisons; votre père a fait condamner le mien à la mort; il m'a réduite à cet état que j'ai voulu vous cacher; et vous son fils! vous! vous osez m'aimer.

LORD MURRAI

Je vous adore, et je le dois; c'est à mon amour à réparer les cruautés de mon père: c'est une justice de la Providence; mon 85 cœur, ma fortune, mon sang est à vous. Confondons ensemble deux noms ennemis. J'apporte à vos pieds le contrat de notre mariage; daignez l'honorer de ce nom qui m'est si cher. Puissent les remords et l'amour du fils réparer les fautes du père!

81 60X*, MS1: nos maisons
84-86 60CR:AC, 60CR*, 60X*, 60AM, MS1: je le dois; mon cœur, ma

LINDANE

Hélas! et il faut que je parte, et que je vous quitte pour jamais. 90

LORD MURRAI

Que vous partiez! que vous me quittiez! vous me verrez plutôt expirer à vos pieds. Hélas! daignez-vous m'aimer?

POLLY

Vous ne partirez point, mademoiselle, j'y mettrai bon ordre; vous prenez toujours des résolutions désespérées. Milord, secondez-moi bien. 95

LORD MURRAI

Eh qui a pu vous inspirer le dessein de me fuir, de rendre tous mes soins inutiles?

LINDANE

Mon père.

LORD MURRAI

Votre père? eh où est-il? que veut-il? que ne me parlez-vous?

LINDANE.

Il est ici; il m'emmène, c'en est fait. 100

LORD MURRAI

Non, je jure par vous, qu'il ne vous enlèvera pas. Il est ici? conduisez-moi à ses pieds.

95 60X*: bien. (*Elle sort.*) / SCÈNE / LORD MURRAI, LINDANE
99 60X*: veut-il? mais que ne
101 60AM: Ah! je jure

LINDANE

Ah! cher amant, gardez qu'il ne vous voie; il n'est venu ici que pour finir ses malheurs en vous arrachant la vie, et je ne fuyais avec lui que pour détourner cette horrible résolution. 105

LORD MURRAI

La vôtre est plus cruelle; croyez que je ne le crains pas, et que je le ferai rentrer en lui-même. (*en se retournant.*) Quoi! on n'est pas encore revenu? Ciel, que le mal se fait rapidement, et le bien avec lenteur!

LINDANE

Le voici qui vient me chercher; si vous m'aimez, ne vous montrez pas à lui, privez-vous de ma vue, épargnez-lui l'horreur de la vôtre, écartez-vous, du moins pour quelque temps. 110

LORD MURRAI

Ah! que c'est avec regret! mais vous m'y forcez; je vais rentrer; je vais prendre des armes qui pourront faire tomber les siennes de ses mains. 115

103 60CR:AC, 60CR*, 60X*, 60AM, MS1: Ah! milord, gardez qu'il
104 60, 60CR: pour finir sa vie en vous arrachant la vôtre, et [60CR:AC, 60CR*, 60X*: β]
106 60X*: est cent fois plus
112 60CR:AC, 60CR*, 60X*, 60AM, MS1: vôtre, éloignez-vous, du moins
113-114 60X*: rentrer et je vais

SCÈNE IV

MONROSE, LINDANE

MONROSE

Allons, ma chère fille, seul soutien, unique consolation de ma déplorable vie! partons.

LINDANE

Malheureux père d'une infortunée! je ne vous abandonnerai jamais. Cependant daignez souffrir que je reste encore.

MONROSE

Quoi! après m'avoir pressé vous-même de partir, après m'avoir offert de me suivre dans les déserts où nous allons cacher nos disgrâces! avez-vous changé de dessein? avez-vous retrouvé et perdu en si peu de temps le sentiment de la nature? 120

LINDANE

Je n'ai point changé, j'en suis incapable;… je vous suivrai;… mais encore une fois, attendez quelque temps; accordez cette grâce à celle qui vous doit des jours si remplis d'orages; ne me refusez pas des instants précieux. 125

MONROSE

Ils sont précieux en effet, et vous les perdez; songez-vous que nous sommes à chaque moment en danger d'être découverts, que vous avez été arrêtée, qu'on me cherche, que vous pouvez voir demain votre père périr par le dernier supplice? 130

LINDANE

Ces mots sont un coup de foudre pour moi; je n'y résiste plus.

119 60AM: encore quelques heures.

L'ÉCOSSAISE

J'ai honte d'avoir tardé:... cependant j'avais quelque espoir;... n'importe, vous êtes mon père, je vous suis. Ah malheureuse!

SCÈNE V

FRIPORT ET FABRICE *paraissent d'un côté, tandis que* MONROSE ET SA FILLE *parlent de l'autre.*

FRIPORT (*à Fabrice.*)

Sa suivante a pourtant remis son paquet dans sa chambre; elles ne partiront point, j'en suis bien aise: je m'accoutumais à elle: je ne l'aime point, mais elle est si bien née, que je la voyais partir avec une espèce d'inquiétude, que je n'ai jamais sentie, une espèce de trouble,... je ne sais quoi de fort extraordinaire.[2] 135

MONROSE (*à Friport.*)

Adieu, monsieur, nous partons le cœur plein de vos bontés; je n'ai jamais connu de ma vie un plus digne homme que vous. Vous me faites pardonner au genre humain. 140

FRIPORT

Vous partez donc avec cette dame: je n'approuve point cela: vous devriez rester: il me vient des idées qui vous conviendront peut-être: demeurez. 145

[2] Palissot: 'Fréeport ne se doute pas lui-même de ce qui se passe au fond de son cœur; sa bonté serait moins respectable s'il n'agissait que par passion; elle existe cependant cette passion, mais comme elle peut exister dans une âme qui se croit supérieure à ces faiblesses, et qui les méconnaît même en les éprouvant. Ces nuances sont très-délicates, et la pièce nous paraît aussi bien conduite qu'elle puisse l'être.'

SCÈNE VI

LES ACTEURS PRÉCÉDENTS, LE LORD MURRAI
dans le fond, recevant un rouleau de parchemin de la main de ses gens.

LORD MURRAI

Ah! je le tiens enfin ce gage de mon bonheur. Soyez béni, ô ciel! qui m'avez secondé.

FRIPORT

Quoi! verrai-je toujours ce maudit milord? que cet homme me choque avec ses grâces!

MONROSE (*à sa fille, tandis milord Murrai parle à son domestique.*)

Quel est cet homme, ma fille? 150

LINDANE

Mon père, c'est... ô ciel! ayez pitié de nous.

FABRICE

Monsieur, c'est milord Murrai, le plus galant homme de la cour, le plus généreux.

MONROSE

Murrai! grand Dieu! mon fatal ennemi, qui vient encore insulter à tant de malheurs! (*il tire son épée.*) Il aura le reste de ma vie, ou 155 moi la sienne.

LINDANE

Que faites-vous, mon père? arrêtez.

145c 60AM: *fond, avec un rouleau de parchemin à la main.*

MONROSE

Cruelle fille, est-ce ainsi que vous me trahissiez?

FABRICE (*se jetant au-devant de Monrose.*)

Monsieur, point de violence dans ma maison, je vous en conjure, vous me perdriez. 160

FRIPORT

Pourquoi empêcher les gens de se battre quand ils en ont envie? les volontés sont libres, laissez-les faire.[3]

LORD MURRAI *toujours au fond du théâtre,*

(*à Monrose.*)

Vous êtes le père de cette respectable personne, n'est-il pas vrai?

LINDANE

Je me meurs!

MONROSE

Oui, puisque tu le sais, je ne le désavoue pas. Viens, fils cruel 165 d'un père cruel, achève de te baigner dans mon sang.

FABRICE

Monsieur, encore une fois...

LORD MURRAI

Ne l'arrêtez pas, j'ai de quoi le désarmer. (*il tire son épée.*)

162a 60AM, MS1, no stage direction
168 60X*: de quoi le satisfaire

[3] Palissot: 'Fréeport est bon, mais il est anglais, et sa bonté conserve un goût de terroir. Cette vérité de mœurs est un mérite de plus'.

LINDANE (*entre les bras de Polly.*)

Cruel!... vous oseriez!...

LORD MURRAI

Oui, j'ose... Père de la vertueuse Lindane, je suis le fils de votre ennemi: (*il jette son épée.*) c'est ainsi que je me bats contre vous. 170

FRIPORT

En voici bien d'une autre!

LORD MURRAI

Percez mon cœur d'une main, mais de l'autre, prenez cet écrit, lisez, et connaissez-moi. (*il lui donne le rouleau.*)

MONROSE

Que vois-je? ma grâce! le rétablissement de ma maison! O ciel! et c'est à vous, c'est à vous, Murrai, que je dois tout? Ah mon bienfaiteur!... (*il veut se jeter à ses pieds.*) vous triomphez de moi plus que si j'étais tombé sous vos coups.[4] 175

169 60AM: (*A lord Murrai.*) Cruel!
174 60AM: (*Après avoir lu il lui donne le rouleau.*)
177 60X*, MS1, no stage direction
177-178 60, 60Y, 60CR: (*il se jette à ses pieds.*) ôtez-moi plutôt cette vie, pour me punir d'avoir attenté à la vôtre. [60CR*, 60X*: β]

[4] Fréron objected to the *dénouement* on the grounds that it is 'trop brusque, trop précipité. Il n'est pas vraisemblable que Monrose, qui, dans tout le cours de la pièce, ne respire que vengeance et veut tuer le fils du destructeur de sa maison, soit tout à coup désarmé, et tombe même à ses genoux, parce qu'il apporte sa grâce' (*Al*, iv.106). After seeing the play performed, however, he admitted that the *dénouement* 'fait tableau' (*Al*, v.283). Palissot stressed its ethical value: 'Voilà de ces dénouemens qui charment toujours, parce qu'ils sont la récompense du malheur et de la vertu'.

LINDANE

Ah que je suis heureuse! mon amant est digne de moi.

LORD MURRAI

Embrassez-moi, mon père. 180

MONROSE

Hélas! et comment reconnaître tant de générosité?

LORD MURRAI (*en montrant Lindane.*)

Voilà ma récompense.

MONROSE

Le père et la fille sont à vos genoux pour jamais.

FRIPORT (*à Fabrice.*)

Mon ami, je me doutais bien que cette demoiselle n'était pas faite pour moi; mais après tout, elle est tombée en bonnes mains, 185 et cela fait plaisir.

Fin du cinquième et dernier acte.

183 60x*: sont à vous pour jamais.
184-185 MS1, 60x*: n'était pas pour moi;

APPENDIX

The 'Avertissement' in the Grasset edition, 1772

The Grasset *Collection complette* (W70L), published in Lausanne from 1770 to 1784, contains a number of short notices supplied by Voltaire, of which this is probably one.

Avertissement de l'éditeur

Cette pièce fut imprimée d'abord en 1759, comme une traduction d'une comédie anglaise, ce qui donna lieu à beaucoup d'assez bonnes plaisanteries. Loin d'être une traduction, elle fut elle-même traduite en anglais quelques années après par monsieur George Colman. On la représenta sur le théâtre de Paris en 1760, 5
et sur celui de Londres en 1766.

Jérôme Carré, sous le nom duquel on avait d'abord donné cet ouvrage, n'est qu'un nom feint. On ne peut en dire autant de celui de Fréron qui ne différait pas beaucoup de celui de Frelon.

On se servit du mot Wasp au lieu de Frelon à la Comédie 
française, parce que Frelon signifie Wasp en anglais.

Anecdotes sur Fréron

édition critique

par

Jean Balcou

INTRODUCTION

1. *Le dossier Thiriot (août 1760)*

Le 31 mai 1760, d'Alembert a claironné la nouvelle: autorisation est donnée de jouer *L'Ecossaise* (D8949). Voltaire est en transes: début juin, il lance *Le Pauvre diable* (D8971); début juillet, la *Requête de Jérôme Carré aux Parisiens* (D9049).[1] Et, pendant ce temps, il corrige *L'Ecossaise*. Tous les amis de Paris veulent participer à l'hallali. Le 25 juillet, ils distribuent la *Requête*; le 26, ils prennent d'assaut la Comédie-Française pour la mise à mort. Un seul objectif, en effet: abattre Fréron, le directeur de l'*Année littéraire*.

Pendant que d'Argental manœuvre au grand jour pour le succès de l'opération, Thiriot se charge de la basse besogne. L'idée lui vient, ou lui est suggérée, d'établir un dossier sur le sieur Fréron. Tout prouve que l'abbé de La Porte a fourni la matière.[2] Il semble aussi que La Harpe ait été dans le coup. Le 20 août, Voltaire a reçu le précieux paquet. Et de s'extasier: 'On peut tirer parti de l'histoire d'Elie Catherine né à Kimper Corentin. Il est bon de faire connaitre les scélérats. La philosophie ne peut que gagner à toutte cette guerre' (D9159). Trois jours auparavant, il avait enfin lu la 'Relation d'une grande bataille' (D9154), ce papier où Fréron, loin de succomber au mauvais coup de *L'Ecossaise*, prenait, en racontant la corrida, une trop belle revanche.[3]

Mais que le journaliste ne redresse pas trop vite le front… 'On m'a envoyé', écrit Voltaire le 29 août à Damilaville, 'des mémoires

[1] D'autres pamphlets, *La Vanité*, *Le Russe à Paris*, *Le Plaidoyer pour Ramponeau*, voient également le jour début juillet.

[2] L'abbé Joseph de La Porte joue, en effet, dans les *Anecdotes sur Fréron* un trop grand et trop beau rôle. Beuchot avait déjà pensé à sa culpabilité (M.xxiv.181-89).

[3] *Al* (27 juillet 1760), v.209-15.

sur sa vie, dont il y a, dit on, plusieurs copies dans Paris. Il paraît par ces mémoires que cet homme appartient plus au Châtelet qu'au Parnasse' (D9173). Pour donner plus de corps à l'apparence, Voltaire envoie le 3 septembre à Cramer le dossier qu'il a arrangé en lui demandant d'en 'tirer au moins deux cent cinquante' exemplaires (D9187). Mais l'imprimeur a préféré remiser le mémoire en question dans ses placards puisque vers la fin de l'année Voltaire revient ainsi à la charge: 'Je prie caro Gabriel de ne plus oublier la vie de s[t] Freron, ouvrage très utile pour former l'esprit et le cœur' (D9467).

2. *Les deux éditions de 1761*

Un nouveau personnage avait surgi à l'horizon: Ponce-Denis Ecouchard Le Brun, secrétaire du prince de Conti, et poète. Comme Fréron avait attiré l'attention du public sur la détresse de la petite-nièce de Corneille et qu'il avait commencé par s'occuper d'elle, Le Brun avait écrit à Voltaire qu'à lui seul revenait cet honneur (*c.* 25 octobre 1760; D9349). Une ode accompagnait son appel. Et voilà comment Voltaire allait devenir le protecteur de Marie Corneille. Fréron est aussi furieux contre Le Brun que contre Voltaire. Le 14 décembre, il maintient que les vers de Le Brun sont un attentat contre la poésie, et le 30, sous le prétexte d'évoquer la biographie de Sadi, que toute la vie de Voltaire est un attentat contre la dignité.[4]

La rage saisit Voltaire. Mais à une nouvelle perfidie, c'est la tempête. Dans son cahier du 14 décembre, en effet, Fréron le félicite d'héberger aussi le sieur L'Ecluse, un ancien acteur. Ainsi, conclut-il, 'il faut avouer qu'en sortant du couvent Mademoiselle Corneille va tomber en de bonnes mains' (viii.164). Ce méchant trait, Voltaire ne peut le pardonner, dont la bonne action se trouve infectée. 'Quoi', s'exclame-t-il, '[Fréron] dira impunément que

[4] *Al* (1760), vi.145-64 et 335-49.

m^lle Corneille est élevée par un danseur de corde dans un bordel!' (D9582). Mais déjà Cramer avait reçu l'ordre d'imprimer enfin, toutes affaires cessantes, le dossier Thiriot. Le 6 février, Le Brun en a reçu 'onze exemplaires'.[5] Telle est la première édition des *Anecdotes sur Fréron* (sigle 61A), et qui contient le 'Supplément' et la première phrase de la note (BV, no.3482).

Mais cela ne suffit pas à Voltaire qui ne décolère plus. Le coquin n'a pas assez payé: 'car ce n'est pas assez de rendre Fréron ridicule', écrit-il le 16 février 1761 à d'Argental, 'l'écraser est le plaisir' (D9630). Bientôt, vers la fin du mois de mars, une seconde édition est prête. Le 3 avril, le philosophe envoie l'ouvrage à d'Argental en s'excusant ainsi (D9719): 'Voicy un mémoire bien bas mais c'est aussi du plus bas des hommes dont il s'agit'. Le 6 il expédie à Damilaville un paquet: s'y trouve la seconde édition des *Anecdotes* destinée à l'inévitable Le Brun (D9726, D9727). Ce dernier regrettera de ne point y lire l'histoire de cette tabatière jadis donnée par Piron à Fréron qui s'était empressé de la revendre.[6] Mais l'histoire de la tabatière ne sera pas enchâssée dans les *Anecdotes*. Cette seconde édition (sigle 61B) reprend le texte de la première.

Mais ces deux éditions de 1761 ont été tirées à un très petit nombre d'exemplaires. Réticences de l'imprimeur, distribution confidentielle, voire quelque ultime inquiétude... Voltaire, en tout cas, s'empresse de dégager sa responsabilité. Il a bientôt trouvé le nom du véritable auteur du libelle contre Fréron. 'Les Anecdotes sur Fréron', écrit-il le 6 mai à Le Brun, 'sont du sieur La Harpe, jadis son associé et friponné par lui. Thiriot m'a envoyé ces anecdotes écrites de la main de La Harpe'. Il envoie, en même temps, à son complice les 'quelques exemplaires' qui lui restent

[5] Le Brun, *Œuvres* (Paris 1811), iv.24. Voir aussi Bengesco, ii.92-96, no.1657.

[6] Le Brun, en revanche, insérera l'histoire de la tabatière dans la *Wasprie*, un lourd pamphlet qu'il lança contre Fréron en 1761 (ii.37). Ce sont ses *Anecdotes* à lui. Le journaliste, muni d'une attestation de Piron lui-même, songea à déférer Le Brun devant les tribunaux. Mais ses amis l'en dissuadèrent. Pour toute cette pauvre histoire, voir Piron, *Œuvres inédites* (Paris 1859), p.197-99.

(D9767). Là-dessus va tomber sur les *Anecdotes* un lourd silence d'une dizaine d'années.

3. *Les Choses utiles et agréables*

L'*Année littéraire* est le cauchemar de Voltaire. Rares sont les œuvres et actions du patriarche qui échappent aux morsures de Fréron. Voltaire a beau jurer, tempêter, multiplier les 'fréronades', il n'arrive pas à jeter, comme il le souhaite, 'le diable dans l'abîme' (D14107). Il a beau invoquer les puissances, user de tous les moyens pour chercher à étouffer l'*Année littéraire*, il perd son temps. Fréron, imperturbable, férocement de sang-froid, continue de dénoncer ses 'plagiats', de dévoiler ses 'turpitudes', d'ironiser sur ses 'prétentions' et son 'incompétence'. Dans sa feuille du 30 août 1769, il a raconté une histoire. 'S Gravesande avait ri au nez de Voltaire qui s'affichait comme un spécialiste de Newton. 'Il a tâché', conclut Fréron, 'de faire oublier l'anecdote par l'assurance avec laquelle il a parlé depuis, mais malheureusement on a de la mémoire' (*Al*, 1769, v.270-71). D'autres articles de la même encre se succèdent,[7] mais nous pensons que c'est l'anecdote de 's Gravesande qui a malheureusement rafraîchi la mémoire de Voltaire.

Le 6 décembre 1769, le patriarche en appelle à Panckoucke: 'Envoyez moi tout ce que vous avez, jusqu'à ce jour, des imbéciles méchancetés de Martin [Fréron], afin que je le fasse pendre avec les cordes qu'il a filées' (D16025). Même recours auprès de Lacombe, l'autre libraire, le 5 janvier 1770 (D16077). Mais comment en finir avec Fréron? Il y a, bien sûr, ce dossier reçu en août

[7] Signalons: le 10 octobre, l'article sur le navire 'le Voltaire' (vi.213-17); le 18 novembre, le commentaire d'une lettre au père Porée (viii.141-53); le 30 novembre, le cinglant compte rendu du *Traité des différentes sortes de preuves qui servent à établir la vérité de l'histoire* du père Griffet (vii.289-329). Voltaire était naturellement au courant de tout ce que Fréron écrivait sur lui.

1760, revu et complété en 1761, et qui lui brûle à nouveau les mains. En réalité, Voltaire ne s'est jamais consolé de n'avoir pu s'en servir comme il l'eût voulu.

Pourtant il n'ose en refaire une édition séparée. Il se décide donc à enfouir ses chères *Anecdotes sur Fréron* dans le tome second des *Choses utiles et agréables* (ii.350-63), en supprimant particulièrement les références à Marin (voir 130*v* et 144*v*). Il ajoute également cette seconde phrase à la note finale:

Si on parle, dans l'histoire naturelle, des aigles et des rossignols, on y parle aussi des crapauds.

Le recueil est sous presse à la fin de janvier (D16115). Il ne paraît sans doute à Paris qu'en mars. Toujours est-il qu'en avril Grimm a lu les *Anecdotes* qu'il signale comme une nouveauté, preuve qu'il ne connaissait pas celles de 1761.[8] Or celles que voilà risquaient à leur tour le même sort. Car, à en croire les *Mémoires secrets* du 27 juillet 1770 elles 'n'avaient encore fait aucun bruit, et n'étaient pas parvenues à la connaissance de ceux qu'elles concernaient' (v.145).

4. *Le mémoire Royou*

Le hasard est quelquefois trop diabolique. Au moment même où le recueil des *Choses utiles et agréables* tombait ainsi à plat, Voltaire reçoit de Londres un document sensationnel. Si tout ce que raconte l'auteur, un certain Royou, avocat, qui se présente comme le propre beau-frère de Fréron, est vrai, le directeur de l'*Année*

[8] CLT, viii.495. Grimm naturellement attribue aussitôt ces *Anecdotes* à Voltaire: 'Il est aisé de reconnaître la main qui a daigné tracer l'histoire des mœurs, faits et gestes de ce folliculaire, qui vient encore d'être emprisonné' (ce qui, du reste, était mensonger: voir J. Balcou, *Fréron contre les philosophes*, Genève 1975, p.300-301). Même appréciation chez Bachaumont: 'on reconnoît parfaitement M. de Voltaire au style & à ce talent particulier qu'il a pour dire des injures' (3 septembre 1770; xix.214).

littéraire est un homme mort. Voici la lettre que, de Londres où il s'était enfui, Royou aurait écrite à Voltaire, un mardi matin, le 6 mars 1770:

Fréron épousa ma sœur il y a trois ans (en Bretagne), mon père donna vingt mille livres de dot. Il les dissipa avec des filles, & donna du mal à ma sœur. Après quoi il la fit partir pour Paris, dans le panier du coche, et la fit coucher en chemin sur la paille. Je courus demander raison à ce malheureux. Il feignit de se repentir. Mais comme il faisait le métier d'espion, & qu'il sut qu'en qualité d'avocat j'avais pris parti dans les troubles de Bretagne, il m'accusa auprès de mr. de.. & obtint une lettre de cachet pour me faire enfermer. Il vint lui même avec des archers dans la rue des Noyers un lundi à dix heures de matin, me fit charger de chaînes, se mit à côté de moi dans un fiacre, & tenait lui même le bout de la chaîne...'

L'original a disparu, mais tel est du moins le texte retenu par Besterman dans sa première édition (Best.15207) et qui fut imprimé dans les *Questions sur l'Encyclopédie* (1770, i.264-65*n*), agrémenté du post-scriptum suivant, avant-dernier paragraphe également du 'Mémoire sur lequel M. Duclos est prié de dire son avis et d'agir selon son cœur et sa prudence', adressé à d'Alembert le 19 mars 1770 (D16241):

Qu'on peut s'informer de toutes les particularités de cette affaire au sieur Royou, père du déposant, lequel demeure à Quimper-Corentin; à M. Dupont, conseiller au parlement de Rennes; à M. Duparc, professeur royal en droit français à Rennes; à M. Chapelier, doyen des avocats à Rennes.[9]

L'embarras est d'autant plus grand que Th. Besterman, dans l'édition définitive, a changé son texte de base (D16202) en préférant la version plus développée telle quelle fut imprimée en 1770 dans l'opuscule *Dieu. Réponse au Système de la nature* et telle qu'elle devait orner les *Anecdotes* elles-mêmes (lignes 223-282).

Il y a en outre deux erreurs dans ce document: le père de Royou

[9] Il y avait alors à Rennes trois conseillers du nom de 'de Pont'; Le Chapelier était le doyen des avocats; Poullain Du Parc est le jurisconsulte bien connu.

habite, non à Quimper, mais à Pont-l'Abbé; aucun avocat ne fut enfermé pour les affaires de Bretagne en 1765. Mais c'est un fait: Royou a bien écrit une lettre de ce genre à Voltaire dût-elle être différente.[10]

Trévédy, un érudit quimpérois du siècle dernier, a identifié l'affreux beau-frère.[11] En même temps, il éclairait cette lamentable histoire. L'aîné des Royou, Guillaume, reçu avocat au parlement de Rennes en 1763, était un fieffé débauché. Il est quasi certain que le père Royou a finalement demandé à Fréron, son gendre, d'intervenir pour obtenir contre Guillaume une lettre de cachet.[12] C'est pour éviter l'arrestation que ce dernier aurait passé la Manche. Plein de rage contre son beau-frère, à qui il attribuait tous ses malheurs, il l'a, comme il l'écrira le 23 septembre 1804 à sa sœur, la veuve de Fréron, dénoncé à Voltaire 'dans un moment d'ivresse et de fureur', sans se douter toutefois que le philosophe allait rendre sa lettre publique. Tous les témoignages, même ceux des amis de Voltaire, concordent: Royou est une crapule, un fou. Guillaume Royou regrettera amèrement d'avoir ainsi cédé à la passion. Sa lettre de 1770 n'était, dira-t-il à sa sœur, 'qu'un libelle affreux et diffamatoire, un tissu énorme de mensonges abominables et de calomnies les plus atroces'.[13]

[10] Signalons que dans le tome 3 du *Corpus des notes marginales*, au no.545, deux fragments manuscrits de la main de Wagnière servent de signets: 1. 'Mémoire sur Fréron'. Au verso de main inconnue: 'Mr. Royou n'a aucun ... / seulement ...'. 2. 'Fréron laisse coucher sur la paille' (p. 689, n.321).

[11] J. Trévédy, *Notes sur Fréron et ses cousins Royou* (Quimper, Rennes 1902), p.95-119. Fréron a épousé en secondes noces, le 4 septembre 1766, Anne-Françoise Royou. Ses quatre beaux-frères: Guillaume, Claude (le futur conventionnel Guermeur), Thomas (l'abbé Royou), Jacques-Corentin. Jusqu'à Trévédy, tout le monde accusait ce dernier d'être l'auteur du mémoire de 1770. Le coupable est, en réalité, Guillaume, l'aîné.

[12] Fréron est, en effet, à Paris, un puissant personnage. Grimm n'hésite pas à parler 'd'une catin, dépositaire des lettres de cachet et sa protectrice' (15 juin 1770; CLT, ix.62).

[13] J. Balcou, *Le Dossier Fréron* (Genève 1975), p.394.

5. *Enquête*

Au reçu de cette accablante dénonciation, Voltaire a dû éprouver l'une des plus sauvages joies de sa vie. Mais il a immédiatement un retour de lucidité. Pris entre la frénésie de la vengeance et la peur d'être dupe, le patriarche en appelle à ses intimes. Le 18 mars, il écrit à d'Argental: 'Je me flatte que vous distribuerez des copies du petit mémoire du beau-frère'. Mais il ajoute aussitôt: 'Tâchez d'approfondir cette affaire' (D16240).

Le 19, il demande à Elie de Beaumont, tout en lui signifiant, que la chose 'touche l'ordre des avocats sensiblement', de faire des copies du mémoire et d'en donner surtout à La Harpe (D16244). Le même jour, il envoie le document à d'Alembert avec de nouvelles précisions dues à son imagination policière.[14] Prudent, malgré tout, il lui demande de confier l'enquête à Duclos, bien au courant des affaires de Bretagne (D16241). Le 21 enfin, il avoue au marquis de Florian (l'oncle du fabuliste) que ce mémoire lui paraît tout de même 'extraordinaire' (D16246).

Les amis de Paris sont bien effrayés. Fréron est fort protégé, et pas seulement, comme Voltaire aimerait trop le croire, de la police. D'Alembert déclare qu'il est toujours le favori de 'la personne de France la plus respectable après le maître', c'est-à-dire Choiseul (26 mars; D16261).

Mais voici que, le 12 avril, est communiqué à Voltaire le résultat de l'enquête menée en Bretagne par Duclos: l'avocat Royou est 'un homme de beaucoup d'esprit mais un très-mauvais sujet'. Suit ce conseil: 'allez *bride en main*' (D16287). Bientôt d'autres renseignements aussi désastreux parviennent à Ferney. Voltaire ne manquera pas d'en aviser Royou lui-même, comme l'avouera ce dernier dans sa lettre de 1804 à sa sœur. Il ne se déclare pas

[14] Ainsi, 'Fréron [...] a accusé [Royou] d'un commerce secret avec M. de La Chalotais [...] par un hasard singulier, le sieur Royou s'est échappé de sa prison [...] Fréron a servi, pendant six mois, d'espion à Rennes; [...] il a, depuis, été espion de la police, et c'est la seule chose qui l'a soutenu' (D16241).

vaincu pour autant, car, comme il l'écrit le 25 avril à d'Argental (D16313): 'quand il s'agit de Fréron, il n'y a rien qu'on ne fasse'.[15] Pourtant le mois de mai, du moins d'après les lettres connues, ne connaît que deux temps forts d'excitation: le 16 à l'adresse de d'Argental et le 23 à celle de La Harpe (D16358). Mais l'idée qu'il ne pourrait pas utiliser la lettre du beau-frère est intolérable à Voltaire. Elle est là, qui lui brûle la bile. Ah! ce sera le couronnement du dossier de 1761, et transition trouvée: 'Il est nécessaire que ces infamies soient constatées par le témoignage de tous ceux qui sont cités dans cet écrit; ils ne doivent pas les refuser à la vengeance publique'. Et quel coup inespéré de brocher les calomnies sur un document authentique! Dès lors tout l'édifice tient debout. Il faut que cela paraisse. Et c'est bien des *Anecdotes*, version définitive, dont parle Marin le 16 juin (D16418). Toujours est-il que le lendemain – c'est assez à sa manière d'annoncer le lendemain ce qui a paru la veille – Voltaire révèle à Thiriot qu'on a fait 'une autre édition particulière des [*Anecdotes*] à laquelle on ajoute la lettre du s^r^ Royou' (D16424), que dans sa revue datée du 15 Grimm lui a consacré une page, et que le 25 cadeau en est fait aux d'Argental. C'est donc dans la seconde quinzaine de juin 1770 que nos *Anecdotes*, telles qu'en elles-mêmes, sont apparues, se sont risquées, dans la capitale.

6. *Réactions*

Rares, semble-t-il, les lecteurs alors. Et l'impression qui domine est de rejet. Seul Marin jubile, heureux surtout que son nom ne figure pas au panégyrique du 'corsaire de Quimpercorentin'

[15] Cette même lettre contenait la réponse de Voltaire à un deuxième envoi de Royou. Il est dommage que le philosophe ait égaré dans son 'tas de paperasses' cette nouvelle lettre de Royou (voir D16346). Il est probable que ce dernier y sollicitait 'les bons offices' de Voltaire 'pour l'aider à rentrer en France' (Cornou, *Elie Fréron*, Paris 1922, p.401).

(D16418). Mais de Dorat, un fréronien plutôt, il est vrai, ce trait, relevé par les *Mémoires secrets* du 27 juillet (v.141), contre le coupable: 'S'il n'avait pas écrit, il eût assassiné'. Grimm, dans sa lettre confidentielle, donne un bref aperçu pour s'en laver en même temps les mains. Mais de reconnaître quand même qu'il y a là 'un tas d'ordures détestables', et qu'en écrivant de telles infamies l'auteur 'a souillé sa plume' (CLT, ix.63). Le Brun lui-même, pourtant ennemi acharné du journaliste et qui soupçonne La Harpe d'en être le responsable, est maintenant scandalisé. Il traite l'ouvrage d''infâme libelle' et de 'libelle si odieux' (D16415). Le Brun, le receleur des *Anecdotes* de 1761, vise, on peut l'espérer, le *Mémoire Royou*.

Quant à Voltaire, sa fureur n'est pas retombée. Il voudrait plus que jamais que la justice se saisît de l'affaire Royou-Fréron, et d'Argental sera obligé de le raisonner, de l'effrayer même (D16487). Sa fureur ne le poussera pourtant pas à avouer son enfant. Après la mort de Fréron, l'opinion accuse encore La Harpe. Comme ce dernier ne cesse de clamer son innocence et de réclamer un démenti, Voltaire le fait volontiers tout en répétant que c'est Thiriot qui lui avait autrefois envoyé ladite brochure (25 février 1777; voir ci-dessous, p.521-22). Le 8 avril 1777, le patriarche blanchit définitivement La Harpe en ces termes: 'Soiez persuadé qu'il n'y a personne dans la Littérature d'assez vil et d'assez insensé pour vous attribuer jamais ces anecdotes sur feu Zoïle Fréron. Il n'y a qu'un colporteur qui puisse les avoir écrites' (D20627). Le même jour, il disait à d'Alembert: 'Les anecdotes [...] sont quelque chose de si bas, de si misérable, de si crasseux; c'est un ramas si dégoûtant d'avantures des halles et de sacristies qu'il n'y a qu'un porte-Dieu, ou un crocheteur qui ait pu écrire une pareille histoire' (D20626). Dont acte.

Une évidence: seul le groupe philosophique a réagi. Mais Elie Fréron, comment a-t-il reçu le coup?

7. *La conspiration du silence*

Malgré la page de Grimm, et Dorat et Marin, tout porte à croire que les 'frères', ont, en réalité, fait l'impossible pour étouffer le mémoire Royou. Ce mot de d'Argental résumerait assez bien la situation (D16487): 'c'est risquer de sa faire gratuitement un grand nombre d'ennemis'. Voltaire, qui est si loin, peut tout se permettre, encore sans rien signer. 'Ce n'est pas à Paris', regrette l'audacieux Marin (D16418), 'qu'on peut imprimer ces anecdotes'. Et même, ne lui en déplaise, les colporter! Notons aussi qu'au 27 juillet les *Mémoires secrets* parlent de la diatribe voltairienne comme s'il s'agissait uniquement de celle qui avait déjà paru dans le recueil des *Choses utiles et agréables*. Seuls, en réalité, quelques initiés ont vu l'édition séparée des *Anecdotes sur Fréron*, et ils ont eu peur. Et cela – l'auteur puni par où il a péché! – à cause du mémoire Royou lui-même dont on voit bien qu'il mettait en jeu trop de politique. C'est pourquoi Voltaire récidive en les intégrant à son pamphlet *Dieu. Réponse au Système de la nature* qui paraît vers le 10 août (D16572): ce qui est assez curieux. Il ira encore jusqu'à glisser, nous le savons, un condensé de la lettre de Royou dans ses *Questions sur l'Encyclopédie*. Un dernier témoignage enfin: c'est seulement le 19 mai 1772 que Fréron demandera à Capperonnier de lui envoyer 'la petite brochure infâme intitulée les *Anecdotes sur Fréron*'.[16]

Trévédy et Cornou[17] se sont interrogés sur l'inexplicable silence du journaliste. Pour eux, si Fréron avait parlé, il souillait à jamais le nom de Royou, le nom de sa femme. Voltaire avait forcé Fréron à se taire. Ou bien encore ce dernier se faisait-il à son tour piéger par le fameux mémoire? Tous les autres critiques qui se sont intéressés au directeur de l'*Année littéraire* ont naturellement déduit

[16] *Le Dossier Fréron*, p.357.

[17] Cornou, p.397-410; Trévédy, *Notes sur Fréron*; *Le Dossier Fréron*, p.107-109.

de son silence sa culpabilité.[18] D'autant plus que le silence comme forme de mépris n'est guère dans sa nature! Pour notre part, nous nous demandons, dût cela paraître un peu énorme, si Fréron n'a pas parlé parce que tout simplement il a alors ignoré l'attaque, qu'on a réussi à la lui cacher.

Mais dès qu'il l'a sue, le ton de l'*Année littéraire* devient d'une violence inhabituelle. Voltaire ne sera plus pour Fréron que le diable de Ferney, un 'scélérat'.[19]

8. *Fabulation*

Les *Anecdotes sur Fréron* se prétendaient 'écrites par un homme à un magistrat qui voulait être instruit des mœurs de cet homme'. Quand il aura lu le dossier, le magistrat en question sera édifié. Car le mot qui revient comme un leitmotiv est le mot 'friponnerie'. Tous les témoins sont à charge: l'abbé de La Porte, un rival de Fréron; Royou, un fou; l'auteur lui-même, juge et partie, qui prend d'ailleurs soin d'user parfois de formules du genre 'je me souviens avoir entendu dire'. Et quand la précision fait défaut, quelques vagues allusions suffisent. Mais l'ensemble, écrit d'un style alerte et piquant, sème l'inquiétude, emporte la conviction. La condamnation sera sans appel.

L'impayable est que rien n'y est vraiment vrai et que tout y paraît vraisemblable. Thiriot, qui connaissait Fréron depuis longtemps et qui était au courant de tout, n'a pas, pour son dossier, recueilli que des ragots. L'abbé de La Porte, qui, nous en sommes convaincu, est le principal pourvoyeur des premières *Anecdotes*, fut, de 1752 à 1758, le bras droit de Fréron; Royou, le

[18] C'est le cas de Nisard (*Les Ennemis de Voltaire*, 1853, p.276), Soury ('Un critique au XVIIIe siècle', *Rdm*, 3e pér., 1877, xx.80-112), ou même Monselet (*Fréron ou l'illustre critique*, 1864).

[19] C'est le mot qu'il lance à Voltaire dans l'un des tout derniers papiers qu'il lui consacre (*Al*, 6 novembre 1775, vi.64).

beau-frère, n'est pas un personnage en l'air. Voltaire a donc puisé à bonne source, même si elle est trouble. Sa calomnieuse imagination ne brode qu'à partir d'éléments du réel. Pour y voir, dans la mesure du possible, plus clair, il faudra donc multiplier, détailler les annotations. Car s'assurer d'abord du fait, c'est le seul moyen de mesurer la part de la fabulation polémique. C'est aussi une question d'honneur.[20]

9. *Appendices*

Nous avons cru bon de compléter les *Anecdotes sur Fréron* par deux textes particulièrement éclairants. Le premier est un *Avis à l'éditeur* conservé à la Bibliothèque municipale de Grenoble (N 1481) et qui est de la main même de Voltaire (voir figure 8). Son intérêt est d'autant plus grand qu'il s'agit, en outre, d'un inédit. Il était fait pour 'lancer' les *Anecdotes*. Le prouvent le ton de la lettre, les allusions aux attaques anti-philosophiques du printemps 1760; et le 'trio' ici visé de Fréron, Palissot et Pompignan renvoie si bien à cet endroit de la lettre du 20 août 1760: 'Le public voit d'un côté Palissot, Freron et Pompignan à la tête de la relligion, et de l'autre les hommes les plus éclairez qui respectent cette relligion encor plus que les Frerons ne la deshonnorent' (D9159). Nous voilà vraiment à l'origine des *Anecdotes*: Voltaire a reçu le paquet de Thiriot, s'est rapidement informé, et tout aussi rapidement réécrit le tout, mais à ras de texte.

Par contraste, la lettre de Voltaire du 25 février 1777 déjà évoquée plus haut (p.482) est une des dernières allusions aux *Anecdotes*. Dans une lettre qui ne nous est pas parvenue d'Alembert

[20] Il est évident que rien n'est plus absurde et plus injuste que de juger Fréron d'après ces *Anecdotes*. Ne s'y trouvent, en effet, accumulés que les éléments susceptibles de donner prise à la calomnie. Il est facile d'imaginer des *Anecdotes sur Fréron* écrites par un ami qui ne tiendrait compte que de ce qu'il y eut de bien dans sa vie, un abbé Prévost, un Rameau ou un Baculard d'Arnaud par exemple.

memoire sur freron

avis de lediteur

les anecdotes suivantes metant parvenues
jay pris des informations exactes; et je
les ay trouvées conformes en tout a la
verité.
peutetre le moment présent et l'indignation
publique que le nommé freron a excitée
qui sans feront lire ces anecdotes,
qui sans ces raisons nattireraient la curio
sité de personne
il est bon quelles fassent connaitre un homme
qui savisait de juger les autres. quelques provinciaux
lisaient ses feuilles et simaginaient avoir par
elles des nouvelles sures des belles lettres
de paris. la premiere qualité dun orateur
dit ciceron, est detre honnete homme.
on peut ajouter que cest la premiere
qualité dun critique. quelle confiance peut

8. *Anecdotes sur Fréron*: la première page du manuscrit holographe de l'"Avis de l'éditeur' (Bibliothèque municipale, Grenoble).

revenait sur la suspicion qui n'avait jamais cessé de peser sur La Harpe d'en être l'auteur. Le lendemain 26 la lettre que nous publions sera envoyée à d'Alembert comme une 'lettre ostensible écrite à qui vous voudrez' (D20578). Elle a été publiée dans la correspondance (D.app.482), mais par sa place et sa destination, ce document méritait de conclure notre édition.

10. *Le texte*

La première édition des *Anecdotes* est sortie des presses de Cramer en 1761 (61A) et la 'seconde édition' (61B) date vraisemblablement de la même année. En 1770 Voltaire a collaboré à une dernière édition séparée (70) et à deux impressions dans des recueils: *Les Choses utiles et agréables* (CU70) et *Dieu. Réponse au Système de la nature* (DR70, notre texte de base). En 1778 ce dernier a été incorporé dans le tome huit de *L'Evangile du jour* (EJ78). Les *Anecdotes* figurent pour la première fois dans les œuvres complètes de Voltaire en 1830, dans l'édition Beuchot (Paris 1829-1840). Le seul manuscrit connu aurait été copié à l'intention de Beuchot sur une des éditions séparées.

MS

Anecdotes / Sur Freron. / Ecrites par un homme de lettres a un / Magistrat qui voulait être instruit / des mœurs de cet homme. /

Copie; 3 feuilles pliées et insérées les unes dans les autres pour en former un cahier de 12 pages, paginées 1 à 12; 136 x 213 mm.

Après le texte figure la note 'copié sur l'imprimé de 15 pages in 12'. On ne connaît pas d'édition in-douze, mais il est peut-être plutôt question d'un petit in-octavo. Quoi qu'il en soit, cette copie renferme quelques variantes, et figure donc dans notre apparat critique.

Bn: N14292, f.19-24 (papiers Beuchot).

61A

[*titre de départ*] (I) / [*filet gras-maigre*] / ANECDOTES / SUR FRÉRON, / *Ecrites par un homme de Lettres à un / Magiſtrat qui voulait être inſtruit des / mœurs de cet homme.* / Elie Catherin Fréron eſt né à Quim- / [...]

8°. sig. *[8]; pag. XV

C'est la première édition de 1761, probablement sortie des presses des Cramer.

Leningrad: BV, no.3482 (Pot-pourri 63, 11-178).

61B

[*titre de départ*] (I) / [*filet gras-maigre, 61 mm*] / ANECDOTES / SUR FRÉRON, / *Ecrites par un homme de Lettres à un / Magiſtrat qui voulait être inſtruit des / mœurs de cet homme.* / Seconde Edition. / Elie Catherin Fréron eſt né à Quim- / [...]

8°. sig. *[8]; pag. XV

Une édition copiée sur 61A, dont elle reproduit le texte et trois des coquilles. On trouve de légères différences textuelles aux lignes 38-39 et 45.

Bn: Ln[27] 8012A.

CU70

LES / CHOSES / UTILES / ET AGRÉABLES. / *TOME SECOND.* /

8°. sig. A-Z[8] Aa[2]; pag. 371; $4 signé, chiffres arabes (– A1-2, L1, O3, P4, Aa2); tomaison '*Tom. II.*'; réclames aux cahiers et aux rubriques.

[1] titre; [2] bl.; [3]-349 autres textes; 350-362 Anecdotes sur Fréron écrites par un homme de lettres à un magistrat qui voulait être instruit des mœurs de cet homme; 363-368 Lettre à messieurs les auteurs des Etrennes de la Saint-Jean; 369-371 Table des pièces contenues dans ce volume.

Le mémoire Royou ne figure pas dans cette édition, dont le texte occupe une position intermédiaire entre les éditions de 61 et notre texte de base, DR70.

Bn: Z 20862.

70

[*titre de départ*] ∗ (I) ∗ / [*filet gras-maigre, 78 mm*] / ANECDOTES / SUR FRERON / *Ecrites par un homme de lettres à un Ma- / giſtrat qui voulait être inſtruit des mœurs / de cet homme.* / ELIE Catherin Fréron eſt né à Quimper-Co- / [...]

8°. sig. A^8; pag. 15; $4 signé, chiffres arabes.

Cette édition est très proche de la suivante (DR70), mais la note à la ligne 48 manque.

L'exemplaire 11-182 de la bibliothèque de Voltaire porte deux annotations autographes: en bas de la p.1 'Pankouke qui est venu chez moy dit que touttes ces anecdotes sont vraies. Tiriot les eut il y a sept ou huit ans de la main de l'autheur. Ne pourait-on pas défaire le public de ce monstre nommé Freron?'; et en note au nom de Laugeon, p.3 (ligne 44 de notre édition) 'il faudrait parler à ce procureur et consulter l'abbé de la porte'; voir figure 9.

Leningrad: BV, no.3484 (trois exemplaires, 9-56, 11-135, 11-182); Bn: Ln^{27} 8012; Taylor: V6 A6 B (3,7).

DR70

[*titre de départ*] DIEU. / *RÉPONSE* / AU / SYSTÊME DE LA NATURE. / [*filet, 77 mm*] / SECTION II. / *Article tiré d'un livre intitulé* Queſtions / ſur l'Encyclopédie, *en quelques volu- / mes in-8°, qui n'a pas encore paru.* / SI après avoir reconnu un DIEU ſuprême, il eſt / [...]

8°. sig. A-B^8 C-D^6; pag. 56; $5 signé, chiffres arabes (– D5); réclames aux cahiers.

[1]-44 autres textes; [45]-56 Anecdotes sur Fréron écrites par un homme de lettres à un magistrat qui voulait être instruit des mœurs de cet homme.

Cette édition (hollandaise) serait la dernière à subir l'influence de l'auteur et pour cette raison nous l'avons choisie comme texte de base. Il y a deux nouvelles notes (p.47 et 51, aux lignes 48 et 170 de notre édition) où sont corrigées des erreurs de l'édition précédente. On trouve parfois des exemplaires de DR70 annexés au tome 8 de l'*Evangile du jour* (1770).

Bn: 8° Z 4252; Rés. Z Beuchot 290 (7-8); Rés. Z Bengesco 278 (les p.45-56 seulement).

(1)

ANECDOTES SUR FRERON

Ecrites par un homme de lettres à un Magistrat qui voulait être instruit des mœurs de cet homme.

ELie Catherin Fréron est né à Quimper-Corentin, son père était orfèvre. Voici un fait qu'on m'a assuré, mais dont je n'ai pas la certitude: on prétend que le père de Fréron a été obligé plusieurs années avant sa mort, de quitter sa profession, pour avoir mis de l'alliage plus que de raison, dans l'or & l'argent.

Fréron commença ses études à Quimper, & fit sa Rhétorique à Paris sous le père Porée. Un oncle qu'il avait aux environs de la ruë St. Jacques, lui donna un azile dans sa maison, & s'en défit en faveur des Jésuites, qui le mirent dans leur noviciat, ruë Pot-de-fer. Ils le nommèrent ensuite régent en sixième au collège de Louis le Grand. Il y resta deux ans & demi, & sa conduite ayant trop éclaté ils l'envoyèrent à Alençon, d'où il quitta tout à fait la société.

Je me souviens d'avoir entendu dire à Fréron

A

Pankouke qui est venu chez moy dit que toutes ces anecdotes sont vraies Tirées les [illegible] il y a sept ou huit ans de la main de l'autheur. ne pourait on pas défaire le public de ce monstre nommé freron!

9. *Anecdotes sur Fréron*: la première page de l'édition de 1770 (sigle 70), avec une note holographe de Voltaire (Bibliothèque d'Etat Saltykov-Schédrine, Leningrad).

EJ78

L'EVANGILE / DU JOUR / CONTENANT / RÉFLEXIONS PHILOSOPHIQUES ſur la Mar- / che de nos Idées / LETTRE d'un AVOCAT à Mr. d'Alembert. / Le SYMBOLE d'un LAÏQUE, ou la profeſſion / de foi d'un homme déſintereſſé. / Diverſes EPITRES écrites de la Campagne. / Les ADORATEURS ou les Louanges de Dieu. / REQUÊTE à tous les Magiſtrats du Royaume. / DÉFENSE de Louïs XIV. / PENSÉES détachées de Mr. l'Abbé de St. Pierre. / DIEU. Réponſe au Syſtême de la Nature. / ART de jetter en Fonte des figures conſidéra- / bles d'Or ou de Bronze. / REQUÊTE au Roi contre les moines de St. Claude. / ANECDOTES ſur Fréron. / [*filet triple, 78 mm*] / *A LONDRES* / M D CC LXXVIII. /

[*faux-titre*] L'EVANGILE / DU / JOUR. / [*filet, 81 mm*] / *TOME HUITIEME.* / [*filet, 70 mm*] /

8°. sig. π^2 *A*^{8} *B-H*^{6} I-N^6 *O*^{6} *P*^{2}; pag. [*4*] 176; $4 signé, chiffres arabes (–*A*1, *D*4, *E*4, I4; + *A*5, I6; I6 signé 'I4', M2 '*M2*', M3 '*B3*', M4 '*M4*'); réclames par cahier.

[*1*] faux-titre; [*2*] bl.; [3] titre; [*4*] bl.; [1]-164 autres textes; [165]-176 Anecdotes sur Fréron écrites par un homme de lettres à un magistrat qui voulait être instruit des mœurs de cet homme.

Une réimpression de l'*Evangile* de 1770, avec une pagination suivie.

ImV: BA 1769/1 (8).

11. *Principes de cette édition*

L'édition retenue comme texte de base est DR70 parce qu'il s'agit de la dernière revue par Voltaire. Elle reprend l'édition séparée de 1770, avec 4 coquilles en moins et une meilleure ponctuation. En outre, l'auteur en a profité pour corriger deux erreurs, l'une sur la date des *Lettres sur quelques écrits de ce temps*, l'autre sur l'identité du nommé Coste (lignes 48 et 170).

Les variantes figurant dans l'apparat critique proviennent du manuscrit (MS) et des éditions 61A, 61B (qui ne diffère de 61A qu'aux lignes c, 38-39 et 45), CU70, 70 et EJ78. Ces variantes ne portent pas sur les différences de ponctuation, sauf quand elles entraînent des modifications de sens.

Traitement du texte

On a conservé l'orthographe des noms propres, ainsi que les italiques du texte de base.

On met la majuscule initiale aux titres d'ouvrages.

On a respecté la ponctuation à une exception près: le point qui suit les chiffres romains et arabes a été supprimé.

Par ailleurs, le texte de DR70 a fait l'objet d'une modernisation portant sur la graphie, l'accentuation et la grammaire. Les particularités du texte de base étaient les suivantes:

1. Graphie
   – absence de *p*: tems
   – absence de *t*: enfans (et: enfants)
   – redoublement de consonnes: appellât, caffé, déshonnorés
   – orthographe étymologique: sçais, sçut, nuds, isles
   – orthographe particulière: azile, cayer, crapeaux, exaler, lézé, satyre, sont citez
   – mots attachés ou séparés: dequoi, quoi qu'il
   – abréviations: Mr., Mrs., Sr., St. deviennent M., MM., sieur, St
   – trait d'union dans: très-bien, très-considérable, très-curieux, très-soigneusement
   – utilisation systématique de la perluette
   – majuscule dans: Abbé, Académicien (-mique), Analyse, Architecte, Audience, Avocat, Censeur, Chevalier, Comédie, Commissaire, Espagnole, Français, Italien (adj.), Jésuite, Journal, Latin (adj.), Lettre, Libraire, Littérateur, Littérature, Livre, Lundi, Madame, Magistrats, Mardi, Mars, Milord, Monsieur, Parlement, Procureur, Rhétorique, Roi, Secrétaire, Sénéchal, Subdélégué

2. Accentuation
   – accent aigu absent dans: societé
   – accent aigu présent dans: Bréton, fripiére, niéce, réflexions
   – accent grave absent dans: déja
   – accent circonflexe absent dans: diner, grace, infame, paraitrai

- accent circonflexe présent dans: bâteleuses, bû, eû, eût (passé simple), mêtier
- tréma présent dans: poëte, poësie; bouë, connuë, continuë, interrompuës, lieuës, suspenduës, vuë
- élision: entr'autres

3. Grammaire
   - 'cent' demeure invariable
   - emploi de *t* au participe passé: il n'a sçut

ANECDOTES SUR FRÉRON

Ecrites par un homme de lettres à un magistrat qui voulait être instruit des mœurs de cet homme

Elie Catherin[1] Fréron est né à Quimper-Corentin,[2] son père était orfèvre. Voici un fait qu'on m'a assuré, mais dont je n'ai pas la certitude: on prétend que le père de Fréron a été obligé plusieurs années avant sa mort, de quitter sa profession, pour avoir mis de l'alliage plus que de raison, dans l'or et l'argent.[3] 5

Fréron commença ses études à Quimper, et fit sa rhétorique à Paris sous le père Porée.[4] Un oncle qu'il avait aux environs de la rue St Jacques, lui donna un asile dans sa maison, et s'en défit en faveur des jésuites, qui le mirent dans leur noviciat, rue Pot-de-fer. Ils le nommèrent ensuite régent en sixième au collège de 10

c-1 61B: *homme.* / SECONDE EDITION. / Elie

[1] En réalité, Elie Catherine. Le parrain de Fréron était Elie Marias, sa marraine Catherine Le Roy.

[2] Fréron est né à Quimper le 20 janvier 1718 (extrait du registre de la paroisse de Saint-Ronan).

[3] Daniel Fréron (1673-1756) exerçait, en effet, la profession d'orfèvre. Deux témoignages des registres de la paroisse de Quimper réfutent la calomnie de Voltaire: en 1750, le père de Fréron figure comme orfèvre au rôle de la capitation roturière (il y est imposé d'une livre); en 1753, il est mentionné, sur un acte de baptême de l'église de Saint-Ronan, comme 'marchand-orfèvre' habitant la rue Obscure (aujourd'hui rue Elie Fréron). Ainsi trois ans avant sa mort, alors qu'il est âgé de 81 ans, Daniel Fréron exerçait toujours sa profession. En 1753, il était 'maître-orfèvre' depuis 57 ans.

[4] C'est sans doute le père Bougeant, un Quimpérois de quelque renom, qui attira à Paris son jeune compatriote. Fréron a quitté sa ville natale à la fin de 1734. Le 24 décembre, en effet, il est inscrit dans la classe du père Porée (*Catalogus triennalis*, S. J. 1737). 'J'ai le même avantage que M. de Voltaire', écrira un jour Fréron, 'celui d'avoir étudié sous ce professeur habile et vertueux' (*Al*, 1768, ii.66).

Louis le Grand.[5] Il y resta deux ans et demi, et sa conduite ayant trop éclaté ils l'envoyèrent à Alençon, d'où il quitta tout à fait la société.[6]

Je me souviens d'avoir entendu dire à Fréron au café de Viseux, rue Mazarine, en présence de quatre ou cinq personnes, après un dîner où il avait beaucoup bu, qu'étant jésuite, il avait été l'*agent* et le *patient*.[7] Comme je ne veux dire que ce que je sais bien certainement, je ne rapporterai pas tout ce qu'on m'a raconté de ses friponneries, vols et sacrilèges, lorsqu'il portait l'habit de jésuite.

Chassé de la société, Fréron se lia avec l'abbé Des Fontaines,[8]

21 MS, 61A: Sorti de la société
21-22 MS, 61A: Desfontaines, sorti des

[5] A la fin de 1735 Fréron entre au noviciat de la rue Pot-de-fer et on lui permet de suivre à Louis-le-Grand les cours de philosophie et de physique. De 1736 à 1737, il est professeur de cinquième à Caen (Cornou, p.18). C'est là qu'il fit paraître sa première œuvre: Elia Frerone, *Ad bellonam, ode* (Caen 1737), in-4°. De la fin de 1737 au début de 1739, il revient à Louis-le-Grand comme régent de cinquième puis de quatrième (et non de sixième). Avec l'épisode de Caen, dont Voltaire ne parle pas, cela fait en gros deux ans et demi (voir Feller, *Dictionnaire historique*, Augsbourg 1781-1783). Fréron gardera le titre d'abbé jusqu'en 1744.

[6] Il dut quitter de lui-même la Société. Toute sa vie, en tout cas, il resta profondément attaché à cette 'patrie' qu'il a, dira-t-il, 'abandonnée' (*Lettres sur quelques écrits*, 21 juin 1753, xi.347). Mais pour Voltaire, il en fut naturellement 'chassé' comme il l'écrit un peu plus loin. On connaît aussi le vers du *Pauvre diable*: 'De Loyola chassé pour ses fredaines' (M.x.97). Quel crime avait-il donc commis? D'après Feller, il donnait 'quelques sujets de mécontentement à ses supérieurs'. Soury (*Rdm*, 1887, ii.82) et Cornou (p.19) précisent qu'il avait été surpris en habit laïque au théâtre. Fréron fut, en conséquence, envoyé au début de l'année 1739 à Alençon: il n'y demeura que jusqu'au 10 avril.

[7] Fréron, ce pédéraste? Est-ce le souvenir de Desfontaines qui aurait ainsi brouillé l'imagination de Voltaire?

[8] Au retour d'Alençon, l'abbé de Boismorand présenta Elie Fréron à Desfontaines, ce grand maître du journalisme. Il se forma à son école et ne l'oubliera jamais. Citons encore le *Pauvre diable* où Voltaire appelle Fréron 'Vermisseau né du cul de Desfontaines'. Fréron collabora aux journaux de Desfontaines (*Observations sur les écrits modernes*, *Jugements sur quelques ouvrages nouveaux*) de

chassé des jésuites comme lui, qui l'employa à son journal moyennant 24 livres la feuille d'impression: c'était toute sa ressource pour vivre. Il portait alors le petit collet; et un jour qu'il était au parterre de la Comédie Française, il se prit de paroles avec un avocat; au sortir du parterre, on en vint aux coups; et les deux champions se vautrèrent dans la boue en présence de six cents personnes.[9] 25

M. Destouteville retira Fréron chez lui, pour l'aider à traduire le chant des *Plaisirs* du chevalier Marin. Ils le traduisirent ensemble, et après la mort de M. Destouteville, Fréron s'attribua l'ouvrage à lui seul. Notez que Fréron ne sait pas l'italien.[11] 30

28-29 MS, 61A: personnes. ¶On ignore assez communément que F..... [MS: Fréron] fut quinze jours lieutenant d'infanterie; le fait est pourtant certain;[10] mais je ne sais s'il est vrai, comme on me l'a assuré, qu'il avait été obligé de quitter le corps pour lâcheté et friponnerie. ¶M. Destouteville

30 MS, 61A: des *vrais Plaisirs*
MS, 61A, CU70: du cavalier Marin

1739 à 1745. C'est seulement à partir de 1743 qu'il signa ses articles du nom de 'l'abbé Fréron'.

[9] Il s'agit probablement de l'histoire du 5 novembre 1749 que Voltaire transpose et déforme ici. Furieux des plaisanteries du journaliste sur son compte (*Lettres sur quelques écrits de ce temps*, 8 avril 1749, i.30-58 et 10 juillet 1749, i.109-26), Marmontel s'est précipité sur Fréron pour l'insulter au foyer de la Comédie-Française. Tous deux finirent par sortir et tirèrent l'épée. Heureusement pour Marmontel, la police vint les séparer (voir Delort, *Histoire de la détention des philosophes et des gens de lettres à la Bastille et à Vincennes*, Paris 1829, ii.169-70). L'événement, on s'en doute, fit beaucoup de bruit.

[10] Vers 1743-1744 Fréron aurait-il songé à une carrière dans l'armée? C'est Palissot qui dans la note 7 du chant IX de *La Dunciade* (mais la première version en 3 chants est de 1764 et la dernière en 10 de 1770) rapporte le fait: Fréron aurait alors acheté un grade de lieutenant et se serait appelé quelque temps le chevalier Fréron.

[11] C'est en 1748 que Fréron, qui connaît fort bien l'italien, a aidé le duc Colbert d'Estouteville à traduire *L'Adone* du chevalier Marino: *Les Vrais plaisirs, ou les amours de Vénus et d'Adonis*. Travail qui rapporta, aux dires de Fréron lui-même, une assez jolie somme (*Opuscules*, 1753, ii.397-99). L'ouvrage fut réédité en 1775 sous le titre *Adonis*, chez Musier fils à Londres et à Paris, 54 p. in-8°. L'épisode se situant en 1748, on voit que Voltaire ne suit pas la chronologie.

A peine l'abbé Des Fontaines tomba malade de la maladie dont il est mort, que Fréron le quitta pour faire des feuilles en son nom. Il les intitula *Lettres d'une comtesse.*[12] 35

Dès le troisième ou quatrième cahier de ce nouveau journal, Fréron eut l'impudence d'attaquer M. l'abbé de Bernis, sur une pension de mille écus, que lui faisait avoir madame de Pompadour.[13] Le fruit de cette insolente plaisanterie, fut le séjour de quelques mois à Vincennes, d'autres disent à Bicêtre; et un exil 40 de huit mois à Bar-sur-Seine.[14]

Il revint à Paris, et je sais que pour vivre, il s'était associé avec des fripons au jeu; qu'ils avaient des dés pipés; et qu'une nuit ils gagnèrent 40 louis au procureur Laugeon, dans la rue des Cordeliers. Ce fait, ainsi qu'un autre de cette nature, est rapporté 45

34 MS, 61A, CU70: Fréron lui donna le chagrin de le quitter, pour
38-39 MS, 61B: avoir Mad^{e} de P......
61A: M. de P......
39 MS, 61A, CU70: cette mauvaise plaisanterie
45 MS, 61A: Cordeliers. Ce Laugeon est le père de celui qui est chez M. le comte de Clermont prince, et qui a fait l'acte [61B: le joli acte] d'Eglé. Ce
MS: de même nature

[12] Desfontaines meurt en décembre 1745. Dès le premier septembre, Fréron a lancé ses premières feuilles, les *Lettres de madame la comtesse de ... sur quelques écrits modernes*. Il y aura, jusqu'au 12 janvier 1746, 19 lettres en tout. Elles sont à lire non dans la réédition falsifiée des *Opuscules* de 1753 mais dans l'édition originale, Genève, les frères Philibert, 240 p. in-12°.

[13] Dans sa dix-neuvième feuille du 12 janvier 1746, Fréron célébrait sous le titre *Pension donnée* la manière dont l'abbé de Bernis, le protégé de Mme de Pompadour, avait forcé les portes de l'Académie française. 'Saisissons l'exemple, concluait la comtesse, faisons nos preuves, s'il le faut cabalons, cabalons'. Cette 'pension donnée' n'avait rien à voir avec une pension ordinaire, fût-elle de 1000 écus.

[14] Son audace valut à Fréron d'être emprisonné à Vincennes du 17 janvier au 12 mars 1746 (ce qui fait quelques 50 jours et non 'quelques mois') et d'être exilé à Bar-sur-Seine du 12 mars au 26 juin (ce qui fait un peu plus de trois mois et non 'huit'). Voir *Le Dossier Fréron*, p.16-23. Quand, en 1750, Voltaire apprendra que Frédéric de Prusse veut faire de Fréron son correspondant à Paris, il lui écrit aussitôt que cet homme est 'dans un décri et dans un mépris général, tout sortant de la prison [il y a 4 ans!] où il a été mis pour des choses assez vilaines' (D4128).

en termes couverts dans l'Observateur littéraire de l'abbé Laporte année 1758. Tome II, page 319.[15]

En 1719,[a] Fréron entreprit un nouveau journal satirique sous le titre de *Lettres sur quelques écrits de ce temps.*[16] Il s'associa, pour cet ouvrage, un nommé Dutertre, auteur de *l'Histoire des Conjurations*, d'un *Abrégé de l'histoire d'Angleterre* etc. Ce Dutertre est mort. Il eut part avec Fréron aux dix premiers volumes des Lettres sur quelques écrits de ce temps.[17] 50

[a] *Il y a erreur dans la date.*

46 MS, 61A: l'abbé de Laporte [partout]
48 MS: En 1739, Fréron
MS, 61A, CU70, 70, note *a* absente
MS, 61A, CU70: journal sous

[15] L'aventure a lieu, non au retour de Bar-sur-Seine mais au retour d'Alençon en 1739. Elle est racontée par Fréron lui-même. Il s'était réfugié chez l'abbé de Boismorand, un parent et un compatriote. Un soir, à l'hôtel de Gèvres, le jeune homme a joué aux dés et gagné 76 louis (mais sans tricher!). Evoquant en 1773 ce souvenir, Fréron croira entendre le vieillard lui enjoindre d'une voix terrible de ne plus se livrer à de tels plaisirs (*Al*, 1773, VIII.119). En 1758, l'abbé de La Porte, que le nom de Fréron rendait fou, relatait en même temps que l'histoire d'un procureur dépouillé par une bande de joueurs, celle d''un homme de lettres' qui, aux dés, s'était comporté comme 'un Grec'. Il s'agit sans doute de Fréron puisque c'est à ce témoignage que renvoie Voltaire (qui combine les deux histoires en une seule!), même si de La Porte n'a désigné ni le coupable ni la victime. L'*Observateur littéraire* de 1758 et l'*Année littéraire* de 1773 rapportaient probablement le même fait. Chose curieuse: le procureur Laugeon, si c'est vraiment lui qui fut ainsi grugé, restera toujours lié avec Fréron.

[16] Les *Lettres sur quelques écrits*, qui devaient paraître tous les dix jours sous la forme d'un cahier de 72 pages, sont le premier grand périodique de Fréron. Elles forment, du 8 avril 1749 au 26 janvier 1754, une collection de 62 cahiers reliés en douze volumes de cinq cahiers chacun, le treizième volume comprenant les deux derniers cahiers.

[17] D'après le témoignage de l'inspecteur Joseph d'Hémery, c'est seulement en octobre 1752 que Du Tertre s'associe avec Fréron. Il est vrai que 27 cahiers seulement ont déjà paru. Du Tertre travaillera donc aux 35 qui restent, c'est-à-dire aux sept derniers volumes des *Lettres sur quelques écrits*. Il mourut en 1759.

Ces Lettres ont été interrompues et reprises plusieurs fois.[18] La première cause qui les fit interdire, est un article concernant la vie de Ninon Lenclos, et cet article de Ninon Lenclos, fait le commencement du tome VI *des Lettres sur quelques écrits de ce temps*.[19] Je ne parle point ici des querelles de Fréron et de son lâche procédé avec M. Marmontel. Cette histoire est trop connue et se trouve imprimée dans la *Bigarrure* en Hollande.[20]

Six mois se passèrent sans que Fréron pût obtenir la permission de reprendre ses feuilles. Mais ayant fait beaucoup de bassesses auprès de Solignac, secrétaire du roi de Pologne et ex-jésuite comme lui, ce Solignac persuada à Sa Majesté, que Fréron était persécuté; qu'il mourait de faim; qu'il avait une femme et des enfants; et qu'enfin Sa Majesté *bienfaisante* ne pouvait pas mieux user de ses bontés, qu'envers Fréron. Il l'engagea à se montrer son protecteur, et Fréron eut le droit de recommencer ses satires.[21]

63-64 MS, 61A, CU70: Pologne, ce Solignac
68-69 MS, 61A, CU70, pas d'alinéa

[18] Il y eut, en tout, six suspensions: 1) du 8 avril au 10 juillet 1749; 2) du 22 février au 9 novembre 1750; 3) du 29 décembre 1750 au 4 juin 1751; 4) du 4 juin au 2 septembre 1751; 5) du 2 septembre au 27 décembre 1751; 6) du 15 avril au 25 octobre 1752 (*Fréron contre les philosophes*, p.39-46).

[19] Voltaire omet de signaler que c'est lui-même qui obtint alors la suspension des *Lettres sur quelques écrits*. Car il n'a pu supporter que le journaliste commençât le compte rendu des *Mémoires sur la vie de Mlle de Lenclos* de Bret en brossant son portrait: Fréron avait malignement rapproché la célèbre courtisane de Voltaire! (*Lettres sur quelques écrits*, 15 avril 1752, vi.3-4). Il s'agit de la sixième suspension du périodique de Fréron, non de la première qui fut obtenue dès le 8 avril 1749 par Marmontel à la suite de l'article sur sa tragédie *Denys le tyran* (*Lettres sur quelques écrits*, 1749, i.30-58).

[20] Pour cette histoire, voir *Fréron contre les philosophes*, p.47-53 et ci-dessus, n.9. Elle défraya la chronique, comme en témoigne *La Bigarrure*, journal qui s'imprimait en Hollande (i.147-51).

[21] La suspension dura, en effet, 6 mois. Ce sont le comte de Tressan et Mme de Graffigny qui intervinrent les premiers en faveur de Fréron (*Le Dossier Fréron*, p.40-41, 43) et qui le firent agréer par Stanislas de Pologne (il sera en 1754 le parrain de Stanislas Fréron). Voltaire ne parle ni de Tressan ni de Mme de Graffigny. Aucun document ne mentionne à ce moment Solignac. Mais il est sans doute intervenu lui aussi. Dès 1752, en tout cas, le roi de Pologne et la

Dans ce temps-là l'abbé Laporte avait quitté ses feuilles, parce que ce métier lui paraissait infâme et indigne d'un littérateur.[22] Fréron vint le trouver; lui proposa de s'associer avec lui; l'abbé Laporte y consentit à la fin, à condition qu'il ne mettrait point son nom, et qu'il ne paraîtrait pas y avoir part. Je veux bien, dit Fréron, me charger de tout l'odieux de la besogne, mais je veux que ce sacrifice de mon honneur me tienne lieu de travail; ainsi en faisant le quart de la feuille, je veux qu'elle me soit payée comme si j'en avais fait la moitié! L'abbé Laporte accepta la proposition, et les voilà associés. Il était dit dans leur traité, que le libraire payerait à l'abbé Laporte le quart du prix de la feuille, lorsqu'il en aurait fait la moitié; et qu'il payerait la moitié du prix, toute la feuille faite. Comme c'était le libraire qui payait, l'abbé Laporte n'a point eu à se plaindre du payement.

Ils travaillèrent ainsi pendant quelques mois.[23] Laporte fit l'extrait des Lettres sur l'histoire par milord Bolinbrocke; Fréron ajouta à cet extrait des personnalités offensantes contre ce milord. Ceux qui s'intéressent encore à sa mémoire, se plaignirent, voilà encore les feuilles de Fréron suspendues.[24]

70 MS, 61A, CU70: paraissait désagréable et indigne d'un vrai littérateur
73 MS, 61A: nom dans l'ouvrage, et
85-86 MS: ce lord. Ceux

reine de France accordent à Fréron une protection qui ne se démentira jamais. Le 22 septembre, le journaliste est présenté à Stanislas le Bienfaisant. Dans cette affaire Voltaire en personne a intercédé pour sa victime (13 juin; D4911). Il préfère taire, dans les *Anecdotes*, sa bonne action.

[22] Les *Observations sur la littérature moderne* de l'abbé de La Porte furent supprimées le 17 août 1752 pour un article sur La Condamine. L'abbé de La Porte s'est consacré au journalisme toute sa vie, métier qui ne devait pas lui paraître si indigne. Le rôle qu'il joue ici montre bien que c'est lui qui a fourni le 'scénario' des premières *Anecdotes*. A Voltaire d'en être le 'metteur en scène'.

[23] Quelques mois? Leur collaboration dura d'octobre 1752 (témoignage de l'inspecteur d'Hémery) à juin 1758 (date de la rupture avec Fréron).

[24] Le compte rendu des *Lettres sur l'histoire* de Bolingbroke paraît dans les *Lettres sur quelques écrits* du 21 novembre 1752 (vi.327). Si le coupable est de La Porte, le responsable en est Fréron. L'article se terminait par cette attaque insupportable pour un grand: 'On peut être né avec un génie supérieur, on peut

Fréron va crier famine chez le magistrat de la Librairie; représente ses enfants et sa femme nus et mourant de faim, il écrit à son protecteur Solignac, et on lui rend ses feuilles.[25] Il les continue jusqu'en 1754 sous le titre de *Lettres sur quelques écrits de ce temps*. Il avait fait un traité avec le libraire Duchesne. Il traita sous main avec le libraire Lambert; et sans se mettre en peine de son marché avec Duchesne, il ôta ces feuilles à ce dernier. Il y a un mémoire imprimé, où Duchesne se plaint de cette friponnerie de Fréron.[26]

Laporte qui n'avait fait aucun traité avec Duchesne,[b] n'en fit aucun avec Lambert, et n'était pour rien dans tout le tripotage; il ne connaissait pas même Lambert, lorsque Fréron fit son traité avec ce libraire. Mais comme l'abbé Laporte devait avoir le quart

[b] On peut interroger l'abbé Laporte, et Duchesne.

96 MS, 61A: L'abbé de Laporte
97 MS: tout ce tripotage

acquérir une infinité de connaissances et conserver en même temps un cœur ulcéré par la disgrâce, un esprit dur, un caractère inflexible: enfin être médiocre'. Sur la pression des amis de Bolingbroke, aucun cahier ne paraît en décembre. Le bruit court même que le journaliste est à la Bastille: 'Ces coquins d'Anglais qui ont été se plaindre de lui l'auraient sans doute bien voulu' (d'Hémery, Bn N22156, f.189-91). Mais tout s'arrange et Fréron réussit à cacher cette interruption en antidatant ses numéros (*Fréron contre les philosophes*, p.42).

[25] Comme il n'y a vraiment pas eu, contrairement à ce qu'avance Voltaire, de suspension lors de cette affaire, il n'y a pas eu non plus sollicitation. Mais il est exact que les lettres envoyées par Fréron à Malesherbes, le directeur de la Librairie, prennent souvent un tour assez pathétique (voir *Le Dossier Fréron*, p.142-301).

[26] Le 26 janvier 1754, Fréron décide de quitter Duchesne, alors que deux cahiers des *Lettres sur quelques écrits* ont déjà paru. Fréron ira fonder chez Lambert (l'éditeur de Voltaire!) l'*Année littéraire* (184 volumes de 360 p. in-12° chacun, de 1754 au 10 mars 1776, date de sa mort). Déception de Duchesne. D'où un 'Avis' de 8 pages qui paraît à la fin du treizième tome des *Lettres sur quelques écrits*. Le fait est que 'Fréron s'est laissé séduire à l'appât des conditions plus avantageuses que celles que lui faisait Duchesne'. Mais le 'mémoire' de Duchesne se terminait sur des protestations d'amitié et l'espérance de voir Fréron revenir bientôt dans la maison qui l'avait lancé. 'Friponnerie'?

du produit des feuilles, il était en droit de demander à voir le nouveau traité, afin d'exiger ce quart du produit. Fréron qui voulait le friponner, fit deux traités avec son nouveau libraire; l'un secret, et l'autre ostensible. Le premier portait qu'il recevrait 500 livres par cahier, l'autre ne portait que 400 livres. On montra ce dernier traité à l'abbé Laporte, et par là on ne lui donnait que cent francs, tandis que réellement Fréron mettait dans sa poche 25 livres qui étaient destinées à son associé. Il y a eu 40 cahiers par an; c'est donc de 100 pistoles dont Laporte était lésé. Il n'a su cela qu'à la fin de l'année; et ce fut la femme du libraire, qui, quelque temps avant que de mourir, lui révéla cette friponnerie, pressée par un remords de conscience, disait-elle, qui l'empêchait de mourir tranquillement.[27]

100 EJ78: du profit des
108 MS, 61A: dont l'abbé de Laporte
110 MS: avant de mourir

[27] La correspondance entre Fréron, Lambert et Malesherbes (*Le Dossier Fréron*, p.208-28) permet de voir un peu clair dans cet imbroglio. En réalité, il y eut, en 1754, deux traités entre Fréron et Lambert: l'un, officiel, donnait au journaliste 400 livres sur lesquelles de La Porte prélevait le quart; l'autre, en sous-main (donc à l'insu de l'abbé de La Porte) lui donnait 100 livres en plus. Là-dessus l'associé ne touchait rien: il aurait dû recevoir ses 25 livres par cahier (c'est-à-dire ses 100 pistoles par an), comme dit Voltaire. Mais les lettres de Fréron à Malesherbes des 12, 13, 17 novembre 1757 peuvent faire croire que ces 100 livres ont été données à Fréron parce que ce dernier a réussi à procurer à Lambert l'impression du *Journal des savants*. Ce dessous de table serait donc pour service personnel rendu. Quant à l'affirmation que de La Porte 'n'a su cela qu'à la fin de l'année [1760] et que ce fut la femme du libraire qui, quelque temps avant de mourir [elle était morte au début de 1757!] lui révéla cette friponnerie, pressée par un remords de conscience, disait-elle, qui l'empêchait de mourir tranquillement', elle est tout à fait inexacte. Le témoignage de Lambert du 17 novembre 1757 est, en effet, formel: 'le peu de discrétion de Fréron trahit bientôt son secret et M. l'abbé a eu la délicatesse de ne m'en jamais parler'. Ainsi de La Porte était dès le début au courant et il semble avoir trouvé cela normal. Ce qui ne l'empêche pas d'avoir le sentiment d'être roulé. En outre, le renom de Fréron, sa fortune, son train de vie, l'impression de n'être pas rémunéré à sa mesure, les reproches que lui adressait le directeur de l'*Année littéraire* sur sa lourdeur et son manque de goût (voir *Le Dossier Fréron*, p.241 et *Al*, 1777, v.283),

Dans les temps des brouilleries de Lambert avec Fréron, Lambert qui avait intérêt de faire connaître les friponneries de Fréron, fit un mémoire présenté à M. de Malesherbe, dans lequel ce trait était rapporté tout au long.[28] 115

Les feuilles de Fréron, en passant de la boutique de Duchesne dans celle de Lambert, prirent le titre d'*Année littéraire*; et comme le nombre des cahiers avait augmenté, Fréron s'associa d'autres gens de lettres pour travailler avec lui, parce qu'il n'était pas en état de faire la moitié de l'ouvrage qui lui était réservé, car Laporte avait déclaré qu'il s'en tiendrait à la moitié de la besogne. Ce fut alors que le nombre des croupiers de Fréron devint très considérable.[29] 120

112-113 MS, 61A, pas d'alinéa
113 MS, 61A: Dans le temps
117 61A: boutique à Duchesne
121 MS, 61A: car l'abbé de Laporte

ont fini par exaspérer de La Porte. Fréron, de son côté, toujours pressé par des besoins d'argent, voudrait revenir au contrat de 1754 que Lambert, parce que l'*Année littéraire*, disait-il, ne rapportait pas autant qu'il en escomptait, ne respectait plus. C'est alors qu'il projette avec de La Porte de s'arranger sur le dos de Fréron. Mais la combinaison échoue: Fugère, le directeur du *Journal des savants*, s'est entremis; Fréron et Lambert signent, le 8 juin 1758, un compromis. L'abbé de La Porte lance aussitôt son *Observateur littéraire* (de juin 1758 à la fin 1761, 17 vols in-12°) pour faire pièce à l'*Année littéraire* (*Le Dossier Fréron*, p.239-44). Aucun doute n'est plus possible: c'est bien l'abbé de La Porte, ce rival aigri, le seul à connaître si bien les dessous du jeu, (qu'il se soit acoquiné avec La Harpe, pourquoi pas?) qui est à l'origine des *Anecdotes sur Fréron*. Cet épisode permet, en outre, de saisir sur le vif le travail de Voltaire: il a terminé le paragraphe par une bêtise sur la femme du libraire, bêtise relevée par la soudaine allégresse de la plume.

[28] Voir le 'Mémoire de Lambert à Malesherbes', *Le Dossier Fréron*, p.210-12.

[29] L'*Année littéraire* connut, en effet, à travers tout le siècle, un succès extraordinaire. Aux heures de gloire, Fréron gagnait 20 000 livres par an et Lambert le double. En 1770, le patriarche de Ferney en grince encore de dépit rageur: 'Il est vrai que les feuilles de maître Aliboron eurent d'abord un cours prodigieux' (D16316). C'est l'unique raison pour laquelle 'le nombre des croupiers de Fréron devint très considérable'. Notons enfin que d'août 1755 à septembre 1756 le chef de l'*Année littéraire* dirigeait en même temps le *Journal étranger*.

A l'exception de quelques injures grossières dont Fréron lardait les extraits qu'on lui apportait, tout était de main étrangère;[30] et voici les noms de ces nouveaux croupiers, avec les extraits qu'ils fournissaient au journaliste en chef. Je ne parlerai pas des extraits de l'abbé Laporte; il suffit de dire qu'il a fait exactement pendant sept ans la moitié de l'ouvrage. Quant à l'autre moitié, outre M. Dutertre dont j'ai déjà parlé, MM. de Caux, de Resseguier, Palissot, Bret, Berlan, de Bruix, Dorat, Louis, Bergier, d'Arnaud, Coste, Blondel, Patte, Poinsinet, Vandermonde, de Rivery, Leroi, Sedaine, Castillon, Colardot, Déon de Beaumont, Gossard, etc. sont ceux qui y ont le plus contribué.[31]

125 130 135

124-125 61A, pas d'alinéa
126-127 MS: étrangère; voici
131-132 MS, 61A: Resseguier, Marin, Palissot
132 61A, CU70: Borat

[30] Autant dire que Diderot n'a rien à voir avec l'*Encyclopédie*!

[31] Il est évident que l'*Année littéraire* est, à l'image de l'*Encyclopédie*, une œuvre collective. Mais sous la variété des articles il y a une remarquable unité de ton et la présence du chef se discerne partout. Bien que les textes ne soient presque jamais signés, il n'est pas trop difficile de reconnaître la touche du maître. Signalons, à ce propos, l'indispensable index de l'*Année littéraire* publié par Dante Lénardon chez Slatkine, Genève, en 1979. La liste donnée ici par Voltaire est certainement faite des principaux croupiers de Fréron de 1754 à 1760, quoique l'auteur de la *France littéraire*, qui n'est autre que l'inévitable de La Porte, ne cite ni Bret, ni Bruix, ni Sedaine. Ce dernier avait été fort apprécié pour *Blaise le savetier* (*Al*, 16 mai 1759, iii.138-44), mais au soir de *L'Ecossaise* il sera parmi les manifestants anti-fréronistes. Aussi Grimm, dans sa feuille du 15 juin, est-il fort surpris de le retrouver dans la compagnie. La plupart des auteurs cités par Voltaire verront aux pages suivantes leurs attributions précisées. Mais tous les autres ont également joué leur rôle, tels Boullenger de Rivery (*Al*, 1754, iv.46-49) et Charles-Augustin Vandermonde (*Al*,1755, vi.122-30; vii.284-86) pour la médecine, le chevalier d'Eon de Beaumont pour les finances (*Al*, 1758, vi.217-34; 1759, vi.56-68), Julien David Leroy pour l'architecture (*Al*, 1756, ii.22-31; 1758, vii.100-24). Quant à Jean-B. Gossart, de l'Académie d'Amiens (ne pas confondre avec l'abbé Gossard de Nyon), c'est un ami de longue date (voir *Le Dossier Fréron*, p.368). C'est surtout après 1760 que Claude-Joseph Dorat deviendra un familier de l'*Année littéraire*, car il était alors bien jeune. Sa première contribution sera de 1763 (*Al*, viii.85-99). Pour Castillon, s'agit-il de l'abbé professeur à Utrecht? Il n'est cité qu'une fois dans l'*Année littéraire*, pour sa

C'est M. de Caux qui a fait les extraits[32] de toutes les tragédies[c] dont l'Année littéraire a fait mention, jusqu'à Iphigénie en Tauride exclusivement, temps auquel il s'est brouillé avec Fréron, parce que Fréron ne le payait pas.[33] Il a fait aussi l'extrait des œuvres de M. de la Mothe,[34] et de tous les poètes latins et français dont il est parlé dans le même ouvrage, jusqu'au temps que je viens de dire. Le chevalier de Resseguier a pris sa place pour les poètes français. Il a fait entre autres extraits, celui des poésies de l'abbé de l'Attaignant, en forme de lettre attribuée à un Breton.[35] J'ignore 140

[c] Il faut interroger M. de Caux et autres.

135-136 MS, 61A, CU70, pas d'alinéa

critique du *Discours sur l'origine de l'inégalité* (1759, vii.43-52). Le plus piquant est de voir certains travailler à la fois à l'*Année littéraire* et à l'*Encyclopédie*, tels Antoine Louis, le chirurgien, ou Pierre Patte et Jacques Blondel, les architectes, qui tous ont, pour leur part, beaucoup collaboré avec Fréron; mais l'ambition de celui-ci était aussi de concurrencer l'*Encyclopédie*.

[32] Voltaire a bien raison de parler d'"extraits'. Car le rôle des 'nègres' est de ne faire que cela. Au rédacteur en chef de les encadrer, de les corriger, de les présenter à point ou, comme il le dira lui-même, de les 'lessiver' (*Le Dossier Fréron*, p.341). Après tout Voltaire reconnaît que Fréron a bien agi ainsi pour les *Lettres sur l'histoire* de Bolingbroke ou pour le livre d'Helvétius.

[33] L'extrait d'*Iphigénie en Tauride* de Guymond de La Touche paraît dans l'*Année littéraire* le 24 août 1758 (v.73-108). Impossible de préciser cette collaboration de Caux de Cappeval.

[34] Extraits publiés dans l'*Année littéraire*, 25 octobre 1754 (vi.123-42) et 9 décembre 1754 (vii.145-64).

[35] Il est exact que le chevalier Clément J. Ignace de Rességuier a écrit de Vannes une lettre où il critiquait l'article trop élogieux, à son avis, consacré par le directeur de l'*Année littéraire* à Lattaignant (30 mai 1758, iii.280-88). Fréron publie la protestation de son pseudo-compatriote (le chevalier est de Toulouse) et se justifie (26 octobre 1759, vi.289-312).

si le chevalier de Resseguier reçoit de l'argent. MM. Blondel et Patte faisaient les extraits des ouvrages d'architecture. Blondel a dirigé l'appartement de Fréron qui lui doit encore et ses extraits et son travail comme architecte. Patte se contentait de quelques louanges fades pour tout payement.[36] On peut voir dans les feuilles de cette année, comment Patte et Fréron se sont déshonorés mutuellement au sujet des planches de l'Encyclopédie.[37] Louis a

145 MS, 61A: l'argent. Marin est celui qui succèda à l'abbé de Laporte. Ce dernier trompé et friponné comme on vient de voir, par Fréron, travaillait avec Laporte [MS omet: travaillait avec Laporte], sans vouloir avoir aucun autre commerce particulier avec son associé. Ils étaient quelquefois six mois sans se [MS: le] voir; mais enfin l'abbé de Laporte ayant refusé d'être la caution de Fréron auprès de son tapissier, ils se brouillèrent tout à fait et Fréron prit Marin d'avec lequel il vient de se séparer, parce qu'il le friponnait comme il avait fait tous les autres. MM. Blondel

[36] Blondel restera toute sa vie un grand ami de Fréron. D'innombrables articles lui sont consacrés dans l'*Année littéraire* depuis 1754 (v.399) jusqu'en 1774 (v.187-98), et surtout Fréron en transcrit les cours. Aurait-il continué si longtemps sa collaboration (on retrouve jusqu'en 1777 la présentation d'un cours commun de Patte et Blondel; *Al*, i.186) si Fréron n'était que cet ingrat décrit ici? Il est vrai que la réputation de Fréron dépensier et mauvais payeur n'était plus à faire (voir 'Le Dossier Fréron: suite', *Rhl* 78, 1978, p.260). Dès 1754 également, Fréron connaissait très bien Patte (*Al*, 1754, vi.59), qui allait bientôt s'illustrer avec lui dans la bataille contre l'*Encyclopédie*.

[37] Le 8 septembre 1759, un privilège pour un *Recueil de planches sur les sciences, les arts libéraux avec leur explication* a été accordé à Le Breton pour compenser la suppression de l'*Encyclopédie*. Or les encyclopédistes comptaient utiliser les dessins faits par l'Académie des sciences pour l'*Histoire* de Réaumur. C'est alors que Fréron déclenche avec Patte, un ancien encyclopédiste, l'affaire des planches: il ne s'agissait ni plus ni moins que de ruiner dans l'œuf l'entreprise de Diderot (*Al*, 1759, vii.344). L'accusation est si bien conduite qu'elle oblige les académiciens à envoyer coup sur coup trois commissions d'enquête chez les libraires: le 14 décembre 1759, le 16 janvier et le 23 février 1760. Pendant que l'*Année littéraire* précisait à nouveau ses attaques (29 janvier 1760, i.246-57), l'abbé de La Porte, de son côté, défendait les encyclopédistes. Même si Fréron et Patte ne réussissent pas leur coup, ils ont mis l'opinion de leur bord. A preuve cet aveu désabusé de Grimm: 'Tout le public a crié contre M. Diderot dès que l'accusation a paru, et lors d'une réponse juridique et formelle, personne n'a dit que Fréron était un menteur et son M. Patte un fripon. Telle est la justice de ce monde' (CLT, iv.224). L'Académie des sciences qui a recruté Patte publiera

donné quelques extraits de livres de chirurgie, non à cause de Fréron qui lui a volé un couteau, mais pour faire plaisir à l'abbé Laporte son ami lorsqu'il travaillait avec Fréron.[38] D'Arnaud a rendu compte du discours sur le maréchal de Saxe[39] qui a remporté le prix à l'Académie française en 1759, il a aussi fait quelques extraits de nos poètes, Palissot a loué l'Anacréon de son beau-frère Poinsinet, et critiqué le Jaloux, comédie du sieur Bret;[40] et celui-ci faisait de son côté l'éloge des Tuteurs, comédie de Palissot.[41] 155 160

C'est ainsi que Fréron, qui mettait son nom à tous les extraits, faisait travailler ses croupiers les uns sur les autres. Il a un peu

158 MS, 61A: comédie de M. Bret

160-161 61A, pas d'alinéa

162-164 MS, 61A, CU70: autres. L'abbé Arnaud a fait la critique du livre de l'Esprit. Bergier, l'extrait de l'Ami

à son tour sa *Description des arts*. Fréron ne cessera de l'utiliser contre le recueil des planches de l'*Encyclopédie*. Pour toute cette affaire, voir *Fréron contre les philosophes*, p.181-85 et 244-45.

[38] Pourtant l'extrait du mémoire de Louis accréditant le suicide du fils Calas paraîtra dans l'*Année littéraire* (24 novembre 1763, vii.268-81), et on retrouve encore sa collaboration en 1760 (iii.115-17), 1766 (iv.60-71) et 1767 (viii.38-50).

[39] L'article qui vise l'*Eloge du maréchal de Saxe*, un des premiers exploits académiques d'Ambroise Léonard Thomas, alors professeur au collège de Beauvais, porte, à notre avis, la marque de Fréron (*Al*, v.242-48). Baculard d'Arnaud n'est, en revanche, que l'auteur d'un autre *Eloge du maréchal de Saxe*, objet d'un compte rendu dans les pages qui suivent (v.252-60). Fréron sera un enthousiaste commentateur de la série des *Epreuves du sentiment*.

[40] Charles Palissot de Montenoy, compagnon d'armes et ami de Fréron jusqu'à 1762 est, en effet, le beau-frère de Louis Poinsinet de Sivry, valet de chambre du duc d'Orléans. L'édition établie par ce dernier des œuvres d'Anacréon est célébrée dans l'*Année littéraire* (1755, v.345-49). Le 14 juin, le journal critique *Le Jaloux*, une comédie d'Antoine Bret (iii.342-54).

[41] Aucun doute: l'article sur *Les Tuteurs*, où il y a quelques critiques, est bien de Fréron (*Al*, 18 décembre 1754, vii.266-88). Voltaire veut opposer la bonne volonté de Bret à la malignité de Palissot. Légère concession au parti philosophique, car, au fond, il ne peut trop en vouloir à Palissot, son adorateur.

travaillé à la critique odieuse du livre de l'Esprit d'Helvetius.[42] Bergier, a fait celle de l'Ami des hommes, et des Annales de l'abbé de St Pierre.[43] Poinsinet a loué sa *Briséis*.[44] Colardot a déchiré Marmontel, et toujours sous le nom de Fréron.[45] Berlan a fait l'analyse de sa traduction du *Praedium rusticum* du P. Vannière.[46] Bruix, celle de ses pensées et réflexions.[47] Coste a parlé lui-même de son *voyage d'Espagne*, et cet extrait a fait mettre Fréron à la 165

168 MS: La Coste [partout]

[42] La critique du célèbre ouvrage d'Helvétius est de l'abbé François Arnaud. Les philosophes le savent très bien. Garat dans ses *Mémoires historiques sur la vie de M. Suard* (p.220) racontera que 'Saint-Lambert barrera de son corps la route de l'Académie à l'abbé Arnaud qui avait écrit à Fréron contre Helvétius'. C'est seulement le 5 janvier 1759 que l'*Année littéraire* consacre un article à *De l'esprit* (i.45-65).

[43] Critique très favorable de l'*Ami des hommes* de Mirabeau dans l'*Année littéraire* (3 février 1758, i.217-32) et des *Annales politiques* de l'abbé de Saint-Pierre (29 janvier 1759, i.217-38). Il ne nous semble pas que le père Nicolas Bergier, déjà directeur du *Journal de Trévoux*, ait collaboré à l'*Année littéraire*. En outre, la politique n'était pas son fort, alors qu'elle passionnait Fréron.

[44] Rapide éloge de la *Briséis* de Poinsinet de Sivry, alors âgé de 23 ans (*Al*, 4 juillet 1759, iv.187-89).

[45] Marmontel avait retouché le *Venceslas* de Rotrou. Mais l'acteur Lekain demanda à Colardeau de rétablir pour son rôle les vers de l'original et de les intégrer au nouveau *Venceslas*. Les articles cinglants que l'affaire a suscités (*Al*, 14 mai 1759, iii.97-129 et 5 juin 1759, iii.289-322) sont tellement de Fréron que Marmontel a remué ciel et terre pour tenter d'étouffer la voix du journaliste (*Le Dossier Fréron*, p.260-66). L'auteur du *Venceslas* retouché faillit ne jamais se relever de sa mésaventure.

[46] Analyse de l'*Economie rurale*, traduction du *Praedium rusticum* du père Jacques Vannière (*Al*, 21 octobre 1756, vi.145-57). Berland d'Halouvry n'a été que le traducteur.

[47] Compte rendu des *Réflexions diverses* du chevalier de Bruix, que l'auteur de l'article oppose à 'nos petits anatomistes du cœur humain' (*Al*, 30 avril 1758, iii.3-10).

Bastille.[48] Ce[d] Coste est un mauvais sujet de Bayonne qui a fait cent lettres de change à Paris où il n'ose plus paraître. Il couchait avec la femme de Fréron,[49] et faisait mettre de l'argent de ce même Fréron sur des corsaires: c'est le seul ami qu'ait eu Fréron.[50] En voilà assez; les autres actions de ce polisson sont assez publiques.

170

175

[d] Il faut savoir si ce La Coste est celui qui a été depuis condamné aux galères. (*Ce n'est pas le même*)[49]

170*n* MS, 61A, CU70, 70: Galères.//
171 MS: cent fausses lettres
174-175 MS, 61A, CU70: de ce scélérat sont assez publiques, et je suis las de souiller du papier de son nom.

[48] Si Coste d'Arnobat a donné à l'*Année littéraire* un extrait de ses *Lettres sur le voyage d'Espagne* (1756, vii.146-59), c'est, en tout cas, Fréron qui est considéré comme le responsable de l'article d'autant plus que l'auteur n'était pas nommé. L'ambassadeur d'Espagne se plaint. Fréron est incarcéré à la Bastille du 24 janvier au 16 février 1757. Motif: 'pour livre injurieux aux Espagnols Navarrais et à la religion' (*Le Dossier Fréron*, p.188-92). Ce motif ne paraît-il pas bien philosophique?

[49] Elie Fréron a épousé Thérèse-Jacqueline Guyomar le 21 janvier 1751. Elle lui donne six enfants. Tous les témoignages montrent à quel point Fréron adorait ses enfants et sa femme qui allait affronter avec lui les horions de l'*Ecossaise*. Sa mort en 1762 va le désespérer. Lisons le mot qu'il envoie alors à son ami Triboudet: 'J'ai perdu Madame Fréron qui dans la fleur de son âge m'a été enlevée d'une maladie de poitrine qui a duré plus de dix mois. Si tu aimes ta femme, comme je n'en doute pas, meurs avant elle ou en même temps qu'elle, car je ne connais rien de plus cruel, de plus affreux que de survivre à quelqu'un que l'on aime' (*Le Dossier Fréron*, p.314). Le seul à calomnier madame Fréron est, avec Voltaire, Chevrier qui, dans son *Colporteur* (édition de 1762, p.386), monte une scène à grand spectacle où le journaliste est présenté comme un 'maquereau' de sa femme. Quant aux amis de Fréron, il suffit de lire l'*Année littéraire* et sa correspondance pour en mesurer le nombre et la qualité: Rameau le musicien, l'abbé Prévost, Triboudet, d'Olivet, Duhamel du Monceau, Blondel, Baculard d'Arnaud, etc., etc.

[50] Le médecin Coste, l'ami de Fréron, n'a évidemment rien à voir avec l'escroc du même nom qui mourra au bagne de Toulon en janvier 1762 (D10270). Voltaire, nous le savons, s'excusera de son erreur.

SUPPLÉMENT

Les feuilles de Fréron furent encore suspendues, pour avoir injurié grossièrement quelques personnes.

Autre suspension pour avoir fait paraître sa feuille sans qu'elle ait été vue par le censeur, lorsqu'il rendit compte du discours académique de M. d'Alembert. Il avait éludé le censeur, pour pouvoir plus librement exhaler sa rage contre cet académicien.[51] 180

Autre suspension à l'occasion des Lettres de son ami Coste dont j'ai parlé plus haut. Dans l'extrait que Fréron fit de ses Lettres, il parla avec une indécence digne de Bicêtre, de la nation espagnole; il n'alla qu'à la Bastille.[52] 185

Vous demandez ce que c'est que son mariage avec sa nièce, et son procès avec sa sœur. Sa nièce est de Quimper-Corentin comme lui. C'est la fille d'un huissier. Elle vint à Paris, il y a 13 ou 14 ans, et fut mise en qualité de servante chez la sœur de

177 MS, 61A: grossièrement M. Crébillon fils, à l'occasion de ses heureux Orphelins.

182-183 MS: à l'occasion de son ami Coste ou La Coste dont

[51] Le compte rendu du discours académique de d'Alembert paraît dans le dernier ordinaire de l'*Année littéraire*, 28 décembre 1754 (vii.349-58). Fréron s'est contenté d'évoquer le peu de talent de l'illustre géomètre pour les lettres et de critiquer son style 'contraint et embarrassé'. Mais d'Alembert, susceptible en diable, réussit à obtenir de Malesherbes la suspension du périodique (du 10 janvier au 10 février 1755). Le censeur Morand était un ami de Fréron et en même temps le confrère de d'Alembert à l'Académie des sciences. Il lut l'article le vendredi 27 décembre et ne dit rien. Le samedi matin étant le jour de vente du journal, Lambert, se croyant à couvert, le fit distribuer. C'est seulement à midi que Morand vint déclarer que l'article ne passerait pas. Manœuvre évidente: 'Je ne me serais pas attendu', proteste Fréron, 'à un pareil procédé de sa part'. De nombreuses et puissantes interventions feront rétablir les feuilles (*Le Dossier Fréron*, p.148-64).

[52] Retour inattendu et maladroit à l'affaire Coste. Seul élément nouveau: c'est bien Fréron qui a fait l'extrait de ses *Lettres sur l'Espagne*.

Fréron.[53] Je l'ai vue balayer la rue devant la boutique de sa tante. 190
Le mauvais traitement qu'elle recevait chez cette même tante, engagea Fréron qui demeurait avec sa sœur, à en sortir, et à prendre avec lui dans une chambre garnie, rue de Bussy, la petite fille avec laquelle il était en commerce, quelque temps après Fréron prit des meubles. Sa nièce devint sa gouvernante. Il lui fit 195
deux enfants; pendant la grossesse du second, il se maria par dispense.[54]

L'histoire du procès de Fréron avec sa sœur est très longue et très compliquée. Le libraire Lambert m'a fait lire un mémoire manuscrit, très curieux, et très bien fait, où le procès est plaisam- 200
ment raconté. Je sais que Lambert conserve très soigneusement ce manuscrit; et l'abbé Laporte en a parlé dans l'Observateur littéraire 1760. Tom. I. page 177; il rapporte le sujet de ce

200 MS: est très plaisamment

[53] Thérèse-Jacqueline Guyomar (1730-1762) était la fille d'Henri Guyomar, sieur de Kerviniou, et de Louise Fréron, née d'un premier mariage de Daniel Fréron (le père de Fréron se maria trois fois). Elle était bien la nièce d'Elie Fréron. Elle avait douze ans de moins que lui. Devenue orpheline en 1748, elle fut envoyée par son grand-père Daniel Fréron chez Marie, une autre fille de ce dernier, la filleule de la mère de Thérèse. Les actes de Plonévez-Porzay qualifient le père de Thérèse de 'général et d'armes' au siège présidial de Quimper, c'est-à-dire 'sergent général', sergent audiencier ayant le droit d'instrumenter dans le ressort du présidial. Le terme 'huissier' est donc assez juste. L'ensemble de ce court 'supplément' se caractérise par sa couleur bretonne et familiale. Même si Voltaire dramatise la situation, même s'il doit se tromper dans le paragraphe suivant sur l'identité d'une sœur de Fréron, il est fort bien renseigné. Et c'est encore signé l'abbé de La Porte.

[54] Jal, dans son *Dictionnaire critique* (1867), a publié les actes de Saint-Sulpice, paroisse où s'est marié Elie Fréron. Les faits rapportés par Voltaire sont exacts. Le 19 novembre 1749 Marie-Catherine-Françoise est baptisée à l'église Saint-Côme, sans nom de famille. Le 16 janvier 1751, François-Elie-Marie est baptisé à Saint-Sulpice sous le nom de Fréron et de Thérèse Guyomar, son épouse. Les deux enfants sont reconnus dans l'acte. Quelques jours après, le 21 janvier, mariage de Fréron à Saint-Sulpice. Depuis trois ans Fréron vivait avec Thérèse rue de Seine. L'acte stipule aussi que le mariage eut lieu 'par décret' (c'est-à-dire par autorisation, Thérèse étant mineure) de la cour des regaires de Cornouaille.

procès.[55] La sœur de Fréron est fripière; son enseigne est au riche Laboureur; pour faire niche à son frère qu'elle déteste bien cordialement, elle m'a dit qu'elle allait mettre une enseigne d'habits et de meubles sur sa boutique, avec ces mots: 205

A L'ANNÉE FRIPIÈRE

FRÉRON.[56]

Fréron a fait faire il y a 12 à 14 ans deux cents paires de souliers pour envoyer aux îles; l'envoi a été fait effectivement; il en a reçu l'argent, et le doit encore au cordonnier.[57] 210

J'ai ouï dire à un procureur du Châtelet, qu'il n'y avait pas de semaine qu'on n'appelât à l'audience quelque procès de ce Fréron, etc. etc. 215

214 MS: de Fréron

[55] En 1744, Fréron est parrain à l'église Saint-André-des-Arts d'un enfant de sa sœur Thérèse, épouse Duché (en réalité demi-sœur, née du deuxième mariage de Daniel Fréron). Il a commandé une caisse de vin de 54 livres 10 sous pour le baptême. Tout le problème est là: est-ce lui ou son beau-frère qui doit payer? En tout cas Fréron refusera toujours de régler la note. Et de s'exclamer: 'Si j'avais à me louer de mon beau-frère et de ma sœur, je paierais encore cette dette'. L'affaire traînera dix ans jusqu'en juin 1754, date du procès. On en ignore l'issue. La *Revue rétrospective* (2e sér., 10, 1837, p.449-57), a raconté cette histoire. Si la référence à l'*Observateur littéraire* est exacte, l'abbé de La Porte se contentait d'y citer 'un cabaretier rançonné par un écrivain fort célèbre' (*Le Dossier Fréron*, p.138-40).

[56] Il ne s'agit pas de Thérèse, épouse Duché, mais de Marie-Louise, née du troisième mariage de Daniel Fréron, deux ans avant Elie (28 novembre 1716). Elle était mercière à l'enseigne du 'Riche laboureur', quartier de Saint-Sulpice. Elle signa, en 1751, l'acte de baptême du second enfant d'Elie Fréron.

[57] Cette histoire de souliers vendus aux Iles n'a laissé aucune trace. Des ennemis de Fréron, Voltaire est, à notre connaissance, le seul à rapporter ce ragot.

NOTE

Celui qui a daigné faire imprimer cet écrit tombé entre ses mains, a voulu seulement faire rougir ceux qui ont protégé un coquin, et ceux qui ont fait quelque attention à ses feuilles. Si on parle dans l'histoire naturelle des aigles et des rossignols on y parle aussi des crapauds.[58] 220

Il est nécessaire que ces infamies soient constatées par le témoignage de tous ceux qui sont cités dans cet écrit, ils ne doivent pas le refuser à la vengeance publique.

COPIE DE LA LETTRE DE MONSIEUR ROYOU,
AVOCAT AU PARLEMENT DE RENNES,
MARDI MATIN 6 MARS 1770

Fréron auteur de l'Année littéraire est mon cousin, et malheureusement pour ma sœur, pour moi et pour toute la famille, mon 225 beau-frère depuis trois ans.[59]

218-284 MS, 61A: feuilles.//
220-284 CU70: crapauds.//

[58] Dresser le catalogue des injures dont Voltaire a abreuvé Fréron est une lourde tâche. Tous les noms d'animaux y passent: âne, cochon, chien, dogue, couleuvre, serpent, chenille, crapaud, Wasp… Toutes les marques d'infamie sont notées: bandit, Cartouche, Mandrin, Raffiat, galérien, maraud, fripon… Les pires châtiments sont envisagés: à la chaîne, à la potence, à l'échafaud, à la Grève, à écraser, à étouffer… Les mœurs les plus scandaleuses sont évoquées: l'agent et le patient, l'escroc, le traître, l'espion (mais voir à ce sujet, car ce sera un mot-clé du mémoire Royou, l'article de Marlinda R. Bruno dans les *Studies* 148 (1976), 'Fréron, police spy', p.177-99, et notre mise au point dans *Rhl* 78, 1978, p.311), l'ivrogne (ah! mais)… Voltaire ne sait plus s'il s'appelle Jean, Martin, Catherin ou Wasp, Aliboron ou Cerbère… On se demande s'il n'est pas à la fin persuadé que Fréron a vraiment ramé sur les galères.

[59] Le 4 septembre 1766, Elie Fréron épousa dans la chapelle du château de Pont-l'Abbé, en secondes noces, Annétic Royou, sixième fille de Louise Campion et de Jacques Royou. Fille d'une cousine germaine de Fréron, elle était sa nièce à la mode de Bretagne.

Mon père, subdélégué et sénéchal du Pont l'abbé à trois lieues de Quimper-Corentin en Basse-Bretagne,[60] quoique dans une situation aisée, n'étant pas riche, ne donna à sa fille que vingt mille livres de dot.[61] Trois jours après les noces[62] M. Fréron jugea à propos d'aller à Brest où il dissipa cette somme avec des bateleuses. 230

Il revint chez son beau-père pour donner à ma sœur sa femme un très mauvais présent,[63] et demander en grâce de quoi se rendre à Paris. Mon père fut assez bon, ou plutôt assez faible pour donner encore mille écus... Il était alors à l'Orient et quoiqu'il reçut cette nouvelle somme par lettre de change, il ne put se rendre qu'à Alençon,[64] et fit le reste de la route jusqu'à Paris comme les 235

[60] Jacques-Corentin Royou était, en 1756, procureur fiscal de la baronnie de Pont-l'Abbé. En 1766, il était 'subdélégué de Monseigneur l'Intendant' (*Archives du Finistère*, voir Trévédy, p.49).

[61] Contre-vérité, comme en témoigne l'enregistrement du 1er septembre 1766 des *Archives de Quimper*: maître Mahieu, notaire royal, et son confrère maître le Gorgeu ont dressé le contrat par lequel M. et Mme Royou constituent à leur fille une dot de 3000 livres.

[62] Trois jours après les noces, Fréron était encore à Pont-l'Abbé chez ses beaux-parents. Des nombreuses lettres écrites alors par Fréron à la famille Royou et aux amis de Quimper, quelques-unes ont été conservées. Elles ont été publiées pour la première fois dans l'*Océan de Brest* en mars-avril 1861 par Armand Du Chatellier et déposées aux archives de Quimper seulement en 1970. Elles ruinent tout ce que Royou-Voltaire écrit du mariage de Fréron (*Le Dossier Fréron*, p.331-44).

Grâce à elles, nous pouvons reconstituer ainsi les faits: du 4 au 9 septembre 1766, Fréron et Annétic sont à Pont-l'Abbé; du 10 au 17, réceptions à Quimper (comptes rendus quotidiens); le 17, retour à Pont-l'Abbé; quelques jours après (sans doute le 21) retour à Paris avec la petite Thérèse (dernière fille du premier mariage) qui avait accompagné son père; le laquais de Fréron, Brei, était aussi du voyage.

[63] Le même mauvais présent dont, selon Voltaire, l'abbé Desfontaines était mort. Aller à Brest (où Fréron n'a jamais mis les pieds), c'était, à coup sûr, attraper la vérole.

[64] Les lettres écrites par Fréron en septembre 1766 rendent invraisemblable ce périple qui fait aller les mariés de Quimper à Lorient, puis à Alençon. Le texte cité dans les *Questions sur l'Encyclopédie* (voir aussi Best.15207) est un peu plus féroce, puisque c'est de Quimper à Paris que la malheureuse Mme Fréron aurait voyagé dans le panier du coche.

capucins,[65] et ne donna pour toute voiture à sa femme qu'une place sur un peu de paille dans le panier de la voiture publique.[66] 240

Arrivé à Paris il n'en agit pas mieux avec elle. Ma sœur après deux ans de patience se plaignit à mon père, qui m'ordonna[67] de me rendre incessamment à Paris pour m'informer si ma sœur était aussi cruellement traitée qu'elle le lui marquait.[68] Alors Fréron chercha et tenta tous les moyens de me perdre. Il sut que 245 pendant les troubles du parlement de Bretagne où je militais depuis plusieurs années en qualité d'avocat, j'ai montré un zèle vraiment patriotique, et toute la fermeté d'un bon citoyen.

Comme il faisait le métier d'espion il ne négligea rien pour

[65] A pied, sinon en mendiant.

[66] Voyager dans le panier, c'est prendre place parmi les bagages. Mais ce Fréron que Voltaire fait aller à pied pour que sa femme puisse prendre place, fut-ce dans les bagages?

[67] Or Royou est alors brouillé avec son père et sa famille. Il est le seul (avec l'abbé Thomas Royou, resté à Paris pour suppléer Fréron à l'*Année littéraire*) à ne pas assister au mariage de sa sœur (voir la liste des présents donnée par Trévédy, p.59).

[68] Quelque temps après son mariage, Fréron invita chez lui Jacques-Corentin Royou, le jeune frère d'Annétic. Jacques épousera le 4 juillet 1773 Louise-Philippine, la propre fille de Fréron. Toutes les lettres rassemblées par Du Chatellier en 1861 montrent à quel point Fréron demeure très lié avec sa belle-famille. Citons ces quelques extraits d'une longue lettre écrite, le 15 février 1772, à sa belle-mère, Mme Royou, qui est en même temps sa cousine: 'Nous avons reçu tout ce que vous nous avez envoyé: douze andouilles, sept bécasses et trois pluviers [...] Je vous envoie une pacotille de lettres pleines de tendresse et de reconnaissance. Ces sentiments vous sont dûs à juste titre. Pour moi, ma très chère et très aimable cousine, je vous ai voué une amitié éternelle et un attachement inviolable. Je vous embrasse un million de fois de toute mon âme'.

Quant à l'amour d'Annétic Royou pour son mari (qui avait pourtant 30 ans de plus qu'elle), il est exemplaire. Sa mort la rendra inconsolable. Elle veut rassembler ses lettres car 'tout lui en est précieux'. Elle demande à Jacob Vernes de lui parler de son mari: 'l'attachement', écrit-elle, 'n'a pas besoin de grands motifs pour se renouveler quand on ne peut plus entendre une personne qu'on aimait'. Dans une autre lettre, elle lui déclare que 'sa reconnaissance ne peut s'expliquer'. Elle souffre trop: 'Je ne persuaderai jamais ce que je sens' dit-elle (lettres à Jacob Vernes des 23 juillet et 19 août 1777, *Le Dossier Fréron*, p.381-84).

obtenir par le moyen de ... une lettre de cachet pour me faire renfermer.[69] 250

Fréron qui voulait être à la fois ma partie, mon témoin et mon bourreau, vint en personne escorté d'un commissaire, et de neuf à dix manants, m'arrêter dans mon appartement à Paris, rue des Noyers. Il me fit traiter de la manière la plus barbare et conduire 255 au petit Châtelet, où je passai dans le fond d'un cachot la nuit du dimanche au lundi de la Pentecôte. Le lundi Fréron se rendit environ les dix heures du matin avec ses affiliés au petit Châtelet. Il me fit charger de chaînes et conduire à ma destination. Il était à côté de moi dans un fiacre et tenait lui-même les chaînes, etc. 260 etc.

On nous a communiqué l'original de cette lettre signée Royou. Ce n'est pas à nous de discuter si le sieur Royou a été coupable ou non envers le gouvernement. Mais quand même il eût été criminel, c'est toujours le procédé du plus lâche et du plus 265 détestable coquin de faire le métier d'archer pour arrêter et pour garrotter son beau-frère.

C'est pourtant ce misérable qui a contrefait l'homme de lettres,[70] et qui a trouvé des protecteurs[71] quand il a fallu déshonorer la littérature. 270

On lui a donné des examinateurs qui tous se sont dégoûtés l'un après l'autre d'être les complices des platitudes d'un homme digne

[69] Rappelons qu'aucun avocat ne fut poursuivi et menacé d'emprisonnement à l'occasion des troubles du Parlement de Bretagne en 1765-1766. Donc c'est pour une autre raison que Royou fut enfermé.

[70] La profession de journaliste était considérée par Voltaire et les philosophes (oubliant qu'ils en tâtaient à l'occasion) comme 'la chambre basse de la littérature' (voir Maurice Pellisson, *Les Hommes de lettres au XVIIIième siècle*, Paris 1911, p.256-64). La grandeur de Fréron est précisément de l'avoir imposée à un siècle hostile mais fasciné.

[71] Voilà qui fait enrager les philosophes. Dès 1750, en effet, Voltaire lançait cette exclamation indignée: 'Et on soufre des Frérons! et ils sont protégez!' (D4294). Les protecteurs de Fréron? Stanislas de Pologne, la reine, le dauphin, Mmes Adélaïde et Victoire, d'Hémery, l'inspecteur de la Librairie... Chaque fois que son journal est suspendu, des voix s'élèvent pour protester.

d'ailleurs de toute la sévérité de la justice. Ce fut d'abord le chirurgien Morand qui après l'avoir guéri d'un mal vénérien cessa d'avoir commerce avec lui. A Morand succéda le sieur Coquelet, 275 de Chausse Pierre avocat, qui rougit bientôt de ce vil métier si peu fait pour lui. Il fut remplacé par le sieur Rémond Ste Albine connu vulgairement sous un autre nom.[72] On ne conçoit pas comment le sieur Rémond a pu donner son attache aux grossièretés que Fréron a vomies contre l'Académie dans je ne sais quelle 280 satire contre l'éloge de Molière excellent ouvrage de M. de Chamfort.[73] Fréron doit rendre grâce au mépris dont il est couvert s'il n'a pas été puni. L'Académie a ignoré ses impertinences: si la police l'avait su, il aurait pu faire un nouveau voyage à Bicêtre.

[72] Les censeurs de Fréron: Morand, le chirurgien, de février 1755 à septembre 1756; Coqueley de Chaussepierre (Fréron ignorait son identité; un tiers servait d'intermédiaire), qui resta en place le plus longtemps. En 1767, Voltaire croit que Coqueley est toujours le censeur de Fréron (13 avril; D14107). Mais le même jour, il parle d'un certain 'd'Albaret' (D14110). Rémond de Sainte-Albine entra en fonction vers 1770. Ici Voltaire fait l'impasse sur le censeur qui surveilla Fréron de 1766 à 1770: pendant ces quatre ans, en effet, le directeur de l'*Année littéraire* a été victime d'une véritable machination. Elle fut montée à la mort de Stanislas de Pologne. Le tiers chargé de remettre les feuilles au censeur inconnu avait été acheté par les philosophes. Tout article qui les visait, il le gardait dans ses tiroirs. C'est seulement en 1770 (*Al*, i.préambule) et surtout en 1772 (i.3-11) que Fréron put dénoncer publiquement le complot. Voir à ce sujet *Fréron contre les philosophes*, p.302-305.

[73] *Al*, 1769, vii.28-55. Les articles de Fréron frappent généralement par une certaine modération: la passion y est presque toujours maîtrisée par l'ironie. Mais reconnaissons que s'il y avait en lui un grand polémiste et un grand critique, le second fut bien souvent la dupe du premier: la rançon du journalisme, et à une telle période de notre histoire? Quant à sa valeur, la permanence de la haine de Voltaire – elle a duré trente ans – suffit déjà à la mesurer. L'intérêt des *Anecdotes* est que cette haine est là, toute condensée, et exemplaire.

APPENDICE I

L'"Avis de l'éditeur'

Sur ce texte inédit, voir ci-dessus, p.485. Nous reproduisons l'autographe de Voltaire avec les modifications suivantes: l'apostrophe a été suppléée là où elle manque; on met la majuscule aux noms propres et au début des phrases.

Memoire sur Freron.
Avis de l'editeur.

Les anecdotes suivantes m'etant parvenues j'ay pris des informations exactes; et je les ay trouvées conformes en tout a la verité.

Peutetre le moment présent et l'indignation publique que le nommé Freron a excitée feront ils lire ces anecdotes, qui sans ces raisons n'attireraient la curiosité de personne.

Il est bon qu'elles fassent connaitre un homme qui s'avisait de juger les autres. Quelques provinciaux lisaient ses feuïlles et s'imaginaient avoir par elles des nouvelles sures des belles lettres de Paris. La premiere qualité d'un orateur dit Cicéron, est d'etre honnete homme. On peut ajouter que c'est la premiere qualité d'un critique. Quelle confiance peut on avoir aux décisions d'un écrivain dont le cœur est aussi corrompu que le goust? Sied il bien a des hommes connus par la bassesse de leurs sentiments et de leurs mœurs de s'ériger en juges, de dire au public, *je* suis d'un tel avis, *je* trouve un tel ouvrage mauvais, *je* prononce que telle entreprise ne reussira pas? Le *moy* comme on sçait est toujours impertinent. Mais que devient il dans un homme infame? et quand un tel homme ose faire le mauvais plaisant, et quand il joint

4 MS: excitée ⟨qui sans⟩ V feront
13-14 MS: et ⟨par des⟩ V↑de leurs+ mœurs ⟨infames⟩ de
16 MS: entreprise ⟨est⟩ ne

l'ignorance et le mauvais goust a la présomption, y a t'il sur la terre un être plus odieux?

Si on n'avait pas toléré de tels misérables nous n'aurions pas eu dans la litterature les scandales qui nous affligent. On a vu presque en meme temps Freron, Palissot et Pompignan insulter les plus honnetes gens, Pompignan au milieu d'une academie[1] dont il s'est attiré le mepris et la haine, Palissot sur le teatre,[2] et Fréron dans ses feuilles. Le public a fait aisément la comparaison de ces trois personnages avec les hommes les plus celebres de L'Europe qu'ils ont osé calomnier, et le cri de la nation s'est élevé contre les calomniateurs. Il est vray que ces trois hommes ne se ressemblent pas; Palissot et Freron, ont barbouillé du papier pour de l'argent et Pompignan n'a eté possedé que de l'orgueuil d'un poete de province qui s'est imaginé qu'on l'écouterait a Paris comme dans sa petite ville,[3] et qu'on prendrait son babil téméraire pour de l'éloquence. Il a du sentir a quel point il a révolté tous les esprits. Pour les Frerons et les gens de cette espece ils ne sentent rien. Ce n'est pas sans doute pour humilier ce personnage que je donne au public le mémoire suivant, c'est pour avertir tous les jeunes gens qu'il est impossible qu'un homme qui s'est fait un metier de dire du mal, ne soit pas d'ailleurs un tres malhonnete homme. Cette reflexion est utile.

21-22 MS: pas ⟨vu⟩ V↑eu
31-32 MS: d'un ⟨provincial ridicule⟩ V↑poete de province

[1] Le discours prononcé le 10 mars 1760 par Lefranc de Pompignan à l'Académie française fut considéré comme une déclaration de guerre aux philosophes et, en particulier, à Voltaire (cf. *Al*, 30 mars 1760, ii.26-77). Aussitôt criblé de traits par Voltaire, le malheureux académicien ne devait plus s'en remettre.

[2] C'est le 2 mai 1760 qu'eut lieu la représentation des *Philosophes*, comédie en 3 actes de Charles Palissot de Montenoy. Cette autre manifestation publique contre les philosophes visait, cette fois, en premier lieu Dortidius/Diderot (cf. *Al*, 16 juin 1760, iv.217-407). De son côté Voltaire avait déjà en chantier *L'Ecossaise*.

[3] Montauban. L'un des leitmotiv des attaques voltairiennes: l'extraordinaire 'vanité' du personnage.

APPENDICE II

La lettre de Voltaire

Voir ci-dessus, p.485. Nous publions cette lettre d'après une copie de la main de Wagnière conservée à la Bibliothèque nationale (F 12940, p.289-90). Elle porte la mention, de la main de Voltaire: 'envoié a mr dalembert pr m de la harpe'.

25e fevr: 1777. a Ferney.

Quoi que je sois bien vieux et bien malade, Monsieur, je n'ai pas absolument perdu la mémoire. Je me souviens qu'il y a environ quinze ans[1] que Mr. Thiriot m'envoia une brochure intitulée, Anecdotes sur Frèron. Il me manda que plusieurs personnes l'attribuaient à Mr. De La Harpe. Il se peut qu'avant de l'avoir éxaminée, j'ai cru et j'ai mandé que cet ouvrage était très véridique, et qu'il était de l'auteur à qui on l'attribuait. Mais je reconnus bientôt que cet ouvrage ne pouvait être ni de Mr. De La Harpe, ni d'aucun homme de Lettres. Il n'y est principalement question que de marchés avec des libraires et des colpo[r]teurs,[2] de querelles et de procez sur les objets les plus bas. Le stile est digne du sujet qu'il traitte.

Mr. L'abbé De La Porte dont il était fort question dans cet ouvrage, et Mr. De Marmontel dont il est aussi parlé peuvent être consultés[3] sur la vérité des faits énoncés dans la brochure. Il y

9 MS, 'principalement' ajouté au dessus de la ligne
10 MS: ⟨querelles⟩ marchés

[1] Près de 17, puisque l'envoi eut lieu en août 1760.

[2] De là à dire à La Harpe quelque temps après (D20627, 8 avril): 'Il n'y a qu'un colporteur qui puisse les [*Anecdotes*] avoir écrites'.

[3] En invoquant ainsi la garantie de l'abbé de La Porte et Marmontel Voltaire ne signe-t-il pas ses sources? On pense surtout au premier.

était dit que le libraire Lambert[4] avait un mémoire manuscrit concernant tout ce qu'on reprochait alors à Fréron.

Voilà, je crois, tous les écclaircissements que je peux vous donner. Si jamais je retrouve un éxemplaire de cette brochure vous verrez si elle est véridique ou non. Mais vous verrez bien plus évidemment qu'elle n'est pas d'un homme de Lettres. Je me souviens qu'il était parlé à la fin de l'ouvrage d'un procez pour des paires de souliers. Toutes ces pauvretés là ne passent pas la cheville du pied.

J'ai l'honneur d'être, Monsr. vôtre

[4] Voir ci-dessus, p.504, note 28.

LIST OF WORKS CITED

Aghion, Max, *Le Théâtre à Paris au dix-huitième siècle* (Paris 1926).

Alasseur, Claude, *La Comédie-Française au dix-huitième siècle* (Paris 1967).

Anseaume, Louis, et Panard, Charles-François, *L'Ecosseuse, parodie de l'Ecossaise, opéra comique en 1 acte, par Mrs P. et A.* (Paris 1760).

Bachaumont, Louis Petit de, *Mémoires secrets pour servir à l'histoire de la république des lettres en France depuis 1762 jusqu'à nos jours* (Londres 1777-1789).

Baker, David Erskine, *Biographica dramatica, or a companion to the playhouse* (London 1782).

Balcou, Jean, 'L'affaire de l'*Ecossaise*', *Information littéraire* (mai-juin 1969), p.111-15.

– *Le Dossier Fréron: correspondance et documents* (Genève 1975).

– 'Le dossier Fréron: suite', *Rhl* 78 (1978), p.260-67.

– *Fréron contre les philosophes* (Genève 1975).

Barthélemy, Anatole de, 'Le droit du seigneur', *Revue des questions historiques* 1 (1866), p.95-123.

Bayle, Pierre, *Dictionnaire historique et critique* (Rotterdam 1697).

Beaumarchais, Pierre Auguste Caron de, *Théâtre complet* (Paris 1964).

– *Théâtre complet* (Paris 1973).

Bengesco, Georges, *Voltaire: bibliographie de ses œuvres* (Paris 1882-1890).

– *Les Comédiennes de Voltaire* (Paris 1912).

Besterman, Theodore, 'A provisional bibliography of Italian editions and translations of Voltaire', *Studies* 18 (1961), p.263-310.

– 'A provisional bibliography of Scandinavian and Finnish editions and translations of Voltaire', *Studies* 47 (1966), p.53-92.

– 'Provisional bibliography of Portuguese editions of Voltaire', *Studies* 76 (1970), p.15-35.

– *Voltaire*, 3rd ed. (Oxford 1976).

Bibliothèque de Voltaire: catalogue des livres (Moscou, Leningrad 1961).

La Bigarrure (La Haye 1749-1753).

Boas, Frederick S., *An introduction to eighteenth-century drama 1700-1780* (Oxford 1953).

Boethius, Hector, *Scotium historiae* (Paris 1527).

Boissy, Louis de, *Le Droit du seigneur ou le mari retrouvé et la femme fidèle* (Bn F9322).

Boswell, James, *Journal of a tour to the Hebrides*, ed. R. W. Chapman (Oxford 1924).

Brenner, Clarence D., *A bibliographical list of plays in the French language 1700-1789*, ed. M. A. Keller and N. Zaslaw (New York 1979).

Brown, Andrew, 'Calendar of Voltaire manuscripts other than correspondence', *Studies* 77 (1970), p.13-101.

Brunetière, Ferdinand, 'La direction de la Librairie sous Malesherbes', *Rdm* (1er février 1882), p.567-612.

Brunetti, *Mémoires des décorations peintes à la Comédie-Française depuis l'ouverture du théâtre de 1769 jusques à la clôture de 1769* (Comédie-Française).

LIST OF WORKS CITED

Bruno, Marlinda R., 'Fréron, police spy', *Studies* 148 (1976), p.177-99.

Casanova, Giacomo, *Mémoires*, ed. R. Abirached (Paris 1959).

Catalogue des pièces choisies du répertoire de la Comédie Française (Paris 1775).

Catalogue hebdomadaire (1763-1782).

Catalogus triennalis (1737).

Caussy, Fernand, *Inventaire des manuscrits de la bibliothèque de Voltaire* (Paris 1913).

Chevrier, François-Antoine, *Le Colporteur* (Londres 1762).

Clément, Jean-Marie-Bernard, et La Porte, Joseph de, *Anecdotes dramatiques* (Paris 1775).

Collé, Charles, *Journal et mémoires*, ed. H. Bonhomme (Paris 1868).

Colman, George, the Elder, *The English merchant* (London 1767).

Colman, George, the Younger, ed., *Posthumous letters addressed to F. Colman and G. Colman the Elder etc.* (London 1820).

Cornou, François, *Elie Fréron (1718-1776), trente années de luttes contre Voltaire et les philosophes du dix-huitième siècle* (Paris 1922).

Coyer, Gabriel-François, *Discours sur la satyre contre les philosophes* (Athènes 1760).

Delort, Joseph, *Histoire de la détention des philosophes et des gens de lettres à la Bastille et à Vincennes* (Paris 1829).

Deschanel, Emile, *Le Théâtre de Voltaire* (Paris 1866).

Descotes, Maurice, *Le Public de théâtre et son histoire* (Paris 1964).

Desfontaines, François-Georges Fouques Deshayes, dit, *Le Droit du seigneur, comédie en trois actes et en prose mêlée d'ariettes* (Paris 1783).

Desnoiresterres, Gustave, *Voltaire et la société au dix-huitième siècle* (Paris 1871-1876).

Diderot, Denis, *Correspondance*, ed. G. Roth et J. Varloot (Paris 1955-1970).

– *Œuvres complètes*, ed. H. Dieckmann, J. Proust et J. Varloot (Paris 1975-).

Dorat, Claude-Joseph, *Epître à un ami dans sa retraite, à l'occasion des Philosophes et de l'Ecossaise* (s.l. s.d.).

Le Droit du seigneur, comédie en un acte pour les Comédiens Français, année 1732 (Bn F9295).

Du Chatellier, Armand, '[Correspondance]', *Océan de Brest* (mars-avril 1861).

Duckworth, Colin R., 'Madame Denis's unpublished *Pamela*: a link between Richardson, Goldoni and Voltaire', *Studies* 76 (1970), p.37-53.

Dufresny, Charles Rivière, *Œuvres* (Paris 1731).

Du Verdier, Antoine, *Diverses leçons* (Lyon 1577).

L'Encyclopédie, ou dictionnaire raisonné des sciences, des arts et des métiers (Paris 1751-1780).

Favart, Charles-Simon, *Mémoires et correspondance* (Paris 1808).

– et Duni, E. G., *Les Moissonneurs, comédie en trois actes et en vers, mêlée d'ariettes* (Paris 1768).

Feller, François-Xavier de, *Dictionnaire historique ou histoire abrégée de tous les hommes qui se sont fait un nom par le génie, les talens, les vertus, depuis le commencement du monde jusqu'à nos jours* (Augsbourg 1781-1783).

Flaubert, Gustave, *Le Théâtre de Voltaire*, ed. Th. Besterman, Studies 50-51 (1967).

Fletcher, John, and Massinger, P., *The Custom of the country* (London 1622).

Fréron, Elie Catherine, *Ad bellonam, ode* (Caen 1737).

– *L'Année littéraire, ou suite des Lettres sur quelques écrits de ce temps* (Paris 1754-1776).

– *Lettres de madame la comtesse de ***, sur quelques écrits modernes* (Genève 1745-1746).
– *Lettres sur quelques écrits de ce temps* (Genève, Paris 1749-1754).
– *Opuscules de M. F**** (Amsterdam 1753).
'Fréron et sa famille', *Revue rétrospective*, 2e sér., 10 (1837), p.449-58.
Fuchs, Max, *Lexique des troupes de comédiens au dix-huitième siècle* (Paris 1944).
Furetière, Antoine, *Dictionnaire universel* (La Haye, Rotterdam 1690).
Gaiffe, Félix, *Le Drame en France au dix-huitième siècle* (Paris 1910).
Garat, Dominique-Joseph, *Mémoires historiques sur la vie de M. Suard, sur ses écrits et sur le dix-huitième siècle* (Paris 1820).
Goldoni, Carlo, *Le Commedie* (Torino 1756-1758).
Green, Frederick C., *Eighteenth-century France: six essays* (London 1929).
Grimm, Friedrich Melchior, *Correspondance littéraire*, ed. M. Tourneux (Paris 1877-1882).
Grosclaude, Pierre, *Malesherbes, témoin et interprète de son temps* (Paris 1962).
Harny de Guerville, *Les Nouveaux calotins* (Paris 1760).
Havens, George R., and Torrey, Norman L., *Voltaire's catalogue of his library at Ferney*, Studies 9 (1959).
Histoire du livre et de l'imprimerie en Belgique (Bruxelles 1923-1934).
Horn-Monval, Madeleine, *Répertoire bibliographique des traductions et adaptations françaises du théâtre étranger du quinzième siècle à nos jours* (Paris 1958-1967).
Howarth, W. D., 'Cervantes and Fletcher: a theme with variations', *Mlr* 56 (1961), p.563-66.
– '*Droit du seigneur*: fact or fantasy?', *Journal of European studies* 1 (1971), p.291-312.
– 'The playwright as preacher: didacticism and melodrama in the French theatre of the Enlightenment', *Forum for modern language studies* 14 (1978), p.97-115.
– 'The theme of the "droit du seigneur" in the eighteenth-century theatre', *French studies* 15 (1961), p.228-39.
Hume, David, *The History of Great Britain under the house of Stuart* (Edinburgh 1754-1757).
Irailh, Augustin S., *Querelles littéraires* (Paris 1761).
Jal, Auguste, *Dictionnaire critique de biographie et d'histoire* (Paris 1867).
Joannidès, A., *La Comédie Française, 1680-1900, dictionnaire général des pièces et des acteurs* (Paris 1901).
Jones, Sir William, *Works* (London 1799).
Journal encyclopédique (Liège, Bouillon 1756-1793).
Kleinschmidt, John R., *Les Imprimeurs et libraires de la république de Genève, 1707-1798* (Genève 1948).
Kölving, Ulla, et Carriat, Jeanne, *Inventaire de la Correspondance littéraire de Grimm et Meister*, Studies 225-227 (1984).
Lafarga, Francisco, *Voltaire en España (1734-1835)* (Barcelona 1975).
La Grange, Nicolas, *L'Ecossaise, comédie en cinq actes, traduite de l'anglais, et mise en vers* (Paris 1761).
La Harpe, Jean-François de, *Commentaires sur le théâtre de Voltaire* (Paris 1814).
Lancaster, H. Carrington, 'The Comédie Française 1701-1774, plays, actors, spectators, finances', *Transactions of the American philosophical society* 41 (1951), p.593-849.

Lang, Andrew, *A history of Scotland* (Edinburgh, London 1900-1907).

La Porte, Joseph de, *L'Observateur littéraire* (Amsterdam 1758-1761).

– *Observations sur la littérature moderne* (Londres, Paris 1749-1752).

– *Les Spectacles de Paris, ou suite du Calendrier historique et chronologique des théâtres* (Paris 1754-1778).

La Ribadière, de, *L'Ecueil du sage, comédie de M. de Voltaire, réduite à 3 actes pour le service de la cour de Vienne* (Vienne 1764).

Le Brun, Ponce-Denis Ecouchard, *L'Ane littéraire, ou les âneries de Me Aliboron, dit Fr...* (Paris 1761).

– *Œuvres* (Paris 1811).

– *La Wasprie, ou l'ami Wasp, revu et corrigé* (Berne 1761).

Le Franc de Pompignan, Jean-Jacques, *Mémoire présenté au roi* (1760).

Lénardon, Dante, *Index de l'Année littéraire (1754-1790)* (Genève 1979).

Léris, Antoine de, *Dictionnaire portatif historique et littéraire des théâtres*, 2nd ed. (Paris 1763).

Lessing, Gotthold Ephraim, *Hamburgische dramaturgie*, ed. Otto Mann (Stuttgart 1958).

Lettre de M. D. R. à M. de S. R. sur la Zulime de M. de Voltaire et sur L'Ecueil du sage du même auteur (Genève 1762).

Lettre sur la comédie de l'Ecossaise (s.l. s.d.).

Lioure, Michel, *Le Drame de Diderot à Ionesco* (Paris 1973).

Loftis, John, *Comedy and society from Congreve to Fielding* (Stanford 1959).

Longchamp, Sebastien, et Wagnière, Jean-Louis, *Mémoires sur Voltaire et sur ses ouvrages* (Paris 1826).

Lynch, Kathleen M., '*Pamela nubile*, *L'Ecossaise* and *The English merchant*', *Mln* 47 (1932), p.94-96.

Manne, Edmond-Denis de, *Galerie historique des comédiens français de la troupe de Voltaire* (Lyon 1877).

Marsy, François-Marie de, *Histoire de Marie Stuart* (Londres 1742).

Maynard, Ulysse, *Voltaire, sa vie, ses œuvres* (Paris 1867).

Le Mercure de France (1724-1794).

Monselet, Charles, *Fréron ou l'illustre critique* (Paris 1864).

Montaigne, Michel Eyquem de, *Essais*, ed. Pléiade (Paris 1958).

Montesquieu, Ch.-L. de Secondat, baron de La Brède et de, *De l'esprit des lois*, ed. G. Truc (Paris 1967).

Mouhy, Charles de Fieux, chevalier de, *Abrégé de l'histoire du Théâtre-Français* (Paris 1780).

Naves, Raymond, *Le Goût de Voltaire* (Paris 1967).

Niklaus, Robert, *A literary history of France: the eighteenth century, 1715-1789* (London 1970).

Nisard, Charles, *Les Ennemis de Voltaire* (Paris 1853).

Origny, Antoine Jean Baptiste Abraham d', *Annales du théâtre italien* (Paris 1788).

Page, Eugene R., *George Colman the Elder* (New York 1935).

Palissot de Montenoy, Charles, *Œuvres* (Liège 1777).

– *Petites lettres sur de grands philosophes* (Paris 1757).

Papon, Jean, *Recueil d'arrêts notables des cours souveraines de France* (Lyon 1568).

Peake, Richard B., *Memoirs of the Colman family* (London 1841).

Pellisson, Maurice, *Les Hommes de lettres au dix-huitième siècle* (Paris 1911).

Piron, Alexis, *Œuvres inédites* (Paris 1859).

Quérard, Joseph-Marie, *La France littéraire, ou dictionnaire bibliographique*

des savants, historiens et gens de lettres de la France (Paris 1827-1864).
– *Les Supercheries littéraires dévoilées* (Paris 1869-1871).
Regnard, Jean-François, *Théâtre*, ed. G. d'Heylli (Paris 1876).
Robertson, William, *The History of Scotland during the reigns of Queen Mary and King James VI* (London 1758).
Rosenfeld, Sybil, *Foreign theatrical companies in Great Britain in the seventeenth and eighteenth centuries* (London 1955).
Rousseau, Jean-Baptiste, *Le Café* (Paris 1695).
Schmidt, Karl, *Jus primæ noctis: eine geschichtliche Untersuchung* (Freiburg im Breisgau 1881).
Simul et singulis: la Comédie-Française racontée par ses comédiens (Paris 1980).
Soury, Jules, 'Un critique au dix-huitième siècle', *Rdm* (1 mars 1877), p.80-112.
Les Spectacles de Paris (1761).
The Spectator, ed. Donald F. Bond (Oxford 1965).
Sutherland, Lucy Stuart, *A London merchant, 1695-1774* (London 1933).
Taylor, S. S. B., 'The definitive text of Voltaire's works: the Leningrad *encadrée*', *Studies* 124 (1974), p.7-132.
Il Teatro moderno applaudito (Venezia 1796-1809).
Todd, Christopher, 'A provisional bibliography of published Spanish translations of Voltaire', *Studies* 161 (1976), p.43-136.
Trapnell, W. H., 'Survey and analysis of Voltaire's collective editions, 1728-1789', *Studies* 77 (1970), p.105-99.
Trévédy, J., *Notes sur Fréron et ses cousins Royou* (Quimper, Rennes 1902).
Vercruysse, Jeroom, 'Bibliographie provisoire des traductions néerlandaises et flamandes de Voltaire', *Studies* 116 (1973), p.19-64.
Veuillot, Louis, *Le Droit du seigneur au Moyen Age* (Paris 1854).
Victor, Benjamin, *A history of the theatres of London* (London 1761-1771).
Voltaire et la culture portugaise, exposition bibliographique et iconographique (Paris 1969).
Voltaire, *Candide*, ed. R. Pomeau, in Voltaire 48 (Oxford 1980).
– *Corpus des notes marginales de Voltaire* (Berlin, Oxford 1979-).
– *Correspondence and related documents*, ed. Th. Besterman, in Voltaire 85-135 (1968-1977).
– *La Défense de mon oncle*, ed. J.-M. Moureaux, in Voltaire 64 (1984).
– *Essai sur les mœurs*, ed. R. Pomeau (Paris 1963).
– *Lettres inédites à son imprimeur Gabriel Cramer*, ed. B. Gagnebin (Genève 1952).
– *Œuvres*, ed. Ch. Palissot (Paris 1792-1797).
– *Œuvres complètes* ([Kehl] 1784-1789).
– *Œuvres complètes*, ed. A. A. Renouard (Paris 1819-1825).
– *Œuvres complètes*, ed. J. Clogenson (Paris 1824-1832).
– *Œuvres complètes*, ed. A. J. Q. Beuchot (Paris 1829-1840).
– *Œuvres complètes*, ed. L. Moland (Paris 1877-1885).
– *Œuvres complètes / Complete works* (Genève, Banbury, Oxford 1968-).
– *Recueil des facéties parisiennes pour les six premiers mois de l'an 1760* (1760).
Willens, Lilian, *Voltaire's comic theatre: composition, conflict and critics*, Studies 136 (1975).
Yashinsky, Jack, 'Voltaire's *L'Ecossaise*: background, structure, originality', *Studies* 182 (1979), p.253-71.

INDEX

Abbeville, 10
Abirached, R., 278*n*, 279*n*
Académie des sciences, 227, 290, 507*n*, 511*n*
Académie française, 498*n*, 508, 509*n*, 518, 520*n*
Acante (*Droit du seigneur*), 16, 17, 22, 23, 25, 28, 30-32, 64
Addison, Joseph, 240*n*
Adélaïde, Marie-Adélaïde de France, known as Mme, 517*n*
Alasseur, Claude, 265*n*
Albaret, d', 518*n*
Albergati Capacelli, marquis Francesco, 12
Alceste (*Misanthrope*), 237*n*, 239
Aldamon (*Tancrède*), 275*n*
Alembert, Jean Le Rond d', 24, 226, 246, 247, 249, 250, 251*n*, 252*n*, 264, 265, 267, 268*n*, 269, 275, 288, 289, 473, 478, 480, 482, 485, 487, 511; 'Genève', 289
Alençon, 496, 499*n*, 515
Almaviva (*Mariage de Figaro*), 17
Alton, Lady (*Ecossaise*), 240, 254*n*, 255, 256, 258, 262, 263, 275, 289, 294, 298, 350, 361
Amadis, 101
Ameno, Francisco Luís, publisher at Lisbon, 277, 329
America, 372*n*
Amiens, évêque d', 7, 10
André (*Ecossaise*), 276, 362
Anitus, 354
Anseaume, Louis, 275, 330; *L'Ivrogne corrigé*, 305
Argenson, Marc-Pierre Voyer de Paulmy, comte d', 227
Argental, Charles-Augustin Feriol, comte d', 13, 18-21, 23, 24, 26, 28, 32, 34, 233, 242*n*, 247*n*, 250*n*, 251-53, 255, 257-61, 263-65, 267, 270, 271, 275, 277, 291, 294, 320, 374*n*, 386*n*, 473, 475, 480, 481, 483
Argental, Jeanne-Grâce Bosc Du Bouchet, comtesse d', 13, 18-20, 23, 24, 26, 259, 277, 481
Argire (*Tancrède*), 275*n*
Ariston, 359*n*
Ariston (*Envieux*), 241
Arlequin (*Ecossaise*, La Grange), 276
Armand, Armand-François Huguet, known as, 262, 263, 361
Arnaud, François, 509*n*
Arnaud, François-Thomas-Marie de Baculard d', 270*n*, 394*n*, 485*n*, 505, 508, 510*n*; *Les Epreuves du sentiment*, 508*n*
Arnould, Madeleine-Sophie, 292
Artois, 66
Asia, 346
Astaingue, Count (*Pamela*, Mme Denis), 230
Athalie (*Athalie*), 343
Aumont, Louis-Marie-Auguste d'Aumont de La Rochebaron, duc d', 259
Auspingh, Count (*Pamela nubile*), 230
Austria, 345*n*

Babylon, 11
Bachaumont, Louis Petit de, *Mémoires secrets*, 22, 29, 477, 482, 483
Le Bailli (*Droit du seigneur*), 20, 23-25, 30, 64
Balcou, Jean, 231, 249*n*, 253*n*, 477*n*, 479*n*
Barbados water, 371, 373
Bar-sur-Seine, 498, 499*n*
Barthélemy, Anatole de, 15*n*

La Bastille, 502*n*, 510, 511
Bayle, Pierre, *Dictionnaire historique et critique*, 6
Bayonne, 510
Beaumarchais, Pierre-Augustin Caron de, 3; *Essai sur le genre dramatique sérieux*, 286; *Le Mariage de Figaro*, 14, 17, 318
Beauvais, collège de, 508*n*
Belise (*Droit du seigneur*), 66
Bellecour, Jean-Claude-Gilles Colson, known as, 12, 21*n*, 263, 275*n*, 361
Belot, Octavie, 19
Bengesco, Georges, 51, 53, 233, 275, 330, 331*n*, 475*n*
Bergier, Nicolas-Sylvestre, 505, 509
Berland d'Halouvry, 505, 509
Berlin, 276
Bernis, François-Joachim de Pierres de, 498
Berryer de Ravenoville, Nicolas-René, 227
Berthe (*Droit du seigneur*), 25, 64
Bertrand, Elie, 249, 321
Besterman, Theodore, 26*n*, 230*n*, 328*n*, 478
Beuchot, Adrien-Jean-Quentin, 257*n*, 260*n*, 272*n*, 276, 304, 331, 345*n*, 373*n*, 473*n*, 487
Bible, book of Tobit, 6
Bicêtre, 498, 511, 518
La Bigarrure, 500
Blainville, Pierre-Jean, 22*n*, 362
Blaise (*Nanine*), 31
Blanford (*Prude*), 237, 239
Blin de Sainmore, Adrien-Michel-Hyacinthe, *Orphanis*, 239*n*
Blondel, Jacques, 505, 506*n*, 507, 510*n*
Boas, Frederick S., 244*n*
Bode, J. J. C., 329, 330
Boetius, Hector, 5
Boileau-Despréaux, Nicolas, 270
Boismorand, Claude-Joseph Chéron de, 496*n*, 499*n*
Boissy, Louis de, *Le Droit du seigneur*, 15; *Le Français à Londres*, 236*n*
Bolingbroke, Henry St John, first viscount, 502*n*; *Lettres sur l'histoire*, 501, 506*n*
Bonneval, Jean-Baptiste-Jacques Gimat de, 296, 362
Bordeaux, 275
Boswell, James, *Journal of a tour to the Hebrides*, 5
Boucher d'Argis, Antoine-Gaspard, 7, 8
Bougeant, Guillaume-Hyacinthe, 495*n*
Boullenger de Rivery, Claude-François-Félix, 505
Boursault, Edme, 270
Bouthier Darcourt, 296
Brei, laquais de Fréron, 515*n*
Brenner, Clarence D., 15*n*, 275, 276*n*, 330
Brest, 515
Bret, Antoine, 505; *Le Jaloux*, 508; *Mémoires sur la vie de Mlle de Lenclos*, 500*n*
Brittany, 478-80, 516, 517
Brizard, Jean-Baptiste Britard, known as, 22*n*, 262, 263, 275*n*, 361
Brosses, Charles de, baron de Montfalcon, 229, 249
Brueys, David-Augustin de, *Le Muet*, 236*n*
Bruix, chevalier de, 505; *Réflexions diverses*, 509
Brunetière, Ferdinand, 268*n*
Brunetti, 259
Bruno, Marlinda R., 514*n*
Brussels, 280
Buchanan, George, 10, 358
Bussy, rue de, 512
Byng, admiral John, 370*n*

Caen, 496*n*
Das Caffeehaus, 329, 330
Caffe-Huset, 330

Il Caffé, o la Scozzese, 329
Le Caffè ossia la Scozzese, 329
Calas, Marc-Antoine, 508*n*
Campion, Louise, 514*n*
Candaux, Jean-Daniel, 305
Candor (*Moissonneurs*), 32
Canongate Theatre, 243*n*
Capperonnier, Jean-Auguste, 483
Caron Du Chanset, 253*n*, 296
Carrage, Marquis du (*Droit du seigneur*), 10*n*, 16, 17, 22, 23*n*, 25, 28, 30, 32, 64
carragio, 10*n*
Carré, Jérôme, 259-61, 271, 289, 291*n*, 302, 306, 307, 309, 313, 316, 319-27, 341, 348, 351-53, 355*n*, 469
Carriat, Jeanne, 30*n*, 35
Carthage, Council of, 6, 10
Cartouche, 514*n*
Casanova, Giacomo, 278-80, 328
Castillon, Jean de, 505; *Discours sur l'origine de l'inégalité*, 506*n*
Catalogue hebdomadaire, 41
Catane (*Tancrède*), 275*n*
Catherine II, empress of Russia, 280*n*
Catinon, Catherine-Antoinette Foulquier, known as Mlle, 276
Caux de Cappeval, N. de, 505, 506
Cervantes Saavedra, Miguel de, *Persiles y Sigismunda*, 4
César (*Mort de César*), 344
César (*Mort de Pompée*), 343
Chambeau, Louis, 304, 310, 330
Chamfort, Sébastien-Roch-Nicolas, *Eloge de Molière*, 518
Champagne (*Droit du seigneur*), 17*n*, 25, 64
Chapman, R. W., 5*n*
Charles V, 86
Charles, Sir (*Pamela*, Mme Denis), 240, 241
Châtelet, 513; –, Petit, 474, 517
Chauvelin, Bernard-Louis, 12, 24
Chavigny, Théodore de Chevignard de, 278
Chevalley, Sylvie, 21*n*
Chevrier, François-Antoine de, *Le Colporteur*, 510*n*
China, 274, 346*n*
Choiseul, Etienne-François de Choiseul-Stainville, duc de, 26, 229, 246, 248-50, 274, 480
Cicero, 519; *Pro Murena*, 347; *De re publica*, 347*n*
Cideville, Pierre-Robert Le Cornier de, 277*n*
Clairon, Claire-Josèphe-Hippolyte Leyris de Latude, known as Mlle, 19*n*, 26, 251*n*, 277*n*
Clement XIII, 226
Clément, Jean-Marie-Bernard, 249*n*, 265*n*
Clermont, Louis de Bourbon-Condé, comte de, 498
Clifort, Lady (*Pamela*, Mme Denis), 240
The Coffee-house, 328, 329
Coimbra Martins, A., 328*n*
Colardeau, Charles-Pierre, 505, 509
Colette (*Droit du seigneur*), 20-25, 30, 64
Collé, Charles, 247*n*, 257*n*, 263, 265*n*, 266*n*, 295, 331
Collingwood, W. G., 328
Colman, George, the Elder, *The English merchant*, 233*n*, 280, 281, 328, 469
Colman, George, the Younger, 281
Comedia nueva, la Escocesa, 329
Comédie-Française, 3, 16, 19-21, 23-25, 28, 29, 41, 225, 233, 244, 246, 247, 249*n*, 250*n*, 253*n*, 259, 264, 267, 277, 283, 289-91, 294, 302, 469, 473, 497
Comédie-Italienne, 32, 259, 275
Congreve, William, 238
Constantinople, 371*n*
Constapel, H., publisher at The Hague, 305
Conti, Louis-François de Bourbon, prince de, 474

Copenhagen, 299, 314
Coqueley de Chaussepierre, Georges Charles, 255*n*, 261*n*, 268, 269, 271, 518
Cordeliers, rue des, 498
Corneille, Marie-Françoise, 13, 23, 273, 284*n*, 474, 475
Corneille, Pierre, 474; *La Mort de Pompée*, 343*n*
Cornou, François, 481*n*, 483, 496*n*
Coste, abbé, 273
Coste d'Arnobat, Charles-Pierre, 491, 505; *Lettres sur le voyage d'Espagne*, 509-11
Covelle, Robert, 355*n*
Covent Garden, 243, 349*n*
Coverley, Sir Roger de, 239
Coyer, Gabriel-François, *Discours sur la satire contre les philosophes*, 273, 274
Cramer, Gabriel, 26, 27, 35, 40, 43-45, 49-55, 230*n*, 242, 243, 245-47, 253*n*, 298, 299, 303, 306, 307, 309, 310, 314, 316, 317, 334, 347*n*, 474, 475, 487, 488
Crébillon, Prosper Jolyot de, 20*n*, 21, 22, 32, 33, 138*n*, 261*n*, 273*n*, 285*n*
Crébillon, Claude-Prosper Jolyot de, *Les Heureux orphelins*, 511*v*
Crispin (*Philosophes*), 263*n*
Croupillac, Baronne de (*Enfant prodigue*), 240*n*
Cruz, Ramón de la, 329
Cuissart, 330
cul-de-sac, 351
Curbrech, Sire (*Pamela nubile*), 236
Cyrus, 127

Daguesseau, Henri-François, 227
Daily post, 234
Damilaville, Etienne-Noël, 12, 20, 21, 23, 24, 26, 281*n*, 331, 473, 475
Dancourt, Florent Carton, 288; *La Maison de campagne*, 300
Dandin, 273
Dangeville, Marie-Anne, 21, 22, 262, 263, 361
Dauberval, Etienne-Dominique Bercher, 22*n*, 275*n*, 362
Davers, Lady (*Pamela*), 240
Davesne, Bertin, 275, 330
Dazincourt, Joseph-Jean-Baptiste Albouy, known as, 25, 318
De Grieck, publishers at Brussels, 300
Delaporte, prompt, 42, 296
Les Délices, 13, 229, 252, 279, 289
Delort, Joseph, 497*n*
Denis, Marie-Louise Mignot, Mme, 19, 23; *Pamela*, 230, 231, 236, 238, 240, 241
Deschanel, Emile, 246*n*
Descotes, Maurice, 17*n*
Desessarts, Denis Deschanet, known as, 25
Desfontaines, François-Georges Fouques Deshayes, known as, 264, 265; *Le Droit du seigneur*, 15
Desfontaines, Pierre-François Guyot, 241, 242*n*, 293, 496, 498, 515*n*; *Jugements sur quelques ouvrages nouveaux*, 496*n*; *Observations sur les écrits modernes*, 496*n*; *La Voltairomanie*, 242
Desnoiresterres, Gustave, 233*n*, 268*n*, 288
Desprez, Louis-Jean, 234*n*
Desprez de Boissy, Charles, 234*n*
Desprez de Crassier, Etienne-Philibert, 234*n*
Diderot, Denis, 21*n*, 247-52, 261, 263, 267, 269, 282, 283-85, 288, 507*n*, 520*n*; *Discours sur la poésie dramatique*, 284-87, 356*n*; *Entretiens sur le Fils naturel*, 284, 356*n*; *Le Neveu de Rameau*, 294; *Le Père de famille*, 286, 294
Didot, François-Ambroise, 319, 326
Dignant (*Droit du seigneur*), 25, 31, 64
Dijon, 19, 20; –, Académie de, 20
Diodati, O., 329
Doligny, Louise-Adélaïde de Berthon de, known as Mme, 25

Dorat, Claude-Joseph, 482, 483, 505; *Epître à un ami dans sa retraite, à l'occasion des Philosophes et de l'Ecossaise*, 273*n*
Dormène (*Droit du seigneur*), 31, 64
Dortidius (*Philosophes*), 261*n*, 267, 520*n*
Le Droit du seigneur, anon., 14
Drouin, Mlle, 22*n*
Drummond, William, 4th viscount of Strathallan, 232
Drury Lane, 243, 280, 349*n*
Du Bocage, Anne-Marie Fiquet, Mme, 293
Dubois, Louis Blouin, known as, 275*n*, 361
Du Châtelet, Gabrielle-Emilie Le Tonnelier de Breteuil, marquise, 241*n*
Du Chatellier, Armand, 515*n*, 516*n*
Duchesne, Marie-Antoinette Cailleau, veuve, 28, 313, 324, 325
Duchesne, Nicolas-Bonaventure, 26-28, 35, 41-43, 45, 47, 308, 312, 314, 318, 326, 328, 330, 502, 504
Duckworth, Colin, 230*n*
Duclos, Charles Pinot, 226, 247, 267, 478, 480
Du Deffand, Marie de Vichy de Chamrond, marquise, 231*n*, 249, 264, 341*n*
Dufresny, Charles Rivière, *Le Faux honnête homme*, 236*n*; *La Noce interrompue*, 14
Dugazon, Jean-Baptiste-Henri Gournaud, known as, 25
Duhamel Du Monceau, Henri-Louis, 510*n*
Duim, Izaak, publisher at Amsterdam, 330
Du Marsais, César Chesneau, 290, 346*n*
Dumas, Alexandre, *fils*, 13
Duni, Egidio Romualdo, 32
Du Plessis-Villette, Reine-Philiberte Rouph de Varicourt, marquise, 235
Durancy, Jean-François Fieuzal, known as, 22*n*, 362
Durancy, Madeleine-Céleste Fieuzal de Froissac, known as Mlle, 22*n*
Durancy, Mme, née Françoise-Marie Dessuslefour, 22*n*
Duras, Emmanuel-Félicité, duc de, 277*n*
Du Tertre, François-Joachim Duport, 505; *Abrégé chronologique de l'histoire d'Angleterre*, 499; *Histoire des conjurations*, 499
Du Verdier, Antoine, *Diverses leçons*, 6

L'Ecosseuse, 275, 330
Edinburgh, 243*n*, 349*n*, 355, 423
Elie de Beaumont, Jean-Baptiste-Jacques, 480
L'Encyclopédie, 7, 226, 252, 254*n*, 267, 274, 283, 356, 505*n*, 507, 508*n*; 'Cependant', 227; 'Critique', 227-28, 252
England, 230, 234, 258, 357, 372*n*, 388*n*, 440*n*
Eon de Beaumont, Charles-Geneviève-Louis-Auguste-André-Timothée, chevalier d', 505
Epinay, Louise-Florence-Petronille de Tardieu d'Esclavelles d', 253, 254, 259*n*, 260*n*
Epinay, Pierrette-Claudine-Hélène Pinet, known as Mlle d', 13
Eraste (*Droit du seigneur*, anon.), 14-15
Eratou, 355*n*
Ernold, Cavaliere (*Pamela nubile*), 236, 240
Escarbagnas, comtesse d', 420*n*
La Escocesa, 329
Estouteville, Colbert, comte d', *Les Vrais plaisirs*, 497
Evenus III, 5, 10

Fabrice (*Ecossaise*), 234-36, 254, 256, 260*n*, 262, 263, 298, 361

INDEX

Fabrizio (*Locandiera*), 236
Falbrige, Lord (*Ecossaise*), 257, 373, 374*n*, 423
Falkirk, battle of, 244
Fanie (*Tancrède*), 275*n*
Fantet, publisher at Besançon, 313
Farquhar, George, 238
Fatéma, 355*n*
Favart, Charles-Simon, 258, 262-64, 270*n*, 276*n*; *Les Moissonneurs*, 31, 32
Feller, François-Xavier de, *Dictionnaire historique*, 496*n*
Ferney, 23, 24, 229, 252, 277*n*, 480, 484, 504, 521
Fierenfat (*Enfant prodigue*), 240*n*
Figaro (*Mariage de Figaro*), 18, 318
Flaubert, Gustave, 17*n*, 294
Fletcher, John, *The Custom of the country*, 4
Fleury, Abraham-Joseph Bénard, known as, 25
Florian, Philippe-Antoine de Claris, marquis de, 480
Fontaine, Marie-Elisabeth de Dompierre de, née Mignot, 22
Fontainebleau, 15
Foppington, Lord (*Relapse*), 420*n*
France, 5, 7, 9, 229, 231, 274, 284, 292, 294, 343, 345*n*, 346*n*, 353, 355, 358, 371*n*, 388*n*, 396*n*, 440*n*
Francport (*Ecosseuse*), 275
Frederick II, king of Prussia, 229, 249, 498*n*
Freeport (or Friport) (*Ecossaise*), 234-40, 260*n*, 263, 264, 270, 275, 280-82, 286, 290, 294, 355, 361
Freeport, Sir Andrew, 239
Frélon (*Ecossaise*), 226, 233, 235, 236, 240-42, 245, 249, 251-55, 260*n*, 261, 275, 276, 278, 281, 283, 284, 286, 287, 292-94, 304, 349, 350, 352, 353, 356, 357, 361, 469
French Theatre, London, 234
Fréron, Anne-Françoise Royou, Mme, 478-480, 514*n*, 515, 516*n*
Fréron, Daniel, 495*n*, 512*n*
Fréron, Elie-Catherine, 233, 241, 242, 246*n*, 247, 248, 251, 253*n*, 254*n*, 255, 260-64, 268-72, 274, 275, 277, 280-82, 285, 288-90, 293-95, 347, 350, 351*n*, 354*n*, 469, 473-91, 495-522; *Ad bellonam*, 496*n*; *L'Année littéraire*, 30, 31, 225-29, 236, 240*n*, 243-45, 252, 253, 256, 258, 259, 265-67, 272, 276, 283, 284, 332, 350*n*, 352, 357*n*, 394*n*, 467*n*, 473, 476, 483, 484, 495*n*, 499*n*, 504-11; *Histoire de Marie Stuart*, 231; *Lettres de madame la comtesse*, 226, 498; *Lettres sur quelques écrits de ce temps*, 227, 347*n*, 491, 496*n*, 497*n*, 499, 500, 502; 'Relation d'une grande bataille', 258, 266-68, 270, 271, 292, 473
Fréron, François-Elie-Marie, 512*n*
Fréron, Louise, 512*n*
Fréron, Louise-Philippine, 516*n*
Fréron, Marie-Catherine-Françoise, 512*n*
Fréron, Marie-Louise, 513
Fréron, Stanislas, 500*n*
Fréron, Thérèse, 515*n*
Fréron, Thérèse, épouse Duché, 512, 513
Fréron, Thérèse-Jacqueline Guyomar, Mme, 263, 266*n*, 510*n*, 512
Fromm, Hans, 328*n*
Fuchs, Max, 304
Fugère, A.-C., 504*n*
Furet (*Ecosseuse*), 275
Furetière, Antoine, *Dictionnaire universel*, 6
Fuzelier, Louis, *Momus exilé*, 305

Gagnebin, Bernard, 243*n*, 299, 307
Gaiffe, Félix, 235, 246*n*, 254*n*, 282*n*, 284*n*, 288*n*
Galilee, 343
Garat, Dominique-Joseph, 509*n*
Garrick, David, 243, 281*n*, 328, 349*n*

Gaussin, Jeanne-Catherine, 22, 262, 263, 361
Geneva, 274, 288, 289, 348
Genoa, 279
Geoffroy, Julien-Louis, 246*n*
Germany, 9
Gernance, Chevalier (*Droit du seigneur*), 17, 22, 25, 29, 30, 64
Gex, 229
Ghelen, printer at Vienna, 44, 306, 315
Gibert y Tutó, Carlos, publisher at Barcelona, 329
Girard, 21*n*
Godefroy, François, 316
Goldoni, Carlo, 240, 248*n*, 284, 355; *La Bottega del caffè*, 235, 236, 241, 243, 270*n*; *Il Cavaliere e la dama*, 270*n*; *Il Filosofo inglese*, 270*n*; *La Locandiera*, 236, 270*n*; *Pamela nubile*, 230, 236, 238; *Le Père de famille*, 248*n*; *La Scozzese*, 278, 279*n*, 329; *Le Véritable ami*, 248*n*
Goodman, Mrs (*English merchant*), 233*n*
Gorgeu, notaire, 515*n*
Gossard, de Nyon, 505*n*
Gossart, Jean. B., 505
Gouvernet, Philippe-Antoine-Gabriel-Victor-Charles, marquis de, 233, 234, 239
Gouvernet, Suzanne-Catherine Gravet de Corsembleu de Livry, marquise de, 233-35
Goveanus, Andreas, 358
Graffigny, Françoise-Paule d'Issembourg d'Happoncourt de, 500*n*; *Cénie*, 286
La Grand'Jeanneton (*Ecosseuse*), 275
Grandval, François-Charles Racot de, 22
Grasset, François, 52, 320, 469
Gravelot, Hubert-François Bourgignon, 237*n*, 316
s'Gravesande, Willem Jacob, 476
Gravier, Jean, 56, 325
Greece, 358
Green, F. C., 246*n*, 250*n*
Grieck, *see* De Grieck
Griffet, Henri, *Traité des différentes sortes de preuves qui servent à établir la vérité de l'histoire*, 476*n*
Grimbergh, Jean-Baptiste, 234
Grimm, Friedrich-Melchior, 242, 247, 267, 269; *Correspondance littéraire*, 22, 29, 30, 32, 35, 58, 233, 244, 245, 253-55, 262, 263, 273, 283, 286, 287, 477, 479*n*, 481-83, 505*n*, 507*n*
Gröll, publisher at Dresden, 310
Grosclaude, Pierre, 226*n*, 248*n*, 268*n*
Guy, Pierre, 26, 27, 33*n*
Guymond de La Touche, Claude, *Iphigénie en Tauride*, 506
Guyomar, Henri, 512*n*
Gyldendal, publisher at Copenhagen, 330

Hampton, 281*n*
Harny de Guerville, *Les Nouveaux calotins*, 276*n*, 330
Havens, George R., 236*n*, 276*n*
Haymarket, 234
Helvétius, Claude-Adrien, 247; *De l'esprit*, 228, 506*n*, 508, 509
Hémery, Joseph d', 499*n*, 501*n*, 502*n*, 517*n*
Henri II, king of France, 64
Henriette (*Droit du seigneur*, anon.), 14-15
Herodotus, 11
Das Herrenrecht oder die Klippe des Weisen, 31
Hesselberg, Pierre, printer at Stockholm, 305
The Highland girl, 328
Home (or Hume), John, 226, 231, 251-54, 257, 260, 274, 278, 283, 287, 289, 290, 296, 299-317, 319-27, 341, 348-53, 355-357; *Agis*, 243, 349; *Douglas*, 243, 244, 348, 349
Homer, 354*n*

Horace, 354*n*
Horn-Monval, Madeleine, 243*n*
Howarth, W. D., 4*n*, 15*n*, 18*n*
Hugo, Victor, 287; *Hernani*, 257*n*, 261*n*
Hume, David, 243*n*, 289, 348, 349, 355; *The History of Great Britain under the house of Stuart*, 231; *Histoire de la maison des Stuart*, 231*n*
Hurtaud, 18

impasse, 351
Irailh, Augustin-Simon, 288*n*
Iriarte, Tomás de, 329
Italy, 258, 279, 344

Jack (*Pamela*), 240
Jacobites, 230, 232, 244
Jal, Auguste, 512*n*
Jamaica, 237, 253, 372
Japan, 346*n*
Joad (*Athalie*), 343
Joannidès, A., 277*n*
Jodelle, Etienne, 18
Joly de Fleury, Omer, 249, 271, 396*n*
Jones, Sir William, 371*n*
Jonval, C. P., 271*n*
Journal de Trévoux, 509*n*
Journal des savants, 357*n*, 503*n*, 504*n*
Journal encyclopédique, 228*n*, 251*n*, 348, 349*n*
Journal étranger, 504*n*
jus primae noctis, 3-14

Kenrick, William, 280
Kleinschmidt, John R., 314
Kölving, Ulla, 30*n*, 35
Korn, publisher at Breslau, 31
Krauss, H. P., 329

La Brie (*Droit du seigneur*, anon.), 14-15
La Chalotais, Louis-René de Caradeuc de, 480*n*
La Chassaigne, Marie-Anne-Hélène Broquin de, 25
La Chaussé, Pierre-Claude Nivelle de, *Mélanide*, 286; *Paméla*, 16
La Cloche, M. de (*Scozzese*), 278
Lacombe, Jacques, 476
La Condamine, Charles-Marie de, 501*n*
Lacoste, Emmanuel-Jean de, 510
Lafarga, Francisco, 328*n*
La Grange, Nicolas, *L'Ecossaise*, 276, 330
La Harpe, Jean-François de, 473, 475, 480-82, 504*n*, 521
Lally, Thomas-Arthur, comte de, 427*n*
La Marck, Marie-Anne-Françoise de Noailles, comtesse de, 251, 252
La Marre, 487
Lambert, Michel, 245, 255*n*, 502-504, 511*n*, 512
La Motte, Antoine Houdar de, 506
Lang, Andrew, 232*n*, 243*n*
La Porte, Joseph de, 249*n*, 267, 268*n*, 473, 484, 489, 501-505, 507, 508, 521; *L'Observateur littéraire*, 262, 499, 504*n*, 512, 513*n*, 521; *Observations sur la littérature moderne*, 501*n*
Larcher, Pierre-Henri, *Supplément à la Philosophie de l'histoire*, 11
Largillière, Nicolas de, 234
La Ribadière, de, *L'Ecueil du sage*, 25
La Rose (*Ecosseuse*), 275
Lattaignant, Gabriel-Charles de, 506
Laugeon (or Laujon), procureur, 489, 498, 499*n*
Laujon, Pierre, *Aeglé*, 498
Lauraguais, Louis-Félicité de Brancas, comte de, 290, 292, 343, 345*n*, 346*n*
Laure (*Droit du seigneur*), 16*n*, 17*n*, 31, 87, 106, 114, 116, 142, 158, 162, 166, 170, 172, 173, 191, 200, 209, 212
Lausanne, 226
Laus de Boissy, M.-A. de, 333
Le Blanc, Jean-Bernard, *Aben-saïd*, 15
Le Breton, André-François, 507*n*
Le Brun, Ponce-Denis Ecouchard,

357*n*, 474, 475, 482; *L'Ane littéraire*, 273*n*; *La Wasprie*, 273, 332, 475*n*
Le Chapelier, avocat, 478
L'Ecluze de Thilloy, Louis, 474
Lefranc de Pompignan, Jean-Jacques, 248*n*, 249, 271, 282*n*, 347*n*, 348, 485, 520; *Mémoire présenté au roi*, 341*n*
Le Goust, 20
Lekain, Henri-Louis Cain, known as, 23, 24, 26, 275*n*, 291*n*, 362, 509*n*
Lénardon, Dante, 505*n*
Lenclos, Ninon, 500
Lenoir, Jean-Charles-Pierre, 34
Léris, Antoine de, 276*n*
Le Roy, Catherine, 495*n*
Leroy, Julien-David, 505
Lesage, Alain-René, 276*n*, 330
Lessing, Gotthold Ephraim, *Hamburgische Dramaturgie*, 233*n*, 235, 278
Lettre de M. D. R. à M. de S. R. sur la Zulime de M. de Voltaire, 30
Lettre sur la comédie de l'Ecossaise, 272
Lillo, George, *The London merchant*, 239
Lindana (*Scozzese*), 278
Lindane (*Ecossaise*), 231-35, 237, 238, 240, 255-59, 260*n*, 262-64, 276, 279, 281, 282, 286, 294, 323, 361
Lintilhac, Eugène, 246*n*, 288*n*
Lioure, Michel, 293
Lisaura (*Bottega del caffè*), 235
Lisbon, 278
Lise (*Enfant prodigue*), 240*n*
Livry, Mlle de, *see* Gouvernet
Livy, 359*n*
Lochaber, 232
Locke, John, 343
Loftis, John, 238*n*, 243*n*
A Loja do café, 277, 329
Lombardy, 9
London, 232-35, 237, 245, 254, 257, 281, 355, 361, 362, 367, 373, 381, 395, 428, 451, 469, 477, 478
London journal, 234
Longchamp, Sébastien, 231
Lorédan (*Tancrède*), 275*n*
Lorient, 515
L'Orme, Baronne de (*Nanine*), 240
Louis, dauphin, 517*n*
Louis xv, king of France, 232
Louis, Antoine, 505, 506*n*, 508*n*
Louis-le-Grand, collège, 396*n*, 496
Louisa Ulrica of Prussia, queen of Sweden, 35
Lovat, Simon Fraser, twelfth Lord, 232
Luzy, Dorothée, 25
Lynch, Kathleen M., 280*n*
Lyon, 259*n*, 275, 363

Les Magots, 305
Mahieu, notaire, 515
Mairan, Jean-Jacques Dortous de, 227
Malesherbes, Chrétien-Guillaume de Lamoignon de, 226, 248, 255, 261*n*, 265, 266*n*, 268-72, 357*n*, 502*n*, 503*n*, 504, 511*n*
Mallard, J. L. R., 319
Mandrin, 514*n*
Manly (*Plain dealer*), 237
Manne, E.-D. de, 263*n*, 291*n*
Marias, Elie, 495*n*
Marie Leszczynka, queen of France, 517*n*
Marin, François-Louis-Claude, 277, 477, 481, 483, 505*v*, 507*v*
Marino, Giovanni Battista Marini, known as chevalier de, 497
Marivaux, Pierre Carlet de Chamblain de, 266*n*, 383*n*
Marmontel, Jean-François, 226, 264, 268*n*, 288, 497*n*, 500, 521; *Aristomène*, 227; 'Critique', 227-28, 252; *Denys le tyran*, 500*n*; *Venceslas*, 509*n*
Marseille, 259*n*, 275, 363
Marsy, François-Marie de, 231
Martinet, engraver, 323
Marylebone, 234
Marzio, Don (*Bottega del caffè*), 235, 236

Massillon, Jean-Baptiste, 343
Massinger, Philip, *The Custom of the country*, 4
Mathurin (*Droit du seigneur*), 15, 18, 25, 31, 32, 64
Maupertuis, Pierre-Louis Moreau de, 293
Mazarine, rue, 496
Maynard, Ulysse, 289
Melitus, 354
mercheta mulierum, 5, 6
Le Mercure de France, 26, 228*n*, 262*n*
Mérope (*Mérope*), 343
Métaprose (*Droit du seigneur*), 64, 99; *see* Le Bailli
Metz, 86, 109
Minorca, 253, 296, 370
Mirabeau, Victor Riquetti, marquis de, *L'Ami des hommes*, 509
Moland, Louis, 246*n*
Molé, François-René, 22, 25, 28
Molière, Jean-Baptiste Poquelin, known as, 3*n*; *Le Misanthrope*, 237*n*; *Monsieur de Pourceaugnac*, 281; *Tartuffe*, 347*n*
Monrose, Lord (*Ecossaise*), 230, 231, 256, 257, 260*n*, 262-64, 275, 278, 279, 286, 361
Monselet, Charles, 246*n*, 259, 267*n*, 484*n*
Montaigne, Michel Eyquem de, 6, 288, 289, 293; *Essais*, 4, 358, 359
Montauban, 348, 351, 520*n*
Montesquieu, Charles-Louis de Secondat, baron de La Brède et de, *De l'esprit des lois*, 7-8
Montrose, place, 232
Montrose, James Graham, second duke of, 232*n*
Moore, Edward, *The Gamester*, 263
Morand, Jean-François-Clément, 511*n*, 518
Mordant (*Ecossaise*, La Grange), 276
Moreau, Jacob-Nicolas, 226
Morellet, André, *La Vision de Charles Palissot*, 250*n*, 292
Mossy, Jean, 322
Moucheron (*Ecosseuse*), 275, 276
Mouhy, Charles de Fieux, chevalier de, 261, 291*n*
Muret, Marc-Antoine, 358
Murray (or Murrai), Lord (*Ecossaise*), 232, 233, 240, 255, 256, 258, 259, 260*n*, 263, 275, 278, 286, 361
Murray, Lord George, 232*n*
Murray, Sir John, 232

Nanine (*Nanine*), 16, 240
Naves, Raymond, 288
Newcastle, Sir Thomas Pelham-Holles, first duke of, 373*n*
Newton, Sir Isaac, 343, 476
Niklaus, Robert, 282*n*
Nisard, Charles, 484*n*
Nomentanus, 354
Norval (*Douglas*), 244
Nougaret, Pierre-Jean-Baptiste, *Le Droit du seigneur*, 15
Noyers, rue des, 478, 517

Olban, Comte d' (*Nanine*), 16, 240
Olivet, Pierre-Joseph Thoulier d', 347*n*, 351*n*, 510*n*
Origny, Antoine-Jean-Baptiste d', 276
Orkney islands, 451

Palissot de Montenoy, Charles, 226, 252, 261, 264, 271, 276, 284, 296, 345*n*, 346*n*, 347*n*, 354*n*, 355*n*, 363*n*, 369*n*, 371*n*, 382*n*, 383*n*, 388*n*, 390*n*, 391*n*, 393*n*, 394*n*, 395*n*, 396*n*, 397*n*, 420*n*, 423*n*, 431*n*, 437*n*, 440*n*, 443*n*, 464*n*, 466*n*, 467*n*, 485, 505, 508, 520; *Le Cercle*, 250*n*; *La Dunciade*, 293, 497*n*; *Petites lettres sur de grandes philosophes*, 248; *Les Philosophes*, 246-51, 253, 254, 262, 263*n*, 265, 266, 272-74, 282, 295, 299, 520*n*; *Supplément*

d'un important ouvrage, 248; *Les Tuteurs*, 508
Pamela (*Pamela*, Mme Denis), 230
Panard, Charles-François, 275, 330
Panckoucke, Charles-Joseph, 34, 40, 54, 322, 476, 489
Pantolabes, 354
Papon, Jean, *Recueil d'arrêts notables des cours souveraines de France*, 6
Paris, 19, 24, 76, 226, 242, 249, 252, 253, 259*n*, 275, 280, 281, 291, 297, 341, 345, 346, 349, 353, 358, 363, 469, 473, 474, 477-80, 483, 495, 498, 511, 515-17, 519, 520
Parnassus, 474
Patte, Pierre, 505-507
Paulin, Louis-François, 22*n*, 362
Peake, Richard B., 280*n*
Pellisson, Maurice, 517*n*
Perdita (*Winter's Tale*), 244
Peru, 4
Philibert, Claude, 314
Phlipe (*Droit du seigneur*), 90
Picardet (Picardin), 20
Picardy, 64, 66, 77
Piferrer, viuda, publisher at Barcelona, 329
Piron, Alexis, 261, 270*n*, 394*n*, 475
Pitt, William, 373*n*
Plomteux, Clément, printer at Liège, 53, 321
Plonévez-Porzay, 512*n*
Poinsinet, Antoine-Alexandre-Henri, 275, 276, 330
Poinsinet de Sivry, Louis, 505; *Anacréon*, 508; *Briséis*, 509
Polly (*Ecossaise*), 256, 260*n*, 262, 263, 294, 323, 361
Pompadour, Jeanne-Antoinette Poisson Le Normand d'Etioles, marquise de, 498
Pont, de, 478
Pont-l'Abbé, 479, 514*n*, 515
Pope, Alexander, 292, 293; *Dunciad*, 354
Porée, Charles, 476*n*, 495
Porter, Sir James, 371*n*
Port Mahon, 253*n*
Pot-de-Fer, rue, 495, 496*n*
Poullin Du Parc, Augustin-Marie, 478
Prault, libraire, 300
Préville, Pierre-Louis Dubus, known as, 22*n*, 262-64, 361
Préville, Mme, 22*n*, 262, 263, 275*n*, 361
Prévost d'Exiles, Antoine-François, 485*n*, 510*n*
Protasov, Aleksandr, 330
Ptolomée (*Mort de Pompée*), 343

Québec, 254*n*
Quérard, Joseph-Marie, 276*n*, 315
Quimper, 273, 473, 478, 479, 495, 511, 512*n*, 515

Racine, Jean, 227*n*, 265, 285*n*
Raffiat, 514*n*
The Rainbow, coffee-house, 234
Rameau, Jean-Philippe, 485*n*, 510*n*
Randolph, Lady (*Douglas*), 349*n*
Raphaël, 287
Réaumur, René-Antoine Ferchault de, 507*n*
Recueil de planches sur les sciences, 507*n*
Regnard, Jean-François, *Le Légataire universel*, 30, 96; *La Sérénade*, 22
Rémond de Sainte-Albine, Pierre, 518
Rennes, 277, 478-80, 514
Renouard, Antoine-Augustin, 233*n*, 234
Rességuier, Clément J. Ignace de, 505-507
Richardson, Samuel, 17, 30; *Clarissa Harlowe*, 16*n*; *Pamela*, 16, 226, 230, 231, 240
Richelieu, Louis-François-Armand, 13, 253*n*, 277, 370*n*, 427*n*
Richoff, François-Canut, publisher at Amsterdam, 47, 48, 50, 308, 311, 313, 315, 317

Ripafratta (*Locandiera*), 236
Robecq, Anne-Marie de Luxembourg de Montmorency, princesse de, 248, 250*n*, 251, 292
Robertson, William, *The History of Scotland*, 231*n*
Rodolfo (*Bottega del caffè*), 235
Rohan, Guy-Auguste Rohan-Chabot, chevalier de, 440*n*
Rome, 346*n*
Roqueville, Joannes de, 303-304
Rosenfeld, Sybil, 234*n*
Rosine (*Moissonneurs*), 32
Rossi, Pietro, 279
Roth, George, 21*n*, 263*n*
Rotrou, Jean, *Venceslas*, 509*n*
Rousseau, Jean-Baptiste, *Le Café*, 243*n*
Rousseau, Jean-Jacques, 247, 250*n*, 282, 289; *Lettre à d'Alembert sur les spectacles*, 288; *La Nouvelle Héloïse*, 308
Royou, Claude, 479*n*
Royou, Guillaume, 477-84, 488, 514, 516*n*, 517
Royou, Jacques, 514*n*
Royou, Jacques-Corentin, 479*n*, 515*n*, 516*n*
Royou, Thomas, 479*n*, 516*n*
Ruault, Nicolas, 325
Rüdiger, publisher at Berlin, 329, 330

Sadi, Muslah-al-Dîn, 474
Saint-Gelais, Mellin de, 20
Saint-Jacques, rue, 405
Saint-Lambert, Jean-François, marquis de, 509*n*
Saint-Laurent, foire, 15, 275
Saint-Omer, 396*n*
Saint-Petersburg, 280, 344
Saint-Pierre, Charles-Irénée Castel de, *Annales politiques*, 509
Saint-Priest, François-Emmanuel Guignard, comte de, 371*n*
Saint-Ronan, 495*n*
Saint-Sulpice, 512*n*, 513*n*
Sarrazin, Pierre-Claude, 262
Sartines, Antoine-Raymond-Jean-Gualbert-Gabriel de, 33
Schmid, Johann Friedrich, 31
Schmidt, Karl, 4*n*
Scotland, 5, 6, 9, 10, 230-32, 355, 369, 380, 381, 399, 413, 440, 441
Scottish rebellion of 1745, 230
Sedaine, Michel-Jean, 267, 505; *Blaise le savetier*, 505*n*; *Le Philosophe sans le savoir*, 286
Seine, rue de, 512*n*
Seven Years' War, 229, 370*n*
Shakespeare, William, 243*n*; *Winter's tale*, 244
Siddons, Mrs, 349*n*
Silesia, 249
Silva, Inocêncio Francisco da, 278*n*, 329
Skottländskan, 330
Socrates, 354*n*
Soleure, 278, 279
Solignac, Pierre-Joseph de La Pimpie, chevalier de, 500, 502
Sophocles, 344
Soury, Jules, 484*n*, 496*n*
Spain, 257, 374, 381
Spatter (*English merchant*), 280
Les Spectacles de Paris, 262*n*
The Spectator, 239, 240
Stanislas Leszczynski, king of Poland, 500, 501*n*, 517*n*, 518*n*
Steele, Sir Richard, 239
Stern, Jean, 246*n*
Stuart, family, 231, 232
Stuart, Charles Edward, 231, 232
Studnitz, Adam, baron de, 35
Suard, Jean-Baptiste, 34
Sully, 233
Sumarokov, Alexandr Petrovich, 3*n*
Surate, 254*n*
Sutherland, Lucy Stuart, 243*n*
Suzanne (*Mariage de Figaro*), 17
Sweden, 345*n*
Swift, Jonathan, 354

Taconet, Toussaint-Gaspard, *La Petite Ecosseuse*, 276*n*, 331
Tancrède (*Tancrède*), 275*n*
Taylor, S. S. B., 55, 335*n*
Teilmann, Andreas Charles, 330
Theatre Royal, 280
Théophraste (*Philosophes*), 252*n*, 267
Thibouville, Henri Lambert d'Herbigny, marquis de, 22
Thiriot, Nicolas-Claude, 19, 23, 26, 228, 248*n*, 250*n*, 263, 264, 270*n*, 271, 275*n*, 292, 331, 473, 475, 481, 482, 484, 485, 489, 521
Thomas, Ambroise-Léonard, *Eloge du maréchal de Saxe*, 508
Thorowgood (*London merchant*), 239
Tillotson, John, 343
Tobias, 6, 7
Todd, Christopher, 328*n*
Torrey, Norman L., 236*n*, 276*n*
Toulouse, 506*n*
Tournay, 229, 289
Trapnell, William, 51
Trattern, J.-Th., printer at Vienna, 315
Tressan, Louis-Elisabeth de La Vergne, comte de, 500*n*
Trévédy, J., 479, 483, 515*n*, 516*n*
Triboudet, Jacques, 510*n*
Tronchin, Théodore, 229
Trublet, Nicolas-Charles-Joseph, 277, 293
Tuileries, 267
Turkey, 371*n*

Ulff, Charles Théophile, publisher at Stockholm, 305, 306

Vadé, Guillaume, 289, 348*n*, 355*n*
Vanbrugh, Sir John, 238; *The Relapse*, 294*n*, 420*n*
Vandermonde, Charles-Augustin, 505
Vanhove, Charles-Joseph, 25
Vannes, 506*n*
Vannière, Jacques, *Praedium rusticum*, 509
Varloot, Jean, 21*n*, 263*n*
Venice, 278
Vercruysse, Jeroom, 328*n*
Vernes, Jacob, 230*n*, 516*n*
Versailles, 277
Veuillot, Louis, 15*n*
Victor, Benjamin, 280*n*
Vienna, 344
Vincennes, 498
Virginia, 370
vis-à-vis, 347
Viseux, café, 496
Voltaire, François-Marie Arouet de, library, 231*n*, 236*n*, 276*n*; collective editions: Geneva 1756, 35, 40, 51, 298; – Lausanne 1770, 469; – *encadrée* (Leningrad copy), 28, 34, 35, 40, 54-56, 323; – Kehl, 10*n*, 28, 40, 56, 345*n*, 346*n*;
Adélaïde Du Guesclin, 41, 310; *Agathocle*, 25, 28; *Anecdotes sur Fréron*, 471-520; – 'Avis de l'éditeur', 485; *Appel à toutes les nations*, 286, 289, 291*n*, 348*n*; *Brutus*, 'Discours sur la tragédie', 344*n*; *Le Café*, see *L'Ecossaise*; *Candide*, 228, 280*n*, 294; *Charlot*, 318; *Les Choses utiles et agréables*, 476, 477, 483, 487; *Commentaire historique sur les œuvres de l'auteur de la Henriade*, 229*n*; *Le Comte de Boursoufle*, 294*n*; *La Défense de mon oncle*, 11, 12*n*, 13; *Des mensonges imprimés*, 228; *La Dévote*, see *La Prude*; *Dieu. Réponse au Système de la nature*, 478, 483, 487; *Discours en vers sur l'homme*, 226; *Discours sur les Welches*, 351*n*; *Le Droit du seigneur*, 3-219, 233*n*, 318; *L'Ecossaise*, 30, 43, 221-469, 473, 505*n*, 510*n*; – 'A messieurs les Parisiens', 259-61, 284, 289-90, 307, 328, 473; – 'Avertissement', 307; – 'Epître dédicatoire', 290-92, 307; – 'Préface', 243, 283, 284, 287; *L'Ecueil du sage*, 3, 12, 13, 21, 22, 29, 32, 33, 62, 63 (see also *Le Droit du seigneur*); *L'Enfant prodigue*,

240*n*, 285, 286; *L'Envieux*, 236, 241; *L'Essai sur les mœurs*, 8, 13; *Evangile du jour*, 487, 489, 491; *Extrait des nouvelles à la main de la ville de Montauban*, 348*n*; *Fanime*, 291; *La Femme qui a raison*, 228, 248*n*, 272, 309, 311; *Les Guèbres*, 289, 348*n*; *La Henriade*, 27; *Histoire de Charles XII*, 49; *Histoire de la guerre de 1741*, 231; *L'Homme aux quarante écus*, 280*n*; *L'Ingénu*, 280*n*; *Irène*, 28; *Lettres philosophiques*, 239; *Manifeste du roi de France en faveur du prince Charles-Edouard*, 232*n*; *Mariamne*, 26; *Médime*, see *Zulime*; *Mérope*, 264, 272; *La Mort de César*, 344*n*; *Nanine*, 3, 16, 17, 19, 30, 31, 226, 230, 231, 238, 240, 241, 285, 286; *Olympie*, 18, 26; *Oreste*, 291, 350*n*; *L'Orphelin de la Chine*, 18, 48, 290; *Le Pauvre diable*, 242*n*, 250*n*, 272, 287, 473, 496*n*; *Le Plaidoyer pour Ramponeau*, 473*n*; *Précis du siècle de Louis XV*, 232*n*; *La Princesse de Babylone*, 280*n*; *La Prude*, 236, 237; *Le Pyrrhonisme de l'histoire*, 12*n*; *Questions sur l'Encyclopédie*, 9, 12*n*, 13, 281*n*, 286, 288*n*, 478, 483, 515*n*; *Recueil des facéties parisiennes*, 252*n*; *Relation du jésuite Berthier*, 228; *Requête à messieurs les Parisiens*, 259-61, 284, 289-90, 306, 328, 473; *Rome sauvée*, 291; *Le Russe à Paris*, 272, 473*n*; *Les Scythes*, 26*n*, 27, 318; *Seconde suite des mélanges*, 292; *Sémiramis*, 344*n*; – 'Dissertation sur la tragédie', 283*n*, 343*n*, 344*n*; *Socrate*, 354*n*; *Supplément du Discours aux Welches*, 351*n*; *Tancrède*, 18, 264, 265*n*, 275, 291, 300, 304, 306; 'Taxe', 10; *La Vanité*, 341, 473*n*; *Zadig*, 294; *Zaïre*, 264, 294; *Zulime*, 26, 27, 30*n*, 247, 250, 251

Wagnière, Jean-Louis, 26, 27, 33, 34, 55, 106, 201-203, 208, 216, 252*n*, 479*n*
Walther, Georg Conrad, 50, 51
Wasp (*Ecossaise*), 226, 252, 255, 260, 261*n*, 262, 263, 269, 271, 273, 275*n*, 281, 282, 304, 349, 350, 361, 469, 514*n*
De Wedergevondene dochter, 330
Wilkie, J., publisher at London, 328
Willens, Lilian, 3*n*, 18*n*
Wilson, Titus, publisher at Kendal, 328
Windsor, 381, 441
Woffington, Peg, 349*n*
Wycherley, William, *The Plain dealer*, 237

Yashinsky, Jack, 230*n*, 294

Zoïle, 242, 280, 354, 482
Zoïlin (*Envieux*), 241, 242, 354*n*
Zoïlos, 354*n*